# Amsterdam

**timeout.com/amsterdam**

**Penguin Books**

PENGUIN BOOKS

Published by the Penguin Group
Penguin Books Ltd, 80 Strand, London WC2R ORL, England
Penguin Books USA Inc., 375 Hudson Street, New York, New York 10014, USA
Penguin Books Australia Ltd, 250 Camberwell Road, Camberwell, Victoria 3124, Australia
Penguin Books Canada Ltd, 10 Alcorn Avenue, Toronto, Ontario, Canada M4V 3B2
Penguin Books (NZ) Ltd, cnr Rosedale and Airborne Roads, Albany, Auckland, New Zealand

Penguin Books Ltd, Registered Offices: Harmondsworth, Middlesex, England

First published 1991
Second edition 1993
Third edition 1995
Fourth edition 1996
Fifth edition 1998
Sixth edition 2000
Seventh edition 2002
10 9 8 7 6 5 4 3 2 1

Colour reprographics by Icon, Crown House, 56-58 Southwark Street, London SE1
and Precise Litho, 34-35 Great Sutton Street, London EC1
Printed and bound by Cayfosa-Quebecor, Ctra. de Caldes, Km 3 08 130 Sta, Perpètua de Mogoda, Barcelona, Spain

**Edited and designed by**
**Time Out Guides Limited**
**Universal House**
**251 Tottenham Court Road**
**London W1T 7AB**
**Tel + 44 (0) 20 7813 3000**
**Fax + 44 (0) 20 7813 6001**
**Email guides@timeout.com**
**www.timeout.com**

## Editorial

**Editor** Will Fulford-Jones
**Deputy Editor** Claire Fogg
**Consultant Editor** Steve Korver
**Listings Editor** Erin Tasmania
**Researchers** Pieter Bakker, Cathy Limb, Jacek Rajewski
**Proofreader** Simon Coppock
**Indexer** Jackie Brind

**Editorial Director** Peter Fiennes
**Series Editor** Ruth Jarvis
**Deputy Series Editor** Jonathan Cox
**Guides Co-ordinator** Jenny Noden

## Design

**Group Art Director** John Oakey
**Art Director** Mandy Martin
**Art Editor** Scott Moore
**Designers** Benjamin de Lotz, Lucy Grant
**Picture Editor** Kerri Littlefield
**Deputy Picture Editor** Olivia Duncan-Jones
**Picture Librarian** Sarah Roberts
**Scanning & Imaging** Dan Conway
**Ad Make-up** Glen Impey

## Advertising

**Group Commercial Director** Lesley Gill
**Sales Director/Sponsorship** Mark Phillips
**International Sales Co-ordinator** Ross Canadé
**Advertisement Sales (Amsterdam)** Boom Chicago
**Advertising Assistant** Sabrina Ancilleri

## Administration

**Publisher** Tony Elliott
**Managing Director** Mike Hardwick
**Group Financial Director** Kevin Ellis
**Marketing Director** Christine Cort
**Marketing Manager** Mandy Martinez
**US Publicity & Marketing Associate** Rosella Albanese
**Group General Manager** Nichola Coulthard
**Production Manager** Mark Lamond
**Production Controller** Samantha Furniss
**Accountant** Sarah Bostock

**Features in this guide were written and researched by:**
**Introduction** Will Fulford-Jones. **History** Will Fulford-Jones (*For Pete's sake* Steve Korver). **Amsterdam Today** Willem de Blaauw (*Take it to the max* Laura Martz). **Architecture** Steve Korver. **Art** Will Fulford-Jones (*Faking it* Steve Korver). **Sex & Drugs** Will Fulford-Jones. **Accommodation** Todd Savage (*Get happy* Steve Korver). **Sightseeing** Steve Korver (*sights and museums reviews, Brits abroad* Will Fulford-Jones; *Of bodies and bloodstains* Carl Guderian; *Baby, let's play house* Laura Martz; *Plane and sinful* Isaac Davis). **Restaurants** Steve Korver (*Something fishy* Laura Martz). **Bars** Pip Farquharson (*Lining the stomach* Steve Korver). **Coffeeshops** Pip Farquharson. **Shops & Services** Kate Holder. **By Season** Steve Korver. **Children** Tim Muentzer. **Film** Willem de Blaauw (*Directors' cuts* Steve Korver). **Galleries** Steve Korver. **Gay & Lesbian** Willem de Blauuw, Pip Farquharson. **Music** Kees Bakhuyzen (*Brood swings* Steve Korver). **Nightclubs** Erin Tasmania & Jacek Rajewski. **Sport & Fitness** Tim Muentzer (*A whole new ballgame, Game on* Will Fulford-Jones). **Theatre, Comedy & Dance** Tim Muentzer (*Location, location, location...* Steve Korver). **Trips Out of Town** Will Fulford-Jones, Steve Korver. **Directory** Will Fulford-Jones, Steve Korver, Cathy Limb (*The euro files* Jonathan Cox).

**The Editor would like to thank:**
Sophie Blacksell, Nyx Bradley, Michael Bruynse and all at the Concert Inn, Tom Fulford-Jones, Sarah Guy, Kevin Hudson, Mariska Majoor at the Prostitution Information Center, Andrew Moskos, Paul Mowat, Jaro Renout, and all the contributors from previous editions, whose work formed the basis for parts of this book.

**Maps** by Mapworld, 71 Blandy Road, Henley on Thames, Oxon RG9 1QB. Amsterdam Transport map by Studio Olykan.

**Photography** by Hadley Kincade, except: pages 7, 10 and 16 (right) AKG London; pages 8, 14, 16 (left) and 17 Mary Evans Picture Library; pages 12 and 19 Hulton Archive; pages 25, 181, 183 and 201 Associated Press; pages 36, 37 and 38 (top) Rijksmuseum Foundation; page 38 (bottom) Museum van Loon; page 39 (top) Bijbels Museum; page 39 (bottom) Van Gogh Museum; page 40 (top) Stedelijk Museum of Modern Art; page 40 (bottom) CoBrA Museum of Modern Art; page 41 Museum of Fake Art; page 179 Netherlands Board of Tourism; page 215 Redferns; page 233 Empics; pages 253, 255, 268 and 265 Getty Images; pages 256, 258, 259, 261, 262, 263, 264, 266 and 270 Corbis Images. The following images were provided by the featured establishments: pages 182, 184 and 233.

# Contents

# Introduction

Everyone knows the clichés and the stereotypes. But exactly which clichés and stereotypes you remember best will depend on your own interests and predilections.

Those after peace and quiet keep in mind images of endless canals, free from the noise and smog of usual city traffic, dotted with impossibly welcoming corner cafés. Culture vultures picture a gallery on every street, bustling with a people who not only accept art but actively love it, feel proud of it. Lovers of kitsch can't wait to dash through fields rich with tulips to a horizon punctuated by rows of windmills, wherein a feast made entirely of cheese awaits. Smokers and tokers envisage a town as dense in the fug of dope as London once was with fog, a city permanently stoned. Naughty boys sit on seat's edge, tongues lollygagging at the thought of all the naked flesh perched in scarlet-lit windows, there for the taking if the money's right.

Like all clichés and stereotypes, they don't tell the whole story. But also like all clichés and stereotypes, they get through an awful lot of its chapters. The truth is that Amsterdam is a lot like the city held in popular imagination. It's beautiful, truly beautiful; a walk along the Keizersgracht or Prinsengracht, with their grand merchants' houses and disconcertingly traffic-free roads, will convince you of that. Art is everywhere, from the grand and globally

known Rijksmuseum to the smaller commercial galleries scattered around town. You want flowers, cheese and windmills? Well, say the Dutch, you can have flowers, cheese and windmills, and we'll even throw in a pair of clogs for good measure. And, yes, sex and drugs are available on tap.

But what the endless lists of Rembrandts and red lights, wasters and waterways can't adequately convey is the atmosphere of the place. Its laid-back, unhurried feel; the warmth of welcome offered by its locals; its eyelids-unbatted tolerance – nay, acceptance – of all kinds of everything. They also don't capture Amsterdam's exciting plans for the future. A walk around the dramatically regenerating waterfront, replete with stunning modern architecture and alive with activity, will show a city more than comfortable with the idea of progress. That said, periodic demonstrations against development in the historic centre illustrate that the locals understand and appreciate what they've got, and that the old school can sit side by side with the futuristic. Yet the stunning juxtaposition of old and new still has to be seen to be believed.

In other words, there are no words that'll pin this place down. Easy conjecture is defied: Amsterdam's a city that just demands to be experienced. Clichéd? Stereotypical? Yeah. But a whole lot more besides.

## ABOUT THE TIME OUT CITY GUIDES

The *Time Out Amsterdam Guide* is one of an expanding series of *Time Out* City Guides, now numbering over 35, produced by the people behind London and New York's successful listings magazines. Our guides are all written and updated by resident experts who have striven to provide you with all the most up-to-date information you'll need to explore the city or read up on its background, whether you're a local or a first-time visitor.

## THE LOWDOWN ON THE LISTINGS

Above all, we've tried to make this book as useful as possible. Addresses, telephone numbers, websites, transport information, opening times, admission prices and credit card details have all been included in the listings. And, as far as possible, we've given details of facilities, services and events, all checked and correct as we went to press. However, owners and managers can change

their arrangements at any time, and they often do. Before you go out of your way, we'd advise you to telephone and check opening times, ticket prices and other particulars. While every effort has been made to ensure the accuracy of the information contained in this guide, the publishers cannot accept responsibility for any errors it may contain.

## PRICES AND PAYMENT

We have noted where venues such as shops, hotels, restaurants, museums, attractions and the like accept the following credit cards: American Express (AmEx), Diners Club (DC), MasterCard (MC) and Visa (V). Many will also accept travellers' cheques, along with other, less widely held credit cards.

As this book was being completed in late 2001, many European countries – including the Netherlands – were gearing up for the introduction of the euro the following year. While many establishments in Amsterdam

were already able to give us their prices in euros, others were less prepared; regardless, there are likely to be some minor fluctuations in prices as Europe grows accustomed to its new currency.

In other words, the prices we've supplied should be treated as guidelines, not gospel. However, if prices vary wildly from those we've quoted, please write and let us know. We aim to give the best and most up-to-date advice, so we always want to know if you've been badly treated or overcharged.

### THE LIE OF THE LAND

Central Amsterdam divides fairly neatly into separate neighbourhoods. The Old Centre is split down the middle into the Old Side and the New Side, and is bordered by a ring of canals known as the *grachtengordel*. Outside these canals lie a number of smaller, primarily residential neighbourhoods, such as the Pijp, the Museum Quarter and the Jordaan. Each of these areas has its own section within the Sightseeing chapter, and these area designations have been used consistently throughout the book.

### TELEPHONE NUMBERS

The area code for Amsterdam is 020. All telephone numbers in this guide take this code unless otherwise stated. We have stipulated where phone numbers are charged at non-standard rates – such as 0800 numbers, which are free, and 0900, which are billed at premium rate. For more details on telephone codes and charges, *see p288*.

There is an online version of this guide, as well as weekly events listings for over 35 international cities, at www.timeout.com.

### ESSENTIAL INFORMATION

For all the practical information you might need for visiting the city – on such topics as visas, facilities and access for the disabled, emergency numbers, Dutch vocabulary and local transport – turn to the Directory chapter at the back of the guide. It starts on page 274.

### MAPS

Wherever possible, map references have been provided for every venue in the guide, indicating the page and grid reference at which it can be found on our street maps of Amsterdam. There are also overview maps of the city and of the Netherlands, and a map of Amsterdam's tram network. The maps start on page 302.

### LET US KNOW WHAT YOU THINK

We hope you enjoy the *Time Out Amsterdam Guide*, and we'd like to know what you think of it. We welcome tips for places that you consider we should include in future editions and take note of your criticism of our choices. There's a reader's reply card at the back of this book for your feedback, or you can email us at amsterdamguide@timeout.com.

## Sponsors & advertisers

# Teamsys.

## A WORLD OF SERVICES

Teamsys is always with you, ready to assure you all the tranquillity and serenity that you desire for your journeys, 365 days a year.

Roadside assistance always and everywhere, infomobility so not to have surprises, insurance... and lots more.

To get to know us better contact us at the toll-free number **00-800-55555555** .

...and to discover Connect's exclusive and innovative integrated infotelematic services onboard system visit us at:

www.targaconnect.com

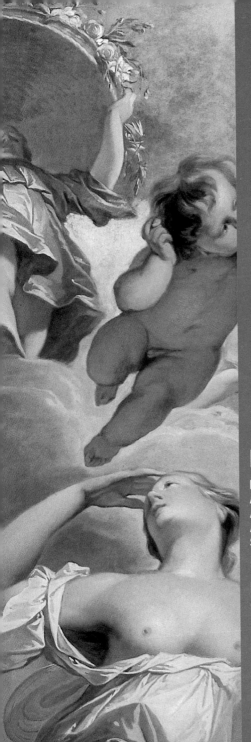

# In Context

# History

Political protests, religious strife and countless wars:
Amsterdam's history is a colourful one.

According to legend, Amsterdam was founded by two fishermen and a seasick dog, which ran ashore and threw up on the site of the city when their ship ran aground. The reality, sadly, is rather more mundane.

Although the Romans occupied other parts of Holland, they didn't reach the north. Waterlogged swampland was not the stuff on which empires were built, so the legions headed elsewhere in northern Europe. Archaeologists have found no evidence of settlement at Amsterdam before AD 1000, though there are prehistoric remains further east in Drenthe. Amsterdam's site, in fact, was partially under water for years, and the River Amstel had no fixed course until enterprising farmers from around Utrecht began to build dykes during the 11th century. Once the peasants had done the work, the nobility took over.

During the 13th century, the most important place in the newly reclaimed area was the tiny hamlet of Oudekerk aan de Amstel. In 1204, the Lord of Amstel built a castle nearby on what is now the outskirts of Amsterdam. After the

Amstel was dammed in about 1270, a village grew up on the site of what is now Dam Square, acquiring the name Aemstelledamme.

The Lord of Amstel at this time was Gijsbrecht, a pugnacious man continually in trouble with his liege lord, the Bishop of Utrecht, and with his nearest neighbour, Count Floris V of Holland. Tension increased in this power struggle when Floris bestowed toll rights – and some independence – on the young town in 1275. Events culminated in Floris's murder by Gijsbrecht at Muiden (where Floris's castle, Muiderslot, can still be seen). Gijsbrecht's estates were confiscated by the Bishop of Utrecht and given to the Counts of Holland. Amsterdam has remained part of the province of North Holland ever since.

In 1323, the Count of Holland, Floris VI, made Amsterdam one of only two toll points in the province for the import of brews. This was no trivial matter at a time when most people drank beer; drinking the local water, in fact, was practically suicidal. Hamburg had the largest brewing capacity in northern Europe, and within 50 years a third of that city's production was flowing through Amsterdam. Thanks to its position between the Atlantic and Hanseatic ports, the city increased its trade in an assortment of essential goods.

However, Amsterdam remained small. As late as 1425, the 'city' consisted only of a few blocks of houses with kitchen gardens and two churches, arranged along the final 1,000-metre stretch of the River Amstel and bordered by what are now known as Geldersekade, Kloveniersburgwal and Singel. Virtually all these old buildings – such as the Houtenhuis, still standing in the Begijnhof – were wooden, so fire was a constant threat; in the great fire of May 1452, three-quarters of the town was razed. Structures built after the fire had to be faced with stone and roofed with tiles or slates. These new architectural developments coincided with urban expansion, as – most notably – foreign commerce led to developments in shipbuilding.

### WAR AND REFORMATION

None of the wealth and glory of Amsterdam's Golden Age would have been possible without the turbulence that preceded it. During the 16th century, Amsterdam's population increased fivefold, from about 10,000 (a low level even by medieval standards) to 50,000 by 1600. The city's first major expansion accommodated the growth, but people flocked to the booming city to find poverty, disease and squalor in the hastily built working-class quarters. Local merchants, however, weren't complaining: during the 1500s, the city started to emerge as one of the world's major trading powers.

Amsterdam may have been almost autonomous as a chartered city, but on paper it was still subject to absentee rulers. Through the intricate and exclusive marriage bureau known as the European aristocracy, the Low Countries (the Netherlands and Belgium) had passed into the hands of the Catholic Austro-Spanish House of Habsburg. The Habsburgs were the mightiest monarchs in Europe and Amsterdam was a comparative backwater among their European possessions, but events in the 16th century soon gave the city a new prominence.

## 'Drunkenness and immorality were punishable by a spell in a house of correction.'

Amsterdam's burgeoning status as a trade centre led to the import of all kinds of radical religious ideas that were flourishing throughout northern Europe at the time, encouraged by Martin Luther's audacious condemnation of the all-powerful Catholic Church in 1517. Though Luther's beliefs failed to catch on with locals, many people were drawn to the austere creeds of the Anabaptists and, later, Calvin. When they first arrived from Germany in about

River of tears: the Anabaptists were persecuted as heretics.

# Captain Kerk

In early medieval society, the Catholic Church permeated every aspect of life throughout Europe, and Amsterdam was no exception. Contemporary chronicles show that the city became an independent parish before 1334. Documents dating from this period also contain the first recorded references to the Oude Kerk (or 'old church').

As Amsterdam expanded, more and more cloisters cropped up around the city: at one point, 18 were dotted around the tiny urban enclave, though the only remaining example is the Begijnhof, just off Spui. Their proliferation is thought, in part, to be down to the inspirational effect of the 'miracle'

of 1345. A dying man was given the last sacrament, which he then vomited up into a fire. However, the host emerged unscathed and, remarkably, the man recovered. The cloisters were to become Amsterdam's principal source of social welfare, providing hospital treatment and acting as orphanages, at least until the Protestant elite – which took over the city after the Reformation – obliterated every trace of popery.

The Heiligeweg (Holy Way) was the road within the city that led to the chapel on Rokin close to where the miracle took place. Its length – roughly 70 metres – is an indication of just how small Amsterdam then was.

1530, the Catholic city fathers tolerated the Anabaptists. But when they seized the Town Hall in 1534 during an attempt to establish a 'New Jerusalem' on the River Amstel, the leaders were arrested and executed, signalling an unparalleled period of religious repression: 'heretics' were burned at the stake on the Dam.

After the Anabaptists were culled, Calvinist preachers arrived in the city both directly from Geneva, where the movement started, and via France. The arrival of the sober Calvinists caused a transformation. In 1566, religious discontent erupted into what became known as the Iconoclastic Fury. This spontaneous uprising led to the sacking of many churches and monasteries. Amsterdam's Zuiderkerk was allocated to the Calvinists, and Philip II of Spain sent an army to suppress the heresy.

## ALTERED STATES

The Eighty Years' War (1568-1648) between the Habsburgs and the Dutch is often seen as a struggle for religious freedom, but there was more to it than that. The Dutch were, after all, looking for political autonomy from an absentee king who represented a continual drain on their coffers. By the last quarter of the 16th century, Philip II of Spain was fighting wars against England and France, in the East against the Ottoman Turks, and in the New World for control of his colonies. The last thing that he needed was a revolt in the Low Countries.

Amsterdam toed the Catholic line during the revolt, supporting Philip II until it became clear he was losing. Only in 1578 did the city patricians side with the rebels, led by the first William of Orange. The city and William then combined to expel the Catholics and dismantle their institutions in what came to be called the

Alteration. A year later, the Protestant states of the Low Countries united in opposition to Philip when the first modern-day European Republic was born at the Union of Utrecht. The Republic of Seven United Provinces was made up of Friesland, Gelderland, Groningen, Overijssel, Utrecht, Zeeland and Holland. Though lauded as the start of the modern Netherlands, it wasn't the unitary state that William of Orange had wanted, but rather a loose federation with an impotent States General assembly.

Each province appointed a Stadhouder (or viceroy), who commanded the Republic's armed forces and had the right to appoint some of the cities' regents or governors. The Stadhouder of each province sent delegates to the assembly, held at the Binnenhof in the Hague. The treaty enshrined freedom of conscience and religion, apart from for Catholics (at least until the Republic's end in 1795).

## CALVIN AND NOBS

From its earliest beginnings, Amsterdam had been governed by four Burgomasters – mayors, basically – and a council representing citizens' interests. By 1500, though, city government had become an incestuous business: the city council's 36 members were appointed for life, 'electing' the mayors from their own ranks. Selective intermarriage meant that the city was, in effect, governed by a handful of families. When Amsterdam joined the rebels in 1578, the only change in civic administration was that the Catholic elite was replaced by a Calvinist faction comprising equally wealthy families.

However, social welfare was transformed. Formerly the concern of the Catholic Church, welfare under the Calvinists was incorporated into government. The Regents, as the Calvinist elite became known, took over the convents and monasteries, starting charitable organisations such as orphanages. But the Regents' work ethic and abstemious way of life would not tolerate any kind of excess: crime, drunkenness and immorality were all punishable offences.

During the two centuries before the Eighty Years' War, Amsterdam had developed a powerful maritime force. Even so, it remained overshadowed by Antwerp until 1589, when that city fell to the Spanish. In Belgium, the Habsburg Spanish had adopted siege tactics, leaving Amsterdam unaffected by the hostilities and free to benefit from the blockades suffered by rival ports. Thousands of refugees fled north, among them some of Antwerp's most prosperous Protestant and Jewish merchants. These refugees brought the skills, the gold and, famously, the diamond industry that would soon lead to Amsterdam becoming the greatest trading city in the world.

### THE GOLDEN AGE

European history seems to be littered with Golden Ages, but in Amsterdam's case, the first six decades of the 17th century deserve the title. The small city on the Amstel came to dominate world trade and establish important colonies, resulting in a population explosion and a frenzy of urban expansion in Amsterdam: the girdle of canals was one of the great engineering feats of that century. This all happened while the country was at war with Spain and presided over not by kings, but by businessmen.

The East India Company doesn't have much of a ring to it, but the name of the Verenigde Oost Indische Compagnie (VOC), the world's first transnational company, loses something in translation. The VOC was created by a States General charter in 1602 to finance the wildly expensive and hellishly dangerous voyages to the East. Drawn by the potential fortunes to be made out of trade in spices and silk, the shrewd Dutch saw sense in sending out merchant fleets, but they also knew that one disaster could leave an individual investor penniless. As a result, the main cities set up trading 'chambers', which evaluated the feasibility (and profitability) of ventures, then sent ships eastwards. The power of the VOC was far-reaching: it had the capacity to found colonies, establish its own army, declare war and sign treaties.

The story of Isaac Lemaire illustrates just how powerful the VOC became. Lemaire fled to Amsterdam from Antwerp in 1589 and became a founder member of the VOC, buying a ƒ90,000 stake in the company (over €40 million in today's money). Later, after being accused of embezzlement, he quit and cast around for ways to set up on his own. However, the VOC had a

**William II** and Scots bride **Mary**. See p11.

monopoly on trade with the East via the Cape of Good Hope; at the time, there was no alternative route. Lemaire was not easily beaten, and heard Portuguese seamen claiming the Cape route was not the only passage to the East: they believed the fabulous spice islands of Java, the Moluccas and Malaya could also be reached by sailing to the tip of South America, where a strait would lead into the Pacific. In 1615, Lemaire financed a voyage, led by his son, that discovered the strait that bears his name.

While the VOC concentrated on the spice trade, a new company received its charter from the Dutch Republic in 1621. The Dutch West India Company (West Indische Compagnie), while not as successful as its sister, dominated trade with Spanish and Portuguese territories in Africa and America, and in 1623 began to colonise Manhattan Island. The settlement was laid out on a grid similar to Amsterdam's, and adopted the Dutch city's name. But although it flourished to begin with, New Amsterdam didn't last. After the Duke of York's invasion in

1664, the peace treaty between England and the Netherlands determined that New Amsterdam would change its name to New York and come under British control. The Dutch got Surinam as a feeble consolation prize.

Though commerce with the Indies became extensive, it never surpassed Amsterdam's European business: the city had soon become the major European centre for distribution and trade. Grain from Russia, Poland and Prussia, salt and wine from France, cloth from Leiden and tiles from Delft all passed through the port. Whales were hunted by Amsterdam's fleets, generating a flourishing soap trade, and sugar and spices from Dutch colonies were distributed to ports throughout Scandinavia and the north of Europe. All this activity was financed by the Bank of Amsterdam, which had been set up in the cellars of the City Hall by the municipal council as early as 1609. It was a unique initiative and led to the city being considered the money vault of Europe, its notes readily exchangeable throughout the trading world.

## WHERE THERE'S A WILL

The political structure of the young Dutch Republic was complex. When the Treaty of Utrecht was signed in 1579, no suitable monarch or head of state was found, so the existing system was adapted to fit new needs. The seven provinces were represented by a 'national' council, the States General. In addition, the provinces appointed a Stadhouder.

The obvious choice for Stadhouder after the treaty was William of Orange, the wealthy Dutchman who had led the rebellion against Philip II of Spain. William was then succeeded by his son, Maurits of Nassau, who was as successful against the Spanish as his father had been, eventually securing the Twelve Years' Truce (1609-21). Though each province could, in theory, elect a different Stadhouder, in practice they usually chose the same person. After William's popularity, it became a tradition to elect an Orange as Stadhouder. By 1641 the family had become sufficiently powerful for William II to marry a British princess, Mary Stuart. It was their son, William III, who set sail in 1688 to accept the throne of England in the so-called Glorious Revolution.

But the Oranges weren't popular with everyone. The provinces' representatives at the States General were known as regents, and Holland's – and therefore Amsterdam's – regent was in a powerful enough position to challenge the authority and decisions of the Stadhouder. This power was exercised in 1650, in a crisis precipitated by Holland's decision to disband its militia after the Eighty Years' War with Spain. Stadhouder William II wanted the militia to be

maintained – and, importantly, paid for – by Holland, and in response to the disbandment, he got a kinsman, William Frederick, to launch a surprise attack on Amsterdam.

After William II died three months later, the leaders of the States of Holland called a Great Assembly of the provinces. Even though there was no outward resistance to the Williams' earlier attack on the city, the provinces – with the exception of Friesland and Groningen, which remained loyal to William Frederick – decided that there should be no Stadhouders, and Johan de Witt, Holland's powerful regent, swore no prince of Orange would ever become Stadhouder again. This became law in the Act of Seclusion of 1653.

During this era, Amsterdam's ruling assembly, the Heren XLVIII (a sheriff, four mayors, a 36-member council and seven jurists), kept a firm grip on all that went on both within and without the city walls. Though this system was self-perpetuating, with the mayors and the council coming from a handful of prominent families, these people were merchants rather than aristocrats, and anyone who made enough money could, in theory, become a member.

The less elevated folk – the craftsmen, artisans and shopkeepers – were equally active in maintaining their position. A guild system had developed in earlier centuries, linked to the Catholic Church, but under the new order, guilds were independent organisations run by their members. The original Amsterdammers – known as *poorters* from the Dutch for 'gate', as they originally lived within the gated walls of the city – began to see their livelihoods being threatened by an influx of newcomers who were prepared to work for lower wages.

Things came to a head when the shipwrights began to lose their trade to competitors in the nearby Zaan region and protested. The shipwrights' lobby was so strong that the city regents decreed Amsterdam ships had to be repaired in Amsterdam yards. This kind of protectionism extended to almost all industrial sectors in the city and effectively meant most crafts became closed shops. Only poorters, or those who had married poorters' daughters, were allowed to join a guild, thereby protecting Amsterdammers' livelihoods and, essentially, barring outsiders from joining their trades.

## GROWING PAINS

Though Amsterdam's population had grown to 50,000 by 1600, this was nothing compared with the next 50 years, when it ballooned fourfold. Naturally, the city was obliged to expand to fit its new residents. The most elegant of the major canals circling the city centre was Herengracht (Lords' Canal): begun in 1613, this was where many of the Heren XLVIII had their homes. So there would be no misunderstanding about who was most important, Herengracht was followed further out by Keizersgracht (Emperors' Canal) and Prinsengracht (Princes' Canal). Immigrants were housed more modestly in the Jordaan.

Despite the city's wealth, famine hit Amsterdam with dreary regularity in the 17th century. Guilds had benevolent funds set aside for their members in times of need, but social welfare was primarily in the hands of the ruling merchant class. Amsterdam's elite was noted for its philanthropy, but only poorters were

eligible for assistance: even they had to fall into a specific category, described as 'deserving poor'. Those seen as undeserving were sent to a house of correction. The initial philosophy behind them had been idealistic: that hard work would produce useful citizens. But soon, the institutions became little more than prisons.

Religious freedom was still not what it might have been, either. As a result of the Alteration of 1578, open Catholic worship was banned in the city during the 17th century, and Catholics were forced to practise in secret. Some Catholics started attic churches, which are exactly what

# For Pete's sake

Hoping to find the means and techniques to drag his rotting corpse of a Russian Empire into the modern world, Peter the Great (1672-1725) came to Holland as 'a student in search of teachers' in 1697, when Amsterdam was near its pinnacle of prestige as the world's capital of imperialistic commerce and culture. Although he only stayed eight months, he left with a fine training as ship's carpenter, an awareness of the importance of a mercantile economy and religious tolerance, and huge collections of artworks and curiosities. Perhaps most importantly, though, he garnered reassurance that it was possible to build a city on a bog; he later built St Petersburg on such a site, following Amsterdam's lead.

Although Pete's plan to learn shipbuilding in the famed shipyards of Zaandam was foiled when he was mobbed by groupies, Burgomaster Nicolas Witsen arranged for him to learn the trade in Amsterdam's usually private VOC shipyards. He refused special treatment: living simply, cooking his own meals and refusing to answer to any name other than 'Carpenter Peter'. While building a 100-foot frigate, he found time to run Russia from afar. But all this graft didn't stop Pete from unwinding in style. He threw a right royal party when he heard of the slaughtering of the Turkish army at Zenta. And his dictatorial tendencies had to be reined in by Witsen on occasions when he thought to execute some wayward lackeys in his entourage.

Pete also tirelessly visited all the great minds of the time, hoping to lure an army of Dutch architects, inventors and scientists to come back to Russia with him. He took up dentistry and surgery as hobbies (and was only too willing to practise on servants), observed sperm under the just-invented microscope of Anton van Leeuwenhoek, hung out with his hero William of Orange, learned how to make slippers and repair his own clothes, and ended most nights as a regular at a whole range of taverns.

As a seven-foot giant of a man, it's also not surprising that Peter became fascinated with the collection of preserved freaks belonging to Frederik Ruysch. Acclaimed as the greatest anatomist and preserver of body-bits of all time, Ruysch was not just content with potting parts in brine and suspending Siamese foetuses in solution: he also constructed moralistic 3-D collages with gall and kidney stones piled up to suggest landscape, dried arteries and veins woven into lush shrubberies and testicles crafted into pottery, scenes that were then animated with skeletal foetuses. After kissing the forehead of a preserved baby, Peter paid Ruysch ƒ30,000 (around €13,500) for the complete collection. With a subsidiary of St Petersburg's Hermitage museum planned to open in Amsterdam in 2006, it can only be hoped that this and other souvenirs will return to their hometown for a visit.

their name suggests: of those set up during the 1600s, the Museum Amstelkring has preserved Amsterdam's only surviving example – Our Lord in the Attic – in its entirety.

## DECLINE AND FALL

Though Amsterdam remained one of the wealthiest cities in Europe until the early 19th century, its dominant trading position was lost to England and France after 1660. The United Provinces then spent a couple of centuries bickering about trade and politics with Britain and the other main powers. Wars were frequent: major sea conflicts included battles against the Swedes and no fewer than four Anglo-Dutch wars, from which the Dutch came off worse. It wasn't that they didn't win any wars; more that the small country ran out of men and money.

Despite – or perhaps because of – its history with the Orange family, Amsterdam became the most vocal opponent of the family's attempt to acquire kingdoms, though it supported William III when he crossed the sea to become King of England in 1688. The city fathers believed a Dutchman on their rival's throne could only be an advantage, and for a while they were proved right. However, William was soon back in Amsterdam looking for more money to fight more wars, this time against France.

The admirals who led the wars against Britain are Dutch heroes, and the Nieuwe Kerk has monuments to admirals Van Kinsbergen (1735-1819), Bentinck (1745-1831) and, most celebrated of all, Michiel de Ruyter (1607-76). The most famous incident, although not prominent in British history books, occurred during the Second English War (1664-72), when de Ruyter sailed up the Thames to Chatham, stormed the dockyards and burnt the *Royal Charles*, the British flagship, as it lay at anchor. The *Royal Charles*'s coat of arms was stolen, and is now displayed in the Rijksmuseum.

Despite diminished maritime prowess, Amsterdam retained the highest standard of living of all Europe until well into the 18th century. The Plantage district was a direct result of the city's prosperity, and tradesmen and artisans flourished: their role in society can still be gauged by the intricate shapes and carvings on gablestones.

The Dutch Republic also began to lag behind the major European powers in the 18th century. The Agricultural and Industrial Revolutions didn't get off the ground in the Netherlands until later: Amsterdam was nudged out of the shipbuilding market by England, and its lucrative textile industry was lost to other provinces. However, the city managed to exploit its position as the financial centre of the world

until the final, devastating Anglo-Dutch War (1780-84). The British hammered the Dutch merchant and naval fleets, crippling the profitable trade with their Far Eastern colonies.

The closest the Dutch came to the Republican movements of France and the United States was with the Patriots. During the 1780s, the Patriots managed to shake off the influence of the Stadhouders in many smaller towns, but in 1787 they were foiled in Amsterdam by the intervention of the Prince of Orange and his brother-in-law, Frederick William II, King of Prussia. Hundreds of Patriots then fled to exile in France, where their welcome convinced them that Napoleon's intentions towards the Dutch Republic were benign. In 1795, they returned, backed by a French army of 'advisers'. With massive support from Amsterdam, they celebrated the new Batavian Republic.

## 'In the Jordaan, riots broke out regularly, canals were used as cesspits and the mortality rate was high.'

It sounded too good to be true, and it was. According to one contemporary, 'the French moved over the land like locusts'. Over $f$100 million (about €50 million today) was extracted from the Dutch, and the French also sent an army, 25,000 of whom had to be fed, equipped and billeted by their Dutch 'hosts'. Republican ideals seemed hollow when Napoleon installed his brother Louis, as King of the Netherlands in 1806, and the symbol of Amsterdam's mercantile ascendancy and civic pride, the City Hall of the Dam, was requisitioned as the royal palace. Even Louis was disturbed by the impoverishment of a nation that had been Europe's most prosperous. However, after Louis had allowed Dutch smugglers to break Napoleon's blockade of Britain, he was forced to abdicate in 1810 and the Low Countries were absorbed into the French Empire.

Even so, government by the French wasn't an unmitigated disaster for the Dutch. The foundations of the modern state were laid in the Napoleonic period, and a civil code introduced. However, trade with Britain ceased, and the cost of Napoleon's wars prompted the Dutch to join the revolt against France. After Napoleon's defeat, Amsterdam became the capital of a constitutional monarchy, incorporating what is now Belgium; William VI of Orange was crowned King William I in 1815. But though the Oranges still reigned in the northern provinces, the United Kingdom of the Netherlands, as it then existed, lasted only until 1830.

## BETWEEN THE OCCUPATIONS

When the French were finally defeated and left Dutch soil in 1813, Amsterdam emerged as the capital of the new kingdom of the Netherlands but very little else. With its coffers depleted and its colonies occupied by the British, Amsterdam would have to fight hard for recovery.

The fight was made tougher by two huge obstacles. For a start, Dutch colonial assets had been reduced to present-day Indonesia, Surinam and the odd island in the Caribbean. Just as important, though, was the fact that the Dutch were slow to join the Industrial Revolution. The Netherlands had few natural resources to exploit and business preferred to use the power of sail. Add to this the fact that Amsterdam's opening to the sea, the Zuider Zee, was too shallow for the new steamships and it's easy to see how the Dutch were forced to struggle.

Prosperity, though, returned to Amsterdam after the 1860s. The city adjusted its economy, and its trading position was improved by the building of two canals. The opening of the Suez Canal in 1869 sped up the passage to the Orient and led to an increase in commerce. But what the city needed most was easy access to the major shipping lanes of northern Europe. When it was opened in 1876, the Noordzee Kanaal (North Sea Canal) enabled Amsterdam to take advantage of German industrial trade and to become the Netherlands' greatest shipbuilding port again, at least temporarily. Industrial machinery was introduced late to Amsterdam. However, by the late 19th century, the city had begun to modernise production of the luxury goods for which it would become famous: chocolates, cigars, beer and cut diamonds.

Of course, not all of Amsterdam's trade was conducted on water, and the city finally got a major rail link and a new landmark in 1889. Centraal Station was designed by PJH Cuypers in 1876, and was initially intended to be in the Pijp. When it was decided that the track should instead run along the Zuider Zee, separating the city from the lifeblood of its seafront, a deluge of objections – ultimately overriden – ensued.

There was also controversy when the Rijksmuseum was situated at what was then the fringe of the city, and about the selection of Cuypers as its architect. The result was, like Centraal Station, uniquely eclectic and led to the museum attracting ridicule as a 'cathedral of the arts'. Still, the city's powers consolidated Amsterdam's position at the forefront of Europe with the building of a number of landmark structures such as the Stadsschouwburg (in 1894), the Stedelijk Museum (1895) and the Tropen Institute (1926). The city's international standing had soon improved to such a point that, in 1928, it hosted the Olympics.

The 1928 **Olympic Games**: a world stage for the reinvigorated Netherlands.

# Diamond geezers

The history of the diamond trade in Amsterdam is also, in some small way, the history of social change in the city. The first records of the industry in Amsterdam date back to 1586; latterly, fabulous stones such as the Koh-i-Noor (Mountain of Light), one of the British crown jewels, were cut by an Amsterdammer.

But as the industry was dependent upon the discovery of rare stones, it was in a constant state of flux. In the early 1870s, diamond cutters could light cigars with ƒ10 notes (the average weekly wage for the rest of the workforce was ƒ8). A decade later, the city prohibited diamond workers from begging naked in the streets. Thankfully for the impoverished workers, however, the working classes had become more politicised in the intervening years, and the ideas behind the old guild system took on a new resonance. Funds were established to protect diamond workers during slumps, a movement that led to the formation of the first Dutch trade union.

In the early days of the union movement, socialists and the upper classes coexisted relatively harmoniously, but by the 1880s things were changing. The movement found an articulate leader in Ferdinand Domela

Nieuwenhuis, who set up a political party, the Social Democratic Union. The SDU faded into obscurity after a split in 1894, but a splinter group, the Social Democratic Labour Party (SDAP), won the first ever socialist city-council seat for the diamond workers' union chief, Henri Polak, in 1901. The SDAP went on to introduce the welfare state after World War II.

## NEW DEVELOPMENTS

Amsterdam's population had stagnated at 250,000 for two centuries after the Golden Age, but between 1850 and 1900 it more than doubled. The increased labour force was needed to meet the demands of a revitalised economy, but the major problem was how to house the new workers. Today, the old inner city quarters are desirable addresses, but they used to be the homes of Amsterdam's poor. The picturesque Jordaan, where regular riots broke out in the 1930s, was occupied primarily by the lowest-paid workers, canals were used as cesspits and the mortality rate was high. Around the centre, new developments – the Pijp, Dapper and Staatslieden quarters – were built: they weren't luxurious, but at least they had simple lavatory facilities. Wealthier city-dwellers, meanwhile, found elegance and space in homes constructed around Vondelpark and in the south of the city.

The city didn't fare badly in the first two decades of the 20th century, but Dutch neutrality during World War I brought problems. While the elite lined their pockets selling arms, the poor were confronted with

food shortages. In 1917, with food riots erupting, especially in the Jordaan, the city had to open soup kitchens and introduce rationing. The army was called in to suppress another outbreak of civil unrest in the Jordaan in 1934. This time the cause was mass unemployment, endemic throughout the industrialised world after the Wall Street Crash of 1929.

Unfortunately, the humiliation of means testing for unemployment benefit meant that many families suffered in hungry silence. Many Dutch workers even moved to Germany where National Socialism was creating new jobs. At home, Amsterdam initiated extensive public works under the 1934 General Extension Plan, whereby the city's southern outskirts were developed for public housing. The city was just emerging from the Depression by the time the Nazis invaded in May 1940.

## WORLD WAR II

Amsterdam endured World War II without being flattened by bombs, but nonetheless its buildings, infrastructure, inhabitants and morale were reduced to a terrible state by the

Graphic depictions of the Holocaust: Nazi propaganda (centre) and local Jewish press.

occupying Nazi forces. The Holocaust also left an indelible scar on a city whose population in 1940 was ten per cent Jewish.

Early in the morning of 10 May 1940, German bombers mounted a surprise attack on Dutch airfields and military barracks in order to destroy the Dutch Air Force. The government and people had hoped that the Netherlands could remain neutral, as they had in World War I, so the armed forces were unprepared for war. Though the Dutch aimed to hold off the Germans until the British and French could come to their assistance, their hope was in vain. Queen Wilhelmina fled to London to form a government in exile, leaving Supreme Commander Winkelman in charge. But after Rotterdam was destroyed by bombing and the Germans threatened other cities with the same treatment, Winkelman gave up the ghost on 14 May. The Dutch colonies of Indonesia and New Guinea were then invaded by the Japanese in January 1942. After their capitulation on 8 March, Dutch colonials were imprisoned in Japanese concentration camps.

During the war, Hitler appointed Austrian Nazi Arthur Seyss-Inquart as Rijkskommissaris (State Commissioner) of the Netherlands, and asked him to tie the Dutch economy to the German one and to Nazify Dutch society. Though it won less than five per cent of the

votes in the 1939 elections, the National Socialist Movement (NSB) was the largest fascist political party in the Netherlands, and was the only Dutch party not prohibited during the occupation. Its doctrine resembled German Nazism, but the NSB wanted to maintain Dutch autonomy under the direction of Germany.

During the first years of the war, the Nazis allowed most people to live relatively undisturbed. Rationing, however, made the Dutch vulnerable to the black market, while cinemas and theatres eventually closed because of curfews and censorship. Later, the Nazis adopted more aggressive measures: Dutch men were forced to work in German industry, and economic exploitation assumed appalling forms. In April 1943, all Dutch soldiers, who'd been captured during the invasion and then released in the summer of 1940, were ordered to give themselves up as prisoners of war. In an atmosphere of deep shock and outrage, strikes broke out, but were violently suppressed.

To begin with, ordinary citizens, as well as the political and economic elite, had no real reason to make a choice between collaboration and resistance. But as Nazi policies became more virulent, opposition to them swelled, and a growing minority of people were confronted with the difficult choice of whether to obey German measures or to resist. There were

**NEDERLAND IN DEN OORLOG ZOOALS HET WERKELIJK WAS**

**ONZE VERNEDERING II**

De Jodenvervolging ingezet - Pogrom in de hoofdstad - Hun ontrechting en uitplundering - Westerbork - Het ghetto van Warschau - Theresienstadt - Vernichtungslager. Minister van Staat, beneden de maat - Ned. Oostcompagnie - Vernedering van de boeren - Moffen en Medici.

A. W. BRUNA & ZOON UITGEVERSMAATSCHAPPIJ UTRECHT

several patterns of collaboration. Some people joined the NSB, while others intimidated Jews, got involved in economic collaboration or betrayed people in hiding or members of the Resistance. Amazingly, a small number even signed up for German military service.

The most shocking institutional collaborations were by the police, who dragged Jews out of their houses for deportation, and by Dutch Railways, which was paid for transporting Jews to their deaths. When the war was over, up to 150,000 people were arrested for collaborating. Mitigating circumstances – NSB members who helped the Resistance, for example – made judgments complicated, but, eventually, over 60,000 were brought to justice.

The Resistance was made up chiefly of Communists and, to a lesser extend, Calvinists. Anti-Nazi activities took several forms, with illegal newspapers keeping the population informed and urging them to resist the Nazi dictators. Underground groups took many shapes and sizes. Some spied for the Allies, others fought an armed struggle against the Germans through assassination and sabotage, and still others falsified identity cards and food vouchers. A national organisation took care of people who wanted to hide, and aided the railway strikers, Dutch soldiers and illegal workers being sought by the Germans, with

other groups helping Jews into hiding. By 1945, more than 300,000 people had gone underground in the Netherlands.

Worse was to follow towards the end of the war, when, in 1944, the Netherlands plunged into the Hunger Winter. Supplies of coal vanished after the liberation of the south and a railway strike, called by the Dutch government in exile in order to hasten German defeat, was disastrous for the supply of food. In retaliation for the strike, the Germans damaged Schiphol Airport and the harbours of Rotterdam and Amsterdam – foiling any attempts to bring in supplies – and appropriated everything they could. Walking became the only means of transport, domestic refuse was no longer collected, sewers overflowed and the population became vulnerable to disease.

To survive, people stole fuel: more than 20,000 trees were cut down and 4,600 buildings were demolished. Floors, staircases, joists and rafters were plundered, causing the collapse of many houses, particularly those left by deported Jews. Supplies were scarce and many couldn't afford to buy their rationing allowance, let alone the expensive produce on the black market. By the end of the winter, 20,000 people had died of starvation and disease, and much of the city was seriously damaged.

But hope was around the corner. The Allies had liberated the south of the Netherlands on 5 September 1944, Dolle Dinsdag (Mad Tuesday), and complete liberation came on 5 May 1945, when it became apparent that the Netherlands was the worst hit country in western Europe. In spite of the destruction and the loss of so many lives, there were effusive celebrations. But tragedy struck on 7 May, when German soldiers opened fire on a crowd who had gathered in Dam Square to welcome their Canadian liberators. Twenty-two people were killed.

### THE HOLOCAUST

'I see how the world is slowly becoming a desert, I hear more and more clearly the approaching thunder that will kill us,' wrote Anne Frank in her diary on 15 July 1944. Though her words obviously applied to the Jews, they were relevant to all those who were persecuted during the war. Granted, anti-Semitism in Holland had not been as virulent as in Germany, France or Austria. But even so, most – though not all – of the Dutch population closed its eyes to the persecution, and there's still a feeling of national guilt as a result.

The Holocaust arrived in three stages. First came measures to enforce the isolation of the Jews: the ritual slaughter of animals was prohibited, Jewish government employees were dismissed, Jews were banned from public places and, eventually, all Jews were forced to wear a yellow Star of David. (Some non-Jews wore the badge as a demonstration of solidarity.) Concentration was the second stage. From early 1942, all Dutch Jews were obliged to move to three areas in Amsterdam, isolated by signs, drawbridges and barbed wire. The final stage was deportation. Between July 1942 and September 1943, most of the 140,000 Dutch Jews were deported, via Kamp Westerbork. Public outrage at the first deportations provoked the most dramatic protests against the anti-Semitic terror, the impressive February Strike of 1941.

## 'The Dutch reverted to the virtues of a conservative society: decency, hard work and thrift.'

The Nazis also wanted to eliminate Dutch Gypsies: more than 200,000 European Gypsies, including many Dutch, were exterminated in concentration camps. Homosexuals, too, were threatened with extermination, but their persecution was less systematic: public morality acts prohibited homosexual behaviour, and gay pressure groups ceased their activities. In addition, men arrested for other activities were punished more severely if they were found to be gay. In Dutch educational history books, the extermination of Gypsies and homosexuals is still often omitted, but Amsterdam has the world's first memorial to persecuted gays: the Homomonument, which incorporates pink triangles in its design, turning the Nazi badge of persecution into a symbol of pride.

### THE POST-WAR ERA

The country was scarred by the occupation, losing ten per cent of all its housing, 30 per cent of its industry and 40 per cent of its production capacity. Though Amsterdam escaped the bombing raids that devastated Rotterdam, it bore the brunt of deportations: only 5,000 Jews, out of a pre-war Jewish population of 80,000, remained. Despite intense poverty and drastic shortages of food, fuel and building materials, the Dutch tackled the task of post-war recovery with a strong sense of optimism. In 1948, people threw street parties, firstly to celebrate the inauguration of Queen Juliana and, later, the four gold medals won by Amsterdam athlete Fanny Blankers-Koen at the London Olympics.

Some Dutch flirted briefly with communism after the war, but in 1948, a compromise was struck between the Catholic party, KVP, and the newly created Labour party, PvdA, and the two proceeded to govern in successive coalitions until 1958. Led by Prime Minister Willem Drees,

the government resuscitated social programmes and laid the basis for a welfare state. The Dutch now reverted to the virtues of a conservative, provincial society: decency, hard work and thrift.

The country's first priority, though, was economic recovery. The city council concentrated on reviving the two motors of its economy: Schiphol Airport and the Port of Amsterdam, the latter of which was boosted by the opening of the Amsterdam–Rhine Canal in 1952. Joining Belgium and Luxembourg in the Benelux also brought the country trade benefits, and the Netherlands was the first to repay its Marshall Plan loans. The authorities dusted off their pre-war development plans and embarked on rapid urban expansion. But as people moved to new suburbs, businesses moved into the centre, worsening congestion on the already cramped roads.

After the war, the Dutch colonies of New Guinea and Indonesia were liberated from the Japanese and pushed for independence. With Indonesia accounting for 20 per cent of their pre-war economy, the Dutch launched military interventions in 1947 and 1948. But these did not prevent the transfer of sovereignty to Indonesia on 27 December 1949, while the dispute with New Guinea dragged on until 1962 and did much to damage the Netherlands' reputation abroad. Colonial immigrants to the Netherlands, including the later arrival of Surinamese, and Turkish and Moroccan 'guest workers', now comprise 16 per cent of the population. Though poorer jobs and housing have usually been their lot, racial tensions were relatively low until the mid-'90s, with the brief rise of the neo-fascist CD party.

Although the economy and welfare state revived in the '50s, there was still civil unrest. Strikes flared at the port and council workers defied a ban on industrial action. In 1951, protesters clashed with police outside the Concertgebouw, angered by the appointment of a pro-Nazi as conductor. In 1956, demonstrators besieged the Felix Meritis Building, home of the Dutch Communist Party from 1946 until the late '70s, outraged at the Soviet invasion of Hungary.

In the late '40s and '50s, Amsterdammers returned to pre-war pursuits: fashion and celebrity interviews filled the newspapers and cultural events mushroomed. In 1947, the city launched the prestigious Holland Festival, while the elite held the Boekenbal, an annual event where writers met royalty and other dignitaries. New avant-garde movements emerged, notable among them the CoBrA art group, whose 1949 exhibition at the Stedelijk Museum of Modern Art caused an uproar, and the vijftigers, a group of experimental poets led by Lucebert. Many of these artists met in brown cafés around Leidseplein.

## FAREWELL TO WELFARE

The '60s was one of the most colourful decades in Amsterdam's history. There were genuine official attempts to improve society. The IJ Tunnel eased communications to north Amsterdam just as the national economy took off. There were high hopes for rehousing developments such as the Bijlmermeer (now Bijlmer), and influential new architecture from the likes of Aldo van Eyck and Herman Herzberger sprang up around town.

Yet the generous hand of the welfare state was being bitten. Discontent began on a variety of issues, among them the nuclear threat, urban expansion and industrialisation, the consumer society and authority in general. Popular movements similar to those in other west European cities were formed, but with a zaniness all their own. Protest and dissent have always been a vital part of the Netherlands' democratic process, yet the Dutch have a habit of keeping things in proportion; so, popular demonstrations took a playful form.

Discontent gained focus in 1964, when pranks around 't Lieverdje statue, highlighting political or social problems, kickstarted a new radical subculture. Founded by anarchist philosophy student Roel van Duyn and 'anti-smoke magician' Robert Jasper Grootveld, the Provos numbered only about two dozen, but were enormously influential. They had a style that influenced the anti-Vietnam demos in the US, and set the tone for Amsterdam's love of liberal politics and absurdist theatre. Their 'finest' hour came in March 1966, when protests about Princess Beatrix's wedding to ex-Nazi Claus van Amsberg turned nasty after the Provos let off a smoke bomb on the carriage route. A riot ensued, though not quite on the scale of that begun by striking construction workers three months later.

Foreign hippies flocked to the city, attracted by its tolerant attitude to soft drugs. Though the possession of up to 30 grams (one ounce) of hash wasn't decriminalised until 1976, the authorities turned a blind eye, preferring to prosecute dealers who also pushed hard drugs. But the focal points of hippie culture in the 1960s were the Melkweg and Paradiso, both of which emitted such a pungent aroma of marijuana that tokers could be smelt way over in Leidseplein. The city soon became a haven for dropouts and hippies from all over Europe until the end of the decade, when the Dam and

Anti-royalists raise a symbolically egalitarian bicycle in protest at police violence in 1966.

Vondelpark turned into unruly campsites and public tolerance of the hippies waned. In the '70s, Amsterdam's popular culture shifted towards a tougher expression of disaffected urban youth. Yet Vondelpark, the Melkweg and the Dam remain a mecca for both ageing and New Age hippies, even today.

Perhaps the most significant catalyst for discontent in the '70s – which exploded into civil conflict by the '80s – was housing. Amsterdam's compact size and historic city centre had always been a nightmare for its urban planners. The city's population increased during the '60s, reaching its peak (nearly 870,000) by 1964. The numbers were swelled by immigrants from the Netherlands' last major colony, Surinam, many of whom were dumped in the Bijlmermeer. It quickly degenerated into a ghetto, and when a plane crashed there in October 1992, the number of fatalities was impossible to ascertain: many victims were illegal residents and not registered.

## 'Squatters were supplanted by yuppies. Flashy cafés and galleries replaced the alternative scene.'

The Metro link to the Bijlmermeer is itself a landmark to some of Amsterdam's most violent protests. Passionate opposition erupted against the proposed clearance in February 1975 of the Jewish quarter of the Nieuwmarkt. Civil unrest culminated in 'Blue Monday', 24 March 1975, when police sparked clashes with residents and supporters. Police fired tear gas into the homes of those who refused to move out and battered down doors. Despite further violence, the first Metro line opened in 1977, with the Centraal Station link following in 1980, though only one of the four planned lines was completed.

City planners were shocked by the fervent opposition to their schemes for large, airy suburbs. It was not what people wanted: they cherished the narrow streets, the small squares and the cosy cafés. The public felt the council was selling out to big business, complaining that the centre was becoming unaffordable for ordinary people. In 1978, the council decided to improve housing through small-scale development, renovating houses street by street. But with an estimated 90,000 people (13 per cent of the population) still on the housing list in 1980, public concern grew.

Speculators who left property empty caused justifiable, acute resentment, which was soon mobilised into direct action: vacant buildings were occupied illegally by squatters. In March 1980, police turned against them for the first

time and used tanks to evict them from a former office building in Vondelstraat. Riots ensued, but the squatters came away victorious. In 1982, as Amsterdam's squatting movement reached its peak, clashes with police escalated: a state of emergency was called after one eviction battle. Soon, though, the city – led by new mayor Ed van Thijn – had taken control over the movement, and one of the last of the city's important squats, Wyers, fell amid tear gas in February 1984 and was pulled down to make way for a Holiday Inn. The squatters were no longer a force to be reckoned with, though their ideas of small-scale regeneration have since been absorbed into official planning.

### BACK TO BASICS

Born and bred in Amsterdam, Ed van Thijn embodied a new strand in Dutch politics. Though a socialist, he took tough action against 'unsavoury elements' – petty criminals, squatters, dealers in hard drugs – and upgraded facilities to attract new businesses and tourists. A new national political era also emerged, with the election in 1982 of Rotterdam millionaire Ruud Lubbers as leader of the then centre-right coalition government of Christian Democrats and right-wing Liberals (VVD). He saw to it that the welfare system and government subsidies were trimmed to ease the country's large budget deficit, and aimed to revitalise the economy with more businesslike methods. In February 1984, though, Van Thijn resigned to become Home Affairs Minister.

The price of Amsterdam's new affluence (among most groups, except the poorest) has been a swing towards commercialism. Yet evidence of his intentions can be seen in the casino, luxury apartments and shopping complex at the Leidseplein and the massive redevelopment of its docklands. Van Thijn also pushed through plans to build the Stadhuis-Muziektheater (City Hall-Opera House) complex, dubbed 'Stopera!' by its opponents.

The hordes of squatters were largely supplanted by well-groomed yuppies. Flashy cafés, galleries and nouvelle cuisine restaurants replaced the alternative scene and a mood of calm settled on the city. Still, a classic example of Dutch free expression was provoked by the city's mid-'80s campaign to host the 1992 Olympics. Amsterdam became the first city ever to send an (ultimately successful) official anti-Olympics delegation. It seems the city isn't ready to relinquish its rebel status just yet.

▶ For more on **maritime history**, *see p101*.
▶ For more on **Anne Frank**, *see p89*.
▶ For more on **the Jordaan**, *see p104*.

# Key events

## EARLY HISTORY

**1204** Gijsbrecht van Amstel builds a castle in the coastal settlement that is eventually to become Amsterdam.
**1270** The Amstel is dammed at Dam Square.
**1300** Amsterdam is granted city rights by the Bishop of Utrecht.
**1306** Work begins on the Oude Kerk.
**1313** The Bishop of Utrecht grants Aemstelledamme full municipal rights and leaves it to William III of Holland.
**1342** The city walls (*burgwallen*) are built.
**1421** The St Elizabeth's Day Flood occurs, as does Amsterdam's first great fire.
**1452** Fire destroys most wooden houses.
**1489** Maximilian grants Amsterdam the right to add the imperial crown to its coat of arms.

## WAR AND REFORMATION

**1534** Anabaptists try to seize City Hall but fail. A period of anti-Protestant repression begins.
**1565** William the Silent organises a Protestant revolt against Spanish rule.
**1566** The Beeldenstorm (Iconoclastic Fury) is unleashed. Protestant worship is made legal.
**1568** The Eighty Years' War with Spain begins.
**1577** The Prince of Orange annexes the city.
**1578** Catholic Burgomasters are replaced with Protestants in a coup known as the Alteration.
**1579** The Treaty of Utrecht is signed, allowing freedom of religious belief but not of worship.
**1589** Antwerp falls to Spain; there is a mass exodus to the north.

## THE GOLDEN AGE

**1602** The inauguration of Verenigde Oost Indische Compagnie (VOC).
**1606** Rembrandt van Rijn is born.
**1611** The Zuiderkerk is completed.
**1613** Work starts on the western stretches of Herengracht, Keizersgracht and Prinsengracht.
**1623** WIC colonises Manhattan Island; Peter Stuyvesant founds New Amsterdam in 1625.
**1642** Rembrandt finishes the *Night Watch*.
**1648** The Treaty of Münster is signed, ending war with Spain.
**1654** England declares war on the United Provinces.
**1667** England and the Netherlands sign the Peace of Breda.

## DECLINE AND FALL

**1672** England and the Netherlands go to war; Louis XIV of France invades.
**1675** The Portuguese Synagogue is built.

**1685** French Protestants take refuge after the revocation of the Edict of Nantes.
**1689** William of Orange becomes King William III of England.
**1696** Undertakers riot against funeral tax.
**1787** Frederick William II, King of Prussia, occupies Amsterdam.
**1795** French Revolutionaries are welcomed to Amsterdam by the Patriots. The Batavian Republic is set up and run from Amsterdam.
**1806** Napoleon's brother is made King.
**1810** King Louis is removed from the throne.
**1813** Unification of the Netherlands. Amsterdam is no longer a self-governing city.
**1815** Amsterdam becomes capital of Holland.

## BETWEEN THE OCCUPATIONS

**1848** The city's ramparts are pulled down.
**1876** Noordzee Kanaal links Amsterdam with the North Sea.
**1880s** Oil is discovered on the east coast of Sumatra. The Royal Dutch Company (Shell Oil) is founded.
**1883** Amsterdam holds the World Exhibition.
**1887** The Rijksmuseum is completed.
**1889** Centraal Station opens.
**1922** Women are granted the vote.
**1928** The Olympics are held in Amsterdam.
**1934** Amsterdam's population is 800,000.

## WORLD WAR II

**1940** German troops invade Amsterdam.
**1941** The February Strike ensues, in protest against the deportation of Jews.
**1944-5** 20,000 die in the Hunger Winter.
**1945** Canadian soldiers free Amsterdam.
**1947** Anne Frank's diary is published.

## THE POST-WAR ERA

**1966** The wedding of Princess Beatrix and Prince Claus ends in riots.
**1968** The IJ Tunnel opens.
**1976** Cannabis is decriminalised.
**1977** First Metrolijn (underground) opens.
**1980** Riots take place on Queen Beatrix's Coronation Day (30 April) in Nieuwe Kerk. This day becomes National Squatters' Day.
**1986** The controversial Stopera is built.
**1992** A Boeing 747 crashes into a block of flats in Bijlmermeer.
**1997** The euro is approved as a European currency in the Treaty of Amsterdam.
**1999** Prostitution is made legal after years of decriminalisation.
**2002** The guilder is dead; long live the euro.

# Amsterdam Today

Despite a new and attention-grabbing urban expansion, many of the same old challenges remain in Amsterdam.

It's a cliché, certainly. But ask a young visitor what they expect from Amsterdam and they'll likely offer up their hopes of finding themselves some sex, drugs and rock 'n' roll. There isn't much left of the latter these days, at least not since notorious local rock star Herman Brood jumped to his death from atop the Hilton in summer 2001... but hey, what a rock 'n' roll way to go. And as for the other ingredients: you won't have to look far to find them.

However, they're not the be-all and end-all. The canals are beautiful. Most places of interest are within walking distance. Then there are the locals: Amsterdammers are friendly and happy to show off their command of the English language. The arts are thriving, and there are many interesting bars, clubs and theatres. Oh, and then there's the Red Light District. While we're on the subject, you can walk into a coffeeshop and buy dope much like you'd buy a carton of milk. Mix all these aspects up, add in the fact that it's cheap both to live here and to visit when compared to the likes of London and Paris, and it's not hard to see why both visitors and inhabitants rate Amsterdam so highly.

## CRIME AND THE CITY SOLUTION

However, Amsterdam's main attraction, its liberal and liberated atmosphere, has also been at the root of its main sources of concern over the past few years. Thanks to the relaxed laws, Amsterdam attracts many people who think that they can get away with almost anything. But the overall feeling among locals is that because, in the recent past, a great deal of illegal activities were left unpunished by police, morals and values drained away, resulting in a large increase in acts of (petty) crime.

Although Amsterdam is a fairly safe city – only 47 murders were committed here in 2000 – recent figures show that robberies, assaults, car thefts and drug-related offences are on the rise. In 2000, 104,238 crimes were reported in Amsterdam, of which 65,125 were street crimes. Although the locals don't want Amsterdam to change into a no-fun city, they also realise that something has to be done.

Mayor Job Cohen, who took office at the beginning of 2001, is continuing the trail drawn out by his predecessor, Schelto Patijn, to clean up the city. A project called Streetwise ensures

Amsterdam's public transport has a few problems, but many walk or cycle anyway.

that, every weekend, portable toilets are set up around Leidseplein and Rembrandtplein to prevent partygoers relieving themselves against buildings. Those who still piss against a wall get a huge fine if caught (as, incidentally, do cyclists who bike through a red traffic light or ride down the pedestrian Leidsestraat). Drinking alcohol on the street is now forbidden in areas such as Waterlooplein, Albert Cuypstraat, Leidseplein and – despite its name – Marie Heinekenplein. As many problems and fights are alcohol-related, there's also been talk of banning happy hours throughout the city.

Having said that, festivities such as Queen's Day attract huge crowds and often pass without incident. Of course, there is a vast police presence there, but for many tourists it comes as a surprise that their attitude is relaxed and friendly; during Gay Pride, it's not unusual to see the cops having a little bop themselves.

### MYSTERY TRAIN

In 2001, the council finally started preparation work on the Noord–Zuidlijn, the new Metro line that will run from Amsterdam North via Centraal Station to the World Trade Centre in the south of the city. The council and the government both believe the new line is vital for the economic health of the city; it certainly seems likely to attract more business. Major companies such as ABN-AMRO have already moved into the area, while others – the ING Bank, for example – will follow as soon as their new building is completed. Then there are the benefits of the actual building of the line, estimated to create jobs for 10,000 people.

However, the line is not without its critics. Some have pointed out that Amsterdam has a perfectly adequate transport system. Moreover,

some claim that the construction will result in many buildings being demolished; and that a lot of businesses – particularly shops – will go broke because large swathes of the city, such as the area around the Albert Cuypmarkt, will be unreachable during the building of the line.

All these points could be moot, though. Despite the fact that initial construction work has been carried out, the council has trouble finding a company to build the tunnels: quotes from Dutch companies have been too high, and the council has been left with no option other than to look abroad. Because of the cash problems, there's been talk of shortening the line or building less stations along it. But given the vast investments already made, it's highly unlikely that the authorities will give up the ghost entirely at this late stage.

### ROUND, ROUND, GET AROUND

Quite aside from the problems with the Noord–Zuidlijn, other means of public transport in Amsterdam are hardly running smoothly. A 2001 survey showed that the Metro's existing fire escapes need to be redesigned. Meanwhile, the local transport authority, the GVB, is losing thousands of euros each day on fare-dodgers, with the honesty ticket-stamp system installed on the trams a major contributing factor.

More seriously, though, the GVB seems to be unable to make the transport network safe. Fights between passengers and drivers are a common occurrence, with pickpockets also a problem; tourists and day-trippers are the major targets. In 2001, the government agreed to spend €14 million over the next few years on safety measures, such as ticket booths in trams, CCTV on trams and buses, ticket barriers at Metro entrances and more ticket

inspectors. If the situation doesn't get any better, police may be posted on trams, buses and Metro trains.

However, in among the bad news, there has been the occasional ray of light. The trains linking Schiphol Airport with Centraal Station have long been a target for pickpockets, with the 300 reported crimes on this stretch each month just the tip of the iceberg. However, after police staked out the Schiphol run in late 2001, 33 people were arrested, and reports of pickpocket crimes were cut in half. While the stated police ambition to banish pickpockets altogether seems over-optimistic, any improvement is certainly cause for applause.

**BUILT TO LAST**

Amsterdam is also cleaning up the city. After renovations that improved the aesthetics and atmospheres (to varying degrees) on the once-seamy Nieuwendijk, the formerly ill-kempt Spui, the still-sleazy Zeedijk and the vastly improved Museumplein, Dam Square and Warmoesstraat have been the latest areas to get an overhaul.

# Take it to the max

Máxima. It's the perfect name for a prominent figure, a potential focus of public adoration. And it's a fitting moniker for someone who's stirred up so much feeling in perennially hard-to-excite Holland.

Despite her splendidly over-the-top name, Máxima Zorreguieta is neither a drag performer (though there are sure to be namesakes by now) nor a fashion designer. In fact, she's the bleached-blonde future queen of the Netherlands, set to marry Crown Prince Willem Alexander (*pictured*, with Máxima) in the Nieuwe Kerk in February 2002. And she's the exciting, photogenic royal-to-be the tabloids have been waiting for.

The woman Alex chose wasn't just a hot tamale: she was a hot potato. From the minute the engagement was announced in early 2001, debate raged. Máxima's father, Jorge Zorreguieta, was Argentina's agriculture minister during the distinctly iffy military dictatorship of the 1970s. Many Dutch were loath to link the royal family to someone from such a politically dubious lineage. Some anti-monarchists tried to rally support for protests, but more press than protestors ended up making appearances. And in any case, Máxima distanced herself from the Videla

regime's crimes in short order, and it was agreed that daddy would stay well away from the wedding ceremony.

The controversy did nothing to quell a wave of Maxploitation which, while it paled in comparison to the Princess Diana industry, stretched from cheap perfume and joke postage stamps to unimaginative ads that played on her name. In return, Máxima rapidly learned Dutch, lost the New York banker look (she worked for Deutsche Bank in Manhattan before the engagement) and began to appear in public in queenishly dowdy linen dresses and matching hats. In summer 2001, the publicity blitz began, with the future queen devoting her days to meet-and-greets and lectures from experts on agriculture and water management.

The wedding and attendant festivities are set for February 2002, in Amsterdam's Beurs van Berlage and Nieuwe Kerk, and hotels are sure to fill up well in advance. The Dutch already love Máxima more than her mother-in-law, Queen Beatrix; indeed, she began to top the most-popular-royal polls long before actually becoming one. And if nothing else, the ordinarily dull Dutch newspapers are finally able to publish photos of a good-looking person smiling.

The latter, a long and narrow thoroughfare in the Red Light District, is Amsterdam's oldest street, but for years was a foreboding and thoroughly scuzzy strip. Much as they did on nearby Zeedijk, the council has begun buying properties on Warmoesstraat in an effort to loosen the grip that criminal groups have in the area. While many coffeeshops, leather bars, porn stores and cheap hostels remain, it's now less seedy and run-down than it was before.

## 'The supply of housing doesn't meet demand, and prices are obscenely high.'

Still, the owners of the shops and bars are not happy, and are understandably outraged by the decision to close down the police station in Warmoesstraat and relocate it. In any case, despite the revamp, the alley is still frequented by hustling junkies, planeloads of stag partiers and assorted other lowlife: the contrast between the smartly redesigned street and its streetlife is indeed a big one. In an attempt to smarten up the area's image, many hotels and hostels have begun to refuse reservations from English groups; enough, they say, is enough.

Outside the city centre, there is a lot of building activity going on. Amsterdam is a small city, and city fathers have come to the conclusion that if they're going to attract more business, they simply have to expand it. Because of spiralling property prices and the fact that it's more or less impossible to reach the city centre by car (let alone park), more and more banks, insurance and telecommunications companies have decided to relocate. Take the Teleport area near Sloterdijk station, for example: once deserted, it's now home to an ever-increasing number of call centres and telecommunications companies, employing 17,000 workers. By the end of 2002, the locale will boast 560,000 square metres of office space.

Another booming area is in the south-east of the city, about 15 minutes from the centre of town by Metro. For the longest time, it was home only to drab high-rise housing. However, it's recently become a major business centre, complete with banks, telecom companies, law firms and accountants. It's attracted a lot of commercial investment, and is fast becoming a (slightly tacky) leisure paradise with a cineplex, a huge mall and a new music venue, with a new theatre in the pipeline. Whether the inner-city inhabitants will take a shine to it remains to be seen – many think it unlikely that people will travel out of town to get their leisure kicks when there's so much on their doorstep already – but it's certainly made the area a lot livelier.

## LIVE AND LET LIVE

Amsterdam is developing new residential areas in an attempt to reduce its housing crisis. The supply of housing in central Amsterdam, where houses are narrow and rarely more than four storeys high, doesn't come close to meeting the demand, and prices are obscenely high.

In the last few years, the eastern edge of Amsterdam next to Centraal Station has been appointed to create more housing space. After the ugly aesthetic mistakes of years gone by – the eyesore high-rises in south-east Bijlmermeer are truly brutal – the authorities made a point of making the blocks on Javakade and KNSM Eiland easy on the eye. And they've largely succeeded: the new buildings are often architecturally striking, especially when set against the waterfront locale, even if the apartments they contain are pretty pricey.

Though work in the area – known as the Eastern Docklands – carries on, it's already home to hip bars and restaurants. However, they're set against the new Passengers' Terminal, built to accommodate cruise ships. The local council is hoping that its presence, and the expected arrival of affluent tourists in town, will give the tourist trade a boost. At the moment, a great many of Amsterdam's visitors are cash-strapped backpackers whose holidays – and money – are spent wandering from coffeeshop to smart shop in a fug of dope.

On the other hand, long-time squat buildings such as the Silo, Vrieshuis Amerika and the Kalenderpanden have all been cleared in the past few years, their grounds sold to property developers in order that they can build new luxury flats. Many young and aspiring artists who had workshops in these evicted squats, along with collectives that ran restaurants, bars or special club nights, are determined to fight the council plans and are continuing trying to find new spaces for their quest. Their success, though, is hardly guaranteed.

Does this mean that Amsterdam is turning into a no-fun zone, a mini-Disneyland for mummy, daddy and their 2.4 kiddies? Is it goodbye to the edge that made the city famous and hello to clean-cut family fun? Fortunately not. All parties want Amsterdam to remain just as liberal and liberated as it is today, loved by locals and the tourists that visit each year. Worry not: the party ain't over. And knowing the locals, it won't be for a long while yet.

► For more on **Amsterdam transport**, see p274.
► For more on **Warmoestraat**, see p84.
► For more on **crime**, see p83.

# Architecture

With its Golden Age gabled houses and Eastern Docklands redevelopment, Amsterdam is a tantalising brick tease.

'The colours are strong and sad, the forms symmetric, the façades kept new,' wrote Eugène Fromentin, the 19th-century art critic, of Amsterdam. 'We feel that it belongs to a people eager to take possession of the conquered mud.' The treacherously soft soil upon which the merchants' town of Amsterdam is built put strictures on most attempts at monumental display. Thanks to the make-up of the land – combined with the Protestant restraint that characterised the city's early developments – it's not palaces and castles that are the architectural high points but, rather, warehouses, domestic architecture, the stock exchange and the City Hall.

Amsterdam's architectural epochs have followed the pulse of the city's prosperity. The decorative façades of wealthy 17th- and 18th-century merchants' houses still line the canals. A splurge of public spending in the affluent 1880s gave the city two of its most notable landmarks in **Centraal Station** and the **Rijksmuseum**. Conversely, social housing projects in the early 20th century stimulated the

innovative work of the Amsterdam School, while Amsterdam's late-'80s resurgence as a financial centre and transport hub led to an economic upturn and to thickets of bravura modern architecture on the outskirts of town.

Prime viewing time for Amsterdam architecture is late on a summer's afternoon, as the sun gently picks out the varying colours and patterns of the brickwork. Then, as twilight falls, the canal houses – most of them more window than wall – light up like strings of lanterns, and you get a glimpse of the beautifully preserved, frequently opulent interiors that lie behind the façades.

### MUD, GLORIOUS MUD

Amsterdam is built on reclaimed marshland, with a thick, soft layer of clay and peat beneath the topsoil. About 12 metres (39 feet) down is a hard band of sand, deposited 10,000 years ago during the Little Ice Age, and below that, after about five metres (16 feet) of fine sand, there is another firm layer, this one left by melting glacial ice after the Great Ice Age. A further

25 metres (82 feet) down, through shell-filled clay and past the bones of mammoths, is a third hard layer, deposited by glaciers over 180,000 years ago.

The first Amsterdammers built their homes on muddy mounds, making the foundations from tightly packed peat. Later, they dug trenches, filled them with fascines (thin, upright alder trunks) and built on those. But still the fruits of their labours sank slowly into the swamp. By the 17th century, builders were using longer underground posts and were rewarded with more stable structures, but it wasn't until around 1700 that piles were driven deep enough to hit the first hard sand layer.

The method of constructing foundations that subsequently developed has remained more or less the same ever since, though nowadays most piles reach the second sand level and some make the full 50-metre (164-foot) journey to the third hard layer. To begin, a double row of piles is sunk along the line of a proposed wall (since World War II, concrete has been used instead of wood). Then, a crossbeam is laid across each pair of posts, planks are fastened longitudinally on to the beams, and the wall is built on top. From time to time, piles break or rot, which is why Amsterdam is full of buildings that teeter precariously over the street, tilt lopsidedly or prop each other up in higgledy-piggledy rows.

### STICKS AND STONES

Early constructions in Amsterdam were timber-framed, built mainly from oak with roofs of rushes or straw. Wooden houses were relatively light and less likely to sink into the mire, but after two devastating fires (in 1421 and 1452), the authorities began stipulating that outer walls be built of brick, though wooden front gables were still permitted. In a bid to blend in, the first brick gables were shaped in imitation of their spout-shaped wooden predecessors.

Amsterdammers took to brick with relish. Granted, some grander 17th-century buildings were built of sandstone, while plastered façades were first seen a century later and reinforced concrete made its inevitable inroads in the 20th century. But Amsterdam is still essentially a city of brick: red brick from Leiden, yellow from Utrecht and grey from Gouda, all laid in curious formations and arranged in complicated patterns. Local architects' attachment to – and flair with – brick reached a zenith in the fantastical, billowing façades designed by the Amsterdam School early in the 20th century.

### TOUCH WOOD

Only two wooden buildings remain in central Amsterdam: one (built in 1460) in the quiet square of **Begijnhof** (No.34, known as the

**Houtenhuis**; *see p85*), and the other on Zeedijk. The latter, **In't Aepjen** (Zeedijk 1; *see p137*), was built in the 16th century as a lodging house, getting its name from the monkeys that impecunious sailors used to leave behind in payment. Though the ground floor dates from the 19th century, the upper floors provide a clear example of how, in medieval times, each wooden storey protruded a little beyond the one below it, allowing rainwater to drip on to the street rather than run back into the body of the building. Early brick gables had to be built at an angle over the street for the same reason, though it also allowed objects to be winched to the top floors without crashing against the windows of the lower ones. Wonky by design, in other words.

## 'Hendrick de Keyser's work gives Amsterdam's skyline an oriental appearance.'

Amsterdam's oldest building, though, is the **Oude Kerk** ('Old Church', Oude Kerksplein 23; *see p83*). It was begun in 1300, though only the base of the tower dates from then: over the ensuing 300 years, the church developed a barnacle crust of additional buildings, mostly in a Renaissance style with a few Gothic additions. Surprisingly, nearly all the buildings retain their original medieval roofs, making the church unique in the Netherlands. The only full Gothic building in town – in the style of towering French and German churches – is the **Nieuwe Kerk** (at Dam and Nieuwezijds Voorburgwal; *see p75*), still called the 'New Church' even though building work on it began at the end of the 14th century.

When gunpowder arrived in Europe in the 15th century, Amsterdammers realised that the wooden palisade that surrounded their settlement would offer scant defence, and so set about building a new city wall. Watchtowers and gates left over from it make up a significant proportion of remaining pre 17th-century architecture, though most have been altered over the years. The **Schreierstoren** (Prins Hendrikkade 94-95; *see p79*) of 1480, however, has kept its original shape, with the addition of doors, windows and a pixie-hat roof. The base of the **Munttoren** (Muntplein; *see p86*) originally formed part of the Regulierspoort, a city gate built in 1490. Another city gate from the previous decade, the **St Antoniespoort** (Nieuwmarkt 4) was converted into a public weighhouse (or 'Waag') in 1617, then further refashioned to become a Guild House. It's now **In de Waag**, a café-restaurant (*see p79 and p137*).

For old times' sake: **Oude Kerk**. *See p28.*

### DUTCH RENAISSANCE

A favourite 16th-century amendment to these somewhat stolid defence towers was the addition of a sprightly steeple. Hendrick de Keyser (1565-1621) delighted in designing such spires, and it is largely his work that gives Amsterdam's present skyline a faintly oriental appearance. He added a lantern-shaped tower with an openwork orb to the Munttoren, and a spire that resembled the Oude Kerk steeple to the **Montelbaanstoren** (Oudeschans 2), a sea-defence tower that had been built outside the city wall. His **Zuiderkerk** (Zuiderkerkhof 72; *see p95*), built in 1603, sports a decorative spire said to have been much admired by Christopher Wren. The appointment of De Keyser as city mason and sculptor in 1595 had given him free reign, and his buildings represent the pinnacle of the Dutch Renaissance style.

Since the beginning of the 17th century, Dutch architects had been gleaning inspiration from translations of Italian pattern books, adding lavish ornament to the classical system of proportion they found there. Brick façades were decorated with stone strapwork (scrolls and curls derived from picture frames and leather work). Walls were built with alternating layers of red brick and white sandstone, a style that came to be called 'bacon coursing'. The old spout-shaped gables were replaced with cascading step-gables, often embellished with vases, escutcheons and masks (before house numbers were introduced in Amsterdam in the 18th century, ornate gables and wall plaques were a means of identifying houses).

The façade of the **Vergulde Dolphijn** (Singel 140-42), designed by De Keyser in 1600 for Captain Banning Cocq (the commander of Rembrandt's *Night Watch*), is a lively mix of red brick and sandstone, while the **Gecroonde Raep** (Oudezijds Voorburgwal 57) has a neat step-gable, with truly riotous decoration featuring busts, escutcheons, shells, scrolls and volutes. However, De Keyser's magnificent 1617 construction, the **Huis Bartolotti** (Herengracht 170-72, now part of the Theatre Instituut; *see p88*), is the finest example of the style.

# By the numbers

### Tallest building
**Rembrandt Tower**, in the south near Amstel Station, tops them all at a height of 135 metres (411 feet).

### Oldest building
The **Oude Kerk**, on which building work started in 1300.

### Skinniest building
**Singel 166**, whose frontage is a mere 1.84 metres (5.5 feet) wide.

# We go out of our way so you don't have to.

**With 15 regional airports to choose from, you can fly to Amsterdam from your doorstep.**

Once you get there, you can then fly on to over 500 worldwide destinations with our network of partner airlines. To book, call 08705 074 074, visit us at www.klmuk.com, or go straight to your travel agent.

From all over the UK, to all over the world.

Aberdeen • Birmingham • Bristol • Cardiff • Edinburgh • Glasgow • Humberside • Leeds Bradf
London City, Heathrow and Stansted • Manchester • Newcastle • Norwich • Teesside

This decorative step-gabled style was to last well into the 17th century. But gradually a stricter use of classical elements came into play; the façade of the Bartolotti house features rows of Ionic pilasters, and it wasn't long before others followed where De Keyser had led. The Italian pattern books that had inspired the Dutch Renaissance were full of the less ornamented designs of Greek and Roman antiquity. This appealed to many young architects who followed De Keyser, and who were to develop a more restrained, classical style. Many, such as Jacob van Campen (1595-1657), went on study tours of Italy, and returned fired with enthusiasm for the symmetric designs, simple proportions and austerity of Roman architecture. The buildings they constructed during the Golden Age are among the finest Amsterdam has to offer.

### THE GOLDEN AGE

The 1600s were a boom time for builders as well as for businessmen. There was no way it could have been otherwise, as Amsterdam's population more than quadrupled during the first half of the century. Grand new canals were constructed, and wealthy merchants lined them with mansions and warehouses. Van Campen, along with fellow architects Philips Vingboons (1607-78) and his brother Justus (1620-98), were given the freedom to try out their ideas on a flood of new commissions.

Stately façades constructed of sandstone began to appear around Amsterdam, but brick still remained the most popular material. Philips Vingboons's **Witte Huis** (Herengracht 168, now part of the Theatre Instituut) has a white sandstone façade with virtually no decoration: the regular rhythm of the windows is the governing principle of the design. The house he built in 1648 at **Oude Turfmarkt 145** has a brick façade adorned with three tiers of classical pilasters – Tuscan, Ionic and Doric – and festoons that were characteristic of the style. However, the crowning achievement of the period was Amsterdam's boast to the world of its mercantile supremacy and civic might: namely, the Stad (City Hall) on the Dam, designed by Van Campen in 1648 and now known as the **Koninklijk Paleis** (*see p74*).

There was, however, one fundamental point of conflict between classical architecture and the requirements of northern Europe. For practical reasons, wet northern climes required steep roofs, yet low Roman pediments and flat cornices looked odd with a steep, pointed roof behind them. The architects solved the problem by adapting the Renaissance gable, with its multiple steps, into a tall, central gable with just two steps. Later, neck-gables were built

**Canal houses:** mansions fit for merchants.

with just a tall central oblong and no steps. The right angles formed at the base of neck-gables – and again at the step of elevated neck-gables – were often filled in with decorative sandstone carvings called claw-pieces.

On very wide houses, it was possible to construct a roof parallel to the street rather than end-on, making a more attractive backdrop for a classical straight cornice. The giant **Trippenhuis** (Kloveniersburgwal 29; *see p81*), built by Justus Vingboons in 1662, has such a design, with a classical pediment, a frieze of cherubs and arabesques, and eight enormous Corinthian pilasters. It wasn't until the 19th century, when zinc cladding became cheaper, that flat and really low-pitched roofs became feasible.

### THE 18TH CENTURY

Working towards the end of the 17th century, Adriaan Dortsman (1625-82) had been a strong proponent of the straight cornice. His stark designs – such as for the Van Loon house at

**Keizersgracht 672-4** – ushered in a style that came to be known as Restrained Dutch Classicism. It was a timely entrance. Ornament was costly, and by the beginning of the 18th century, the economic boom was over.

The merchant families were prosperous, but little new building went on. Instead, the families gave their old mansions a facelift or revamped the interiors. A number of 17th-century houses got new sandstone façades (or plastered brick ones, which were cheaper), and French taste – said to have been introduced by Daniel Marot, a French architect living in Amsterdam – became hip. As the century wore on, ornamentation regained popularity. Gables were festooned with scrolls and acanthus leaves (Louis XIV), embellished with asymmetrical rococo fripperies (Louis XV) or strung with disciplined lines of garlands (Louis XVI). The baroque grandeur of **Keizersgracht 444-6**, for example, hardly seems Dutch at all. Straight cornices appeared

# Back to school

Amsterdam is not really renowned for the monuments and palaces of past rulers and the ruling classes. Its Golden Age gabled houses were mere merchants' residences, while its other great architectural legacies were built for the working classes. The Amsterdam School, which peaked by 1925 and whose swoopy expressiveness is akin to a gentler version of Gaudí, worked with socialist vision in a time of prosperity.

While due credit can be given to the stonemasons who had practised non-geometrical brickwork when repairing the canals' sinking houses, it was Hendrik Berlage who formed the nexus of the movement. Not only did his work strip things down, rejecting all the neo-styles that had defined most 19th-century Dutch architecture, but he also provided the opportunity to experiment with new forms by coming up with Plan Zuid, an urban plan meant to provide housing for the working classes whose population had grown in the city since the Industrial Revolution.

Although the school was short-lived – it was forced to simplify within a decade when the money ran out, the Functionalism-obsessed De Stijl school started to diss the school's more self-indulgent tendencies, and its greatest proponent, Michel de Klerk, died – examples of the school's work remain. The Rivierenbuurt, Spaarndammerbuurt and

Concertgebouwbuurt, plus the area around Mercantorplein, all offer ample gazing opportunity; what follows, though, are some of the school's highlights.

Located along the waterfront, the eerie and epic **Scheepsvaarthuis** (Prins Hendrikkade 108-114) is generally considered to be the school's first work. Completed in 1916, it was the work of three big names: JM van der Mey, Piet Kramer and de Klerk. Among the school's hallmarks on show are obsessively complex brickwork, infinite and allegorical decorations (reflecting its use as offices for shipping companies) , sculptures and wrought-iron railings fused as one with the building.

Behind Westerpark lies the Spaarndammer neighbourhood, which sports the school's most frolicsome and bizarre work. The **Ship**, as locals like to call it, takes up a whole block bound by Zaanstraat, Hembrugstraat and Oostzaanstraat. Completed in 1919, it was commissioned by the Eigen Haard housing association and includes 102 homes and a school. Be sure to poke your head through the archway at Oostzaan 1-21, where you can see the courtyard and its central meeting hall, before swinging by **Poste Restante** next door (www.posterestante.nl; open 2-5pm Wed, Thur, Sun). This former post office is now an exhibition space with videos and computers even on narrow buildings, and became extraordinarily ornate: a distinct advantage, this, as it hid the steep roof that lay behind, with decorative balustrades adding to the deception. The lavish cornice at **Oudezijds Voorburgwal 215-17** is a prime example.

## ONE FOOT IN THE PAST

Fortunes slumped further after 1800, and during the first part of the century, more buildings were demolished than constructed. When things picked up after 1860, architects raided past eras for inspiration. Neo-classical, neo-Gothic and neo-Renaissance features were sometimes lumped together in the same building in mix-and-match eclectic style. The **Krijtberg church** (Singel 446) from 1881, for example, has a soaring neo-Gothic façade and a high, vaulted basilica, while the interior of AL van Gendt's **Hollandse Manege** (Vondelstraat 140), also 1881, combines the classicism of the Spanish Riding School in Vienna with a state-of-the-art iron and glass roof.

On the other hand, the **Concertgebouw** (Van Baerlestraat 98; *see p219*), a Van Gendt construction from 1888, borrows from the late Renaissance, with 1892's **City Archive** (Amsteldijk 67) little more than De Keyser revisited. But the period's most adventurous building is the **Adventskerk** (Keizersgracht 676), which crams in a classical rusticated base, Romanesque arches, Lombardian moulding and fake 17th-century lanterns.

The star architect of the period was PJH Cuypers (1827-1921), who landed the commissions for both the **Rijksmuseum** (Stadhouderskade 41; *see p107*) of 1877-85 and **Centraal Station** (Stationsplein), built from 1882 to 1889. Both are in traditional red brick, adorned with Renaissance-style decoration in sandstone and gold leaf. Responding to those who thought his tastes too catholic, Cuypers decided to organise each building according to a single coherent principle. This idea became the basis for modern Dutch architecture.

Sail of the century: the **Ship**. *See p32.*

that tell the tale of the school. While you're here, take a peek at the adjoining Spaarndammerplantsoen and Zaanhof.

However, the school's heartland is in Plan Zuid district, at the border of the Pijp and the Rivierenbuurt. The Josef Israelkade, betweeen 2e Van der Helststraat and Van Woustraat, is a pleasant stretch along the Amstelkanaal; enter PL Takstraat and circle Burg Tellegenstraat without forgetting to pop into the courtyard of **Cooperatiehof**. Socialist housing association de Dageraad ('the Dawn') allowed de Klerk and Kramer to do their hallucinatory best and employ their favourite sculptor, Hildo Krop. Kramer, incidentally, went on to design over 200 bridges; after visiting this area, you shouldn't have any problem recognising his work elsewhere in the city.

It's a different story elsewhere, though. Backtrack and cross the Amstelkanaal, and then walk down Waalstraat; here you'll find later examples of the school's work. Things are noticeably more restrained here, a fact primarily due to the necessary tightening of purse-strings. Nearby, on Vrijheidslaan and its side-streets, are some more classic school buildings, all freshly scrubbed and renovated.

Conclude your tour by heading to Roelof Hartplein, where a window seat at the Wildschut (*see p147*) affords a panorama

of school goodies. Look out for **House Lydia** (across the street at No.2), which served as home to Catholic girls; finished in 1927, it stands as one of the school's last constructs in which wacky window shapes and odd forms were still allowed.

## THIS IS THE MODERN WORLD

Brick and wood – good, honest, indigenous materials – appealed to Hendrik Petrus Berlage (1856-1934), as did the possibilities offered by industrial developments in the use of steel and glass. A rationalist, he took Cuypers' ideas a step further in his belief that a building should openly express its basic structure, with a modest amount of ornament in a supportive role. His **Beurs van Berlage** (Beursplein; *see p74*), built 1898-1903 – all clean lines and functional shapes, with the mildest patterning in the brickwork – was startling at the time, and earned him the reputation of being the father of modern Dutch architecture.

## 'After World War II, Functionalist ideology became an excuse for dreary, derivative eyesores.'

Apart from the odd shopfront and some well-designed café interiors, the art nouveau and art deco movements had little direct impact on Amsterdam, though they did draw a few wild flourishes: HL de Jong's **Tuschinski** cinema (Reguliersbreestraat 26; *see p192*) of 1918-21, for example, is a delightful piece of high-camp fantasy. Instead, Amsterdam architects developed a style of their own, an idiosyncratic mixture of art nouveau and Old Dutch using their favourite materials: wood and brick.

This movement, which became known as the Amsterdam School, reacted against Berlage's sobriety by producing whimsical buildings with waving, almost sculptural brickwork. Built over a reinforced concrete frame, the brick outer walls go through a complex series of pleats, bulges, folds and curls that earned the work the nickname 'Schortjesarchitectuur' ('apron architecture'). Windows may be trapezoid or parabolic; doors are carved in strong, angular shapes; brickwork is decorative and often polychromatic; and brick and stone sculptures are in abundance.

The driving force behind the school came from a two young architects, Michel de Klerk (1884-1923) and Piet Kramer (1881-1961). Commissions for social housing projects – one for the **Dageraad** (constructed around PL Takstraat, 1921-23), one for **Eigen Haard** (in the Spaarndammerbuurt, 1913-20) – allowed them to treat entire blocks as single units. Just as importantly, the pair's adventurous clients gave them freedom to express their ideas.

In the early 1920s, a new movement emerged that was the antithesis of the Amsterdam School. Developing on rather than reacting

against Berlage's ideas, the Functionalists believed that new building materials such as concrete and steel should not be concealed, but that the basic structure of a building should be visible. Function was supreme; ornament anathema. Their hard-edged concrete and glass boxes have much in common with the work of Frank Lloyd Wright in the USA, Le Corbusier in France and the Bauhaus in Germany.

Unsurprisingly, such radical views were not shared by everyone, and the period was a turbulent one in Amsterdam's architectural history. Early Functionalist work, such as 1937's **Round Blue Teahouse** (in Vondelpark) and the **Cineac Cinema** (Reguliersbreestraat 31) of 1934, has a clean-cut elegance, and the Functionalist garden suburb of **Betondorp** (literally, 'Concrete Town'), built between 1921 and 1926, is more attractive than the name might suggest. But after World War II, Functionalist ideology became an excuse for dreary, derivative, prefabricated eyesores. The urgent need for housing, coupled with town-planning theories that favoured residential satellite suburbs, led to the appearance of soulless, high-rise horrors on the edge of town, much the same as in the rest of Europe.

A change of heart during the 1970s refocused attention on making the city centre a pleasant jumble of residences, shops and offices. At the same time, a quirkier, more imaginative trend began to show itself in building design. The **ING Bank** (Bijlmerplein 888), built in 1987 of brick, has hardly a right angle in sight. A use of bright colour, and a return to a human-sized scale, is splendidly evident in Aldo van Eyck's **Moederhuis** (Plantage Middenlaan 33) from 1981. New façades – daringly modern, yet built to scale – began to appear between the old houses along the canals. The 1980s also saw, amid an enormous amount of controversy, the construction of what became known as the **Stopera**, a combined city hall (**Stadhuis**) and opera house on Waterlooplein (*see p221*). The eye-catching brick and marble coliseum of the **Muziektheater** is more successful than the dull oblongs that make up the City Hall.

Housing projects of the 1980s and 1990s have provided Amsterdam with some imaginative modern architecture. The conversion of a 19th-century army barracks, the **Oranje Nassau Kazerne** (Sarphatistraat and Mauritskade), into studios and flats, with the addition of a row of rather zanily designed apartment blocks, is one of the more successful examples. Building on the KNSM Eiland and other islands in the derelict Eastern Docklands has combined an intelligent conversion of existing structures with some inventive new architecture.

Blummin' Ecyk: Aldo's **Moederhuis**. *See p34.*

## THE FUTURE

At the municipal information centre for planning and housing in the **Zuiderkerk** (Zuiderkerkhof 72), one can see various models of the many current and future developments set to transform Amsterdam in the next decades. Those interested are advised to pay a visit to the website of **ARCAM** – the Architecture Centrum Amsterdam (*see p198*) – at www.arcam.nl; **Bureau Monumentenzorg Amsterdam**, meanwhile, offers an obsessive overview of the city's architecture up to 1940 at www.amsterdam.nl/bmz.

Architectural travesties of the past have politicised the populace, who now keep a sharp eye on development. As such, referendums are now held prior to many new developments. Though 130,000 votes against the construction of IJburg – a residential community currently being built on a series of man-made islands in the IJmeer, just east of Amsterdam – was not enough to stop development around this ecologically sensitive area, it did inspire the promise that ƒ15 million (now around €7 million) would be invested in 'nature-development'. When completed, the six islands will be home to some 45,000 people in 18,000 dwellings, complete with a total infrastructure of commercial and industrial premises, shops, schools and other facilities. Parts of the area will also be a showcase for the recently hyped Dutch concept of *wilde wonen* – 'wild living', as it were – where residents themselves get to design and build their own houses.

Similarly, the referendum result against the laying of the new Noord–Zuidlijn on the Metro network didn't halt the project – still set to begin – but it did establish that the city needed to be considerably more diligent in its thinking. The powers that be, after all, apparently skimmed over such significant details as financing, loss of revenue for proximate shopkeepers and the potential for all this digging to cause the speedier sinking of above-lying historical buildings when planning the line, none of which endeared them to voters.

Now that the facelift of **Museumplein** has at last been completed, all eyes are on the **Eastern Docklands**. It's hoped that redevelopments will turn it into a stunning photogenic harbourfront not unlike that in Sydney, Australia. Similarly, construction around the **ArenA** stadium will hopefully pump some much needed economic life into the nearby architectural prison known as the Bijlmermeer. This boulevard, due to be completed in 2006 but already sporting a huge Pathé cinema and rows of lighting poles by Philippe Starck, should become home to many businesses, a huge multifunctional concert hall and – thanks to the recent leaps and bounds made in building vertically on bog – the largest residential tower in the country.

Currently, Dutch architecture – thanks in part to such pundits as Rem Koolhaas – is very much in vogue. International periodicals, no longer casting LA and Hong Kong as the primary visionaries, now regard the 'Dutch Model' – where the boundaries between building, city and landscape planning have long blurred beyond recognition – as both pragmatic and futuristic. After all, ecological degradation is now a worldwide phenomenon, and the space-constrained Netherlands had long ago begun regarding nature as an artificial construct that needed to be nurtured. Expect this principle to define some of the Dutch architecture of the future, although knowing what's gone before, it'll likely be incorporated in unexpected, eyebrow-raising fashion.

▶ For more on the **Oude Kerk**, *see p83*.
▶ For more on the **Eastern Docklands**, *see p100*.
▶ For more on **new buildings**, *see p102*.

# Art

In the Golden Age, painting became central to the Dutch way of life. More than 350 years later, it remains that way.

The first two-thirds of the 17th century in the Netherlands are known as the Golden Age because of the economic upturn in the country. In these 60-odd years, bookended roughly by the founding of the East India Company (VOC) in 1602 and the English takeover of what is now New York in 1664, Amsterdam's population quadrupled, the city went through a financial upswing, the still-lovely canals that ring the town were built, and the country became one of the world's leading trading powers.

However, the Golden Age nickname applies in equal measure to the Dutch art of the period, art that has long outlasted the country's trading dominance. Although the Low Countries had been home to a number of noteworthy artists prior to 1600 (many of them Flemish), the boom in art in the Netherlands was directly tied into its economic successes. The affluent classes' demand for paintings meant that many artists were able to make a decent living from the period. Names like Frans Hals, Rembrandt van Rijn and Jan Vermeer are only the most famous of the bunch: other, less-known artists such as Jan Steen and Jacob van Ruisdael were also able to thrive both creatively and economically against this unfailingly optimistic background.

Though the end of the Golden Age meant the end of art's heyday, the Dutch had learned to feel proud of their artists (even today, young artists are more readily accepted than in other cities). And still the art developed: the 18th century brought forward Jacob de Wit and Johan Jongkind; the 19th century offered George Breitner (whose impression of the bridge over the Singel at Paleisstraat, now on display at the Rijksmuseum, is pictured above) and Vincent van Gogh; while the 20th century produced such varied talents as MC Escher, Piet Mondriaan and Karel Appel. Certainly, the Netherlands has been responsible for far more great art than you'd expect from a country its size.

Best of all, much of the finest Dutch art is still on show at Amsterdam's museums, which range from the traditional (a visit to Amsterdam without checking out the Rijksmuseum is like going to Dublin and skipping out on the drinking Guinness bit) to the cosy and residential (the Museum van Loon) via the spikily modern (the Stedelijk Museum). On the following pages are some of the highlights of these museums, a cherry-picked selection of works spanning over 500 years and myriad styles. But trust us: there are plenty more where these came from…

## Geertgen tot Sint Jans ▶

Little is known about Dutch artist Geertgen tot Sint Jans (c1465-c1493). He died aged 28 in the monastery where he had lived for the preceding decade or thereabouts, and has had only a dozen works attributed to him. However, these 12 pieces are extremely striking, and he's come to be regarded as the most important of all Dutch medieval painters. **The Holy Kinship** (c1485), a panel painting detailing the supposed extended family of St Anne, is wholly representative of his deft, detailed style. It's also among his most famous pieces, and not only because it took the Rijksmuseum the best part of two decades to restore. Dirty and part-wrecked by over-painting (undertaken years ago in a bid to disguise water damage), it was removed from display in 1983. Eighteen years later and as good as new, it was put back on display in 2001.
**On display:** room 203 of the Rijksmuseum (*see p107*).

## ▼ Rembrandt van Rijn

*The Company of Captain Frans Banning Cocq and Lieutenant Willem van Ruytenburch* (1642) isn't the snappiest title for a painting. **The Night Watch**, though, is rather more memorable, and it's by this name that the most famous work by Rembrandt van Rijn (1606-69) is now known. Amsterdam's civic guard commissioned this group portrait to decorate their new building. But rather than conjure up a neat, unexciting portrait, Rembrandt went for spontaneity, capturing a moment of lively chaos, the captain issuing an order as his men jostle to his rear. It's now the most popular work in the most popular museum in Amsterdam.
**On display:** room 229 of the Rijksmuseum (*see p107*).

## ◄ Johannes Vermeer

Delft artist Vermeer (1632-75) specialised in straightforward, honest representations of 17th-century Dutch domestic life. **The Kitchen Maid** (1658-60) is classic Vermeer: a working woman is depicted in a strong and direct fashion, drawing the viewer into her everyday mundanities. The subdued colouring is typical of Dutch painting of this period, a tradition later explored in Van Gogh's early work before he moved to France where, influenced by the clearer light, his painting developed into the more expressionist style for which he became famous. Vermeer is known to have painted only around 30 works, dying while only in his forties. **On display:** room 218 of the Rijksmuseum (*see p107*).

## ▼ Jan Miense Molenaer

The family of Willem van Loon, co-founder of the VOC, went on to become important players in the Dutch political scene. Although Willem never lived at Keizersgracht 672 – he died several decades before it was built in 1672 – his descendants owned and occupied the house from 1884 to 1945. Since then, it's been turned into a museum whose main attraction is a collection of portraiture. Taking pride of place is **The Marriage of Willem van Loon and Margaretha Bas** (1637) by relatively minor genre artist Jan Miense Molenaer (1610-68), who is believed to have studied with Frans Hals. The painting is a grand portrayal of a predictably swanky occasion.

**On display:** Museum van Loon (*see p93*).

### ◀ Jacob de Wit

Jordaan-born decorative artist Jacob de Wit (1695-1754) was influenced, during his formative years, by Rubens's ceiling paintings in an Antwerp church. However, you wouldn't necessarily know it to look at De Wit's work, which is airier and more sympathetic than that of Rubens. De Wit's handiwork can be seen in a number of Amsterdam buildings, among them the Theater Instituut (*see p88*), the attic church at the Museum Amstelkring (*see p82*), the Rijksmuseum (*see p107*) and the Pintohuis (now a library; *see p95*). However, they're trumped by the two ceiling paintings at the Bijbelsmuseum. One was painted for local merchant Jacob Cromhout, while the other, entitled **Apollo and the Four Seasons**, was salvaged in the 1950s from another property on Herengracht. After falling into relative disrepair in recent years – blocked gutters led to water damage – both paintings have recently been restored to stylish and lively effect.

**On display:** Bijbels Museum (*see p88*).

### Vincent van Gogh ▶

In Arles in the late 1880s, Vincent van Gogh (1853-90) painted a series of sunflower paintings to decorate the room where his friend Paul Gauguin was to stay on a prospective visit. He completed four of a planned 12, only two of which he felt were good enough to hang. He later painted three copies, **Sunflowers** (*right*; 1889) being one of them. Gauguin loved the paintings, and decided to depict Van Gogh in a moment he thought typical of his friend. The end result was **Vincent van Gogh Painting Sunflowers** (*below*; 1888), a beguiling companion piece to the real thing.

**On display:** Van Gogh Museum (*see p108*).

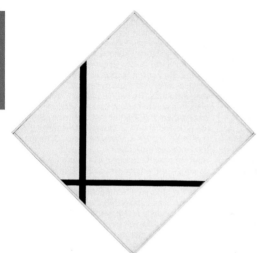

## ◀ Piet Mondriaan

Piet Mondriaan (1872-1944) experimented with impressionist and cubist techniques early in his career. However, it was as part of the movement known as De Stijl (The Style) that his work found recognition. Mondriaan coined the term neo-plasticism to describe his work, which was composed of horizontal and vertical lines and blocks of colour (white, black and primary colours) and which was meant to disavow any pretence towards individualism. By 1931's **Compositie met Twee Lijnen** (*Composition with Two Lines*), he'd pared the form down to its minimum components, though a playful touch can be seen in his turning of the canvas 45 degrees.

**On display:** Stedelijk Museum of Modern Art (*see p108*).

## Karel Appel ▶

When a show by the CoBrA group – who took their name from the three cities where their artists were based, Copenhagen, Brussels and Amsterdam – opened at the Stedelijk Museum of Modern Art in 1949, the normally unshockable Dutch art establishment was taken aback by the wild and chaotic primitivism of the exhibits on display. At the centre of the movement was Amsterdam-based Karel Appel (b.1921), whose works are among the most striking of all; **Figure with Bird** (1948) is typical of his childlike oeuvre. The CoBrA group – which also counted the likes of Pierre Alechinsky, Asger Jorn and Lucebert among its number – disbanded in 1951, but has since found belated and permanent recognition in the naming of a café after them on the super-establishment Museumplein (*see p132*). Appel, meanwhile, has spent the last four decades living in the US, but is still arguably the best-known living Dutch artist.

**On display:** CoBrA Museum of Modern Art (*see p112*).

# Faking it

As a Mount Zion of the arts since its Golden Age, the Dutch have long dealt with forgers. But while fakers have long been denounced by the establishment, there's a case to be made that a thing's 'realness' should be based more on the quality of the tale it tells and the emotions it inspires. This being the case, the art produced by two of Holland's most famed forgers is every bit as real as the stuff they imitated; indeed, their fakes ever now have their own museum in Drenthe (*see p264*).

## Hans van Meegeren

During World War II, the art market was revitalised by German units commissioned by Hermann Göring to buy, trade and/or plunder Europe's art treasures. After the war, when the booty was unearthed, the Allies found a Vermeer entitled *Christ with the Adulteress* and tried to trace its origins. Investigations led to art dealer Hans van Meegeren, but he couldn't explain where he had obtained it and was arrested for collaboration.

When it occurred to Van Meegeren that collaboration was an offence punishable by death, he changed his tune in a hurry. At his trial, he claimed he'd painted the 'Vermeer' himself; what's more, he maintained he should be treated like a hero for scamming the Nazi scum. While the jury agreed on the former point, they disagreed on the latter, and Van Meegeren was sentenced to a year in jail, where he died in 1947. It was reported that while on trial in Nuremberg, Göring cried the salty tears of a knee-scuffed child when he heard that his cherished 'Vermeer' was a mere Van Meegeren. The story spread and Hollywood began planning a film version.

But that wasn't the end of it: historians discovered that Van Meegeren had actually pulled the same scam many times. His success derived not from greed, but from revenge. In the '20s, his own efforts were dissed by critics, one of whom was a leading Vermeer authority. Van Meegeren set about tricking him using the critic's own theories; and it was check and then checkmate as the critic authenticated his fakes.

With money rolling in during the '30s to feed his alcohol and morphine habits, Van Meegeren kept his secret private. However, he exacted a public revenge on his detractors with articles explaining their 'lack of taste' in terms of their racial inferiority. Hollywood continues to struggle with the screenplay.

## Geert Jan Jansen

At the height of his creativity, a typical day for Geert Jan Jansen would produce 'before breakfast a couple of Chagall drawings, during the morning a couple of hefty Appels and during the afternoon a couple of Picassos. Only then would I feel satisfied.' Jansen skilfully manipulated a vast variety of media to produce thousands of works 'by' the likes of Beuys, Cocteau, Miro, Hockney, Magritte, Matisse (*pictured*) and Warhol.

Greed aside, Jansen's was a real talent. Appel himself has verified several of Jansen's works as his own, and it is said that Andy himself once gleefully witnessed Jansen signing a Warhol. Dubbed by French and German police as the 'forger of the century', this Amsterdam art history school drop-out betrays little regret in his interviews. 'At least,' he dryly remarks, 'I wasn't selling carcinogenic french fries.'

Charges against him were first made in 1994 when, following a tip from a Muncih gallery owner who noticed a spelling mistake in the authentication certificate of a 'Chagall', his castle in Orleans was raided by French police. Jansen was arrested and his collection impounded. He spent the next six months in jail making a Picasso for the warden and writing his pithy art dealer-baiting memoirs, *Magenta: Adventures of a Master Forger*.

With no one willing to file a complaint – one can only assume his customers were happy ones – the French finally decided in 2000 to search out some customers and threaten them with charges of accessory. The result for Jansen may be another year in jail and the burning of his collection. However, said collection apparently includes bona fide works by many notables, and rich irony now has Stedelijk director Rudi Fuchs championing the cause to save this treasure trove.

# Sex & Drugs

Liberal Dutch attitudes have turned vices and taboos into veritable tourist traps in Europe's Sin City.

Amsterdam's liberal attitudes are known the world over. They've long attracted the attentions of the curious and the naughty. But an increasing number of visitors are drawn to the town purely by the lure of sex and drugs, the Red Light District and the coffeeshops, the promise of things to fuck and things to fuck you up. You might even be one of them.

The local authorities would prefer it if their town's reputation rested on the art, the canals and the all-around easy charm. Fat chance. When a city's policies on sex and drugs are as forward-thinking as Amsterdam's, they're going to find fame. And so it goes that outside the Netherlands, Amsterdam's image is dominated by sex and drugs, by prostitutes and joints, by visions of mile upon mile of nubile and naked women in red-lit windows offering come-ons to passers-by, as the air grows denser in a spliffy fog. A Bacchanalian, orgiastic feast for the senses. The truth of the matter is a little different to this. But only a little.

## SEX

It doesn't really matter where in the world you are: as long as there are men, there'll be demand for prostitutes. The only real difference from city to city, country to country, continent to continent, is how the local government chooses to deal with the world's oldest profession.

Most condemn it. Traditional definitions of morality being what they are, governments have always had a lot more to lose than gain by loosening the legal screws that tightly forbid prostitution in most countries. Others turn a blind eye, tacitly accepting it's going to go on but maintaining its illegality, making no great effort to eradicate it but making fewer attempts to solve the social problems it causes or fosters.

The Netherlands is very different. But although prostitution has been almost entirely decriminalised in Amsterdam since 1912, it wasn't until the turn of the 21st century that it became truly legal. For years, prostitutes worked under an ambivalent law that permitted prostitution while still designating brothels illegal. The law was never strictly enforced, though, and the anachronism was finally corrected in October 2000. The government's desire to monitor the sex industry more closely meant it first had to legalise brothels.

The history of prostitution in Amsterdam, though, goes back centuries. Some have put the prevalence of prostitution in the city down, at least in part, to the high proportion of sailors and tradesmen that passed through the city, and there's some truth in this. These were single men looking for a good time, of course, but the trade was doubtless helped along by the fact that local sailors left their wives for weeks and months at a time; with no money to support themselves in their husbands' absence, the women were forced to find themselves work, and many turned to prostitution.

Although the brothels on what is now Damstraat were controlled by the city's sheriff during the Middle Ages, prostitution hasn't always been legal. But it has always been around. Prostitutes have worked the area around Zeedijk since the 15th century: the street was for years favoured by sailors as a party strip, riddled with drinking dens and working women. Brothels were still confined to certain areas of the city, but were largely allowed to go about their business (many also operated as gambling dens) outside the law.

By the 17th century, prostitutes were walking through the Old Side with red lanterns, hoping to pick up trade. Soon after, other enterprising women turned to advertising themselves in the windows of their own homes, especially by the Oude Kerk; it's this practice from which today's rather more garish window trade is directly descended. More traditional methods of carrying out business continued to operate, though. Streetwalkers once worked on Rembrandtplein and Kalverstraat (now the city's main shopping drag), while traditional brothels have been in operation for many years: a luxurious one used to stand on the site of what is now Café Fonteyn on Nieuwmarkt for more than a century.

But it's the red-lit windows that have garnered Amsterdam notoriety for its liberal sex laws. And no matter how prepared you are, you'll be taken aback the first time you visit. Street after street of huge picture windows, each decorated with red velvet-effect soft furnishings, each lit sparingly, each dominated by the figure of a nearly-naked woman. Some sit looking glum filing their nails and counting the hours, others gossip to their colleagues in neighbouring windows like workmates at a water cooler, others dance and cavort, teasing passers-by. They come in all shapes and sizes,

colours and ages. But all are prostitutes, and all are available at the drop of a few notes and a little negotiation (the going rate at the end of 2001 was ƒ100 for 15 minutes, which will likely translate to around €40 or €50).

Amsterdam's most famous red light district is centred around Oudezijds Voorburgwal and Oudezijds Achterburgwal, in the maze of streets between Oude Kerk and Nieuwmarkt. However, smaller, less heralded red-light areas sit on the New Side (around Singel and Nieuwezijds Voorburgwal between Lutherse Kerk and Lijnbaanssteeg) and in the Pijp (Ruysdaelkade, from Albert Cuypstraat to 1e Jan Steenstraat).

### 'Coach parties have stripped the area of its down-and-dirty seediness.'

Nor is this the only way in which prostitutes work in Amsterdam. Escort services are just as common here as in cities where the sex trade is illegal. Streetwalkers, too, still work in assorted spots in town, most notoriously behind Centraal Station (one of several 'tippelzones', where streetwalking is tolerated and monitored by police). There are plenty of brothels scattered around the city, the most famous and most expensive being Yab Yum (Singel 295).

Of course, savvy businessmen realised years ago that not everyone after titillation would want to go so far, and thoughtfully provided entertainment for the millions of visitors each year happy to look but reluctant to touch. The Casa Rosso (Oudezijds Achterburgwal 106) is the most famous of the dozen or so live sex shows, just as Female and Partners (Spuistraat 100) is the nicest of the town's countless sex shops. And then there are a handful of strip clubs, two or three peep shows, a clutch of sex cinemas, plenty of shops offering private video booths, and even a few sex clubs.

On the surface, it seems to work. Violent crime is lower than you'd expect of an area so dominated by the sex industry and all its encumbent sleaziness. Police patrol the area with just enough presence to dissuade most troublemakers. The atmosphere throughout the area is largely unthreatening (although that can change in a hurry when tourists start taking pictures of the girls, a massive no-no).

The prostitutes, too, are very well organised. Thanks to the deterrent of push-button alarm systems in almost every window, few get harmed by their clients. Healthcare is taken seriously: almost all the window prostitutes insist their clients use a condom, and there's an STD clinic in the Old Side's Red Light District where sex workers can go anonymously for check-ups and information. They even have a union: De Rode Draad (the Red Thread).

That said, it's by no means perfect. Although the aforementioned changes in the law in 2000 were aimed in part at reducing the number of illegal immigrants (and, to a lesser extent, under-age girls) working the windows, and although it seems to have succeeded in the limited time it's been in effect, a significant minority of prostitutes are here illegally. Many have been coerced into working against their will, in some cases by organised criminal rings. Others are in the clutches of 'boyfriends', who are little better – and sometimes worse – than pimps. And you only have to take a drive behind Centraal Station to see that Amsterdam still has a serious problem with drug-dependent streetwalkers.

What's more, for the Dutch women working voluntarily as prostitutes, life outside their job – which, contrary to popular male fantasy, few enjoy – is difficult. Despite the legality of the industry and the relaxed ease with which the liberal Dutch have grown accustomed to its visibility, many sectors of society have been slow to catch up and still regard sex workers as second- or third-class citizens. Despite being liable for taxes, prostitutes still find it nigh-on impossible to get bank accounts, mortgages and insurance. The laws may be forward-thinking, but the attitudes in society definitely aren't.

As for the potential consumers, opinions vary. It's an extraordinary area, certainly. But despite the number of mouth-agape tourists who stroll the Red Light District staring at the women as if they were pictures at an exhibition – or even animals in a zoo – people do buy. In the 1990s, the business was estimated to be worth a staggering $f$1 billion (around €450 million) a year. Whatever your preference or fetish, you'll find it catered for here. Unless, of course, you're a woman on the lookout for a man. An intriguing experiment in the mid 1990s to put men in the windows – by Mariska Majoor, an ex-prostitute who now runs the Prostitution Information Centre near Oude Kerk – didn't last long; now the only male prostitutes in the city are rent boys, working from streetcorners in other parts of town and through escort agencies.

The Red Light District is an incredible sight, a freakish tourist attraction in its own right. But while there might be fun to be had behind the red velvet curtains drawn in windows, signalling that business is being conducted behind them, whether the area is actually erotic or arousing is a moot point. Certainly, the coach parties that descend upon the area have stripped the area of some of its down-and-dirty seediness. Visit a sex cinema expecting fun, and

Love for sale. Kinda.

you'll likely find yourself in a damp-smelling room watching a 30-year-old print flicker on a screen, its dubbed-German audio bearing little relation to its half-heartedly erotic visuals, its only other audience a coughing drunk and a panting Belgian businessman wanking himself raw two seats away. Walk the Red Light District on Friday or Saturday night, hoping to be entertained and perhaps a little titillated by the wall-to-wall women, and you'll soon find yourself swamped by a sea of British stag parties, hammered on Heineken, singing filthy songs, taunting girls and picking fights.

Even the sex shows depress, unless watching a put-upon woman perform gynaecologically implausible acts with fruit before an audience of aggressively drunk bachelor partiers is your idea of erotica. And as you stand in a peep-show booth, shovelling coins into a slot to watch a mulleted fortysomething distractedly fuck an unnatural blonde on a revolving podium, avoid the pale white dispatch deposited by the booth's previous occupant that'll be inexorably dribbling down the glass towards your shoe.

Certainly, the locals' liberal, grown-up attitudes merit applause, and the methods they've employed to deal with the inevitability of a sex industry have arguably resulted in a better deal for both customer and sex worker. It's true, too, that the Dutch method for dealing with prostitution might prove to be the way of the future for many of its European neighbours. But when it comes down to it, Amsterdam's fabled sex industry is not really all that sexy.

### DRUGS

Amsterdam celebrated a quarter-century of decriminalised dope in 2001. But no flags were hung from the rafters, no street parties blocked off traffic; in fact, the anniversary passed all but unnoticed in the media. Despite the goggle-eyed, slack-jawed amazement with which the rest of the world eyes the Dutch drugs policy, the locals barely give it a second thought these days. They've moved on. Long before the rest of the world has even caught up.

Amsterdam's reputation as a druggie's paradise precedes discussion of almost any other of its characteristics. It's a reputation, too, that's muddied by hearsay, exaggeration and overstatement. Those in favour of the Dutch legal position believe that soft drugs are neither harmful nor addictive, that legalising them is the only fair and just way to deal with a problem that isn't going to go away even if it's illegal, and in any case it's not a problem anyway. Those against suggest that use of soft drugs leads, inevitably, to hard drugs, and that in any case, all drugs are bad.

But before the argument, a little background. Strange as it may sound, the Netherlands' tolerant policy on soft drugs stems from a large increase in heroin addiction in the 1970s. In the early part of the decade, the country became swamped with heroin brought in by Chinese triads. Recognising that smack represented more of a problem within society than cannabis, the fight against wimpy drugs came to be regarded by the always-progressive and liberal Dutch authorities as a waste of time and money.

In 1976, a vaguely worded law defined a difference between hard and soft drugs, separating these markets from each other's influence. In so doing, it allowed the use and sale of small amounts of soft drugs, legitimising the euphemistically named 'coffeeshops'. These outlets – there are around 2,000 throughout the country, with close on 20 per cent of them in Amsterdam – are permitted to sell soft drugs in amounts of up to five grams per buyer, while individuals can possess up to 30 grams (or one ounce) and remain safe from prosecution.

However, soft drugs were never officially legalised, only decriminalised, and then only in certain places (though selling the stuff in coffeeshops is legal, street-dealing is not). What's more, the law still has a huge loophole. While the 'front door' of the coffeeshop has been opened up for sale of the drugs to the public, the 'back door', where produce arrives by the kilo, is still a gateway to an illegal distribution system. Basically, the people who supply the coffeeshops are working outside the law.

## 'The new breed of tourist comes here purely to get so fucked up they can't remember a thing about it.'

That said, the system seems to work. Time passed without the increase of drug use that doomsayers predicted, while the coffeeshop became a permanent part of the Amsterdam streetscape. The government, as they promised, has maintained concerted efforts against harder drugs – mostly heroin, but also cocaine and ecstasy – with policies that treat addicts less as criminals and more as patients.

So far, so straightforward. Yet the fact that the rest of the world doesn't quite see it the same way as the Dutch is perfectly illustrated by the difference between how the locals treat the easy availability of soft drugs and how visitors approach it. In a nutshell, it's the difference between a father having a quiet glass of wine with dinner and a teenager sneaking away to a friend's house party to find the absent parents have left a ton of alcohol in the house. You can probably guess the rest.

The majority of locals who smoke treat soft drugs in a matter-of-fact way; just something else to do. Dope tourists, though, hit the scene with a wild, giggling abandon, an abandon usually followed by a painful comedown when they belatedly realise that Amsterdam's drugs are considerably stronger than those they're used to at home. Oh, and perhaps that third spacecake might have been two too many…

Breathe deeply...

The easy availability of soft drugs has led to a new breed of tourist: those who come to the city purely to get so fucked up they can't remember a thing about it. And it's this new breed that has led the tourist authorities to look upon their city's most famous law with a pronounced ambivalence. On the one hand, the very presence of the coffeeshops attracts many visitors to the city. On the other, the kind of visitors the law attracts are, not to put too fine a point on it, hardly the kind of tourists the authorities welcome with open arms.

Although many of Amsterdam's weekending funseekers only go to blight certain areas of the city with their stag-party antics – the Red Light District predictably chief among them – the authorities' disdain for them is down to a simple matter of economics. Many visitors simply show up on Friday, spend three days getting wasted on spliffs, spacecake and Amstel, then go home again on Monday. The positive effects on the Dutch economy are negligible; the local authorities would rather their city was visited by more affluent tourists keener on seeking out the museums and restaurants than the backpackers' holy grail of coffeeshops and fast food outlets.

Despite the happy-go-lucky image projected by those in favour of the Dutch laws, things aren't perfect. Although pressure from neighbouring nations has meant coffeeshops are monitored more closely, from time to time one gets busted for selling hard drugs under the counter. The aforementioned legal loophole – the coffeeshops supply the public, but who supplies the coffeeshops? – is a mess. And in any case, coffeeshops aren't the only places in Amsterdam selling drugs. Anyone walking from Centraal Station on to Damrak will be greeted by wild-eyed dealers, offering everything from (impure and often fake) heroin to (overpriced and often fake) marijuana. It's the same story in the Red Light District, especially around the bridges and the alleyways that link them. Junkies patrol the area, on the lookout for unsuspecting tourists to pickpocket and poorly locked bicycles to thieve. It's not unusual to see them injecting themselves in full view of the public and, their inactivity leads one to suspect, the police.

Then there's the thorny, underpublicised issue of organised crime. Every country has it in some form, of course, but the gangs in the Netherlands are able to go about their drug-running businesses with considerably more ease than the government would like. Worse still, many Dutch gangs are believed to be freely trafficking drugs both hard and soft all over Europe, a fact that hasn't exactly endeared the Netherlands to its neighbours.

And yet, and yet, and yet… The policy still works. The country has a smaller proportion of hard drugs addicts than many neighbouring countries with stricter laws in place. The government simply realised early on that drugs are never just going to vanish because of their illegality, and it's better to confront them head-on. And to its credit, this confrontation doesn't stop with soft drugs: heroin addicts are treated with sympathy here, for example, while clubgoers can get their ecstasy tablets tested for safety at clubs. In 2002, the Dutch government are expected to completely legalise cannabis as a prescription medicine and make it available at chemists for sufferers of some diseases.

A forward-thinking approach, but 25 years after it was put into practice, other countries – Britain among them – are coming around. The days of Europe-wide coffeeshops are a way off, but they're closer now than ever. And while they won't want to push their luck, the Dutch may be entitled to whisper a little 'told you so' into their neighbours' ears.

> ▶ For more on **prostitution**, *see p77*.
> ▶ For more on **coffeeshops**, *see p147*.
> ▶ For more on **sex shops**, *see p176*.

# Accommodation

# Accommodation

Amsterdam's hottest hotels book out quick and the temperatures are rising, so get in fast before there's no room at the inn.

Which of Amsterdam's many personalities best reflects your travelling agenda? Are you a museum-hopping culture vulture, a Golden Age prince or princess, or a party monster with red lights in your eyes? Whatever your answer, there are hotels and hostels to suit your moods and predilections, from back-to-basics setups in the city's partying heart to stately canalside houses with peaceful, antique-filled rooms and backyard garden terraces.

Space, however, has always been at a premium in Amsterdam, and this becomes immediately clear in many older hotels with modestly-sized rooms and curious ladder-like stairs. (It's wise to inquire whether a hotel has a lift, if that's a concern.) While there tends to be a number of high-end choices, room rates have continued to rise, and fewer budget choices have opened in recent years. The result? Room options quickly diminish the longer you wait to make your booking. Amsterdam can be a maddeningly difficult place in which to find a room – any room – during the busy spring and summer months and, indeed, during much of the year, especially when conventions are on. So booking ahead is imperative.

That said, hoteliers can be friendly and willing to help, often referring you to another hotel if theirs is full. Gay and lesbian couples should be assured that, since 1998's Gay Games, most hotels won't bat an eye at same-sex couples. (For gay-operated hotels, see p203.) Another convenience is that the vast majority of hostels don't require IYHF membership. For the two that do, pay about €2 extra per night and get a nightly stamp on an IYHF card; after six nights, you can trade this in for membership.

Prices listed are inclusive of the five per cent visitors' tax, although they may vary – up or down – from what's stipulated here: in early 2002, no one was really too sure how the introduction of the euro would affect those economies entering into it. So be warned.

## RESERVATIONS

Aside from going direct to the hotels – and if you do this, be sure to book well in advance – or booking a travel-and-hotel package with your travel agent, there are several ways of making reservations. The **Nederlands Reserverings Centrum** (aka the Dutch Hoteliers' Reservation Service) handles bookings for the whole of the country, as do the **Amsterdam Tourist Board** offices at Centraal Station and Schiphol Airport (see p289); both organisations only take enquiries in person. A third source for the Netherlands is **www.bookings.nl**, dealing with online reservations only. The Amsterdam Tourist Board also produces a comprehensive guide to hotels in the city, priced at around €2.

## Nederlands Reserverings Centrum

*Nieuwe Gouw 1, 1442 LE Purmerend (0299 689144/www.hotelres.nl).*
All bookings must be made online: the phone number listed can only be used for cancelling or making changes to prior reservations.

---

**The best** Hotels

**For canal house charm**
Canal House Hotel (*see p57*) and Toren (*see p58*).

**For canal house chic**
Blakes (*see p57*) and **717** (*see p59*).

**For a smokers' paradise**
The Greenhouse Effect (*see p53*).

**For breakfast in bed**
Seven Bridges (*see p61*).

**For a quiet refuge from the chaos**
Zosa (*see p53*).

**For a theme night**
Hotel de Filosoof (*see p66*) and Winston Hotel (*see p53*).

**For backpacker central**
Hans Brinker Budget Hotel (*see p62*).

**For classic comfort**
Hôtel de l'Europe (*see p49*).

**For family-run hospitality**
Estheréa (*see p58*).

**For leather lovers**
Black Tulip Hotel (*see p203*).

---

# Hotels

## The Old Centre

### Deluxe

#### Barbizon Palace
*Prins Hendrikkade 59-72, 1012 AD (556 4564/ fax 624 3353/www.goldentuliphotels.nl). Tram 1, 2, 4, 5, 7, 9, 13, 17, 20, 24, 25/Metro Centraal Station.* **Rates** €278-€341 single/double; €446-€892 suite. **Credit** AmEx, DC, MC, V. **Map** p306 D2.
Part of the Golden Tulip chain that also includes the Schiller (*see p59*) and the Krasnapolsky (*see below*). The lavish surroundings are apparent from first walking into the hall. A canopy creates an exotic impression, enhanced by the swanky fitness centre, complete with sauna, Turkish bath and solarium; indulge further at the award-winning Vermeer restaurant. The hotel even has its own landing stage for canal boats. Breakfast is €19.
**Hotel services** *Air-conditioning. Babysitting. Bar. Beauty services. Concierge. Disabled: adapted room. Gym. Limousine service. No-smoking floor. Parking. Restaurants.* **Room services** *Dataport. Minibar. Room service (24hrs). TV: satellite/pay movies/VCR (by request).*

#### The Grand
*Oudezijds Voorburgwal 197, 1012 EX (555 3111/ fax 555 3222/www.thegrand.nl). Tram 4, 9, 14, 16, 20, 24, 25.* **Rates** €378 single; €415-€462 double; €562-€1,522 suite. **Credit** AmEx, DC, MC, V. **Map** p306 D3.
Prince William of Orange was one of the first illustrious guests to stay in this centrally located building when it opened as an inn in the late 16th century. Since then, the site has been home to the great Dutch Admiralty and, contradictorily, the dull city council. You get a taste of the history as soon as you enter the spacious courtyard of this five-star hotel, and the 182 rooms, suites and apartments are decorated accordingly. The restaurant's fine chef is directed by Albert Roux (*see p119*). Breakfast is €20-€25.
**Hotel services** *Air-conditioning. Babysitting. Bar. Business services. Concierge. Garden. Gym. Limousine service. No-smoking rooms. Parking. Restaurant. Swimming pool.* **Room services** *Dataport. Minibar. Room service (24hrs). TV: cable/pay movies/VCR (by request).*

#### Grand Hotel Krasnapolsky
*Dam 9, 1012 JS (554 9111/fax 622 8607/ www.krasnapolsky.nl). Tram 1, 2, 4, 5, 9, 13, 14, 16, 17, 20, 24, 25.* **Rates** €341-€394 single; €367-€420 double; €474-€735 suite; €63 extra bed. **Credit** AmEx, DC, MC, V. **Map** p306 D3.
This enormous hotel boasts 468 rooms, including 36 fully furnished apartments and two national monuments. One of these is the Winter Garden, with a high, glass-roofed atrium where guests can breakfast (€20) and lunch orangerie-style. There are

Making an entrance at the **Barbizon Palace**.

restaurants for every palate: Mediterranean-influenced dining can be had at Brasserie Reflet, Japanese cuisine at Edo and Kyo, and there are also Italian, Mexican and Middle Eastern options. After a meeting in one of the 100 convention rooms, business types can stroll to the Lounge, which presides over Dam Square, its long windows providing perfect viewing across to the Palace.
**Hotel services** *Air-conditioning. Babysitting. Bar. Beauty salon. Business services. Concierge. Disabled: adapted rooms. Garden. Gym. No-smoking floors. Parking. Restaurants.* **Room services** *Dataport. Minibar. Room service (24hrs). TV: satellite/pay movies.*

#### Hôtel de l'Europe
*Nieuwe Doelenstraat 2-8, 1012 CP (531 1777/fax 531 1778/www.leurope.nl). Tram 4, 9, 14, 16, 20, 24, 25.* **Rates** €294 single; €336-€378 double; €446-€976 suite. **Credit** AmEx, DC, MC, V. **Map** p306 D3.
Looking out from one of the 100 individually decorated Victorian rooms, you might think this five-star hotel has a moat. It doesn't; it's just that its location on the Amstel gives a front-row view of the city centre's main functional waterways. Its grandeur is further enhanced by the Excelsior restaurant (jacket required), serving haute cuisine and champagne on its river-level terrace. With its Victorian-period lounge and foyer, this truly is an elegant place, and caters for all, from business types to just-marrieds (the bridal suite comes complete with jacuzzi). Breakfast costs from €22.50.
**Hotel services** *Air-conditioning. Babysitting. Bar. Business services. Concierge. Gym. Limousine service. No-smoking rooms. Parking. Restaurants. Swimming pool.* **Room services** *Dataport. Minibar. Room service (24hrs). TV: cable/pay movies/ VCR (by request).*

Victorian grandeur at the **Hôtel de L'Europe**. *See p49.*

## Sofitel Amsterdam

*Nieuwezijds Voorburgwal 67, 1012 RE (627 5900/ fax 623 8932/www.sofitel.nl). Tram 1, 2, 5, 13, 17, 20.* **Rates** €304-€378 single/double; €351-€424 triple; €499 suite. **Credit** AmEx, DC, MC, V. **Map** p306 C2.

Built on the site of a former monastery, the 148-room Sofitel is remarkably understated, with muted, classical furnishings blending subtly together. Its Duke of Windsor bar is decorated with lamps and panelling from the Orient Express, reminding drinkers of trans-Europe travel. As the Sofitel is a mere five-minute walk from Centraal Station and located between Kalverstraat and the canals, guests won't have to do much travelling to make the most of the superb location. Breakfast is €17.50.

**Hotel services** *Air-conditioning. Babysitting. Bar. Concierge. Disabled: adapted room. No-smoking rooms. Parking (paid). Restaurant.* **Room services** *Dataport. Minibar. Room service (24hrs). TV: cable/pay movies.*

## Victoria Hotel Amsterdam

*Damrak 1-5, 1012 LG (623 4255/fax 625 2997/ www.parkplazaww.com). Tram 1, 2, 4, 5, 9, 13, 14, 16, 17, 20, 24, 25.* **Rates** €298-€310 single; €325-€345 double; €477-€525 suite; €52 extra bed. **Credit** AmEx, DC, MC, V. **Map** p306 D2.

Conveniently located opposite Centraal Station, this deluxe four-star hotel makes a perfect business person's palace. There are so many comforts to enjoy after work, including an indoor pool and a health club. If that all sounds like far too much effort, you

can enjoy a leisurely afternoon tea on Vic's Terrace atop a perch overlooking the Damrak. Breakfast is charged at an extra €19.

**Hotel services** *Air-conditioning. Babysitting. Bar. Beauty salon. Business services. Concierge. Disabled: adapted rooms. Gym. No-smoking rooms. Parking nearby (paid). Restaurants. Swimming pool (indoor).* **Room services** *Dataport (suites). Minibar. Room service (6.30am-11pm). TV: satellite/pay movies.*

## Expensive

### Hotel Inntel

*Nieuwezijds Kolk 19, 1012 PV (530 1818/fax 422 1919/www.hotelinntel.com). Tram 1, 2, 5, 13, 17, 20.* **Rates** €199-€283 single/double; €295-€379 suite. **Credit** AmEx, DC, MC, V. **Map** p306 D2.

Its location on a small pedestrian square means the Inntel is quiet enough to ensure a good night's rest. However, it's also just one minute away from the shopping on Kalverstraat and close to Centraal Station. All 236 guest rooms are simply but tastefully decorated, with a designer-cool edge. The conservatory-style breakfast room overlooks a terrace, and Inntel guests can use two neighbouring restaurants, then add dinner to the hotel bill. Friendly staff ensure your stay is pleasant. Breakfast is €16.

**Hotel services** *Air-conditioning. Bar. Disabled: adapted rooms. Limousine service. No-smoking floors. Parking (paid).* **Room services** *Dataport. Minibar. Room service (6.30-10am Mon-Fri; 7-11am Sat, Sun). TV: satellite/pay movies.*

# AMS HOTELS

The Art of Hospitality

# 12 HOTELS IN THE CENTRE OF AMSTERDAM

**AMS HOTEL GROUP** manages 12 hotels in the city centre of Amsterdam. Surrounded by the world-famous museums, the most sophisticated shoppingstreets, the Concert Hall, theatres and close to the Amsterdam nightlife. Within easy reach are the World Trade Centre, the RAI conference & exhibition centre, the airport Schiphol and all important business districts.

**AMS HOTEL GROUP** provides you with different classes and rating: Tourist Class, Superior Tourist Class and Business Class. We aim to offer you and your guests the best product with the best quality in a most pleasant and personal atmosphere, in which we always focus our attention on:

## "The Art of Hospitality"

For Reservations:
Phone: + 31 (0)20 683 18 11
Fax: + 31 (0)20 616 03 20
Site: www.ams.nl  E-mail: info@ams.nl

## Moderate

### Hotel Citadel

*Nieuwezijds Voorburgwal 98-100, 1012 SG (627 3882/fax 627 4684). Tram 1, 2, 4, 5, 9, 13, 14, 16, 17, 20, 24, 25.* **Rates** €80-€103 single; €112-€148 double; €148-€180 triple. **Credit** AmEx, DC, MC, V. **Map** p306 C2.

This bright, modern three-star hotel is a two-minute walk from the station, and near the Royal Palace on Dam Square. It's very handy for strolls along the canals into the Jordaan and, in the opposite direction, the Kalverstraat shopping area. All of the 38 rooms are comfortable and clean, in a generic hotel kind of way (the quietest rooms in back are on the dark side), and most have baths.

**Hotel services** *Bar.* **Room services** *TV: cable/pay movies.*

### Zosa

*Kloveniersburgwal 20, 1012 CV (330 6241/fax 330 6241/www.zosa-online.com). Tram 4, 9, 17, 20, 24, 25/Metro Nieuwmarkt.* **Rates** €113 single; €136 double; €23 extra bed. **Credit** AmEx, MC, V. **Map** p306 D3.

Right off the Nieuwmarkt, Zosa is tucked away above a restaurant. Six modestly proportioned rooms with whimsical themes (Dutch Design, Lollypop and so on) overlook either the canal or a private garden. The young, international staff look fit for a fashion shoot and do a fine job of making you feel part of the scene. A tasty breakfast is served in the ground-floor soup and salad restaurant.

**Hotel services** *Bar. Restaurant.* **Room services** *Telephone. TV: cable.*

## Budget

### Amstel Botel

*Oosterdokskade 2-4, 1011 AE (626 4247/fax 639 1952). Tram 1, 2, 5, 9, 13, 17, 20, 24, 25.* **Rates** €81-€86 single/double/twin; €90-€95 triple. **Credit** AmEx, DC, MC, V. **Map** p307 E1.

The three-star Botel is moored in an unlikely spot. Were it a little to the north-east – ie north of the station – it would get fine views of the man-made islands on the IJ. As it is, the vistas aren't that interesting; take the watery side of the boat for the best views. Still, it does offer relative comfort at reasonable prices. Breakfast is an extra €8.

**Hotel services** *Bar.* **Room services** *TV: cable.*

### Greenhouse Effect

*Warmoesstraat 55, 1012 HW (624 4974/fax 489 0850/www.the-greenhouse-effect.com). Tram 4, 9, 17, 20, 24, 25.* **Rates** €27 dorm bed; €39 single; €70-€113 double/twin; €93 triple. **Credit** MC, V. **Map** p306 D2.

These guest rooms in the heart of Amsterdam's party district are where the owner of Zosa (*see p53*) first got into the hospitality business. One building contains seven rooms and another across the street has a further two. The feel is basic and lived-in, but

vastly improved by the themes (Arabian Nights and the Sailor's Cabin, for example) and friendly staff. A big plus is the groovy bar and coffeeshop of the same name (*see p151*) where hotel guests get money off smokes and drinks.

**Hotel services** *Bar.* **Room services** *TV: cable.*

### Hotel Internationaal

*Warmoesstraat 1-3, 1012 HT (624 5520/fax 624 4501/michdel@wxs.nl). Tram 1, 2, 4, 5, 9, 13, 16, 17, 20, 24, 25.* **Rates** €40-€75 single; €55-€75 double; €85-€120 triple. **Credit** AmEx, DC, MC, V. **Map** p306 D2.

We might be talking small, but if lively is what you want, then staying at this hotel above a traditional Dutch pub puts you in the thick of the Red Light District, with all the joy that brings. The eight simple rooms are pretty light, and the shared bathrooms have been newly refurbished. Breakfast sets you back around €5.

**Hotel services** *Bar. Concierge.* **Room services** *Dataport.*

### Winston Hotel

*Warmoesstraat 129, 1012 JA (623 1380/fax 639 2308/www.winston.nl). Tram 4, 9, 14, 16, 20, 24, 25.* **Rates** €57-€69 single; €71-€92 double; €108-€123 triple; €121-€142 quad; €142-€158 5-person room; €166-€188 6-person room. **Credit** AmEx, DC, MC, V. **Map** p306 D2.

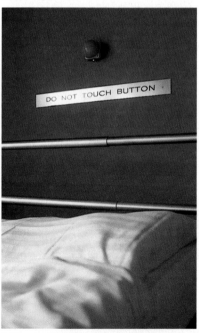

Art's out of the frame at the **Winston Hotel**.

Right in the bustle of the Red Light District, with a 24-hour bar for guests and decent club nights (*see p214 and p223*), the Winston is a fun place to stay. Ask if you can have one of the 26 funky art rooms: the hotel's philosophy is to get art out of frames and into your head, and these spicily decorated rooms succeed. The atmosphere is laid-back and friendly. **Hotel services** *Bar. Disabled: adapted room.*

### Young Budget Hotel Kabul
*Warmoesstraat 38-42, 1012 JE (623 7158/ fax 620 0869). Tram 4, 9, 14, 16, 20, 24, 25.* **Rates** €20-€29 dorm bed; €48-€52 single; €68-€91 double; €86-€113 triple; €125 suite. **Credit** AmEx, DC, MC, V. **Map** p306 D2.

Don't be put off the Kabul by its daunting exterior: staff here are friendly and the aroma of cannabis smacks of the classic backpacker experience. Some big rooms look out over Damrak and let in loads of light, though others in this no-frills labyrinth are more than a little gloomy. Better news is the fact that the hotel doesn't operate a curfew and is only a two-minute walk from Centraal Station. **Hotel services** *Bar.*

## Hostels

### Bob's Youth Hostel
*Nieuwezijds Voorburgwal 92, 1012 SG (623 0063/fax 675 6446). Tram 1, 2, 5, 13, 17, 20.* **Rates** €16 dorm bed; €68 2-person apartments. **No credit cards. Map** p306 D3.

A mellow place in which to meet fellow travellers. Make sure you don't miss the entrance, down a short flight of steps underground to the breakfast bar. Dorms range in size from four to 16 beds, and there are even apartments for two people sharing. Most of the dorms are mixed, but one is women-only. **Hotel services** *Bar. TV room: cable.*

### Bulldog Budget Hotel
*Oudezijds Voorburgwal 220, 1012 GJ (620 3822/ fax 627 1612/www.bulldog.nl). Tram 4, 9, 14, 16, 20, 24, 25/Metro Nieuwmarkt.* **Rates** €17-€24 dorm bed; €49-€59 single; €61-€74 double; €87-€96 triple; €112-€124 quad. **Credit** AmEx, MC, V. **Map** p306 D3.

Stroll out from the Bulldog, one of a chain of nine bars and coffeeshops, and you'll be bang in the city centre. Currently offering 100 beds, the hotel has plans to expand by the summer of 2002. All private rooms and smaller dorms have TVs, and a spacious lounge offers Internet terminals and movies on DVD. **Hotel services** *Internet. Parking (street).* **Room services** *TV: cable (selected rooms only).*

### Flying Pig Hostels
**Flying Pig Downtown** *Nieuwendijk 100, 1012 MR (420 6822/group bookings 421 0583/ fax 428 0802/www.flyingpig.nl). Tram 1, 2, 3, 5, 13, 17, 20.* **Flying Pig Palace** *Vossiusstraat 46-7, 1071 AJ (400 4187/group reservations 421 0583/fax 421 0802/www.flyingpig.nl). Tram 2, 5, 20.*

The immensely popular **Flying Pig Hostels**.

**Rates** *Downtown* €15.50-€23.50 dorm bed; €57.50-€68 single/twin. *Palace* €15.75-€23 dorm bed; €54.50-€56 single; €56.50-€64 twin; €67.50 triple. **Credit** *Both* MC, V. **Map** *Downtown* p306 D2. *Palace* p310 C6.

The Flying Pigs – one (Flying Pig Downtown) on Nieuwendijk, the other (Fling Pig Palace) in the Museum Quarter – are so popular that reservations can only be made online, or by calling reception the morning of the night you want to stay and going on the waiting list. Both sites are clean and laid-back, with staff who understand the needs of backpackers. Both also have an equipped kitchen and offer a range of tourist info, and most rooms have showers and loos. There's no curfew, but if you want to stay in, both sites have lively bars (guests only). Come summer, consider a night at the Pig's seaside outpost at Nordwijk, reachable for a small charge via shuttle. **Hotel services** *Bar.*

# Get happy

She was once the Netherlands' most infamous export, but Xaviera Hollander has long since retired from being New York City's most enthusiastic bordello madam. Such work requires a certain sense of anonymity and that all disappeared after she wrote *The Happy Hooker*. Published in 1971 (and due to be republished in summer 2002), it proved a landmark in sexual frankness, selling over 17 million copies, spawning several sequels and movie adaptations, and introducing countless innocents to the sheer breadth of the human sexual landscape. Bless.

Hollander, though, still retains a madam's zest for making people happy. As a happy booker, she has hosted – both in her home and in special locations – regular English-language dinner theatre productions featuring solo performers (Earl Okin, Cindy Freeman, Lisa Lipkin, Linda Marlowe and Stephen Rappaport, to name a few) that catch her eye during her annual pilgrimage to the Edinburgh Festival.

More recently, she's turned her hostessing skills to offering B&B in her own home, a quiet, residential dwelling dense with art, musical instruments, mementos and a steady stream of visiting friends. Whether in an upstairs bedroom – complete with terrace – or in a 'chalet' out in the backyard, it's hard to underestimate the sheer uniqueness of these accommodations, which also happen to be fairly centrally located. While the opportunity certainly exists to tap her for

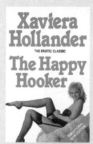

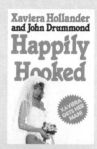

some outrageous stories, you don't have to be a sexual libertine to feel at home here. But, you suspect, it probably helps...

## Xaviera Hollander Bed & Breakfast
*Stadionweg 17, Zuid, 1077 RV (673 3934/ fax 664 3687/www.xaviera-theatre.com/ sleeper). Tram 5, 24.* **Rates** *from €100 double.* **No credit cards.**

## Meeting Point
*Warmoesstraat 14, 1012 JD (tel/fax 627 7499/ www.hostel-meetingpoint.nl). Tram 4, 9, 16, 20, 24, 25.* **Rates** *€16-€20 dorm bed; €20-€25 per person 4/5/6-bed private room.* **No credit cards.** **Map** p306 D2.

The dark reception area at Meeting Point leads up to rooms with four, five, six, 12 or 18 beds. The hostel is basic but cheap, with breakfast for €2.50. As with most hostels, reservations have to be made in person. Plenty of fun is to be had right on your doorstep: the spliff-friendly bar is open 24 hours but is for guests only.
**Hotel services** *Bar. No-smoking rooms.*

## NJHC Hostels
**Stadsdoelen** *Kloveniersburgwal 97, 1011 KB (624 6832/fax 639 1035/www.njhc.nl). Tram 4, 9, 14, 16, 20, 24, 25.*
**City Hostel Vondelpark** *Zandpad 5, 1054 GA (589 8996/fax 589 8955/www.njhc.nl). Tram 1, 2, 5, 6, 7, 10, 20.*

**Rates** *Stadsdoelen €15-€18.50 dorm bed. City Hostel Vondelpark €19-€27 dorm/quad bed; €53.50-€71 single/twin. Both hostels non-members €2.25 extra.* **Credit** *Both* MC, V. **Map** *Stadsdoelen* p306 D3. *City Hostel Vondelpark* p310 C6.

The Stadsdoelen branch of the NJHC is just a few moments away from the steamy Red Light District, but is also ideally situated for Waterlooplein or Rembrandtplein. If you're looking for surrounds that offer a fair bit of green space, then try the Vondelpark branch instead. Both the hostels are kept totally spotless, and both are friendly and open right round the clock. The bar at Stadsdoelen offers light meals and snacks. The newly renovated Vondelpark site, meanwhile, constitutes one of Europe's largest and most modern hostels. Facilities include a restaurant overlooking the park, Internet access and a TV room.
**Hotel services** *Bar (both). Courtyard (Stadsdoelen only). Disabled: adapted rooms (Vondelpark only). No-smoking rooms (both). Restaurant (both).*

## Western Canal Belt

### Deluxe

#### Amsterdam Marriott Hotel

*Stadhouderskade 12, 1054 ES (607 5555/
fax 607 5567/www.marriotthotels.com). Tram 1, 2,
5, 6, 7, 10, 20.* **Rates** €217-€278 room (holds 1-4
people); €478-€525 suite (holds 1-4 people).
**Credit** AmEx, DC, MC, V. **Map** p310 C5.
This five-star hotel is in the centre of the city, overlooking Leidseplein and near the big museums. The
comfortable 392 rooms and suites all offer a feeling
of spaciousness: there are no singles, so you'll just
have to sit back and let yourself be pampered. Of
the two restaurants, Port O' Amsterdam offers a
luxurious menu, while Characters includes Pizza
Hut pizzas for lunch and dinner, plus a jukebox and
a pool table. Breakfast is €12.50-€17.50.
**Hotel services** *Air-conditioning. Babysitting. Bars.
Business services. Concierge. Disabled: adapted
rooms. Gym. No-smoking floors. Parking (€25/day).
Restaurants.* **Room services** *Dataport. Minibar.
Room service (24hrs). TV: satellite/pay movies.*

#### Blakes

*Keizersgracht 384, 1016 GB (530 2010/fax 530
2030/www.blakesamsterdam.com). Tram 1, 2, 5.*
**Rates** €236-€289 single; €367-€472 double; €682-
€1,312 suite. **Credit** AmEx, DC, MC, V. **Map** p310 C4.
This building is something of a local landmark: it
dates back to 1617 and was originally a theatre.
These days, though, it's found a new lease of life as
Anouska Hempel's Amsterdam hotel. And what a
hotel. Opened in 1999, Blakes is the epitome of modern luxury: dramatic, elegant decor complemented
by sensational service, a model for anyone looking
to start a fashionable boutique hotel. The restaurant
is equally winning (*see p123*), serving a menu
inspired by the 16th-century merchant venturers.
Breakfast costs €16.
**Hotel services** *Air-conditioning. Babysitting. Bar.
Concierge. Garden. Limousine service. Parking (valet).
Restaurant.* **Room services** *Dataport. Minibar.
Room service (24hrs). TV: cable/VCR.*

#### Hotel Pulitzer

*Prinsengracht 315-31, 1016 GZ (523 5235/fax 316
4398/www.sheraton.nl). Tram 13, 14, 17, 20.*
**Rates** €220 single; €386-€398 double; €758-€822
suite; €47 extra bed. **Credit** AmEx, DC, MC, V.
**Map** p306 C3.
One of the more centrally located five-star hotels,
the Pulitzer is also one of the more traditional. The
hotel consists of 230 guest rooms, and occupies an
entire block of canal houses (25 in total), with a
labyrinth of connecting corridors incorporating the
covered walkway through the central courtyard
gardens. What's more, the cultural significance of
the Pulitzer goes far beyond its architecture: a
gallery holds regular exhibitions, and an annual
music festival is held on canal barges in front of the
hotel. Breakfast is around €22.

Anouska Hempel's **Blakes**: heaven.

**Hotel services** *Air-conditioning. Babysitting.
Bar. Business services. Concierge. Garden. Limousine
service. No-smoking rooms. Parking (valet).
Restaurant.* **Room services** *Dataport. Minibar.
Room service (24hrs). TV: cable/pay movies/VCR
(by request).*

### Expensive

#### Ambassade Hotel

*Herengracht 341, 1016 AZ (555 0222/fax 555
0277/www.ambassade-hotel.nl). Tram 1, 2, 5.*
**Rates** €152 single; €180 double; €210 triple;
€250-€315 suite; €285 apartment; €32 extra bed.
**Credit** AmEx, DC, MC, V. **Map** p310 C4.
The differing structures of the ten ancient houses at
the beautiful canalside Ambassade mean that no two
rooms are alike. To complement this, each bedroom
has been individually and exquisitely decorated in
keeping with the historic surroundings. Visiting publishers and authors often stay here (Salman Rushdie
and Umberto Eco have both been spied), while the
hotel's new library, consisting of 1,000 signed books,
adds to the literary feel. Breakfast is €14.
**Hotel services** *Babysitting. Business services.
Concierge. Limousine service. No-smoking rooms.*
**Room services** *Internet. Room service (24hrs).
TV: cable/VCR.*

#### Canal House Hotel

*Keizersgracht 148, 1015 CX (622 5182/fax 624
1317/www.canalhouse.nl). Tram 13, 14, 17, 20.*
**Rates** €140-€190 single/double. **Credit** DC, MC, V.
**Map** p306 C3.

The culture-friendly **Hotel Pulitzer**. See p57.

The Canal House is one of the few hotels to refuse children who are under 12: a relief if you don't have any, and the serenity is carried over with the absence of any TVs. That said, the new Irish owners, Brian and Mary Bennett, have definitely snapped up a treasure. This is a gorgeous 17th-century building, with ornate ceilings and antiques liberally sprinkled throughout the 26 rooms. Stay here and you'll have the illusion of inhabiting the set of a costume drama.

**Hotel services** *Bar. Garden.* **Room services** *Dataport. Telephone.*

### Estheréa

*Singel 303-9, 1012 WJ (624 5146/fax 623 9001/ www.estherea.nl). Tram 1, 2, 5.* **Rates** €143-€198 single; €152-€255 double; €211-€283 triple; €238-€310 quad. **Credit** AmEx, DC, MC, V. **Map** p306 C3.

Tucked round the corner from the Spui and still owned and run by the same family that founded it almost 60 years ago, this charming four-star haven is ideal for those who love being looked after. From the luxurious breakfast room overlooking the canal, where tea and coffee are served (free) all day and breakfast costs €14, to the 70 individually and traditionally renovated rooms, meticulous attention to detail is evident. Some 20 rooms spread throughout the plot of eight canal houses are even more deluxe, with the additional bonus of glorious views over the Singel canal. You have to pay a supplement for these, but it's worth the extra.

**Hotel services** *Babysitting. Bar. Concierge. No-smoking rooms.* **Room services** *Dataport. Minibar. Room service (7.30am-10pm). TV: cable.*

### Toren

*Keizersgracht 164, 1015 CZ (622 6352/fax 626 9705/www.toren.nl). Tram 13, 14, 17, 20.* **Rates** €110 single; €126-€215 double; €194 triple; €241 suite. **Credit** AmEx, DC, MC, V. **Map** p306 C3.

Erik Toren's eponymously named four-star has fantastic detailing, and with 30-plus staff looking after the 40 rooms, the ultra-high standards are maintained effortlessly. Located on the site where the Free University was founded, the hotel's historic features have been carefully preserved. However, the hotel is equipped with all modern amenities, combining 17th-century atmosphere with 21st-century comfort. The garden suites open out into a green oasis, while the nine rooms overlooking the canal have jacuzzis. A terrific hotel, and great value, too. Breakfast is €12.

**Hotel services** *Air-conditioning (selected rooms). Babysitting. Bar. Garden. Parking (paid). Restaurant.* **Room services** *Minibar. TV: cable/pay movies.*

## Moderate

### Amsterdam Wiechmann

*Prinsengracht 328-32, 1016 HX (626 3321/fax 626 8962/www.hotelwiechmann.nl). Tram 1, 2, 5, 7, 17, 20.* **Rates** €70-€90 single; €115-€137 double; €170-€180 triple/quad; €230 suite. **Credit** MC, V. **Map** p310 C4.

The owner of Amsterdam Wiechmann prides himself on his antiques, the wooden beams and panelling of the three restored canal houses that make up the hotel. Accommodations here are basic, but the prices are decent, and it's located in a charming part of town not far from Leidseplein.

**Hotel services** *Babysitting. Bar.* **Room services** *TV: cable.*

### Singel Hotel

*Singel 15, 1012 VC (626 3108/fax 620 3777). Tram 1, 2, 5, 13, 17, 20/Metro Centraal Station.* **Rates** €64-€89 single; €109-€129 double; €136-€170 triple. **Credit** AmEx, DC, MC, V. **Map** p306 C2.

This sister of the Hotel Citadel (*see p53*) shares its sibling's welcoming atmosphere. Located on the Singel, just a short walk from the Jordaan, many of the 32 rooms have a view of the canal.

**Hotel services** *Babysitting. Bar. Concierge.* **Room services** *Room service (24hrs). TV: cable.*

## Southern Canal Belt

### Deluxe

### American Hotel

*Leidsekade 97, 1017 PN (556 3000/fax 556 3110/ www.amsterdam-american.crowneplaza.com). Tram 1, 2, 5, 6, 7, 10, 20.* **Rates** €320-€373 single; €346-€399 double; €26 extra bed. **Credit** AmEx, DC, MC, V. **Map** p310 C5.

A classic art deco exterior, modernised interior and plush rooms make the American – now owned by Crowne Plaza – an attractive option. Numerous rock stars seem to enjoy the hotel's proximity to the Melkweg (*see 213*) and the Paradiso (*see p214*), along with the Stadsschouwburg (*see p243*). Situated on the ground floor is Café Américain (*see p124*), the hotel's focal point, which overlooks the bustling Leidseplein. In contrast, the wonderfully tranquil reaches of Vondelpark are just a couple of minutes' walk away. Breakfast is €20.

**Hotel services** *Air-conditioning. Babysitting (by request). Bars. Business services. Concierge. Disabled: adapted room. Gym. Limousine service (by request). No-smoking floors. Parking (paid). Restaurants.* **Room services** *Dataport. Minibar. Room service (24hrs). TV: cable/pay movies.*

### Amstel Inter-Continental Amsterdam

*Professor Tulpplein 1, 1018 GX (622 6060/fax 622 5808/www.interconti.com). Tram 6, 7, 10, 20.* **Rates** €493-€546 single/double; €703-€2,467 suite. **Credit** AmEx, DC, MC, V. **Map** p311 F4.

The alluring Grand Hall foyer gives a hint of what lies beyond in the city's most luxurious, formal five-star hotel. With a ratio of two staff to each of the 79 antique- and Delft-adorned rooms and suites, you can expect to be pampered. Guests' high expectations seem to be met, too, given the number of returning celebs and royals. The hotel's superb cuisine can be enjoyed either in sumptuous indoor surroundings or on the riverside terraces. Breakfast is €21.

**Hotel services** *Air-conditioning. Bars. Business services. Concierge. Gym. Limousine service. No-smoking rooms. Parking. Restaurants. Swimming pool.* **Room services** *Dataport. Minibar. Room service (24hrs). TV: cable/pay movies/VCR.*

### Schiller Hotel

*Rembrandtplein 26-36, 1017 CV (554 0700/fax 624 0098/www.goldentulip.com). Tram 4, 9, 14, 20.* **Rates** €189-€215 single; €231-€283 double; €313 triple. **Credit** AmEx, DC, MC, V. **Map** p311 E4.

Amid the touristy tack of Rembrandtplein lies the refined covered terrace of the Schiller, a four-star that's been faithfully restored to its former art deco Jugendstil style. The hotel was originally renowned for the artists and poets who lingered over drinks while hotly debating contemporary art. Alas, those days have gone and the artistic types have given way to business visitors, though some 40 per cent of the hotel's guests are still tourists. The restaurant serves French cuisine. Breakfast is around €15.

**Hotel services** *Babysitting (by request). Bar. Business services. No-smoking rooms. Restaurant.* **Room services** *Minibar (selected rooms). Room service (7am-11pm). TV: cable/pay movies.*

### 717

*Prinsengracht 717, 1017 JW (427 0717/ fax 4230 717/www.717hotel.nl). Tram 1, 2, 5.* **Rates** €345 single; €370 double; €417-€595 suite. **Credit** AmEx, DC, MC, V. **Map** p310 D4.

Luxury, straight from the old school: the **American Hotel**. *See p58.*

Do it the deco way at the **Schiller Hotel**.

Discreet could be the watchword for this early 19th-century canal house's exterior, but the refurbished interior yields something of a timeless romanticism. Original owner, Dutch designer and decorator Kees van der Valk, has carefully arranged beautiful objects (in classical, primitive and contemporary styles), from the inviting sitting room and library to eight suites furnished with pieces from all over Europe. Breakfast, afternoon tea and wine can be enjoyed in the secluded patio out back and are included in your bill. Impressive.

**Hotel services** *Air-conditioning (suites only). Business services. Garden. No-smoking rooms. Parking (paid).* **Room services** *Dataport. Minibar. Room service (7.30am-1am). TV: cable/pay movies/VCR.*

## Expensive

### Eden Hotel

*Amstel 144, 1017 AE (530 7878/fax 624 2946/ www.bestwestern.nl). Tram 4, 9, 14, 20.*
**Rates** €116-€154 single; €134-€205 twin/double; €186-€236 triple; €210-€273 quad; €184-€256 apartment (min 7 nights). **Credit** AmEx, DC, MC, V. **Map** p307 C3.

As Amsterdam's largest three-star hotel – 340 rooms, with a further 70 to follow after renovations are completed – the Eden offers stacks of variety. Talented students from the Rietveld Art Academy have even designed three special art rooms: ask for the interpretation of Rembrandt's *Night Watch* (though if you stay in one of these rooms, prepare to pay a supplement of around €15). There are also 13 apartments available for longer stays. Its location right on the banks of the Amstel, practically around the corner from Rembrandtplein, makes it an easy jump to virtually anywhere in the city. Breakfast is charged at €13.50 extra.

**Hotel services** *Babysitting. Bar. Business services. Concierge. Disabled: adapted room. No-smoking rooms. Parking nearby. Restaurant.* **Room services** *Dataport (selected rooms). Minibar (selected rooms). TV: cable/pay movies.*

### Hotel Dikker & Thijs Fenice

*Prinsengracht 444, 1017 KE (620 1212/fax 625 8986/www.dikkerenthijsfenice.nl). Tram 1, 2, 5.*
**Rates** €145-€195 single; €195-€245 double; €245-€345 suite. **Credit** AmEx, DC, MC, V. **Map** p310 C5.

This four-star hotel on the corner of Prinsengracht and Leidsestraat is just a two-minute walk from Leidseplein, making it extremely handy for shopping and social festivities, and for Museumplein. Many of the 42 rooms have a nice canal vista over the Prinsengracht. The adjacent restaurant, De Prinsenkelder, serves French and Italian cuisine for dinner or a late supper, and guests can charge their meals to the hotel bill.

**Hotel services** *Babysitting. Bar. Business services. Concierge. Parking (paid). Restaurant.* **Room services** *Dataport. Minibar. Room service (during restaurant hrs). TV: cable/pay movies.*

Ask for an art room at the **Eden Hotel**.

## Moderate

### Bridge Hotel

*Amstel 107-11, 1018 EM (623 7068/fax 624 1565/www.thebridgehotel.nl). Tram 4, 6, 7, 9, 10, 20.* **Rates** €85 single; €85-€130 double; €130 triple; €180 apartment/quad. **Credit** AmEx, DC, MC, V. **Map** p307 E3.

Located on the Amstel with a view of the city's locks and nearly next door to the Carré Theatre, the 30-room Bridge Hotel is ideal for romantic walks on the Magerebrug (Skinny Bridge). Friendly staff make a stay here pleasant and, for the cheery country-pine rooms, prices are reasonable (although at some times, the hotel cheekily insists that weekend bookings run for three nights). The top-floor apartment offers a spacious home away from home if you can manage the endless stairs to reach it.

**Hotel services** *Bar.* **Room services** *TV: cable.*

### Hotel Agora

*Singel 462, 1017 AW (627 2200/fax 627 2202/www.hotelagora.nl). Tram 1, 2, 5.* **Rates** €66-€95 single; €79-€125 double; €147 triple; €170 quad. **Credit** AmEx, DC, MC, V. **Map** p310 D4.

It's easy to see why this cosy two-star hotel usually has a full house: its owners are personable, the location terrific (near the Bloemenmarkt; *see p162*), and the canal house itself is a lovely historic treasure (though there isn't a lift). Five of the 16 rooms look out over Singel, and renovations have left the bathrooms in tiptop condition with pretty ceramic tilework (only one room has a shower off the hall). Breakfast in bed is gratis; or take it in the convivial lounge and garden area.

**Hotel services** *Garden.* **Room services** *Room service (8am-10.30pm). TV: cable.*

### Seven Bridges

*Reguliersgracht 31, 1017 LK (623 1329). Tram 16, 24, 25.* **Rates** €90-€150 single; €110-€170 double. **Credit** AmEx, MC, V. **Map** p311 E4.

Seven Bridges is strewn with enough lightly coloured antique furnishings to dispel the myth that old-fashioned styling means sombre tones and dark wood. Both the proprietors take great pride in their small hotel, and the eight rooms contain some charming pieces: how about preening in a Napoleonic mirror while your toes sink into a deep, handwoven carpet? Breakfast is served in guests' rooms.

**Hotel services** *No-smoking rooms.* **Room services** *TV: cable.*

## Budget

### De Admiraal

*Herengracht 563, 1017 CD (626 2150/fax 623 4625). Tram 4, 9, 14, 20.* **Rates** €48-€70 single; €61-€93 double; €118-€172 triple/quad. **Credit** AmEx, DC, MC, V. **Map** p311 E4.

A friendly and homely hotel by Rembrandtplein. Eight of De Admiraal's nine rooms have canal views, and room six boasts five windows with a stunning view of the lovely Reguliersgracht and Herengracht. Note that the hotel closes from mid November to mid March, except for Christmas and New Year. The big Dutch breakfasts are about €5 extra.

**Room services** *TV: cable.*

### Euphemia Hotel

*Fokke Simonszstraat 1-9, 1017 TD (622 9045/fax 638 9673/www.euphemiahotel.com). Tram 16, 24, 25.* **Rates** €62-€138 double/triple; €92-€140 quad. **Credit** AmEx, DC, MC, V. **Map** p311 E5.

Located on a quiet sidestreet handy for both the Heineken Experience (*see p114*) and Rembrandtplein, this former monastery now contains 30 cheap and comfy rooms. Fortunately, the management doesn't expect guests to behave like monks: there's a relaxed attitude towards visitors who want to sample Amsterdam's coffeeshops or gay nightlife. Most rooms are en suite and there's a communal sitting room with TV and video.

**Hotel services** *Internet (not in rooms). No-smoking rooms.*

### Hans Brinker Budget Hotel

*Kerkstraat 136-8, 1017 GR (622 0687/fax 638 2060/www.hans-brinker.com). Tram 1, 2, 5, 16, 24, 25.* **Rates** €21-€24 dorm bed per person; €52 single; €70 double; €90 triple. **Credit** AmEx, DC, MC, V. **Map** p311 E4.

A sizeable presence on Kerkstraat, this centrally located hostel with a gift for self-promotion has over 530 beds. One of its clever ad campaigns proclaimed

Rooms with a view at **De Admiraal**.

that Hans Brinker is 'close to the best hospitals in Amsterdam' – not exactly the most reassuring of statements, but a good indication that it won't be dull staying here. There's a large bar, cantina and disco, staff are friendly, and everything is clean and looked after. The main drag? No advance bookings in busy summer months.

**Hotel services** *Bar. Restaurant.*

### Hotel ITC

*Prinsengracht 1051, 1017 JE (623 0230/fax 624 5846/www.itc-hotel.com). Tram 4.* **Rates** €60-€64 single; €81-€92 double; €105-€122 triple. **Credit** MC, V. **Map** p311 E4.

Fans of this small, gay-friendly hotel will be pleased to learn that another 12 rooms were being added in late 2001. Located in one of the prettiest areas of Amsterdam, ITC is conveniently near the gay bar scenes of the Amstel and Reguliersdwarsstraat, and its inexpensive rates mean guests can spend their savings in their choice of the smart restaurants on Utrechtsestraat. Rooms are spartan, but some have attractive beamed ceilings; doubles are all en suite, while singles share bathrooms on the hallway. Breakfast, €6, is served in the hotel's canalside lounge. No children or pets allowed.

**Room services** *Dataport. TV: cable/pay movies.*

### Hotel Prinsenhof
*Prinsengracht 810, 1017 JL (623 1772/fax 638 3368/www.hotelprinsenhof.com). Tram 4.*
**Rates** €40-€75 single; €60-€80 double; €85-€100 triple; €100-€135 quad. **Credit** AmEx, MC, V. **Map** p311 E4.
Hotel Prinsenhof is a pretty canal house with beamed ceilings and wood furnishings. Facilities are basic: there's no lift, but a motorised hook in the central stairway makes hoisting your luggage up almost fun, and only three of the 11 rooms have en suite toilet and shower. Staff are friendly and the place is incredibly clean to boot. Good value.
**Room services** *Dataport. Telephone.*

### Hotel Quentin
*Leidsekade 89, 1017 PN (626 2187/fax 622 0121). Tram 1, 2, 5.* **Rates** €34-€75 single; €66-€116 double; €86-€134 triple; €113 quad; €136 5-person room. **Credit** AmEx, DC, MC, V. **Map** p310 C5.
Quentin Crisp once stayed in this small laid-back hotel, and his legendary presence has been honoured in its name. Something of his eccentric spirit seems to live on here, attracting touring rock bands, artsy types, gays and lesbians. Rooms are clean with decent furnishings, and many are quite spacious. There's a friendly lounge in which to satisfy your munchies 24 hours a day, and the canalside location is a winner. Breakfast is €3-€9.
**Hotel services** *Bar/lounge.* **Room services** *TV: cable.*

## Hostels

### International Budget Hostel
*Leidsegracht 76, 1016 CR (624 2784/fax 772 4825). Tram 1, 2, 5.* **Rates** €61-€71 twin; €80-€92 quad. **Credit** AmEx, MC, V. **Map** p310 C4.
International Budget Hostel is the only inexpensive youth hostel to offer rooms with a canal view. Most of the facilities are shared (though four doubles offer private bathrooms) and dorms are mixed unless you ask in advance. There isn't a curfew, so you can party late in Leidseplein. Breakfast is €1.60-€3.60.
**Hotel services** *TV room: cable.*

## Jodenbuurt, the Plantage & the Oost

## Moderate

### Arena
*'s Gravesandestraat 51, 1092 AA (694 7444/ 850 2410/www.hotelarena.nl). Tram 3, 6, 9, 10, 14.* **Rates** €125-€173 double; €169 triple; €202 quad. **Credit** AmEx, MC, V. **Map** p312 G3.
Once an orphanage, then a youth hostel, this landmark building has been converted into a modish hotel, with airy rooms that are minimally furnished with hardwood floors and designer furniture. While the Arena isn't central, the facilities mean you may

not want to go elsewhere in the evening: a swanky restaurant, To Dine, serves fine food, and the café lounge has a terrace in front and a large garden behind. Guests also get a discount to the newly renovated night club (*see p225*). Avoid guest rooms facing the entrance if you want a quiet night's sleep.
**Hotel services** *Bar. Concierge. Disabled: adapted rooms. Garden. Parking (paid). Restaurant.* **Room services** *Telephone. TV: cable/DVD/Playstation.*

## The Jordaan

## Budget

### Hotel van Onna
*Bloemgracht 102-108, 1015 TN (626 5801/ www.netcentrum.nl/onna). Tram 10.* **Rates** €40 single; €80 double; €120 triple. **No credit cards.** **Map** p305 B3.
The charm of Hotel van Onna comes from its pleasant setting overlooking a quiet Jordaan canal and the delightfully informal feel created by the eponymous Loek van Onna, the laid-back owner. The 41 rooms, housed in three 17th-century houses, are modern and basic but clean and warm. All rooms have an en suite bathroom and the price includes a Dutch breakfast.
**Hotel services** *No-smoking rooms.*

## The Museum Quarter, Vondelpark & the South

## Deluxe

### Hilton Amsterdam
*Apollolaan 138, 1077 BG (710 6000/fax 710 9000/ www.hilton.com). Tram 5, 24.* **Rates** €294-€357 single; €315-€378 double; €441-€919 suite. **Credit** AmEx, DC, MC, V.
Despite being famed for John and Yoko's 'bed-in' of 1969, the huge five-star Hilton looks pretty unexciting. However, it does offer 271 air-conditioned rooms and a restaurant with great Mediterranean cuisine. The John and Yoko suite can be hired for weddings, and is very popular with honeymooners. The hotel's location – *waaaay* south – is not ideal, but then again, there's no room for a yacht club and marina in the city centre (though these are not part of the hotel, just a backdrop). Breakfast is €22 or so.
**Hotel services** *Air-conditioning. Babysitting. Bar. Beauty salon. Business services. Concierge. Disabled: adapted rooms. Garden. Gym. Limousine service. No-smoking floors. Parking. Restaurant.* **Room services** *Dataport. Minibar. Refrigerator (suites only). Room service (24hrs). TV: cable/pay movies/web TV.*

### Hotel Okura Amsterdam
*Ferdinand Bolstraat 333, 1072 LH (678 7111/fax 671 2344/www.okura.nl). Tram 12, 25.* **Rates** €336-€373 single; €373-€409 double; €388-€1,732 suite; €73 extra bed. **Credit** AmEx, DC, MC, V.

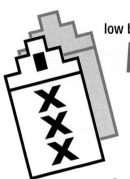

Perfectly situated and equipped for business, the luxury five-star Okura boasts 321 rooms, 49 suites and 16 banqueting and conference rooms. Granted, the location isn't very central, but the fact that it's only a ten-minute walk from the RAI Congress and the World Trade Centre is an obvious advantage to business travellers. Commerce aside, there are two bars and four restaurants, one of which is on the 23rd floor and offers an incredible panoramic view of the entire city. Breakfast is an extra €22.
**Hotel services** *Air-conditioning. Babysitting. Bar(s). Beauty salon. Business services. Concierge. Disabled: adapted rooms. Gym. Limousine service. No-smoking rooms. Parking (paid). Restaurant(s). Swimming pool (indoor).* **Room services** *Dataport. Minibar. Room service (24hrs). TV: satellite/pay movies/VCR (suites only).*

## Expensive

### Best Western AMS Hotel Terdam

*Tesselschadestraat 23, 1054 ET (612 6876/fax 683 8313/www.bestwestern.nl). Tram 1, 2, 3, 5, 6, 12, 20.* **Rates** €133-€180 single; €148-€199 double; €236 triple; €30 extra bed. **Credit** AmEx, DC, MC, V. **Map** p310 C5.
The long-winded name might be a mouthful to say to a taxi driver, but don't let that put you off. This hotel has 89 comfortable rooms in the vicinity of the Vondelpark close to Leidseplein. One wing has been renovated, and now features air-conditioning and revamped bathrooms.
**Hotel services** *Air-conditioning (selected rooms). Babysitting. Bar. Concierge. Disabled: adapted rooms. Limousine service. Parking nearby.* **Room services** *Dataport. Minibar (selected rooms). TV: cable/pay movies.*

### Hotel Vondel

*Vondelstraat 28-30, 1054 GE (612 0120/ fax 685 4321/www.srs-worldhotels.com). Tram 1, 3, 6, 12.* **Rates** €220 single/double; €385 suite. **Credit** AmEx, DC, MC, V. **Map** p310 C5.
This stylish four-star hotel, located in a quiet area, takes its name from Joost van den Vondel (1587-1679), the 'Prince among Poets' who doubled as the Netherlands' most acclaimed playwright. The interior is astounding: lots of the 70 rooms are sumptuously decorated in crimson and cream, with detailing in walnut wood. Many rooms that look out over the Vondelstraat have balconies, enabling guests to hear the occasional busking flautist. Breakfast is €15.
**Hotel services** *Bar. Business services. Concierge. Garden.* **Room services** *Dataport. Minibar. TV: cable/pay movies/VCR.*

### Jan Luyken Hotel

*Jan Luijkenstraat 58, 1071 CS (573 0730/fax 676 3841/www.janluyken.nl). Tram 2, 3, 5, 12, 20.* **Rates** €182 single; €205-€283 double; €42 extra bed. **Credit** AmEx, DC, MC, V. **Map** p310 D6.
On a quiet street between the Vondelpark and the museums, this friendly but formal four-star hotel caters for the more mature, refined customer, and

**Hans Brinker Budget Hotel.** *See p62.*

for business travellers. An authentic townhouse atmosphere pervades in the reception area: the hotel has done a good job of largely retaining its original 19th-century style – though there are also some quirky decorative elements. The spa is a perfect place to unwind, while the 62 well-furnished rooms come with renovated bathrooms, so you can still bathe in luxury if someone else has just booked the hot tub. Breakfast is €24.
**Hotel services** *Air-conditioning. Babysitting. Bar. Business services. Garden. No-smoking floors.* **Room services** *Dataport. Minibar. Refrigerator. Room service (7am-midnight). TV: cable/pay movies.*

### Omega Hotel

*Jacob Obrechtstraat 33, 1071 KG (664 5182/fax 664 0809/www.omegahotel.nl). Tram 2, 3, 5, 12, 20.* **Rates** €147-€181 single; €199-€215 double; €236 triple. **Credit** AmEx, DC, MC, V. **Map** p310 C6.
The four-star Omega, located on a quiet square in the well-to-do Old South, now belongs to the AMS hotel group, but thankfully has retained its individual character. Interior decor is a rich array of reds and oranges with a smattering of antiques in the lobby, while rooms are clean and modern with vibrant striped walls. Breakfast (around €13) goes on until 11am, enabling late sleepers to catch up on their zzzs. In summer, enjoy drinks in the garden or on the rooftop, which boasts a terrific panoramic view of the city.
**Hotel services** *Air-conditioning (selected rooms). Bar. Business services. Concierge. Garden. No-smoking rooms.* **Room services** *Dataport. Minibar. Room service (24hrs). TV: cable.*

## Park Hotel

*Stadhouderskade 25, 1071 ZD (671 7474/fax 664 9455/www.parkhotel.nl). Tram 1, 2, 5.* **Rates** €194-€241 single; €241-€289 double; €289-€336 triple; €294-€341 suite; €45 extra bed. **Credit** AmEx, DC, MC, V. **Map** p310 D5.

This four-star hotel is perfectly positioned for local nightlife, with the casino just across the canal and Leidseplein only a few minutes away. During the daytime, culture vultures can make their way to nearby Museumplein. The hotel completed renovations in late 2001, and offers wide-ranging facilities, especially for business travellers. There are five small boutiques – accessible from inside the hotel – and offering hairstyling, Gucci accessories and the like. Breakfast is €17.50.

**Hotel services** *Air-conditioning (selected rooms). Babysitting. Bar. Business services. Limousine service. No-smoking floors. Parking (paid). Restaurant.* **Room services** *Dataport (selected rooms). Minibar (selected rooms). Room service (24hrs). TV: satellite/pay movies.*

# Moderate

## Concert Inn

*De Lairessestraat 11, 1071 NR (305 7272/fax 305 7271/www.concert-inn.nl). Tram 16.* **Rates** €104 single; €141 double; €327 studio; €361 apartment. **Credit** AmEx, DC, MC, V.

The rooms at the Concert Inn – named for its proximity to the Concertgebouw – are absolutely fine, with redecoration having taken on new TVs, new carpets and drapes that give total blackout; there are also some apartments in an adjoining building. However, the hotel really sells itself on its pleasant garden, perfect for summer, and the splendid warmth of the welcome you'll receive. The hotel makes a feature of its location just out of the centre by renting out an excellent little fleet of bikes at very reasonable rates.

**Hotel services** *Garden. Internet (not in rooms).* **Room services** *TV: cable.*

## Hotel de Filosoof

*Anna van den Vondelstraat 6, 1054 GZ (683 3013/ fax 685 3750/www.xs4all.nl/~filosoof). Tram 1, 6.* **Rates** €98-€108 single; €115-€130 double; €160-€170 triple.* **Credit** AmEx, MC, V. **Map** p309 B6.

Thoughtful types will find themselves absorbed by this fascinating themed hotel. Each of the 25 rooms is dedicated to a philosopher or philosophy: the Aristotle room is dreamy, while the Zen room is serene in the extreme. Even the spiral staircase that leads out into the garden encourages guests to pause and look, papered, as it is, in sheet music. It comes as little surprise, then, to find that charming owner Ida Jongsma welcomes a local philosophy group to the bar for a monthly evening of philosophical chat. A delight.

**Hotel services** *Babysitting. Bar. Garden.* **Room services** *TV: cable.*

## Hotel V

*Victorieplein 42, 1078 PH (662 3233/fax 676 6398/www.hotelv.nl). Tram 4, 12, 25.* **Rates** €70-€85 single; €95-€120 double; €135-€145 triple. **Credit** AmEx, DC, MC, V.

What was once a rather dowdy hotel has been transformed with a minimalist style. Design aficionados on a budget will love the location – near Hendrik Berlage's boulevard district, with a statue opposite the hotel paying homage to the renowned Dutch architect. Each of the 24 twin-bed rooms sport an upbeat slogan on the wall ('Love don't hate', 'Have fun') amid an otherwise clean and simple IKEA-type look. The clubby-looking breakfast room boasts cow-print stools and a long white banquette.

**Hotel services** *Bar. Garden. Parking (street).* **Room services** *TV: cable.*

## Hotel van de Kasteelen

*Frans van Mierisstraat 34, 1071 RT (679 8995/fax 670 6604/hotel@kastele.a2000.nl). Tram 3, 5, 12, 16, 20.* **Rates** €54-€91 single; €91-€136 double; €32 extra bed. **Credit** AmEx, MC, V. **Map** p310 D6.

On a quiet, tree-lined street close to Museumplein, this small, friendly hotel is popular with visitors to the cultural epicentre of the city. The peaceful lounge and garden decorated with orchids, candles and Asian artwork is a welcome sight after a day battling with crowds in the Rijksmuseum, as are the recently renovated rooms

**Hotel services** *Garden.* **Room services** *TV: cable.*

## Owl Hotel

*Roemer Visscherstraat 1, 1054 EV (618 9486/fax 618 9441/www.owl-hotel.demon.nl). Tram 1, 3, 6, 12.* **Rates** €73-€89 single; €89-€112 double; €114-€140 triple; €130-€167 quad. **Credit** AmEx, DC, MC, V. **Map** p310 C5.

A small and super-friendly family-run hotel on a quiet back street along the Vondelpark, five minutes from the Museumplein and the Rijksmuseum (*see p107*). The 34 rooms are all furnished in contemporary style and have en suite facilities. Guests can unwind in a quiet terrace out back.

**Hotel services** *Babysitting. Bar. Disabled: adapted room. Garden.* **Room services** *Dataport. Room service (breakfast only). TV: cable.*

## Prinsen Hotel

*Vondelstraat 36-8, 1054 GE (616 2323/fax 616 6112/www.prinsenhotel.demon.nl). Tram 1, 2, 3, 5, 6, 12, 20.* **Rates** €84-€102 single; €113-€125 double; €154-€163 triple; €177-€193 quad; €147 suite; €7 baby bed. **Credit** AmEx, DC, MC, V. **Map** p310 C6.

Gracious and friendly service is on hand at this pleasant hotel, conveniently located on a quiet street across from the Vondelpark and minutes away from Leidseplein. This three-star is bright with sunny colours, up-to-date yet certainly hip, and has a secluded garden in which to unwind. Of the 45 modest rooms, two have balconies and two have terraces, both offered at no extra charge.

**Hotel services** *Bar. Garden. Internet (not in rooms).* **Room services** *TV: cable.*

the park and major museums. Unfortunately, it's closed between November and March, save for the Christmas and New Year holidays.
**Hotel services** *Babysitting*. **Room services** *Dataport*.

### PC Hooft

*PC Hooftstraat 63, 1017 BN (662 7107/fax 675 8961). Tram 2, 3, 5, 12.* **Rates** €45-€52 single; €61-€68 double; €81-€88 triple; €93-€100 quad. **Credit** MC, V. **Map** p310 D5.
Addresses don't come much posher than this: PC Hooftstraat is where Amsterdam's beautiful people buy their designer clobber. Though not a patch on its chic surroundings, the hotel is pleasant and clean; it's also conveniently close to the city's major museums. Three rooms are en suite and most are modest-sized with newish furnishings (avoid the back rooms with high windows). Incidentally, Mr Hooft was a historian who hung out with friend and poet Joost van den Vondel, himself immortalised in the name of the neighbouring park.
**Room services** *TV: cable*.

## Hostels

For **Flying Pig Hostels**, *see p54*; for **NJHC Hostels**, *see p55*.

## The Pijp

**Hotel de Filosoof**: think about it... *See p66*.

## Budget

### Hotel Acro

*Jan Luijkenstraat 44, 1071 CR (662 0526/fax 675 0811/www.acro-hotel.nl). Tram 2, 5, 20.* **Rates** €41-€73 single; €57-€95 double; €75-€116 triple; €97-€123 quad. **Credit** AmEx, DC, MC, V. **Map** p310 D6.
This comfortable, modern hotel on a leafy sidestreet is handy for the museums and Leidseplein, but if you don't want to go out, the bar is open 24 hours and does basic snacks. Renovations have expanded Acro to 64 rooms, decking many of them out with hardwood floors and newer furnishings. The managers often have off-peak offers, so call ahead to check.
**Hotel services** *Bar. Concierge. Parking (on street). Internet (not in rooms)*. **Room services** *TV: cable/pay movies*.

### Parkzicht

*Roemer Visscherstraat 33, 1054 EW (618 1954/fax 618 0897). Tram 1, 2, 3, 5, 6, 12, 20.* **Rates** €45 single; €75-€80 double; €110 triple; €120 quad. **Credit** AmEx, MC, V. **Map** p310 C5.
The panelled breakfast room at this good-value Dutch country house offers the timeless charm of lace curtains and parquet floors covered with oriental rugs. Furnishings are fairly basic in all 14 rooms, but most are quite spacious – some with very high ceilings – and the location is sublimely peaceful, near

## The Pijp

## Budget

### Van Ostade Bicycle Hotel

*Van Ostadestraat 123, 1072 SV (679 3452/fax 671 5213/www.bicyclehotel.com). Tram 3, 12, 24, 25.* **Rates** €91-€93 single/double. **No credit cards.** **Map** p311 F6.
No need to worry about Van Ostade's location off the beaten path in the Pijp: it's a two-wheel savvy hotel that has bicycles for hire. The 16 rooms are clean and basic and there's a cosy communal area. Good value all round.
**Hotel services** *Internet (not in rooms). No-smoking rooms. Parking*. **Room services** *TV: cable*.

# Other Options

## Apartment rentals

For details on how to find somewhere permanent to live, *see p290* **Moving in**.

### Amsterdam Apartments

*Kromme Waal 32, Old Centre: Old Side (626 5930/ fax 622 9544). Tram 4, 9, 16, 20, 24, 25.* **Open** 9am-5pm Mon-Fri. **Map** p307 E2.
About 20 furnished, self-contained flats in central areas of town. Rates start from €600 a week for a one-person studio or one-bed flat. The minimum let is for one week and the maximum one month.

Accommodation

## Apartment Services AS

*Maasstraat 96, South (672 3013/672 1840/fax 676 4679/info@apartmentservices.nl). Tram 4, 12, 25.* **Open** 10.30am-5pm Mon-Fri.

A wide variety of mainly furnished accommodation, from simple short-let flats to apartments and whole houses. Rentals start at around €1,000 per month and a minimum let of two months is usual.

## Intercity Room Service

*Van Ostadestraat 348, the Pijp (675 0064). Tram 3, 4.* **Open** 10am-5pm Mon-Fri. **Map** p311 F6.

The place to try if you require something quickly. Intercity specialises in flatshares, but occasionally offers entire apartments; flatshares in the centre of town cost from €230 per month, with self-contained flats from €680. The minimum stay is six months, with one month's rent payable as commission.

# Bed & breakfast

The B&B ideal is growing in the Netherlands, but due to restrictions on the number of rooms and people allowed to stay (four is the maximum), it's still not as popular as in the UK. The best way to find a B&B is through **City Mundo** or **Holiday Link**, both of which deal with private accommodation and longer stays.

## City Mundo

*Schinkelkade 47 II, 1075 VK (676 5270/fax 676 5271/www.citymundo.com).*

This fine network, founded as recently as 1998, provides visitors with short-term private accommodation (three to 21 nights), from B&Bs and studios to flats on boats and even in windmills. Prices vary according to location and amenities and duration of stay (the longer you stay, the cheaper it becomes). The focus is less on budget prices and more on providing a specific service for people who really relish their surroundings.

## Holiday Link

*Postbus 70-155, 9704 AD Groningen (050 313 2424/313 3535/313 4545/ fax 050 313 3177/ www.holidaylink.com).*

Holiday Link is an organisation dealing with B&B and budget accommodation. Its annual guide to B&Bs is available in bookshops, tourist offices, by post or from its website for €15 (plus €2.50-€5 postage), and has stacks of information on all types of accommodation, from B&Bs to holiday home swaps. Worth investigating.

## Marcel van Woerkom

*Leidsestraat 87, Southern Canal Belt, 1017 NX (tel/fax 622 9834/www.marcelamsterdam.nl). Tram 1, 2, 5.* **Rates** €68 per person. **Credit** V. **Map** p310 D4.

Graphic artist Marcel van Woerkom provides a creative exchange in his pristine city-centre home, where four en suite rooms are available. Van Woerkom's favourite art is on the walls; all of it by

his friends. Guests with an appreciation of creative arts are especially welcome. Breakfast isn't included, but that's hardly the point. Book well ahead. **Hotel services** *No-smoking rooms.* **Room services** *Fridge (selected rooms). TV: cable.*

# Camping

**Vliegenbos** and **Zeeburg** are classified as youth campsites, while the other two are more family-oriented campsites with separate areas for youth camping.

## Gaasper Camping Amsterdam

*Loosdrechtdreef 7 (696 7326/fax 696 9369). Metro Gaasperplas/bus 15, 59, 60.* **Open** *July-Aug* 9am-10pm daily. *Sept-Dec, mid Mar-June* 9am-8pm daily. Closed Jan-mid Mar. **Rates** *Per person per night* €1.50-€4. *Vehicles* €2-€7. **No credit cards**.

A great campsite on the edge of Gaasperplas park, which has a lake with a watersports centre and facilities for canoeing, swimming (for kids, too), rowing and sailing, plus a surfing school. Ground facilities include a shop, café, bar and restaurant, a terrace, launderette, supermarket and service station for fuel.

## Het Amsterdamse Bos

*Kleine Noorddijk 1 (641 6868/fax 640 2378/ camping@dab.amsterdam.nl). Bus 171.* **Open** *Apr-mid Oct* 9am-9pm daily. **Rates** *Per person per night* €9. *Vehicles* €2.50-€6. **Credit** MC, V.

The site is a way from Amsterdam, but half-hourly buses for the 30-minute trip into town stop 300m from the grounds, on the edge of Amsterdamse Bos (*see p110*). Wooden cabins for up to four people are around €27 per night. Site facilities include a shop, bar and restaurant, lockers and bike hire (July and August only). In high season, the campsite has its own express bus service one-way to Centraal Station (about €3).

## Vliegenbos

*Meeuwenlaan 138 (636 8855/fax 632 2723). Bus 32, 36, 110, 111, 114.* **Open** *Apr-Sept* 9am-9pm daily. **Rates** *Per person per night* €4-€8. *Vehicles* €4-€8. **Credit** AmEx, DC, MC, V.

The grounds are close to the IJ, a five-minute bus journey from Centraal Station. Facilities include a bar, a restaurant, a safe at reception, and a small shop with exchange service. Guests staying for less than three nights have to pay a small supplement.

## Zeeburg

*Zuider IJdijk 20 (694 4430/fax 694 6238/ www.campingzeeburg.nl). Tram 14/bus 22.* **Open** *Summer* 8am-11pm daily. *Winter* 9am-noon, 5-8pm daily. **Rates** *Per person per night* €1.60-€3.65. *Vehicles* €2.25-€6.50. **No credit cards**.

Facilities at these grounds, north of the IJ, include a bar, a restaurant, a shop and bike hire. Log cabins sleeping two or four people cost about €11 per person including bedding (book during high season), and there's also a 24-bed dorm (€8 per person).

# Sightseeing

## Features

# Introduction

Welcome to Amsterdam.

Amsterdam has one great advantage above all other cities: its size. The compact nature of the town makes it easily negotiable, especially if you're prepared to take your life into your hands and rent a bike for the duration of your stay. And if you're not, the city's layout means you'll rarely be more than a half-hour's walk from wherever you're going, with trams providing back-up if you don't fancy the exertion.

Within the centre of town are Amsterdam's medieval buildings, its old port, the red lights that denote the presence of the world's oldest trade, the earliest and prettiest canals, the grand 17th-century merchants' houses, and many of its most famous sights. Slightly further out are neighbourhoods built to accommodate the various waves of incoming workers: the Jordaan, the Pijp, Amsterdam Oost, and various suburbs further south and west.

Except to stroll Museumplein and its three major art museums, few visitors go beyond the *grachtengordel*, the calming belt of canals – exaggeratedly tagged in Albert Camus' *The Fall* as the 'circles of hell' – that ring the historic and fascinating Old Centre. Don't make the same mistake. While the primarily residential Jordaan and the Pijp are largely attraction-free, at least in traditional terms, they're still hugely attractive places. Further out, too, there's plenty to enjoy, both to the north and north-east on the redeveloping Waterfront, and way south down around the idyllic Amsterdamse Bos. For more on Amsterdam's various areas, *see p72* **Neighbourhood watch**.

## TICKETS AND INFORMATION

While most Amsterdam museums charge for admission, prices are reasonable: rarely more than €5. However, if you're thinking of taking in a fair few, the **Museumjaarkaart** ('Annual Museum Card') is a steal: it costs €31.75 for adults and €13.60 for under-25s (€35 and €15 from July 2002), and is arguably better value than the various all-in cards offered by the Amsterdam Tourist Board. The card offers free or discounted admission to over 400 attractions in the Netherlands and is valid for a year from date of purchase; where reduced or free entry is offered to holders of the Museumjaarkaart, it's denoted in our listings by the phrase 'MJK'. You can buy the card at any participating museum; take a passport-size photo.

The deals don't end there. During **National Museum Weekend** every April (*see p179*), about 200 small museums around the country offer free or reduced admission, though many get very busy. Also jam-packed are temporary exhibitions at major museums on weekends, and many museums on Wednesday afternoons, when primary schools let the kids out early.

Two final tips. If you're planning on visiting a museum on a public holiday, call to check it will be open, as many shut for the day. And if you're worried about the language barrier, don't be. In Amsterdam, at least, almost all the main museums (and many of the smaller ones) have captions and/or guidebooks in impeccable English, and those that don't usually have English-speaking staff on hand to help.

# The best Things to do in Amsterdam

## For putting one foot in the past
A morning in **Amsterdams Historisch Museum** (*see p86*), an afternoon in the **Museum Amstelkring** (*see p82*) and an evening at the **Concertgebouw** (*see p219*).

## For going back to the future
A morning in **Nemo** (*see p101*), an afternoon walk around the **Eastern Docklands** (*see p102*) and a night in **More** (*see p225*).

## For art both ancient and modern
The museums on **Museumplein** (*see p107*) or the galleries in the **Jordaan** (*see p199*).

## For a religious experience
The **Oude Kerk** (*see p83*), the **Joods Historisch Museum** (*see p96*) or the **Chinese Fo Kuang Shan Buddhist Temple** (*see p79*).

## For a triple-bill of Dutch clichés
A drink at the **Brouwerij 't IJ**, next to a windmill (*see p143*); shopping at cheese emporium **Wegewijs** (*see p167*); and a wander around **Bloemenmarkt**, the floating flower market on Singel (*see p165*).

## For the party to end all parties
The canals on **Queen's Day** (*see p181*) or **New Year's Eve** on Nieuwmarkt (*see p184*).

## For creature comforts
Artis (*see p98*), the **Poezenboot** (*see p87*) or one of the city's **urban farms** (*see p187*).

## For the desperate, the horny or the just plain curious
A walk around the **Red Light District** (*see p77*), a visit to the **Sexmuseum** (*see p77*) or an evening in the **Casa Rosso** (*see p81*).

## For smoke without fire
PGC Hajenius (*see p176*) or a trip to a coffeeshop (*see p147*).

## For the longest queues in town
Anne Frankhuis (*see p89*), the **Van Gogh Museum** (*see p108*) or **boat tours from near Centraal Station** (*see p71*).

## For getting away from it all
Hortus Botanicus (*see p98*), Flevopark (*see p99*) or **Amsterdamse Bos** (*see p110*).

## Tours

### Bike tours
Fear not, worried would-be cyclists. If you follow your guide's instructions, you'll be OK on two wheels here. Rental of a bike is included in the prices listed. For bike hire, *see p278*.

#### Yellow Bike
*Nieuwezijds Voorburgwal 66, Old Centre: New Side (620 6940). Tram 1, 2, 5, 13, 17, 20.* **Open** *Apr-Nov* 8.30am-5.30pm daily. **No credit cards. Map** p306 C2. A three-hour City Tour departs at 9.30am and 1pm daily from Nieuwezijds Kolk 29 and costs €17. A six-hour Waterland Tour, leaving 11am daily (€22.50), includes a visit to a windmill and a pancake house.

### Boat tours
There's little to choose between the variety of boat tours that rove Amsterdam's waterways for an hour at a time: you're best off just going with the one that has the shortest queues. In addition to day cruises, all these firms run night cruises at 9pm daily in summer (less often in winter), costing €20-€25; Lindbergh, Lovers and Holland International offer dinner cruises for €65-€75. Booking is required for both.

Lovers also runs the **Museumboot**, for which tickets last a full day (10am-5pm) and entitle the holder to get on or off at any one of seven stops, each near several museums; see its website for full details. It costs €13.50, with 4-12s paying €9 and under-4s riding for free. Prices drop by €2 after 1pm, and all tickets include discounts of up to 50 per cent on usual museum admission. For boat hire, *see p278*.

#### Best of Holland
*Damrak 34; depart by Centraal Station, Old Centre: New Side (623 1539). Tram 4, 9, 16, 20, 24, 25.* **Open** 8.30am-10pm daily. **Cruises** every 30min, 10am-5pm daily. **Cost** €8; €4 under-13s. **Credit** AmEx, DC, MC, V. **Map** p305 D2.

#### Holland International
*Prins Hendrikkade 33A; depart by Centraal Station, Old Centre: New Side (622 7788). Tram 4, 9, 16, 20, 24, 25.* **Cruises** *Summer* every 30min, 9am-10pm daily; *Winter* every 30min, 10am-6pm daily. **Cost** €8; €4.50 under-13s. **Credit** AmEx, MC, V. **Map** p305 D2.

#### Lindbergh
*Damrak 26; depart by Centraal Station, Old Centre: New Side (622 2766/www.lovers.nl). Tram 4, 9, 16, 20, 24, 25.* **Cruises** *Summer* every 15min, 10am-6pm daily. *Winter* every 30min, 9.30am-4pm daily. **Cost** €6. **Credit** AmEx, DC, MC, V. **Map** p305 D2.

# Neighbourhood watch

## THE OLD CENTRE

Amsterdam's ground zero of consumerism, vice, entertainment and history, the Old Centre has boundaries of Prins Hendrikkade to the north, Oudeschans and Zwanenburgwal to the east, the Amstel to the south and Singel to the west.

Within these borders, the Old Centre is split into the **New Side** (west of Damrak and Rokin) and the **Old Side** (east of Damrak and Rokin). Within the Old Side, roughly in an area bordered by Zeedijk, Kloveniersburgwal, Oude Hoogstraat, Damstraat and Warmoesstraat, is the Red Light District (only one of several in the city, but the most famous).

## THE CANALS

The *grachtengordel* ('girdle of canals') that guards the Old Centre is idyllic, pleasant and quintessentially Amsterdam. In the listings for shops, restaurants and the like in this guide, we've split the canals in half. **Western Canal Belt** denotes the stretch of canals to the west and north of Leidsegracht, while **Southern Canal Belt** covers the area east of here, taking in **Leidseplein** and **Rembrandtplein**.

## JODENBUURT, THE PLANTAGE AND THE OOST

The area around Waterlooplein were settled by Jews two centuries ago, and took its name – **Jodenbuurt** – from them. The **Plantage**, which lies east and south-east of Waterlooplein, holds many delights, among them the Hortus Botanicus and Artis. Further east – or **Oost** – lies the Tropenmuseum, before the city opens up and stretches out.

## THE WATERFRONT

Once the gateway to the city's prosperity, Amsterdam's waterfront is now the setting for one of Europe's most exciting architectural developments. Traditional sights are few, but before long this stretch will be home to thousands of new residents.

## THE JORDAAN

Bordered by Brouwersgracht, Prinsengracht, Leidsegracht and Lijnbaansgracht, the Jordaan is arguably Amsterdam's most charming neighbourhood. Working-class stalwarts rub shoulders with affluent newcomers in an area that, while lacking the grandiose architecture of the canals, wants for nothing in terms of character.

## THE MUSEUM QUARTER, VONDELPARK AND THE SOUTH

Highlighted by its world-class museums and some stupendously posh fashion emporia, Amsterdam's **Museum Quarter** is a mix of culture and couture. South of Singelgracht, with approximate borders at Overtoom (west) and Hobbemakade (east), it's also home to many pleasant hotels and, at its northernmost tip, is within a stone's throw of Leidseplein. South of it is the **Vondelpark**.

## THE PIJP

Against all odds, the Pijp has managed to remain a wonderful melting pot of cultures and nationalities. Located east of the Museum Quarter and south of the canals, it's an area short on traditional sights but defiantly long on character and fun.

### Lovers

*Prins Hendrikkade (opposite 25-7, nr Centraal Station), Old Centre: New Side (622 2181). Tram 4, 9, 16, 20, 24, 25.* **Cruises** every 30min, 10am-5pm daily. **Cost** €8; €5.50 under-13s. **Credit** AmEx, MC, V. **Map** p305 D2.

### Rondvaarten

*Rokin (opposite 125, at corner of Spui), Old Centre: New Side (623 3810). Tram 4, 9, 16, 20, 24, 25.* **Cruises** *Summer* every 30min, 9am-10pm daily. *Winter* every 30min, 10am-5pm daily. **Cost** €6.50; €3.75 under-13s. **No credit cards.** **Map** p306 D3.

## Walking tours

Amsterdam is a great city to explore on foot, though its uneven streets and tramlines mean it isn't great if you're wearing stilettos, pushing pushchairs or in a wheelchair. The **Amsterdam Tourist Board** (*see p289*) publishes brochures (in English) with easy-to-follow walks.

### Archivisie

*Postbus 14603, 1001 LC (625 9123).* Tailor-made architectural tours, and regular theme tours. Phone for appointments and details of prices.

### Mee in Mokum

*Hartenstraat 18, Western Canal Belt (625 1390). Tram 13, 14, 17, 20.* **Tours** (last 2-3hrs) 11am Tue-Sun. **Cost** €2.50; free under-12s. **Map** p306 C3. Residents of Amsterdam, all over 55, give personal tours of the Old Centre and the Jordaan: each has his or her own route and stories (told in English and Dutch). Tours leave from the Amsterdams Historisch Museum (*see p86*); booking is required, and mention if you intend to bring children when you call.

# The Old Centre

Part notorious Red Light District, part clean and innocent shoppers' paradise: to say opposites attract in the Oud Centrum is a pretty big understatement.

On one side are myriad shopping treats, yet on the other it's sex that's for sale: both sides are dense with history. Amsterdam's Old Centre is both contradictory and compelling.

With boundaries of Centraal Station, Singel and Zwanenburgwal canals, the area is bisected by Damrak, which turns into Rokin south of Dam Square. Within the Old Centre (aka Oud Centrum), the area to the east containing the Red Light District is the ancient Old Side (Oude Zijde), while the area to the west – whose most notable landmark is Spui Square – is the not-really-that-new New Side (Nieuwe Zijde).

## The Old Side

### Around the Dam

#### Map p308

Straight up from Centraal Station, just beyond the once-watery and now-paved and touristy strip named Damrak, lies **Dam Square**, the heart of the city since the first dam was built here across the Amstel in 1270. Today, it's a convenient meeting point for many tourists, the majority of whom convene under its mildly phallic centrepiece, the **Nationaal Monument**. This 22-metre (70-foot) white obelisk is dedicated to the Dutch servicemen who died

in World War II. Designed by JJP Oud, with sculptures by John Raedecker, it incorporates 12 urns, 11 filled with earth collected from the then-11 Dutch provinces and the 12th containing soil from war cemeteries in longtime Dutch colony Indonesia.

Following the refurbishment of the monument in recent years, the square itself has now received a much-needed facelift: the roughness of the new cobblestones has deterred errant bikers, and their lighter colour disguises the Jackson Pollock-splodges of pigeon shit. Especially in the quiet traffic-free moments of dawn, the square now reflects a once long-lost sense of the epic; appropriate, since the Dam has hosted such singular social and political activities as Anabaptists running naked through the square to test the boundaries of religious freedom in 1535, hippies chilling in the name of peace in the '60s, and an endless array of protests, coronations and executions.

The west side of Dam Square is flanked by the **Koninklijk Paleis** (literally, 'Royal Palace'; *see p74*); next to it is the 600-year-old **Nieuwe Kerk** ('New Church', so named as it was built a century after the Oude Kerk, or 'Old Church', in the Red Light District; *see p83*). In kitsch contrast, on the south side, is **Madame Tussaud's Scenerama** (*see p74*).

**Centraal Station**: a crucial landmark for visitors to Amsterdam.

## Beurs van Berlage

*Damrak 277, entrance at Beursplein 1*
*(museum 530 4141/Artiflex tours 620 8112/*
*www.beursvanberlage.nl). Tram 4, 9, 14, 16,*
*20, 24, 25.* **Open** *Museum* 11am-5pm Tue-Sun.
**Admission** *Museum* prices vary with exhibition;
discount with MJK. **No credit cards. Map** p306 D2.
Designed in 1896 by Hendrik Berlage as the city's
palatial stock exchange, the Beurs, while incorporating many traditional building styles, represents
a break with 19th-century architecture and prepared the way for the modernity of the Amsterdam
School (*see p32* **Back to school**). It is now considered the country's most important piece of architecture from the 20th century. By exposing the
architectural structures and fusing them with the
stunning decorations, it celebrates the workers and
artisans that built it. In fact, it's a complete socialist statement – much of the artwork warns against
blind capitalism and each of the nine million bricks
were envisioned by Berlage to represent the individual and the resulting monolith, society at large.

Having long alienated the stockbrokers, the Beurs
is now all things to all other people: a conference and
exhibition centre, concert halls (*see p219*), a café, a
restaurant and a rather pricey museum, whose exhibitions range from Karel Appel to supermarket
memorabilia (a recent exhibition focused on the history of Hema). In addition, tours of the building are
conducted by art historians from Artiflex, though
booking is compulsory; call the number above.

## Koninklijk Paleis (Royal Palace)

*Dam (624 8698/www.kon-paleisamsterdam.nl).*
*Tram 1, 2, 4, 5, 9, 13, 14, 16, 17, 20, 24, 25.*
**Open** *Jul-Aug* 11am-5pm daily. *Sept-June* 12.30-5pm
days vary. **Admission** €4.5; €3.60 5-16s, over-60s;
free under-4s. **No credit cards. Map** p306 C3.
Designed by Jacob van Campen in the 17th century
along classical lines and famously built on 13,659
wooden piles that were rammed deep into the sand,
the Royal Palace was originally used as the city hall.
The poet Constantijn Huygens hyped it as 'the
world's Eighth Wonder', a monument to the cocki-
ness Amsterdam felt at the dawn of its Golden Age.
It was meant as a smug and epic 'screw you' to
visiting monarchs, a species that the people of
Amsterdam had happily done without.

The exterior is only really impressive when
viewed from the rear – where Atlas holds his load
from a great height. However, it's grander inside
than out: the Citizen's Hall, with its decoration in
grand marble and bronze that images a miniature
universe, is meant to make you feel about as
worthy as the rats seen carved in stone over the
Bankruptcy Chamber's door.

Though much of the art on display here reflects
the typically jaded humour of a people who have
seen it all, the overall impression is one of deadly
seriousness: one screw-up and you could end up
among the grotesque carvings of the Tribunal and
sentenced to die in some uniquely torturous and
public way. Kinder, gentler displays of creativity,

The phallic **Nationaal Monument**. *See p73.*

though, can be seen in the chimney pieces, painted
by artists such as Ferdinand Bol and Govert Flinck,
both pupils of Rembrandt (who, ironically, had his
own sketches rejected). The city hall was transformed into a royal palace in 1808, shortly after
Napoleon had made his brother, Louis, King of the
Netherlands, and a fine collection of furniture from
this period can be viewed on a guided tour. The
Palace became state property in 1936 and is still
used occasionally by the royal family.

## Madame Tussaud's Scenerama

*Peek & Cloppenburg, Dam 20 (622 9239/*
*www.madame-tussauds.com). Tram 4, 9, 14,*
*16, 20, 24, 25.* **Open** 10am-5.30pm daily.
**Admission** €12; €10 over-60s; €8 5-16s; free under-
5s. **Credit** AmEx, DC, MC, V. **Map** p306 D3.
London's version might be the most popular, the
recently opened New York branch might be the most
expensive (it cost US$50 million to open), but as far
as queasy kitsch goes, it's hard to believe anywhere
tops the Amsterdam outpost of Madame Tussaud's,
on the south side of Dam Square in the top two
floors of the Peek & Cloppenburg department store.
Cheese-textured representations from Holland's own
Golden Age of commerce are all depicted alongside
a more contemporary golden shower of hits: the
Dutch royal family, local celebs and global super-
stars. It all ends in the Dome of Fame, the selection
process of which defies easy analysis. Some of the
models look like their subjects, some don't. But while

there's some kitsch fun to be had here, it comes at a price, and it's hard not to leave with the feeling that the materials used should really have been put towards making candles.

### Nieuwe Kerk (New Church)

*Dam (626 8168/recorded information 638 6909/ www.nieuwekerk.nl). Tram 1, 2, 4, 5, 9, 13, 14, 16, 17, 20, 24, 25.* **Open** hours vary. **Admission** varies with exhibition. **No credit cards. Map** p306 C3.

While the 'old' Oude Kerk in the Red Light District was built in the 1300s, the sprightly 'new' Nieuwe Kerk dates from 1408. It is not known how much damage was caused by the fires of 1421 and 1452, or even how much rebuilding took place, but most of the pillars and walls were erected after that time. Iconoclasm in 1566 left the church intact, though statues and altars were removed in the Reformation. The sundial on its tower was used to set all of the city's clocks until 1890.

In 1645, the Nieuwe Kerk was gutted by the Great Fire; the ornate oak pulpit and great organ (the latter designed by Jacob van Campen) are thought to have been constructed shortly after the blaze. Also of interest here is the tomb of naval hero Admiral de Ruyter (1607-76), who initiated the ending of the Second Anglo-Dutch war – wounding British pride in the process – when he sailed up the Thames in 1667, inspiring a witness, Sir William Batten, to observe: 'I think the Devil shits Dutchmen.' Behind the black marble tomb of De Ruyter is a white

**Koninklijk Paleis.** *See p74.*

# Brits abroad

There's a lot to be said for the Easy Life. We'd all live it if we could. No more work worries, no more emotional crises, always a smile and never a frown. Sounds like a dream, doesn't it? Well, it's one that's found its reality in Amsterdam's British and Irish expat community.

First things first, though: not all British and Irish expats fit this happy-go-lucky bill. Many have assimilated into Dutch culture with alacrity, drinking in Dutch bars, observing Dutch customs, even learning the language, perhaps now feeling more European than British. But then there are the hardcore expats from the old school, for whom the Easy Life is a holy grail. You'll find this breed in bars around Warmoesstraat, Nieuwendijk and beyond. Their Sundays are spent glued to Sky Sports, their idea of integration is drinking Heineken, their Dutch-language skills consist of 'bier, alstublieft'.

'And why not?' they might reply. 'It's an Easy Life, ain't it?' On that point, there's no argument: you'll never see an unsmiling face in the Old Quarter, or the Sower, or the Shamrock. The world for these expats is good and simple, appearing to consist entirely of drinking, with the occasional bit of singing thrown in for good measure. Indeed, the outsider is left wondering when they fit in work around all the beers... until it dawns on you that those that do work are all employed by each other, in the various expat bars frequented by their mates. To say it's an insular existence is a splendidly spectacular understatement: these expats could be anywhere and they'd live the same way. But in Amsterdam, they found drink on tap and drugs in shops and sex in windows and... well, why leave? Life just doesn't get any easier.

They even have a house publication: the 36-page *Amsterdam Stun* (the title a pun on the *Sun*, Britain's most popular tabloid), which details, in endearing but ultimately catatonia-inducing detail, the antics of the same crop of expats in the same crop of bars, month after month after month. 'Propping up their favourite part of the bar in Mister Coco's,' reads one not untypical caption, 'it's Mickey and Pat.' Raising a glass, it's safe to say, to the Easy Life.

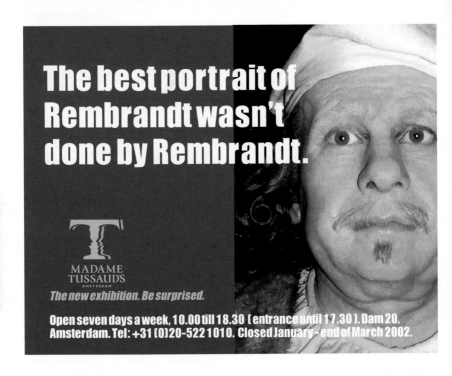
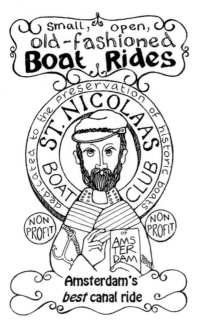

marble relief depicting the sea battle in which he died. Poets and Amsterdam natives PC Hooft and Joost van den Vondel are also buried here. These days, the Nieuwe Kerk hosts organ recitals, state occasions and consistently excellent exhibitions.

### Sexmuseum

*Damrak 18 (622 8376). Tram 4, 9, 14, 16, 20, 24, 25.* **Open** 10am-11.30pm daily. **Admission** €2.50. **Map** p306 D2.

The Sexmuseum is one of two museums devoted to doin' the dirty in Amsterdam, and a tawdry little operation it is, too. The Damrak location, just by Centraal Station, is designed to lure in masses of passing tourists, and on this count it succeeds. But with the exception of a splendid and often hilarious collection of pornographic Victorian photographs, the exhibition is largely botched. The potentially interesting stuff is skimmed over or poorly annotated: there's a fascinating exhibition on the history of porn movies to be staged, but the all-too-brief one here ain't it. Otherwise, it's a mess of ivory dildos, filthy porcelain, joyless cartoons, peeling pin-ups and ugly art, any potential eroticism rendered moot by the context and the leering gangs of gigglers that make up the majority of the punters. The minuscule admission charge might be worth it for the fun of telling your mates you've been there when you get back, but otherwise, don't bother.

## The Red Light District

### Maps p306 & p307

The Red Light District, situated in an approximate triangle formed by Centraal Station, the Nieuwmarkt and the Dam, is at the root of Amsterdam's international notoriety. The world's desperate and horny imagine breasts eagerly pancaked against red neon-framed windows, canals awash with bodily fluids. As if to give weight to this image, the postcards on sale in local shops depict a sort of small, cutesy Vegas. If truth be told, though, the cheesy joke shop has here become the cheesy sex shop, with electric palm buzzers and comedy nose glasses being replaced by multi-orificed inflatables and huge orbital dildos.

Most of the history of the Red Light District – of which there is plenty, this being the oldest part of Amsterdam – has been greasily veneered with that other of oldest trades: marketing. Sex, while the hook upon which the area hangs its reputation, is actually secondary to window-shopping. People do buy – it's estimated to be a €500-million-per-year trade – but mostly they wander in groups, stopping here and there to gawp open-mouthed at the countless live exhibits.

Most window girls are self-employed, and even though prostitution was only defined as a legal profession in 1988 and bordellos have only

The new **Buddhist Temple**. *See p79.*

been officially legit since October 2000 (a tactic hoped to make taxation easier), the women have had their own union, De Rode Draad, since 1984. The prostitutes are, indeed, mostly women: despite attempts to launch male and transsexual prostitution, men have so far found it difficult to get their dicks into this particular door of opportunity. With legality has come a plethora of new rules: from the temperature at which lingerie must be washed, to the cleansers that must be used to ensure that the adjoining showers are free of 'liquid-loving insects'.

As at more traditional markets such as the **Albert Cuypmarkt** (*see p166*), where cheese merchants line up alongside cheese merchants and fishmongers group with fishmongers, women of similar specialisations also tend to clump together. Sultry Latins gather on the Molensteeg and the beginning of Oudezijds Achterburgwal, ambiguously sexed Thais on Stoofstraat, and the model-ish and skinny on Trompettersteeg, Amsterdam's smallest street (where you will have trouble passing other punters if you happen to be sporting a woody). But there is much else to absorb in this most iconoclastic of neighbourhoods. Prostitutes, clerics, schoolkids, junkies, carpenters and cops all interact with a strange brand of social cosiness, and the tourists are mere voyeurs. It's all good fun and pretty harmless, just so long as you remember that window girls do not like having their pictures taken and that drug dealers react to eye contact like dogs to bones.

## Zeedijk

Facing away from Centraal Station to the left are two churches, the **St Nicolaaskerk** (whose interior of funky darkness can be viewed from Easter to mid October, 1.30-4pm Mon, 11am-4pm Tue-Sat and where one can vibrate to Gregorian chanted vespers every Sunday at 5pm from September to June ) and the dome and skull-adorned exterior of the **St Olafkerk** (known locally as the 'Cheese Church', having

Sightseeing

# Of bodies and bloodstains

Like any decent city, Amsterdam's history has been alternately blighted and enlivened by murder, mayhem and madness. And like any decent city, remnants and leftovers from said acts of murder, mayhem and madness are still scattered around town. The most famous such site is the **Waag** on Nieuwmarkt, whose name – it translates as 'weigh house' – belies its rather nastier occupations.

If what motivates you are humankind's darkest sides, then try to imagine the body parts that used to garnish the Waag's south-east side: this is where the majority of Amsterdam's many public executions took place. There were always corpses for the medical guild to dissect in the Waag's Anatomical Theatre, or for Rembrandt to study and paint: *The Anatomy Lesson of Dr Nicolaes Tulp* stands as evidence. However, the theatre is now scrubbed clean and is open to the public by appointment, as is a trendy café (**In de Waag**; *see p137*) and the Society for Old and New Media, complete with free Internet room. The building's 500-year passage from torture to technology is now complete.

Taking pride of place is the **House with the Bloodstains** (*pictured bottom*), the former mayor Coenraad van Beuningen's residence at Amstel 216, near the Herengracht. Van Beuningen (1622-93) was a brilliant politician who ably handled the crises of 1672, but later went insane. In the winter of 1689, he saw visions – red fireballs and a rainbow-coloured coffin floating above the Reguliersgracht – and then scribbled graffiti on the front wall of his house. Faint, cryptic stars, a sailing ship, and the names of him and his wife are still visible, scrawled maniacally in a bloody reddish-brown. Van Beuningen died four years later, owning only a few clothes and a small oval

mirror. While attempting to decipher the graffiti, ponder as to what that mirror saw and to just who has it now.

Closer to the present but farther from the centre of town is the **Van Heutsz Monument** (*pictured top*) at Olympiaplein, the former tomb of Johannes Benedictus van Heutsz (1851-1924). As Governor-General of Sumatran kingdom Acheh, Van Heutsz quickly suppressed a decades-long rebellion with a policy that amounted to a simple instruction: 'Lop off their heads!' Queen Wilhelmina dedicated the pacificator's monument in 1935, but it has since declined along with his reputation. At night, the empty tomb, the stylised sunburst atop the pillar and the empty reflecting pool suggest an abandoned sacrificial altar. The monument may soon be rededicated in a more culturally sensitive fashion, so see it before the renovation happens.

'It is worthy to subdue that which frightens us,' reads the inscription on the **Rasphuispoortje** at Heiligeweg 19, a remnant of the city workhouse founded in 1603 for vagabonds, debtors and other men of ill repute. A frieze depicts two lions pulling a wagonload of wood. For the less classically minded is added a blunter message: the legend 'CASTIGATIO' and a woman holding a scourge over two men in chains. In the Rasphuis, the first modern penitentiary, inmates ground prickly logs of Brazil wood into red dye powder and lived by a schedule of work and moral education. The labourers afforded visitors an amusement-park version of Hell. Women, mostly prostitutes, were locked in the Spinhuis, across the Damrak. The Rasphuis was pulled down in the 1890s during the development of the Kalverstraat, and the only criminals now passing through the gate are sartorial.

housed the cheese exchange for many years). Between the two, you can enter Zeedijk, a street with a rich and tattered history.

Before this dyke was built around 1300, Amsterdam was a fishing village with barely enough bog to stand on. But by the 15th and 16th centuries, with the East India Company raking in the imperialist dollars, Zeedijk was where sailors came to catch up on their boozing, brawling and bonking (or 'doing the St Nicolaas', as it was fondly termed in those days, as a tribute to their patron saint, a busy chap who also patrons children, thieves, prostitutes and the city of Amsterdam).

Sailors who had lost all their money could trade in their pet monkey for a flea-infested bed at Zeedijk 1, which still retains its old name – **In't Aepjen**, meaning 'In the Monkeys' – and is one of the oldest wooden houses in the city (*see p137*). Just off the street down Oudezijds Kolk, you can spot the **Schreierstoren**, aka the 'Weeping Tower' (*see p28*). It is said that wives would cry there, perhaps with relief, when husbands set off on a voyage, then cry again if the ship returned with news that the husband was lost at sea. If the latter ever happened, then – conveniently – it was but a short walk to Zeedijk, where the bereaved lady would often continue life as a 'merry widow'. Prostitution was often the female equivalent of joining the navy: the last economic option.

During the 20th century, Zeedijk has been sparked by cultural diversity. In the 1930s, the first openly gay establishments appeared, and at the now-closed – though a replica is on display in the **Amsterdams Historisch Museum** (*see p86*) – Café t'Maandje (Zeedijk 65), there's a window shrine to legendary owner Bet van Beeren (1902-67), who has gone down in local mythology as the original Lesbian Biker Chick (*see p207* **Wanna Bet?**). In the '50s, jazz greats such as Chet Baker and Gerry Mulligan, came to jam and hang out in the many after-hours clubs here, among them the still-functioning **Casablanca** (Zeedijk 26; *see p216*).

Unfortunately, this subculture marked Zeedijk as a place where heroin could be scored with comparative ease. By the 1970s, the street had become crowded with dealers, junkies and indifferent cops, with most of the restaurants and cafés renting their tables to dealers. The junkies' magic number back then was 27: *f*25 for the drugs themselves, and *f*2 for the drink the owners insisted the junkies purchase to maintain the façade of legality.

Amsterdam's reputation became littered with needles and foil, never more so than when a wasted Chet Baker made his final moody decrescendo in 1988 on to a cement parking pole from a window (second floor on the left) of the

Prins Hendrik Hotel at the entrance of the Zeedijk. A brass plaque commemorating the crooning trumpeter has been installed to the left of the hotel's entrance. But though there was a time when a German tour operator's 'criminal safari' was not even allowed on the Zeedijk, police claim to have cleaned the street up in recent years; indeed, the scene is today infinitely less intimidating and packed with new and new-ish businesses and restaurants. Famed dance label Outland Records has a store at No.22; **Demask** offers its posh line of leathers and latexes at No.64 (*see p205*); excellent cheap Chinese food can be found at **Nam Kee** at Zeedijk 111-13 (*see p117*); and **Latei** is half junk shop, half café and totally charming. Across the street from Nam Kee, the new **Chinese Fo Kuang Shan Buddhist Temple** (open noon-5pm Mon-Sat, 10am-5pm Sun), where monks and nuns service a library, Internet café and vegetarian restaurant, speaks much of this street's continued spiritual growth.

## Nieuwmarkt

At the bottom of Zeedijk, your eyes will be drawn to the huge and menacing castle-like **De Waag**, or 'the Weigh House'. The Waag, previously called St Antoniespoort, stands in the centre of the Nieuwmarkt and dates from 1488, when it was built as a gatehouse for the city defences (*see p137*). In the dark days of the Nazi occupation, the square itself was surrounded by

Weigh it up at **De Waag**.

## BIKE TOURS:

Bike Rentals and Internet Lounge available seven days a week. Located at 302a Lijnbaansgracht. (Easy to find, from the Rijksmuseum cross the street at the traffic lights, at the second canal, Lijnbaansgracht, turn right.)

**meet at 11:30 & 4:00**
May 1 - August 31

**meet at 12:30**
March 1 - April 30 &
September 1 - November 30
*December - February reservations only*

**Tour meets in front of main entrance of the Rijksmuseum.**

Call us at +31 (0)20-6227970 or +31 (0)6-25400218 for more info and reservations
email: egg77@hotmail.com  website: www.mikesbiketours.com

barbed wire and used as one of the collection points to hold those from the Jewish quarter who were to be shipped off to concentration camps via the **Hollandse Schouwburg** (*see p98*). More recently, in 1980, Nieuwmarkt was the site of riots when the city was busy demolishing housing in order to build the Metro.

The streets leading north-east from Nieuwmarkt contain Amsterdam's small Chinatown, while the colourfully named sidestreets – among them Monnikkenstraat (Monk Street), Bloedstraat (Blood Street) and Koestraat (Cow Street) – on the south-west lead into the reddest part of the Red Light District. Heading south from the Nieuwmarkt along the Kloveniersburgwal canal, though, makes for a more interesting stroll.

At Kloveniersburgwal 29 is the **Trippenhuis**, now home to the Dutch Academy of Sciences, who formerly shared it in the 18th century with the original Rijksmuseum collection. During the Golden Age, the building was owned and equally shared (witness the bisecting wall in the middle window) by the two Trip brothers and their respective families. Their fortune was made by arms dealing (witness, now, the mortar-shaped chimneys and the cannons engraved on the gable) and their riches meant they could easily afford the imposing gunpowder grey exterior. They even – or so the story goes – indulged themselves in building the **House of Mr Trip's Coachman** at No.26, erected in response to a one-liner the coachman reputedly made about being happy with a house as wide as the Trips' front door. He got his wish. The house, capped with golden sphinxes, is now home to a clothing store complete with appropriately anorexic display figures.

## 'De Wallen'

The canals Oudezijds Voorburgwal and Oudezijds Achterburgwal, with their interconnecting streets, are where carnal sin screams loudest. So it's with splendid irony that, right in the middle of Sin City, you'll stumble across a pair of churches. The **Oude Kerk** (*see p83*), Amsterdam's oldest building, is literally in the centre of the sleazy action, with hookers in windows ringing the mammoth church like bullies taunting the class geek. Keep your eyes peeled for the small brass bosom inlaid into the pavement outside. The **Museum Amstelkring** (*see p82*), meanwhile, is tucked away a little distance from the red-lit action, but shouldn't be overlooked on your journey around the area.

The Oudezijds Voorburgwal was known as the 'Velvet Canal' in the 16th century due to the obscene wealth of its residents. Now, though, at least along its northern stretch, the velvet has been replaced by red velour, illuminated by scarlet fluorescent lighting and complemented by bored-looking girls sat in the windows of the lovely canal houses. It's rather ironic, then, that this canal should be so densely populated with churches, chapels and orders. Reps from the Salvation Army lurk on every corner near the **Agnietenkapel** (*see p83*) to the south of the street, with the aforementioned Oude Kerk and Museum Amstelkring to the north.

The parallel Oudezijds Achterburgwal offers some of the more 'tasteful' choices for the eroto-clubber. The **Casa Rosso** nightclub (Oudezijds Achterburgwal 106-108, 627 8954) is certainly worth a look, if only for the peculiar marble cock-and-rotary-ball water fountain at its entrance. A short walk away at No.37 is the **Bananenbar** (622 4670), where Olympic-calibre genitalia can be witnessed night after night working out; and, incidentally, spitting out an average of 15 kilograms (33 pounds) of fruit each evening in the process. A former owner of the Bananenbar once attempted to stave off the taxman – and get round the fact his drinking licence had lapsed – by picking Satan as a deity and registering the Bananenbar as a church. It was a scam that worked for years; until 1988, when the 'Church of Satan' started to claim a membership of 40,000 overseen by a council of nine anonymous persons. Tax police were called in to find the loopholes and bust the joint, but the bar was tipped off just in time, and the 'church' disbanded. Now under a new owner, the Bananenbar has kept its name and returned to its roots as a purveyor of specialised sleaze.

If your urges are more academic than participatory, then you can conduct some, um, research at the **Erotic Museum** (*see p82*), following it in semi-traditional fashion with a smoke of sorts over at the **Hash Marihuana Hemp Museum** (which doesn't actually sell dope, but you get the picture; *see p82*). Other than that, sleaze and stag parties dominate this strip, with it becoming particularly unpleasant and busy on weekends.

It's a far cry from the Spinhuis, a former convent tucked away at the southern end of the canal (on Spinhuissteeg) that used to set 'wayward women' to work spinning wool as their penance. The male equivalent was at Heiligeweg 9 – now an entrance to the Kalvertoren shopping complex – where audiences used to watch the prisoners being branded and beaten with a bull's penis. In a further historical foreshadowing of Amsterdam's contemporary S&M scene, the entrance gate sports a statue that bears a striking resemblance to a scolding dominatrix.

Do ya think it's sexy? **Erotic Museum**.

## Erotic Museum

*Oudezijds Achterburgwal 54 (624 7303). Tram 4, 9, 16, 20, 24, 25/Metro Nieuwmarkt.* **Open** 11am-1am Mon, Thur, Sun; 11am-2am Fri, Sat.
**Admission** €2.50. **No credit cards. Map** p306 D2.
While the Sexmuseum (*see p77*) benefits from its Damrak location in terms of the passing trade it receives, the Erotic Museum is in the more appropriate location: slap bang in the Red Light District. That's not to say, though, that it's any more authentic or interesting. Its prize exhibits are a few of John Lennon's erotic drawings, while lovers of Bettie Page (and there are many) will enjoy the original photos of the S&M muse on display. However, other than those two, there's little of interest here, and the name of the museum is scandalously inaccurate: despite its best intentions, it's as unsexy as can be. All in all, you're probably best off going to one of the many nearby sex shops for your kicks and your education.

## Hash Marihuana Hemp Museum

*Oudezijds Achterburgwal 148 (623 5961). Tram 4, 9, 14, 16, 20, 24, 25/Metro Nieuwmarkt.* **Open** 11am-10pm daily. **Admission** €6.
**No credit cards. Map** p306 D3.
Amsterdam's been home to loads of notable artists, so it follows that it should have several big art museums. Amsterdam's got more liberal laws on sex than any other city, so it follows that it has a couple of sex museums. And given the decriminalised preponderance of dope here, it figures that Amsterdam should have a museum devoted to hash.

It's just a pity that it has to be this slightly shabby, ridiculously named operation, which tries to be all things to all people and ends up being nothing to anyone, aside from a pricey way for a backpacker to waste around half an hour in the Red Light District. There's some interesting information here, sure: the display on the medical benefits of the drug is enlightening, as are a few nuggets on the history of hemp. But the small exhibition lacks cohesion and entertainment value, and comes across alternately as hippyish and – surprisingly – po-faced. Definitely a missed opportunity.

## Museum Amstelkring

*Oudezijds Voorburgwal 40 (624 6604/ www.museumamstelkring.nl). Tram 4, 9, 14, 16, 20, 24, 25.* **Open** 10am-5pm Mon-Sat; 1-5pm Sun.
**Admission** €4.50; €3.50 5-18s; €2 students, over-65s; free MJK, under-5s. **No credit cards. Map** p306 D2.
The Amstelkring takes its name from that of the group of historians who succeeded in saving it from demolition in the late 1800s. Good job they did save it, too, for what remains is one of Amsterdam's most unique spots, and one of its best kept secrets. The lower floors of the house have been wonderfully preserved from the late 17th century, and offer a sneak look at what life might have been like back in the day. But the main attraction is upstairs, and goes by the name of Ons' Lieve Heer op Solder, or 'Our Lord in the Attic'.

Built in 1663, this attic church was used by Catholics during the 17th century when they were banned from worshipping after the Alteration. It's been beautifully preserved, too, the altarpiece featuring a painting by 18th-century artist Jacob de Wit. The church is often used for services and a variety of other meetings. Don't miss it in.

## Oude Kerk (Old Church)

*Oudekerksplein 1 (625 8284/www.oudekerk.nl).
Tram 4, 9, 16, 20, 24, 25, 26.* **Open** 11am-5pm
Mon-Sat; 1-5pm Sun. **Admission** €4; €3 over-65s;
€2 MJK; free under-12s. **No credit cards.**
**Map** p306 D2.

Originally built in 1306 as a wooden chapel, and constantly renovated and extended between 1330 and 1571, the Oude Kerk is the city's oldest and most interesting church. Its original furnishings were removed by iconoclasts during the Reformation, but the church has retained its wooden roof, which was painted all the way back in the 15th century with figurative images. Keep your eyes peeled for the Gothic and Renaissance façade above the northern portal, and the stained-glass windows, parts of which date from the 16th and 17th centuries. Rembrandt's wife Saskia, who died in 1642, is buried under the small organ. The inscription over the bridal chamber, which translates as 'Marry in haste, mourn at leisure', is in keeping with the church's location in the heart of the Red Light District, though this is more by accident than design. The church is now as much of an exhibition centre as anything, with shows covering everything from Aboriginal art to the annual World Press Photo (*see p179*).

## Universiteitsmuseum de Agnietenkapel

*Oudezijds Voorburgwal 231 (525 3339). Tram 4, 9, 14, 16, 20, 24, 25.* **Open** 9am-5pm Mon-Fri (ring bell for entry). **Admission** free. **No credit cards.**
**Map** p306 D3.

Of Amsterdam's 17 medieval convents, this Gothic chapel is one of a few remnants to have survived intact. Built in the 1470s and part of the university since its foundation in 1632, the chapel has an austere, Calvinistic beauty highlighted by stained-glass windows, wooden beams and benches, and a collection of paintings of humanist thinkers. The Grote Gehoorzaal ('Large Auditorium'), the country's oldest lecture hall, is where 17th-century scholars Vossius and Barlaeus first taught; its wooden ceiling is painted with soberly ornamental Renaissance motifs including angels and flowers. Exhibitions are held here only occasionally.

# Call the cops

In a country where it often seems crime is dealt with in an overly pragmatic way – whenever a certain crime becomes a problem, it is immediately condoned – it's not especially surprising that the local police are unique creatures. Amsterdam is the only place in the world where you're guaranteed a cop's friendly and helpful response in impeccable English to such queries as 'Where is the nearest reputable supplier of big fat joints?' or 'Where might I find the leggy blonde section?'

Unlike the military police, who are only called in from out of town to deal with such pesky details as rioting and the flushing out of squats, Amsterdam police are justifiably proud of their sweet, huggable reputation. Forget homegrow peyote kits or porn postcards: the best souvenir you can take home to induce a drop in the jaws of all your friends is one of the pamphlets that cops distribute to tourists via various bars, cafés and police stations (which are also oh-so-sensitively open to members of the public whose bladders are ready to burst).

These lists of 'rules/information' cover some obvious basics – such as 'parking is not free' – geared to those whose travelling experience has not ventured much further than their backyard. And it graciously informs you of the fine for those caught 'wild-pissing' (peeing in the street). But most fascinating is the sustained subtext that positively screams 'WE ARE USED TO WEIRD THINGS!', which gives the impression that the blurb was written not by a uniformed official but, rather, by some sage-like retired bordello madam who's out to nobly dispense a lifetime of accumulated street smarts. Did you know, for example, that in the Red Light District, 'if you visit one of the women… they are not always women'?

What these informative little booklets fail to mention, however, is a far more common local form of mistaken identity: namely, that police in the Red Light District are not always police. Sometimes they're just a couple of uniformed gents out for some frisky frolicking at the Cockring. But then again, they could also just be off-duty and unwinding…

## Warmoesstraat & Nes

It's hard to believe that Warmoesstraat, Amsterdam's oldest street, was once the most beautiful of lanes, providing a sharp contrast to its then-evil and rowdy twin, Zeedijk. The poet Vondel ran his hosiery business at Warmoesstraat 101; Mozart's dad would try to scalp tickets at the posh bars for his young son's concerts; and Marx would later come here to write in peace (or so he would claim: cynics point out that he was much more likely to be in town to borrow money from his cousin-by-marriage, the extremely wealthy Gerard Philips, founder of the globe-dominating Philips corporate machine).

But with the influx of sailors, the laws of supply and demand dictated a sizeable fall from grace for Warmoesstraat. Adam and Eve in their salad days can still be seen etched in stone at Warmoesstraat 25, but for the most part, this street has fallen to accommodating only the low-end traveller. However, hip hangouts such as gay bar **Getto** (*see p208*) and the **Winston Hotel** (*see p53*), shops including the **Condomerie het Gulden Vlies** (*see p176*) and gallery **W139** (*see p196*) have ensured that the strip has retained some brighter and less commercial colours, while the council's serial clean-up operation reached the street quite recently and has at least had some of the desired cosmetic effect.

Just as Warmoesstraat stretches north from the Nationaal Monument into the Old Side, so Nes leaves the same spot to the south, parallel and to the west of Oudezijds Achterburgwal. Dating from the Middle Ages, this street was once home to the city's tobacco trade and the Jewish quasi-Buddhist Spinoza (1623-77), who saw body and mind as the two aspects of a single substance. Appropriate, then, that you can now witness the alignment of body and mind on the stages of the many theatres that now grace this street. You can also stop, recharge and realign your own essence at one of the many charming cafés hereabouts. At the end of the Nes, either take a turn left to cross a bridge where the junkies are often out making a pretty penny by selling freshly thieved bicycles for next to nothing – though be warned that buying one will have you risking jail and deportation, and in any case the bike you're purchasing has been thieved from some poor bastard only a few minutes earlier – towards the exceedingly euro-scenic **Oudemanhuis Book Market** (*see p166*) situated on the University of Amsterdam campus; or turn right and end up near the archaeologically inclined **Allard Pierson Museum** (*see below*).

Back in time to the **Allard Pierson Museum.**

### Allard Pierson Museum

*Oude Turfmarkt 127 (525 2556/www.uba.uva.nl/apm). Tram 4, 9, 14, 16, 20, 24, 25.* **Open** 10am-5pm Tue-Fri; 1-5pm Sat, Sun. **Admission** €4.30; €3.20 over-65s; €1.40 12-15s; €0.45 4-11s; free MJK, under-4s. **No credit cards. Map** p306 D3.
Established in Amsterdam in 1934, the Allard Pierson claims to hold one of the world's richest university collections of archaeological exhibits, gathered from ancient Egypt, Greece, Rome and the Near East. So far, so good. And, if archaeological exhibits are your thing, then it probably is. However, if you didn't spend several years at university studying stuff like this, then you'll likely be bored witless. Many of the exhibits (statues, sculptures, ceramics, et cetera) are unimaginatively presented, as if aimed solely at scholars. English captions are minimal – though for the record, the Dutch ones are scarcely any more advanced – and few staff are on hand to help explain exactly what you're looking at. The invaluable and historic collection of glass antiquities, for example, might as well be the shattered contents of a bottle bank for all the descriptive fanfare they're given. Some items are instantly accessible and interesting – the full-size sarcophagi, the model of a Greek chariot – but mostly, this is a frustrating experience.

## The New Side

### Map p306

Rhyming, near enough, with 'cow', the Spui is the square that caps the three main arteries that start down near the west end of Centraal Station: the middle-of-the-road walking and shopping street Kalverstraat (called Nieuwendijk before it crosses the Dam), Nieuwezijds Voorburgwal and the Spuistraat.

Coming up Nieuwezijds Voorburgwal – translated literally as 'the New Side's Front of the Town Wall', to distinguish it from the Oudezijds Voorburgwal ('the Old Side's Front of the Town Wall') found in near mirror image in the Red Light District, though both fortress walls have long since been destroyed – the effects of tragically half-arsed urban renewal are immediately noticeable. The Crowne Plaza hotel at Nieuwezijds Voorburgwal 5 was formerly the site of the large Wyers squat, which was dramatically emptied by riot police in 1985 after a widely supported campaign by squatters against the mass conversion of residential buildings into commercial spaces (or, in the case of the domed Koepelkerk at Kattengat 1, a Lutheran church painted by Van Gogh, turned into a hotel convention centre).

The multinational, perhaps predictably, proved victorious, as did the ABN-Amro Bank slightly further up, with its in-your-face glass plaza at the corner with Nieuwezijds Kolk. It is perhaps as an antidote to this that the nearby Pompoen Theater Cafe Restaurant Multimedia now screens an excellent multimedia and multilanguage presentation, Het Mirakel van Amsterdam, that covers Amsterdam's long and rebellious history (Spuistraat 2/Kattengat 10, 521 3000, 10am-5pm daily).

But urban renewal does have its plus sides, in that it allows an opportunity for city archaeologists to dig down and uncover Amsterdam's sunken history (in general, every 50 centimetres downwards represents a century backwards). For instance, while the underground car park was being dug on the ABN-Amro site, researchers uncovered 13th-century wall remains which were, for a short time, hypothesised to be the remains of a marsh-surrounded castle belonging to the Lords of the Amstel. While this proved to be jumping the gun, it did prove that the so-called 'New Side' is not new at all.

A quiet backwater accessible via the north side of Spui square or, when that entrance is closed, via Gedempte Begijnensloot (the alternating dual entrances have been brought in to appease residents), the **Begijnhof** is a group of houses built around a secluded courtyard and garden. Established in the 14th century, it

originally provided modest homes for the Beguines, a religious sisterhood of unmarried women from good families who, though not nuns, lived together in a close community and often took vows of chastity. The last sister died in 1971, though one of her predecessors never left, despite dying back in 1654: she was buried under a red granite slab that's still visible – and often still adorned with flowers – on the path. Nowadays, it's merely the best-known of the city's numerous *hofjes* (almshouses); for details of others, *see p104*.

Most of the neat little houses in the courtyard were modernised in the 17th and 18th centuries. In the centre stands the **Engelsekerk** (English Reformed Church), built as a church in around 1400 and given over to Scottish (no, really) Presbyterians living in the city in 1607; many came to be Pilgrims when they decided to travel further to the New World in search of religious freedom. Now one of the principal places of worship for Amsterdam's English community, the church is worth a look primarily to see the pulpit panels, designed by a young Mondriaan.

Also in the courtyard is a Catholic church, secretly converted from two houses in 1665 following the banning of the Roman Catholic faith after the Reformation. It once held the vomited bread that starred in the Miracle of Amsterdam (*see p179*), a story depicted in the church's beautiful stained glass windows. The wooden house at Begijnhof 34, known as the Houtenhuis, dates from as early as 1477 and is the oldest house still standing in the city, while Begijnhof 35 is an information centre. The Begijnhof is also close to one of the several entrances to **Amsterdams Historisch Museum** (*see p86*), which in turn is the starting point for the informal **Mee In Mokum** walking tours (*see p38*).

The Spui square itself plays host to many markets – the most notable being the busy book market on Fridays – and was historically an area where the intelligentsia gathered for some serious browbeating and alcohol abuse, often after doing an honest day's graft at one of the many newspapers that were once located on the Spuistraat. The Lieverdje ('Little Darling') statue in front of the **Athenaeum Newscentrum** store (*see p155*), a small, spindly and pigeon shit-smeared statue of a boy in goofy knee socks, was the site for Provo 'happenings' in the mid '60s.

You can leave the Spui by going up either the Kalverstraat, Amsterdam's main shopping street, or the Singel past Leidsestraat: both routes lead to the **Munttoren** (Mint Tower) at Muntplein. Just across from the floating flower market (the **Bloemenmarkt**; *see p162*), this medieval tower was the western corner of the

Sightseeing

Bulbs and biographies at two New Side spots: **Bloemenmarkt** (*left*) and the **Spui book market**.

Regulierspoort, a gate in the city wall in the 1480s; in 1620, a spire was added by Hendrick de Keyser, the foremost architect of the period. The tower takes its name from the time when it was used to mint coins after Amsterdam was cut off from its money supply during a war with England, Munster and France. There's now a shop on the ground floor selling fine Dutch porcelain (**Holland Gallery de Munt**; *see p171*), but the rest of the tower is closed to visitors. The Munttoren is prettiest at night when it's floodlit, though daytime visitors may be able to hear its carillon, which often plays for 15 minutes at noon.

Clubbers may want to stop in the area and pay tribute to the former site of the infamous Roxy nightclub (Singel 465) that burned down in 1999; rather eerily, in fact, since the fire started during the wake that was taking place there for its deceased designer, the artist and poet Peter Giele. His colourful vision can still be sampled pretty much across the street at the jet-set eaterie **Inez IPSC** (*see p125*).

From here, walk down Nieuwe Doelenstraat from the **Hôtel de l'Europe** (featured in Hitchcock's *Foreign Correspondent; see p49*). This street connects with the scenic – so scenic, in fact, that it's rated the city's most popular film location, having appeared in everything from *The Diary of Anne Frank* to *Amsterdamned* – Staalstraat. Walk up here and you'll end up at **Waterlooplein** (*see p95 and p166*).

### Amsterdams Historisch Museum

*Kalverstraat 92 (523 1822/www.ahm.nl). Tram 1, 2, 4, 5, 9, 14, 16, 20, 24, 25.* **Open** 10am-5pm Mon-Fri; 11am-5pm Sat, Sun. **Admission** €6; €3 6-16s; free MJK, under-6s. **No credit cards. Map** p306 D3.

A note to all those historical museums around the world who struggle to present their exhibits in engaging fashion: head here to see exactly how it's done. Amsterdam's Historical Museum is a gem: illuminating, interesting and entertaining.

It starts with the buildings in which it's housed: a lovely, labyrinthine collection of 17th-century constructions built on the site of a 1414 convent. You can enter it down Sint Luciensteeg, just off Kalverstraat, or off Spui, walking past the Begijnhof (*see p85*) and through the grand Civic Guard Gallery, a small covered street hung with massive 16th- and 17th-century group portraits of wealthy burghers.

And it continues with the first exhibit, a computer-generated map of the area showing how Amsterdam has grown (and shrunk) throughout the last 800 years or so. The museum then takes a chronological trip through Amsterdam's past, using archaeological finds (love those 700-year-old shoes), works of art (by the likes of Ferdinand Bol and Jacob Corneliszoon) and plenty of quirkier displays: tone-deaf masochists may care to play the carillon in the galleried room 10A, while lesbian barflies will want to pay homage to Bet van Beeren, late owner of legendary Café t'Mandje. It's all linked together with informative, multilingual captions and the occasional audio-visual exhibit. Amsterdam has a rich history, and this wonderful museum does it justice.

# The Canals

Amsterdam's idyllic, image-defining waterways are awash with funky houseboats, arty shops and pavement cafés.

The Dutch call them *grachten*. There are 165 of them in Amsterdam. They stretch for 75.5 kilometres (47 miles) around the city, and reach an average depth of three metres (ten feet). They keep the sea and the surrounding bog at bay. About 10,000 bicycles, 100 million litres of sludge and grunge and 50 corpses (usually tramps, who trip while pissed and pissing) are dredged from their murky depths each year.

The major canals and their radial streets are where the real Amsterdam exists. What they lack in sights, they make up for as a focus for scenic coffee slurping, quirky shopping, aimless walking and meditative gable gandering. The Grachtengordel – 'girdle of canals' – rings the centre of town, with its waterways providing a trekkable border between the tourist-laden centre and the sedate, artsier locales of the Museum Quarter, the Jordaan and the Pijp.

The **Singel** was the original medieval moat of the city, while the other three canals that follow its line outward were part of a Golden Age urban renewal scheme; by the time building finished, Amsterdam had quadrupled in size. The **Herengracht** (named after the gentlemen who initially invested in it), the **Keizersgracht** (named for Holy Roman Emperor Maximilian I) and the **Prinsengracht** (named after William, Prince of Orange) are canals where the rich once lived, but though parts are still residential, many properties have been given over to offices, hotels, museums and banks.

The connecting canals and streets, originally built for workers and artisans, have a higher density of cafés and shops, while the shopping stretches of **Rozengracht**, **Elandsgracht**, **Leidsestraat** and **Vijzelstraat** are all former canals, filled in to deal with the traffic. Smaller canals worth seeking out include **Leliegracht**, **Bloemgracht**, **Spiegelgracht**, **Egelantiersgracht** and **Brouwersgracht**.

In this guide, for the sake of ease of use, we've split venues on the canals into the **Western Canal Belt** (between Singel and Prinsengracht, south of Brouwersgracht, north and west of Leidsegracht) and **Southern Canal Belt** (between Singel and Prinsengracht, from Leidsegracht south-east to the Amstel). This splitting is historically backed by the fact that the Western girdle was completely finished before work began on the Eastern half.

## The Western Canal Belt

### Map p306

### Singel

One of the few clues to Singel's past as the protective moat surrounding the city's wall is the bridge that crosses at Oude Leliestraat. It's called the **Torensluis** and did, indeed, once have a lookout tower; the space under the bridge, now ironically populated with drinkers on its terraces, was supposedly used as a lock-up for medieval drunks. The statue of Multatuli on it, depicting his head coming genie-like from a bottle, shadows the nearby **Multatuli Museum** (*see p88*).

While you're wandering this lazy canal, you may want to join the debate on whether Singel 7 or Singel 166 is the smallest house in town. Located between them, and adored by pussy-lovers, is the **Poezenboot** (Cat Boat, 625 8794; www.pandemic.com/catboat) opposite Singel 40, home to stray and abandoned felines. Slightly further down, and always good for a snort, is the **House with Noses** at Singel 116, though arty types may be more interested in Singel 140-42, once the home of Banning Cocq: the principal figure of Rembrandt's *Night Watch*, he was, in his time, poetically referred to as 'the stupidest man in Amsterdam'. A little further south, you may also want to stake out the town's poshest sex club, **Yab Yum** (Singel 295, 624 9503), to watch the country's elite enter for a good old-fashioned servicing.

**Poezenboot**'s pussy galore.

## Multatuli Museum

*Korsjespoortsteeg 20 (638 1938). Tram 1, 2, 5, 13, 17, 20.* **Open** 10am-5pm Tue; noon-5pm Sat, Sun; also by appointment. **Admission** free. **No credit cards. Map** p306 C2.

Located just off Singel, in the house where he was born, the life of 19th-century writer Eduard Douwes-Dekker, aka Multatuli, is illustrated by assorted literaturabilia. There's also a small library here.

## Herengracht

Cross Singel at Wijde Heisteeg, and opposite you on Herengracht is the **Bijbels Museum** (Bible Museum; *see below*). A few doors south, at Herengracht 380, stone masons kept themselves busy by knocking up an exact copy of a Loire mansion, complete with coy reclining figures on the gable and frolicking cherubs and other mythical figures around its bay window.

The northern stretch of Herengracht, from here up to Brouwersgracht, is fairly sight-free; the canal also wants for cafés and decent shops. Still, it's a very pleasant walk. Try to peek into the windows of the **Van Brienenhuis** at Herengracht 284: the excesses of bygone eras will soon become apparent. Keep walking, and you'll reach a Vingboons building at No.168, dating from 1638. Along with De Keyser's Bartolotti House, this architectural gem now houses the **Theater Instituut** (*see below*).

### Bijbels Museum (Bible Museum)

*Herengracht 366-8 (624 2436/ www.bijbelsmuseum.nl). Tram 1, 2, 5.* **Open** 10am-5pm Mon-Sat; 1-5pm Sun, public holidays. **Admission** €5; €2.50 6-18s; free MJK, free under-6s. **No credit cards. Map** p310 C4.

Housed in two handsome Vingboons canal houses, Amsterdam's Bible Museum aims to illustrate life and worship in biblical times with archaeological

**Theater Instituut**: displays to surprise.

finds from Egypt and the Middle East, several models of ancient temples, and a slideshow. As you'd expect from the name, there's also a fine collection of Bibles from several centuries (including a rhyming Bible from 1271). However, not all the displays are in English, and those that are tend to be fairly dry affairs. Restoration of the houses and the splendid Jacob de Wit paintings on the ceilings were completed in 2000. Try to allow time to relax in the grand garden, whose focus is on a wild Martie van der Loo sculpture entitled *Apocalypse*.

### Theater Instituut

*Herengracht 168 (551 3300/www.tin.nl). Tram 13, 14, 17, 20.* **Open** 11am-5pm Tue-Fri; 1-5pm Sat, Sun. **Admission** €3.85; €2.90 students, 7-16s, over-65s; free MJK, under-6s. **Credit** AmEx, MC, V. **Map** p306 C3.

It's hard to know exactly what'll be on display at Amsterdam's Theatre Institute before you show up. The exhibits change regularly: displays are largely drawn from the institute's collection of costumes, props, posters, memorabilia and ephemera, a collection they're in the process of digitally categorising. Keep your fingers crossed that the museum commissions more pieces like 2000's fabulous *A House Full of Voices*, an interactive journey through several canal rooms conceived by Orkater. Upstairs is a massive library with over 100,000 books and more than 6,000 videos; call ahead for information on hours and prices. Inside is a ceiling painting by Jacob de Wit; outside is a lovely, idyllic garden.

## Keizersgracht

Walk down Keizersgracht from its northern tip (by Brouwersgracht), and you'll soon encounter the **House with the Heads** at Keizersgracht 123, a classic of pure Dutch Renaissance. The official story has these finely chiselled heads representing classical gods, but the real scoop is supposed to be that these are actually the heads of burglars, chopped off by a vigilante and a lusty maidservant. She decapitated six and married the seventh, or so the story goes.

Another classic is at **Keizersgracht 174**, an art nouveau masterpiece by Gerrit van Arkels and currently the headquarters of Greenpeace International. Similarly hard to ignore is the **Felix Meritis Building** at Keizersgracht 324, given that it's a neo-classical monolith with 'Happiness through achievement' chiselled over its door. And achieve it did: after housing a society of arts and sciences in the 1800s, it went on to house the Communist Party and is now the European Centre for Art and Science. This stretch was also once the site of the Slipper Parade every Sunday, where the posh-footed rich strolled about to see and be seen. From here, take a right down Molenpad and you'll reach Prinsengracht.

Get in line at the **Anne Frankhuis**.

## Prinsengracht

The most charming of the canals. Pompous façades have been mellowed with shady trees, cosy cafés and some of the town's funkier houseboats. One of the funkiest is a short stroll away – the **Woonbootmuseum** *Hendrika Maria* (Houseboat Museum; *see p90*) – but also around this area are some delightful shopping thoroughfares. Working northwards, Runstraat, Berenstraat and Reestraat all link Prinsengracht and Keizersgracht, and all offer a delightfully diverse selection of smaller, artsier speciality shops that perfectly complement a leisurely stroll down by the water.

On your way up Prinsengracht, a large spire will loom into view before too long. This is the **Westerkerk** (*see p90*), a 370-year-old landmark church whose tower is easily the tallest structure in this part of town. Tours of the tower afford views that, while worth a look, are considerably less impressive than you'd hope after expending so much effort on reaching the summit. The problem is that few buildings in Amsterdam top four floors, and so the skyline panorama is good rather than great.

A short saunter away from the Westerkerk is the expanded – but still less than expansive – **Anne Frankhuis** (*see below*). A statue of Anne Frank by Mari Andriessen (dated 1977)

stands nearby, at the corner of Westermarkt and Prinsengracht. Meanwhile, any Descartes fans – and if you think, you therefore probably are – can pay tribute by regarding his former house around the corner at Westermarkt 6, which looks out on the pink granite triangular slabs that make up the **Homomonument** (*see p202*), the planet's first memorial to persecuted gay men and lesbians.

If it's a Monday and you're at the weekly **Noordermarkt**, inside the Jordaan on the west side of Prinsengracht (*see p166* **Amsterdam's markets**), stop for coffee at the **Papeneiland** (Prinsengracht 2). Reputedly, a tunnel used to go under the canal from here to a Catholic church that was located at Prinsengracht 7 at the time of the Protestant uprising. Also on this uneven numbered side of the canal, one can check in to see if the doors to the courtyards of the **Van Briennen** hofje (No.85-133) or the **De Zon** hofje (No.159-71) are open.

### Anne Frankhuis

*Prinsengracht 263 (556 7100/www.annefrank.nl).*
*Tram 13, 14, 17, 20.* **Open** *Jan-Mar, Sept-Dec* 9am-7pm daily. *Apr-Aug* 9am-9pm daily.
**Admission** €6.50; €3 10-17s; free under-10s.
**Credit** MC, V. **Map** p306 C2.
Prinsengracht 263 was the 17th-century canalside house where the young Jewish girl Anne Frank spent two years in hiding during World War II, from June 1942 to August 1944, and is now one of the most

# Bridging the gaps

With so many canals, it's logical that Amsterdam should also have a fair number of bridges: there are, in fact, over 1,400 of them. Try to stop off at the point on **Reguliersgracht**, at the junction with **Keizersgracht**, where you can see seven parallel bridges. Floodlit by night, it's one of Amsterdam's most beautiful scenes.

One of Amsterdam's odder bridges is the **Magerebrug** ('Skinny Bridge'), constructed in the 17th century. The story goes that two sisters who lived either side of the Amstel were bored by having to walk all the way round to visit each other, so the bridge was built for them. Uniquely, it's made from wood, and has to be repaired every 20 years. The bridge links Kerkstraat and Nieuwe Kerkstraat, and is opened by hand when a boat needs to pass. The main other bridge of note is the **Blauwbrug**, which links Amstelstraat with Waterlooplein and was inspired by the elaborate Pont Alexandre III in Paris.

# XXX-rated

When you're walking the canal belt or the Jordaan, your eyes could well be drawn to the **Westerkerk** (*pictured*); unsurprising, as it's one of the city's tallest buildings. Staring up at its tower, you'll see a gaudy gold, blue and red crown marked 'XXX'. 'What's this?' you may think. 'A church of porn?' Sadly not: the truth is more prosaic.

The story goes that in 1489, Maximilian, the Holy Roman Emperor, was in need of medical help during a pilgrimage. He found sanctuary in Amsterdam, and was so grateful he granted the city the right to include his crown on its coat of arms. The triple-X came to be used by the city's traders as a seal to denote quality. That said, after catching sight of the remarkably phallic 'XXX'-marked parking poles scattered throughout the city – they're called *Amsterdammertjes*, and you can even buy used ones for around €50 from Pieter Braaijweg 10, 8am-3pm Mon-Fri – you'd be forgiven for putting two and two together and making a particularly filthy five.

popular attractions in Amsterdam. Visitor numbers have been rising consistently for years at this tiny but globally known property; before long, they'll reach the magic figure of a million visitors a year.

Having fled from persecution in Germany in 1933, Anne Frank, her sister Margot, her parents and four other Jews went into hiding on 5 July 1942. Living in an annexe behind Prinsengracht 263, they were sustained by friends who risked everything to help them; a bookcase marks the entrance to the sober, unfurnished rooms that sheltered the eight inhabitants for two long years. Eventually, on 4 August 1944, the occupants of the annexe were arrested and transported to concentration camps, where Anne died along with Margot and their mother. Her father, Otto, survived, and decided that Anne's diary should be published. The rest, as they say, is history.

The house is now home to an involving exhibition on the Jews and the persecution they suffered during the war, as well as displays charting developments in racism, neo-Fascism and anti-Semitism (all with English texts). However, the compact nature of the building (despite the addition of a new building, it's still no Rijksmuseum), when coupled with the huge numbers of visitors drawn here, means that queues can be prohibitively long. Your best bet for avoiding the lines is to get there first thing in the morning, or (in summer) after 7pm: although the museum is now open until 9pm nightly five months of the year, many tourists and tour groups haven't picked up on this yet, and queues are usually a lot shorter in the early evening than in mid-afternoon.

## Westerkerk

*Prinsengracht 279 (624 7766/tower 612 6856/ www.westerkerk.nl). Tram 13, 14, 17, 20.*
**Open** *Church* Apr-Jun 11am-3pm Mon-Fri. July-Sept 11am-3pm Mon-Sat. *Services* 10.30am Sun. *Tower* Apr-Sept 10am-5pm Mon-Sat. **Admission** *Tower* €1.50. **No credit cards. Map** p306 C3.

Before noise pollution, it was said that if you could hear the bells of the Westerkerk, built in 1631 by Hendrick de Keyser, you were in the Jordaan. These days, its tower is just a good place from which to view its streets and canals, provided you don't suffer from vertigo: the 85m (278ft) tower sways 3cm in a good wind. Although the last tour up the 186 steps is at 5pm, and tours are only scheduled in summer, groups may be able to book at other times; call for details.

While you recover from the exertion of the climb, ponder the fate of Amsterdam's Rembrandt van Rijn. It's thought that the painter is buried here, though no one is sure where. Rembrandt died a pauper, and is commemorated inside with a plaque. Though his burial on 8 October 1669 was recorded in the church register, the actual spot was not specified; there's a good chance he shares a grave with his son, Titus, who died the previous year and is buried here.

## Woonbootmuseum (Houseboat Museum)

*Prinsengracht, near no.296 (427 0750/ www.houseboatmuseum.nl). Tram 13, 14, 17, 20.*
**Open** *Mar-Oct* 11am-5pm Wed-Sun. *Nov-Feb* 11am-5pm Fri-Sun. **Admission** €2.50; €2.05 children under 152cm (5ft). **No credit cards. Map** p310 C4.

For 'Woonboot', read 'Houseboat', and then take the translation literally. The Houseboat Museum is not just a museum about houseboats: it's actually one. In fact, it more or less is one: aside from some discreet explanatory panels, a small slide show and a ticket clerk, the *Hendrika Maria* is laid out as a houseboat would be, in an attempt to educate visitors on what it's like to live on the water. It's more spacious than you might expect, certainly, and does a good job of selling the lifestyle afforded by its unique comforts. Until, that is, you notice the pungent stench of piss emanating from the public urinoir right by the boat, and feel glad that you don't have to live by such an inconvenient convenience.

## The Southern Canal Belt

### Map p310

### Around Rembrandtplein

It might not be much to look at now, but back in the day, Rembrandtplein was called Reguliersmarkt and hosted Amsterdam's butter market. In 1876, the square was renamed in honour of Rembrandt; a statue – the oldest in the city – of the Dutch master, looking more fancy than he does in his self-portraits, stands in the centre of the gardens, gazing in the direction of the Jewish quarter. Though there's no longer a market here, it's still the centre of probably more commercial activity than ever, with neon signs and loud music blaring out from the cafés, bars, pubs and restaurants on all sides.

The area is unashamedly, unconscionably, unbearably tacky. Full of sunbathers by day and funseekers by night, the square is home to a variety of establishments, from the faded and fake elegance of the traditional striptease parlours to the seedy peep-show joints and nondescript cafés. Nevertheless, there are a few exceptions, such as the zoological sample-filled grand café **De Kroon** and HL de Jong's colourful deco masterpiece, the **Tuschinski** cinema on Reguliersbreestraat (*see p192*). Carry on past here and you'll end up at **Muntplein** (*see p86*), by the floating flower market at the southern tip of Singel (the **Bloemenmarkt**; *see p165*). Meanwhile, along Reguliersdwarsstraat and round the corner on the Amstel is a stretch of lively and largely popular gay cafés and bars (*see p207*); and on the façade of Amstel 216, the city's freakiest graffiti (*see p78* **Of bodies and bloodstains**).

From Rembrandtplein, walk south along the prime mid-range shopping and eating street **Utrechtsestraat**, or explore the painfully scenic **Reguliersgracht** and the grotesquely pleasant oasis of **Amstelveld**. Whichever you choose, you'll cross Herengracht as you wander.

## The canals

As the first canal to be dug in the glory days, **Herengracht** attracted the richest of merchants, and this southern stretch is where you'll find the most stately and overblown houses on any of Amsterdam's canals. The **Museum Willet-Holthuysen** (*see p93*) is a classic example of such a 17th-century mansion.

However, it's on the stretch built later between Leidsestraat and Vijzelstraat, known as the 'Golden Bend', that things get out of hand. By then, the rich saw the advantage of buying two adjoining lots so they could build as wide as high. Excess defines the Louis XVI style of **Herengracht 475**, while tales of pre-rock 'n' roll excess are often told about Herengracht 527, whose interior was trashed by Peter the Great (*see p12* **For Pete's sake**). Mischievous types, meanwhile, may like to annoy the mayor: to do so, simply park your boat on his personal and pleasantly scenic dock in front of his official residence at Herengracht 502. If you're caught, quickly douse your spliff and try palming off the authorities with the excuse that you're just visiting the **Kattenkabinet** (Cat Cabinet; *see p93*).

It's a similarly grand story on this southern section of **Keizersgracht**, too. For evidence, pop into the **Museum van Loon** (*see p93*), on Keizersgracht just east of Vijzelstraat. But for

Log on at **Reguliersbreestraat**.

Sightseeing

# The **Time Out City Guides** spectrum

Available from all good bookshops and at www.timeout.com/shop

www.timeout.com    www.penguin.com

an alternative view of this area, head half a block south to **Kerkstraat**, parallel to and directly between Keizersgracht and Prinsengracht. The houses here are less grand, but what they lack in swank they more than make up for in funkiness, with galleries and shops – including smart drugs central **Conscious Dreams** (*see p157*) – only adding to the community feel. The pleasant oasis of Amstelveld helps, too, with the **Amstelkerk** – the white wooden church that once took a break from its holy duties to act as a stable for Napoleon's horses – worth a nose around.

Heading east along Kerkstraat will get you to the **Magerebrug** (or 'Skinny Bridge'; *see p89* **Bridging the gaps**) over the Amstel and on down Nieuwe Kerkstraat towards the Plantage (*see p97*). Alternatively, turn right at Amstel and right again down **Prinsengracht** if you can't get enough of grand canal houses, peace and quiet, and a general loveliness.

### Kattenkabinet (Cat Cabinet)
*Herengracht 497 (626 5378/www.kattenkabinet.nl).* Tram 4, 9, 14, 16, 20, 24, 25. **Open** 9am-2pm Mon-Fri; 1-5pm Sat, Sun. **Admission** €4.50; €3 under-12s. **No credit cards**. **Map** p310 D4.
Housed in a grand 17th-century canal house but not opened until 1990, the Cat Cabinet differs wildly from Amsterdam's more notorious pussy palaces. It's a veritable temple to the feline form: it boasts that it's the world's only museum with a permanent exhibition devoted to cats, and no one's yet come forward to argue. Paintings, statues, posters and ephemera fill the vast rooms, guarded (after a fashion) by moggies who spend the whole time lying disinterestedly around, cocking a silent snook at guests. Fun, especially for cat-lovers, even if the admission price seems a little steep for such a slight enterprise.

### Museum van Loon
*Keizersgracht 672 (624 5255/www.musvloon.box.nl).* Tram 16, 24, 25. **Open** 11am-5pm Mon, Fri-Sun. **Admission** €4.50; €3 students; free MJK, under-12s. **No credit cards**. **Map** p311 E4.
Amsterdam's waterways are chock-a-block with grand canal houses. Few of their interiors have been preserved in anything approaching their original state, but the former Van Loon residence is one that has. Designed by Adriaan Dortsman – whose other notable local buildings include the New Lutheran Church on Singel – the house was originally the home of artist Ferdinand Bol. Hendrik van Loon, after whom the museum is named, bought the house in 1884; it was opened as a museum in 1973.

The posh mid 18th century interior is terrifically grand, and admirers of Louis XV and XVI decor will find much that excites. However, so will art-lovers. The house holds a collection of family portraits from the 17th through 20th centuries; perhaps more unexpectedly, it hosts a modern art show every two years, featuring the likes of Steve McQueen and

Richard Wright. The 18th-century garden, laid out in the French style, contains Ram Katzir's striking sculpture of a headless man, *There*.

### Museum Willet-Holthuysen
*Herengracht 605 (523 1870/www.ahm.nl/english/willet).* Tram 4, 9, 14, 20. **Open** 10am-5pm Mon-Fri; 11am-5pm Sat, Sun. **Admission** €6; €4.50 over-65s; €3 6-16s; free MJK, under-6s. **Credit** MC, V. **Map** p311 E4.
Built in the 1680s, this mansion was purchased in the 1850s by the Willet-Holthuysen family. When Abraham died in 1889, wife Sandrina Louisa left the house and its contents to the city on the condition it was preserved and opened as a museum. The family followed the fashion of the time and decorated it in the neo-Louis XVI style: it's densely furnished, with the over-embellishment extending to the collection of rare objets d'art, glassware, silver, fine china and paintings. English texts accompany the exhibits, and there's also an English-language video explaining the history of the house and the city's canal system. The view from the first floor into the recently renovated 18th-century garden almost takes you back in time, but the illusion is disturbed somewhat by the adjoining modern buildings.

### Torture Museum
*Singel 449 (320 6642).* Tram 1, 2, 5. **Open** 10am-11pm daily. **Admission** €4; €3 students (summer holidays only). **No credit cards**. **Map** p310 D4.
Tucked away on Singel, the Torture Museum is one of those attractions you might stumble across while walking around town and be tempted to visit. Don't bother. Though there are a few interesting nuggets of information contained within its walls, this is mostly just a frustrating experience, riddled with tattily maintained exhibits and uninvolving captions. The whole place can easily be done in 20 minutes, and really isn't worth the money. The impression with which you'll likely leave is that of yet another Amsterdam tourist trap (cf Sexmuseum, Hash Marihuana Hemp Museum) that could have been a lot more informative, engaging and – most importantly – fun than it actually is.

## Around Leidseplein

**Leidseplein**, which from Prinsengracht is reached via the chaotic pedestrian- and tram-packed Leidsestraat, is the tourist centre of Amsterdam. The bastard child of Times Square in New York City and London's Leicester Square, it's permanently packed with merrymakers drinking at pavement cafés, listening to buskers and soaking up the atmosphere (and the Amstel Light).

Leidseplein lies on the south-west edge of the Canal Belt; although it's called a square, it is, in fact, shaped like an L-shape, running from the end of Leidsestraat to the Amsterdam

On and around **Leidseplein**: by day, full of drinkers; by night... um, still full of drinkers.

School-styled bridge over Singelgracht. In today's current climate of city-centre traffic reduction schemes, Leidseplein is a striking reminder that such ideas are not new: during the Middle Ages, carts and wagons were banned from the centre of Amsterdam, and people heading for the city had to leave their vehicles in *pleinen*, or squares. At the end of the road from Leiden was a 'cart park', which was surrounded by warehouses and businesses that catered for this captive clientele.

The area has more cinemas, theatres, clubs and restaurants than any other part of town. It's dominated by the **Stadsschouwburg** (the municipal theatre; *see p243*) and by the cafés that take over the pavements during summer. This is also when fire-eaters, jugglers, acrobats, musicians and small-time con-artists fill the square, but watch out for pesky pickpockets. However, the development of Leidseplein in recent years has meant that there are now fast food restaurants on every corner, and many locals feel that the essential Dutch flavour of the district has been destroyed for a quick buck.

Leidseplein has always been a focal point of the town for one reason or another. Artists and writers used to congregate here in the 1920s and 1930s, when it was the scene of clashes between Communists and Fascists. During the war, it was a focus for protests, ruthlessly broken up by the occupying Nazis: there's a commemorative plaque on nearby Kerkstraat. But Leidseplein's contemporary persona is more jockstrap than political, especially when Ajax, the local football team, win anything and their

fans take over the square. The police take the mini-riots that usually ensue in their stride, and so they should: they've had enough practice at dealing with them by now.

The café society associated with Leidseplein began in earnest with the opening of the city's first bar incorporating a terrace, the Café du Théâtre. It was demolished in 1877, 20 years before completion of Kromhout's impressive **American Hotel** – now a meeting place for the posh tourist; *see p58* – at the south-west end of the square. Opposite the American is a building, dating from 1882, that reflects Leidseplein's transformation: once grand, it's now illuminated by huge, vile adverts.

Just off the square, in the Leidsebos, is the Adamant, a white pyramid-type sculpture given to Amsterdam by the city's diamond industry in 1986 to commemorate 400 years of the trade. Designed by Joost van Santen at a cost of ƒ75,000 (€34,000), it uses light to form a rainbow hologram. Further south is the Max Euweplein and its **Max Euwe Centrum** (*see below*).

### Max Euwe Centrum

*Max Euweplein 30A (625 7017/www.maxeuwe.nl).* *Tram 1, 2, 5, 6, 7, 10.* **Open** 10.30am-5pm Tue-Fri; 10am-4pm first Sat of mth. **Admission** free. **No credit cards. Map** p310 D5.
Named after the only chess world champion the Netherlands has ever produced and housed in the city's old House of Detention – it held Resistance leaders during World War II – the Max Euwe Centrum harbours a library of works in dozens of languages, various chess artefacts from Euwe's legacy, vast archives, and chess computers that visitors can use and abuse at their leisure.

# Jodenbuurt, the Plantage & the Oost

An assortment of intriguing museums, a mammoth park and monkey business at Amsterdam's impressive zoo.

## Jodenbuurt

**Map p307**

South-east of the Red Light District, Amsterdam's old Jewish neighbourhood is a peculiar mix of old and new architectural styles. If you leave the Nieuwmarkt along **Sint Antoniesbreestraat**, you'll pass several bars, coffeeshops and chic clothes stores: it's a good escape route out of the throbbing Red Light District. The modern yet tasteful council housing that lines the street was designed by local architect Theo Bosch, while the Italian renaissance-styled **Pintohuis** at No.69 was renovated by the Jewish refugee and a VOC founder, Isaac de Pinto, and is now a public library where you can browse under Jacob de Wit ceiling paintings.

Pop through the skull-adorned entrance across the street between Sint Antoniesbreestraat 130 and 132, and enter the former graveyard and now restful square around **Zuiderkerk** (South Church). Designed by De Keyser and built between 1603 and 1614, the first Protestant church to appear after the Reformation. Now, it's the municipal information centre for the physical planning and housing of Amsterdam. Development plans are made to look promising with interactive scale models, but as you walk around the neighbourhood – or view it from the church's tower (689 2565, tours 2pm, 3pm, 4pm Wed-Sat) – it becomes obvious that shiny ideals can often create obtuse realities.

Crossing the bridge at the end of Sint Antoniesbreestraat, you'll arrive at the obtuse reality of performing arts school, the Arts Academy (aka De Hogeschool voor de Kunsten), on the left and the **Rembrandthuis** (*see p97*) on the right, next door to the **Holland Experience** (*see p96*). Immediately before this, though, some steps will take you to **Waterlooplein Market** (*see p166* **Amsterdam's markets**). Though touristy, it can be a bargain-hunter's dream if you're a patient shopper.

Nearby is the 19th-century **Mozes en Aäronkerk**, built on the spot of Spinoza's birth home. This former clandestine Catholic church on the corner where Waterlooplein meets Mr Visserplein – the square-cum-traffic roundabout that has as its new showcase the obtuse reality of the copper-green Film and Television Academy – is where Liszt reportedly played his favourite concert in 1866, and has been used as a social and cultural centre since 1970. It could be worth checking to see if the plans to temporarily revamp the abandoned traffic tunnel underneath the square as a skateboarding park by day and a nightclub by night have finally been realised. Also close by is the **Joods Historisch Museum** (the Jewish Historical Museum; *see p96*).

Dominating Waterlooplein is the **Stadhuis-Muziektheater** (the City Hall-Music Theatre; *see p221*). It wasn't always thus, though: the area where it stands was once a Jewish ghetto, and later, in the 1970s, home to dozens of gorgeous squatted 16th- and 17th-century buildings. The building was dogged by controversy: first mooted in the 1920s, it was not until 1954 that the council chose Waterlooplein as the site, and it was 1979 before it was agreed that the civic headquarters should be combined with an opera house.

The decision was controversial, as was the actual design by Wilhelm Holtzbauer and Cees Dam, and locals showed their discontent by protesting: in 1982, a riot caused damage estimated at ƒ1 million (€450,000) to construction equipment. These displays of angered displeasure are the reasons why the ƒ300-million (€136-million) building, home to the **Nederlands Opera** and the **Nationale Ballet** (*see p250*), is still universally known as the 'Stopera'.

It's rare that science and art meet on the level, but in the passage between City Hall and the Muziektheater, the **Amsterdam Ordnance Project** includes a device showing NAP (normal Amsterdam water level) and a cross-section of the Netherlands detailing its geological structure. Close by is the **Blauwbrug** (Blue Bridge), which links Waterlooplein with Amstel. Years ago, it was the main route into the city from the east.

Souvenir kitsch: **Waterlooplein**, Amsterdam's biggest tourist market. *See p166.*

The current bridge was built in 1873, but a plaque depicting the original (taken from a demolished house) has been placed at the entrance of the Muziektheater car park. Recent renovation work has returned the bridge to the same state as Dutch Impressionist painter Breitner saw it at the turn of the century. However, you won't see much blue: that was the colour of the original wooden one…

### Holland Experience
*Waterlooplein 17 (422 2233/www.holland-experience.nl). Tram 9, 14, 20/Metro Waterlooplein.* **Open** 10am-6pm daily. **Admission** €8; €6.85 over-65s, under-16s. **Credit** AmEx, DC, MC, V. **Map** p307 E3.

A monumentally peculiar attraction, this, and one it's hard to recommend, unless you have more money than sense and a blinkered fetish for Euro-kitsch. For your hard-earned, you get to sit on an undulating platform wearing 3-D glasses and watch a half-hour film that basically acts as a roll-call of Dutch clichés. Windmills? Check. Canals? Check. Clogs? Check. Tulips? Check. Cheese? Yep, it's cheesy all right. Heaven only knows what Rembrandt, whose old house adjoins the Holland Experience (*see p97*), would have thought of it.

Plus points? Children may enjoy it, and the actual technology isn't unimpressive. But coming to Amsterdam and forking out to see the Holland Experience is roughly akin to visitors in London taking a £1 ride on a red double-decker bus to a theatre so they can then pay £7 in order to watch a film about riding red double-decker buses, or heading to New York so they can look at photographs of the Statue of Liberty. And as one big cornball simulation, it raises the question: why? The real Holland experience is, after all, right outside the door.

### Joods Historisch Museum (Jewish Historical Museum)
*Jonas Daniël Meijerplein 2-4 (626 9945/www.jhm.nl). Tram 9, 14, 20/Metro Waterlooplein.* **Open** 11am-5pm daily. **Admission** €5; €3 students, over-65s; €2.50 13-18s; €1.50 6-12s; free MJK, under-6s. **No credit cards. Map** p307 E3.

Housed since 1987 in four former synagogues in the old Jewish quarter (before that, it was housed in De Waag; *see p79*), the Jewish Historical Museum is full of religious items, photographs and paintings detailing the history of Judaism in the Netherlands. The interesting if unexciting permanent displays concentrate on religious practice and Dutch Jewish culture; among the more striking exhibits is the painted autobiography of artist Charlotte Salomon, killed in Auschwitz aged 26. An excellent new kids' wing opened in 2000, and crams interactive exhibits on aspects of Jewish culture (including a nice one on music) into its galleried space. Temporary shows explore various aspects of Jewish culture; the Jonas Daniël Meijerplein with its Dock Worker statue commemorating the February Strike of 1941 in protest against Jewish deportations sit across the street, beside the Portuguese Synagogue (*see p96*).

## Portuguese Synagogue

*Mr Visserplein 3 (624 5351/www.esnoga.com).*
*Tram 4, 9, 14, 20.* **Open** *Apr-Oct* 10am-4pm
Mon-Fri, Sun. *Nov-Mar* 10am-4pm Mon-Thur, Sun;
10am-3pm Fri. **Admission** €4.50; €3.50 10-15s;
free under-10s. **No credit cards. Map** p307 E3.
Architect Elias Bouwman's mammoth synagogue,
reputedly inspired by the Temple of Solomon, was
inaugurated in 1675. It's built on wooden piles, and
surrounded by smaller buildings (offices, archives,
a library, the rabbinate). Renovation that took place
in the late 1950s restored the synagogue nicely, and
the low-key tours are informative and interesting.

## Rembrandthuis

*Jodenbreestraat 4 (520 0400/www.rembrandthuis.nl).*
*Tram 9, 14, 20/Metro Waterlooplein.* **Open** 10am-
5pm Mon-Sat; 1-5pm Sun. **Admission** €7; €5
students; €1.50 6-16s; free MJK, under-6s.
**Credit** AmEx, DC, MC, V. **Map** p307 E3.
The renovation of Rembrandt van Rijn's old pad
near Waterlooplein was a long time in coming: all in
all, over 340 years. Rembrandt bought the house in
1639 for ƒ13,000 (around €6,000), a massive sum at
the time. Indeed, the pressure of the mortgage pay-
ments eventually got to the free-spending artist, who
went bankrupt in 1656 and was forced to move to
a smaller house (Rozengracht 184). When he was
declared bankrupt, clerks inventoried the house
room by room; it's these bankruptcy records that
provided researchers with clues as to what the house
might have looked like in Rembrandt's time.

However, while you can't help but admire the skill
and effort with which craftsmen tried to recreate the
house, walking through it is a disappointment. The
house is full of antiquities, objets d'art (Rembrandt
was a compulsive collector) and 17th-century furniture. However, the presentation is, on the whole, dry
and unengaging. Nagging at you all the time is the
fact that this isn't really Rembrandt's house, but
rather a touch-wood mock-up of it, which lends an
unreal air to the place. And anyway, if it's his art
you're after, head to the Rijksmuseum; the collection
found here is primarily made up of etchings and
drawings, but, while showing Rembrandt at his
most experimental, it's only of marginal interest to
non-scholars. A strangely hollow experience.

# The Plantage

## Map p307 & p312

The mostly residential area known as the
Plantage lies south-east of Mr Visserplein and
is reached via Muiderstraat. The attractive
**Plantage Middenlaan** winds past the Hortus
Botanicus, passes close by the Verzetsmuseum,
runs along the edge of the Artis Zoo, and heads
towards the Tropenmuseum.

After a period during which the area was
largely populated by rich citizens, Jews began
to settle here some 200 years ago; the area was
soon redeveloped on 19th-century diamond

money. The headquarters of the diamond
cutters' union, designed by Berlage as a more
outward expression of his socialism than his
Stock Exchange (aka **Beurs van Berlage**;
*see p74*), still stands on Henri Polaklaan, and
other extant buildings such as the Gassan, the
Saskiahuis and the Coster act as reminders that
the town's most profitable trade was once based
here (*see p15* **Diamond geezers**). However, the
spectre of World War II again raises its head at
the **Hollandse Schouwburg** (*see p98*).

The Plantage is still wealthy, even though
its charm has faded over the years. Graceful
buildings and tree-lined streets provide a
residential area much sought after by those
who want to live centrally but away from the
more touristy areas. The area has undergone
extensive redevelopment and work is still
continuing. As one would expect, results have
been mixed: while the housing association flats
and houses erected where the army barracks
and dockside warehouses once stood (just
past Muiderpoort city gate) are unattractive,
**Entrepotdok** works far better.

To wander down this stretch is to admire a
delicate balance between the new and the old,
with docked post-hippie houseboats and the
views of Artis providing a charmed contrast
to the condominiums. Still, the area has
maintained some of its heritage: the brightly
coloured **Van Eyck's Moedershuis** at
Plantage Middenlaan 33 was a mother and child
refuge during World War II, while on the other
side of the road is the attractive **Huize Sint**

**Joods Historisch Museum**. *See p96.*

Hortus Botanicus: an oasis of calm.

**Jacob**, an old people's home that has been rebuilt on the site of an earlier one using the original stone portal.

For most visitors, the stretch of Plantage Middenlaan is notable mostly for the lovely collection of attractions that dots its sidings and surrounds: the **Hortus Botanicus** (*see below*), the **Verzetsmuseum** (the Museum of the Dutch Resistance, located in an old choral society building near Waterlooplein; *see p99*), and the nearby **Artis**, with all its encumbent attractions (*see below*).

### Artis

*Plantage Kerklaan 38-40 (523 3400/www.artis.nl).* Tram 6, 9, 14, 20. **Open** 9am-5pm daily. **Admission** €14; €12 over-65s; €10 4-11s; free under-4s. **No credit cards. Map** p312 G3.
A great day out for children, this, along with adults who don't mind hanging out with the hordes of tourists who head here each year. Along with the usual range of animals, Artis has an indoor 'rain forest' for nocturnal creatures and a 120-year-old aquarium that includes a simulated Amsterdam canal (the main difference is the clear water, which means the eels are clearly visible). The 160-year-old zoo expanded a couple of years ago after a long battle for extra land and now features a mock-up of an African savannah that wraps around a new woody and light-infused restaurant. Also notable – and typically Amsterdam – are the gay animal tours that

allow the pleasures of not only seeing the zoo's resident gay elephants, monkeys and dolphins, but also witnessing flamingos' same-sex orgies.

Elsewhere in here, there are also other attractions. The narration in the planetarium is in Dutch, but an English translation is available. Further extras are a geological museum, a zoological museum, an aquarium and, for kids, a petting zoo and playgrounds; all this combined makes Artis the kind of attraction that could easily take up a whole day of your trip.

### Hollandse Schouwburg

*Plantage Middenlaan 24 (626 9945).* Tram 7, 9, 14, 20. **Open** 11am-4pm daily. **Admission** free. **No credit cards. Map** p307 F3.
In 1942, this grand theatre became a main point of assembly for between 60,000 and 80,000 of the city's Jews before they were transported to the transit camp Westerbork. It's now a monument with a small but very impressive exhibition and a memorial hall with 6,700 surnames paying tribute to the 104,000 Dutch Jews who were exterminated. The façade has been left intact, with most of the inner structure removed to make way for a memorial.

### Hortus Botanicus

*Plantage Middenlaan 2A (625 9021/www.hortus-botanicus.nl).* Tram 9, 14, 20/Metro Waterlooplein. **Open** *Apr-Oct* 9am-5pm Mon-Fri; 11am-5pm Sat, Sun. *Nov-Mar* 9am-4pm Mon-Fri, 11am-4pm Sat, Sun. **Admission** *Apr-Oct* €5; €2.30 5-14s; free under-5s. *Nov-Mar* €3.40; €2 5-14s; free under-5s. **No credit cards. Map** p312 G3.
You don't have to be the green-fingered type to enjoy these beautiful gardens. The Hortus has been at this location since 1682, although it was set up 50 years earlier when East India Company ships brought back tropical plants and seeds originally intended to supply doctors with medicinal herbs. Some of those specimens are still here in the palm greenhouse, which dates from 1912, while three other greenhouses maintain desert, tropical and subtropical climates. The terrace is one of the nicest in town: only the distant sounds of the city remind you where you are. The Hortus was part of the University of Amsterdam until 1989, when funding was tightened; now it's run by a foundation and partly supported by the city.

### Vakbondsmuseum (Trade Unions Museum)

*Henri Polaklaan 9 (624 1166/www.deburcht-vakbondsmuseum.nl).* Tram 7, 9, 14, 20. **Open** 11am-5pm Tue-Fri; 1-5pm Sun. **Admission** €5. **No credit cards. Map** p307 F3.
The Trade Unions Museum offers a permanent exhibition showing the progress and history of unions in Dutch history. If you think that sounds interesting, you'll enjoy it; if not, don't make a special trip, unless for the fascinating collection of posters. That said, for those whose interest in labour relations is casual, the building's worth a peek: it was designed by Berlage to house the offices of the country's first trade union, that of diamond workers.

## Verzetsmuseum
### (Museum of the Dutch Resistance)
*Plantage Kerklaan 61 (620 2535/*
*www.verzetsmuseum.nl). Tram 6, 9, 14, 20.*
**Open** 10am-5pm Tue-Fri; noon-5pm Sat, Sun.
**Admission** €4; €2.50 6-16s; free MJK, under-6s.
**No credit cards. Map** p307 F3.

One of several spots devoted to the events of World War II, the Verzetsmuseum is one of Amsterdam's most illuminating museums, and perhaps its most moving. It takes a chronological journey through its subject, with myriad artefacts telling the story of the Resistance. False ID papers, clandestine printing presses and illegal newspapers, spy gadgets and an authentic secret door behind which Jews hid all help to detail the ways people in the Netherlands faced up to and dealt with the Nazi occupation. The engaging presentation is enhanced by the constant use of personal testimony; indeed, the museum's disparate exhibits are linked effectively by these stories, told by those who lived through the war on small panels that act as adjuncts to the main displays. Temporary shows explore wartime themes and modern-day forms of oppression, and there's a small research room, too. An excellent enterprise.

## The Oost

### Map p312

South of Mauritskade is Amsterdam Oost (East), where the Arena complex (*see p63 and p225*) is located along the edge of a former graveyard that was long ago transformed into **Oosterpark**. While hardly Amsterdam's most beautiful park, it's not without its charms, not least because the neighbourhood in which it sits isn't notable for much else, the **Tropenmusem** (*see below*) and the **Dappermarkt** (*see p166* **Amsterdam's markets**) excepted.

It's a similar story in the **Indische Buurt** (Indonesian neighbourhood) north-east of here, although the **Brouwerij 't IJ**, a brewery in a windmill (*see p143* **Roll out the barrels**), is a good place to sip on a culturally reflective beer. North and a little to the west of here are the Eastern Docklands (*see p100*), but as you head further east from the centre of Amsterdam, you'll find little of interest save for the pleasant green expanses of **Flevopark**. The peace and quiet is the main attraction here, though added bonuses come with the two open-air swimming pools that, though popular in summer, always seem to have enough space on the surrounding grass for the late-coming sunbather.

## Tropenmuseum
*Linnaeusstraat 2 (568 8215/www.tropenmuseum.nl).*
*Tram 9, 10, 14/bus 22.* **Open** 10am-5pm daily.
**Admission** €6.80; €4.55 over-65s; €3.40 6-17s; free MJK, under-6s. *Children's museum* €1.60 extra (6-12s only). **Credit** MC. **Map** p312 H3.

It's a handsome building, this, sitting grandly in a slightly out-of-the-way (for Amsterdam, at any rate) location. But better than that: the exhibitions in the Tropical Museum are terrific, too. Through a series of informative and lively displays – the majority of which come with English captions – the visitor is offered a vivid, interactive glimpse of daily life in the tropical and subtropical parts of the world (ironically, given that the vast three-storey building was originally designed and erected in the 1920s to glorify the colonial activities of the Dutch). Artefacts from religious items and jewellery to washing powder and vehicles have pride of place among the exhibits, divided by region and broad in their catchment. A musical display allows visitors to hear a variety of different instruments at the push of a button (the Tropenmuseum is also the city's leading venue for world music); walk-through environments include simulated African and South Asian villages and a Manilan street; and a Latin American exhibit is highlighted by a fun cultural room complete with videos of sporting highlights and a jukebox. Temporary arts and photographic exhibitions fill a large central space on the ground floor, while the shop has a good selection of souvenirs and books. Attached to the main museum is the all-Dutch **Kindermuseum**, for children aged six to 12, and a small cinema showing foreign films.

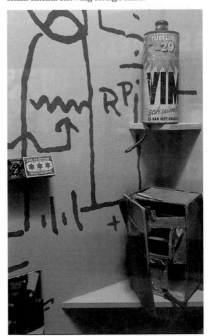

**Verzetsmuseum** tells of the Resistance.

# The Waterfront

The prosperity of the Golden Age was largely due to its existence. These days, missing out on the half-historic, half-futuristic harbour would be water torture.

Map p307

Amsterdam's historic wealth owes a lot to the city's waterfront, for it was here that all the goods were unloaded, weighed and prepared for storage in the warehouses still found in the area. During Amsterdam's trading heyday in the 17th century, most maritime activity was centred east of Centraal Station, along Prins Hendrikkade and on the artificial islands east of Kattenburgerstraat. At the time, the harbour and its arterial canals – many of which have been filled in since the rise of land traffic – formed a whole with the city itself. A drop in commerce slowly unbalanced this unity, and the construction of Centraal Station late in the 19th century served as the final psychological cleavage. This neo-Gothic monument to modernity – as it was seen then – blocked both the city's view of the harbour and its own past.

However, the harbour never started slacking. While Rotterdam is the world's largest port, Amsterdam and the nearby North Sea Canal ports of Zaanstad, Beverwijk and IJmuiden rank among the world's top 15. Amsterdam is the centre of Nissan's European distribution, and is still the world's largest cocoa port, something that leads to week-long spewings of dark smoke whenever a storage warehouse for these most oily of nuts catches fire.

Since 1876, access to the sea has been via the North Sea Canal. Because the working docks are also to the west, there is little activity on the IJ behind Centraal Station beyond a handful of passenger ships and the free ferry that runs across to Amsterdam Noord.

The **Schreierstoren**, or 'Weeping Tower', is the first thing you'll notice on the right if you walk east from Centraal Station, and is the most interesting relic of what's left of Amsterdam's medieval city wall. Built in 1487, it was successfully restored in 1966. In 1927, though, a bronze memorial plaque was added by the Greenwich Village Historical Society of New York: its text states that it was from this point, on 4 April 1609, that Henry Hudson departed in search of shorter trade routes to the Far East. He ended up colonising a small island in the mouth of a river in North America. The river was later named after him and the colony was called New Amsterdam, only to have its name changed by the English to New York.

(Today, some of the boroughs still have a nederstamp on them: in particular, Harlem, after Haarlem, and Brooklyn, after Breukelen.) The next eye-opener you'll see is the renamed **Nemo** (see p101), a science museum whose stunning green building dominates the horizon. It positively dwarfs the nautically inclined **Nederlands Scheepvaartmuseum** (see p101), itself a very grand structure and a major draw for tourists, especially the Dutch.

However, the old harbour is now virtually disused and the IJ-Oevers (docklands) are undergoing massive redevelopment, a big issue that concerns both locals and environmental groups in the city. It is said to be the country's only remaining upmarket area for new housing and office development, and plans for the new developments – estimated to cost €3 billion – are continually subject to alteration because of the lack of financial backing, pressure from local residents and new *stadsdeelraden* (local councils), and the ever-changing traffic control plans. Certainly, the city's subculture has lost out badly with the demise of both the sprawling Silo and Vrieshuis Amerika squats, but the city hopes that a transformed harbourfront will be as image enhancing as that in Sydney, Australia.

Going east, you'll espy **KNSM Eiland**, where the KNSM shipping company originally docked its boats and unloaded cargo. In recent years, it's been transformed from a squatters' paradise to a largely residential area, featuring some striking architecture and some newish bars and entertainment venues, such as **Kanis & Meiland** (see p144). As for the squatters in this area, many of them have had to look towards Amsterdam Noord or have made the harsh transition to being legal tenants and homeowners. Further east, you can watch the controversial building of the artificial residential island of IJburg (see p102 **On the waterfront**).

The **Westelijke Eilanden** (Western Islands), north-west of Centraal Station, are also artificial islands, created in the 17th century for shipping-related activities. While there are now trendy warehouse flats and a yacht basin on Realeneiland, Prinseneiland and Bickerseiland, where once shipyards, tar distillers, fish-salters and -smokers were once located, the area – thanks in part to its large artist community – remains the city's best setting for a scenic stroll.

## Nederlands Scheepvaartmuseum (Dutch Maritime Museum)

*Kattenburgerplein 1 (523 2222/*
*www.scheepvaartmuseum.nl). Bus 22, 32.*
**Open** *late Sept-early June* 10am-5pm Tue-Sun.
*Mid June-mid Sept* 10am-5pm daily.
**Admission** €7; €6 over-65s; €4 6-17s; free MJK,
under-6s. **Credit** AmEx, MC, V. **Map** p307 F2.

The Dutch nautical history is a rich and fascinating one. The city's prosperity was largely built on the seas, especially back in the Golden Age of the 1600s, but the tradition encompasses more than just the East India Company. It follows, then, that the country should boast one of the world's finest nautical museums; second only, say experts, to the National Maritime Museum in London.

However, non-Dutch speakers will likely find the Netherlands Maritime Museum a frustrating experience. There's no doubt as to the importance of the collection of models, portraits, boat parts and other naval ephemera; nor can there be any quibbling with the wonderful building in which it's housed (built 350 years ago by Daniel Stalpaert). But while the Dutch captions are excellent, the British, French and German ones are brief and unilluminating. For example, many of the portraits on display are captioned in Dutch with mini-biographies, or at least details of why the subjects merit inclusion in the museum; the non-Dutch captions consist only of a name and the dates the subject was alive. It's a similar deal with the objects: displaying a rudderhead from a 17th-century yacht is all very well, but without any context or explanation – in contrast to the detailed Dutch caption, the English labelling reads only 'Rudderhead from yacht, 17th century' – it's merely an old, junky lump. Only the huge replica VOC ship at the rear, complete with costumed 'sailors', really excites.

It may be unreasonable to expect a museum in a country where English isn't the first language to offer full English descriptions of its exhibits. However, given the prevalence of full English captioning in almost all Amsterdam's other major museums, it seems fair to criticise, because for non-Dutch speakers without a broad knowledge of maritime history, it's an oversight that turns a potentially fascinating museum into a largely dull one.

## Nemo

*Oosterdok 2 (531 3233/0900 919 1100*
*premium rate/www.e-nemo.nl). Bus 22.*
**Open** 10am-5pm Tue- Sun. **Admission** €10;
€8 students; free under-3s. **Credit** AmEx, DC,
MC, V. **Map** p307 F2.

The impossibly striking newMetropolis opened in 1998 to all sorts of fanfare. Fast forward a couple of years, though, and the attraction found itself in all sorts of financial trouble – largely due to poor visitor numbers – from which it's still struggling to recover. In an attempt to entice more visitors, it's rebranded itself, most conspicuously by changing its name. However, given that the new moniker, Nemo, is as unclear, anti-descriptive and frankly inexplicable as the old one – it's actually a science museum – it seems rather unlikely that it'll have much bearing on the museum's future.

Get ship-shape at the **Nederlands Scheepvaartmuseum.**

That said, it' a fine attraction, at least if you have kids. It's aimed squarely at children, eschewing traditional exhibits in favour of all manner of hands-on trickery, gadgetry and tomfoolery (in English and Dutch): you can mess around on a virtual stock market, play a hi-tech happy families game and use the Internet (albeit on oddly archaic gear). The museum's open-plan interior means that aside from the plush film theatre, there's no escape from the young 'uns, who run riot in hair-raising fashion. Some floors have the feel of a vast, high-budget crèche, and adults without kids should save their money. However, those with children in tow (particularly under-12s) should find their kids leave with smiles.

Childless adults, however, should at least check out the building. Renzo Piano's mammoth structure resembles a green ship rising from the water, and never fails to raise a gasp from people seeing it for the first time. Energetic types will enjoy the climb all the way to the top via the long, sloping roof, where you'll get a breathtaking view of the city. In summer, the outdoor café way up top is as lovely a place to spend an afternoon and early evening as anywhere in town. Best of all, it's free to get up there.

### Open Havenmuseum

*KNSM-Laan 311 (418 5522). Bus 22, 28, 32, 59.* **Open** 11am-5pm Tue-Sun. **Admission** €3.40. **No credit cards.**

# On the waterfront

Amsterdam's Eastern Docklands is the city's up-and-coming eating and entertainment hot-spot. But, perhaps more interestingly, it's also a fantastic showcase for the Netherlands' rather out-there experiments in residential living. If you want to explore the future of Amsterdam, hop on a bike, grab a map and get moving.

Hugging the water eastward from Centraal Station, hook up with and follow Oostelijk Handelskade and its parallel boardwalk to pass the glass wave-shaped **Passenger Terminal** for luxury cruise-ships; the rising **MuziekGebouw**, which will be home to the likes of the Bimhuis (*see p216*) and the IJsbreker (*see p220*) from late 2003; and **Pakhuis Amsterdam**, a former warehouse now transformed into a showcase for Europe's top interior designers. But before heading further on to nightspot **Panama** (*see p128 and p225*), **Odessa** (*see p128*) and the **Lloyd Hotel** (soon set to return to its former role after years as a youth prison), take the spacey Jan Schaeferbrug to the left that begins by going through the de Zwijger warehouse to the tip of Java Eiland. (The less energetic can travel on the free ferry which departs every 20 minutes from Steiger 8 directly behind Centraal Station.)

At first glance, **Java Eiland** may look like a dense designer prison. But it's not hard to be charmed while on the island's bisecting walking street, which will have you crossing canals on funkily designed bridges and passing a startling variety of architecture. At Azartplein, the island changes its name to **KNSM Eiland**, named for the Royal Dutch Steam Company that was once located here (and whose history is documented at the **Open Havenmuseum**; *see p102*).

Jag north and follow Surinamekade with its houseboats on one side and the visible interiors of artist studios on the other. Pass the 'Black Widow' tower – you'll know it when you see it – then loop around the island's tip and head back along KNSM-Laan, hanging left into Barcelonaplein and then right when you pass through the abstract but strangely suggestive sculpted steel archway. You may want to stop for refreshment at one of the waterside bars and restaurants or invest in an art coffin at the alternative burial store, but definitely linger and check out the imposingly dark-brown residential Piraeus building of German architect Hans Kollhoff, and its eye-twisting inner courtyard.

The two peninsulas to the south are **Borneo-Sporenburg**, designed by the urban planners and landscape architects of West 8. The lots are all sized differently, in an attempt to inspire the many participating architects – a veritable who's who of the internationally acclaimed – to come up with creative solutions for low-rise living. Cross to Sporenburg via the Verbindingsdam to the building that has probably already caught your eye: the raised silver **Whale** residential complex, designed by architect Frits van Dongen, on Baron GA Tindalplein. For folksy contrast, a floating styrofoam park produced by onetime Provo Robert Jasper Grootveld has been placed in front of it on Panamakade.

From here, cross to **Borneo** via a very red and very swoopy bridge. Turn left up Stuurmankade, past yet an even swoopier walking bridge. At the end, enjoy the view, but imagine the view enjoyed by those living in the blue and green glassed cubes that jut out of the building. Then head back via **Scheepstimmermanstraat**, Amsterdam's

Located in the former passenger hall of the KNSM, the Open Havenmuseum puts on exhibitions that focus on the history of Amsterdam's haven, whether it be shipping technology or the role of prostitution. The building was designed by ship's architect Johan van Tienhoven, and recalls the atmosphere on board a ship of yore that once sailed the seven seas.

### Persmuseum (Press Museum)
*Zeeburgerkade 10 (692 8810/www.persmuseum.nl).* Bus 22, 28, 32, 59. **Open** 10am-5pm Tue-Fri; noon-5pm Sat, Sun. **Admission** €3.50. **No credit cards.** This newly revamped museum covers in its permanent exhibition the 400-year history of the press in Amsterdam and the Netherlands. Temporary shows

are usually focused more on graphics, photography and magazines, though one in late 2001 covered the fascinating history of the Provos.

### Werf 't Kromhout
*Hoogte Kadijk 147 (627 6777/ www.machinekamer.nl/museum/index.html).* Bus 22. **Open** 10am-3pm Tue. **Admission** €4.5; €2.75 under-15s. **No credit cards.** A nostalgic museum, full of old, silent ship engines and tools. The shipyard is proud of the fact that it's one of the few remaining original yards still in use, but its 18th-century heritage is no longer very apparent, nor is the yard especially active. Worth a peek, though, if you're in the area or are of a nautical bent.

**Sightseeing**

most eccentric architectural street. Each façade, whether with twisting steel rods or with wilfully haphazard plywood, seems more odd than the next.

From here, energetic types might want to take a 20-minute bike trek to IJburg, heading south via O van Eesterenlaan and Veelaan and then left down Zeeburgerdijk. This connects up with Zuiderzeeweg, which then turns into a bridge that ends at a set of traffic lights. Here, follow the bike path to the right and hang a left just before the Shell Station. Follow the undulations of the path until you reach the steel shack that houses the **Kaap Kot** restaurant (*see p128*). Here you will also see the floating **IJburg Information Centre** (680 6806/www.ijburg.nl; open 11am-5pm Thur-Sun), and a lookout tower from which you can watch the state of construction arising from the sand banks that are arising from the water. When it's completed in 2012, the seven islands will be home to 45,000 people in 18,000 residences, many of which will float. It will also be a showcase for Dutch landscape and residential architecture, with houses that combine thrilling aesthetics with all the latest environmentally friendly mod-cons.

On the way back to town explore the south end of the eastern half of **Zeeburg** island, one of the few 'free' places where squatters and artists are still allowed to make funky homes of trailers and boats and throw some of the city's more eccentric parties. The vibe that permeates Zeeburg once defined the whole area, before the yuppies came to town a few years ago. Since they arrived, the atmosphere's not as lively as it used to be, but the architecture, as you'll have seen on your trip, is a vast improvement.

You'll have a **Whale** of a time checking out the new buildings here.

For more information on architectual tours of these areas, call **Arcam** (*see p198*). In addition, a classic old ferry (423 1100) sails from Steiger 9 behind Centraal Station on Sundays and holidays between mid April and the end of October at noon, 2pm, 4pm and 6pm, stopping at Wilhelminadok, Java Eiland, KNSM Eiland, Sporenburg, Entrepotdokhaven and Nieuwendam. The same ferry also does a tour around IJburg that leaves from Steiger 9 on Saturdays between mid April and the end of October at 2pm and returns around three hours later. KNSM Eiland and Java Eiland are both served by assorted buses (28, 32, 59 and 61 among them), though a tram line linking the islands with Centraal Station should be completed by 2002.

# The Jordaan

Probably Amsterdam's most charming neighbourhood, the Jordaan presents a relaxing change from the city's crowded tourist areas.

The Jordaan is roughly sock-shaped, with borders at Brouwersgracht, Prinsengracht, Leidsegracht and Lijnbaansgracht. The area emerged when the city was extended in the 17th century and was designated for the working classes and the smellier of industries, while also providing a haven for victims of religious persecution, such as Jews and Huguenots. In keeping with the modest circumstances of the residents, houses are small and densely packed, at least when compared to the dwellings along the swankier canals to the east.

The area is a higgledy-piggledy mixture of old buildings, bland modern social housing and the occasional eyesore. Despite its working-class associations, properties here are now highly desirable, and though the residents are mainly proud, community-spirited Jordaansers, the *nouveaux riches* have long moved in to yuppify the 'hood: once one of the most densely populated neighbourhoods in Europe with 80,000 residents at the end of the 19th century, it now houses under a fifth of that number.

There are several theories as to the origin of the name 'Jordaan'. Some believe it to be a corruption of *joden*, Dutch for Jews, while others think it's from the French word for garden, *jardin*. The latter seems more plausible: the area was formerly a damp meadow, and many streets are named after flowers or plants. Other streets are also named after animals

whose pelts were used in tanning, one of the main – and certainly stinkiest – industries in the Jordaan in the 17th century. Looiersgracht ('Tanner's Canal') is surrounded by streets such as Hazenstraat ('Hare Street'), Elandsgracht ('Elk Canal') and Wolvenstraat ('Wolf Street').

## North of Rozengracht

**Map p305**

The Jordaan has no major sights; it's more of an area where you just stumble across things. It's also constantly surprising to wander through its streets and hardly see a soul. In general, the area north of the shopping-dense Rozengracht, the Jordaan's approximate mid-point, is more interesting and picturesque, with the area to the south more commercial.

Much of the area's charm comes from what is hidden from the uninformed eye. Chief among these treats are the *hofjes* or almshouses, many of which are pretty and deliciously peaceful. As long as you remain restrained, the residents don't mind folks admiring their inner garden courtyards. The best known are **Claes Claesz Hofje** (1e Egelantiersdwarsstraat 3), **Karthuizerhof** (Karthuizerstraat 21-31), **Sint Andrieshofje** (Egelantiersgracht 107-14), **Suyckerhofje** (Lindengracht 149-63), **Venetiae** (Elandsstraat 106-36, the only one on this list south of Rozengracht), and the oldest,

# On the pull

One occurrence that helped gel the Jordaan's fierce sense of community occurred in 1886. Before Lindengracht was filled in, it was the city's premier venue for the indigenous sport of eel-pulling. The trick to this most peculiar of games was to yank an eel off a rope from which it was dangling over the canal, while standing in a tipsy – an adjective that could also probably be applied to the participants – boat. The banning of the sport led to the day when a passing policeman elected to cut the rope from which the eel was hanging. This was, perhaps, not the wisest idea: the residents of the Jordaan had long felt generally hard done by, and the cop's interference was the final straw. The Eel Riot of 1886, as the incident came to be known, escalated so quickly that the army had to be called in. After a few days, it was announced that 26 Jordaansers had died and 136 were wounded. And the eel? Astonishingly, it survived the event, and its dry husk was auctioned in 1913 for the princely sum of ƒ1,75 (less than €1 in today's money).

**Linden Hofje** (Lindengracht 94-112). Hofje-hopping is a gamble, as entrances are sometimes locked in deference to the residents. But take a chance, and you'll be rewarded.

The area north of Rozengracht is easy to get a little lost in, albeit in a lovely, wasteful way. Little lanes and alleys link the already quiet main streets in a mazy haze, and it's no surprise that such a chilled atmosphere incorporates some of the city's best cafés: **'t Smalle** (Egelantiersgracht 12; see p145), for example, set on a small, picturesque canal, where Peter Hoppe (of Hoppe & Jenever, the world's first makers of gin) founded his distillery in 1780.

**Claes Claesz Hofje**. See p104.

Between scenic coffees or decadent daytime beers, check out one of the many specialist shops tucked away on these adorable sidestreets. Some of the best of the outdoor markets are found nearby: Monday's bargain-packed **Noordermarkt** and Saturday's foodie paradise **Boerenmarkt** (for both, see p166 **Amsterdam's markets**) are held around the Noorderkerk, the city's first Calvinist church, built in 1623. The remains of the former livestock market that occasionally sets up next to the Boerenmarkt can be a disturbing sight, with cages crammed with birds, ducks and even kittens. Adjacent to the Noordermarkt is the **Westermarkt**, while another general market fills Lindengracht on Saturdays (see p166 **Amsterdam's markets**).

More quirky shopping opportunities are found on **Haarlemmerdijk**, just north of Brouwersgracht. Though not officially part of the Jordaan, the street and its alleys share an ambience. Where it ends at Haarlemmerplein, you can see the imposing **Haarlemmerpoort**, built as a city gate for William II's visit in 1840. Behind it is the wanderable Westerpark, which connects to the **Westergasfabriek** (see p245), a large terrain that's evolved from gas factory to squat village to cutting-edge arts centre.

## Rozengracht & further south

### Map p305, p309 & p310

As its name suggests, **Rozengracht** was once a canal. It's now filled in, and scythes through the heart of the Jordaan in unappealing fashion. It's unlikely it was so traffic-clogged back when Rembrandt lived at No.184 from 1659 until his death a decade later; all that remains of his former home is a plaque on the first floor bearing the inscription 'Hier Stond Rembrandts Woning 1410-1669' ('Here Stood Rembrandt's Home 1410-1669'). While you're here, look up

Sightseeing

the gable of Rozengracht 204 to spy an iron stickman wall anchor. In addition to such folksy flourishes, the Jordaan's association with art is still alive, with many galleries and resident artists (*see p199*).

The area south of Rozengracht is notable for its shops, especially two browse-worthy antique markets; what's more, both **Rommelmarkt** and **Looier** (*see p166* **Amsterdam's markets**) have cafés. Nearby, Elandsgracht 71-7 used to be home to the maze-like Sjako's Fort. Sjako is often referred to as the 'Robin Hood of Amsterdam', glossing over the fact he usually neglected to give to the poor after stealing from the rich. Still,

he had style: robbing houses dressed in white, accompanied by black-clad henchmen. His 24-year-old head ended up spiked on a pole in 1718 where the Shell Building now stands, but a local band (Sjako!), an anarchist-oriented bookstore (**Fort van Sjako**; Jodenbreestraat 24; 625 8979), and a shrine in the window of the building that replaced his fort keep his name alive. Another tribute can be paid where Elandsgracht hits Prinsengracht: here you'll find statues of Tante Leni, Johnny Jordaan and Johnny Meijer, who personified the spirit of the Jordaan by crooning of lost love and spilt beer in local cafés (*see below* **Going for a song**).

# Going for a song

Imagine a neighbourhood where the hungry feed the hungrier, the broke buy beer for the broker, a dodgy money-making scheme is something to be shared, and the sense of family extends to all your neighbours. Sounds like *EastEnders*? Well, it's not far off.

It's not hard to pin the folk of the Jordaan as clog-wearing versions of the good old-fashioned Cockney community. Brought up as working class in cramped living spaces, developing a fierce sense of identity renowned cross-country, speaking in a unique and rich dialect... it's Albert Square all over. But while many echoes remain, this Jordaan disappeared when much of its original population moved to the garden towns out west. With gentrification having taken hold, songs have proven to be the strongest force in keeping this past alive and mythologised.

If not for its local repertoire of songs, the Jordaan may have disappeared instead of just cheerfully evolving. In the 1950s, these songs won the propaganda war being waged with the local government, who were mulling over razing and rebuilding this once socialist working-class bastion. Sing-a-long drinking tunes glorifying poverty, community bonds and the simple pleasures of issuing curses, making babies, drinking coffees and hanging out on the front step became nationwide hits. Soon, the whole country was singing along to tributes to the 'long stiff tower' of Westerkerk.

While there were a suspicious number of songs glorifying Westerkerk's all-knowing omnipotence, it was not down to any superannuated sense of *double entendre*: these were, after all, more innocent times. No: the attraction had more to do with the fact that the Jordaan had long been the most musical of neighbourhoods, where one could not walk a block without an open window providing an Italian opera soundtrack. Talents such as the duo of Louis Davids and Margie Morris had already spent the 1920s and '30s writing some timeless songs, and it only required individual talents such as Johnny Jordaan, with his throat of gold and heart pinned on sleeve, and Tante Leni, the personification of matronly love and wisdom, to make the Jordaan's thoroughly unique take on Caruso exportable beyond its borders.

Most of the watering holes where these songs were bellowed out are now sadly silent; no more does legendary accordionist Johnny Meijer squeeze out notes of love and loss in exchange for free beer in local taverns. Still, a few remain, and **Café Nol** (*pictured; see p144*) and **De Twee Zwaantjes** (Prinsengracht 114; 625 2729) both offer glimpses of a bygone era. In the Jordaan, the working classes have been replaced by the middle classes, and accordions have been ditched in favour of synths, but the themes – love, loss and spilt beer – remain hardy perennials.

# The Museum Quarter, Vondelpark & the South

Cash meets culture in the quarter where art, diamonds and greenery abound; less swanky, though, is the residential Zuid.

## The Museum Quarter

**Map p310**

A century ago, the area now known as the Museum Quarter was still officially outside the city limits and consisted of little more than vegetable patches. Towards the end of the century, though, the city expanded rapidly and the primarily upper-class city fathers decided to erect a swanky neighbourhood between the working-class areas to the west and south. Most of the beautiful mansions, with their deco gateways and stained-glass windows, were built around the turn of the century.

The heart of the area is **Museumplein**, the city's largest square, bordered by the **Rijksmuseum** (*see below*), the **Stedelijk Museum of Modern Art**, the **Van Gogh Museum** (for all, *see p108*) and the **Concertgebouw** (*see p219*). The Museumplein is not really an authentic Amsterdam square, its recent revamping accenting its more 'park' – or, rather, cow field – aspects. Developed in 1872, it served as a location for the World Exhibition of 1883, and was then rented out to the Amsterdam ice-skating club between 1900 and 1936. During the Depression, the field was put to use as a sports ground, and during World War II the Germans built four bunkers and a concrete shelter on it. Further annoyance followed with the laying of the country's 'shortest motorway', Museumstraat, in 1953, which cut the *plein* in two and remained until its recent resurrection with grass, wading pool, skate ramp, café and wacky new addition to the Van Gogh Museum.

As you'd expect given its high-falutin' cultural surroundings, property here doesn't come cheap, and the affluence of the residents is reflected in both architecture and consumerism. **Van Baerlestraat** and, especially, **PC Hooftstraat** are as close as Amsterdam gets to Rodeo Drive, their clothing boutiques offering shopping solace to ladies who would otherwise be lunching. It's little surprise that this neck of the woods is also where you'll find the majority of Amsterdam's diamond retailers.

Nearby **Roemer Visscherstraat**, which leads to Vondelpark, is notable not for its labels but for its buildings. The houses from Nos.20 to 30 each represent a different country and are built in the appropriate 'national' style: Russia comes with a miniature dome, Italy has been painted pastel pink, and Spain's candy stripes have made it one of the street's favourites.

### Rijksmuseum

*Stadhouderskade 42 (674 7047/*
*www.rijksmuseum.nl). Tram 2, 5, 6, 7, 10, 20.*
**Open** 10am-5pm daily. **Admission** €8; free MJK, under-19s. **Credit** AmEx, MC, V. **Map** p310 D5.
Designed by PJH Cuypers and opened in 1885, the Rijksmuseum holds the largest collection of art and artefacts in the Netherlands. The collection was started when William V started acquiring pieces just

There's no escape from cyclists in Amsterdam, not even on **Museumplein**.

**PC Hooftstraat** or Rodeo Drive? *See p107.*

for the hell of it, and has been growing ever since: it includes Dutch paintings from the 15th century until 1900, as well as decorative and Asian art. But if you only have a limited amount of time, head for the Dutch Masters section on the top floor. Here's where you'll find Rembrandt's *Night Watch* (room 229), the jewel of the collection, and Vermeer's *The Kitchen Maid* and *Woman Reading a Letter* (room 218), each capturing a moment in the life of a woman from a different background. There are also selections by the likes of Frans Hals (room 209), Jacob de Wit (room 220) and Ferdinand Bol (room 231).

Room after room at the Rijks holds a wealth of decorative arts, including 17th-century furniture and intricate silver and porcelain (rooms 162-65). A room devoted to 17th- and early 18th-century dolls' houses (room 164) and craftsmen-made furniture gives a glimpse of how canal-house interiors looked. Over near the east entrance, the Dutch history collection spans the 15th to mid 20th centuries (rooms 102-12). The South Wing, meanwhile, provides a home for 18th- and 19th-century paintings; art objects from Asia, including statues, lacquer work, paintings, ceramics, jewellery, weaponry and bronze; and the Textile and Costume collection.

Since the arrival of the ARIA computer system, it's much easier to find your way around this enormous place. ARIA offers information on 1,250 items from the collection in sound, film, text and image, and lets you design your own customised museum route around the pieces you want to see. Located in a room behind the *Night Watch*, it's free unless you want to make a printout, and is also available online.

In autumn 2003, much of the Rijksmuseum is scheduled to close for urgent and expensive (€200 million) restoration and renovation works; things are unlikely to get back to normal until 2006 or thereabouts. While this work is ongoing, the Philips Wing will display over 200 of the museum's most famous works (*The Night Watch* et al); it's also possible – though by no means confirmed as of early 2002 – that the museum will mount some joint exhibitions with the Stedelijk. However, it's advisable to check the museum's excellent website for more details on all these matters nearer the time of your visit.

## Stedelijk Museum of Modern Art

*Paulus Potterstraat 13 (573 2911/www.stedelijk.nl).*
*Tram 2, 3, 5, 12, 16, 20.* **Open** 11am-5pm daily.
**Admission** €5; €2.50 7-16s; free MJK, under-7s.
**Credit** (shop only) AmEx, MC, V. **Map** p310 D6.
The Stedelijk offers the best collection of modern art in Amsterdam. Displays change regularly: some exhibitions are drawn from the collection, while others are made up from works loaned to the museum, but each tends to focus on a particular trend or the work of a specific artist. After occupying various locations around the city, the Stedelijk finally settled in its present neo-Renaissance abode, designed by AW Weissman, in 1895. In time, the building became too small for the ambitions of its directors and an ugly new wing was tacked on in 1954.

However, the museum is now expanding further. New plans call for the building of two new wings, both designed by Portuguese architect Alvaro Siza; extensive renovations of the current building; and the construction of a new building elsewhere in the city to be used for research. The total cost will be around €90 million; work is scheduled to start at the end of 2002 and last for two and a half years. During this period, the museum will be closed, but it's hoped that there'll be a permanent Stedelijk display elsewhere in the city. Be sure to call before setting out, or check the website for more information.

When it's open, though, the museum is a real winner. Pre-war highlights include works by Cézanne, Picasso, Matisse and Chagall, plus a prized collection of paintings and drawings by Malevich. Post-1945 artists represented include De Kooning, Newman, Ryman, Judd, Stella, Lichtenstein, Warhol, Nauman, Middleton, Long, Dibbets, Kiefer, Polke, Merz and Kounellis. The Nieuwe Vleugel (New Wing) is used as a temporary space for exhibitions often focusing on design and applied art. CoBrA artist Karel Appel decorated the Appelbar and restaurant; the latter is still in use, and its picture windows make it an ace place to sit on a sunny day.

## Van Gogh Museum

*Paulus Potterstraat 7 (570 5200/*
*www.vangoghmuseum.nl). Tram 2, 3, 5, 12, 16, 20.*
**Open** 10am-6pm daily. **Admission** €7; €2.25 13-17s; free MJK, under-13s. *Temporary exhibitions* prices vary. **Credit** MC, V. **Map** p310 D6.
Aside from the bright colours of his palette, Vincent van Gogh is also known for his productivity, and both are clearly reflected in the 200 paintings and 500 drawings that form part of the permanent exhibition here. Aside from this large collection, there are also examples of his Japanese prints, as well as works by the likes of Toulouse-Lautrec that add perspective to Van Gogh's own efforts. Changing exhibitions, created from the museum's archives and private collections, also feature here; in February 2002, for example, a terrific show on the relationship between Gauguin and Van Gogh opened. After a major and impressive refurbishment, the enlarged Rietveld building remains the base for the permanent collec-

tion, while Japanese architect Kisho Kurokawa's new wing has been devoted to temporary exhibitions. Do yourself a favour and get there early in the morning, though: the queues in the afternoon can get frustratingly long, and the gallery unbearably busy.

## Vondelpark

### Map p310

Amsterdam's largest green space is named after the city's most famous poet, Joost van den Vondel (1587-1679), whose controversial play *Lucifer* caused a backlash from the religious powers of the time against those who engaged in what was quaintly termed 'notorious living'. The concerted campaign from the moral majority helped bring about the downfalls of both Rembrandt and Vondel, who forlornly ended his days as a pawnshop doorman.

Vondelpark is the most central of the city's major parks, its construction inspired after the development of Plantage, which had formerly provided the green background used by the rich for their leisurely walks. It was designed in the 'English style' by Zocher, with the emphasis on natural landscaping; the original ten acres opened in 1865. There are several ponds and lakes in the park – no boating, though – plus a number of children's play areas and cafés; the most pleasant are **Het Blauwe Theehuis** (Round Blue Teahouse; *see p146*) and **Café Vertigo**, at the **Nederlands Filmmuseum** (*see p194*). The NFM is less a museum and more a cinema with a café attached and a library

nearby, though this didn't stop local movie fans rejoicing when a recent decision to move it to Rotterdam was overturned.

Vondelpark gets fantastically busy on sunny days and Sundays, when bongos abound, dope is toked and football games take up any space that happens to be left over. The dicky-tickered can avoid a seizure by keeping one eye out for Rollerbladers, who meet here weekly for the Friday Night Skate. Films, plays and concerts are also held here, including a free festival of open-air theatre in summer (*see p246*).

## Further south

The Museum Quarter is the northernmost tip of Amsterdam's **Oud Zuid** (Old South), which stretches down beyond Vondelpark. This area is defined by residential housing, with the more bohemian streets around the park contrasting nicely with their smarter equivalents by the museums and comparing favourably with the uglier modern buildings nearby.

### Nieuw Zuid

Stretching out in a ring beneath Vondelpark is a fairly indeterminate region known as **Nieuw Zuid** (New South), bordered to the north by Vondelpark, to the east by the Amstel and to the west by **Olympisch Stadion** (www.olympisch-stadion.net; recently renovated and notable for visitors primarily for its restaurant **Vakzuid**, for which *see p133*).

Kick back in **Vondelpark**.

Sightseeing

The New South was planned by Berlage and put into action by a variety of Amsterdam School architects, who designed both private and public housing for the area. It's the former that's given the New South what character it has, most notably around the likes of Apollolaan (where you'll find the Hilton from which legendary rocker Herman Brood tossed himself in 2001; *see p215* **Brood swings**) and Beethovenstraat (worth visiting simply for the **Oldenburg** bakery at No.17; *see p167*).

The few visitors this area draws are here on business, especially around the World Trade Centre. The controversial Noord–Zuidlijn is set to link this district with the centre of town and Amsterdam Noord. East of here is another staple of Amsterdam business life: the ugly **RAI Exhibition and Congress Centre**, which holds numerous trade fairs, conventions and public exhibitions throughout the year.

However, in between the RAI and the WTC lies one of Amsterdam's loveliest parks. Extended and renovated in 1994, **Beatrixpark** is a wonderfully peaceful place, handy if you

want to avoid the crowds in town on a summer's day. The Victorian walled garden is worth a visit, as is the pond, complete with geese, black swans and herons. Amenities include a wading pool and play area for kids; there are concerts in July and August.

Still further south, **Amstelpark** was created for a garden festival in 1972, and now offers recreation and respite to locals in the suburb of Buitenveldert, near the RAI. A formal rose garden and rhododendron walk are among the seasonal floral spectacles, and there are also a labyrinth, pony rides and a children's farm, plus tours on a miniature train. The Rosarium Restaurant serves expensive meals, though its outdoor café is less pricey.

## Amstelveen

Of all Amsterdam's southern suburbs, Amstelveen is the most welcoming to the casual visitor. Though the **CoBrA Museum** (*see p112*) helps, the main attraction here is the **Amsterdamse Bos**, a mammoth wood that's

# Baby, let's play house

A decade or more ago, all the cool guidebooks to Amsterdam mentioned the squats. For the leftists of the 1980s, they were a clever solution: an act of protest against the housing shortage and property speculation that also netted free, central bases for the movement. Many a visitor who was hard up and down with the cause found him- or herself bedded down in one of Amsterdam's squatted buildings.

Nowadays, though, there's precious little underground left. The squats have been swept aside in a wave of EU-minded, pro-business values. Loopholes that made it easy to occupy and stay in a building closed; property speculators got wise, installed guards and tore floors out. As jobs boomed and unemployment benefits were cut to please other EU nations, the masses returned to work and had less time and energy to squat. Squatting is no longer a housing solution but a radical and – in most cases – ultimately futile act.

The most mourned squat may be the Graansilo, a vast industrial-age fortress that housed everything from a pirate radio station to a bakery before it fell to the mighty real estate market in 1998. In a now-familiar scenario, its residents were evicted, its vast spaces were renovated and the harbour views

that gave its restaurant so much atmosphere were handed over to wealthy flat-owners. Vrieshuis Amerika, another big waterfront squat famous for its parties and indoor skateboard park, followed in 1999. And the Kalenderpanden, overlooking a canal behind the zoo, was evicted in 2000 despite protests that garnered broad support.

Some really entrenched squatters have won a few compromises. The artists who have occupied the nearby village of Ruigoord since the 1970s saw a long land dispute with the port authority end in a partial victory: they can keep their studio spaces, but they can't live there. And in an 11th-hour reprieve, venerable squatters' bar **Vrankrijk** (Spuistraat 216; www.vrankrijk.org) got the city to compromise on a sudden licensing crackdown: cops still won't be allowed inside, but safety rules will be observed.

Even in the current climate, a few newer squats are thriving. The **Academie** (*pictured*; Overtoom 301; 779 4912), an old film school building near Vondelpark, shows quality movies on its big screen while also serving drinks and dinner (the latter on Tuesday, Friday and Sunday only). The **ADM**, a former dry-dock site in the western harbour (Hornweg 6; 411 0081), has a restaurant (open Wednesday, Friday and Sunday) and often treasured by locals yet neglected by visitors (which, you suspect, probably makes the locals treasure it even more).

The 2,000-acre site sprawls out beautifully, and comes with a great many attractions in case the tranquility isn't worthwhile enough. The man-made Bosbaan is used for boating and swimming, with canoe and pedalo rental available. Other attractions include play areas, a horticultural museum, jogging routes, a buffalo and bison reserve, a bike-hire centre (open March to October), a watersports centre, stables and a picnic area. The non-subsidised goat farm sells cheese, milk and ice-cream: you can even feed the goats while you're there. Happily, the wood feels a lot further away from **Schiphol Airport** than it actually is: the airport is less than a mile from the wood's western edge.

## Ajax Museum

*ArenA Boulevard 3 (311 1469/www.ajax.nl).* *Metro Bijlmer.* **Open** *Apr-Sept* 10am-6pm daily. *Oct-Mar* 10am-5pm daily. Opening hours on match days vary. **Admission** €8; €7 under-12s. **Credit** MC, V.

A great outing for footie fans, the Ajax Museum – located way out south-east in the Bijlmer; *see p112* **Plane and sinful** – takes you on a tour through the long and rich history of this legendary club. The exhibitions trace the development of the team from their humble beginnings to the big business enterprise of today. Unique photographs and memorabilia taken from the club's and players' collections are on display, as are all the cups, in the trophy cabinet. An eight-minute film offers footage of the all-time great goals scored in the last 25 years. Given the scarcity of tickets – and the fact that they're an absolute bugger to get hold of if you don't have a Personal Club Card – it'll likely be the closest you'll get to seeing the team in action.

## Aviodome

*Schiphol Centre (406 8000/www.aviodome.nl).* *NS rail Schiphol Airport.* **Open** *Apr-Sept* 10am-5pm daily. *Oct-Mar* 10am-5pm Tue-Fri; noon-5pm Sat, Sun. **Admission** €6.80; €5.70 students, 4-12s, over-65s; free under-4s. **No credit cards.**
Aeroplane enthusiasts will loop the loop over the fascinating displays in this exhibition: over 30 historic aircraft are neatly parked or suspended at the

holds festivals. The **CIA Infocafé** (Vijzelstraat 5; 683 1021; open 1-7pm Sat, Sun) continues the tradition of dispensing activist information and cheap beer, and the squatted Internet café **ASCII** (Jodenbreestraat 24; open 2-7pm daily), located underneath anarchist bookstore **Fort van Sjako**, offers free access for activists, although this pair were fighting a massive rent hike in late 2001 and may be forced to move.

In a show of traditional Dutch compromise, or maybe appeasement, the city has decided to create 'cultural breeding grounds'; basically, subsidised studio spaces for young artists. But critics argue that these won't have the energy of the squats, which were spontaneously generated, user-built hybrid spaces for all manner of experimentation. And they won't have the magic that squats derived from their unexpected locations, which ranged from old factories to mansions.

However, the squat scene is alive and kicking in one part of Amsterdam: its webspace. There's still free real estate online, and anyone interested in finding out about the latest developments in the squat scene should log on to http://squat.net or www.underwateramsterdam.com.

# Plane and sinful

The suburb of **Bijlmermeer**, to the south-east of Amsterdam, is known for one event above all others, and it's not a pretty one. In 1992, a 747 crashed into one of the hideous high-rises in this long-downtrodden corner of the city. The official death toll was pinned at 43, although it's believed that more lives were lost: many of the block's residents were illegal immigrants, and not registered with the authorities.

Once the shock of the crash had worn off, though, so did the public's interest in the area. The Bijlmermeer had long been decorated with an unshakeable reputation as one of Amsterdam's seamiest suburbs, riddled with crime, drugs and general deprivation, and not an area to which locals readily journeyed.

However, change is afoot. In recent years, the Bijlmermeer has been the subject of massive investment from big business and the local council. For years, the only thing of note anywhere near here was Ajax's stadium; recently, though, businesses have moved in, attracted by the cheaper-than-average rents and encouraged by the local council.

Even more strangely, the Bijlmer is currently being converted into a clean 'n' corporate entertainment district, complete with a cineplex (**Pathé Arena**; *see p192*), a music venue (**Heineken Music Hall**; *p213*) and a mall. The old, seedy character of the neighbourhood hasn't evaporated entirely, but it's well on its way to vanishing after one of the most unlikely salvage projects in the city's history.

Aviodome museum. The exhibition has everything from the first motorised plane – the 1903 Wright Flyer – and the Spider, designed by Dutch pioneer Anthony Fokker, to much more recent aeronautical developments and even space travel. There are also film screenings and collections of models, photographs and aeroplane parts. The Aviodome organises markets and fairs, as well as some occasional theme weekends.

## Bosmuseum

*Koenenkade 56, Amsterdamse Bos (676 2152).*
*Bus 170, 171, 172.* **Open** 10am-5pm daily.
**Admission** free. **No credit cards**.
The Bosmuseum recounts the history and use of the Amsterdamse Bos. Its mock woodland grotto, which turns from day to night at the flick of a switch, is wonderful for kids (*see p185*).

## CoBrA Museum of Modern Art

*Sandbergplein 1 (547 5050/www.cobra-museum.nl).*
*Tram 5/Metro 51.* **Open** 11am-5pm Tue-Sun.
**Admission** €5; €3.50 over-65s; €2.50 5-16s;
free MJK, under-5s. **Credit** (shop only) MC, V.
The CoBrA group attempted to radically reinvent the language of paint in 1948, preaching an ethos of participation and believing everyone should make art, regardless of ability or education. Artists such as Dane Asger Jorn and Dutchmen Karel Appel and Corneille were once regarded as little more than eccentric troublemakers. However, they've now been absorbed into the canon; this museum provides a sympathetic environment in which to trace the development of one of the most influential Dutch art movements of the 20th century.

## Electrische Museumtramlijn Amsterdam (Electric Tram Museum)

*Haarlemmermeerstation, Amstelveenseweg 264 (673*
*7538/www.trammuseum.demon.nl).* *Tram 6, 16.*
**Open** *Easter-Oct* 11am-5pm Sun, public holidays.
*July-Aug* also Wed afternoons; phone for times.
**Admission** €3 round trip; €1.50 children.
**No credit cards**.
Both the pride and *raison d'être* of the Electric Tram Museum, housed in a beautiful 1915 railway station, is its rolling stock. The main 'exhibitions' are the outings, at which colourful antique streetcars, gathered from several cities, make their way along their own track through the nearby and surprisingly rural Amsterdamse Bos. As of 2000, the museum's 25th anniversary year, the volunteer staff have mounted exhibitions in the Haarlemmermeerstation building, which also houses an atmospheric bar-restaurant.

## Hortus Botanicus (Vrije Universiteit)

*Van der Boechorststraat 8, Zuid (444 9390/*
*www.hortus-vu.nl).* *Tram 5/bus 69, 169, 170, 171,*
*172.* **Open** 8am-4.30pm Mon-Fri. **Admission** free.
**No credit cards**.
This small but perfectly formed garden is, rather curiously, wedged between the high buildings of a university and a hospital. Built in 1967, it doesn't have the charm of its counterpart in the city centre (*see p98*), but it's a pleasant enough place for a stroll if you're in the neighbourhood. The fern collection is one of the largest in the world, while the Dutch garden next door shows the great variety of flora found in this country.

## Museum Vrolik

*Entrance on south side of AMC medical faculty,*
*Meibergdreef 15 (566 9111).* *Bus 59, 60, 61, 120,*
*126/Metro Holendrecht.* **Open** 2-5pm Mon-Fri; also*
by appointment. **Admission** free. **No credit cards**.
This anatomical embryological laboratory way out in the south-east of the city contains 18th- and 19th-century specimens of human embryos, human anatomy and congenital malformations collected by Professor Gerardus Vrolik and his son. Needless to say, not recommended for those with weak stomachs.

Sightseeing

# The Pijp

Suck on this: artists, hookers, cheap ethnic eats, a temple to the local adult beverage and the best market in town.

**Map p311**

Not to be confused with the suggestive slang in Dutch for the act of 'piping' – 'giving a blow job' – doing the Pijp can still be a colourful experience: the district definitely has a spunky verve about it. Although it's hardly a treasure trove of history and traditional sights, the Pijp's time is the present, with over 150 different nationalities keeping its global village vibe alive and the recent economic upturn seeing the opening of more upmarket and trendy eateries and bars than the area's used to hosting.

The Pijp is the best known of the working-class quarters built in the late 19th century, when a population boom burst the city's seams. Harsh economics saw the building of long, narrow streets, which probably inspired the change in name from the official double yawn-inducing 'Area YY' to its more appropriate nickname, 'the Pipe'. Because rents were too high for many tenants, they were forced to let rooms out to students, who then went on to give the area its bohemian character.

That said, the numerous Dutch writers who lived here helped add to it. Among the locals were such luminaries as Heijermans, De Haan and Bordewijk, who famously described World War I-era Amsterdam as a 'ramshackle bordello, a wooden shoe made of stone'. Many painters had studios here, too – such as Piet Mondriaan, who lived for a time in the attic of Ruysdaelkade 75 – and the area was packed with brothels and drinking dens. In the basement of Quellijnstraat 64, the Dutch cabaret style, distinguished by its witty songs with cutting social commentary for lyrics, was formulated by Eduard Jacobs and continues to live on through the likes of Freek de Jonge and Hans Teeuwen.

At the turn of the century, the Pijp was a radical socialist area. Although the area has lost much of its bite since those halcyon days, the students remain, even though many families with children have fled to suburbia. The number of cheap one- and two-bedroom places, combined with the reasonably central location, makes the area very attractive to students, young single people and couples. The area also has the densest gay population in Amsterdam.

During the last 40 years, many immigrants have found their way into the Pijp to set up shop and inspire the general economic upswing of the area. The Pijp now houses a mix of nationalities, providing locals with plenty of Islamic butchers, Surinamese, Spanish, Indian and Turkish delicatessens, and restaurants offering authentic Syrian, Moroccan, Thai, Pakistani, Chinese and Indian cuisine. Thanks to all these low-priced exotic eats, the Pijp is the best place in town for quality snacking treats, the ingredients for which are mostly bought fresh from the largest daily market in the Netherlands.

**Albert Cuypmarkt** is the hub around which the Pijp turns, attracting thousands of customers every day. It's the core of the Pijp street life and spills merrily into the adjoining roads: the junctions of Sweelinckstraat, Ferdinand Bolstraat and 1e Van der Helststraat, north into the lively Gerard Douplein, and south towards Sarphatipark. The chaos will undoubtedly be enhanced over the next few years by the construction of the Metro's controversial Noord–Zuidlijn that will run pretty much underneath Ferdinand Bolstraat.

Staying on Albert Cuypstraat, cross Ferdinand Bolstraat and you'll find a cluster of fine cheap Chinese-Surinamese-Indonesian restaurants. After passing the coach-party attraction of the **Van Moppes & Zoon Diamond Factory** (*see p162* **A girl's best friend**), diamond turns to ruby around the corner along Ruysdaelkade, on the Pijp's very own mini red light district. Watch horned-out motorists caught in their own traffic gridlock while you lounge casually around an otherwise restful canal.

**Albert Cuypmarkt** is on a roll.

Close by, at Ruysdaelkade 149, is the **Jan Steen Café**. Steen (1625-79) was a barkeeper and painter of rowdy bar scenes, and this locals' hangout represents him well: the beer's cheap and the crowd is loud. And why view his work in the Rijksmuseum when you can see it in action? The Pijp, of course, didn't even exist in Steen's day, but artists have since found it much to their liking. It's estimated that over 250 artists currently live in the area, and the current crop is gaining more status in a district where most streets are named after their illustrious forebears' Steen, Ferdinand Bol, Gerard Dou and Jacob van Campen are just a few of the artists honoured in this way.

Head back away from the water (and the red lights) a few blocks along 1e Jan Steenstraat, passing splendid bric-a-brac shop Nic Nic as you go, and you'll soon run across the Pijp's little green oasis: the grass-, pond- and duck-dappled **Sarphatipark**, designed and built as a mini Bois de Boulogne by the inspired and slightly mad genius Samuel Sarphati (1813-66). Aside from building the Amstel InterContinental hotel and the Paleis voor Volksvlijt, Sarphati showed philanthropic tendencies as a baker of inexpensive bread for the masses, and as initiator of the city's garbage collection. The centrepiece fountain comes complete with a statue of Sammy himself.

Edging along and beyond the south edge of Sarphatipark, Ceintuurbaan offers little of note for the visitor, with the exception of the buildings at Nos.251-5. Why? Well, there aren't many other houses in the city that incorporate giant ball-playing green gnomes with red hats

in their wooden façades. The unique exterior of the **Gnome House** was inspired by the owner's name: Van Ballegooien translates literally (and somewhat clumsily) as 'Of the ball-throwing'. Around the corner from here, on the Amstel river, is the city's archive, **Gemeentearchief Amsterdam** (Amsteldijk 67, 572 0202), at which you can peruse the library or one of its excellent exhibitions.

After a stroll through the park, wander north up 1e Van der Helststraat towards Gerard Douplein. This little square, with its cafés, coffeeshops, chip shops and authentic Italian ice-cream parlour, turns into one big terrace during the summer, and is hugely popular with the locals. Bargain second-hand Euro knick-knacks can be bought at the nearby Stichting Dodo (No.21; trivia hounds should know that the Dutch – or rather their egg-eating animals – were responsible for this bird's extinction after colonising the island of Mauritius in 1598), while the cheapest raw herring in town can be gotten for the gullet at Volendammer Vis Handel at No.60. On the corner of 1e Van der Helststraat and Govert Flinckstraat is one of the area's best bakeries, **Runneboom** (*see p167*); a few streets away, overlooking Singelgracht from the decidedly unappealing Stadhouderskade, is the old **Heineken Brewery** (*see below*), now a self-aggrandising interactive museum of sorts.

## Heineken Experience

*Stadhouderskade 78 (523 9666/ www.heinekenexperience.com). Tram 6, 7, 10, 16, 20, 24, 25.* **Open** 10am-6pm (last entry 5pm) Tue-Sun. **Admission** €5. **Credit** MC, V. **Map** p311 E5.

Once upon a time, this vast building was the main Heineken Brewery. We know this from the blurb by the entrance that hyperbolically states that the building is 'where Heineken was actually brewed'. In 1988, Heineken stopped brewing here, but kept the building open for endearingly unflashy tours: for a charitable donation of ƒ2 (less than €1 in today's money), you got an hour-long guided walk through the site, then as much Heineken as you could neck down. It's safe to say that more punters were there for the free beer than the brewing education.

Unfortunately, Heineken have cottoned on to this, and recently renovated the huge building so tourists can enjoy the Heineken Experience. And while it's a lot flashier, it's a little less illuminating and a lot less fun. There's an interesting story to be told here, but this botched affair fails to narrate it. Plus points: the quasi-virtual reality ride through a brewery from the perspective of a Heineken bottle is easily the most ludicrous exhibit in Amsterdam, and you still get three free beers plus a surprise free gift (and not a bad one at that) at the end. But all in all, you're probably better off just going to a bar.

Gnomes play ball on **Ceintuurbaan** façades.

# Eat, Drink, Smoke, Shop

# Restaurants

World-class, globally inspired eateries and New Dutch Cuisine:
Amsterdam certainly has a lot to chew on.

It's a tragic story, really. One of the few plus points of Napoleonic rule at the dawn of the 19th century was that the wealthier population became seduced by innovations such as herbs and spices, and the concomitant awareness that over-boiling and over-frying are hardly tantalising to tastebuds. But a century later, some well-meaning bourgeoisie developed simplified recipes for the working classes that proved popular only with the next generation of bourgeoisie. The subtleties of southern cuisine were eradicated from the home and passed down via only a few restaurants.

While a French influence is felt in the town's top-end restaurants, the culinary void elsewhere allowed the spicy food of Indonesia to colonise the Dutch palate after World War II, when this former colony was granted independence and the country grew full of Indonesian immigrants. Today, take your pick from the various cheap Surinam-Chinese-Indonesian snackbars or visit the purveyors of the 'rice-table', where every known fish, meat and vegetable is reworked into a gut-filling micro-extravaganza. Along with fondue – a 'national' dish stolen from the Swiss because its shared pot appealed to the Dutch sense of the democratic – Indo is certainly the food of choice for any celebratory meals. The pheasants and hogs that decorated Golden Age paintings have long been replaced with sticks of satay and mountains of rice.

Waves of other immigrants helped create a vortex of culinary diversity. Not only is there a vast choice of traditional dishes from Asia, the Middle East and the Mediterranean, but there's also a whole new generation of chefs who take inspiration from the world and ingredients from the freshest of local – and often organic – products. The once mocking term 'New Dutch Cuisine' now actually means something. And vegetarians should be more than satisfied with the decent range of food on offer (*see p127* **Living on the veg**).

If you prefer to stroll and sniff out your own sustenance, here are a few tips… Head directly to the Pijp if you crave econo-ethnic; cruise Utrechtsestraat, Nieuwmarkt, the 'Nine Streets' area (the thoroughfares linking Prinsengracht, Keizersgracht and Herengracht between Leidsegracht and Raadhuisstraat) and Reguliersdwarsstraat if you want something

posher; and only surrender to Leidseplein if you don't mind being overcharged for a leathery steak or a porridge-like pasta.

In addition to the restaurants listed below, there are many cafés and bars serving decent – even inspired – food at reasonable prices; for these, *see p136*. For gay-friendly and gay-owned restaurants and cafés, *see p208*.

### LEISURELY DINING

Dining in Amsterdam is a laid-back affair, though the Dutch do tend to eat early: many kitchens close by 10pm. All bills should by law include 17.5 per cent tax and a 15 per cent service charge, though it's customary to leave some small change as well if the service merits it. If you have any special requirements, such as high chairs or disabled access, it's always best to phone the restaurant before setting out. For more places to take the kids, *see p186*.

Given the introduction of the euro in 2002 and the financial flux that will bring, the prices listed here should only be used as a guideline. Head to www.dinnersite.nl/amsterdam or www.diningcity.nl for online menus and, in some cases, reservations for a variety of restaurants. Local foodies weigh in at www.specialbite.nl to discuss the city's hotspots, and www.underwateramsterdam.com nobly covers the world of squat dining.

## The Old Centre: Old Side

### Cafés & snack stops

#### 1e Klas
*Centraal Station, Line 2B (625 0131). Tram 1, 2, 4, 5, 9, 13, 16, 17, 20, 24, 25.* **Open** 8.30am-11pm daily. **Main courses** €15-€22. **Credit** AmEx, DC, MC, V. **Map** p306 D1.
This former brasserie for first-class commuters is now open to anyone who wants to kill some time in style – with a full meal or with snackier fare – while waiting for a train. The art nouveau interior will whisk you back to the turn of the 19th century.

#### Tisfris
*Sint Antoniesbreestraat 142 (622 0472). Tram 9, 14, 20/Metro Nieuwmarkt.* **Open** *Summer* 9am-8pm Mon-Sat; 10am-8pm Sun. *Winter* 9am-7pm Mon-Sat; 10am-7pm Sun. **Main courses** €4-€8. **No credit cards. Map** p307 E3.

Catch a supreme fish dish at **Nam Kee**.

A trendy but undaunting split-level café that's popular with a young and arty clientele. It's *the* place for a healthy breakfast or lunch (quiches, salads, soups) in the area. Bonus: the music is bang up-to-date.

## Chinese & Japanese

### Morita-Ya
*Zeedijk 18 (638 0756). Tram 1, 2, 5, 13, 17, 20.* **Open** 6-9.30pm Mon, Tue, Thur-Sun. **Main courses** €16-€21. **Credit** AmEx, MC, V. **Map** p306 D2.
A cheap and cheerful Japanese place near Centraal Station. The opening hours are a little erratic, but if you do manage to get there when it's serving, you'll enjoy some fantastic sushi and sashimi.

### Nam Kee
*Zeedijk 111-13 (624 3470/www.namkee.nl). Bus 51, 53, 54.* **Open** 11.30am-midnight daily. **Main courses** €6-€15. **No credit cards. Map** p306 D2.
A small Chinese joint with regulars who adore the cheap and terrific food: the oysters in black bean sauce have achieved classic status. If it's busy, try the **New King** (Zeedijk 115-17; 625 2180) next door.

### Oriental City
*Oudezijds Voorburgwal 177-9 (626 8352). Tram 4, 9, 14, 16, 20, 24, 25.* **Open** 11.30am-10.30pm daily. **Main courses** €8-€23. **Credit** AmEx, DC, MC, V. **Map** p306 D2.
The views overlook Damstraat, the Royal Palace and the canals. And that's not even the best bit: some of Amsterdam's most authentic dim sum can be had at Oriental City. Popular with Chinese locals.

## Dutch & Belgian

### De Brakke Grond
*Nes 43 (626 0044). Tram 4, 9, 14, 16, 20, 24, 25.* **Open** *May-Sept* noon-1am daily. *Oct-Apr* noon-1am Tue-Sun. **Main courses** €10-€18. **Credit** AmEx, DC, MC, V. **Map** p306 D3.
Though **Lieve** (Herengracht 88; 624 9635) offers a more sophisticated rendering of Belgian cuisine, De Brakke Grond shows somewhat more sensitivity to those pre-equipped with an abiding love for Belgian beers by recommending the best choice of beverage to accompany each dish.

### Café Bern
*Nieuwmarkt 9 (622 0034). Tram 4, 9, 14, 16, 20, 24, 25/Metro Nieuwmarkt.* **Open** 4pm-1am daily. *Kitchen* 6-11pm daily. **Main courses** €9-€13. **No credit cards. Map** p306 D2.
Despite its Swiss origins, the Dutch long ago appropriated the cheese fondue as their own national dish. This is a suitably cosy brown bar for some communal culinary conviviality: the menu is easily affordable and the bar stocked with a variety of grease-cutting agents.

## French & Mediterranean

### Blauw aan de Wal
*Oudezijds Achterburgwal 99 (330 2257). Tram 9, 16, 24.* **Open** 6-11.30pm Mon-Sat. **Main courses** €20-€25. **Credit** AmEx, DC, MC, V. **Map** p306 D2.
Down an alley and in the carnal heart of the Red Light District lies this oasis of reverence to the finer things in life. Tempting dishes (French in origin), an inspired wine list: this is a new culinary landmark.

# Restaurants

### Inez IPSC
A perfect fusion of food, decor and views. *See p125.*

### Keuken van 1870
Farmers' fare served with a grandmother's flair. *See p120.*

### Nam Kee
Cheap Chinese, divine oysters, central location. *See p117.*

### Riaz
The Surinamese with the best rice and beans. *See p133.*

### Vossius
Robert Kranenborg's joint is a wallet-weakener, but well worth it. *See p132.*

**Eat, Drink, Smoke, Shop**

### Café Roux
*The Grand, Oudezijds Voorburgwal 197 (555
3560/www.thegrand.nl). Tram 4, 9, 14, 16, 20,
24, 25.* **Open** noon-3pm, 6.30-10.30pm daily.
**Main courses** €15-€25. **Credit** AmEx, DC, MC, V.
**Map** p306 D3.
The food here is identical to that of the Grand Hotel
itself, and is overseen by Albert Roux. Despite
Roux's stellar status, meals here are value for money,
especially for lunch and afternoon tea. *See also p49.*

### Centra
*Lange Niezel 29 (622 3050). Tram 4, 9, 14, 16, 20,
24, 25.* **Open** 1-11pm daily. **Main courses** €7-€22.
**No credit cards. Map** p306 D2.
Good, wholesome, homely Spanish cooking with
an unpretentious atmosphere to match. The tapas,
lamb and fish dishes are all great.

### Excelsior
*Hôtel de l'Europe, Nieuwe Doelenstraat 2-8
(531 1701/531 1705/www.leurope.nl). Tram 4, 9,
14, 16, 20, 24, 25.* **Open** 12.30-2.30pm, 7-10.30pm
Mon-Fri; 7-10.30pm Sat, Sun. **Main courses** €35-
€45. **Credit** AmEx, DC, MC, V. **Map** p306 D3.
Indulgently elegant with a city view to swoon over,
this purveyor of formality features the mainly classical French menu of Jean-Jacques Menanteau.

## Indonesian & Thai

### Raad Phad Thai
*Kloveniersburgwal 18 (420 0665). Tram 4, 9, 14,
16, 20, 24, 25/Metro Nieuwmarkt.* **Open** 2-10.30pm
daily. **Main courses** €7-€11. **No credit cards.**
**Map** p306 D2.
A gaggle of friendly ladies cook up a storm behind
the counter, pumping out fish cakes and chicken pad
thai to die for. It couldn't be more unpretentious.

### Thaise Snackbar Bird
*Zeedijk 72 (snack bar 420 6289/restaurant 620
1442). Tram 1, 2, 4, 5, 9, 13, 14, 16, 17, 20, 24,
25.* **Open** *Snack bar* 3-10pm daily. *Restaurant*
5-10.30pm daily. **Main courses** €10-€17.
**Credit** (restaurant only) AmEx, DC, MC, V.
**Map** p306 D2.
The most authentic and cheapest Thai place in town.
It's also the most crowded, but it's worth the wait,
whether you settle on a tom yam soup or a full-
blown meal. If you want to linger, go to their restaurant almost directly opposite.

## South American

### Poco Loco
*Nieuwmarkt 24 (624 2937). Tram 4, 9, 14, 20.*
**Open** 5.30-11.30pm Mon-Thur, Sun; 11am-4am
Fri, Sat. *Kitchen* 5.30-10.30pm daily. **Main courses**
€10-€17. **Credit** AmEx, DC, MC, V. **Map** p307 E2.
This Mexican/Cajun café sports a patio with a prime
view of the wonderfully scenic Nieuwmarkt square.
As a bonus, staff cook it right and serve it quick.

## Cafés & snack stops

### Al's Plaice
*Nieuwendijk 10 (427 4192). Tram 1, 2, 4, 5, 9,
14, 16, 17, 20, 24, 25.* **Open** 4-10pm Mon, Tue;
noon-10pm Wed-Sun. **Main courses** €3-€8.
**No credit cards. Map** p306 D2.
Brits will spot the pun from 50 paces: yep, it's an
English fish 'n' chip tent. Besides fish, there's a selec-
tion of pies, pasties, peas and downmarket tabloids.

### Helder
*Taksteeg 7 (320 4132). Tram 4, 9, 14, 16, 20, 24, 25.*
**Open** noon-6pm Mon-Sat; dinner by reservation only
after 7.30pm. **Main courses** €8-€15. *Sandwiches*
€2.30-€3.50. **No credit cards. Map** p306 D3.
The 'Clear', in an alley off Kalverstraat, has an
inspired chef who only uses the freshest ingredients
in his salads, sandwiches, pastas and blinis (takeaway is available). One of the city's best lunch spots.

### De Jaren
*Nieuwe Doelenstraat 20-22 (625 5771/www.cafe-de-
jaren.nl). Tram 4, 9, 14, 16, 20, 24, 25.* **Open**
*Café* 10am-1am Mon-Thur, Sun; 10am-2am Fri, Sat.
*Restaurant* 5.30-10.30pm daily. **Main courses** *Café*
€3-€5. *Restaurant* €11-€16. **Credit** V. **Map** p306 D3.
The grand De Jaren lies in a beautifully restored,
building that was once a bank, and has retained a
slightly sterile business feel. The food in the ground-
floor café is OK; upstairs in the restaurant (with terrace) service can be painfully slow, but worth it.

Get in touch with the Dutch:
**Keuken van 1870.** *See p120.*

## Chinese & Japanese

For **Stereo Sushi**, *see p128* **Something fishy**.

## Dutch & Belgian

### Keuken van 1870

*Spuistraat 4 (624 8965). Tram 1, 2, 5, 20.*
**Open** 12.30-8pm Mon-Fri; 4-9pm Sat, Sun.
**Main courses** €5-€11. **Credit** (above €15)
AmEx, MC, V. **Map** p306 C2.
Eating here will put you in touch with the Dutch pop-
ulace: you may have to share a table with locals, and
the menu is mostly staunch Dutch favourites such
as endive with rashers of bacon. Cheap mussels!

### De Roode Leeuw

*Damrak 93-4 (555 0666/www.restaurant
deroodeleeuw.com). Tram 4, 9, 14, 16, 24, 25.*
**Open** 10am-11.30pm daily. *Kitchen* 10am-10pm
daily. **Set menu** €25-€35. **Credit** AmEx, DC,
MC, V. **Map** p306 D2.
This brasserie, housed in one of the oldest heated
terraces in Amsterdam, takes a step back to classier
times. It specialises in Dutch fare and even has a
selection of Dutch wine on offer.

### D'Vijff Vlieghen

*Spuistraat 294-302 (624 8369/
www.d-vijffvlieghen.com). Tram 1, 2, 5, 13, 17, 20.*
**Open** 5.30-10pm daily. **Main courses** €22-€28.
**Credit** AmEx, DC, MC, V. **Map** p306 C3.
'The Five Flies' tries to pump up a grand old Golden
Age vibe – it even has a Rembrandt's Room, which
features some of the great artist's etchings – but in

actual fact it does rather better as a purveyor of
interactive kitsch. The food here is probably best
described as poshed-up Dutch.

### Vlaamse Friteshuis

*Voetboogstraat 31 (no phone). Tram 1, 2, 5.*
**Open** 11am-6pm Mon-Sat; noon-5.30pm Sun.
**No credit cards**. **Map** p310 D4.
A great Belgian chip shop: chunky potatoey good-
ness, served with your pick of toppings. Go for *oor-
log* ('war'): chips with mayo, peanut sauce and onions.

## Fish

### Lucius

*Spuistraat 247 (624 1831/www.lucius.nl).
Tram 1, 2, 5.* **Open** 5pm-midnight daily.
**Main courses** €18-€20. **Credit** AmEx, DC,
MC, V. **Map** p306 C3.
Lucius serves a dinner of fresh ocean fish (not the
normal North Sea variety), poached, grilled or fried,
and shellfish in season. Order lobster in advance.

## Global

### Supper Club

*Jonge Roelensteeg 21 (344 6400/www.supperclub.nl).
Tram 1, 2, 5, 13, 17.* **Open** 8pm-1am daily.
**Set menu** €57 (5 courses). **Credit** AmEx, DC,
MC, V. **Map** p306 D3.
With its white backdrop, beds for seating, irrever-
ent food combos and themed acts, the arty Supper
Club is casual to the point of narcoleptic. The lounge
is similarly chilled and just as hip.

Nurse your arty instincts at the chilled **Supper Club**.

# Western Canal Belt

## Cafés & snack stops

### Gary's Muffins

*Prinsengracht 454 (420 1452). Tram 1, 2, 5.*
**Open** 8.30am-5.30pm Mon-Fri; 9am-6pm Sat, Sun.
**Main courses** *Sandwiches* €2.30-€4.20.
**No credit cards. Map** p310 C5.
One of the best snack stops in town, serving bagels, brownies and muffins. In good weather, sit outside by the canal and share your food with the sparrows. Branches at Jodenbreestraat 15, Marnixstraat 121 and Reguliersdwarsstraat 53, the latter late-opening.

### Goodies

*Huidenstraat 9 (625 6122). Tram 1, 2, 5.*
**Open** noon-10.30pm Mon, 9.30am-4.30pm, 6-10.30pm Tue-Sat; 11am-4.30pm, 6-10.30pm Sun.
**Main courses** €10-€16.50. *Sandwiches* €4-€6.
**Credit** AmEx, DC, MC, V. **Map** p310 C4.
A sandwich and bagel stop by day, with sarnies named after famous couples and bagels after cartoon characters (the 'Cartman' is tuna, onions and pickle). In the evening, it serves cheap but ace pasta.

### Greenwoods

*Singel 103 (623 7071). Tram 1, 2, 5.*
**Open** 9.30am-7pm daily. **Main courses** €4.50-€11.50. **No credit cards. Map** p306 C3.
Service at this teashop is friendly but can be slow. Everything is freshly prepared, however, so forgive them. Cakes, scones and muffins are baked daily on the premises. In summer, sit at the canalside terrace.

### 't Kuyltje

*Gasthuismolensteeg 9 (620 1045). Tram 1, 2, 9, 24, 25.* **Open** 7am-4pm Mon-Fri. *Sandwich* €1.70-€3.30.
**No credit cards. Map** p306 C3.
The world of Dutch *broodjes* (sandwiches) has its greatest champion in this takeaway, one of the very few that still features home-made – as opposed to factory-prepared – meat and fish salads in your bun.

### Lanskroon

*Singel 385 (623 7743). Tram 1, 2, 5.* **Open** 8am-5.30pm Tue-Fri; 8am-5pm Sat; 10am-5pm Sun.
**No credit cards. Map** p310 D4.
The best *banketbakkerij* (pâtisserie) in town? It's a brave man or woman who disagrees. The mouthwatering sacher torte, cakes, savouries, ice-creams and chocolates can be wolfed down in the cramped tearoom or bought as takeaway. No smoking.

### New Deli

*Haarlemmerstraat 73 (626 2755). Tram 1, 2, 5, 13, 17, 20.* **Open** 9am-9pm daily. **Main courses** €4-€14.50. **No credit cards. Map** p306 C2.
A fabulous yet tightly designed café that's more typical of London than Amsterdam. The airy and spartan surrounds evoke a vision of Japan, as does the sandwich and salad menu, which features unusual ingredients like yakitori and shitake. DJs spin on Sundays during the winter.

Sweet sensation: **Gary's Muffins**.

### Pompadour

*Huidenstraat 12 (623 9554). Tram 1, 2, 5.*
**Open** 9.30am-5.45pm Mon-Fri; 9am-5.30pm Sat.
**Credit** MC, V. **Map** p310 C4.
The cakes are ace, but it's the chocolates for which Pompadour is most famous. You can take your food away, but stop to enjoy a bite in the remarkable gilt-and-mirrors interior of the raised tearoom.

## Dutch & Belgian

### Pancake Bakery

*Prinsengracht 191 (625 1333/www.pancake.nl).*
*Tram 13, 17, 20.* **Open** noon-9.30pm daily.
**Main courses** €5-€10. **Credit** AmEx, MC, V.
**Map** p306 C2.
Visit this quaint restaurant in one of Prinsengracht's lovely gabled houses for the best pancakes in town. With Dutch recipes stressing the importance of both thinness and density, it's hard to go wrong.

## French & Mediterranean

### Belhamel

*Brouwersgracht 60 (622 1095/www.belhamel.nl).*
*Tram 1, 2, 5, 13, 17, 20.* **Open** 6-10pm daily.
**Main courses** €17-€21. **Credit** AmEx, MC, V.
**Map** p306 C2.
Imagine a fresh approach to French food, which dips into Italy and Holland for inspiration: Belhamel gives you innovation at a good price/quality ratio and a high art nouveau quotient.

**Eat, Drink, Smoke, Shop**

### Café Cox
*Marnixstraat 429 (620 7222). Tram 1, 2, 5, 6, 7, 10, 20.* **Open** 10am-1am Mon-Thur, Sun; 10am-2am Fri, Sat. *Kitchen* 11am-3.30pm, 6-10.30pm daily. **Main courses** €15-€18. **Credit** AmEx, DC, MC, V. **Map** p310 C5.
Imaginative French and modern Dutch cooking in a lively theatrical crowd environment. The prices are eminently reasonable, especially given its proximity to Leidseplein.

### Christophe
*Leliegracht 46 (625 0807/www.christophe.nl). Tram 13, 14, 17, 20.* **Open** 6.30-10.30pm Tue-Sat. **Main courses** €25-€35. **Credit** AmEx, DC, MC, V. **Map** p306 C3.
Hyper-posh and mega-expensive, Christophe serves inspired French cuisine with flourishes from Algeria to movers and shakers with ample expense accounts. Strap a booster to your taste buds and blast off to those Michelin stars.

### Lof
*Haarlemmerstraat 62 (620 2997). Tram 1, 2, 4, 5, 9, 13, 16, 17, 20, 24, 25.* **Open** 6.45pm-1am Tue-Sun. *Kitchen* 7-11pm Tue-Sun. **Set menu** €31-€37. **No credit cards. Map** p306 C2.
During the day, you could mistake Lof for a soup kitchen. At night, though, it's a different story: the lighting works miracles, as does the chef, who improvises dishes drawn equally from Mediterranean tradition and Far East cuisine.

## Global

### Blakes
*Keizersgracht 384 (530 2010). Tram 1, 2, 5.* **Open** 6.30-11pm Mon-Sat. **Main courses** €24-€88. **Credit** AmEx, DC, MC, V. **Map** p310 C4.
All the critics were right to lavish praise on this elegant restaurant of Anoushka Hempel's modish hotel (*see p57*). The menu is East meets West, though leaning towards Japan (as does the decor). Book ahead, sit down and be Zen.

## Indian

### Himalaya
*Haarlemmerstraat 11 (622 3776). Tram 1, 2, 5, 20.* **Open** 5-11pm daily. **Main courses** €10-€23. **Credit** AmEx, DC, MC, V. **Map** p306 C2.
Excellent Indian cuisine at nice prices. The staff can make any dish more or less spicy than usual and the service is invariably welcoming and friendly, matching the wonderful art and designs on the walls.

## Indonesian & Thai

### Sjaalman
*Prinsengracht 178 (620 2440/www.sjaalman.nl). Tram 13, 14, 17, 20.* **Open** 5.30-10.30pm daily. **Main courses** €11-€15. **No credit cards. Map** p306 C3.

**Himalaya**: the peak of cheap Indian cuisine.

This trendy Thai restaurant sits on the edge of the Jordaan. The woody and subtle designer atmosphere and personable service are finely tuned to evoke a relaxed and hip ambience, where mellow, grooving modern dance beats accompany conversation.

## Southern Canal Belt

## Cafés & snack stops

### Café Kalvertoren
*Singel 457 (427 3901). Tram 1, 2, 4, 5, 9, 14, 16, 20, 24, 25.* **Open** 10am-7pm Mon-Wed, Fri; 10am-9pm Thur; 10am-6pm Sat; 11am-6pm Sun. **Main courses** €3-€11. **Credit** (above €8) AmEx, MC, V. **Map** p310 D4.
A so-so café at the top of the Kalvertoren shopping centre, meriting a mention here for its spectacular vistas, especially as the sun goes down. Bring plenty of cash, but don't forget your camera, either.

### Pulitzers
*Keizersgracht 234 (523 5283). Tram 13, 14, 17, 20.* **Open** 7am-11pm daily. **Main courses** €18-€25. **Credit** AmEx, DC, MC, V. **Map** p306 C6.
Spoil yourself with a posh breakfast in this early-opening hotel restaurant (*see p57*). Sit under a Frans Hals painting; or, rather, a modernised version of one that features mobile phones and Heineken cans.

## Chinese & Japanese

For **Zushi**, *see p128* **Something fishy**.

### Japan Inn
*Leidsekruisstraat 4 (620 4989). Tram 1, 2, 5, 6, 7, 10, 20.* **Open** 5-11.45pm daily. **Main courses** €8-€35. **Credit** AmEx, DC, MC, V. **Map** p310 D5.

Japan Inn offers both quality and quantity. The great fresh sushi and sashimi are served quickly from the open kitchen in the back; both are popular with students (who dig the quantity) and Japanese tourists (who head there for the quality).

### Sherpa

*Korte Leidsedwarsstraat 58 (623 9495). Tram 1, 2, 5, 6, 7, 10.* **Open** 5-11pm daily. **Main courses** €7-€14. **Credit** AmEx, MC, V. **Map** p310 D5.

Amid the mediocrity of this tourist-frenzied area is one very special Tibetan restaurant. Relive your favourite Kathmandu moment by enjoying Sherpa's trad food and service. The Polish might call them pierogi, the Italians ravioli, but the Tibetan momo – at least as served here – is in a class of its own.

### Wagamama

*Max Euweplein 10 (528 7778/www.wagamama.com).* **Open** noon-11pm daily. **Main courses** €8-€15. **Credit** AmEx, DC, MC, V. **Map** p310 D5.

Amsterdam's branch of this popular London franchise of quick 'n' cheap noodle bars. You may not feel compelled to linger in the minimalist canteen setting, but you can't complain about the speedy service and the tasty noodle dishes and soups.

## Fish

### Le Pêcheur

*Reguliersdwarsstraat 32 (624 3121). Tram 1, 2, 5.* **Open** noon-2.30pm, 6-10.30pm Mon-Fri; 6-10.30pm Sat. **Main courses** €18-€39. **Credit** AmEx, DC, MC, V. **Map** p310 D4.

Menus in Dutch, French and English enable you to choose from à la carte or the menu of the day with the minimum of effort. The service is friendly but formal. The mussels and oysters are particularly excellent, as is the Golden Age patio.

## French & Mediterranean

### La Rive

*Amstel Hotel, Prof Tulpplein 1 (520 3264/ www.amstelhotel.nl). Tram 6, 7, 10, 20/Metro Weesperplein.* **Open** noon-2pm, 6.30-10.30pm Mon-Fri; 6.30-10.30pm Sat. **Main courses** €33-€50. **Credit** AmEx, DC, MC, V. **Map** p311 F4.

Despite Robert Kranenborg's departure to open Vossius (*see p132*), this elegant eaterie in the Amstel Hotel has held on to its reputation as an unparalleled purveyor of refined, regional French cuisine. It's all thanks to the able hands of rising star Edwin Kats.

### La Storia Della Vita

*Weteringschans 171 (623 4251). Tram 6, 7, 10, 16, 20, 24, 25.* **Open** 7-10.15pm daily. **Set menu** €21-€35 (7 courses). **Credit** MC. **Map** p311 E5.

After a chat, the engaging proprietor will decide which combination of whatever his original Italian kitchen happens to be fixing that night you'll enjoy. Sit back in grand brasserie style and enjoy both the food and the animated piano player. Great for a date.

### 't Swarte Schaep

*Korte Leidsedwarsstraat 24 (622 3021). Tram 1, 2, 5, 6, 7, 10, 20.* **Open** 5-11pm daily. **Main courses** €21-€35. **Credit** AmEx, DC, MC, V. **Map** p310 C5.

Based in this 300-year-old building since 1937, and noted for its wines, authentic antiques and blend of classic, nouvelle and postmodern cuisine. An occasional hangout of the Dutch royal family.

## Global

### Café Américain

*Leidseplein 97 (556 3232/www.amsterdam- american.crowneplaza.com). Tram 1, 2, 5, 6, 7, 10, 20.* **Open** 10am-midnight daily. *Kitchen* 11am-11pm daily. **Main courses** €12-€18. **Credit** AmEx, DC, MC, V. **Map** p310 C5.

Café Américain's glorious deco interior is a listed monument decorated with murals, stained glass and marbled lampshades: Mata Hari is said to have held her wedding reception here. Now mostly tourists meet here for a coffee and a pastry.

### Eat at Jo's

*Marnixstraat 409 (638 3336). Tram 1, 2, 5, 6, 7, 10, 20.* **Open** 2-9pm Wed-Sun. **Main courses** €4.50-€13. **No credit cards**. **Map** p310 C5.

Each day sees a different fish, meat and vegetarian dish on the menu of this cheap and tasty international kitchen on Marnixstraat. Starspotters take note: whichever act is booked to play at the Melkweg (*see p213*) may chow down here first.

**Café Américain:** gloriously deco.

Got designs on dinner? Head to the New Side, for swanky **Inez IPSC** (*left*) or kooky **Kitsch**.

### Inez IPSC

*Amstel 2 (639 2899/www.diningcity.nl/inezipsc).*
*Tram 4, 9, 20.* **Open** 7-10.30pm daily (lunch by
reservation only). **Main courses** €20-€23.
**Credit** DC, MC, V. **Map** p307 E3.
Featuring fantastic urban views and snappy decor
(from designer Peter Giele of the late, lamented
Roxy), Inez is a hotspot of the moneyed artistic set.
The food matches the setting: the refined taste and
presentation are taken to new aesthetic heights. Ace.

### Kalinka

*Korte Leidsedwarsstraat 49A (330 5996).* Tram 6,
*7, 10.* **Open** 5-10.30pm daily. **Main courses** €12-
€20. **Credit** AmEx, DC, MC, V. **Map** p310 D5.
To dwell on cultural clichés, Russian eaterie Kalinka
serves potent and palate-cleansing vodka. It also has
endearing service and something else… Right: food,
in the form of trad dishes such as stroganoff.

### Kitsch

*Utrechtsestraat 42 (625 9251). Tram 4, 6, 7, 10.*
**Open** 7pm-1am Mon-Thur, Sun; 6.30pm-3am Fri,
Sat. **Main courses** €15-€25. **Credit** AmEx, MC, V.
**Map** p311 E5.
A Barbie room, crocodile wallpaper, a ceiling that
drops confetti, a floor with glass holes where you
can watch the kitchen action, fountain-equipped
tables… Happily, the food isn't as kitsch, with the
menu running the gamut from lobster to foie gras.

### Moko

*Amstelveld 12 (626 1199/www.moko.nl). Tram*
*16, 24, 25.* **Open** 11.30am-1am Mon-Thur, Sun;
11.30am-2am Fri, Sat. *Kitchen* noon-4pm, 6-11pm
daily. **Main course** €16-€18. **Credit** AmEx, DC,
MC, V. **Map** p311 E4.

With one of the most scenic terraces in Amsterdam,
this wooden church – once the stable for Napoleon's
horses – is a lovely place in which to munch posh
sandwiches on a sunny day. Evenings see it transform into a highly regarded purveyor of fusion food.

### Noa

*Leidsegracht 84 (626 0802/www.withnoa.com). Tram*
*1, 2, 5.* **Open** 5.30pm-midnight Mon-Wed, Thur, Fri;
1pm-1am Sat; 1pm-midnight Sun. **Main courses** €7.
**Credit** AmEx, DC, MC, V. **Map** p310 C4.
This lounge is geared towards the international jet-
set and their aspiring disciples. Besides an excellent
complement of beers, wines and champagnes, you
can enjoy pan-Asian cooking (everything from udon
noodles to pad thai) from their open kitchen while
lounging on comfortable couches. No reservations.

## Indian

### Shiva

*Reguliersdwarsstraat 72 (624 8713). Tram 4, 9,*
*14, 16, 20, 24, 25.* **Open** 5-11pm daily. **Main**
**courses** €12-€16. **Credit** AmEx, DC, MC, V.
**Map** p310 D4.
Air-conditioning keeps the heat down in the relaxed
and elegant Shiva. The menu has carefully selected
dishes, from classic curries to speciality plates.

## Indonesian & Thai

### Bojo

*Lange Leidsedwarsstraat 49-51 (622 7434). Tram*
*1, 2, 5.* **Open** 4pm-2am Mon-Fri; noon-4am Sat, Sun.
**Main courses** €8-€12. **Credit** MC, V. **Map** p310 C5.

restaurant **nomads** rozengracht 133-I www.restaurantnomads.nl 020 344 64 01

club **More...** rozengracht 133 www.expectmore.nl 020 344 64 02

# Living on the veg

As mentioned in the introduction, vegetarians are very well catered for in Amsterdam. Though the rule isn't hard and fast, you can be pretty confident of finding at least a couple of vegetarian options on most menus.

However, there are a few specialist veggie eateries in town. Few are more venerable than **De Vliegende Schotel** in the Jordaan (Nieuwe Leliestraat 162; 625 2041), which serves a splendid array of dishes from a blackboard menu nightly. Back up Prinsengracht, the kitschy **De Bolhoed**

(Prinsengracht 60; 626 1803) deals in hearty vegan dishes from noon-10pm daily, while over in the Pijp, **Waaghals** offers a quirky menu and kid-friendly vibe every evening except Monday. South of the Pijp, the unique **Betty's** (Rijnstraat 75; 644 5896) cooks up fine vegetarian dishes of the Jewish diaspora, from falafel to enchiladas to curries, every evening except Monday and Friday. And don't forget squat restaurant **Academie** near Vondelpark (see p110 **Baby, let's play house**), which dishes up fine veggie nosh.

Bojo multitasks as both a fine Indo-eaterie and one of the few places – regardless of type – that stays open into the small hours. The price is right and the portions are large enough to glue your insides together after an evening of excess.

### Sahid Jaya

*Reguliersdwarsstraat 26 (626 3727). Tram 4, 9, 16, 20, 24, 25.* **Open** noon-3pm, 6-11pm daily. **Main courses** €12-€46. **Credit** AmEx, DC, MC, V. **Map** p310 D4.

Light, spacious, intrinsically chic and complete with a Golden Age terrace, Indonesian hangout Sahid Jaya also comes up trumps with their delicious rice table: its spice factor is up to you – choose to ladle from three different types of *sambal* (a chilli concoction). Stellar.

### Tempo Doeloe

*Utrechtsestraat 75 (625 6718/ www.tempodoeloerestaurant.nl). Tram 4, 6, 7, 10.* **Open** 6-11.30pm daily. **Main courses** €18-€44. **Credit** AmEx, DC, MC, V. **Map** p311 E4.

This cosy and rather upmarket Indonesian restaurant (heck, it even has white linen) is widely thought of as one of the city's best and spiciest purveyors of rice table, and not without good reason. Book ahead.

### Tujuh Maret

*Utrechtsestraat 73 (427 9865). Tram 4, 6, 7, 10.* **Open** 5-10pm Tue-Sun (open for lunch by request). **Main courses** €12-€23. **No credit cards. Map** p311 E4.

A relaxed and rattan-chaired Indo gaff whose champions claim is superior to posher neighbour Tempo Doeloe (see above), Tujuh Maret also does takeaway.

## South American

### Rose's Cantina

*Reguliersdwarsstraat 38-40 (625 9797/ www.rosescantina.com). Tram 4, 9, 16, 20, 24, 25.* **Open** 5pm-1am daily. *Kitchen* 5-11pm daily. **Main courses** €7-€23. **Credit** AmEx, MC, DC, V. **Map** p310 D4.

It's definitely not the place for a quiet night out and it's more Tex-Mex than Mexican, but the ingredients are good enough and the portions are generous. Combining a burrito with pitchers of Margarita makes for a merry meal.

## Jodenbuurt, the Plantage & the Oost

### Global

### De Kas

*Kamerlingh Onneslaan 3 (462 4562/ www.restaurantdekas.nl). Tram 9/bus 59, 69.* **Open** Mon-Fri noon-2pm, 6.30-10pm; Sat 6.30-10pm. **Set menu** €30 lunch; €40 dinner (5 courses). **Credit** AmEx, DC, MC, V.

In the heart of Frankendael Park, way out east, lies a renovated greenhouse that dates from 1926. It's now a restaurant, though, and has created much fevered talk among Amsterdam's foodies. A posh and peaceful place, its international menu changes daily based on what was harvested on location earlier that very day.

## The Waterfront

### French & Mediterranean

### Iberia

*Kadijksplein 16 (623 6313). Bus 22.* **Open** 6-11pm daily. **Set menu** €25. **Credit** AmEx, DC, MC, V. **Map** p307 F2.

Close by the Nederlands Scheepvaartmuseum and Nemo (for both, see p101), Iberia offers Spanish and Portuguese dishes in an authentic ambience. Indulge in sherry, fresh from the keg, during your meal.

### A Tavola

*Kadijksplein 9 (625 4994). Tram 6, 9, 14/bus 22.* **Open** 6-10.30pm daily. **Main courses** €10-€17. **No credit cards. Map** p307 F2.

*Eat, Drink, Smoke, Shop*

# Something fishy

The Netherlands and Japan have long had a certain kinship – cramped conditions, watery surroundings, a love for stuff both neat and small – so it's all the more surprising that Amsterdammers came to sushi so late. They're trying to make up for it now, though, in their newfound predilection for all things fast, fresh and fishy.

The best thing about Amsterdam sushi bars is that the fish is fresh. But the portions tend to be tiny, and the price of a decent-sized meal high. Selection, too, is usually diminutive: you won't find fairly pedestrian items such as sea urchin, pea pods and salmon roe at most of the downtown places, which tend to emphasise a limited number of practical, popular items such as shrimp and fake crabmeat. Finally, since the Dutch tend to go places in herds, booking is advisable on weekends if you want a table.

The coolest of the new school is **Stereo Sushi** (Jonge Roelensteeg 4; 777 3010), with a tiny but loungey interior, a DJ some nights and late opening (1am weeknights, 3am at weekends). Although the menu is small, it's a great place to eat before a night out, with good, fresh fish and chill-out music and lighting. Two of the city's trendiest sushi bars are best known for their use of the conveyor-belt gimmick. It's nice to grab what you want off the carousel, but don't look too closely at the dishes rolling by, or before you know it you'll be (1) €50 poorer and (2) dizzy. The Pijp's **Zento** (Ferdinand Bolstraat 17-19; 471 5316; www.zento.nl) is a yuppie after-work favourite, though elegant **Zushi** (Amstel 20; 330 6882) has a broader selection.

To go really cheap, casual and crunchy, pick up a sushi box to go from **Albert Heijn** (*see p170*). Pure it ain't – most of the items are made from cooked fish or vegetables – but decent and good value it certainly is. But if you want to go for the original sushi of the Lowlands – and, perhaps, the real reason why sushi took such a long time to catch on here – go to a fish stall and slide a nice bit of raw herring down your throat. It doesn't get much purer or cheaper.

It might be handy to bring along an Italian phrasebook to communicate with the staff here, but that's just part of the authentic charm you'll find at A Tavola. All the dishes are perfectly prepared and you can even round off your meal with a leisurely stroll along the waterfront.

### Wilhelmina-Dok
*Noordwal 1 (632 3701/www.wilhelminadok.nl). Restaurant boat leaves from Pier 9, or take ferry from Pier 8 to Amsterdam Noord.* **Open** noon-midnight daily. *Kitchen* 6-10pm daily. **Main courses** €13-€16. **Credit** AmEx, MC, V.
Through the large windows of this cube-shaped building, you get remarkable views of KNSM Eiland and Oostelijk Handelskade. Visit for soup and sandwiches by day and a daily-changing menu of Mediterranean dishes by night.

## Global

### Kaap Kot
*IJdijk 9 (692 9816/www.kaapkot.nl). Taxi from Centraal Station.* **Open** 11am-midnight Tue-Sun. *Kitchen* noon-3pm, 6-9pm Tue-Sun. **Main courses** €15-€19. **Credit** MC, V.
Don't let the fact that 'Cape Cod' is housed in a corrugated metal shed scare you. Soon it will be in the heart of a most singular neighbourhood: IJburg (*see p102* **On the waterfront**). Enjoy fish while checking out the state of construction.

### Kilimanjaro
*Rapenburgerplein 6 (622 3485). Bus 22.* **Open** 5-10pm Tue-Sun. **Main courses** €10-€18. **Credit** AmEx, MC, DC, V. **Map** p307 F2.
This relaxed and friendly pan-African eaterie offers an assortment of traditional recipes from Senegal, the Ivory Coast, Tanzania and Ethiopia that can be washed down with the fruitiest of cocktails or the strongest of beers.

### Odessa
*Veemkade 259, (419 3010/www.deodessa.nl). Bus 28, 39.* **Open** 6pm-1am Mon; 11am-1am Tue-Sun. **Main courses** €14-€16. **Credit** AmEx, VC, MC.
Hip diners head here to enjoy fusion food within the revamped interior of this Ukrainian fishing boat. The vibe is '70s Bond, accompanied by DJs and filtered through a modern lounge sensibility. On warmer nights, dine on the funkily lit deck and gaze out at the residential architecture on KNSM Island.

### Panama
*Oostelijke Handelskade 4 (311 8686/ www.panama.nl). Bus 32, 39.* **Open** 11am-1am Mon-Thur, Sun; 11am-3am Fri, Sat. *Kitchen* noon-4pm, 6-10.30pm daily. **Main courses** €18-€21. **Credit** AmEx, DC, MC, V.
Panama's 19th-century industrial architecture has been updated with modern furnishings. It serves authentic, globally inspired dishes, with an emphasis on fish. Stick around to experience the nostalgia-free programming in their club (*see p214 and p225*).

**Eat, Drink, Smoke, Shop**

**Amsterdam**. No points for the name.

### Pier 10
*De Ruijterkade, Steiger 10 (624 8276). Tram 1, 2, 5, 9, 13, 14, 16, 17, 20, 24, 25.* **Open** 6.30pm-1am daily. **Main courses** €15-€20. **Credit** AmEx, MC, V. **Map** p306 D1.
Functional decor, watery vistas and innovative fish dishes are all available at the relaxed Pier 10, a former shipping office behind Centraal Station.

## The Jordaan

### Cafés & snack stops

#### Small World Catering
*Binnen Oranjestraat 14 (420 2774).* **Open** 10.30am-8pm Wed-Sat; noon-8pm Sunday. **Main courses** €6-€10. **No credit cards. Map** p305 B2.
The home-base for this catering company is a tiny deli, which feels like you are in the kitchen of the lovely proprietor. Besides superlative coffee and fresh juices, enjoy salads, lasagne and quiches.

## Dutch & Belgian

### Amsterdam
*Watertorenplein 6 (682 2666/www.cradam.nl). Tram 10.* **Open** 11.30am-10.30pm Mon-Sun. **Main courses** €10-€21. **Credit** AmEx, DC, MC, V.

This spacious monument to industry a half-mile west of the Jordaan pumped water from the coast's dunes for around a century. Now, eat honest Dutch and French dishes here, under a mammoth ceiling and floodlighting culled from the old Ajax stadium. A unique – and child-friendly – experience.

### Groene Lantaarn
*Bloemgracht 47 (620 2088/www.fondue.nl). Tram 10, 13, 17, 20.* **Open** 6-9pm Thur-Sun. **Main courses** €14-€24. **Credit** AmEx, MC, V. **Map** p305 B3.
For posh fondues, try the old world vibe of Groene Lantaarn. Bread comes pre-chunked, the desserts are suitably and deliciously decadent, and the menu even stretches out globally to include dim sum.

### Moeder's Pot
*Vinkenstraat 119 (623 7643). Tram 3, 10.* **Open** 5-9.30pm Mon-Sat. **Main courses** €4-€11. **No credit cards. Map** p305 B1.
Mother's Pot serves up – you guessed it – simple and honest Dutch farmers' fare in woody and kitsch surrounds. It's not bad, either.

## Fish

### Albatros
*Westerstraat 264 (627 9932/www.seafoodhouse.net). Tram 10.* **Open** 6-midnight Mon, Tue, Thur-Sun. **Main courses** €18-€23. **Credit** AmEx, DC, MC, V. **Map** p305 B2.
Great fishy cuisine in a fishy setting. All dishes are cooked to perfection, and the fine wine can be bought by the centimetre. The tiramisu is to die for.

## French & Mediterranean

### Bordewijk
*Noordermarkt 7 (624 3899). Tram 3.* **Open** 6.30-10.30pm Tue-Sun. **Set menu** €33-€46. **Credit** AmEx, DC, MC, V. **Map** p305 B2.
Ideal for sampling some of the city's finest original food and palate-tingling wines in a designery interior. The service and atmosphere are both relaxed, and Bordewijk has a very reliable kitchen. A perfectly balanced restaurant.

### Duende
*Lindengracht 62 (420 6692/www.cafeduende.nl). Tram 3.* **Open** 4pm-1am Mon-Thur, Sun; 4pm-3am Fri, Sat. **Average** *Tapas* €2.50-€8.50. **No credit cards. Map** p305 B2.
Taste the spirit of Andalusia with the good tapas at Duende. Place your order at the bar and prepare to share your table with an amorous couple or a flamenco dancer who might just offer you free lessons.

### Hostaria
*2e Egelantiersdwarsstraat 9 (626 0028). Tram 10, 13, 14, 17, 20.* **Open** 7-10.30pm Tue-Sun. **Main courses** €11-€16. **No credit cards. Map** p305 B3.

**Eat, Drink, Smoke, Shop**

Owners Marjolein and Massimo Pasquinoli serve a wonderful selection of classic Italian dishes, including the lieks of salmon carpaccio and a spectacular insalata di polipo (squid salad). A fine place for excellent, unpretentious food.

### Tapasbar a la Plancha

*1e Looiersdwarsstraat 15 (420 3633). Tram 1, 2, 5, 7, 10, 20.* **Open** 2pm-1am Tue-Thur, Sun; 2pm-3am Fri, Sat. **Main courses** €3-€12. **Credit** MC, V. **Map** p310 C4.

The bull's head barely fits into this tiny spot, but its extended opening hours allow you more than enough time to squeeze in and experience the delicious flavours of some of the best tapas in town. Bring your Spanish phrasebook.

### Toscanini

*Lindengracht 75 (623 2813). Tram 3, 10.* **Open** 6-10.30pm daily. **Main courses** €16-€18. **Credit** AmEx, DC, MC, V. **Map** p305 B2.

The authentic and invariably excellent Italian food at this bustling spot is prepared in an open kitchen. Don't go expecting pizza, and make sure that you book early (from around 3pm) if you want to be sure of getting a table.

### Yam-Yam

*Frederik Hendrikstraat 90 (681 5097/ www.yamyam.nl). Tram 3.* **Open** 6-10pm Tue-Sun. **Main courses** €7-€15. **No credit cards.** **Map** p305 A3.

Unparalleled and shockingly inexpensive pastas and pizzas in a hip and casual atmosphere: no wonder Yam-Yam is a favourite of clubbers and locals alike. Easily worth the trip.

## Global

### Nomads

*Rozengracht 131-33 (344 6401/ www.restaurantnomads.nl). Tram 13, 14, 17, 20.* **Open** 8pm-1am Mon-Thur, Sun; 8pm-3am Fri; 8pm-midnight Sat. **Set menu** €48 (4 courses). **Credit** AmEx, EC, MC, V. **Map** p305 B3.

With a wonderfully evocative decor of curtains, mosaics and marbles, Nomads (from the people that brought you Supper Club; *see p120*) has taken lounging back to its oriental roots. Diners sit on cushions, from where they enjoy masses of Middle Eastern delights. After 11pm, it's time for drinking, dancing or some more lounging.

## Indian

### Balraj

*Haarlemmerdijk 28 (625 1428). Tram 3.* **Open** 5-10pm daily. **Main courses** €9-€13. **No credit cards.** **Map** p305 B2.

A small, cosy eating house with several decades of experience. The food is reasonably priced and particularly well done, with vegetarians generously catered for. Highly recommended.

Say 'cheese!' **Groene Lantaarn.** *See p129.*

## Indonesian & Thai

### Pathum

*Willemsstraat 16 (624 4936). Tram 3/bus 18, 22.* **Open** 5-10pm Mon, Wed-Sun. **Main courses** €9-€15. **Credit** AmEx, DC, MC, V. **Map** p305 B2.

Lovely Thai food at low prices. Ask the waiters for advice on how hot the dishes are if you don't want your head blown off. Which you probably don't.

# The Museum Quarter, Vondelpark & the South

## Cafés & snack stops

### Bakkerswinkel van Nineties

*Roelof Hartstraat 68 (662 3594). Tram 3, 12, 20, 24, 25.* **Open** 7am-6pm Tue-Fri; 7am-5pm Sat; 10am-4pm Sun. **Main courses** €2-€11. **No credit cards.**

A bakery-tearoom where you can indulge in lovingly prepared hearty sandwiches, soups and the most divine slabs of quiche you've ever had. Civilised.

## Dutch & Belgian

### Eetcafé Loetje

*Johannes Vermeerstraat 52 (662 8173). Tram 16.* **Open** 11am-1am Mon-Fri; 5.30pm-1am Sat. *Kitchen* 11am-10pm Mon-Fri; 6-10pm Sat. **Main courses** €5-€16. **No credit cards.** **Map** p310 D6.

Sometimes, after an honest day of sightseeing – or for the regulars, ad exec slavery – there's nothing better than a fillet of beef steak, salad, fries and mayo. A fine antidote to the rarefied air you may have inhaled while gandering at a Rembrandt nearby.

## Fish

### Vis aan de Schelde
*Scheldeplein 4 (675 1583/www.visaandeschelde.nl).*
*Tram 5, 25.* **Open** noon-2pm, 5.30-11pm Mon-Fri;
5.30-11pm Sat, Sun. **Main courses** €21-€37.
**Credit** AmEx, MC, V.
This eaterie out near the RAI convention centre has become a fish temple for the connoisseur. The menu sees classy French favourites colliding with more exotic dishes such as Thai fish fondue.

## French & Mediterranean

### Bodega Keyzer
*Van Baerlestraat 96 (671 1441). Tram 3, 5, 12, 16,*
*20.* **Open** 9am-midnight Mon-Sat; 11am-midnight
Sun. **Main courses** €21-€30. **Credit** AmEx, DC,
MC, V. **Map** p310 D6.
Bodega Keyzer caters mainly for posher concertgoers keen on the upscale French fare. Don't commit a social blunder by trying to order from a concert violinist, who often have the same style sense as the waiters. The fish is terrific, especially the sole.

### Eetcafé I Kriti
*Balthasar Floriszstraat 3 (664 1445). Tram 3, 5, 12,*
*16, 20.* **Open** 5pm-1am Mon-Thur, Sun; 5pm-3am
Fri, Sat. **Main courses** €11-18. **No credit cards**.
Eat and party Greek style in this superior invocation of Crete, where a standard choice of dishes is lovingly prepared. Bouzouki-picking legends drop

in on occasion and pump up the frenzied atmosphere with a few well-picked tunes, further aided by the plate-lobbing option.

### Le Garage
*Ruysdaelstraat 54-6 (679 7176). Tram 3, 5, 6, 12,*
*16, 20.* **Open** noon-2pm, 6-11pm Mon-Fri; 6-11pm
Sat, Sun. **Main courses** €24-€39. **Credit** AmEx,
DC, MC, V. **Map** p311 E6.
Don your favourite glad rags in order to blend in at this fashionable brasserie, which is great for emptying your wallet while watching a selection of Dutch glitterati do precisely the same. The authentic French regional cuisine – and 'worldly' versions thereof – is pretty darn fine.

### Vossius
*Vossiusstraat 1 (577 4100). Tram 2, 3, 5, 12,*
*20.* **Open** noon-2pm, 7-10.30pm Mon-Sat. **Main**
**courses** €18-€50. **Credit** AmEx, DC, MC, V.
**Map** p310 C5.
Robert Kranenborg, the Netherlands' most famous chef, opened this luxurious restaurant in a bid to earn that elusive third Michelin star. Believe the hype and be sure to book your table far, far ahead.

## Global

### CoBrA Café
*Hobbemastraat 18 (470 0111/www.cobracafe.com).*
*Tram 3, 5, 12, 20.* **Open** 10am-9pm Mon, Tue;
10am-midnight Wed-Sun. *Kitchen* 10am-9pm daily.
**Main courses** €12-€19. **Credit** AmEx, MC, V.
**Map** p310 D6.
Named, with unintentional irony, after an art movement that worshipped spontaneity, the CoBrA Café is a tight ship anchored in Museumplein. Pop in for salads, sushi, yoghurt and snacks by day, or indulge in the highly regarded menu by night.

# Grease is the word

Vending machines: every country has them, but how many use them as a futuristic fast food solution? In Amsterdam, it's possible to walk up to a hole in the wall, slip a few coins in the slot, and get a hot meal out. That said, 'meal' may not be exactly the right word for the prefab globs of grease that are the speciality at **Febo**, branches of which are scattered all around town like pimples on the face of an adolescent boy.

For the uninitiated, a visit to Febo (pronounced 'Fay-bo') can give a slightly eerie edge to a Saturday night out. Witness a near-religious moment: the quietening of a loud, beer-fuelled crowd as they line up to put their change into a glowing hole in the wall and, in exchange, receive a sacrament of grease in

the form of hamburger, *kroket* (a deep-fried meat and potato product), *bamibal* (a deep-fried spicy noodle product) or *kaas soufflé* (a deep-fried cheese product).

While some people may find this an odd sight, it is, when you think about it, the next logical step in the evolution of the fast-food industry. The whole point of the fast-food ritual is that quality should never come into play. Instead, Febo constitutes an appropriate representation of the culmination of modern eating habits: humanoid employees have lost their identities to the greater cause of speedy service and corporate growth. Febo is a taste of the future, where automation stands as a realised dream of the 20th century.

### Genet

*Amstelveenseweg 152 (673 4344). Tram 1, 6.*
**Open** 5-11pm daily. **Main courses** €7-€25.
**No credit cards**.
A great spot to sample the *injera* pancake-based
food of Ethiopia after a day of leisure in the greenery. The proprietor is quick to make you feel at home,
and the veggie-friendly food calls for restraint: you'll
want to keep eating regardless of how full you feel.

### Vakzuid

*Olympisch Stadion 35 (0900 825 9843 premium
rate/www.vakzuid.nl). Tram 24/bus 15, 63.*
**Open** 10am-1am Mon-Thur, Sun; 10am-3am Fri,
Sat. *Kitchen* noon-2.30pm, 6-10.30pm daily.
**Main courses** €14-€27. **Credit** AmEx, DC, MC, V.
Dubbed 'Fuck Zuid' by waggish locals, this lounge
restaurant, located in the revamped 1928 Olympic
Stadium, is hugely popular with the working tren-
doids. With modish cons and views over the track
field, it's a stunning site; hopefully the food – call it
Med-Oriental – will come to match it in time.

## Indonesian & Thai

### Djago

*Scheldeplein 18 (664 2013). Tram 4.* **Open**
5-9.30pm Mon-Fri, Sun. **Main courses** €7-€23.
**Credit** AmEx, DC, MC, V.
Djago's West Javanese eats are praised to the hilt by
Indo-obsessives. Located near the RAI convention
centre, it's a bit out of the way, but well worth the
journey south.

### De Orient

*Van Baerlestraat 21 (673 4958). Tram 2, 3, 5, 12,
20.* **Open** 5-10pm daily. **Main courses** €12-€19.
**Credit** AmEx, DC, MC, V. **Map** p310 C6.

A folklore-decorated Indonesian restaurant with a
large, vegetarian-friendly menu. Fifty years of experience has taught them to mellow the spices and
hence makes for a gentler introduction to rice table.

### Sama Sebo

*PC Hooftstraat 27 (662 8146). Tram 2, 3, 5, 12, 20.*
**Open** noon-2pm, 6-10pm Mon-Sat. **Set menu** €25
(16 dishes). **Credit** AmEx, DC, MC, V. **Map** p310 D5.
Mellow out at this comfortable and spacious Indo
restaurant with a brown café-style vibe. There's no
minimum charge, so even if you just fancy a coffee
and a snack between museums, it's a good choice.

## South American

### Riaz

*Bilderdijkstraat 193 (683 6453). Tram 3, 7,
12, 17.* **Open** noon-9pm Mon-Fri; 2-9pm Sun.
**Main courses** €5-€14. **No credit cards**.
**Map** p309 B5.
Amsterdam's finest Surinamese restaurant is where
Ruud Gullit scores his rotis when he's in town. The
Indian edge to the menu sees the inclusion of some
curries. If the skies are sunny, take away a takeaway
to nearby Vondelpark.

## The Pijp

## Cafés & snack stops

### Bagels & Beans

*Ferdinand Bolstraat 70 (672 1610). Tram 16, 24,
25.* **Open** 8.30am-6pm Mon-Fri; 9.30am-6pm Sat;
10am-6pm Sun. **Main courses** €3-€5. **Credit**
(over €20) AmEx, DC, MC, V. **Map** p311 E6.
B&B has consolidated its position in Amsterdam,
thanks in part to this patio-equipped success story.
Perfect for an econo-breakfast, lunch or snack; sun-
dried tomatoes are employed with particular skill.

### Soepwinkel

*1e Sweelinckstraat 19F (673 2293/
www.soepwinkel.nl). Tram 16, 24, 25.* **Open** *Apr-Oct*
11am-9pm Mon-Sat. *Oct-Mar* 11am-8pm Mon-Sat.
**Average** €3.50-€9. **No credit cards**. **Map** p311 F5.
'The Soup Shop' specialises in – yes, folks – soup.
On any given day, there are nine globe-embracing
recipes, including veggie versions. Whether or not
you take them to Sarphatipark, this makes a forti-
fying escape from the chaos of Albert Cuypmarkt.

## Chinese & Japanese

For **Zento**, *see p128* **Something fishy**.

### Albine

*Albert Cuypstraat 69 (675 5135). Tram 16, 24, 25.*
**Open** 10.30am-10pm Tue-Sun. **Main courses** €4-
€12. **No credit cards**. **Map** p311 E6.
One in a row of three cheap Suri-Chin-Indo spots,
Albine – where a Chinese influence predominates –
gets top marks for both its service and its solid

Eat, Drink, Smoke, Shop

vegetarian or meat meals of roti, rice or noodles. Gel your belly back together here after you've experienced the Heineken tour.

## Yamazato
*Okura Hotel, Ferdinand Bolstraat 333 (678 8351/ www.okura.nl/html/yamazato.html). Tram 12, 25.* **Open** 7.30-9.30am, noon-2pm, 6-9.30pm daily. **Main courses** €25-€37. **Credit** AmEx, DC, MC, V.
If you want class, head out here and surrender to the charming kimono-ed service, the too-neat-to-eat presentation and the restful views over a fishpond. The lunches are priced more attractively than the dinners.

## French & Mediterranean

### L'Angoletto
*Hemonystraat 18 (676 4182). Tram 3, 4, 6, 7, 10.* **Open** 6-11pm Mon-Fri, Sun. **Main courses** €5-€9. **Credit** V. **Map** p311 F5.
The most authentic trattoria in town has a Felliniesque edge. It gets very busy, but the food – often hyped as the best pizza and pasta in Amsterdam – makes the wait for a table worthwhile.

### District V
*Van der Helstplein 17 (770 0884). Tram 12, 25.* **Open** 6pm-1am daily. *Kitchen* 6.30-10.30pm daily. **Set menu** €25 (3 courses). **No credit cards.** **Map** p311 F6.
District V not only offers a divine and econo Frenchinspired, daily changing menu, but also sells the locally designed plates, cutlery and tables it is served on. The patio is a lovely spot to sit in summer.

## Global

### Aleksandar
*Ceintuurbaan 196 (676 6384). Tram 3, 20.* **Open** 5-10pm daily. **Main courses** €16-€31. **No credit cards.** **Map** p311 E6.
Balkan food comes in huge heaps here, along with heaps of hospitality. Surrender to the grilled selections and the *slivovic*, a plummy and poetic hard liquor that will soon have you reciting odes to the excellent frog's legs and escargot starters.

### Eufraat
*1e Van der Helststraat 72 (672 0579/www.eufraat.nl).* *Tram 3, 12, 24, 25.* **Open** Tue-Sun. **Main courses** €7-€13. **Credit** AmEx, DC, MC, V. **Map** p311 E5.
This family-run Assyrian restaurant is named after one of the rivers that's said to have flowed through the Garden of Eden. The ancient recipes are brought to life with care and loving attention: Eufraat even makes its own pittas and yoghurts from scratch. Don't miss the supreme Arabic coffee.

### Koerdistan
*Ferdinand Bolstraat 23 (676 1995). Tram 16, 24, 25.* **Open** 5pm-11.30pm Tue-Sun. **Main courses** €7-€13. **Credit** DC, MC, V. **Map** p311 E6.

This small and cosy restaurant is also friendly, and rarely disappoints with its top-notch Middle Eastern cookery. If you lay off the snacks all day, you'll be in perfect shape for trying its generously portioned daily three-course menu, priced at around €12.

### Lokanta Ceren
*Albert Cuypstraat 40 (673 3524). Tram 4, 16, 20, 24, 25.* **Open** 6-10.30pm daily. **Main courses** €9-€15. **No credit cards.** **Map** p311 E6.
A friendly Turkish/Kurdish restaurant. The numerous tasty meze will quickly disappear when accompanied by the fresh, warm Turkish bread and a glass of raki. Round off your feast with some fresh fruit for a quick and tasty health kick.

### Ondeugd
*Ferdinand Bolstraat 13-15 (672 0651/ www.ondeugd.nl). Tram 3, 6, 7, 10, 12, 16, 20, 24, 25.* **Open** 6pm-1am Mon-Thur, Sun; 6pm-3am Fri, Sat. *Kitchen* 6-11pm daily. **Main courses** €15-€20. **Credit** AmEx DC, MC, V. **Map** p311 E6.
A popular restaurant in the Pijp, perfect for a casual and potentially raucous evening out. The menu is primarily French, but with many outside influences. Pop in for the lobster on Mondays.

## Indian

### Balti House
*Albert Cuypstraat 41 (470 8917). Tram 6, 7, 10, 16, 20, 24, 25.* **Open** 5-11pm daily. **Main courses** €10-€21. **Credit** AmEx, MC, V. **Map** p311 E6.
Balti and tandoori dishes at Amsterdam's only balti house come in big portions, which are usually mildly seasoned to suit the typical Dutch palate. If you make a special request for something hotter, however, you'll really land the full spicy works.

## Indonesian & Thai

### Cambodja City
*Albert Cuypstraat 58-60 (671 4930). Tram 16, 24, 25.* **Open** 5-10pm Tue-Sun. **Main courses** €6-€14. **No credit cards.** **Map** p311 E6.
Don't let the name mislead you, the dishes served here are culled from Thailand, Vietnam and Laos as well as Cambodia. Aside from the 3-D moving waterfall painting, the surrounds are plain and simple, and both the helpful service and the food itself never fail to please.

### Warung Spang-Makandra
*Gerard Doustraat 39 (670 5081). Tram 6, 7, 10, 16.* **Open** 11am-10pm Mon, Tue, Thur-Sun. **Main courses** €2-€7. **No credit cards.** **Map** p311 E6.
A Java-Suri restaurant out in the Pijp, where the Indo influence always comes up trumps with the great Javanese rames. The decor is kept simple, but the relaxed vibe and beautifully presented dishes will make you want to sit down for your meal as opposed to taking it away.

**Eat, Drink, Smoke, Shop**

# Bars

Raise a glass to old-style *bruin cafés* and traditional Dutch tasting houses.

Amsterdam is home to Heineken, the second-biggest brewer on the planet. The government funds scientists to research whether beer helps protect against heart disease. And while it's well known that the city's biggest draws are its dope and dames, there is also an absolute abundance of bars. The streets are truly paved in gold; or, at least, in amber nectar.

The most common sort of watering hole is the old-style *bruin café* or brown bar, so called because over the years, nicotine has stained their walls. Wood, warmth and well-worn *gezelligheid* (a uniquely Dutch type of social cosiness) typifies the best. Brown bars have a good range of local and national brews, but enthusiasts should head to speciality bars such as **'t Arendsnest** or **In de Wildeman** (for both, *see p141*); and for fine, locally produced beer visit **Maximiliaans** (*see p137*) or **Brouwerij 't IJ** (*see p143* **Roll out the barrels**).

However, there's much more to Amsterdam's bars than boozing. Some simply ooze history, such as **In 't Aepjen** or **In de Waag** (for both *see p137*). Others form an important Dutch tradition: *proeflokaal* (tasting houses) specialise in jenever (a gin-like spirit made from juniper berries), *brandewijn* (literally, burnt – or distilled – wine), and other old Dutch liquors.

Recent years have seen a steady growth in designer/lounge bars, but other types of bar – geared towards political, literary, musical, trad or rad crowds – are still out there. Finally, a word of warning. When someone gives you 'two fingers', don't respond in kind: a regular beer here (in rather pitiful 250ml glasses) comes with a sizeable head of froth. It's the custom; get used to it.

## The Old Centre

### The Old Side

#### De Buurvrouw
*St Pieterspoortsteeg 29 (625 9654/ www.debuurvrouw.nl). Tram 4, 9, 14, 16, 20, 24, 25.* **Open** 9pm-3am Mon-Thur, Sun; 9pm-4am Fri, Sat. **No credit cards. Map** p306 D3.
Lively, alternative and popular. A sawdust-strewn floor, quirky art – plus a figure of de Buurvrouw, 'the woman neighbour' who watches over proceedings below – give the place its atmosphere. DJs spin on Saturday and there are also occasional performances by bands.

Give a monkeys for **In 't Aepjen**. *See p137*.

#### Café Cuba
*Nieuwmarkt 3 (627 4919). Tram 4, 9, 14, 16, 20, 24, 25/Metro Nieuwmarkt.* **Open** 1pm-1am Mon-Thur, Sun; 1pm-3am Fri, Sat. **No credit cards. Map** p306 D2.
One of Nieuwmarkt's most beautiful cafés, Cuba is spacious with plenty of snug seating. DJs play some weekends, it serves wicked Mojitos, and there's a pool table in the 'chill out space' at the back where you can spliff up. Hemingway would have loved it.

#### Café Fonteyn
*Nieuwmarkt 13-15 (422 3599). Tram 4, 9, 14, 16, 20, 24, 25/Metro Nieuwmarkt.* **Open** 9.30am-1am Mon-Thur, Sun; 9.30am-3am Fri, Sat. **No credit cards. Map** p306 D2.
Something of a home-from-home, the 'Fountain' is perpetually popular for its warm drawing-room feel (they also have a heated terrace) and is a good place for breakfasts, light snacks and cosy conversations.

#### Café Stevens
*Geldersekade 123 (620 6970). Tram 4, 9, 20/Metro Nieuwmarkt.* **Open** 11.30am-1am Mon-Thur, Sun; 11.30am-3am Fri, Sat. **No credit cards. Map** p306 D2.

Set on a corner of the Nieuwmarkt, huge picture windows catch the sun and look out on to the bustle of the square. Inside is calm, rustic and cosy; both service and food are good.

### De Diepte
*St Pieterspoortsteeg 3 (06 2900 5926 mobile). Tram 4, 9, 14, 16, 20, 24, 25.* **Open** 10pm-3am Mon-Thur, Sun; 10pm-4am Fri, Sat. **No credit cards. Map** p306 D3.
Its name – the Depths – refers to the bowels of damnation. In this unholy hole, with its walls seemingly on fire, you can toss back beers to a soundtrack of randy rockabilly, snotty punk and filthy rock 'n' roll. Hell has never seemed so *gezellig*.

### Engelbewaarder
*Kloveniersburgwal 59 (625 3772). Tram 4, 9, 14, 16, 20, 24, 25/Metro Nieuwmarkt.* **Open** noon-1am Mon-Sat; 2pm-1am Sun. **No credit cards. Map** p306 D3.
Engelbewaarder is popular with quasi-academics and beer lovers enjoying the fine brews. Others simply admire the views from the huge picture windows. Live jazz brightens up Sunday afternoons.

### De Hoogte
*Nieuwe Hoogstraat 2A (626 0604). Tram 4, 9, 14, 16, 20, 24, 25/Metro Nieuwmarkt.* **Open** 10am-1am Mon-Thur, Sun; 10am-3am Fri, Sat. **No credit cards. Map** p307 E3.
A small but characterful drinking joint close to the Red Light District, catering to an alternative crowd. Drinks are cheap compared to most hangouts in the neighbourhood, and they have seven high-speed Internet terminals at around €1 for 20 minutes.

### In de Olofspoort
*Nieuwebrugsteeg 13 (624 3918). Tram 4, 9, 14, 16, 20, 24, 25.* **Open** 5pm-1am Tue-Thur; 5pm-2am Fri, Sat. **No credit cards. Map** p306 D2.
Jenevers and liquors from Oud Amsterdam can be found at In de Olofspoort, a renaissance-type building dating from the 17th century and granted monument status. Worth a look.

### In de Waag
*Nieuwmarkt 4 (422 7772/www.indewaag.nl). Tram 4, 9, 14, 16, 20, 24, 25/Metro Nieuwmarkt.* **Open** 10am-1am daily. **Credit** AmEx, DC, MC, V. **Map** p306 D2.
The building can seem imposing, but walk through the doors of this former weigh house (*see p79*), and you'll be transported back in time. There's no music here, and candles are the only lighting. There's also a restaurant here.

### In 't Aepjen
*Zeedijk 1 (626 8401). Tram 4, 9, 14, 16, 20, 24, 25.* **Open** 3pm-1am daily. **No credit cards. Map** p306 D2.
Located in one of the oldest wooden houses in town, this is a terrific bar. The name – 'In the Monkeys' – comes from when Zeedijk was frequented by sailors: those who couldn't pay their bills would bring back a monkey from the Dutch East Indies. *See also p79.*

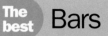

## The best Bars

**Het Blauwe Theehuis**
In the heart of Vondelpark. *See p146.*

**Brouwerij 't IJ**
For the best local beer. *See p143.*

**Sassoon**
Casual, arty and oddly romantic. *See p145.*

**Wolvenstraat 23**
A hip but homely lounge bar. *See p142.*

**Wynand Fockink**
It oozes Old Amsterdam charm. *See p138.*

### Kapitein Zeppos
*Gebed Zonder End 5 (624 2057/www.zeppos.nl). Tram 4, 9, 14, 16, 20, 24, 25.* **Open** 11am-1am Mon-Thur, Sun; 11am-2am Fri, Sat. **Credit** AmEx, MC, V. **Map** p306 D3.
Formerly a horse-carriage store and a cigar factory, Kapitein Zeppos has retained an olde worlde feel. There's music every Sunday, with Café Chantant, on the first Sunday of the month, hugely popular. There's a charming restaurant in the conservatory.

### Lime
*Zeedijk 104 (639 3020). Tram 4, 9, 14, 16, 20, 24, 25/Metro Nieuwmarkt.* **Open** 5pm-1am Mon-Thur; 5pm-3am Fri, Sat. **No credit cards. Map** p306 D2.
The minimalist Lime is perhaps the trendiest bar in the area. However, it's also surprisingly unpretentious; it almost feels like you could be in someone's home. DJs play regularly, the cocktails are fab, and it's popular at weekends as a pre-club destination.

### Lokaal 't Loosje
*Nieuwmarkt 32-4 (627 2635). Tram 4, 9, 14, 16, 20, 24, 25/Metro Nieuwmarkt.* **Open** 9.30am-1am Mon-Thur, Sun; 9.30am-2am Fri, Sat. **No credit cards. Map** p306 D2.
Market traders, locals, artists and writers all convene at this typically Dutch brown café that was formerly a waiting room from the days when trams used to run around the Nieuwmarkt.

### Maximiliaan
*Kloveniersburgwal 6-8 (626 6280). Tram 4, 9, 14, 16, 20, 24, 25.* **Open** 3pm-1am Tue, Wed, Sun; 3pm-2am Thur-Sat. **Credit** AmEx, DC, MC, V. **Map** p306 D3.
In 1544 at this former cloister, nuns began producing beer as the drinking water was so bad. Almost 450 years later, Maximiliaan opened to carry on this worthy tradition. It produces ten different types, and taps on the bar run directly from huge copper vats.

**Eat, Drink, Smoke, Shop**

Age and beauty combine at **Wynand Fockink**.

### The Tara

*Rokin 89 (421 2654/www.thetara.com). Tram 4, 9, 14, 16, 20, 24, 25.* **Open** 11am-1am Mon-Thur, Sun; 11am-3am Fri, Sat. **Credit** AmEx, MC, V. **Map** p306 D3.

This large yet cosy Irish bar has three bars, two pool tables and a couple of log fires. DJs play at weekends, there's regular live music, the food is superb, and TVs – mainly screening football – remain unobtrusive to the non-fan. The best Irish pub in town.

### 't Tuinfeest

*Geldersekade 109 (620 8864). Tram 4, 9, 14, 16, 20, 24, 25/Metro Nieuwmarkt.* **Open** 4pm-1am Mon-Thur, Sun; 4pm-3am Fri, Sat. **Credit** AmEx, DC, MC, V. **Map** p306 D2.

This split-level corner café serves delicious, well-presented food at decent prices. Music is loud but not intrusive, and the place attracts a young crowd. Its popularity means that it can be hard to get a table.

### Van Kerkwijk

*Nes 41 (620 3316). Tram 4, 9, 14, 16, 20, 24, 25.* **Open** 11am-1am Mon-Thur, Sun; 11am-3am Fri, Sat. **No credit cards. Map** p306 D3.

Formerly Amsterdam's 'wine café', Van Kerkwijk still attracts customers with discerning taste. The atmosphere here is warm and welcoming, from the surroundings down to the staff and the friendly cat at the bar. Meals, which are served all day, are delicious and varied.

### VOC Café

*Schreierstoren, Prins Hendrikkade 94-5 (428 8291/www.schreierstoren.nl). Tram 4, 9, 14, 16, 20, 24, 25.* **Open** 10am-1am Mon-Thur; 10am-3am Fri, Sat; noon-8pm Sun. **No credit cards. Map** p306 D2.

Housed in the city's oldest defence tower (*see p79*), the VOC Café is a cosy bar with two terraces overlooking Geldersekade. Further pluses come in the shape of regular live music and good ranges of jenevers and liqueurs.

### Wynand Fockink

*Pijlsteeg 31 (639 2695/www.wynand-fockink.nl). Tram 4, 9, 14, 16, 20, 24, 25.* **Open** *Tasting room* 3-9pm daily. *Lunch/garden terrace* 10am-7pm daily. **No credit cards. Map** p306 D3.

Dating from 1679, this is the most charming tasting house in town. Around 50 old Dutch liquors and 20 jenevers are served (the former are produced just next door); their adjoining 'lunchlokaal', with a beautiful hidden garden (complete with waterfall), is one of the town's best kept secrets. Strictly no mobile phones.

# Lining the stomach

Forget museums and canals: Amsterdam's sweetest pleasure is chilling in a local café. If weather permits, exploit a terrace; otherwise, pick a place with the brownest of woods and the most nicotine-stained of ceilings. Such hangouts – the likes of **Katte in 't Wijngaert** (*see p145*) and **De Prins** (Prinsengracht 124; 624 9382/www.deprins.nl) – often provide the most culturally satisfying of experiences.

As settings for excess for eons, such places have learned to offer a series of snacks – known as **borrel hapjes** ('booze bites') – formulated to gel the belly back together. Inevitably, the menu begins with the strongest of stereotype reinforcers: **kaas** (cheese), which can be ingested either via **tostis** (grilled cheese sandwiches) or pure in the form of a plate of young, rich Gouda or Edam, cut into cubes and served with a dipping bowl of mustard. Other mustard-dipping options may include cubed salami and liverwurst.

But there are also more complex options; ones that even deserve the respect of being preceded by the palate-cleansing powers of jenever (Dutch gin). The most universal in the Netherlands are **bitterballen** ('bitter balls'), spherical deep-fried blobs of potato and meat that are remarkably tasty and addictive. Essentially, they're the cocktail version of the **kroket**, sold in every snack bar across the country. They go with any liquid, but really come into their own when washed down with dark beer (for instance, Palm or De Koninck). A rather rarer deep-fried snack – though it's gaining popularity almost by the second – are **vlammetjes** ('little flames'), filo-wrapped packets of spicy meat. These potential tongue-scorchers are perhaps best enjoyed with tapped **witbier** ('white beer'), the ultimate summer beer: its sweetish edge acts as a happy antidote to the tang of the meal. As the Dutch say: 'Eet smakelijk!'

# The New Side

## Absinthe

*Nieuwezijds Voorburgwal 171 (320 6780/ www.absinthe.nl). Tram 1, 2, 5.* **Open** 8pm-3am Mon-Thur, Sun; 8pm-4am Fri, Sat. **No credit cards.** **Map** p306 D3.

We can thank Henri-Louis Pernod for popularising the wormwood-infused liquid hallucinogenic. And we can thank this grotto-like lounge for home-brew absinthe on tap and highly palatable absinthe cocktails. An upbeat late-opener in the heart of clubland.

## Belgique

*Gravenstraat 2 (625 1974/www.xs4all.nl/~phj). Tram 1, 2, 4, 5, 9, 13, 14, 16, 17, 20, 24, 25.* **Open** noon-1am Mon-Thur, Sun; noon-3am Fri, Sat. **No credit cards.** **Map** p306 C3.

As the name suggests, this cosy bar deals in beer from the Netherlands' neighbours. Eight Belgian brews are on tap, with around 30 served by the bottle; Trappist cheese will make you thirsty for more.

## Bep

*Nieuwezijds Voorburgwal 260 (626 5649). Tram 1, 2, 5.* **Open** *Apr-Oct* noon-1am Mon-Thur, Sun; noon-3am Fri, Sat; *Oct-Apr* 4.30pm-1am Mon-Thur, Sun; 4.30pm-3am Fri, Sat. **No credit cards.** **Map** p306 D3.

A painfully fashionable New Side hangout that sits nicely with its similarly cool neighbours Diep (*see below*) and the Seymour Likely Lounge (*see p141*). Go there to be seen, sure, but don't miss the terrific bar food or cocktails.

## Café het Schuim

*Spuistraat 189 (638 9357). Tram 13, 14, 17, 20.* **Open** 11am-1am Mon-Thur; 11am-3am Fri, Sat; 1pm-1am Sun. **No credit cards.** **Map** p306 C2.

Low, comfy jelly mould-shaped chairs enhance the relaxing atmosphere at this un-signposted café, and the juxtaposition of styles entertains all-comers: a glitzy chandelier hangs by a big glitterball. Chilled music makes it a dreamy hangout on a rainy day.

## Café Luxembourg

*Spui 22 (620 6264/www.cafeluxembourg.nl). Tram 16, 24, 25.* **Open** 9am-1am Mon-Thur, Sun; 9am-2am Fri, Sat. **Credit** AmEx, DC, MC, V. **Map** p310 D4.

Ignore the aloof service and enjoy people-watching, chuckling at the model-wannabes and bespoke suits. This elegant spot has a well-placed terrace for people who need to see and be seen. Afternoons are best.

## Café-Galerie Dante

*Spuistraat 320 (638 8839/www.dante.nl). Tram 4, 9, 14, 16, 20, 24, 25.* **Open** 11am-1am Mon-Thur, Sun; 11am-3am Fri, Sat. **Credit** AmEx, DC, MC, V. **Map** p306 D3.

Dante's bright lighting makes it a spirit-lifting place. But hopefully it won't raise the spirit of Herman Brood (*see p215* **Brood swings**), whose upstairs gallery remains open. Posh nosh, good wine and decent beer.

## Diep

*Nieuwezijds Voorburgwal 256 (420 2020/www.diep.tv). Tram 1, 2, 5.* **Open** 5pm-1am Mon-Thur, Sun; 5pm-3am Fri, Sat. **No credit cards.** **Map** p306 D3.

Watch the world go by from **Het Molenpad**'s canalside terrace. *See p141.*

Though it doesn't quite offer something for everyone, Diep's brown café-meets-opulent disco palace interior should ring bells with anyone who likes their bars eclectic and camp. DJs play on Fridays.

### De Drie Fleschjes

*Gravenstraat 18 (624 8443/www.driefleschjes.nl).*
*Tram 1, 2, 4, 5, 9, 13, 14, 16, 17, 20, 24, 25.*
**Open** noon-8.30pm Mon-Sat; 3-7pm Sun. **No credit cards**. **Map** p306 C3.
Opened in 1650, the friendly De Drie Fleschjes is one of the oldest tasting houses in Amsterdam. It's situated on a calm, picturesque street, and specialises in jenever, traditional Dutch liquors and wine.

### Henri Prouvin

*Gravenstraat 20 (623 9333). Tram 1, 2, 4, 5, 9, 13, 14, 16, 17, 20, 24, 25.* **Open** 3-11pm Tue-Fri; 2-9pm Sat. **No credit cards**. **Map** p306 C3.
This dark, elegant but slightly snooty café offers a spectacular variety of good wines and champagnes either by the bottle or the glass at reasonable prices. It also serves snacks and a few meat dishes.

### Hoppe

*Spui 18-20 (420 4420). Tram 1, 2, 5.* **Open** 8am-1am Mon-Thur, Sun; 8am-2am Fri, Sat. **Credit** AmEx, DC, MC, V. **Map** p310 D4.
This brown café is always popular, though the left-hand entrance leads to the more easygoing of the two bars. A haunt of radicals in the '60s, its old-fashioned decor is now a refreshing change from the chrome fittings or generic tawdriness in most New Side haunts.

### In de Wildeman

*Kolksteeg 3, nr Nieuwezijds Kolk (638 2348/www.indewildeman.nl). Tram 1, 2, 5, 13, 17, 20.* **Open** noon-1am Mon-Thur; noon-2am Fri, Sat. **No credit cards**. **Map** p306 D2.
The Wildeman's main bar offers 200 bottled brews from around the world and 18 draughts (including a monthly special). There's no music, but there can be a lot of noise from loud male pissheads. Happily, the small no-smoking room is a lot quieter.

### Seymour Likely Lounge

*Nieuwezijds Voorburgwal 250 (627 1427). Tram 1, 2, 5.* **Open** 8pm-3am Mon-Thur, Sun; 8pm-4am Fri, Sat. **No credit cards**. **Map** p306 D3.
'It's a bar', proclaims Seymour's in its window. Very handy if you've just got Dieply Bepped at its neighbours (*see p139*). DJs play good music and, despite the place's perpetually hip reputation, the crowd here is chilled and approachable.

### De Still

*Spuistraat 326 (620 1349/www.whisky-destill.nl). Tram 4, 9, 14, 16, 20, 24, 25.* **Open** 3pm-1am Mon-Thur, Sun; 3pm-3am Fri, Sat. **No credit cards**. **Map** p306 D3.
De Still's selling point is its giant range of whiskies: just under 600 in total. Arrange your own tastings at the bar, priced around €11 for a selection of four or €20 for a selection of six (minimum two people). The bar also runs a whisky festival in November.

A happy **Hoppe**.

## The Canals

## Western Canal Belt

### 't Arendsnest

*Herengracht 90 (421 2057/www.arendsnest.nl). Tram 1, 2, 5, 13, 17, 20.* **Open** 4pm-midnight Mon-Thur, Sun; 4pm-2am Fri, Sat. **No credit cards**. **Map** p306 C2.
There's nothing but Dutch beer served at 't Arendsnest; over 130 different kinds. A regular pils, six guest beers and a special recipe from De Schans brewery in Uithoorn are all on tap. Between 3pm and 5pm on the last Sunday of every month, there's a tasting session of ten different beers for around €15. A must.

### Café de Koe

*Marnixstraat 381 (625 4482/www.cafedekoe.nl). Tram 7, 10.* **Open** 4pm-1am Mon-Thur, Sun; 4pm-3am Fri, Sat. *Kitchen* 6-10.30pm daily. **Credit** AmEx, DC, MC, V. **Map** p305 B2.
The decor at this lively two-level bar-restaurant is themed after its name, 'Cow'. Drinkers go upstairs and diners down, to a restaurant serving good food at reasonable prices.

### Het Molenpad

*Prinsengracht 653 (625 9680/www.goodfoodgroup.nl/amsterdam.html). Tram 7, 10, 20.* **Open** noon-1am Mon-Thur, Sun; noon-2am Fri, Sat. *Kitchen* noon-4pm, 6-10.30pm daily. **No credit cards**. **Map** p310 C4.
Mellow music wafts through the smoke at this hangout, as literary types stroll past towards the library a few doors up. Het Molenpad's charming staff serve delicious lunches and dinners, the artists' exhibits change monthly, and there's a delightful canalside terrace.

### Van Puffelen

*Prinsengracht 375-7 (624 6270). Tram 1, 2, 5, 7, 10.* **Open** 3pm-1am Mon-Thur; 3pm-2am Fri, Sat; noon-1am Sun. *Kitchen* 6-10pm daily. **Credit** AmEx, DC, MC, V. **Map** p306 C3.
The biggest brown café in Amsterdam and a haunt of the beautiful people, particularly on summer evenings. Arrive by boat to make an impression, perhaps for the occasional performances by jazz musicians on Sundays.

Eat, Drink, Smoke, Shop

### De Vergulde Gaper

*Prinsenstraat 30 (624 8975). Tram 3, 10.*
**Open** 10am-1am Mon-Thur, Sun; 10am-3am Fri,
Sat. **No credit cards. Map** p306 C2.

A spacious, upmarket bar with an excellent selection of drinks, plus some sofas on which to snuggle up on a cold winter's evening. In the summer, sit by the huge doors or on the terrace. Great for lunches and dinner, though the kitchen's shut on Fridays.

### Wolvenstraat 23

*Wolvenstraat 23 (320 0843). Tram 1, 2, 5.*
**Open** 8am-1am Mon-Thur; 8am-2am Fri;
9am-2am Sat; 10am-1am Sun. **No credit cards.
Map** p310 C4.

This seemingly anonymous haunt is actually a far-from-forgettable lounge bar: affluent beings sink into its sofas, attracted by fab music and art exhibitions. It's great for breakfast and lunch; at night, take a culinary trek from Shanghai to Beijing.

### De Zotte

*Raamstraat 29 (626 8694). Tram 1, 2, 5.*
**Open** 4pm-1am Mon-Thur, Sun; 4pm-3am Fri,
Sat. **Credit** AmEx, DC, MC, V. **Map** p310 C4.

Appropriately, de Zotte is Belgian for 'drunken fool', an inevitability after sampling from their giant selection of 130 beers. As luck would have it, however, you can soak up any excesses with the great food from the kitchen. Incomparably *gezelligheid*.

**Sassoon.** Happily, most food and drink arrives the right way up. *See p145.*

## Southern Canal Belt

### Het Land van Walem

*Keizersgracht 449 (625 3544). Tram 1, 2, 5.*
**Open** 10am-1am daily. **Credit** AmEx, DC, MC, V.
**Map** p310 D4.

One of the first designer bars in Amsterdam, this long, narrow and bright filling station was the work of renowned Dutch architect Gerrit Rietveld. There are two terraces, one out front by the canal, the other out back in the small garden.

### Morlang

*Keizersgracht 451 (625 2681/www.morlang.nl). Tram
1, 2, 5.* **Open** 10am-1am Mon-Thur, Sun; 10am-2am
Fri, Sat. **Credit** AmEx, MC, V. **Map** p310 D4.

The two-floor Morlang, with large canalside terrace, lacks the bright designer looks of Het Land van Walem next door, but it's still a stylish hangout. The food's good, and the selection of spirits awesome. Incidentally, psychological drama *Morlang* was written here by the film's director, Tjeboo Penning.

## Around Leidseplein

### Aroma

*Leidsestraat 96 (624 2941/www.cafe-aroma.nl). Tram
1, 2, 5, 6, 7, 10, 20.* **Open** 9am-1am Mon-Thur, Sun;
9am-3am Fri, Sat. **No credit cards. Map** p310 D4.

Completely out of place on Leidsestraat, this spacious café-bar makes a welcome respite from its surrounds. Its two floors are done out in white, and its Mediterranean-influenced food is very healthy. Happy hour runs 5-7pm daily.

### De Balie

*Kleine Gartmanplantsoen 10 (553 5130/restaurant
553 5131/www.balie.nl). Tram 1, 2, 5, 6, 7, 10, 20.*
**Open** 11am-1am Mon-Thur, Sun; 11am-2am Fri, Sat.
**No credit cards. Map** p310 D5.

The café serving the cultural and political centre of the same name is big and open, crowded with artsy types and the politically involved. Meet here before attending a lecture or movie, or simply enjoy the elevated view across the hectic Leidseplein.

### Boom Bar

*Leidseplein 12 (530 7303/www.boomchicago.nl).
Tram 1, 2, 5, 6, 7, 10, 20.* **Open** noon-1am Mon-
Thur, Sun; noon-3am Fri, Sat. **Credit** AmEx, MC, V.
**Map** p310 C5.

Stand-up fans pause for a drink at Boom's bar before adjourning to the theatre out back (*see p246*). The pre-theatre dinner is popular, but you can't go wrong with the pitchers of beer or cocktails. DJs play Wed-Sat, and there are happy hour promos and themed nights such as karaoke (first Sun of the month).

### Kamer 401

*Marnixstraat 401 (320 4580) Tram 1, 2, 5, 6, 7,
10, 20.* **Open** 4pm-1am Mon-Thur, Sun; 4pm-3am
Fri, Sat. *Kitchen* 6-10.30pm daily. **No credit cards.**
**Map** p310 C5.

# Roll out the barrels

The career transition from sports star to bar owner is a global standard. Before football got rich in the UK, leading players would often take over pubs when they retired; the USA, meanwhile, is full of bars owned by sports stars past and present. However, the road from pop star to master brewer is less well travelled. Kaspar Peterson, in fact, is the only documented example. After a couple of hits in the 1980s, Peterson abandoned music for beer, opening **Brouwerij 't IJ** in 1985.

But while brewing is the main purpose of the operation – free tours are held every Friday at 4pm – drinking plays a part, too. Since 1987, the IJ has been open to the public as a tasting house. The building was once a bathhouse, and retains much of its macho edge. That said, the steam that once fugged the air here has been replaced by cigarette smoke, and the communal troughs have given way to modern urinals. Perhaps pissing out the 180,000 litres of beer produced here annually proved something of a strain on the old cisterns.

The range of beers is broad. There are three seasonal specials (produced in winter, spring and autumn) and one retail-only brew (de Vlo, sold exclusively through Amsterdam's **De Bierkoning** off licence; *see p169*), but it's perhaps best to start with the five standard

beers, offered all year-round. The standard brew is Plzen, a tasty pils which, with an alcohol content of 5%, is the weakest of the lot. There's also the darker 'double beer' Natte, blonde 'triple beer' Zatte, the first ever beer to be produced here, and Columbus and Struis, both 'special beers', rate a hefty 9%.

Finally, despite claims in practically every tourist guide, the brewery is not located in a windmill; in fact, it's adjacent to one, known locally as De Gooyer. But while the prominent 1814 landmark helps in locating the place, finding your way home after a few of its highly alchoholic wares is another matter entirely.

## Brouwerij 't IJ

*Funenkade 7 (622 8325/http:// people.a2000.nl/skip/-bier/brouwerij.htm).* Tram 6, 10/bus 22. **Open** 3-8pm Wed-Sun. **No credit cards**.

---

This lounge, with its 1960s-looking black and grey interior, is dead stylish. A sophisticated pre-theatre/cinema crowd arrive in the early evening for dinner, while a younger, trendier crowd populates the place later on.

## Lux

*Marnixstraat 403 (422 1412) Tram 1, 2, 5, 6, 7, 10, 20.* **Open** 8pm-3am Mon-Thur, Sun; 8pm-4am Fri, Sat. **No credit cards**. **Map** p310 C5.
One of the best late-opening hangouts, this split-level designer bar has DJs every night and draws an alternative and trendy crowd. Lux's owners also run the quieter Weber, at No.397, and Kamer 401 (*see p142*).

## Los Pilones

*Kerkstraat 63 (320 4651). Tram 1, 2, 5, 11.* **Open** 4pm-1am Tue-Thur, Sun; 4pm-2am Fri, Sat. **Credit** AmEx, DC, MC, V. **Map** p310 D4.
A splendid Mexican cantina with an anarchic bent, Los Pilones is run by two young and friendly Mexican brothers; one of them does the cooking, so expect authentic dishes from the homeland rather than standard Tex-Mex fare. The best place in town for tequila.

## Around Rembrandtplein

### De Duivel

*Reguliersdwarsstraat 87 (626 6184/www.deduivel.nl).* Tram 4, 9, 14, 20. **Open** 8pm-3am Mon-Thur, Sun; 8pm-4am Fri, Sat. **No credit cards**. **Map** p311 E4.
Cypress Hill, the Roots and Gang Starr have all popped by this small but lively hip hop bar since it opened a decade ago. Nowadays, DJs at 'the Devil' mix it up with funk, rare groove and breakbeats.

### 't Madeliefje

*Reguliersdwarsstraat 74 (622 2510/www.madeliefje.nl).* Tram 4, 9, 14, 16, 20, 24, 25. **Open** 9pm-3am Tue, Thur; 8pm-3am Wed; 9pm-4am Fri, Sat. **No credit cards**. **Map** p310 D4.
A rarity: a smallish, trendy bar that maintains a relaxed vibe in the middle of a frenzied nightlife district. The music ranges from '70s R&B to soul.

### Mulligans

*Amstel 100 (622 1330/www.mulligans.nl).* Tram 4, 9, 14, 16, 20, 24, 25. **Open** 4pm-1am Mon-Thur; 4pm-3am Fri; 2pm-3am Sat; 2pm-1am Sun. **No credit cards**. **Map** p307 E3.

Eat, Drink, Smoke, Shop

Yet another theme bar, but this one more Irish than Oirish. The beer and the craic are both good, and there's a fine live music programme with an open session on Sundays.

### Schiller
*Rembrandtplein 26 (624 9846). Tram 4, 9, 14, 20.* **Open** 4pm-1am Mon-Thur, Sun; 4pm-2am Fri, Sat (opens at 2pm in winter). *Kitchen* 5.30-10pm daily. **Credit** AmEx, DC, MC, V. **Map** p311 E4.
An absolute godsend for anyone feeling like a fish out of water amid Rembrandtplein's crass, packed terraces, this renowned deco café maintains a high-browed festivity on weekends. Incidentally, Schiller belongs to the hotel of the same name (*see p59*).

## Jodenbuurt, the Plantage & the Oost

For **Brouwerij 't IJ**, *see p143* **Roll out the barrels.**

### Café de Sluyswacht
*Jodenbreestraat 1 (625 7611/www.welcome.to/ sluyswacht). Tram 9, 14, 20/Metro Waterlooplein.* **Open** 11.30am-1am Mon-Thur; 11.30am-3am Fri, Sat; 11.30am-7pm Sun. **Credit** MC, V. **Map** p307 E3.
Built in 1695, this former lock-keeper's house has retained much of its charm, as well as its foundations: the building leans heavily. It's situated across from the Rembrandthuis (*see p97*), and the terrace at the back is one of the most peaceful in town.

### Dantzig
*Zwanenburgwal 15 (620 9039). Tram 9, 14, 20/ Metro Waterlooplein.* **Open** 9am-1am Mon-Fri; 9am-2am Sat; 10am-1am Sun. *Kitchen* 11am-10pm daily. **Credit** AmEx, DC, MC, V. **Map** p307 E3.
A Parisian-style grand café frequented during the day by visitors to the adjacent Waterlooplein market, tourists waiting for their canal boats, and councillors from the city hall. The terrace is large and has great views over the Amstel.

### De Druif
*Rapenburgerplein 83 (624 4530). Tram 7, 20.* **Open** 11am-1am Mon-Thur, Sun; 11am-3am Fri, Sat. **No credit cards. Map** p307 E2.
Originally a jenever distillery, 'the Grape' specialises in wine, imbibed mostly by locals on account of the location near the old harbour. The regulars are a friendly bunch, however, so you should feel at home.

### East of Eden
*Linnaeusstraat 11 (665 0743). Tram 6, 9, 10, 14.* **Open** 11am-1am Mon-Thur, Sun; 11am-2am Fri, Sat. **No credit cards. Map** p312 H3.
One of the few stylish, youthful bars in a rapidly gentrifying workaday neighbourhood across from the Tropenmuseum (*see p99*), the spacious East of Eden is a good place in which to sit and read or write over a restorative coffee or pils.

### Eik & Linde
*Plantage Middenlaan 22 (622 5716). Tram 7, 9, 14, 20.* **Open** 11am-1am Mon-Thur; 2pm-2am Fri, Sat. **No credit cards. Map** p307 F3.
'The Oak & Lime Tree' is an old-fashioned, family-run, tourist-free neighbourhood bar. Local memorabilia on the walls, including posters from radio shows held on the premises, give it historical appeal; low prices and a laid-back air make it user-friendly.

## The Waterfront

### Kanis & Meiland
*Levantkade 127 (418 2439/www.kanisenmeiland.nl). Bus 28, 32, 59.* **Open** 10am-1am Mon-Thur, Sun; 10am-3am Fri, Sat. **No credit cards.**
K&M is in the middle of Amsterdam's redeveloping Eastern Docklands. The bright and spacious café is perfect for summer – and the food's terrific.

## The Jordaan

### Café Nol
*Westerstraat 109 (624 5380). Tram 10.* **Open** 9pm-3am Mon-Thur, Sun; 9pm-4am Fri, Sat. **No credit cards. Map** p305 B2.
Kitsch doesn't come any more hardcore: this over-the-top Jordaan bar/institution, with red leatherette interiors and crowds of lusty-voiced locals, is supposed to sum up the true 'spirit' of the neighbourhood. Be warned: this brand of social cosiness comes with much jolly spittle flying through the air.

### Café Soundgarden
*Marnixstraat 164-6 (620 2853). Tram 10, 13, 14, 17, 20.* **Open** 1pm-1am Mon-Thur; 1pm-3am Fri; 3pm-3am Sat; 3pm-1am Sun. **No credit cards. Map** p305 B3.
Popular with a grungy crowd, Café Soundgarden has one of the best terraces in town, along a quiet stretch of canal. Pool, darts, pinball and table football are on hand to while away those rainy afternoons.

### Café Tabac
*Brouwersgracht 101 (622 4413). Tram 1, 2, 5, 13, 17, 20.* **Open** 10am-1am Mon; 11am-1am Tue-Thur, Sun; 11am-3am Fri; 10am-3am Sat. **No credit cards. Map** p305 B2.
Tabac evokes the vibe of a restful brown café, with modishness coming from an inventive menu and a youthful but relaxed local crowd. Great location, too: on the corner of two scenic canals and bridges.

### Café West Pacific
*Polanceaukade 3 (488 7778/www.westpacific.nl). Tram 10/bus 18, 22.* **Open** 11.30am-1am Mon-Thur, Sun; 11.30am-3am Fri, Sat. *Restaurant* 6-10pm Tue-Sun. Members only after 10pm Thur-Sat. **No credit cards. Map** p305 A2.
This large café-club has a huge fire, a dancefloor and a decent menu. After 11pm there's a cover charge and an emphasis on jazz-funky dance music. Part of the Westergasfabriek (*see p245*).

GOOOOOOOOAAAAAAAAAAAAAAAALLLLLLLLLL!!!!!!!! **Café Soundgarden**. *See p144.*

### Dulac
*Haarlemmerstraat 118 (624 4265). Bus 18, 22.*
**Open** 4pm-1am Mon-Thur, Sun; 4pm-3am Fri, Sat.
**No credit cards. Map** p306 C2.
A wildly OTT grand café fitted out in an outrageously surrealistic deco style (stuffed alligators, mutant trees and more besides). The cosy snugs, the raised gallery and the glass-walled conservatory pack in trendies by the hundred. DJs spin at weekends.

### Finch
*Noordermarkt 5 (626 2461). Tram 1, 2, 5, 13, 17, 20.*
**Open** 7pm-1am Mon; 11am-1am Tue-Thur, Sun; 11am-3am Fri; 9am-3am Sat. **No credit cards. Map** p305 B2.
Located in one of the city's more scenic squares, Finch attracts the hip and artistic to its vaguely *Wallpaper**-like interior, happily muted by the inclusion of a carefree vibe. Excellent eats, grooving tunes and charming staff make it a top hangout.

### De Kat in 't Wijngaert
*Lindengracht 160 (622 4554). Tram 1, 2, 5, 13, 17, 20.* **Open** 10am-1am Mon-Thur, Sun; 10am-3pm Fri, Sat. **No credit cards. Map** p305 B2.
From the 'the Cat in the Vineyard', you can spy the spot of the Eel Riot (*see p105* **On the pull**). It's a neighbourhood café that evokes a truer image of the spirit of the Jordaan than even Café Nol (*see p144*), with locals drawn from every walk of life. Purrrfect.

### De Reiger
*Nieuwe Leliestraat 34 (624 7426). Tram 10, 13, 14, 17, 20.* **Open** 11am-1am Mon-Thur, Sun; 11am-2am Fri, Sat. *Kitchen* 6-10.30pm daily. **No credit cards. Map** p305 B3.

This light and airy brown bar is one of the most popular watering holes in the Jordaan, especially among the vaguely style-conscious. Get here early, particularly if you want to eat from its much-hyped menu.

### Sassoon
*Marnixstraat 79 (420 4075). Tram 7, 10, 17, 20.* **Open** 6pm-1am Mon-Thur, Sun; 3pm-3am Fri, Sat. **No credit cards. Map** p305 B3.
Comfortable sofas and chairs sit among the wonderfully cluttered and intensely arty interior of this alternabar (formerly SAS). Good, homely meals at low prices – and in big portions – are served downstairs, with food by Suzy Cream Cheese on Fridays.

### 't Smalle
*Egelantiersgracht 12 (623 9617). Tram 13, 14, 17, 20.* **Open** 10am-1am Mon-Thur, Sun; 10am-2am Fri, Sat. **No credit cards. Map** p305 B3.
In 1786, Pieter Hoppe (of Hoppe & Jenever) opened his liquor distillery here. Though a few remnants remain, including an original jenever pump on the bar, it's no retro spot. New ownership at the start of 2001 has seen it earn a reputation as a delightful and quiet wine café/brown bar.

### De Tuin
*2e Tuindwarsstraat 13 (624 4559). Tram 3, 10, 13, 14, 17, 20.* **Open** 10am-1am Mon-Thur; 10am-2am Fri, Sat; 11am-1am Sun. **No credit cards. Map** p305 B3.
A classic brown café frequented by slightly alternative locals, 'the Garden' is stone-floored, dark and always lively. There's always someone looking for a game of chess or backgammon.

Café West Pacific. *See p144.*

## The Museum Quarter, Vondelpark & the South

### Het Blauwe Theehuis
*Vondelpark (662 0254/www.blauwetheehuis.nl).*
*Tram 1, 2, 6.* **Open** 9am-1am Mon-Thur, Sun;
9am-3am Fri, Sat. *Kitchen* 9am-4pm, 5-10pm.
**Map** p310 C6.
Resembling a flying saucer, the Blue Teahouse –
designed by HAJ Baanders and J Baanders in
1936 – is a charming and romantic spot. There are
two bars (one upstairs, one down) and snacks are
available all day. It's the place to be in summer,
though it can get very crowded.

### Café Ebeling
*Overtoom 50-52 (689 4858/www.cafeebeling.com).*
*Tram 1, 3, 6, 12.* **Open** 11am-1am Mon-Thur;
11am-3am Fri, Sat; noon-1am Sun. *Kitchen* 11am-9pm
daily. **Credit** AmEx, MC, V. **Map** p310 C5.
Located in an old bank – the toilets are in the safe –
Café Ebeling is a split-level bar that aims itself at
the young without being snobby or needing to have
the music so loud you can't think. Another plus –
it's also one of the few non-Irish bars here that serves
a decent Guinness.

### De Peper Bar
*Academie, Overtoom 301 (779 4912/*
*http://squat.net/overtoom301). Tram 1, 6.*
**Open** 6pm-late Tue, Fri, Sun; 10pm-late Thur.
*Kitchen* 7-8.30pm Tue, Fri, Sun (must reserve from
4pm same day). **No credit cards.**
De Peper is a squat bar that's housed in the former
film academy (*see p193*). The place is only open on
four nights a week, but for a late-night drink in a
relaxed atmosphere, you could do a great deal
worse. *See p110* **Baby, let's play house.**

### De Ruimte Cultureel Media-Café
*1e Constantijn Huygensstraat 20 (489 3619).*
*Tram 1, 3, 6, 12.* **Open** noon-1am Tue-Thur, Sun;
noon-3am Fri, Sat. *Kitchen* 7-10pm daily. **No credit
cards. Map** p310 C6.
Though the building was voted one of Amsterdam's
ugliest by readers of *Het Parool*, it retains its 1960s
utopian ideals and is home to a range of creative
ventures. The ground-floor bar-cum-restaurant
attracts arty thirtysomethings and happens to serve
great food.

### Toussaint
*Bosboom Toussaintstraat 26 (685 0737). Tram
1, 3, 6, 7, 12, 17.* **Open** 10am-midnight Mon-Thur,
Sun; 10am-1am Fri, Sat. **No credit cards.**
**Map** p310 C5.
Rustic charm abounds at this welcoming café-bar.
It's to be found on a quiet street just a ten-minute
walk from Leidseplein, and is worth a detour.
Toussaint's small open kitchen serves super nosh
all day and night (and there's plenty of choice for
vegetarians). A better bet than the unfortunately
named Wanka just down the road.

## The Pijp

### Carel's Café
*Frans Halsstraat 76 (679 4836). Tram 16, 24, 25.*
**Open** 10am-1am Mon-Thur; 10am-3am Fri, Sat;
11am-1am Sun. **No credit cards. Map** p311 E6.
Basically a large neighbourhood café, but worth a
trip for its excellent lunches and dinners. While
you're there, hop about to some of the ever-evolving
selection of bars on this mellow, scenic street.

### Gambrinus
*Ferdinand Bolstraat 180 (671 7389). Tram 16, 24,
25.* **Open** 11am-1am Mon-Thur, Sun; 11am-2am Fri,
Sat. **No credit cards. Map** p311 E6.
Listen to the crunch of salt underfoot as you enter
this pleasant local brown – yet light-infused – café,
popular with couples of the young urban professional variety. The snacks and dinners are tasty.

### Kingfisher
*Ferdinand Bolstraat 24 (671 2395). Tram 6, 7, 10.*
**Open** 1pm-1am Mon-Thur; 1pm-3am Fri, Sat. **No
credit cards. Map** p311 E6.
Of the many local-ish brown cafés that actually let
in fresh light and international style, the Kingfisher
does the best job, balancing impeccable and neigh-
bourly service with inventive snacks and a daily dinner special that'll take your tastebuds on a global
rollercoaster ride. The archetype of the locals' local.

### Wildschut
*Roelof Hartplein 1-3 (676 8220). Tram 3, 5, 12,
24, 25.* **Open** 10am-1am Mon-Thur; 9am-3am Fri;
10.30am-2am Sat; 9.30am-1am Sun. **Credit** (over
€15) AmEx, DC, MC, V.
This chic, cavernous joint is still one of the places to
be seen in town. In summer, take a seat on the large
terrace overlooking the Roelof Hartplein.

# Coffeeshops

A friend with weed is a friend indeed: here's the score on the draw.

All that's missing is a cannabis drip: **Abraxas**. *See p151.*

## The best Coffeeshops

**Abraxas**
A multi-sensory goblin heaven. *See p151.*

**Barney's**
Bangers and hash – the fry high. *See p152.*

**Greenhouse**
For weed and seed connoisseurs. *See p149.*

**T-Boat**
The coffeeshop to float your boat. *See p151.*

**La Tertulia**
Smoke grass amid the greenery. *See p152.*

If you're reading this chapter, you doubtless knew this already. But it still bears repeating. Not to put too fine a point on it, the Netherlands has some of the most progressive laws on cannabis in the world. Possession of soft drugs was decriminalised – not, as many believe, legalised – in 1976, when the government allowed establishments that have become known as coffeeshops to openly trade in da 'erb.

Aside from the facts that retailers must have special dispensation from the local authorities in order to sell soft drugs, that under-18s can't legally buy gear, and that each transaction is limited to five grams per person (still more than enough to get Patsy and Edina through an episode of *Ab Fab*), sales of soft drugs have few restrictions here. Cannabis is still not yet strictly legal – although it may be legalised as a prescription medicine in 2002 – but this is of

Eat, Drink, Smoke, Shop

# Roll up, roll up...

What all coffeeshops have in common is the manner in which hashish and marijuana are sold. Almost all coffeeshops have a menu card either on the bar or just behind it. Most hash and weed is sold in bags of around one gram (about €5), as well as in larger packages. Prices are much of a muchness, although the introduction of the euro may cause a little short-term disparity. However, the quality of the product can vary hugely.

Good coffeeshops have a bewildering array of comestibles. Each shop stocks a number of varieties, detailed on a menu written out with all the plain-as-day disinterestedness you'd see on a restaurant's specials board. The hash side of things is fairly clear, as varieties are usually named after the country of origin. Weed, though, is a bit more complicated. It divides roughly into two categories: bush weeds grown naturally, such as Thai; and Nederwiet or skunk, an indigenous Dutch product grown under UV lights for maximum THC (the active ingredient). As with Guinness in Ireland – well, kinda – the skunk here is worlds away from anything available elsewhere, and caution is advised if you are at all interested in remembering anything. The same caution should be exercised when it comes to most of the spacecake on offer: effects can take an hour or longer to kick in, and return to planet Earth can be a protracted affair.

If you're not used to it, don't drink and draw – note that the majority of coffeeshops don't sell alcohol – and, if you do overdo it, eat or drink something sweet. Tourists passed out on the street from too much spliff are an all too common sight here. Sure, it'll make for a funny story when you get back home, but at the time, you'll never have felt so ill in your life.

The only 'don't' that really needs to be stressed, however, is that you should never buy anything from street dealers. Junkies proliferate in certain areas of town, and if a street deal is not a precursor to a mugging, then you can count yourself lucky. Common sense is all that's needed: there are coffeeshops everywhere. It's also important to bear in mind that there are places where smoking is frowned upon. Not everyone in Amsterdam is going to smile and wave a peace sign if you have a joint in your hand. If in doubt, ask: the worst you'll get is a 'no'. But in the meantime, happy smoking...

---

little concern to the average visitor. If individuals are found with up to 30 grams for their own personal use, then police say it 'will still have no priority as far as investigation is concerned'; translated, this means that you have nothing to worry about. Not only can you openly buy gear at numerous legit establishments all over town, but Dutch police will even turn a blind eye if they see you smoking a 'tulip', a big fat joint resembling the national emblem.

For the first-time visitor, such tolerance can, naturally, take a bit of getting used to. However, it sure as hell beats phoning your dealer on his cellphone and meeting up in some dodgy bar on the other side of town. And though it's tempting to arrive at Centraal Station and head straight for the nearest smoking establishment, however touristy and gaudy it may be, make your first toke in Amsterdam a truly pleasurable experience by checking out one of the fine joints (pun most

definitely intended) described during the course of this chapter. For a survey of the Dutch drugs culture, see p42.

## Coffeeshops

For the **Otherside**, Amsterdam's one and only gay coffeeshop, see p209; for details of women's bar **Saarein II**'s home-growing contest, see p210.

### The Old Centre: Old Side

#### Greenhouse
*Oudezijds Voorburgwal 191 (627 1739/ www.greenhouse.org). Tram 4, 9, 14, 16, 20, 24, 25.* **Open** 9am-1am Mon-Thur, Sun; 9am-3am Fri, Sat. **No credit cards. Map** p306 D3.
The Greenhouse has a worldwide reputation for its menu, which will bring grins of sheer delight to the faces of connoisseurs: it's won countless awards at the Cannabis Cup (*see p184*). Knowledgeable staff

Troubles drift away on the **T-Boat**. *See p151.*

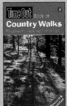

will talk you through the highs of each purchase, which you can accompany with a beer. They also sell seeds by mail order.
**Branches**: Waterlooplein 345 (622 5499); Tolstraat 91 (673 7430).

### Greenhouse Effect

*Warmoesstraat 53 (623 7462). Tram 4, 9, 16, 20, 24, 25.* **Open** 9am-1am Mon-Thur, Sun; 9am-3am Fri, Sat. **No credit cards**. **Map** p306 D2.

Not to be confused with the Greenhouse (*see p149*), this is a small but hip joint that also sells alcohol. However, for some live DJs, a bit more chill-out space, and the delightfully named Cream in your Pants cocktail, take a trip next door to their bar-hotel of the same name (*see p53*). On the other side is Getto, arguably the best gay bar in town (*see p208*).

### T-Boat

*Oudeschans, by No.143 (423 3799). Tram 9, 14, 20.* **Open** 11am-6pm Mon-Thur, Sun; 10am-midnight Fri, Sat. **No credit cards**. **Map** p307 E2.

This is, perhaps, the ultimate 'Amsterdam' experience: a coffeeshop on a boat. A tad tacky, perhaps, and cheap deals are few and far between, but there are great views to be had from the deck, it catches the last of the afternoon sun, and it's conveniently close to Waterlooplein market.

## The Old Centre: New Side

### Abraxas

*Jonge Roelensteeg 12-14 (625 5763/www.abraxas.tv). Tram 4, 9, 16, 20, 24, 25.* **Open** 10am-1am daily. **No credit cards**. **Map** p306 D3.

Comfortable and colourful, this veritable goblin's house is located down a small alley. As well as alcohol, they sell cannabis-infused spacecakes, shakes, bonbons, tea… all that's missing, in fact, is a cannabis drip. There are two Internet terminals (access is free for customers) and DJs play from Thursday to Saturday.

### Dampkring

*Handboogstraat 29 (638 0705/www.dampkring.nl). Tram 1, 2, 5.* **Open** 10am-1am Mon-Thur; 10am-2am Fri, Sat; 11am-1am Sun. **Map** p310 D4.

Dampkring, whose name translates as both 'atmosphere' and 'circle of smoke', shares the same owners as Tweede Kamer (*see p152*); both places sell around 80% organically grown weed. The colourful, ornate coffeeshop – both indoors and out – is handily located just behind the chaotic reaches of Kalverstraat: grab your bags and head here when the chaotic bustle of all those crowds gets too much to handle, as it surely will.

### Homegrown Fantasy

*Nieuwezijds Voorburgwal 87A (627 5683/www.homegrownfantasy.com). Tram 1, 2, 5, 13, 17, 20.* **Open** 9am-midnight Mon-Thur, Sun; 9am-1am Fri, Sat. **No credit cards**. **Map** p306 D2.

When in Rome and all that, for Homegrown Fantasy has one of the widest selections of Dutch-grown weed in Weedsville. The menu and its pleasant environment make it a very popular smokers' venue. The owners also manage the spacious Hartelust next door, a mostly veggie restaurant and one of only a very few eateries in town where you are more than welcome to spliff up.

Pastures new at **La Tertulia**. *See p152.*

Pipe dreams...

## Kadinsky

*Rosmarijnsteeg 9 (624 7023). Tram 1, 2, 5.*
**Open** 10am-1am daily. **No credit cards**.
**Map** p306 D3.
Pastels, plants and sofas decorate this popular hangout. The menu lists a wide range of hash and grass, including descriptions, tastes and effects (from 'well high' to 'very stoned'). The prices are above average, but so is the quality; one day in eight, all deals are discounted by 20%. Try the decent spacecake.

## Tweede Kamer

*Heisteeg 6 (422 2236/www.detweedekamer.nl). Tram 1, 2, 5.* **Open** 10am-1am Mon-Sat; 11am-1am Sun.
**No credit cards**. **Map** p306 D3.
Tweede Kamer is frequented by locals as a result of its deserved reputation for having a wide range of imported grass. Smoky, poky and old Dutch style, you might do well to purchase your grass here but head elsewhere to actually smoke the stuff.

# Western Canal Belt

## Barney's

*Haarlemmerstraat 102 (625 9761/
www.barneys-amsterdam.com). Tram 13, 14,
17, 20.* **Open** *Nov-Feb* 8am-8pm daily. *Mar-Oct* 7am-8pm daily. **No credit cards**. **Map** p306 C2.
This popular, psychedelic cavern serves a range of international breakfasts (from English to Italian) with vegetarian and vegan options. Its closeness to Centraal Station and early opening make it a great post-Schiphol stop-off for that first toke of the trip.

## Siberië

*Brouwersgracht 11 (623 5909/www.siberie.nl). Tram 1, 2, 4, 5, 13, 17, 20.* **Open** 11am-11pm Mon-Thur, Sun; 11am-midnight Fri, Sat. **No credit cards**. **Map** p306 C2.
The friendly and interactive Siberië has regular free horoscope readings, open mic nights, exhibitions and occasional jazz gigs; DJs spin at weekends, too.

But if you want to chill, there are also plenty of board games and on-site net access. The same owners run the small but bright **De Supermarkt** (Frederik Hendrikstraat 69; 486 2479; www.desupermarkt.net) and well-established neighbourhood coffeeshop **De Republiek** (2e Nassaustraat 1a; 682 8431; www.republiek.nl), both just west of the Jordaan.

## La Tertulia

*Prinsengracht 312 (no phone). Tram 7, 10, 13, 14, 17, 20.* **Open** 11am-7pm Tue-Sat. **No credit cards**. **Map** p310 C4.
A stoned-looking Van Gogh is painted on the outer walls of this charming split-level corner coffeeshop where Michelle from *EastEnders* took her first toke years ago. Inside it's bright and airy, weed brownies are served from the sunken counter and there's a miniature garden, complete with fountain. In summer, the canal terrace is a peaceful place to spliff up.

# Southern Canal Belt

## De Rokerij

*Lange Leidsedwarsstraat 41 (622 9442/
www.coffeeshop-nl.com). Tram 1, 2, 5, 6, 7, 10, 20.*
**Open** 10am-1am Mon-Thur, Sun; 10am-3am Fri, Sat.
**No credit cards**. **Map** p310 D5.
A marvellous discovery on an otherwise hideously touristy street by Leidseplein, De Rokerij is a veritable Aladdin's cave: lit by wall-mounted candles and beautiful metal lanterns, it's decorated with colourful Indian art and a variety of seating ranging from mats on the floors to decorative 'thrones'. In line with its central location, it gets very busy on evenings and weekends.
**Branches**: Amstel 8 (620 0484); Singel 8 (422 6643).

# The Jordaan

## Brandend Zand

*Marnixstraat 92 (528 7292/www.brandendzand.nl).
Tram 3, 10.* **Open** 9am-1am Mon-Fri; 10am-1am Sat, Sun. **No credit cards**. **Map** p305 B2.
This friendly and spacious split-level coffeeshop is a real find on this otherwise ugly street. Downstairs is cushion heaven, while upstairs there is Internet access, a pool table and big-screen MTV. The upright designer aquarium may be an aesthetically pleasing addition, but chances are the fish don't really like having to swim so vertically.

## Grey Area

*Oude Leliestraat 2 (420 4301/www.greyarea.nl).
Tram 1, 2, 5, 13, 14, 17, 20.* **Open** noon-8pm Tue-Sun. **No credit cards**. **Map** p306 C3.
A super-friendly atmosphere pervades at Grey Area, with top-quality weed and free refills of organic coffee. Its size means you can enjoy individual attention from the wacky American owners: while you get high, they work the bar and give you the lowdown on parties. On the same street is **Foodism** (No.8; 427 5103), ideal for when you get the munchies.

### Paradox

*1e Bloemdwarsstraat 2 (623 5639). Tram 10, 13, 14, 17, 20.* **Open** 10am-8pm daily. **No credit cards. Map** p305 B3.

When judged next to the many dingy coffeeshops in Amsterdam, Paradox lives up to its name. A bright, characterful contradiction, it serves healthy food, fruit shakes and fresh fruit/vegetable juices on top of all the usual dope. Comfortable and cosy, it's ideal for deep-and-meaningfuls, yet you could probably bring your mum here, too.

### Samenentereng

*2e Laurierdwarsstraat 44 (624 1907). Tram 10, 13, 14, 17, 20.* **Open** *Summer* noon-midnight daily. *Winter* noon-7pm Mon-Thur, Sun; noon-midnight Fri, Sat. **No credit cards. Map** p309 B4.

If you're after a strange experience on a par with one of Mr Benn's visits to the fancy dress shop, then pop into what is ostensibly a bric-a-brac store crammed to the nines. However, tucked away all the way at the back of the store is an unusual African hut-style coffeeshop-cum-conservatory, complete with reggae, rastas and table football. Definitely worth a ganja.

## The Museum Quarter, Vondelpark & the South

### Kashmir Lounge

*Jan Pieter Heijestraat 85-87 (683 2268). Tram 1, 6.* **Open** 10am-1am Mon-Thur; 10am-3am Fri, Sat; 11am-1am Sun. **No credit cards. Map** p309 B6.

Kashmir Lounge's non-central location means cheaper drinks (including alcohol) and more flexible deals on weed. Spacey and spacious, the cushioned area is a great place for a horizontal smoke, especially with DJs playing upbeat lounge in the background (Thur-Sun). The coffeeshop featured in Kees van Ostrum's 2001 movie *Dial 9 for Love*.

## The Pijp

### Yo-Yo

*2e Jan van der Heijdenstraat 79 (entrance on Hemonystraat) (664 7173). Tram 3, 4.* **Open** noon-8pm daily. **No credit cards. Map** p311 F5.

A popular neighbourhood coffeeshop situated out in the Pijp, the women-run Yo-Yo is spacious and simply but pleasingly designed. The atmosphere is intrinsically mellow and chilling all day, and the weed is organic. Don't leave without trying the home-made apple pie.

## Events

For details of the **High Times Cannabis Cup**, *see p184.*

### Global Days Against the Drug War

*Stichting Legalize, Postbus 225, 2300 AE Leiden (070 380 8433/www.legalize.net).*

Events are organised concurrently, usually in late May or early June, in around 30 cities worldwide in an attempt to raise awareness of drugs issues. In Amsterdam, the event includes a remembrance ceremony in Dam Square for victims of drug warfare and a 'Legalize' street party, attracting both party and political animals. Check its website for details nearer the time.

### Highlife Hemp Exhibition

*Highlife, Discover Publishers BV, Huygensweg 7, 5482 TH Schijndel (073 549 8112/fax 073 547 9732/www.highlife.nl).*

Organised by *Highlife* magazine, this event celebrates the cannabis plant, with an emphasis on the industrial uses of hemp. The exhibition holds displays detailing the many uses for the plant, and there are around 100 stalls selling smart drugs, weed tea and coffee, and all sorts of soft drugs paraphernalia. The event's location – it's usually held outside Amsterdam – and dates vary each year, but you can visit the aforementioned *Highlife* website for further details.

## Information

For the **Hash Marijuana Hemp Museum**, *see p82.*

### BCD (Cannabis Retailers Association)

*627 7050.*

Not all coffeeshops belong to the BCD, but members can be identified by a green and white rectangular sticker usually placed near, or on, their door. The BCD also produces a marginally useful free map, available from their members, showing the locations of member coffeeshops.

### Cannabis College

*Oudezijds Achterburgwal 124, Old Centre: Old Side (423 4420/www.cannabiscollege.com).* **Open** noon-7pm Mon-Wed; noon-8.30pm Thur-Sun.

Housed over two floors in a 17th-century registered monument in the Red Light District, the Cannabis College aims to provide the public with objective information about the cannabis plant (including its medicinal use). Run by volunteers, admission is free, but staff do request a small donation if you take a look at their indoor garden.

### Drugs Information Line

*0900 1995.* **Open** 1-9pm Mon-Fri; Dutch recorded message at other times.

A national advice and information number of the Trimbos Institute (Netherlands Institute of Mental Health and Addiction). When you get through, press '0'; you'll then hear a message in Dutch. Press '4' or stay on the line and you'll be connected to an operator, many of whom speak good English. The DIL deals with a wide variety of enquiries, from questions concerning the law to the effects and risks of taking drugs.

*Eat, Drink, Smoke, Shop*

# Shops & Services

Coffeeshops aren't Amsterdam's only retail temptation: there's a wealth of more conventional stores in which to spend, spend, spend.

The Dutch may have decriminalised dope, but shopping is Amsterdam's 100 per cent legal high. Sure, the city doesn't have a reputation as to rival Paris or London, but what it lacks in recognition factor it makes up for in bargains and sheer convenience. Whatever size your wallet, you'll be able to score some nifty gear, often from one-off shops rather than sterile high-street stores.

Perhaps the best way to snag top deals is to saunter around Amsterdam's many sidestreets and canals (for shop-rich areas, *see p157* **Where to head**). Fortunately, the land is so flat and the city centre so compact that even dedicated consumer junkies are unlikely to suffer common ill-effects such as aching feet and legs. And naturally, all the lovely lucre saved by snapping up cheap goodies can always be used for holiday splurges in the city's other, more celebrated types of shops and, um, services.

## Antiques & auctions

**Sotheby's** (550 2200/www.sothebys.com) and **Christie's** (575 5255/www.christies.com) have branches in Amsterdam. *See also p166.*

### Veilinghuis de Nieuwe Zon

*Elandsgracht 68, the Jordaan (623 0343/ www.veilinghuis-de-eland.nl). Tram 7, 10, 17, 20.* **Open** *Viewings* wknd before auctions. *Auctions* every 2mths. **Map** p310 D4.

Auctions of art, antiques and household goods once a month, less frequently in summer. The organisers claim their household auctions are unique: fine antiques are mixed with house clearance items such as furniture and utensils sold off in boxed lots.

## Art & art supplies

For commercial galleries, *see p195.* In addition to these and the shops listed below, it's worth checking the shops at the major museums if it's prints and postcards you're after.

### Art Unlimited

*Keizersgracht 510, Southern Canal Belt (624 8419/www.artunlimited.nl). Tram 1, 2, 5, 20.* **Open** 10am-6pm Mon-Wed, Fri, Sat; 10am-9pm Thur. **Credit** AmEx, DC, MC, V. **Map** p310 C4.

The most comprehensive collection of international photographs and posters in the Netherlands, and the largest collection of postcards in western Europe: a jaw-dropping 40,000, arranged by artist and subject.

Send one back to the folks at home via **Art Unlimited**, but you've got a choice of 40,000.

# The best Shops

### For a bloomin' good time
Bloemenmarkt (see p165).

### For a sparkling smile
De Witte Tandenwinkel (see p172).

### For a stinky stogey
PGC Hajenius (see p176).

### For high flyers
Joe's Vliegerwinkel (see p170).

### For cheeseheads
De Kaaskamer (see p167).

## J Vlieger
*Amstel 34, Southern Canal Belt (623 5834).*
*Tram 4, 9, 14, 16, 20, 24, 25.* **Open** noon-6pm
Mon; 9am-6pm Tue-Fri; 11am-5.30pm Sat.
**Credit** AmEx, DC, MC, V. **Map** p307 E3.
Papers and cards of every description monopolise
the ground floor; upstairs are paints, pens and inks,
as well as small easels and hobby materials.

## Peter van Ginkel
*Bilderdijkstraat 99, Oud West (618 9827). Tram 3,*
*7, 12, 17.* **Open** 10am-5.30pm Mon-Fri; 10am-4pm
Sat. **Credit** MC. **Map** p309 B5.
All creative ilks are catered for by Peter van Ginkel.
Shelves are loaded with paints and pigments, can-
vas, stretcher parts and many types of paper.

## Bookshops

Dutch literature is celebrated with events and
offers in the third week in March. Bookshops
focus on children's books during the second
week in October. Note: English-language books
are pricey here. For book markets, *see p178.*

### General

## American Book Center
*Kalverstraat 185, Old Centre: New Side (625 5537/*
*www.abc.nl). Tram 1, 2, 4, 5, 9, 14, 16, 20, 24, 25.*
**Open** 10am-8pm Mon-Wed, Fri, Sat; 10am-10pm
Thur; 11am-7pm Sun. **Credit** AmEx, DC, MC, V.
**Map** p306 D3.
Since 1972, this shop has dealt in English-language
books and magazines from the UK and US.

## Athenaeum Nieuwscentrum
*Spui 14-16, Old Centre: New Side (bookshop 622*
*6248/news centre 624 2972/www.athenaeum.nl).*
*Tram 1, 2, 5.* **Open** *Bookshop* 11am-6pm Mon;
9.30am-6pm Tue, Wed, Fri, Sat; 9.30am-9pm Thur;
noon-5.30pm Sun. *News centre* 8am-9pm Mon-Sat;
10am-6pm Sun. **Credit** AmEx, MC, V. **Map** p310 D4.

Where Amsterdam's high-brow browsers hang out,
Athenaeum stocks newspapers from all over the
world, as well as a fine choice of magazines, periodicals and books in many languages.

## Book Exchange
*Kloveniersburgwal 58, Old Centre: Old Side (626*
*6266). Tram 4, 9, 14, 20/Metro Nieuwmarkt.*
**Open** 10am-6pm Mon-Fri; 10am-5.30pm Sat;
11.30am-4pm Sun. **No credit cards. Map** p306 D3.
The owner of this book lovers' treasure trove is a
shrewd buyer who'll do trade deals. Choose from a
plethora of second-hand English and American titles
(mainly paperbacks).

## English Bookshop
*Lauriergracht 71, the Jordaan (626 4230). Tram 7,*
*10, 17, 20.* **Open** 1-6pm Tue-Fri; 11am-5pm Sat.
**Credit** AmEx, DC, V. **Map** p309 B4.
Fiction, non-fiction, children's books and cookbooks.
If you're after reading suggestions, try the propri-
etor, who really knows her stuff.

## Waterstone's
*Kalverstraat 152, Old Centre: New Side (638 3821/*
*www.waterstones.co.uk). Tram 1, 2, 4, 5, 9, 14, 16,*
*20, 24, 25.* **Open** 11am-6pm Mon, Sun; 9am-6pm
Tue, Wed; 9am-9pm Thur; 9am-7pm Fri; 10am-7pm
Sat. **Credit** AmEx, MC, V. **Map** p306 D3.
Thousands of book titles, plus magazines and videos,
all in English. The children's section is delightful.

### Specialist

## Architectura & Natura
*Leliegracht 22, Western Canal Belt (623 6186/*
*www.archined.nl/architectura). Tram 13, 14, 17,*
*20.* **Open** noon-6.30pm Mon; 9am-6.30pm Tue-Fri;
9am-6pm Sat. **Credit** AmEx, MC, V. **Map** p306 C3.
The stock here, much in English, includes books
on architectural history, plant life, gardens and
animal studies. Leliegracht 22 is also home to
**Antiquariaat Opbouw**, which deals in antiquar-
ian books on architecture and associated topics.

## Au Bout du Monde
*Singel 313, Western Canal Belt (625 1397/www.au-*
*bout-du-monde.nl). Tram 1, 2, 5.* **Open** noon-6pm
Mon; 10am-6pm Tue, Wed, Fri; 10am-9pm Thur;
10am-5pm Sat. **Credit** MC, V. **Map** p306 C3.
Au Bout du Monde specialises in Eastern philosophy and religion, and stocks a daunting selection of
titles on subjects ranging from psychology to sexuality. There are also magazines, plus related paraphernalia such as incense, cards and videos.

## Intertaal
*Van Baerlestraat 76, Museum Quarter (575 6756/*
*www.intertaal.nl). Tram 3, 5, 12, 16, 20.* **Open** 9am-
6pm Mon-Wed, Fri; 9am-9pm Thur; 10am-5pm Sat.
**Credit** AmEx, MC, V. **Map** p310 D6.
Dealing in language books, CDs and teaching aids,
Intertaal will be of use to all learners, whether grap-
pling with basic Dutch or advancing their English.

### Lambiek

*Kerkstraat 78, Southern Canal Belt (626 7543/*
*www.lambiek.nl). Tram 1, 2, 5.* **Open** 11am-6pm
Mon-Fri; 11am-5pm Sat; 1-5.30pm Sun.
**Credit** AmEx, DC, MC, V. **Map** p310 D4.
Lambiek, founded in 1968, claims to be the world's
oldest comic shop and has thousands of books from
around the world. Its on-site cartoonists' gallery
hosts exhibitions of comic art every two months.

### Pied-à-Terre

*Singel 393, Old Centre: New Side (627 4455/*
*www.piedaterre.nl). Tram 1, 2, 5.* **Open** *Sept-Mar*
11am-6pm Mon-Fri; 10am-5pm Sat. *Apr-Aug* 11am-
6pm Mon-Wed, Fri; 11am-9pm Thur; 10am-5pm Sat.
**No credit cards. Map** p310 D4.
Travel books, international guides and maps for
active holidays. Adventurous walkers should talk
to the helpful staff here before a trip out of town.

## Department stores

### De Bijenkorf

*Dam 1, Old Centre: New Side (621 8080/*
*www.bijenkorf.nl). Tram 1, 2, 4, 5, 9, 13, 14, 16, 17,*
*20, 24, 25.* **Open** 11am-6pm Mon; 9.30am-6pm Tue,
Wed, Fri, Sat; 9.30am-9pm Thur; noon-6pm Sun.
**Credit** AmEx, DC, MC, V. **Map** p306 D3.
Amsterdam's most notable department store has a
great household goods department and a decent mix
of clothing – both designer and own-label – kidswear,
jewellery, cosmetics, shoes and accessories. The Chill
Out department caters to funky youngsters in need
of streetwear, clubwear, wacky foodstuffs and kitsch
accessories, while the store's restaurant, La Ruche,
is a good lunch spot. The Sinterklaas and Christmas
displays are extravagant and hugely popular.

### Hema

*Kalvertoren, Singel 457, Southern Canal Belt*
*(422 8988/www.hema.nl). Tram 1, 2, 4, 5, 9, 14,*
*16, 20, 24, 25.* **Open** 11am-7pm Mon; 9.30am-7pm
Tue, Wed, Fri; 9.30am-9pm Thur; 9.30am-6pm
Sun. **No credit cards**. **Map** p306 D3.
Imagine an American five-and-dime store with a
slightly upmarket take on things. Given the prices,
quality is high: canny buys include casual clothes,
kids' clothing, swimwear, underwear, household
items and stationery. Hema also sells deli foods and
wines. Three main branches are listed here, but there
are seven others in town: call 311 4411 for details.
**Branches:** Ferdinand Bolstraat 93A, the Pijp (676
3222); Borgerstraat 142, Oud West (683 4511);
Nieuwendijk 174-6, Old Centre: New Side (623 4176).

### Maison de Bonneterie

*Rokin 140-2, Old Centre: New Side (531 3400).*
*Tram 1, 2, 4, 5, 9, 14, 20, 24, 25.* **Open** 1-5.30pm
Mon; 10am-5.30pm Tue, Wed, Fri, Sat; 10am-9pm
Thur; noon-5.30pm Sun. **Credit** AmEx, DC, MC, V.
**Map** p306 D3.
This venerable institution stocks quality men's and
women's clothing 'By Appointment to Her Majesty
Queen Beatrix'. As you might expect, it's a pretty

A comic turn: **Lambiek**.

conservative affair: the in-store Ralph Lauren boutique is about as outlandish as it gets. There's also
a fine household goods department.

### Metz & Co

*Leidsestraat 34-6, Southern Canal Belt (520 7020).*
*Tram 1, 2, 5.* **Open** 11am-6pm Mon; 9.30am-6pm
Tue, Wed, Fri, Sat; 9.30am-9pm Thur; noon-5pm Sun.
**Credit** AmEx, DC, MC, V. **Map** p310 D4.
Metz is wonderful for upmarket gifts: designer fur-
niture, glass and Liberty-style fabrics and scarves
are all available. For lunch with a terrific view of the
city make for the top-floor restaurant, which is pop-
ular for business lunches. During the festive season,
Metz & Co's Christmas shop will put the holiday
spirit back into even the most Scroogeian customer.
**Branch:** Schiphol Airport, Zuid (653 5060).

### Vroom & Dreesmann

*Kalverstraat 203, Old Centre: New Side (622*
*0171/www.vroomendreesmann.nl). Tram 4, 9, 14,*
*16, 20, 24, 25.* **Open** 11am-7pm Mon; 10am-7pm
Tue, Wed, Fri; 10am-9pm Thur; 10am-6pm Sat; noon-
6pm Sun. **Credit** AmEx, MC, V. **Map** p306 D3.
V&D means good quality at prices just a step up
from Hema (*see above*). There's a staggering array
of toiletries, cosmetics, leather goods and watches,
clothing and underwear for the whole family,
kitchen items, suitcases, CDs and videos. The bakery, Le Marché, sells delicious bread, quiches and
sandwiches, with La Place restaurant offering all
kinds of other morsels for you to scoff.

## Drugs

### Chills & Thrills

*Nieuwendijk 17, Old Centre: New Side (638 0015).*
*Tram 13, 14, 17, 20.* **Open** noon-8pm Mon-Wed;
11am-9pm Thur; 11am-10pm Fri-Sun. **No credit
cards. Map** p306 C2.

# Where to head

Although reckless abandon and aimless drifting can make for some memorable shopping trips, sometimes having a plan of action doesn't hurt. So, here's a cheat sheet detailing the general characteristics of Amsterdam's main shopping districts to help make your spending spree a breeze.

## DAMSTRAAT

A street at war with its former self, Damstraat is fighting to ditch the sleaze and grow into a boutique-lined oasis. Alas, its proximity to the Red Light District means laddish types can impinge on this otherwise lovely neighbourhood.

## MAGNA PLAZA

Right behind Dam Square, this architectural treat was once a post office. Its reincarnation as a five-floor mall is beloved by tourists, though locals are less keen.

## KALVERSTRAAT AND NIEUWENDIJK

Kalverstraat (*pictured*) and Nieuwendijk are where locals come for consumer kicks. Shops here are largely unexciting, yet they still get insanely busy on Sundays. Still, it's pedestrian-only, so you can forget the dreaded bike menace and focus on the tills.

## LEIDSESTRAAT

Connecting Koningsplein and Leidseplein, Leidsestraat is peppered with fine shoe shops and boutiques. Even though the street had a facelift in 2001, you'll still have to dodge trams to shop there. Cyclists: note that bikes aren't allowed here... and police do notice.

## NINE STREETS

The small streets connecting Prinsengracht, Keizersgracht and Herengracht between Raadhuisstraat and Leidsegracht offer a diverse density of boutiques, antiques and speciality stores.

## THE JORDAAN

Tiny backstreets laced with twisting canals, cosy boutiques, lush markets, bakeries, galleries, restful and old fashioned cafés and bars... the Jordaan captures the spirit of Amsterdam like nowhere else.

## PC HOOFTSTRAAT

What was once Amsterdam's elite shopping spot has taken a turn for the worse. PC Hooftstraat's designer stores remain, but the street reeks of new money and B-list celebs.

## SPIEGELKWARTIER

Across from the Rijksmuseum and centred on Spiegelgracht, this area is packed with antiques shops selling authentic treasures at accordingly high prices. Dress for success and keep your nose in the air.

## THE PIJP

This bustling district is notable mainly for the Albert Cuypmarkt and its ethnic food shops.

A wide selection of pipes and bongs sits alongside the likes of postcards, T-shirts, mushrooms and seeds. The staff will happily show you the portable mini-vaporiser that vaporises pure THC, giving you a clean, smokeless hit.

### Conscious Dreams

*Kerkstraat 93, Southern Canal Belt (626 6907/ www.consciousdreams.nl). Tram 1, 2, 5.* **Open** 11am-7pm Mon-Wed; 11am-8pm Thur-Sat; 2-6pm Sun. **No credit cards. Map** p310 D4.
Conscious Dreams was the original proponent of the smart drugs wave in Amsterdam. The staff here really know their stuff – the owner worked as a drugs adviser for five years – and you're more or less guaranteed to find whatever you're after. **Branch**: *Kokopelli* Warmoesstraat 12, Old Centre: Old Side (421 7000).

### Head Shop

*Kloveniersburgwal 39, Old Centre: Old Side (624 9061/www.headshop.nl). Tram 4, 9, 14, 16, 20, 24, 25/Metro Nieuwmarkt.* **Open** 11am-6pm Mon-Sat. **No credit cards. Map** p306 D3.
Little has changed at the Head Shop since the 1960s – aside from the irritatingly whizzy website – and the store is worth a visit for nostalgic reasons, if nothing else. There are wide selections of pipes, bongs, jewellery, incense and books, and mushrooms and spores – so greenfingered types can cultivate their own – can be had here. Like, *maaan.*

### Hemp Works

*Niewendijk 13, Old Centre: New Side (421 1762/ www.xs4all.nl/~hemp). Tram 1, 2, 5, 13, 17, 20.* **Open** 11.30am-7pm daily. **Credit** AmEx, DC, MC, V. **Map** p306 C2.

**Vroom & Dreesmann.** *See p156.*

It's one of the last retailers targeting hemp clothes and products, but Hemp Works has had to diversify into seed sales and hallucinogenic mushrooms.

### Interpolm

*Prins Hendrikkade 11, Old Centre: Old Side (627 7750/www.interpolm.nl). Tram 1, 2, 4, 5, 9, 16, 17, 20, 24, 25/Metro Centraal Station.* **Open** 11.30am-7pm daily. **Credit** AmEx, MC, V. **Map** p306 D2.
Everything needed to set up a grow centre at home. For those who think we only mean drugs, guess again: Interpolm carries hydroponics equipment and bio-growth books and videos that cross over for green-fingered folk with other crops in mind.

## Electronics

### Expert Mons

*Utrechtsestraat 80-2, Southern Canal Belt (624 5082). Tram 4/Metro Waterlooplein.* **Open** 9am-6pm Mon-Fri; 10am-5pm Sat. **Credit** AmEx, MC, V. **Map** p311 E4.
Washing machines, TVs, stereos, blenders, refrigerators and all other electronic appliances both big and small, most at competitive prices.

## Fabrics & trimmings

### Capsicum

*Oude Hoogstraat 1, Old Centre: Old Side (623 1016). Tram 4, 9, 14, 16, 20, 24, 25.* **Open** 1-6pm Mon; 10am-6pm Tue, Wed, Fri, Sat; 10am-9pm Thur. **Credit** AmEx, DC, MC, V. **Map** p306 D3.
All the fabrics here are made from natural fibres, such as cotton woven in India. Staff spin the provenance of each fabric into the sale. A gem.

### Knopen Winkel

*Wolvenstraat 14, Western Canal Belt (624 0479). Tram 1, 2, 5.* **Open** 1-6pm Mon (except summer); 11am-6pm Tue-Fri; 11am-5pm Sat. **No credit cards. Map** p310 C4.
This unusual specialist boasts a vast selection of buttons – both old and new – from all over the world. If it's beads you're after, try **Copenhagen 1001 Kralen** (Rozengracht 54; 624 3681).

### Stoffen & Fourituren Winkel a Boeken Nieuwe

*Hoogstraat 31, Old Centre: Old Side (626 7205). Tram 4, 9, 16, 20, 24, 25.* **Open** noon-6pm Mon; 10am-6pm Tue, Wed, Fri; 10am-8pm Thur. **Credit** MC, V. **Map** p307 E3.
The Boeken family has been hawking theatrical fabrics since 1920, but always keeps astoundingly up to date. Just try to find somewhere else with this kind of variety: latex, Lycra, fake fur and sequins galore.

## Fashion

### Children

The shops listed below carry new/quality kids' togs. Funky vintage clothes can be found at **Noordermarkt**; those on a budget should try **Albert Cuypmarkt** (for both, *see p166*).

### Geboortewinkel Amsterdam

*Bosboom Toussaintstraat 22-4, Museum Quarter (683 1806). Tram 3, 7, 10, 12.* **Open** 1-5.30pm Mon; 10am-5.30pm Tue-Fri; 10am-5pm Sat. **Map** p310 C5.
A beautiful range of maternity and baby clothes (including premature sizes) in cotton, wool and linen. You'll also find baby articles, cotton nappy systems and videos about childbirth.

### 't Klompenhuisje

*Nieuwe Hoogstraat 9A, Old Centre: Old Side (622 8100). Tram 4, 9, 14/Metro Nieuwmarkt.* **Open** 10am-6pm Mon-Sat. **Credit** AmEx, DC, MC, V. **Map** p307 E3.
Delightful crafted and reasonably priced shoes, traditional clogs and handmade leather and woollen slippers from baby sizes up to size 35.

### 't Schooltje

*Overtoom 87, Museum Quarter (683 0444). Tram 1, 2, 5, 6.* **Open** 1-6pm Mon; 9am-6pm Tue, Wed, Fri; 9am-9pm Thur; 9.30am-5.30pm Sat. **Credit** AmEx, DC, MC, V. **Map** p309 B6.
Well-heeled and well-dressed kids (babies and children aged up to 16) are clothed and shod here. The ranges are attractive but costly.

### Clubwear

For hardcore club aficionados, life has just become a whole lot easier. Not only are the number and size of Amsterdam's clubwear shops growing, but they have all gravitated to the Spuistraat, making this the official cyber-strip one-stop-shopping trip.

### Clubwear House
*Spuistraat 242, Old Centre: New Side (622 8766/ www.clubwearhouse.nl). Tram 1, 2, 5.* **Open** 1-6pm Mon, Sun; 11am-6pm Tue, Wed, Fri, Sat; 11am-9pm Thur. **Credit** AmEx, DC, MC, V. **Map** p306 C3.
Clubby clothes from all around the world, plus from its own label, Wearhouse 2000, and an in-house designer. The staff of clubbers know their proverbial onions and will be able to help you out with flyers or pre-sale tickets. DJ tapes are also available.

### Cyberdog
*Spuistraat 250, Old Centre: New Side (330 6385/ www.cyberdog.net). Tram 1, 2, 5.* **Open** 2-6pm Mon; 11am-7pm Tue, Wed, Fri, Sat; 11am-9pm Thur. **Credit** AmEx, DC, MC, V. **Map** p306 C3.
Their mission is 'to stay one step ahead in the future of fashion', but to infinity and beyond is more like it. Rack after rack of spacey trippy tech creations for the most dedicated clubbers.

### Housewives on Fire
*Spuistraat 102, Old Centre: New Side (422 1067). Tram 1, 2, 5.* **Open** 10am-7pm Mon-Wed, Fri, Sat; 10am-9pm Thur. *May-Aug* also noon-6pm Sun. **Credit** MC, V. **Map** p306 C3.
New and second-hand clothes and accessories, an in-house hair salon offering colours, extensions and dreads, henna tattoos and gaudy make-up, nail polishes and body paints, plus in-house DJs and flyers.

## Designer

### Cora Kemperman
*Leidsestraat 72, Southern Canal Belt (625 1284). Tram 1, 2, 5.* **Open** noon-6pm Mon, Sun; 10am-6pm Tue, Wed, Fri, Sat; 10am-9pm Thur. **Credit** MC, V. **Map** p310 D4.
Garments here are about reams of fine fabric used to create a voluminous avant-garde look. Whether you've got something you'd prefer to hide or just like to shroud yourself in layers, let Cora do the honours.

### Khymo
*Leidsestraat 9, Southern Canal Belt (622 2137). Tram 1, 2, 5.* **Open** noon-6pm Mon; 10am-6pm Tue, Wed, Fri, Sat; 9.30am-9pm Thur; 1-5pm Sun. **Credit** AmEx, DC, MC, V. **Map** p310 D4.
Twenty- to fortysomethings, both male and female, go for the trendy garb here. Among the labels on offer are Plein Sud, Evisu and Amaya Arzuaga.

### Megazino
*Rozengracht 207, the Jordaan (330 1031). Tram 13, 14, 17, 20.* **Open** 10am-6pm Tue, Wed, Fri, Sat; 10am-9pm Thur; noon-6pm Sun. **Credit** AmEx, DC, MC, V. **Map** p305 B3.
Huge discounts on big names like Versace, DKNY, Cerruti, Guess and Armani. There are no shoddy duds here, just classics from last season's collections.

### Razzmatazz
*Wolvenstraat 19, Western Canal Belt (420 0483/ www.razzmatazz.nl). Tram 13, 14, 17, 20.* **Open** 1-6pm Mon, Sun; noon-6pm Tue, Wed, Fri, Sat; noon-7pm Thur. **Credit** AmEx, DC, MC, V. **Map** p310 C4.
Despite the staff being a pain, Razz is still a must-see on account of its designers, from Westwood's Anglomania line to Masaki Matsushima.

### 21R
*Oude Hoogstraat 10-12, Old Centre: Old Side (421 6329). Tram 4, 9, 14, 16, 24, 25.* **Open** noon-7pm Mon; 10.30am-7pm Tue, Wed, Fri, Sat; 10.30am-9pm Thur; noon-6pm Sun. **Credit** AmEx, DC, MC, V. **Map** p306 D3.
This funky number's just for the boys. Two shops side by side on Oude Hoogstraat offer urban streetwear and killer threads from the likes of Helmut Lang, Psycho Cowboy and Anglomania.

## Glasses & contact lenses

### Brilmuseum/Brillenwinkel
*Gasthuismolensteeg 7, Western Canal Belt (421 2414). Tram 1, 2, 5.* **Open** noon-5.30pm Wed-Fri; noon-5pm Sat. **No credit cards. Map** p306 C3.
Officially this 'shop' is an opticians' museum, but don't let that put off. The fascinating exhibits are of glasses through the ages, and most of the pairs you see are also for sale.

**Cyberdog**. Glowsticks optional.

### Donald E Jongejans
*Noorderkerkstraat 18, the Jordaan (624 6888).*
*Tram 3, 10.* **Open** 11am-6pm daily.
**No credit cards. Map** p305 B2.
Friendly staff at this vintage frame specialist stress
that they sell unworn frames dating from the mid-
1800s to the present day. Most pairs are at fabulously
low prices, and are built to last. A complete treat.

### Hans Anders Optitien
*Van Woustraat 161, the Pijp (676 8995/*
*www.hansanders.nl). Tram 4, 20.* **Open** 8.30am-6pm
Mon-Wed, Fri; 8.30am-6pm, 7-9pm Thur; 9am-5pm
Sat. **Credit** V. **Map** p311 F6.
The cheapest contact lenses in town. For under €40
you'll get an off-the-peg pair that lasts six months.
**Branches**: Jan Evertsenstraat 84, West (683 4791);
Ferdinand Bolstraat 118, the Pijp (664 1879).

## Hats & handbags

Many outdoor markets have huge selections of
hats and bags. For warm winter gear and knock-
off bags at low prices, hit **Albert Cuypmarkt**.

### Cellarrich Connexion
*Haarlemmerdijk 98, the Jordaan (626 5526).*
*Tram 1, 2, 4, 5, 13, 14, 16, 17, 20, 24, 25.*
**Open** 1-6pm Mon; 10am-6pm Tue-Fri; 10am-5pm
Sat. **Credit** AmEx, DC, MC, V. **Map** p305 B2.
Nab a sophisticated Dutch handbag in materials
from leather to plastic. Many (but not all) of the cre-
ations are produced locally by four Dutch designers.

### De Hoed van Tijn
*Nieuwe Hoogstraat 15, Old Centre: Old Side (623
2759). Tram 4, 9, 14, 16, 24, 25.* **Open** 11am-6pm
Mon-Sat. **Credit** AmEx, DC, MC, V. **Map** p307 E3.
Mad hatters can delight in this vast array of som-
breros, Homburgs, bonnets and caps. The range
includes period hats dating from 1900, as well as a
range of second-hand, new and handcrafted items.

### De Petsalon
*Hazenstraat 3, the Jordaan (624 7385). Tram 1,
2, 5, 13, 14, 17, 20.* **Open** noon-6pm Mon-Sat.
**Credit** AmEx, DC, MC, V. **Map** p310 C4.
Don some instant individuality with a kooky handmade hat from local designer Ans Wesseling, available in this small shop close to Prinsengracht.

## High street

### America Today
*Ground floor, Magna Plaza, Spuistraat 137, Old
Centre: New Side (638 8447/www.americatoday.nl).
Tram 1, 2, 5, 13, 14, 17, 20.* **Open** 11am-7pm Mon;
10am-7pm Tue, Wed, Fri-Sun; 10am-9pm Thur.
**Credit** AmEx, DC, MC, V. **Map** p306 C2.
This money-spinning giant started as the tiniest of
ventures; today it sells American classics (Converse,
Timberland and the like) at incredibly cheap prices.
**Branch**: Sarphatistraat 48, Southern Canal Belt
(638 9847).

Hats off to **De Hoed van Tijn**.

### Exota
*Hartenstraat 10, Western Canal Belt (620 9102).
Tram 1, 2, 5, 13, 14, 17, 20.* **Open** 11am-6pm Mon;
10am-6pm Tue-Sat; 1-5pm Sun. **Credit** AmEx, DC,
MC, V. **Map** p306 C3.
Tread the fine line between high street and street
fashion with this funky little shop's original selec-
tion of simple yet stylish clothes and accessories.
**Branch**: Nieuwe Leliestraat 32, the Jordaan (420 6884).

### Hennes & Mauritz
*Kalverstraat 125-9, Old Centre: New Side (624 0624).
Tram 1, 2, 4, 5, 9, 14, 16, 20, 24, 25.* **Open** noon-
6pm Mon, Sun; 10am-6pm Tue, Wed, Fri, Sat; 10am-
9pm Thur. **Credit** AmEx, DC, MC, V. **Map** p306 D3.
Prices range from reasonable to ultra low; quality,
too, is variable. Clothes for men, women, teens and
kids are trend-conscious, plus there are often updates
of classics. Branches at Kalverstraat 114-18 and
Nieuwendijk 141 have Big is Beautiful departments.
**Branches** are numerous; check the phone book.

### Sissy Boy
*Kalverstraat 199, Old Centre: New Side (638
9305/www.sissy-boy.nl). Tram 1, 2, 4, 5, 9, 14, 16,
20, 24, 25.* **Open** noon-6pm Mon, Sun; 10am-6pm
Tue, Wed, Fri, Sat; 10am-9pm Thur. **Credit** AmEx,
DC, MC, V. **Map** p306 D3.
Pared-down, urban garb for both sexes. An own-
label range is cleverly crafted by a team of interna-
tional and Dutch designers. Chic staples like French
Connection and Migel Stapper are also available.

### Zara
*Kalverstraat 67-9, Old Centre: New Side (530 4050).
Tram 1, 2, 4, 5, 9, 14, 16, 20, 24, 25.* **Open** noon-
6pm Mon, Sun; 10am-6pm Tue, Wed, Fri, Sat; 10am-
9pm Thur. **Credit** AmEx, MC, V. **Map** p306 D3.

**Eat, Drink, Smoke, Shop**

# A girl's best friend

Amsterdam is well known for its long and remarkable heritage in the diamond industry (for the full story, *see p15* **Diamond geezers**). Indeed, it's a heritage that's still marketed heavily to this day. To be honest, Amsterdam's famed diamond shops – with their incredible sparklers – are as much tourist attractions as they are retail outlets. However, to experience an aspirational brush with luxury, take a tour around any one of them. Just remember: falling in love with a sparkler is the easy bit – figuring out how you're going to pay for it may prove to be a little more tricky...

### Amsterdam Diamond Centre
*Rokin 1-5, Old Centre: New Side (624 5787).* Tram 4, 9, 14, 16, 20, 24, 25. **Open** 10am-6pm Mon-Wed, Fri-Sun; 10.30am-8.30pm Thur. **Credit** AmEx, DC, MC, V. **Map** p306 D2.

### Coster Diamonds
*Paulus Potterstraat 2-6, Museum Quarter (305 5555/www.costerdiamonds.com).* Tram 2, 3, 5. **Open** 9am-5pm daily. **Credit** AmEx, DC, MC, V. **Map** p310 D6.

### Gassan Diamond BV
*Nieuwe Uilenburgerstraat 173-5, Old Centre: Old Side (622 5333).* Tram 9, 14, 20. **Open** 9am-5pm daily. **Credit** AmEx, DC, MC, V. **Map** p307 E2.

### Stoeltie Diamonds
*Wagenstraat 13-17, Western Canal Belt (623 7601).* Tram 4, 9, 14, 20. **Open** 8.30am-5pm daily. **Credit** AmEx, MC, V. **Map** p307 E3.

### Van Moppes & Zoon
*Albert Cuypstraat 2-6, the Pijp (676 7601).* Tram 16, 24, 25. **Open** 9am-5pm daily. **Credit** AmEx, DC, MC, V. **Map** p311 E6.

---

Three cheers for entering the European shopping community: Zara has finally arrived in Amsterdam. Rifle through clothes that are off-the-runway fresh and shoes duplicating the hottest new styles, all at absurdly reasonable prices.

## Jewellery

For diamonds, *see above* **A girl's best friend**.

### De Blue Gold Fish
*Rozengracht 17, the Jordaan (623 3134). Tram 13, 14, 17, 20.* **Open** 11am-6.30pm Mon-Sat. **Credit** AmEx, DC, MC, V. **Map** p305 B3.
A great selection of funky jewellery and housewares for those lucky enough to have it all. Sometimes the staff can get a little arsey.

### Grimm Sieraden
*Grimburgwal 9, Old Centre: Old Side (622 0501). Tram 16, 20, 24, 25.* **Open** 11am-6pm Tue-Fri; 11am-5pm Sat. **Credit** AmEx, DC, MC, V. **Map** p306 D3.
Elize Lutz's appealing gallery shop features the freshest jewellery designers; she always makes a point of stocking the most wearable pieces from the latest cutting-edge ranges.

### Jorge Cohen Edelsmid
*Singel 414, Southern Canal Belt (623 8646). Tram 1, 2, 5, 10.* **Open** 10am-6pm Mon-Fri; 11am-6pm Sat. **Credit** AmEx, DC, MC, V. **Map** p310 D4.
Get your mitts on the kind of art deco-inspired jewellery you'd be proud to pass off as the real thing. The shop creates its charming pieces using a combination of salvaged jewellery, antique and new stones and silver.

## Large sizes

### G&G Special Sizes
*Prinsengracht 514, Southern Canal Belt (622 6339). Tram 1, 2, 5.* **Open** 9am-5.30pm Tue, Wed, Fri; 9am-5.30pm, 7-9pm Thur; 9am-5pm Sat. **Credit** AmEx, DC, MC, V. **Map** p310 D5.
The big news is that G&G stock a full range of men's clothing from sizes 58 to 75. Pay a bit extra and sales assistants will also tailor garments to fit.

### Mateloos
*Bilderdijkstraat 62, Oud West (683 2384). Tram 3, 12, 13, 14, 17, 20.* **Open** 1-6pm Mon; 10am-6pm Tue, Wed, Fri; 10am-9pm Thur; 10am-5pm Sat. **Credit** AmEx, DC, MC, V. **Map** p309 B5.
Two fabulous shops cater for curves with an enormous variety of clothing for women from sizes 44 to 60. Mateloos I offers sumptuous eveningwear and business clothes, while Mateloos II (Kinkerstraat 77, 689 4720) has a dizzying array of leisure- and sportswear, fake furs, hip hop pants and denims.

## Lingerie

### Hunkemöller
*Kalverstraat 162, Old Centre: New Side (623 6032). Tram 1, 2, 4, 5, 9, 14, 16, 20, 24, 25.* **Open** 11am-6pm Mon; 9.30am-6pm Tue, Wed, Fri, Sat; 9.30am-9pm Thur; noon-6pm Sun. **Credit** AmEx, DC, MC, V. **Map** p306 D3.
Female fancy pants should check out this chain with six branches in and around Amsterdam (call 035 646 5413 for details of others). The undies are attractive, yet simply designed and reasonably priced.

Eat, Drink, Smoke, Shop

### Robin's Bodywear

*Nieuwe Hoogstraat 20, Old Centre: Old Side (620 1552). Tram 4, 9, 14, 16, 24, 25.* **Open** 1-6pm Mon-Wed; 11am-6pm Thur, Fri; 11am-5.30pm Sat. **Credit** AmEx, MC, V. **Map** p307 E3.

Larger than the typical women's lingerie shop, Robin's has underwear, swimwear and hosiery by Naf-Naf, Calvin Klein, Lou and others.

### Tothem Underwear

*Nieuwezijds Voorburgwal 149, Old Centre: New Side (623 0641). Tram 1, 2, 4, 5, 9, 13, 14, 16, 17, 20, 24, 25.* **Open** 1-5.30pm Mon; 9.30am-5.30pm Tue, Wed, Fri; 9.30am-9pm Thur; 9.30am-5pm Sat. **Credit** AmEx, DC, MC, V. **Map** p306 D3.

This men's underwear shop mainly sells designer items by well-known names along the lines of Hom, Calvin Klein and Body Art.

## Repairs & cleaning

### Clean Brothers

*Kerkstraat 56, Southern Canal Belt (622 0273). Tram 16, 24, 25.* **Open** 7am-7pm daily. **No credit cards.** **Map** p311 E4.

Washing and dry-cleaning in a relatively central location. Prices are reasonable.

### Luk's Schoenservice

*Prinsengracht 500, Southern Canal Belt (623 1937). Tram 1, 2, 5, 6, 7, 10.* **Open** 9am-5.30pm Tue-Fri; 9am-5pm Sat. **No credit cards.** **Map** p310 D5.

Reliable and speedy shoe repairs.

## Shoes

The best selections of men's and women's shoes can be had at shops on **Leidsestraat** or **Kalverstraat**, while the best bargains in second-hand shoes are to be found at **Waterlooplein**, and **Noordermarkt** on Mondays; for both, *see p166*.

### Big Shoe

*Leliegracht 12, Western Canal Belt (622 6645). Tram 13, 14, 17, 20.* **Open** 10am-6pm Wed, Fri, Sat; 10am-9pm Thur. **Credit** AmEx, DC, MC, V. **Map** p306 C3.

Fashionable footwear for men and women in large sizes only. Every women's shoe on display is available in sizes 42-46.

### Kenneth Cole

*Leidsestraat 20-22, Southern Canal Belt (627 6012/ www.kencole.com). Tram 1, 2, 5.* **Open** noon-6pm Mon-Wed, Fri, Sat; 10am-9pm Thur; 1-5pm Sun. **Credit** AmEx, MC, V. **Map** p310 D4.

Kenneth Cole stocks its own conservatively styled shoes, plus boots from the likes of Timberland and Doc Martens. Stock changes often, and bargains can be had during the frequent sales.

### Paul Warmer

*Leidsestraat 41, Southern Canal Belt (427 8011). Tram 1, 2, 5.* **Open** noon-6pm Mon-Wed, Fri, Sat; 10am-9pm Thur; 1-5pm Sun. **Credit** AmEx, MC, V. **Map** p310 D4.

**Eat, Drink, Smoke, Shop**

The art deco-inspired jewellery at **Jorge Cohen Edelsmid**. *See p162.*

Fashionista heaven, Paul Warmer caters to men and women with very refined tastes in footwear. Expect to find top stylings from Gucci, YSL, Roberto Cavalli and Charles Jourdan among others.

### Seventy Five
*Nieuwe Hoogstraat 24, Old Centre: Old Side (626 4611). Tram 4, 9, 14, 20/Metro Nieuwmarkt.* **Open** noon-6pm Mon; 10am-6pm Tue-Sat. **Credit** MC, V. **Map** p307 E3.
Trainers for folk who don't have sporting in mind: high fashion styles from Nike, Puma, Converse, Acupuncture, Diesel and many more.

### Shoe Baloo
*Koningsplein 7 (men's shoes) and Leidsestraat 10 (women's shoes), Southern Canal Belt (626 7993). Tram 1, 2, 5.* **Open** noon-6pm Mon; 10am-6pm Tue, Wed, Fri, Sat; 10am-9pm Thur; noon-5pm Sun. **Credit** AmEx, DC, MC, V. **Map** p310 D4.
Amsterdam's best shop for designer shoes has expanded. You'll now find men's and women's footwear from Costme Nationale, Prada and Miu Miu in two separate stores, a couple of blocks apart. **Branch:** PC Hooftstraat 80, Museum Quarter (671 2210).

Shoe heaven: **Paul Warmer**. *See p163.*

## Street

Those interested in looking good but paying less can find relaxed streetwear styles in **Waterlooplein Market** (*see p166*).

### Henxs Sint
*Sint Antoniesbreestraat 136, Old Centre: Old Side (416 7786). Tram 4, 9, 14/Metro Nieuwmarkt.* **Open** 1-6pm Mon, Sun; 11am-6pm Tue-Sat. **No credit cards. Map** p307 E3.
A skater's paradise of graffiti magazines and hip hop styles. DJs spin as you scan the urban gear from local label g.sus, stacked on rails alongside casual duds from Carhartt.

### Independent Outlet
*Vijzelstraat 77, Southern Canal Belt (421 2096/ www.outlet.nl). Tram 16, 24, 25.* **Open** 1pm-6pm Mon; 11am-6pm Tue,Wed, Fr, Sat; 11am-9pm Thur. **No credit cards. Map** p310 D4.
Customised boards, Vans shoes and labels such as Fred Perry are some of the things in store at this temple to street cool. The great selection of punk imports is the finishing piercing through the brow of this skate-punk heaven.

### RDLFS
*Magna Plaza, Spuistraat 137, Old Centre: New Side (623 1214/www.rdlfs.nl). Tram 1, 2, 5, 13, 17, 20.* **Open** 11am-7pm Mon; 10am-7pm Tue, Wed, Fri, Sat; 10am-9pm Thur; noon-7pm Sun. **Credit** AmEx, MC, V. **Map** p306 C3.
An inline skate and skateboard outlet with its ear to the street. T-shirts and trainers are mainstays among its desperately hip customers. **Branches** are numerous; check the phone book.

### RMF Streetwear
*Oudezijds Voorburgwal 189, Old Centre: Old Side (626 2954/www.rmfstreetwear.demon.nl). Tram 4, 9, 14, 16, 20, 24, 25.* **Open** 10am-6pm Mon-Wed, Fri; 10am-9pm Thur; 10am-5pm Sat, Sun. **Credit** AmEx, DC, MC, V. **Map** p306 D3.
RMF stocks American brands that can be tricky to find over here, such as Sir Benni Miles and Menace. It's no place for bargains, but the gear here is unique.

## Vintage & second-hand

Loads of fab vintage clothes and accessories can be found (and often at cheaper prices) at **Noordermarkt** and **Waterlooplein**.

### Lady Day
*Hartenstraat 9, Western Canal Belt (623 5820). Tram 1, 2, 5, 20.* **Open** 11am-6pm Mon-Wed, Fri, Sat; 11am-9pm Thur; noon-5pm Sun. **Credit** AmEx, MC, V. **Map** p306 C3.
Beautifully tailored second-hand and period suits, and sportswear classics. Period wedge shoes, pumps and accessories complete the stylish ensemble.

### Laura Dols
*Wolvenstraat 7, Western Canal Belt (624 9066). Tram 1, 2, 5.* **Open** 11am-6pm Mon-Wed, Fri, Sat; 11am-9pm Thur. **No credit cards. Map** p310 C4.
A treasure trove of period clothing, much of it from the '40s and '50s. Mostly it's womenswear (including sumptuous dresses), but there's some menswear, too.

### Wini
*Haarlemmerstraat 29, Western Canal Belt (427 9393). Tram 1, 2, 4, 5, 9, 13, 14, 16, 17, 20, 24, 25.* **Open** noon-6pm Mon; 10am-6pm Tue, Wed, Fri, Sat; 10am-9pm Thur. **Map** p306 C2.

Wini's retro clothes are flavour of the month in Amsterdam's hugely competitive second-hand market. The store sizzles with original pimp jackets, hipsters, Adidas and lots of polyester.

### Zipper

*Huidenstraat 7, Western Canal Belt (623 7302). Tram 1, 2, 5.* **Open** 11am-6pm Mon-Wed, Fri, Sat; 11am-9pm Thur; 1-5pm Sun. **Credit** AmEx, MC, V. **Map** p310 C4.

It's not cheap, but the jeans, cowboy shirts, '80s gear and 1970s hipsters are certainly worth a gander; with luck, you'll turn up some unusual treasures. **Branch**: Nieuwe Hoogstraat 8, Old Centre: Old Side (627 0353).

# Flowers

It's tempting to bring home a selection of bulbs from Amsterdam. However, though travellers to the UK and Ireland will be absolutely fine, some other countries' import regulations either prohibit the entry of bulbs or, in the case of the US, require them to have a phytosanitary certificate. You'll find that some of the packaging is helpfully marked with flags indicating the countries into which the bulbs can safely be taken, but most Dutch wholesalers know the regulations and can ship bulbs to your home. In terms of cut flowers, travellers to the UK and Ireland can take an unlimited quantity, as long as none are chrysanthemums or gladioli, while US regulations vary from state to state.

### Bloemenmarkt (Flower market)

*Singel, between Muntplein and Koningsplein, Southern Canal Belt. Tram 1, 2, 4, 5, 9, 14, 16, 20, 24, 25.* **Open** 9.30am-5pm Mon-Sat. **No credit cards. Map** p310 D4.

This fascinating collage of colour is the world's only floating flower market, with 15 florists and garden shops permanently ensconced on barges along the southern side of Singel. The plants and flowers usually last well and are good value.

### Plantenmarkt (Plant market)

*Amstelveld, on Prinsengracht between Utrechtsestraat and Vijzelstraat, Southern Canal Belt. Tram 4, 6, 7, 10.* **Open** 9.30am-6pm Mon. **No credit cards. Map** p311 E4.

Despite the market's predominant emphasis on plants, pots and vases, the Plantenmarkt also has some flowers for sale. In spring, most plants are meant for the balcony or living room, while later in the year, there are more garden plants and bedding plants suitable for flower boxes.

## Florists

### Jemi

*Warmoesstraat 83A, Old Centre: Old Side (625 6034). Tram 4, 9, 16, 20, 24, 25.* **Open** 9am-6pm Mon-Sat. **No credit cards. Map** p306 D2.

Amsterdam's first stone-built house is now occupied by a delightfully colourful florist. Jemi puts together splendid bouquets, provides tuition in flower arranging, throws floral brunches and stocks loads of pots and plants.

Streetwear for skaters: **Henxs Sint**. *See p164.*

# Amsterdam's markets

### Albert Cuypmarkt

*Albert Cuypstraat, the Pijp. Tram 4, 16, 24, 25.* **Open** 9.30am-5pm Mon-Sat.
**No credit cards. Map** p311 E5.
Amsterdam's largest general market sells everything from pillows to prawns at great prices. Clothes tend to be run-of-the-mill cheapies, with the odd bargain.

### Boerenmarkt

*Westerstraat/Noorderkerkstraat, the Jordaan. Tram 3, 10.* **Open** 9am-3pm Sat.
**No credit cards. Map** p306 B2.
Every Saturday, the Noordermarkt turns into an organic farmers' market. Groups of singers or medieval musicians sometimes make a visit feel more like a day trip than a shopping binge.

### Dappermarkt

*Dapperstraat, Oost. Tram 3, 6, 10, 14.*
***Open*** *9am-5pm Mon-Sat.* **No credit cards.**
**Map** p312 H3.
Dappermarkt is a locals' market: for one thing, prices don't rise in accordance with the number of visitors. It sells the usual market fodder, with plenty of cheap clothes and underwear.

### Looier

*Elandsgracht 109, the Jordaan (624 9038).
Tram 7, 10, 17, 20.* **Open** 11am-5pm Mon-Thur, Sat, Sun. **Credit** AmEx, DC, MC, V.
**Map** p310 C4.
Mainly antiques here, with plenty of collectors' items. It's easy to get lost in the quiet premises and find yourself standing alone by a stall crammed with antiquated clocks eerily ticking.

### Noordermarkt

*Noordermarkt, the Jordaan. Tram 3, 10.*
**Open** 7.30am-1pm Mon. **No credit cards.**
**Map** p306 B2.

Tagged on to the end of the Westermarkt, the Noordermarkt is compact and frequented by the serious shopper. The stacks of (mainly second-hand) clothes, shoes, jewellery and hats need to be sorted with a grim determination, but there are real bargains to be had here. Arrive early or the best stuff may have been nabbed.

### Oudemanhuis Book Market

*Oudemanhuispoort, Old Centre: Old Side.
Tram 4, 9, 14, 16, 20, 24, 25.* **Open** 11am-4pm Mon-Fri. **No credit cards. Map** p306 D3.
People have been buying and selling books, prints and sheet music at this arcade since the 19th century.

### Postzegelmarkt

*Nieuwezijds Voorburgwal, by No.276, Old Centre: New Side. Tram 1, 2, 5, 13, 17, 20.*
**Open** 11am-4pm Wed, Sun. **No credit cards.**
**Map** p306 D3.
A specialist market for collectors of stamps, coins, postcards and medals.

### Rommelmarkt

*Looiersgracht 38, the Jordaan. Tram 7, 10, 17, 20.* **Open** 11am-5pm daily.
**No credit cards. Map** p310 C4.
A flea market where, nestled among the junk, you're likely to stumble across dubious bargains such as a boxed set of Demis Roussos discs.

### Waterlooplein

*Waterlooplein, Jodenbuurt. Tram 9, 14, 20/Metro Waterlooplein.* **Open** 9am-5pm Mon-Sat. **No credit cards. Map** p307 E3.
Amsterdam's top tourist market is basically a huge flea market with the added attraction of loads of clothes stalls (though gear can be a bit pricey and, at many stalls, a bit naff). Bargains can be had, but they may be hidden under crap toasters and down-at-heel (literally) shoes.

### Westermarkt

*Westerstraat, the Jordaan. Tram 3, 10.*
***Open*** *9am-1pm Mon.* **No credit cards.**
**Map** p306 B2.
A general market, selling all sorts of stuff. The amount of people packing the pavement is proof as to the entirely reasonable prices and the range of goods, which includes new watches, pretty (and not so pretty) fabrics and cheap factory reject clothes.

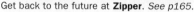

Get back to the future at **Zipper**. *See p165.*

# Food & drink

## Bakeries

For bread, rolls and packaged biscuits, go to a *warmebakker*; for pastries and wickedly delicious cream cakes, you need a *banketbakker*.

### Mediterranee
*Haarlemmerdijk 184, the Jordaan (620 3550). Tram 3/bus 18, 22.* **Open** 8am-8pm daily. **No credit cards. Map** p305 B2.
French, Moroccan and Dutch baking traditions are all practised under this one roof, with mouthwatering results. The finest croissants in town, too.

### Oldenburg
*Beethovenstraat 17, Oud West (662 5520). Tram 5.* **Open** 9am-6pm Mon-Fri; 9am-5pm Sat. **No credit cards.**
Dessert cakes, bavarois and chocolate mousse tarts, plus great choccies, marvellous marzipan confections in winter and chocolate eggs at Easter. **Branch**: Maasstraat 84, Zuid (662 2840).

### Puccini Bomboni
*Staalstraat 17, Old Centre: Old Side (626 5474). Tram 9, 14, 20/Metro Waterlooplein.* **Open** noon-6pm Mon; 9am-6pm Tue-Sat; noon-5pm Sun. **No credit cards. Map** p307 E3.
A great bakery specialising in sweets and desserts made on the premises without artificial ingredients. **Branch**: Singel 184, Western Canal Belt (427 8341).

### Runneboom
*1e Van der Helststraat 49, the Pijp (673 5941). Tram 16, 24, 25.* **Open** 7am-5.30pm Mon-Fri; 7am-5pm Sat. **No credit cards. Map** p311 E5.
This Pijp bakery is a staunch favourite with locals. A huge selection of French, Russian, Greek and Turkish loaves is offered, with rye bread the house speciality. Delicious cakes and pastries are also sold.

## Cheese

In general, the younger (*jong*) the cheese, the creamier and milder it will be, while riper cheeses (*belegen*) will be drier and sharper,

especially the old (*oud*) cheese. The most popular are Goudse (from Gouda), Leidse, flavoured with cumin seeds, and Edammer (aka Edam), with its red crust. However, don't miss Kernhem, a dessert cheese; and Leerdammer and Maaslander, both mild with holes.

### De Kaaskamer
*Runstraat 7, Western Canal Belt (623 3483). Tram 1, 2, 5.* **Open** *Oct-Mar* noon-6pm Mon; 9am-6pm Tue-Fri; 9am-5pm Sat. *Apr-Sept* noon-6pm Mon; 9am-6pm Tue-Fri; 9am-5pm Sat; noon-5pm Sun. **No credit cards. Map** p310 C4.
Over 200 domestic and imported cheeses, plus pâtés, olives, pastas and wines. Have fun quizzing staff on cheese types and trivia: they know their stuff.

### Kef, French Cheesemakers
*Marnixstraat 192, the Jordaan (626 2210). Tram 3, 10.* **Open** 10am-6pm Tue-Thur; 9am-6pm Fri; 9am-5pm Sat. **No credit cards. Map** p305 B3.
This business has been run by French cheesemaker Abraham Kef for over 40 years, and his shop still imports the best French cheeses in Amsterdam. The range of goat's cheeses is especially good.

### Wegewijs
*Rozengracht 32, the Jordaan (624 4093). Tram 13, 14, 17, 20.* **Open** 8.30am-6pm Mon-Fri; 8.30am-5pm Sat. **No credit cards. Map** p305 B3.
The Wegewijs family started running this shop more than 100 years ago. On offer are around 50 foreign cheeses and over 100 domestic types, including *gras kaas*, a grassy-tasting cheese that is available in summer. Pleasingly, you can try the Dutch ones before you buy.

## Chocolate

### Australian
*Leidsestraat 101, Southern Canal Belt (412 4089) . Tram 1, 2, 5.* **Open** noon-6pm Mon-Wed, Fri, Sat; 10am-9pm Thur; 1-6pm Sun. **No credit cards. Map** p310 D4.
Check out the delicious selection of bonbons, ice-cream and coffees with all natural ingredients as you ponder how the Amsterdam branch of a Belgian chain ended up with this name.

### Huize van Wely

*Beethovenstraat 72, Oud West (662 2009). Tram 5.*
**Open** 9am-6pm Mon-Fri; 8.30am-5pm Sat. **Credit** V.
Since 1922, Huize van Wely has been hand-making confections at its factory in Noordwijk, on the west coast of Holland. Indeed, so sublime are its sweet creations that it has been rewarded with the honour of being the sole Dutch member of the prestigious Relais Desserts and Académie Culinaire de France.

### Pâtisserie Pompadour

*Huidenstraat 12, Western Canal Belt (623 9554).*
*Tram 1, 2, 5, 7.* **Open** 9.30am-5.45pm Tue-Fri; 9am-5.30pm Sat. **Credit** MC, V. **Map** p310 C4.
This fabulous bonbonnerie and tearoom – with an 18th-century interior imported from Antwerp – is likely to bring out the little old lady in anyone, even men. The shop is due to close for renovations in 2002, when it will relocate to Kerkstraat 148.

## Delicatessens

### Eichholtz

*Leidsestraat 48, Southern Canal Belt (622 0305).*
*Tram 1, 2, 5.* **Open** 10am-6.30pm Mon; 9am-6.30pm Tue, Wed, Fri; 9am-9pm Thur; 9am-6pm Sat; 1-5pm Sun. **Credit** (over €23 only) AmEx, MC, V.
**Map** p310 D4.
Beloved of expats for its UK and US imports, this is where Yanks can find their chocolate chips and Brits their Christmas puddings. Dutch souvenirs, too.

### De Peperwortel

*Overtoom 140, Museum Quarter (685 1053/*
*www.peperwortel.nl). Tram 1, 6.* **Open** 4-9pm daily. **No credit cards**. **Map** p309 B6.
Stop here en route to Vondelpark. There are luscious sandwiches and salads, a tasty selection of wines and picnic hampers from late spring until early autumn.

## Ethnic/speciality

### Casa Molero

*Gerard Doustraat 66, the Pijp (676 1707). Tram 16,*
*24, 25.* **Open** 10am-6pm Tue-Fri; 8.30am-5.30pm Sat. **No credit cards**. **Map** p311 E6.
Aside from stocking cheeses, spices, sausages and hams from Spain, Casa Molero is also an exclusive distributor for some Spanish and Portuguese wines.

### Olivaria

*Hazenstraat 2A, the Jordaan (638 3552). Tram 7,*
*10.* **Open** 1.30-6pm Mon; 11am-6pm Tue-Sat.
**No credit cards**. **Map** p310 C4.
What's in a name? Quite a lot, judging by Olivaria's devotion to olive oils. There's a vast array of them from around the world, both on show and for sale.

### Oriental Commodities

*Nieuwmarkt 27, Old Centre: Old Side (638 6181).*
*Tram 4, 9, 14, 16, 20, 24, 25/Metro Nieuwmarkt.*
**Open** 9am-6pm Mon-Sat. **No credit cards**.
**Map** p306 D2.

Say cheese: **De Kaaskamer**. *See p167.*

Visit Amsterdam's largest Chinese food emporium for the full spectrum of Asian foods and ingredients, from shrimp- and scallop-flavoured egg noodles to fried tofu balls and fresh veg. There's also a fine range of Chinese cooking appliances and utensils.

### A Taste of Ireland

*Herengracht 228, Western Canal Belt (638 1642).*
*Tram 13, 14, 17, 20.* **Open** 11am-6pm Mon-Fri; 11am-5pm Sat. **No credit cards**. **Map** p306 C3.
Stop homesickness in its tracks by stocking up on fresh sausages, bacon and puddings, flown in from Ireland every week. Impressive selections of British and Irish beers and ciders are also on sale.

### Toko Ramee

*Ferdinand Bolstraat 74, the Pijp (662 2025). Tram*
*16, 20, 24, 25.* **Open** 9am-6pm Tue-Fri; 9am-5pm Sat. **No credit cards**. **Map** p311 E6.
All the unusual spices and interesting ingredients used in Indonesian cooking are available here, along with Chinese and Thai ingredients and a selection of takeaway options.

### Waterwinkel

*Roelof Hartstraat 10, Museum Quarter (675 5932/*
*www.springwater.nl/pages/winkel/winkel.htm).*
*Tram 3, 24.* **Open** 1-6pm Mon; 10am-6pm Tue-Fri; 10am-5pm Sat. **Credit** AmEx, DC, V.
Mineral water galore, both native and imported. Both product variety and shop decor are enough to make the weak of bladder want to head straight for the nearest toilet.

## Fish

### Viscenter Volendam

*Kinkerstraat 181, Oud West (618 7062). Tram 7,*
*17.* **Open** 9am-6pm Mon-Fri; 9am-5pm Sat. **No credit cards**. **Map** p309 B5.
This popular shop is run by a family that commutes from Volendam, a fishing village on the east coast. Choose from selections of freshwater and sea fish, shellfish, cured fish (try the smoked eels, or *gerookte paling*), takeaway snacks and seafood salads.

Eat, Drink, Smoke, Shop

# Health food

*See also p166* **Amsterdam's markets**.

## De Bast

*Huidenstraat 19, Western Canal Belt (624 8087).*
*Tram 1, 2, 5.* **Open** 11.30am-6.30pm Mon; 9.30am-
6.30pm Tue-Fri; 9am-5pm Sat. **No credit cards.**
**Map** p310 C4.
Overdo it at Febo (*see p132* **Grease is the word**)
and you'll be glad of this centrally located health
food shop. Its organic fruit and veg and excellent
freshly baked bread, cakes and savouries are just
the thing to get your body back on an even keel.

## Deshima Freshop

*Weteringschans 65, Southern Canal Belt (423 0391).*
*Tram 6, 7, 10, 16, 24, 25.* **Open** 10am-6pm Mon-
Fri; 10am-5pm Sat. **No credit cards. Map** p310 D5.
This basement macrobiotic shop sells foods that
contain no dairy products, meat or sugar, and also
offers macrobiotic cookery courses in Friesland.
Above the shop is a subdued restaurant serving
macrobiotic lunches (noon-2pm Mon-Fri).

## De Natuurwinkel

*Weteringschans 133, Southern Canal Belt (638*
*4083/www.denatuurwinkel.nl). Tram 6, 7, 10.*
**Open** 7am-8pm Mon-Wed, Fri, Sat; 7am-9pm Thur;
11am-6pm Sun. **Credit** AmEx, MC, V. **Map** p311 E5.
The largest health food supermarket in Amsterdam,
with branches across town. You'll find everything
wholesome here, from organic meat, fruit and veg
(delivered fresh daily) to surprisingly tasty sugar-
free chocolates and organic wine and beer.

# Night shops

It's 11pm, and you're in dire need of ice-cream/
cigarettes/toilet roll/condoms/beer/chocolate
(delete as applicable). This is where the city's
night shops come in handy. Although prices are
often steep, you're paying for the convenience.

## Avondmarkt

*De Wittenkade 94-6, West (686 4919). Tram 10.*
**Open** 4pm-midnight Mon-Fri; 3pm-midnight Sat;
2pm-midnight Sun. **No credit cards. Map** p305 A2.
The biggest and best of all night shops, Avondmarkt
is basically a supermarket, albeit a late-opening one.
Worth the trek out just west of the Jordaan.

## Big Bananas

*Leidsestraat 73, Southern Canal Belt (627 7040).*
*Tram 1, 2, 5.* **Open** 10am-1am Mon-Fri, Sun; 10am-
2am Sat. **No credit cards. Map** p310 D4.
A passable selection of wine, some dodgy-looking
canned cocktails and a variety of sandwiches are
stocked here. Expensive, even for a night shop.

## Dolf's Avondverkoop

*Willemstraat 79, the Jordaan (625 9503).*
*Tram 3.* **Open** 4pm-1am daily. **No credit**
**cards. Map** p306 B2.

One of the best night shops in the Jordaan, Dolf's
stocks all the urgent products you might suddenly
need late at night, including toilet paper, toothpaste
and bread. As pricey as most night shops.

## Sterk

*Waterlooplein 241, Old Centre: Old Side (626 5097).*
*Tram 9, 14, 20/Metro Waterlooplein.* **Open** 8am-
2am daily. **Credit** MC, V. **Map** p307 E3.
Less of a night shop and more of a deli: quiches, pastries and salads are made on site, and there's also
fruit and veg. Be prepared to ask for what you want
here – there's no self-service. Its branch is known as
'Champagne Corner', which hints at what's on offer.
**Branch**: De Clercqstraat 1-7, Oud West (618 1727).

# Off-licences (Slijterijen)

## De Bierkoning

*Paleisstraat 125, Old Centre: New Side (625 2336/*
*www.bierkoning.nl). Tram 1, 2, 5, 13, 14, 16, 17,*
*20, 24, 25.* **Open** 1-7pm Mon; 11am-7pm Tue, Wed,
Fri; 11am-9pm Thur; 11am-6pm Sat; 1-5pm Sun.
**Credit** AmEx, DC, MC, V. **Map** p306 C3.
Named for its location behind the Royal Palace, 'The
Beer King' stocks a trifling 850 brands of beer from
around the world, and a range of nice glasses.

## De Cuyp

*Albert Cuypstraat 146, the Pijp (662 6676). Tram 4,*
*16, 24, 25.* **Open** 9am-6pm Tue-Sat. **Credit** MC, V.
**Map** p311 F5.
De Cuyp is big on international wines and spirits,
including drinks from Brazil, Surinam and Chile. It
also goes in for extremes: there are over 3,000 minia-
tures in stock, plus huge bottles such as a 21-litre
bottle of champagne. There's free delivery, and
rental glasses are on offer for all you partying types.

# Supermarkets

A few tips for Dutch supermarket shopping…
unless a per piece (*per stuk*) price is given, fruit
and veg must be weighed by the customer. Put
your produce on the scale, press the picture of
the item, and press the 'BON' button to get the
receipt. You must pack your groceries yourself,
and if you want a plastic bag, you have to ask
(and pay) for it. For **Hema**, *see p156*.

## Albert Heijn

*Nieuwezijds Voorburgwal 226, Old Centre: New Side*
*(421 8344/www.ah.nl). Tram 1, 2, 4, 5, 9, 13, 14,*
*16, 17, 20, 24, 25.* **Open** 8am-10pm Mon-Sat; 11am-
7pm Sun. **No credit cards. Map** p306 D3.
This massive 'Food Plaza', just behind Dam Square,
is one of over 40 branches of Albert Heijn in
Amsterdam. It contains virtually all the household
goods you could ever need, though some of the
ranges are more costly than at some of its competitors. Note: most branches do not have extended
opening hours such as these.
**Branches** are numerous; check the phone book.

*Eat, Drink, Smoke, Shop*

### Dirk van den Broek

*Marie Heinekenplein 25, the Pijp (673 9393).* Tram
*16, 24, 25.* **Open** 8am-9pm Mon-Fri; 8am-8pm Sat;
1-7pm Sun. **No credit cards. Map** p311 E5.
Decidedly unflashy but a perfectly decent grocery
store nonetheless; cheaper, though with less choice
and less luxury, than Albert Heijn (*see p169*).
**Branches** are numerous; check the phone book

## Tea & coffee

### Geels & Co

*Warmoesstraat 67, Old Centre: Old Side (624 0683).*
*Tram 4, 9, 14, 16, 20, 24, 25.* **Open** *Shop* 9.30am-
6pm Mon-Sat. **No credit cards. Map** p306 D2.
Coffee beans and loose teas, plus a large range of
brewing contraptions and serving utensils. Upstairs
is a small museum of brewing equipment, which is
open only on Saturday afternoons.
**Branch**: *'t Zonnetje* Haarlemmerdijk 45, the Jordaan
(623 0058).

### Simon Levelt

*Prinsengracht 180, Western Canal Belt (624 0823/
www.amsterdamcoffeeandtea.com).* Tram 13, 14,
17, 20. **Open** noon-6pm Mon; 9am-6pm Tue-Fri;
9am-5pm Sat. **No credit cards. Map** p305 B3.
Anything and everything to do with brewing and
serving in a remarkable old shop. The premises date
from 1839 and the place is still replete with much of
the original tiled decor.
**Branches** are numerous; check the phone book

## Furniture

### Bebob Design Interior

*Prinsengracht 764, Southern Canal Belt (624
5763/www.bebob.nl).* Tram 4. **Open** 1-6pm Mon;
10am-6pm Tue-Fri; 10am-5pm Sat. **Credit** AmEx,
DC, MC, V. **Map** p311 E4.
Bebob stocks highly sought-after vintage furnish-
ing from the likes of Eames on up. The quality of
pieces is fantastic, the selection superb and the
prices accordingly high.

### Frozen Fountain

*Prinsengracht 629, Southern Canal Belt (622 9375).*
*Tram 1, 2, 5.* **Open** 1-6pm Mon; 10am-6pm Tue-Fri;
10am-5pm Sat. **No credit cards. Map** p310 D4.
Frozen Fountain defies adequate description, though
its thing is largely cutting-edge designer furnishings
that are deeply seated in tradition. Don't miss.

### Galerie KIS

*Paleisstraat 107, Old Centre: New Side (620
9760/www.house-of-design.nl/kis/).* Tram 1, 2, 4, 5,
9, 11, 13, 16, 17, 20, 24, 25. **Open** noon-6pm Wed-
Sun. **No credit cards. Map** p306 C3.
Despite stocking masses of furniture, lighting and
houseware from independent designers, artists and
architects, Galerie KIS goes to great lengths to
always keep the numbers in each series small and
therefore exclusive.

Vintage furnishings: **Bebob Design Interior**.

## Games, models & toys

### Joe's Vliegerwinkel

*Nieuwe Hoogstraat 19, Old Centre: Old Side
(625 0139).* Tram 4, 9, 16, 20, 24, 25/Metro
Nieuwmarkt. **Open** 1-6pm Mon; 11am-6pm Tue-Fri;
11am-6pm Sat. **Credit** AmEx, DC, MC, V.
**Map** p307 E3.
Kites, kites and more kites, plus a quirky array of
boomerangs, yo-yos and kaleidoscopes can be found
at this spectacularly colourful shop.

### Kramer/Pontifex

*Reestraat 18-20, Western Canal Belt (626 5274).*
*Tram 13, 14, 17, 20.* **Open** 10am-6pm Mon-Fri;
10am-5pm Sat. **No credit cards. Map** p306 C3.
Broken Barbies and battered bears are restored to
health by Mr Kramer, a doctor for old-fashioned dolls
and teddies who has practised here for 25 years.
Pontifex, on the same premises, is a candle retailer.

### Schaak en Go het Paard

*Haarlemmerdijk 147, the Jordaan (624 1171/
www.xs4all.nl/~paard/).* Tram 3/bus 18, 22.
**Open** 10.30am-5.30pm Tue-Sat. **Credit** MC, V.
**Map** p305 B1.
The place to go for a glorious selection of chess sets.
Encompassing the beautiful and the exotic, sets for
sale range from African to ultra-modern.

### Schaal Treinen Huis

*Bilderdijkstraat 94, Oud West (612 2670/
www.schaaltreinenhuis.nl).* Tram 3, 7, 12, 13, 14,
17, 20. **Open** 1-5pm Mon; 9.30am-5.30pm Tue-Sat.
**Credit** AmEx, DC, MC, V. **Map** p309 B5.

Eat, Drink, Smoke, Shop

DIY kits and a ready-made parade that includes electric trains, modern and vintage vehicles and some adorable dolls' houses.

## Gifts & souvenirs

### C-Cedille
*Lijnbaansgracht 275, Southern Canal Belt (624 7178). Tram 6, 7, 10.* **Open** noon-6pm Thur, Fri; 11am-6pm Sat. **Credit** AmEx, DC, MC, V. **Map** p310 D5.
Part of this lovely shop is devoted to designer jewellery, mostly made by hand in the Netherlands. The other section is given over to wooden toys and the like, plus etchings and aquarelles of typical (for which read tourist-friendly) Amsterdam scenes.

### Glasgalerie Kuhler
*Prinsengracht 134, Western Canal Belt (638 0230). Tram 13, 14, 17, 20.* **Open** noon-6pm Wed-Sat; 1-4pm first Sun of mth. **Credit** AmEx, DC, MC, V. **Map** p305 B3.
Contemporary European glass and crystal, with most pieces unique, dated and signed by the artists. Glass-blowing is well represented, along with pate verre, fused pieces and cold laminated sculptures. Prices range from cheap to bankrupting.

### Holland Gallery de Munt
*In the Munttoren, Muntplein 12, Old Centre: New Side (623 2271). Tram 4, 9, 14, 16, 20, 24, 25.* **Open** 10am-6pm Mon-Sat. **Credit** AmEx, DC, MC, V. **Map** p310 D4.
This gallery stocks a selection of antique Delftware and royal and Makkumer pottery, plus other hand-painted objects such as traditional tiles and decorated wooden trays and boxes. Other highlights include miniature ceramic canal houses and dolls in traditional Dutch costume.

### Het Kantenhuis
*Kalverstraat 124, Old Centre: New Side (624 8618/www.kantenhuis.nl). Tram 4, 9, 14, 16, 20, 24, 25.* **Open** 11.45am-6pm Mon; 9.15am-6pm Tue, Wed, Fri, Sat; 9.15am-9pm Thur; noon-5pm Sun. **Credit** AmEx, DC, MC, V. **Map** p306 D3.
The 'Lace House' sells laces in all its forms. There are tablecloths, place mats, doilies and napkins that are embroidered, appliquéd or printed with Delft blue designs. You'll also find lace curtain materials, and kits with which to cross-stitch pictures of cutesy Amsterdam canal houses.

### Tesselschade: Arbeid Adelt
*Leidseplein 33, Southern Canal Belt (623 6665). Tram 1, 2, 5, 6, 7, 10, 20.* **Open** 10am-6pm Tue-Fri; 10am-5pm Sat. **Credit** AmEx, MC, V. **Map** p310 D5.
Everything at this unusual operation is sold on a non-profit basis by Arbeid Adelt ('work ennobles'), an association of Dutch women. There are plenty of toys and decorations, as well as some more utilitarian household items such as tea cosies and decorated clothes hangers.

## Health & beauty

### Body Shop
*Kalverstraat 157-9, Old Centre: New Side (623 9789/www.thebodyshop.co.uk). Tram 4, 9, 14, 16, 20, 24, 25.* **Open** 11am-6pm Mon; 9.30am-6pm Tue, Wed, Fri; 9.30am-9pm Thur; 10am-5.30pm Sat; 1-5pm Sun. **Credit** AmEx, DC, MC, V. **Map** p306 D3.
All the usual lotions and potions for pampering your body, along with gift-wrapping and refill services.

### Douglas
*Kalvertoren, Singel 457, Southern Canal Belt (422 8036/www.douglas.nl). Tram 1, 2, 4, 5, 9, 14, 16, 20, 24, 25.* **Open** 11am-7pm Mon; 9.30am-7pm Tue, Wed, Fri; 9.30am-9pm Thur; 9.30am-6pm Sat; noon-6pm Sun. **Credit** AmEx, MC, V. **Map** p306 D3.
The scents and labels you'd expect from any good high street parfumerie, as well as some special brands not readily available in Amsterdam such as La Prairie, Urban Decay and Versace.
**Branches** are numerous; check the phone book

### Homeopathie De Munt
*Vijzelstraat 1, Southern Canal Belt (624 4533). Tram 4, 9, 14, 16, 20, 24, 25.* **Open** 9.30am-6pm Mon-Wed, Fri, Sat; 9.30am-9pm Thur; 1-6pm Sun. **Credit** AmEx, DC, MC, V. **Map** p310 D4.
It's easy to turn your bathroom into a tranquil spa after stocking up on the essential oils and treatment products that are available from this tiny store. If you've a taste for herbs you can't find in coffeeshops, come here for Celestial Seasonings teas and bee pollen in capsule form.

Fresh and colourful cosmetics that also smell **Lush**. *See p172.*

# Shops by area

## The Old Centre: Old Side

**Absolute Danny** (Sex shops, p176); **Book Exchange** (Bookshops, p155); **Capsicum** (Fabrics & trimmings, p159); **Condomerie het Gulden Vlies** (Sex shops, p176); **Dam Apotheek** (Pharmacies, p176); **Gassan Diamond BV** (Diamonds, p162); **Geels & Co** (Food & drink, p170); **Grimm Sieraden** (Fashion, p162); **Head Shop** (Drugs, p157); **Henxs Sint** (Fashion, p164); **Himalaya** (New Age & eco, p176); **De Hoed van Tijn** (Fashion, p161); **Jacob Hooy & Co** (New Age & eco, p176); **Jemi** (Flowers, p165); **Joe's Vliegerwinkel** (Games, models & toys, p170); **'t Klompenhuisje** (Fashion, p159); **Oriental Commodities** (Food & drink, p168); **Oudemanhuis Book Market** (Markets, p166); **Puccini Bomboni** (Food & drink, p167); **RMF Streetwear** (Fashion, p164); **Robin's Bodywear** (Fashion, p163); **Seventy Five** (Fashion, p164); **Sterk** (Food & drink, p169); **Stoffen & Fourituren Winkel A Boeken Nieuwe** (Fabrics & trimmings, p159); **21R** (Fashion, p160).

## The Old Centre: New Side

**Albert Heijn** (Food & drink, p169); **America Today** (Fashion, p161); **American Book Center** (Bookshops, p155); **Amsterdam Diamond Centre** (Diamonds, p162); **Athenaeum Nieuwscentrum** (Bookshops, p155); **De Bierkoning** (Food & drink, p169); **De Bijenkorf** (Department stores, p156); **Blue Note from Ear & Eye** (Music, p175); **Body Shop** (Health & beauty, p171); **Boudisque** (Records, p175); **Chills & Thrills** (Drugs, p156); **Christine le Duc** (Sex shops, p176); **Clubwear House** (Fashion, p160); **Cyberdog** (Fashion, see p160); **Fame** (Music, p175); **Female & Partners** (Sex shops, p176); **Galerie KIS** (Furniture, p170); **Hemp Works** (Drugs, p157); **Hennes & Mauritz** (Fashion, p161); **Holland Gallery de Munt** (Gifts & souvenirs, p171); **Housewives on Fire** (Fashion, p160); **Hunkemöller** (Fashion, p162); **Het Kantenhuis** (Gifts & souvenirs, p171); **Lush** (Health & beauty, p172); **Maison de Bonneterie** (Department stores, p156); **Midtown** (Music, p175); **PGC Hajenius** (Tobacconists, p176); **Pied-à-Terre** (Bookshops, p156); **Postzegelmarkt** (Markets, p166); **RDLFS** (Fashion, p164); **Sissy Boy** (Fashion, p161); **Soul Food Records** (Music, p175); **Tothem Underwear** (Fashion, p163); **Vitals Vitamine-Advieswinkel** (New Age & eco, p176); **Vroom & Dreesmann** (Department stores, p156); **Waterstone's** (Bookshops, p155); **Zara** (Fashion, p161).

## Western Canal Belt

**Architectura & Natura** (Bookshops, p155); **De Bast** (Food & drink, p169); **Big Shoe** (Fashion, p163); **Au Bout du Monde** (Bookshops, p155); **Brilmuseum/Brillenwinkel** (Fashion, p160); **Exota** (Fashion, p161); **Glasgalerie Kuhler** (Gifts & souvenirs, p171); **De Kaaskamer** (Food & drink, p167); **Knopen Winkel** (Fabrics & trimmings, p159); **Kramer/Pontifex** (Games, models & toys, see p170); **Lady Day** (Fashion, p164); **Laura Dols** (Fashion, p164); **Nic Nic** (Home accessories, p173); **Pâtisserie Pompadour** (Food & drink, p168); **Quadra Original Posters** (Home accessories, p175); **Razzmatazz** (Fashion, p160); **Santa Jet** (Home accessories, p173); **Simon Levelt** (Food & drink, p170); **Stoeltie Diamonds** (Diamonds, p162); **Stout** (Sex shops, p176); **A Taste of Ireland** (Food & drink, p168); **What's Cooking** (Home accessories, p173); **Wini** (Fashion, p164); **De Witte Tandenwinkel** (Health & beauty, p172); **Zipper** (Fashion, p165).

## Lush

*Kalverstraat 98, Old Centre: New Side (330 6376). Tram 4, 9, 14, 16, 20, 24, 25.* **Open** 11am-6pm Mon; 9am-6pm Tue, Wed, Fri; 9am-9pm Thur; 9am-5.30pm Sat; noon-5pm Sun. **Credit** MC, V. **Map** p306 C3. Lush looks lovely and smells divine. Friendly staff help you pick which products suit you best.

## De Witte Tandenwinkel

*Runstraat 5, Western Canal Belt (623 3443). Tram 1, 2, 5.* **Open** 1-6pm Mon; 10am-6pm Tue-Fri; 10am-5pm Sat. **Credit** AmEx, DC, MC, V. **Map** p310 C4. The store that's armed to the teeth with brushes, pastes and other gimmickry to ensure your gnashers are whiter than white and ready to bite.

## Home accessories

### Kitsch Kitchen

*Rozengracht 183, the Jordaan (622 8261). Tram 13, 14, 17, 20.* **Open** 10am-6pm Mon-Sat. **Credit** AmEx, DC, MC, V. **Map** p306 B3. Even the hardiest tat queen will love the culinary and household objects here (including wacky wallpapers). **Branch:** 1e Bloemdwarsstraat 21 (428 4969).

### Marañón Hangmatten

*Singel 488-90, Southern Canal Belt (420 7121/ www.maranon.net). Tram 1, 2, 5, 20.* **Open** 9am-6pm Mon-Sat; 10am-5.30pm Sun. **Credit** AmEx, DC, MC, V. **Map** p310 D4.

**Eat, Drink, Smoke, Shop**

## Southern Canal Belt

**Art Unlimited** (Art & art supplies, *p154*); **Australian** (Food & drink, *p167*); **Bebob Design Interior** (Furniture, *p170*); **Big Bananas** (Food & drink, *p169*); **Bloemenmarkt** (Flowers, *p165*); **C-Cedille** (Gifts & souvenirs, *p171*); **Charles Klassiek en Folklore** (Music, *p175*); **Clean Brothers** (Repairs & cleaning, *see p163*); **Concerto** (Music, *p175*); **Conscious Dreams** (Drugs, *p157*); **Cora Kemperman** (Fashion, *p160*); **Deshima Freshop** (Food & drink, *p169*); **Douglas** (Health & beauty, *p171*); **Eichholtz** (Food & drink, *p168*); **Expert Mons** (Electronics, *p159*); **Frozen Fountain** (Furniture, *p170*); **G&G Special Sizes** (Fashion, *p162*); **Get Records** (Music, *p175*); **Hema** (Department stores, *p156*); **Homeopathie de Munt** (Health & beauty, *p171*); **Independent Outlet** (Fashion, *p164*); **Interpolm** (Drugs, *p159*); **J Vlieger** (Art & art supplies, *p155*); **John N Andringa** (Tobacconists, *p176*); **Jorge Cohen Edelsmid** (Fashion, *p162*); **Kenneth Cole** (Fashion, *p163*); **Khymo** (Fashion, *p160*); **Lambiek** (Bookshops, *p156*); **Luc's Schoenservice** (Repairs & cleaning, *see p163*); **Marañón Hangmatten** (Home accessories, *p172*); **Metz & Co** (Department stores, *p156*); **De Natuurwinkel** (Food & drink, *p169*); **Paul Warmer** (Fashion, *p163*); **Plantenmarkt** (Flowers, *p165*); **Shoe Baloo** (Fashion, *p164*); **Sound of the Fifties** (Music, *p176*); **Tesselschade** (Gifts & souvenirs, *p171*).

## Jodenbuurt, the Plantage & the Oost

**Dappermarkt** (Markets, *p166*); **Waterlooplein** (Markets, *p166*).

## The Jordaan & Oud West

**Avondmarkt** (Food & drink, *p169*); **De Blue Gold Fish** (Fashion, *p162*); **Boerenmarkt** (Markets, *p166*); **Cellarrich Connexion** (Fashion, *p161*); **Dolf's Avondverkoop** (Food & drink, *p169*); **Donald E Jongejans** (Fashion, *p161*); **English Bookshop** (Bookshops, *p155*); **Huize van Wely** (Food & drink, *p168*); **Kef, French Cheesemakers** (Food & drink, *p167*); **Kitsch Kitchen** (Home accessories, *p172*); **Looier** (Markets, *p166*); **Mateloos** (Fashion, *p162*); **Mediterranee** (Food & drink, *p167*); **Megazino** (Fashion, *p160*); **Noordermarkt** (Markets, *p166*); **Oldenburg** (Food & drink, *p167*); **Olivaria** (Food & drink, *p168*); **Peter van Ginkel** (Art & art supplies, *p155*); **De Petsalon** (Fashion, *p161*); **Rommelmarkt** (Markets, *p166*); **Schaal Treinen Huis** (Games, models & toys, *p170*); **Veilinghuis de Nieuwe Zon** (Antiques & auctions, *p154*); **Viscenter Voldendam** (Food & drink, *p168*); **Wegewijs** (Food & drink, *p167*); **Westermarkt** (Markets, *p166*).

## The Museum Quarter, Vondelpark & the South

**Coster Diamonds** (Fashion, *p162*); **Geboortewinkel Amsterdam** (Fashion, *p159*); **Intertaal** (Bookshops, *p155*); **De Pepperwortel** (Food & drink, *p168*); **'t Schooltje** (Fashion, *p159*); **Waterwinkel** (Food & drink, *p168*).

## The Pijp

**Albert Cuypmarkt** (Markets, *p166*); **Casa Molero** (Food & drink, *p168*); **De Cuyp** (Food & drink, *p169*); **Dirk van den Broek** (Food & drink, *p170*); **Hans Anders Optitien** (Fashion, *p161*); **Runneboom** (Food & drink, *p167*); **Toko Ramee** (Food & drink, *p168*); **Van Moppes & Zoon** (Diamonds, *p162*).

Europe's biggest collection of hammocks. The hand-woven ones from South America are the dearest.

### Santa Jet

*Prinsenstraat 7, Western Canal Belt (427 2070). Tram 1, 2, 5, 20.* **Open** 11am-6pm Mon-Fri; 10am-5pm Sat; noon-5pm Sun. **Credit** AmEx, DC, MC, V. **Map** p306 C2.
Live *la vida loca* with Mexican housewares, mini altars and much more Mexican kitsch madness. Olé!

### What's Cooking

*Reestraat 16, Western Canal Belt (427 0630). Tram 13, 14, 17, 20.* **Open** noon-6.30pm Tue-Fri; 11am-6pm Sat. **Credit** AmEx, MC, V. **Map** p306 C3.

Pink salad bowls, green sauces, orange peppermills: culinary gifts don't come any more retina-searing.

# Vintage

### Nic Nic

*Gasthuismolensteeg 5, Western Canal Belt (622 8523). Tram 1, 2, 5, 13, 17, 20.* **Open** noon-6pm Mon-Fri; 10am-5pm Sat. **Credit** AmEx, MC, V. **Map** p306 C3.
The best shop of its ilk in Amsterdam, selling '50s and '60s furniture, lamps, ashtrays and kitchenware, mostly in mint condition. Opening times can vary. **Branch:** 1e Jan Steenstraat 131, the Pijp (675 6805).

# THREE FLOORS TO EXPLORE

FAME music is the home entertainment store with the largest collection in Europe.
We've got three floors packed with your favourite CD's, vinyl, games, videos, DVD's,
books and merchandise. The ground floor holds Charts, Books, Pop and Dance.
In the basement you'll find an impressive collection of Rock music, Classical music
and Movies and Games. On the first floor are the Roots and International music.

We import from Japan,
Australia and the United
States. Visit FAME music in
the heart of Amsterdam!

WWW.FAME.NL

**Open:**
10am-7pm Friday-Wednesday,
10am-9pm Thursday

FAME

### Quadra Original Posters

*Herengracht 383-9, Western Canal Belt (626 9472).*
*Tram 1, 2, 4, 5, 14, 16, 20, 24, 25.* **Open** 10.30am-
4.30pm Tue-Sat. **Credit** MC, V. **Map** p310 D4.
Why not nab yourself an original fin de siècle advertising poster, or decorate your room with a '30s circus poster? Whatever your tastes stretch to – from
beer adverts to B-movies – you're sure to find the
poster you want here.

## Music

Vintage vinyl collectors should also head to the
**Noordermarkt** and **Waterlooplein**.

### Blue Note from Ear & Eye

*Gravenstraat 12, Old Centre: New Side (428 1029).*
*Tram 1, 2, 4, 5, 9, 13, 16, 20, 24, 25.* **Open** 11am-
7pm Mon-Sat; noon-5pm Sun. **Credit** AmEx, DC,
MC, V. **Map** p306 C3.
The full spectrum of jazz, from '30s stompers to
mainstream, avant-garde and Afro jazz, can be seen
on the packed shelves here. Mmmm. Niiiice.

### Boudisque

*Haringpakkerssteeg 10-18, Old Centre: New Side*
*(623 2603/www.boudisque.nl). Tram 1, 2, 4, 5, 9,*
*13, 14, 16, 17, 20, 24, 25.* **Open** noon-6pm Mon,
Sun; 10am-6pm Tue, Wed, Fri, Sat; 10am-9pm Thur.
**Credit** AmEx, DC, MC, V. **Map** p306 D2.
Pop, rock, heavy metal, ambient, house, techno,
world music... the whole gamut, basically, plus
T-shirts, CD-Roms and other malarkey.

### Charles Klassiek en Folklore

*Weteringschans 193, Southern Canal Belt (626*
*5538). Tram 6, 7, 10, 16, 24, 25.* **Open** 1-6.30pm
Mon; 10am-6.30pm Tue, Wed, Fri; 10am-9pm Thur;
10am-5.30pm Sat. **Credit** AmEx, DC, MC, V.
**Map** p311 E5.
Literally, 'classical and folk'. A good place for some
of the smaller German and French labels, and, buck-
ing trends, for good, old-fashioned vinyl.

### Concerto

*Utrechtsestraat 54-60, Southern Canal Belt*
*(626 6577/624 5467). Tram 4.* **Open** 10am-6pm
Mon-Wed, Fri, Sat; 10am-9pm Thur; noon-6pm
Sun. **Credit** (over €12 only) AmEx, DC, MC, V.
**Map** p311 E4.
Head here for classic Bach recordings, obscure
Beatles items, or that fave Diana Ross album that
got nicked from your party. There are also second-
hand 45s and new releases at decent prices.

### Fame

*Kalverstraat 2, Old Centre: New Side (638 2525/*
*www.fame.nl). Tram 1, 2, 5, 13, 14, 17, 20.* **Open**
10am-7pm Mon-Wed, Fri, Sat; 10am-9pm Thur; noon-
6pm Sat. **Credit** AmEx, DC, MC, V. **Map** p306 D3.
It comes as little surprise that the biggest record
store in Amsterdam sits bang on its busiest shopping thoroughfare. Fame offers a vast array of stock
in a variety of genres.

Yum! **Soul Food Records**.

### Get Records

*Utrechtsestraat 105, Southern Canal Belt (622*
*3441). Tram 4.* **Open** 10am-6pm Mon-Wed, Fri, Sat;
10am-9pm Thur; noon-6pm Sun. **Credit** AmEx, DC,
MC, V. **Map** p311 E4.
Much of the vinyl here has been cleared out to
make room for a decent selection of alternative and
independent CDs; it's also good for roots, Americana
and dance. Just be sure to investigate the little
corner at the front of the shop: it's partially dedicated to cheapies.

### Midtown

*Nieuwendijk 104, Old Centre: New Side (638 4252).*
*Tram 1, 2, 5, 13, 17, 20, 24, 25.* **Open** 1-6pm Mon,
Sun; 10am-6pm Tue, Wed, Fri, Sat; 10am-9pm Thur.
**Credit** AmEx, DC, MC, V. **Map** p306 D2.
Dance music galore: hardcore, gabber, trance, club,
mellow house and garage are among the styles on
the shelves. Midtown is also a good source of infor-
mation and tickets for hardcore parties.

### Soul Food Records

*Nieuwe Nieuwstraat 27C, Old Centre: New Side (428*
*6134). Tram 1, 2, 5, 13, 17.* **Open** 10am-6pm Mon-
Wed, Fri, Sat; 10am-9pm Thur; noon-6pm Sun.
**Credit** AmEx, DC, MC, V. **Map** p306 D2.
Hit the spot where local DJs go for hip hop, soul and
R&B imports. Staff are up on all that's in, but check
your ego at the door: these people know their stuff,
and prima donnas are not tolerated.

Eat, Drink, Smoke, Shop

## Sound of the Fifties

*Prinsengracht 669, Southern Canal Belt (623 9745).*
*Tram 6, 7, 10, 20.* **Open** 1-6pm Mon; noon-6pm
Tue-Sat. **Credit** AmEx, MC, V. **Map** p310 C4.
This specialist store sells collectable vinyl from the
'50s, from Liberace to Yma Sumac. Records and
sleeves are in good nick, but that does mean prices
are accordingly high.

# New Age & Eco

## Himalaya

*Warmoesstraat 56, Old Centre: Old Side (626*
*0899/www.himalaya.nl). Tram 1, 2, 4, 5, 9, 16, 17,*
*20, 24, 25/Metro Centraal Station.* **Open** 1-6pm
Mon; 10am-6pm Tue, Wed, Fri, Sat; 10am-8.30pm
Thur; 12.30-5pm Sun. **Credit** AmEx, MC, V.
**Map** p306 D2.
Shop-gallery-teahouse Himalaya is a haven of calm
amid seedy, bustling surroundings. Come here for
an extensive range of books and magazines, crys-
tals, tarot cards and jewellery.

## Jacob Hooy & Co

*Kloveniersburgwal 12, Old Centre: Old Side (624*
*3041/www.jacobhooy.nl). Tram 4, 9, 14, 16, 20,*
*24, 25/Metro Nieuwmarkt.* **Open** 10am-6pm Mon;
8.15am-6pm Tue-Fri; 8.15am-5pm Sat. **Credit** V.
**Map** p306 C3.
Established in 1743, this chemist sells around 600
kitchen and medicinal herbs, spices, natural cosmetics, health foods and homeopathic remedies.

## Vitals Vitamine-Advieswinkel

*Nieuwe Nieuwstraat 47, Old Centre: New Side (625*
*7298). Tram 1, 2, 5, 13, 17, 20.* **Open** 9.30am-6pm
Mon-Fri; 11am-5pm Sat. **Credit** AmEx, DC, MC, V.
**Map** p306 C2.
The emphasis at this friendly shop is on educating
yourself about food supplements and vitamins.

# Pharmacies

## Dam Apotheek

*Damstraat 2, Old Centre: Old Side (624 4331).*
*Tram 4, 9, 14, 16, 20, 24, 25.* **Open** noon-6pm
Mon; 9.30-6pm Tue, Wed, Fri, Sat; 9.30am-9pm Thur;
noon-5pm Sun. **No credit cards. Map** p306 D3.
This centrally located pharmacy is notable for its
extended opening hours. Should you find yourself
in desperate need of a pharmacy in the middle of
the night, *see p283.*

# Sex shops

## Absolute Danny

*Oudezijds Achterburgwal 78, Old Centre: Old Side*
*(421 0915/www.absolutedanny.com). Tram 4, 9, 16,*
*20, 24.* **Open** noon-8pm Mon-Wed, Sat; noon-9pm
Thur; noon-10pm Fri; noon-7pm Sun. **Credit** AmEx,
DC, MC, V. **Map** p306 D2.
Everything from rubber clothes to erotic tooth-
brushes, all under one saucy roof.

## Christine le Duc

*Spui 6, Old Centre: New Side (624 8265/*
*www.christineleduc.nl). Tram 1, 2, 4, 5, 9, 14,*
*16, 20, 24, 25.* **Open** noon-8pm Mon-Wed, Sat;
noon-9pm Thur; noon-10pm Fri; noon-7pm Sun.
**Credit** AmEx, MC, V. **Map** p306 D3.
One of the more plebian erotic shops, Christine le
Duc is trashy but never seedy. Staff sell crotchless
red panties in an array of synthetics, porn mags and
novelties such as an elephant's head G-string.

## Condomerie het Gulden Vlies

*Warmoesstraat 141, Old Centre: Old Side (627*
*4174/www.condomerie.com). Tram 4, 9, 14, 16, 20,*
*24, 25.* **Open** 11am-6pm Mon-Sat. **Credit** AmEx,
DC, MC, V. **Map** p306 D2.
No surprises for guessing this jolly emporium's location. An astounding variety of rubbers will tame
trouser snakes of all shapes and sizes.

## Female & Partners

*Spuistraat 100, Old Centre: New Side (620 9152/*
*www.femaleandpartners.nl). Tram 1, 2, 5, 13, 17,*
*20.* **Open** 1-6pm Mon, Sun; 11am-6pm Tue, Wed, Fri,
Sat; 11am-9pm Thur. **Credit** AmEx, DC, MC, V.
**Map** p306 C2.
The polar opposite of most Red Light District enter-
prises, the ten-year-old Female & Partners welcomes
women (and, yes, their partners) with an attractively
presented array of clothes, videos and toys.

## Stout

*Berenstraat 9, Western Canal Belt (620 1676).*
*Tram 13, 14, 17, 20.* **Open** noon-7pm Tue-Fri;
11am-6pm Sat; 1-5pm Sun. **Credit** AmEx, DC, MC,
V. **Map** p310 C4.
This is the kind of friendly haven where women can
leisurely ponder which erotic toy, video or book
they'd like to buy. Fellas should also note that the
staff love helping a bloke select that special present
for her indoors.

# Tobacconists

## John N Andringa

*Reguliersbreestraat 2, Southern Canal Belt (623*
*2836/www.compaenen.nl/andringa/eng.htm). Tram*
*4, 9, 16, 20, 24, 25.* **Open** noon-6pm Mon; 9.30am-
6pm Tue, Wed, Fri, Sat; 9.30am-9pm Thur; noon-5pm
Sun. **Credit** MC, V. **Map** p310 D4.
John N Andringa and family have been keeping the
masses supplied with big stinky stogies from
around the world since 1902.

## PGC Hajenius

*Rokin 92-6, Old Centre: New Side (625 9985/*
*www.hajenius.com). Tram 4, 9, 14, 16, 20, 24, 25.*
**Open** noon-6pm Mon; 9.30-6pm Tue, Wed, Fri, Sat;
9.30am-9pm Thur; noon-5pm Sun. **Credit** AmEx,
DC, MC, V. **Map** p306 D3.
A smoker's paradise (tobacco, not dope) for well
over 250 years, Hajenius offers all manner of ciga-
rabilia, from traditional Dutch pipes (14in or 20in
stem) to own-brand cigars.

# Arts &
# Entertainment

# By Season

Desperate for a date? Check your diary against dozens of fanciable events.

After working flat out to keep the sea at bay and their bellies filled, Amsterdammers of yore recognised the therapeutic benefits of letting their hair down in a frenzy of song, dance and drink. But with modern life a much gentler proposition, the locals now just go sporadically nuts and act, as the saying goes, as if they got 'hit on the head by a windmill blade' (trust us, it loses something in the translation).

Today, the only occasions to inspire old-fashioned pagan mass psychosis are **Oudejaarsavond** (New Year's Eve; *see p184*) and **Koninginnedag** (Queen's Day; *see p181* **A right royal knees-up**). Otherwise, the year's calendar is filled with more cultural shenanigans. But happily such events often betray the kind of cutting-edge savvy usually associated with New York and London. And herein lies the city's charm: it's a dinky town with the gall to host ambitious, globe-embracing offerings. Both connoisseurs and dilettantes – whether favouring music, art or cannabis – are looked after well.

The **AUB** (0900 0191; *see p279* **Tickets, please**) and the **Amsterdam Tourist Board** (0900 400 4040; *see p289*) list upcoming events in *Uitkrant* and *Day by Day* respectively, and www.timeout.com/amsterdam previews the best. For a list of public holidays, *see p290*. Unless stated, all events are free.

## Frequent events

### Arts & crafts markets
*Spui, Old Centre: New Side (tram 1, 2, 4, 5, 9, 14, 16, 20, 24, 25) & Thorbeckeplein, Southern Canal Belt (tram 4, 9, 14, 20).* **Map** p310 D4 (Spui); p311 E4 (Thorbeckeplein). **Date** *Mar-Oct* 10am-5pm Sun.
Two open-air arts and crafts markets are held every Sunday for half the year, depending on weather. They're decent places to browse, but don't come here to buy elephant dung, a bovine in brine or a crucifix in urine: most of the jewellery, paintings, vases and bargain ornaments are more mediocre. Buskers touting CDs and tapes enhance the laid-back vibe.

### Rowing contests
*Amsterdamse Bos, Bosbaan 6 (646 2740). Bus 170, 171, 172.* **Date** *Apr-June.*
Visit this lovely green expanse to watch participants get wet. There are various rowing contests held here from April through to December; check local press or phone the Amsterdam Tourist Board for details.

### Book markets
*Various locations (626 5783).* **Date** May-Aug.
Besides the year-round Friday book stalls on the Spui, four more fleeting but sprawling book markets spring up in summer: two along the Amstel (art book market, mid June; religion, mid Aug) and two on Dam (children's, mid May; mysteries, mid July).

### Antiques market
*Nieuwmarkt, Old Centre: Old Side. Tram 9, 14, 20/ Metro Nieuwmarkt.* **Map** p306 D2. **Date** *Mid May-Sept* 9am-5pm Sun.
Lovers of antiques and bric-a-brac should head for this small antiques market. There's a fair amount of naffness, but also a few gems, especially books, furniture and objets d'art.

## Spring

Spring is when the tulips and crocuses start cracking through the earth, and a winter's worth of doggy-do defrosts: those who know about this sort of thing estimate the amount at 20 million kilograms. However, it's also when Amsterdam shrugs off the weight of existential drag that defines the northern European mindset in winter. Motivated by a visible sun, the city-dwellers take on the shiny *joie de vivre* vibe that's more readily associated with the southern European terrace-café cultures. On the downside, bicycle paths start to clog up, not only with increased

## The best Events

### Koninginnedag
Sodom and Gomorrah in orange.
*See p181* **A right royal knees-up**.

### Museum Night
Sleep in the zoo or party among Rembrandt's finest. *See p183*.

### Open Monument Days
Go behind the gabled façades. *See p183*.

### Parade
Acting up with the spirit of carnival in the summer heat. *See p180*.

### World Press Photo
New pics in the Old Church. *See p179*.

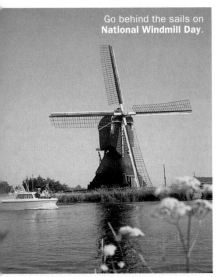

Go behind the sails on **National Windmill Day**.

traffic, but also with lost, doe-eyed tourists stopping to check maps. Relax and enjoy the city at a time when lounging in a park or on a terrace is seen as a respectable thing to do after a long winter's cold rain and mental drain.

### Next Five Minutes: Conference on Tactical Media Information

*Various locations in Amsterdam & Rotterdam (557 9898/www.n5m.org).* **Admission** prices vary. **Date** Mar.

Theorists, artists, activists and media-makers from around the world meet to exchange ideas and strategies for social change in the digital age. Workshops, exhibitions and performances take place in a variety of locations, but most of the action is at the Paradiso (*see p214*) and De Balie (*see p241*).

### Stille Omgang (Silent Procession)

*Through the city, beginning Sat 11.30pm at Spui, Beginhof (information 023 524 6229 after 7pm/write to Gezelschap van de Stille Omgang, Zandvoorterweg 59, 2111 GS Aerdenhout).* **Date** wknd after 10 Mar.

Local Catholics commemorate the 1345 Miracle of Amsterdam (*see p9*) with a silent night-time procession. The route begins and ends at Spui, via Kalverstraat, Nieuwendijk, Warmoesstraat and Nes; the sight of the procession moving through the Red Light District at night is decidedly surreal.

### World Press Photo

*Oude Kerk, Oudekerksplein 23, Old Centre: Old Side (625 8284/www.worldpressphoto.nl).* Tram 4, 9, 16, 20, 24, 25. **Admission** €5; €4 concessions. **Map** p306 D2. **Date** *Apr-May* 10am-6pm Mon-Sat; 1-6pm Sun.

The world's largest photo competition, with exhibits chosen from tens of thousands of photos taken by thousands of different photojournalists, takes place in the already sight-worthy confines of the Oude Kerk (*see p83*). After kicking off in Amsterdam, it moves on to another 70 locations around the world.

### National Museum Weekend

*Around the Netherlands (670 1111).* **Admission** mostly free. **Date** mid Apr.

Many state-run museums have discounted or free admission and special activities during National Museum Weekend. Hours are often extended, but most museums are still busy. Phone the Vereniging Museum Jaarkaart on the above number for information, or pick up the *Museum Weekend* paper at the Amsterdam Tourist Board, the ANWB (auto association) and the museums themselves.

### Koninginnedag (Queen's Day)

*Around the city.* **Date** 30 Apr.
*See p181* A right royal knees-up.

### Herdenkingsdag & Bevrijdingsdag (Remembrance Day & Liberation Day)

**Remembrance Day** *National Monument, Dam, Old Centre: Old Side.* Tram 1, 2, 4, 5, 9, 13, 14, 16, 17, 20, 24, 25. **Map** p306 D3. **Date** 4 May.
**Liberation Day** *Vondelpark (tram 1, 2, 3, 5, 6, 12, 20) & Museumplein (tram 1, 2, 5, 6, 7, 10, 20), Museum Quarter.* **Map** p310 C6. **Date** 5 May.

Those who lost their lives during World War II are remembered at the National Monument on Dam Square on 4 May at 7.30pm. Homosexuals who died in the war are also remembered at a gay remembrance service at the Homomonument (*see p201*).

Liberation Day is celebrated on 5 May. Rokin, Vondelpark, Museumplein and Leidseplein are the best places to head: expect live music, speeches and information stands for political groups, and a market where you can sell everything you bought in a drunken stupor on Queen's Day a week earlier.

### Oosterpark Festival

*Oosterpark, Oost.* Tram 3, 6, 9, 14. **Map** p312 H3. **Date** first wk in May.

The culturally eclectic east of Amsterdam makes a perfect setting for this one- or two-day free festival emphasising community between nationalities. It has its own links with Remembrance Day, since many local Jews were deported during World War II, but this fact isn't commemorated here: the festival is really just a great opportunity to experience different music, customs, food, games and sports.

### National Windmill Day

*Around the Netherlands (075 621 5148).* **Admission** free; donations welcome. **Date** 2nd Sat in May.

Members of the public are welcome at about 75 watermills and 600 of the country's 1,035 windmills, including Amsterdam's half-dozen working mills. Those open to the public carry a blue banner; for full details, call the above number.

## National Cycling Day

*Around the Netherlands (071 560 5959).*
**Date** 2nd Sat in May.
National Cycling Day means the roads are even more full of cyclists than usual. More than 200 routes of varying lengths are set up especially for the occasion, and if you want to saddle up for some two-wheeled action – or, alternatively, avoid it – contact the Amsterdam Tourist Board for details.

## KunstRAI (RAI Arts Fair)

*RAI Congresgebouw, Europaplein, Zuid (549 1212). Tram 4, 25/NS rail RAI station.* **Open** *Office* 8am-6pm Mon-Fri. **Admission** €10-€15.
**No credit cards.** **Date** mid May-early June.
Every artform from ceramics and jewellery to paintings and sculpture are featured at this huge (and hugely mainstream) annual exhibition of contemporary art. All in all, about 100 Dutch and international galleries take part.

## Open Ateliers (Open Studios): Kunstroute de Westelijke Eilanden

*Prinseneiland, Bickerseiland & Realeneiland (627 1238).* **Date** late May/early June.
Many neighbourhoods with large artist populations and artists' studio complexes hold open days in spring and autumn, when, over a weekend or more, dozens of artists – both starving and successful – open their doors to the public. The annual Westelijke Eilanden is the most popular, situated on the picturesque and peaceful islands around Prinseneiland, all connected by traditional 'skinny bridges'. Be sure, also, to check out the Jordaan event, which is usually held on the same weekend. Find out about times and venues for all the Open Ateliers – aka Open Studios – by picking up the Kunstladder (the official list), available at the Amsterdam Tourist Board or the AUB Ticketshop.

## Europerve

*Information: Demask, Zeedijk 64, Old Centre: Old Side (620 5603/www.demask.com).* **Admission** prices vary. **Date** last Sat in May.
Organised by Demask (*see p205*), Europerve brings together thousands of Europe's most sexually adventurous folks – with the Germans and English seemingly the most needy of a buttock blushing – for a long evening of fashion, performance, dancing, naughty games and friction fun. Leather, latex, PVC and/or adult-sized nappies are required dress.

# Summer

With the consistent sunshine that summer brings, Amsterdammers move outdoors for their leisure time. Liberally undressed bodies pack like sardines on the nearby beaches at Bloemendaal and Zandfoort, and Vondelpark gets gridlocked with skaters, joggers, sun-worshippers and bongo players. Many locals dash off to vacationsville, while the city's tourist load reaches critical density.

## Echo Grachtenloop (Canal Run)

*Around Amsterdam (585 9222).*
**Admission** around €5 participants; free spectators. **Date** late May/early June.
Close on 5,000 people take part in either a 5.5-, 9.5- or 18km (three-, six- or 11-mile) run along the city's canals (Prinsengracht and Vijzelgracht). Would-be participants can sign up from mid May at VSB banks (there's one at Rozengracht 207; 638 8009) or register a mere half-hour before the 11am start at the Stadsschouwburg (*see p221*). If you'd rather – perhaps understandably – sit outside with a beer and observe the runners getting knackered, there are plenty of decent vantage points. Avoid the usually crowded Leidseplein and head, instead, for the banks of Prinsengracht.

## Holland Festival

*Stadsschouwburg, Leidseplein, Southern Canal Belt (530 7110/www.holndfstvl.nl). Tram 1, 2, 5, 6, 7, 10, 20.* **Admission** €8-€40. **Credit** AmEx, MC, V.
**Map** p310 C5. **Date** early-mid June.
A fixture in the diaries of the Netherlands' cultured folk, the Holland Festival features art, dance, opera, theatre and a whole lot more. The programme includes both mainstream and oddball works, and is held in the Stadsschouwburg (*see p221*) and other venues, with some events in the Hague. Tickets are sold from May from the AUB Ticketshop, Amsterdam Tourist Board offices and theatres.

## Open Garden Days

*Around Amsterdam (422 1870).* **Date** mid June.
Similar to the Open Monument Days (*see p183*), this weekend event sees owners of beautiful, hidden backyard gardens open their doors to the general public, who file in and emit admiring 'oohs' and 'aahs' in honour of their hosts' landscaping skills.

## Kwakoe

*Bijlmerpark, Bijlmer (416 0894/www.kwakoe.nl). Metro Bijlmer.* **Date** mid July-mid Aug.
The name of this family-oriented multicultural festival, which means 'slave', refers to the emancipation of the people of Surinam. Every weekend in summer you can drop in and usually find some form of theatre, music, film, literature or sport and – perhaps most enticingly – a large range of exotic food stalls.

## Parade

*Martin Luther Kingpark, Zuid (033 465 4577/ www.mobilearts.nl). Tram 25/Metro Amstel.*
**Admission** free-€10. **No credit cards.**
**Date** 1st 2wks of Aug (3pm-1am Mon-Thur, Sun; 3pm-2am Fri, Sat).
One of the highlights of the cultural year, this outdoor theatre festival (*see also p245*) comes pretty darn close to re-enacting the vibes of ancient carnivals. Enter into another – alcohol-fuelled – world, where a beer garden is surrounded by kitschily decorated tents that each feature a different cabaret, music or theatre act. Afternoons are child-friendly. There's also a Winter Parade (*see p184*) in December on the grounds of the Westergasfabriek.

# A right royal knees-up

Party-lovers, crap collectors and students of the stupendously surreal, listen up. If you only go to Amsterdam once in your life, make sure your visit coincides with 30 April. Queen's Day, aka **Koninginnedag** in the local lingo, is, in theory, a one-day celebration of Beatrix's birthday (actually in winter; the ever-pragmatic Dutch choose to celebrate it on her mother's birthday). In reality, though, the Queen is soon forgotten amid the revelry. More than a million folk pour into the city, making every single street and canal dense with different sounds, suspicious smells and hopeful stallholders in the process.

It's a day of excess. You might discover a leather-boy disco party on one sidestreet, boogie through and get to an old-school Jordaan crooner on another, when suddenly a boat bellows by with a heavy metal band on deck, whose amps get short-circuited at the next bridge when a gang of boys dressed in head-to-toe orange urinate on to it. If nothing else, you'll at least come away with a few stories to tell your grandkids.

If you've got kids in tow, head straight to Vondelpark, dedicated to children; gay and lesbian celebrations are focused around Reguliersdwaarsstraat and the Homomonument (*see p201*); and Dam becomes a fairground. The mind gets clogged with an overdose of sensations and pockets slowly empty as punters get tricked into buying just what they always (read: never) wanted: a fetching pair of orange clogs, a brain implant or some processed uranium.

Former Mayor Patijn played party pooper a few years ago by banning street-selling on the Queen's Eve (29 April), but he does have a point: you should try to get some rest before the big day. With performances, markets, crowds and, of course, alcohol, the scenic streets of Amsterdam have it all for one day only. Come and see what the fuss is all about. But don't make too many plans for 1 May.

## Amsterdam Gay Pride Boat Parade

*Prinsengracht (620 8807/www.amsterdampride.nl).
Tram 13, 14, 17, 20.* **Map** p306 C1. **Date** 1st Sat
in Aug, 2-5pm.
If the weather's fine, there might be as many as 250,000 spectators lining the Prinsengracht and its bridges to watch the spectacular Gay Pride Boat Parade. Eighty boats with over-the-top decorations and blasting sound systems crewed by incredibly extravagant sailors set sail at this carnivalesque climax to a whole weekend of special activities (check the website for other events). *See also p203.*

## Hartjesdag

*Zeedijk, Old Centre: Old Side (625 8467/
www.zeedijk.nl). Tram 4, 9, 14, 16, 20, 24, 25.*
**Map** p306 D2. **Date** mid Aug.
An ancient Amsterdam celebration, 'Heart Day' was traditionally held on the last Monday of August and involved a great deal of drinking, cross-dressing and firecrackers. The event wasn't held for decades, but some resourceful folk resurrected it in 1999, primarily to focus on the boozing and dragging side of things. Marvel at the parade of boys dressed as girls and girls dressed as boys: it's predictably popular with the city's burgeoning transvestite population, as are its associated theatrical and music events.

## Uitmarkt

*Various locations, including Museumplein, Dam
& Amstel (www.uitmarkt.nl).* **Date** last wknd
of Aug.
The chaotic Uitmarkt previews the coming cultural season with a fair on and around Museumplein, Leidseplein, Dam and Nes, giving information on theatre, opera, dance and music. From Friday to Sunday, several outdoor stages are set up in squares around the centre of Amsterdam, presenting free music, dance, theatre and cabaret shows. Not surprisingly, it gets very crowded.

**Arts & Entertainment**

Amsterdam has been known to have the occasional Indian summer, but otherwise this season's stormy disposition is a warning of the winter's despair that is sure to follow; it's a time when Amsterdammers start storing any razor blades out of sight.

As a visitor, though, this might be just the right time to visit the city. With the tourist tide finally beginning to depart and touring bands arriving in their droves to play the Melkweg or Paradiso, the true spirit of Amsterdam comes bubbling to the surface. Just bring a strong brolly and be prepared to pop into a pub to wait the weather out – hardly a hardship.

## Bloemen Corso (Flower Parade)

*Around Amsterdam: route usually via Overtoom, Leidseplein, Leidsestraat, Spui, Spuistraat, Dam, Rembrandtplein, Vijzelstraat, Weteringschans (029 732 5100/www.bloemen corsoaalsmeer.nl).* **Date** 1st Sat of Sept.

Since the 1950s, a spectacular parade of floats bearing all kinds of flowers – except tulips, amazingly, as they're out of season – has made its way from Aalsmeer (*see p254*), the home of Holland's flower industry, 15km (9 miles) to the south-west, up the waterways to Amsterdam. Crowds line the pavements to get a glimpse of the beautiful and fragrant displays as they arrive in town; then, at 4pm, the parade reaches a packed Dam to be the guest of honour at a civic reception. At 9pm, it begins an hour-long illuminated cavalcade back through Aalsmeer.

# Read all about it

The literary festival that rocks, **Crossing Border** (www.crossingborder.nl) is – say the organisers – a 'composition where writers, musicians, filmmakers and artists are all programmed next to each other'. Actually, 'authors' in the strictest sense of the word are fairly thin on the ground. Most participants come from the world of music and perform a combination of music and spoken word.

After years in The Hague, the festival's 120-odd acts now take over all the major venues around Leidseplein for two nights in late October. The billing's an inspired mix: in 2001, for example, you could dart between performers as diverse and talented as Eels, Mercury Rev, Jill Scott (*pictured*), Douglas Coupland, Jim White, Rick Moody, Giant Sand and that grand old rebel of American letters, Norman Mailer. Folks grumble about the queues for the bigger acts, but that's just the price you pay to see somebody like Balkan superstar – and Emir Kusturica's favoured soundtrack composer – Goran Bregovic, who was accompanied by

a 40-piece orchestra consisting of a Polish string ensemble, a Serbian Orthodox choir, a Gypsy brass band, three Bulgarian female vocalists, a player of a goat-turned-bagpipe and a skinhead percussionist.

Nor is Bregovic the only one to kick up a storm: a posse of American writers associated with the literary magazine *McSweeney's* (edited by Dave Eggers of *A Heartbreaking Work of Staggering Genius* fame) ended up treating a mostly greying literary crowd to a show they'll never forget. The gilding and red velvet plushness of the historical Stadsschouwburg had never been privy to such an assault: Arthur Bradford smashed his guitar at the climax of a story, Neal Pollack screamed about his 'huge Jewish cock', and David Byrne accompanied a mentally handicapped lad in the singing of an ode to Holland. In other words, if your tastes tend towards the obscure, or you have no problem taking a chance with an up-and-comer, then these two days will likely rate among the most quirky and memorable you've ever had.

It's *fun* judging the **High Times Cannabis Cup**? You must be toking.

## Open Monument Days

*Around Amsterdam (552 4888/*
*www.openmonumentendag.nl).*
**Date** 2nd wknd of Sept.
Every year, the owners of some of Amsterdam's most historic buildings open their doors to the public, who can open their eyes to the past as they gander behind the gabled façades and into the lives lived and living in Golden Age grandeur. It's a national event: wherever you find yourself in the Netherlands, look out for the flying Monumenten flag.

## Jordaan Festival

*The Jordaan (626 5587/www.jordaanfestival.nl).*
**Map** p310 C4. **Date** 3rd wknd of Sept.
This annual neighbourhood festival, usually focused along Elandsgracht, features local talents following in the footsteps of Johnny Jordaan and Tante Leni.
*See p106* **Going for a song**.

## Dam tot Damloop

*Prins Hendrikkade, Amsterdam, to Peperstraat,*
*Zaandam (072 533 8136).* **Date** mid Sept.
The annual 'Dam to Dam Run' stretches 16.1km (ten miles) from Amsterdam to Zaandam. Up to 150,000 gather to watch 25,000 participants, many of whom are world-class athletes. Bands line the route and there's also a circus and various mini-marathons in Zaandam for children.

## Chinatown Festival

*Nieuwmarkt, Old Centre: Old Side (mobile 06*
*2476 0060/www.zeedijk.nl). Tram 9, 14, 20/*
*Metro Nieuwmarkt.* **Map** p306 D2. **Date** mid Sept.
The ancient square of Nieuwmarkt gets covered with stalls of Chinese food and enlivened with many acts and artists in this traditional celebration.

## Kunstroute/Exchange WG Terrein

*WG Terrein, Marius van Bouwdijk Bastiaansestraat,*
*Oud West (618 7848). Tram 1, 3, 6, 12.* **Map** p309
A6. **Date** mid Sept.
Held in a former women's hospital turned artists' studios/living complex, this event changes with each year. One year it's a Kunstroute, meaning that an exhibition of local work is shown here, and the next year it's an exchange exhibition with another city. A route map and catalogue can be obtained from the Amsterdam Tourist Board or the AUB Ticketshop.

## High Times Cannabis Cup

*Melkweg, Lijnbaansgracht 234A (624 1777/*
*www.hightimes.com).* **Admission** prices vary.
**No credit cards. Map** p310 C5. **Date** Nov.
Harvest time means it's time for *High Times'* annual (and heavily commercialised) Cannabis Cup, where all things related to wastedness are celebrated over five days or so. There are banquets, bands, cultivation seminars and a competition where hundreds of judges (you too, if you wish) ascertain which of the hundreds of weeds are the wickedest, dude. The event is scattered – as are the minds – all over town, but is invariably focused around the Melkweg at night.

## Crossing Border

*Venues around Leidseplein (627 4985/*
*www.crossingborder.nl).* **Map** p310 D5. **Date** Oct.
*See p182* **Read all about it**.

## Museum Night

*Around Amsterdam (523 1822/www.de-n8.nl).*
**Admission** €12-€16. **Credit** varies. **Date** 2nd
Sat in Nov.
A night when almost all Amsterdam's museums and galleries stay up late and party, many organising special events to run alongside regular exhibits.

Anyone seen my sleigh? **Sinterklaas Intocht.**

Recent years have seen the Rijksmuseum transformed into a nightclub, the Joods Historisch Museum turned into a lounge and the Amsterdams Historisch Museum putting on a fashion show.

### Amsterdam Dance Event
*Around Amsterdam (035 621 8748/ www.amsterdam-dance-event.nl).* **Admission** prices vary. **Date** mid Nov.
Schmooze by day and party by night during this annual music conference concerned with all things disco. Felix Meritis is the location for daytime convention activities and workshops where over 1,000 delegates come to discuss the business of boogie. During the evening, venues such as the Melkweg and Paradiso host DJs from around the world.

### Sinterklaas Intocht
*Route via Barbizon Palace on Prins Hendrikkade, Damrak, Dam, Raadhuisstraat, Rozengracht, Marnixstraat, Leidseplein.* **Date** mid Nov.
In mid November, Sinterklaas (St Nicholas) marks the beginning of the Christmas season by stepping ashore from a steamboat at Centraal Station. St Nick – with his white beard, robes and staff – is every Dutch kid's favourite patron saint, distributing sweets during this annual parade of the city. Meanwhile, his Zwarte Pieten (Black Peter) helpers represent a threat to any naughty kids. Depending on which story you believe, either Black Peter was originally the devil – the colour and predilection for mischief-making are the only leftovers of an evil vanquished by Sinterklaas – or Zwarte Pieten helpers have dark skin from climbing down chimneys to deliver sweets.

## Winter

With a little luck, the canals turn solid enough for scenic skating in the typical Amsterdam winter. Otherwise, though, it's only the two family-oriented festivals – St Nicholas's Day, as important to the Dutch as Christmas, and New Year's Eve – that break up the monotony of this most sleety of seasons.

### Sinterklaas
*Around Amsterdam.* **Date** 5, 6 Dec.
While the St Nicholas prototype, Sinterklaas, is directing his Black Peter helpers down chimneys on the eve of his day, 6 December, families celebrate by exchanging small gifts and poems. This tradition started when the Church decided to tame the wild pagan partying that had always accompanied the end of the slaughter season. It began by ruling that the traditional celebration should be based around the birthday of St Nicholas – or 'Sinterklaas' – the patron saint of children (and, ironically, also prostitutes, thieves and the city of Amsterdam); a once-violent tradition was reborn as a Christian family feast. Sinterklaas eventually emigrated to the States, mutated into Santa Claus and shifted his birthday to 25 December in order to fill in for Jesus' failings of character when it came to the spirit of capitalism.

### Winter Parade
*Westergasfabriek, Haarlemmerweg 8-10 (033 465 4577/www.mobilearts.nl).* **Admission** prices vary. **No credit cards**. **Date** last 2 wks of Dec.
Such is the success of the August prototype (*see p180*) that the carnivalesque theatrical and musical acts of Parade now bring cheer to winter. Laughter, chaos and drinking are still the defining features, the only differences being that the tents and industrial buildings are heated and the heftier admission price permits entrance to all the festivities.

### Oudejaarsavond (New Year's Eve)
*Around Amsterdam.* **Date** 31 Dec.
Along with Queen's Day (*see p181* **A right royal knees-up**), New Year's Eve is Amsterdam's wildest celebration. There's happy chaos throughout the city, but the best spots are Nieuwmarkt and Dam, both of which get crowded and noisy: the ample use of firecrackers is suggestive of the fall of Saigon. The Dutch often begin with an evening of coffee, spirits and *oliebollen* ('oil-balls', which taste better than they sound: they're deep-fried blobs of dough, apple and raisins, with a sprinkle of icing sugar) with the family; many bars don't open until the witching hour.

### Chinese New Year
*Nieuwmarkt, Old Centre: Old Side (mobile 06 2476 0060/www.zeedijk.nl).* **Map** p306 D2. **Date** end Jan/start Feb.
Lion dances, firecrackers and Chinese drums 'n' gongs may scare away evil spirits, but your children will have a roaring good time chasing the dragon through Amsterdam's scenic Chinatown.

# Children

In town with youngsters in tow? No problem. Keeping children happy in kid-friendly Amsterdam is easy-peasy lemon squeezy.

Hanging tough – in a fluffy kind of way – at **Artis**. *See p98.*

## The best Kids' stuff

### Amsterdamse Bos
A forest and more, at five metres below sea level. *See p110.*

### Canal rides
The trip's more important than the destination. *See p72.*

### Efteling
Pitch your rubbish into talking trash bins. *See p188.*

### Street performers
Captivating, plus the price is right: free. *See p187.*

### Vondelpark
Respite and action for an easy escape from urban stress. *See p109.*

In Amsterdam with children in tow? Follow your whims, sure, but do a little strategic planning, too. Happily, Amsterdam packs a surprising amount of activities for the young and the young at heart into a small space. Indeed, its compact size means parents can easily devise itineraries accommodating the whole family without too much trouble.

Amsterdam has a substantial population of under-18s and – aside from activities obviously geared towards adults – children are welcome almost everywhere. And should the charms of canals and crooked houses wear off, there's plenty specifically for youngsters. The **AUB Ticketshop** (0900 0191; *see p279* **Tickets, please**) in Leidseplein is a great place for ideas, while *Uitkrant* (look under 'Jeugd') can also be enlightening if you can navigate the primarily Dutch text. Note, though, that as with almost everything else in Amsterdam, restrooms are tiny; in the few places changing facilities are available, they're usually only in the ladies.

For kids' clothes and shoe stores, *see p159*; for toy shops, *see p171*.

## Getting around

Few cities compare to Amsterdam when it comes to public transport. Effective and cheap, trams, buses and the Metro penetrate most of the existing city (IJburg and the Eastern Docklands have only limited infrastructure, but service should be extended in the near future). A tram ride can also be a great way to catch your breath, entertain the kids and find your bearings, but fold pushchairs before boarding to lessen congestion. A more pleasurable ride can be taken in the antique electric tram carriages at the **Electrische Museum Tramlijn Amsterdam** (*see p112*) at the edge of the Amsterdamse Bos.

Children love Amsterdam's waterways. A pricey but fun way of getting around is by water taxi, but a decent free alternative is to take a trip on the River IJ ferry to Amsterdam Noord; boats leave from behind Centraal Station about every ten minutes. If you have older kids, you may enjoy renting a canal bike, but remember to navigate on the right-hand side of the waterway. For more information on all transport in Amsterdam, *see p274*.

## Indoor entertainment

### Applied arts

#### Hobbywinkel Oude Badhuis
*Meteorenweg 158, Amsterdam Noord (633 6911/ www.oudebadhuis.nl). Bus 35, 38.* **Open** 1-5pm Mon; 9am-5pm Tue-Sat. **No credit cards.**
This hobby shop doubles up as an art studio where 6-11s can try their hand at being the next Van Gogh. A small fee includes the cost of materials.

#### Keramiekstudio Color Me Mine
*Roelof Hartstraat 22, Museum Quarter (675 2987/www.colormemine.nl). Tram 3, 5, 10, 12, 24.* **Open** 11am-9pm Tue-Sat; noon-6pm Sun. **Credit** MC, V.
All the family can try their hand at creating personal crockery masterpieces at this ceramic studio.

### Films

Most films for children are dubbed (indicated by 'Nederlands Gesproken'), though original versions are often shown at non-matinée times. The **Kriterion** (*see p192*), the **Rialto** (*see p193*) and the **Nederlands Filmmuseum** (*see p194*) cinemas all have screenings for kids. Check local listings for times and other information. During the autumn holidays (mid October), the **Cinekid** film festival (531 7890) takes place nationwide, offering quality kids' films from across the globe (including many in English).

## Go-cart racing

### Race Planet Amsterdam
*Herwijk 10 (0900 722 3752/www.raceplanet.nl). Sloterdijk rail (direction IJmuiden), then bus 82, 182 (bus stop Herwijk).* **Open** 1-11pm Mon-Fri; noon-11pm Sat, Sun. *8-16s* 1-6pm Mon-Fri; noon-6pm Sat, Sun. **Admission** from €14 per person/12min. **Credit** MC, V.
In town with bigger kids (taller than 1.40m) and after something more exhilarating than a canalside stroll? Indoor go-cart racing may pump up the adrenaline and placate any adventure-seeking young 'uns. And you might ket a kick out of it, too.

## Museums

Good bets for children include the interactive, non-Western exhibitions – mostly in Dutch – aimed at ages six to 12 at the **Kindermuseum**, part of the **Tropenmuseum** (*see p99*), and the interesting array of scientific activities designed to appeal to over-fours at **Nemo** (*see p101*). Any of Amsterdam's big museums should hold children's attention in small doses, but the city's smaller, quirkier museums might prove more interesting for youngsters: why not take them to the **Woonbootmuseum** (*see p90*) to see what life on a houseboat is like? Or go to the **Kattenkabinet** (*see p93*) and find out everything there is to know about cats?

## Restaurants

Aside from the restaurants listed below, most cheaper restaurants and pizzerias welcome kids. Youngsters are normally allowed in bars and cafés, as long as they don't run amok. When in doubt, ask staff if kids are welcome. Be warned, though, that most Dutch restaurants and cafés do not have changing facilities, and toilets are often in the cellar. *See also p116*.

### Amsterdams Historisch Museum
*Kalverstraat 92, Old Centre: New Side (523 1822/www.ahm.nl). Tram 1, 2, 4, 5, 9, 14, 16, 20, 24, 25.* **Open** 10am-5pm Mon-Fri; 11am-5pm Sat, Sun. **Admission** €6; €3 6-16s; free MJK, under-6s. **No credit cards.** **Map** p306 D3.
This museum has a reasonably priced restaurant on a peaceful courtyard where kids can play before and after their pancakes or fries. The restaurant has a separate entrance from the museum (*see p86*).

### KinderKookKafé
*Oudezijds Achterburgwal 193, Old Centre: Old Side (625 3257). Tram 1, 2, 4, 5, 9, 14, 17, 20, 24, 25/Metro Nieuwmarkt.* **Open** *Reservations & information* 1-5pm Mon-Fri. *Dinner & high tea* Sat, Sun; phone for details and book ahead. **No credit cards.** **Map** p306 D3.

Nemo memo: it's great for kids. *See p101.*

The Children's Cooking Café runs cooking courses in Dutch for children during the week. But the real fun is to be had at weekends, with kids running the entire place: they cook, serve, present the bill and wash up – all with a little help from the grown-up staff, of course. The simple set menu includes a main course and dessert: ingredients are fresh, the food is healthy and prices for diners are very low.

### Pizzeria Capri
*Lindengracht 63, the Jordaan (624 4940). Tram 3, 10/bus 18, 22.* **Open** 5-10pm daily. **No credit cards.** **Map** p305 B2.
Children are welcome at this pizzeria-cum-gelateria with a small pavement terrace. Staff and customers remain unfazed by kids dropping pasta on the floor, and there's plenty of real Italian ice-cream on hand for blackmail purposes. High chairs are available.

## Swimming pools & saunas

Good for kids are **De Mirandabad** (a sub-tropical pool with a wave machine, whirlpool, toddler pool and slide), the **Zuiderbad** and **Marnixbad** indoor pools, and the **Brediusbad** and **Flevoparkbad** outdoor pools. For local pools, check the phone book under 'Zwembad' and call for special children's hours. Most saunas tolerate quiet children, especially at off-peak hours. For saunas and pools, *see pp237-8*.

## Theatre & circus

The Dutch pride themselves on their cultural development, something that holds true for the way they stimulate their children's appreciation of art and entertainment. The **Children's Theatre Phoneline** (622 2999) offers recorded information in Dutch on kids' theatre, though you can also check under 'Jeugd' in *Uitkrant*. In addition to specialised children's theatre groups, many theatres and music venues hold kid's concerts and the like during the year; the Concertgebouw's *Kijk met je Oren*, for example, which combines classical music and puppetry. Check with **Uitlijn** (0900 0191) for details.

### Circustheater Elleboog
*Passeerdersgracht 32, Western Canal Belt (626 9370/www.elleboog.nl). Tram 1, 2, 5, 7, 10.* **Open** *Bookings* 10am-5pm Mon-Fri. *Activities* times vary Sat, Sun. *Shows* times vary. **Admission** prices vary. **No credit cards.** **Map** p310 C4.
Kids aged between four and 17 can learn circus and clowning skills, tricks, make-up skills, juggling and tightrope walking. Activity days end in a performance for parents and friends. The non-member sessions are always busy, mostly with Dutch kids, but staff speak English.

### De Krakeling
*Nieuwe Passeerdersstraat 1, Western Canal Belt (625 3284/reservations 624 5123/ www.krakeling.nl). Tram 7, 10.* **Shows** 2pm Wed, Sun; 8pm Thur-Sat. **Admission** €8; €7 over-65s; €6 adult accompanying child; €5 under-18s. **No credit cards.** **Map** p310 C4.
De Krakeling is the only Dutch theatre that produces programming exclusively for children. This unique venue has separate productions for over-12s and under-12s: phone to check what's going on at any given time. It also hosts childrens' parties. For non-Dutch speakers, there are puppet and mime shows, and sometimes musicals. Shows are listed in the programme, as well as in *Uitkrant*.

## Outdoor entertainment

Amsterdam is one of those beautiful cities that is just quirky enough to appeal to kids. The leaning houses, canals, bridges, boats, bikes, windmills and stands on every other streetcorner all form an enticing backdrop to whatever might be going on, whatever the season. Street performers abound; there's almost certain to be something going on at Dam Square, Leidseplein and Rembrandtplein if the weather's decent. Keep an eye open for Jan Klaasen, Punch and Judy-style puppet theatre, on Dam Square during the week.

When winter arrives, many local parents take their children skating at the **Jaap Edenhal** rink (*see p237*), though the more daring among them prefer to head for the city's canals: when the weather's cold enough, many of them freeze over. However, as an outsider, you should always check with the locals if it's safe to skate.

## Urban farms

Children's farms dot the Netherlands, and Amsterdam is no exception. **Artis** (*see p98*) is home to surprisingly tame pigs, goats, sheep and chickens, and also has great playgrounds. All Amsterdam's neighbourhoods have at least one urban farm; check the *Yellow Pages* under 'Kinderboerderijen'. With the exception of Artis, admission is usually free.

**Arts & Entertainment**

# Out of Amsterdam

On the beaten track but out of town, these attractions appeal to kids of all ages and are easy to reach by train or car. Check with the local Amsterdam Tourist Board, ANWB shops or the Netherlands Railways (NS) for ideas on day trips. The NS also has walking and cycling routes available for those who want to take advantage of good weather; tickets for **NS Rail Idee** (*see p252*), which runs to all the following attractions, cover the cost of transport and maps to and from the walking or cycling location. For details of other out-of-town attractions, *see p253*.

## Archeon

*Archeonlaan 1, Alphen aan den Rijn (0172 447744/ www.archeon.nl). 50km (31 miles) from Amsterdam; A4 to Leiden, then N11 to Alphen aan den Rijn.* **Open** *Apr-July, Sept, Oct* 10am-5pm Tue-Sun. *Aug* 10am-5pm daily. Closed Nov-Mar. **Admission** €12.75; €10 over-65s; €9.75 5-12s; free under-5s. 50% discount on all prices after 4pm. **Credit** MC, V.
Take a trip through history: from when dinosaurs walked the earth via the Bronze Age to Roman times. There are loads of interactive and hands-on displays here, plus an open-air plunge pool. Great fun.

## Efteling

*Europalaan 1, Kaatsheuvel, Noord Brabant (0416 288111/www.efteling.nl). 110km (68 miles) from Amsterdam; take A27 to Kaatsheuvel exit, then N261.* **Open** *Apr-June, Sept, Oct* 10am-6pm daily.

Party hearty at **De Krakeling**. *See p187.*

*July-late Aug* 10am-9pm Mon-Fri, Sun, 10am-midnight Sat. **Admission** €21; €19 over-60s, disabled; free under-4s. **Credit** AmEx, MC, V.
This enormous fairytale forest is peopled with dwarves and witches, characters from the Grimms' stories and the *Arabian Nights*, enchanted and haunted castles... even talking rubbish bins. The massive (and massively popular) amusement park is packed with state-of-the-art thrills, as well as more traditional fairground rides for tinies. Kids and kitsch-lovers will adore it. Busy in summer.

## Linnaeushof

*Rijksstraatweg 4, Bennebroek (023 584 7624/ www.linnaeushof.nl). 20km (13 miles) from Amsterdam; take A5 to Haarlem, then south on N208.* **Open** *Mar-Sept* 10am-6pm daily. Closed Oct-Feb. **Admission** €6; €5 over-65s, disabled; free under-2s. **No credit cards**.
A staggering 300 attractions are located in this huge leisure park near Haarlem: there's a Wild West train, cable cars, mini-golf, trampolines, a water play area and go-carts. Children under five are happy in the new play area, and the price is most certainly right.

## Madurodam

*George Maduroplein 1, The Hague (070 355 3900/www.madurodam.nl). 57km (35 miles) from Amsterdam; take A4 to The Hague.* **Open** *Mid Mar-June* 9am-8pm daily. *July, Aug* 9am-10pm daily. *Sept-mid Mar* 9am-6pm daily. **Admission** €10; €9 over-60s; €7 4-11s; free under-4s. **Credit** AmEx, DC, MC, V.
It claims to be the largest miniature village in the world, and we're not about to argue. Kids love the detailed models of the country's famous sights – from Rotterdam's Erasmus Bridge to Schiphol Airport – all of which are built to scale on a 1:25 ratio. Go on a summer's evening and see the models enchantingly lit from the inside by over 50,000 tiny lamps.

## Museum van Speelklok tot Pierement

*Buurkerkhof 10, Utrecht (030 231 2789/ www.museumspeelklok.nl). 38km (24 miles) from Amsterdam; take A2 to Utrecht.* **Open** 10am-5pm Tue-Sat; noon-5pm Sun. **Admission** €6; €4 4-12s; under-4s free. **Credit** MC, V.
Mechanical music boxes, circus, fairground and street organs, and wondrous tin toys take pride of place in this unique antique collection. A great double day out for junior machine freaks.

## Nederlands Spoorwegmuseum

*Maliebaanstation 16, Utrecht (030 230 6206/ www.spoorwegmuseum.nl). 38km (24 miles) from Amsterdam; take A2 to Utrecht.* **Open** 10am-5pm Tue-Fri; 11.30am-5pm Sat, Sun. **Admission** €7; €5.75 over-65s; €4.50 4-12s; free under-4s. **No credit cards**.
The Netherlands Railway Museum is housed in an historic station, where over 60 old and new locos can be admired inside and out. There are also rides on a miniature Intercity and TGV line for under-12s.

# A walk in the park

Amsterdam's numerous parks offer an outlet for energy pent up by frazzled city-goers. True tranquility may not be found there, but you can recharge while the kids run a little freer than they might do on busy streets. Most parks have at least a spartan café, handy if you left the picnic basket at home. And almost all of them have a playground with a sandpit and, sometimes, a paddling pool. Be vigilant, however, for the ubiquitous dog droppings.

With its popular summer programme of free afternoon entertainment, an excellent playground and a wading pool, **Vondelpark** (see p109) is the most convenient and dynamic of Amsterdam's parks, as well as the most popular. Check local listings to find out what's planned; most children's events take place on Wednesdays. Among the attractions at **Amstelpark** (see p110), in the south of the city, are a miniature train, a maze, a farm and pony rides; **Rembrandtpark**, way out west, offers similar activities and is also home to

Bouwspeelplaats 't Landje (618 3604), which organises a number of afternoon activities tailor-made for six- to 14-year-olds.

**Flevopark** (see p99) is the wildest and least used of the city's parks, and, as such, is a nice peaceful spot for a picnic or a kickabout. The adjacent Flevoparkbad has two fantastic outdoor swimming pools and a toddlers' paddling pool in a spacious grassy recreation area. **Westerpark**'s renovation is scheduled for completion in 2003 and promises a large wading pond for children (see p105). **Gaasperplas Park** has some superb sports and playground facilities, including a paddling pool and lake for swimming (see 239).

**Amsterdamse Bos** (bos means forest) is more than a park. Boating lakes, bicycle and canoe hire, tennis courts, open-air theatre, large playgrounds, new wading pools, a recreation island and petting zoos all make this reserve fantastic for kids. There's also the magical Bosmuseum, which has park maps, and the Geitenboerderij Ridammerhoeve, where you can pet goats. For more, see p110.

## Six Flags Holland

*Spijkweg 30, Biddinghuizen (0321 329991/329999/ www.sixflags.nl). 72km (45 miles) from Amsterdam; take A1 towards Amersfoort, then A6 towards Lelystad, then follow signs for Six Flags.*
**Open** *Apr-Aug* from 10am daily, closing times vary. *Sept, Oct* from 10am Fri-Sun, closing times vary. **Admission** €21 over 1.4m; €17 over-65s, disabled; €11 1m-1.40m; free under 1m. **Credit** AmEx, MC, V.
Six Flags caters to bigger kids, with the Netherlands' largest collection of rollercoasters, including one made of wood. Tots are sure to be entertained by the Looney Tunes characters and some tamer attractions. Opening hours are complicated and change often, though it's always open until at least 5pm and, during peak season, until 10pm.

## Parenting

### Babyminders

Check the *Yellow Pages* under 'Oppascentrales' for babysitting in the suburbs.

### Oppascentrale Kriterion

*624 5848.* **Rates** from €4.50/hr; €3.50 additional charge Fri, Sat; €3 administration charge. **No credit cards**.
Up and running for 45 years, this ever-reliable service uses male and female students aged over 18, all of whom are individually vetted. Book in advance.

## Children's rights

### Kinderrechtswinkel

*Staalstraat 19, Old Centre: Old Side (626 0067/ info@krwa.demon.nl). Tram 4, 9, 14, 16, 20, 24, 25.* **Open** *Walk-in consultations* 3-6pm Mon; 2-5pm Wed, Sat. **Map** p307 E3.
Under-18s in need of information about legal matters and the responsibilities of teachers, parents and employers will find the folk at this children's rights office very helpful. Kids may phone or visit, and while staff will answer questions from adults, they prefer dealing directly with the children involved.

### Kindertelefoon (Childline)

*0800 0432/office 672 2411/www.kindertelefoon.nl.* **Open** 2-8pm daily.
Young people from eight to 18 are welcome to phone this free line to get information on bullying, sexual abuse, running away from home and so on. Staff are keen to stress that they do not give details about children's entertainment.

### Toy libraries

There are several toy libraries in Amsterdam. You will have to pay a registration fee, and a small borrowing charge for each use. For details of your nearest toy library, consult the *Yellow Pages* under 'Speel-o-theek'.

# Film

Verhoeven and De Bont have stormed Hollywood, but domestic movie-making is also on the up. No wonder cinema-going is popular in the Netherlands.

The good news? Cinema is growing more popular in the Netherlands. Around 23 million Dutch people visited a cinema in 2001, six per cent up on 2000. The bad news? The majority of them go to see big-budget Hollywood flicks or trashy Dutch crowd-pleasers; quality home-grown films often disappear in weeks. The lack of exhibitors for non-Hollywood films make it tough for films to survive on word of mouth.

It's little wonder that Dutch moviemakers often aim for a career abroad. Paul Verhoeven is the most famous, but don't forget Robby Muller (Wim Wenders' cameraman), screenwriter Menno Meyes, and Jan de Bont, a former cameraman who cleaned up as director of *Speed* and *Twister*. Of the Dutch actors that have tried to make it abroad, Famke Janssen has made a living in the likes of *X-Men* and *Don't Say a Word* after her breakthrough role in *GoldenEye*.

Mainstream Dutch films, many tailor-made for a young audience, usually do well at the box office, if not with critics. *Costa!*, about a group of youngsters living it up in Spain, was huge for months. Helped by the presence of popular Dutch soap stars clad in bikinis, it attracted more viewers in its first weekend than *Hannibal* and went on to become the biggest Dutch cinematic success since Paul Verhoeven's 1973 film *Turks Fruit* (*Turkish Delight*).

Luckily, there are other filmmakers working on more worthwhile movies, aided by a tax law designed to encourage local and international investment in Dutch film. That said, it doesn't ensure everything gets made. *Ocean Warrior*, a biopic of Greenpeace founder Paul Watson that, with a budget of ƒ72 million (€33 million), would have been the costliest Dutch film in history, was cancelled due to cash problems.

Of those films that did make it to the big screen in recent years, the most notable have included *The Discovery of Heaven*, based on the bestseller by Harry Mulisch and starring Stephen Fry (still the most expensive Dutch film ever); *Down*, from actor-turned-director Jeroen Krabbé (*The Fugitive*); Dick Maas's silly remake of his '80s flick *The Lift*; and Laurence Malkin's fast-paced but corny thriller *Soul Assassin*. Other attention-grabbing directors include Jean van de Velde (*All Stars*, *Lek*), Eddy Terstall (*Hufters & Hofdames*, *Rent-a-Friend*) and Theo van Gogh (yes, he is related; *Blind Date*,

Loungin' in the **Cinecenter**. *See p192.*

*Baby Blue*), with Alex van Warmerdam (*Abel*, *The Dress*) and Robert Jan Westdijk (*Zusje*) holding up the artier side. For more on young movie-makers, *see p193* **Directors' cuts**.

## The cinemas

Amsterdam's cinemas offer as balanced and substantial a diet as any European city. As in many cities, cinemas can be divided into two categories: first-run houses and art houses (aka 'filmhuizen'). Amsterdammers have a healthy appetite for foreign and art house fare, and these venues offer a cosmopolitan mix of art films, documentaries and retrospectives (as well as an informed selection of more intelligent Hollywood flicks). With the exception of the **Uitkijk**, all have marvellous cafés, while **The Movies**, especially notable for its lavish art deco interior, also has an enchanting restaurant.

*Arts & Entertainment*

The opening of Amsterdam's first multiplex, the 14-screen **Pathé ArenA** out in the Bijlmer suburb, has grabbed both headlines and customers, but there are several other cinemas that prove as much of an attraction as the movies they screen. The **Pathé Tuschinski**, with its sumptuous deco architecture and fittings, is a marvel. Also interesting is the plan to build an art house cinema on water, aptly named **CineShip** and designed to contain four screens, a terrace and a restaurant. Located on Veemkade, near Oostelijke Handelskade by Centraal Station, the glass building should be open within the next few years.

### TICKETS & INFORMATION

Cinema programmes in the multiplexes change every Thursday. Weekly listings for all cinemas except those owned by Pathé (for which, *see below*) can be found in *Filmladder*, printed in the Wednesday editions of all major newspapers and displayed in many cafés, bars and cinemas. Other reliable sources of information include the 'Saturday PS' supplement of *Het Parool*, the *Amsterdams Stadsblad*, Dutch listings site www.filmfocus.nl, and, for indie and art house films, free listings mag *Shark*. Look out, too, for fine monthly Dutch film mag *De Filmkrant*, whose movie information is mostly in Dutch but easily understood by non-natives.

Since their various multiplexes opened in the Netherlands, **Pathé** no longer advertise in the *Filmladder*. The company claims that it has become too expensive a proposition, although that sounds suspiciously like an excuse to get people to log on to their website (www.pathe.nl) and, in particular, call their premium-rate phone line (0900 1458). Both are solely in Dutch.

It's advisable to reserve tickets if you think the movie will be popular (opening weekends, for example). Cinemas usually charge a nominal booking fee, though none accept credit cards. Worse still for those who count English as a first language, Pathé-owned cinemas – all of those listed under **First run** below – now use a computer-operated, premium-rate telephone bookings line in Dutch only. If you don't speak Dutch and can't get online (you can book at www.pathe.nl), then you may have to journey to the cinema itself to reserve tickets.

While art houses go straight into the movie without the unwelcome appetiser of ads, the starting time in multiplexes allows 15 minutes' grace for commercials. All films are shown in the original language (normally English) with Dutch subtitles. Films in Dutch are indicated by the words 'Nederlands Gesproken' after the title. Some cinemas offer student discounts with ID. Purists should also note that for some inexplicable reason, a great many Dutch

**The best** Cinemas

### Het Ketelhuis
Dutch films, docs and discussions near the Westergasfabriek. *See p192.*

### Kriterion
Catch a surprise film at Thursday's weekly preview slot. *See p192.*

### The Movies
Dinner and a movie? You can have both at this restaurant-cinema. *See p193.*

### Nederlands Filmmuseum
Summer's outdoor screenings are the city's closest thing to a drive-in. *See p194.*

### Tuschinski Arthouse
This reliable old stager is pure heaven in an otherwise touristy area. *See p192.*

cinemas stick an interval in the middle of every film. Call ahead to check if you really can't deal with such an unwelcome interruption.

## Cinemas

### First run

### Bellevue Cinerama/Calypso
*Marnixstraat 400-2, Southern Canal Belt (0900 1458 premium rate/www.pathe.nl). Tram 1, 2, 5, 6, 7, 10, 20.* **Tickets** €5-€9. **Screens** 2 each. **No credit cards. Map** p310 C5.
Two adjacent Pathé complexes with a shared box office. As with all cinemas in this section, the cheapest price is for screenings before noon; tickets for evening shows cost top price, with daytime screenings around €2 cheaper. The basement Cinerama is now part of the Nederlands Filmmuseum (*see p194*) and shows art house films both old and new. Tickets must be booked at the above address or number.

A Pathé pair: the glitzy **City** near Leidseplein (*left*), and the more austere **Pathé de Munt**.

## City

*Kleine Gartmanplantsoen 15-19, Southern Canal Belt (0900 1458 premium rate/www.pathe.nl).* **Tram** 1, 2, 5, 6, 7, 10, 20. **Tickets** €4-€8. **Screens** 7. **No credit cards. Map** p310 D5.
The large frontage and huge advertisement hoardings of City dominate Kleine Gartmanplantsoen. Inside, TVs in the foyer run a constant diet of trailers. Its central location and Hollywood-or-bust policy make it hugely popular with loud youngsters.

## Pathé ArenA

*ArenA Boulevard 600, Bijlmermeer (0900 1458 premium rate/www.pathe.nl).* **Tickets** €5-€9. **Screens** 14. **No credit cards**.
This glitzy multiplex, next to the Ajax stadium, offers 14 screens, 3,250 seats, digital sound and spacious foyers. Expect blockbusters, action films and other Hollywood success stories, playing to crowds drawn largely from the surrounding suburbs.

## Pathé de Munt

*Vijzelstraat 15, Southern Canal Belt (0900 1458 premium rate/www.pathe.nl).* **Tram** 4, 9, 14, 16, 20, 24, 25. **Tickets** €5-€9. **Screens** 7. **No credit cards. Map** p310 D4.
Housed in a horrible brick building, this complex near the Tuschinski boasts seven screens, comfy seats and offers mainly Hollywood flicks.

## Pathé Tuschinski

*Reguliersbreestraat 26-8, Southern Canal Belt (0900 1458 premium rate/www.pathe.nl).* **Tram** 4, 9, 14, 16, 20, 24, 25. **Tickets** €5-€9. **Screens** 4. **No credit cards. Map** p311 E4.
Built in 1921 as a variety theatre, the Tuschinski is Amsterdam's most prestigious cinema, which means queues at evenings and weekends. The choice of films here is inspired, while the stunning deco design (*see p34*) attracts visitors to guided tours. If you've come with a group, splash out on the eight-person box, with champagne all round. The cinema's due to reopen in April 2002 following renovations.

## Pathé Tuschinski Arthouse

*Reguliersbreestraat 34, Southern Canal Belt (0900 1458 premium rate/www.pathe.nl).* **Tram** 4, 9, 14, 16, 20, 24, 25. **Tickets** €5-€9. **Screens** 3. **No credit cards. Map** p310 D4.

Another Pathé cinema, next to its older brother the Tuschinski. This one offers artier films, though it also shows intelligent Hollywood flicks.

## Art houses

### Cinecenter

*Lijnbaansgracht 236, the Jordaan (623 6615).* **Tram** 1, 2, 5, 6, 7, 10, 20. **Tickets** €5-€8. **Screens** 4. **No credit cards. Map** p310 C4.
The Cinecenter is a welcoming venue, with a hip 'lounge' decor. Each screen has its own name – check out the tiny 52-seater Jean Vigo room – and the programme is pleasingly international. It's very popular on Sunday afternoons.

### Filmhuis Cavia

*Van Hallstraat 521, West (681 1419/www.filmhuiscavia.nl).* **Tram** 3, 10. **Tickets** €5. **Screens** 1. **No credit cards. Map** p305 A3.
Housed in a former squatted school, Cavia specialises in obscure and political pictures. It also puts on festivals, ranging from gay and lesbian flicks to films from the former Yugoslavia. Irregular Friday night get-together Club Index sees political themes discussed, along with films and documentaries.

### Het Ketelhuis

*Haarlemmerweg 8-10, the Jordaan (684 0090/www.ketelhuis.nl).* **Bus** 18, 22. **Tickets** €7. **Screens** 1. **No credit cards. Map** p305 A1.
Devoted to Dutch films and documentaries – sometimes with subtitles – this project of producer Marc van Warmerdam is a favourite among local film fans. Along with films, it also offers lively film-related discussions and forums.

### Kriterion

*Roetersstraat 170, Oost (623 1708/www.kriterion.nl).* **Tram** 6, 7, 10/Metro Weesperplein. **Tickets** €6-€8; €5 children's matinées, previews. **Screens** 2. **No credit cards. Map** p312 G3.
Run by volunteer students, this local knows how to pick 'em: the intriguing programme includes kids' matinées (Wednesdays, Saturdays and Sundays) and preview screenings (Thursdays). Student flicks are also screened, while late shows cover cult US movies or erotic French films.

## The Movies

*Haarlemmerdijk 161, the Jordaan (624 5790/ www.themovies.nl). Tram 3.* **Tickets** €7.50; €6.35 students. **Screens** 4. **Credit** *Restaurant* MC, V. **Map** p305 B1.

Don't be fooled by the insipid name: the Movies is a great place to visit if you like, um, the movies. Built in 1928, it's a fine building: the '30s-style café is worth a visit even if you're not catching a flick, which will probably be international in origin and interesting in content. Make an evening of it: if you eat in the restaurant, your seats for the show will be reserved, allowing you to slip in at the last minute.

## Rialto

*Ceintuurbaan 338, the Pijp (662 3488/ www.rialtofilm.nl). Tram 3, 12, 24, 25.* **Tickets** €5.50-€7.50; €28 5-visit card; €50 10-visit card. **Screens** 2. **No credit cards**. **Map** p311 F6.

This stylish, alternative cinema in the Pijp is one of the few with disabled access. It offers a mix of new and old international flicks and the occasional European première. Thematic blocks change monthly, but there's always at least one classic oldie on their schedule.

## De Uitkijk

*Prinsengracht 452, Southern Canal Belt (623 7460/www.uitkijk.nl). Tram 1, 2, 5, 6, 7, 10, 20.* **Tickets** €5.50-€7. **Screens** 1. **No credit cards**. **Map** p310 D5.

Amsterdam's oldest cinema – the set-up dates from 1913 – is a charming 158-seat converted canal house; films that prove popular tend to stay put for a while. De Uitkijk doesn't serve snacks, so you won't be disturbed by popcorn-crunching or Coke-slurping.

## Multimedia centres

### Academie Cinema

*Overtoom 301, Oud West (779 4913/http:// squat.net/overtoom301). Tram 1, 6.* **Tickets** €2. **Screens** 1. **No credit cards**. **Map** p309 B6.

The former Nederlandse Filmacademie was squatted in 2000 and turned into, among other things, an organic vegan restaurant, a club, and a cinema offering indie and experimental videos (sometimes films), plus gay and lesbian flicks. Though the future looks promising, it's not known how long the squatters will be allowed to stay, so email, call or check its website before setting out. It's also closed in summer.

### De Balie

*Kleine Gartmanplantsoen 10, Southern Canal Belt (553 5100/www.debalie.nl). Tram 1, 2, 5, 6, 7, 10, 20.* **Tickets** €5-€7. **Screens** 1. **No credit cards**. **Map** p310 D5.

The films shown in the cinema of this highbrow cultural centre (*see p241*) couldn't be more different from those offered opposite at City (*see p192*). Expect documentaries and obscure, frequently arty films from Europe and beyond, both old and new.

# Directors' cuts

Having long looked jealously at the string of successes accrued by low-budget Belgian and Danish films, the Dutch film industry recently began to ask itself what it could do to improve the international hit rate of its movies. While there have been some success stories – a minor hit here and a foreign film Oscar there – at the end of the day, genuine global hits have been few and far between. Hopefuls such as Alex van Warmerdam and Eddy Terstall have yet to break through with an international product as exciting as their potential.

But thanks to an innovative new funding programme that focuses on finding and nurturing home-grown auteurs, the number of Dutch cinematic hopefuls working in the country has increased dramatically. Under the Route 2000 and No More Heroes banners, the Netherlands Film Fund has provided the opportunity for up-and-comers to strut their celluloid stuff. There are only two rules: keep the budget at around €500,000 and wrap up shooting in 23 days.

These limits, however, haven't seemed to hinder the production of such worthwhile, personal and refreshingly genre-free films as Karim Traïdia's *De Poolse Bruid* (*The Polish Bride*), Paula van der Oest's *De Trip van Teetje* (*Tate's Trip*), Nanouk Leopold's *Iles Flottantes* and Lodewijk Crijns's *Met Grote Blijdschap* (*With Great Joy*). And even those who haven't gained financially from the scheme have reaped rewards in other ways. Erik de Bruyn, for example, did not make the final cut for the fund, but he surely benefited from the process of being a contender and ably employed what he learned on his excellent *Wilde Mossels* (*Wild Mussels*) using other funding. Similarly, Martin Koolhoven, while not quite hitting his stride on the fund-produced *AmnesiA*, followed it in 2001 with the rather better *De Grot* (*The Cave*). What's more, the flowering of low-budget films has also provided a showcase for such obviously gifted actors as Fedja van Huêt and the country's best cameraman, Joost van Gelder. The future, at last, looks bright.

## Melkweg

*Lijnbaansgracht 234A, Southern Canal Belt (531 8181/www.melkweg.nl). Tram 1, 2, 5, 6, 7, 10, 20.* **Tickets** €6; €5 students (incl membership). **Screens** 1. **No credit cards. Map** p310 C5.

The Melkweg (*see p198, p213 and p225*) runs a consistently imaginative film programme in its cosy first-floor cinema, taking in anything from mainstream trash to cult fare and art house flicks.

## Tropeninstituut

**Kleine Zaal** *Linnaeusstraat 2, Oost;* **Grote Zaal** *Mauritskade 63, Oost (568 8500/www.kit.nl/ tropentheater). Tram 9, 10, 14, 20.* **Tickets** €6-€7. **Screens** 2. **Credit** MC, V. **Map** p312 H3.

Located way out east just next to the excellent Tropenmuseum (*see p99*), this venue stages regular ethnic music and theatre performances, alongside interesting documentaries and feature films from developing countries. A thoroughly worthwhile enterprise, and often a fascinating one, too.

Park life: the **Nederlands Filmmuseum**.

# Film museum

## Nederlands Filmmuseum (NFM)

*Vondelpark 3, Museum Quarter (589 1400/library 589 1435/www.filmmuseum.nl). Tram 1, 2, 3, 5, 6, 12, 20.* **Open** *Library* 10am-5pm Tue-Fri; 11am-5pm Sat. **Tickets** €6.25; €5 students; €3.50 members. *Membership* €15/yr. **Screens** 3. **No credit cards. Map** p310 C6.

Don't be fooled: this government-subsidised enterprise is really more of a cinema than a museum; established in the 1940s, it has over 35,000 films in its vaults, culled from every period, cinematic style and corner of the world. Dutch films and children's matinées screen on Sundays, and occasional showings of silent movies come with piano accompaniment. On Thursdays at 10pm in summer, there are outdoor screenings on the terrace. Students of cinema can be found poring over the archives. The museum's Café Vertigo, in the basement, has one of Amsterdam's most charming terraces.

# Film festivals

## Amnesty International Film Festival

*626 4436/www.amnesty.nl/filmfestival.* **Date** Mar-Apr 2003.

This five-day biennial event on human rights is held in various locations, including De Balie (*see p193*) and features films, documentaries, lectures, discussions and a workshop.

## Festival van de Fantastische Film

*623 1708/www.fff2000.nl.* **Date** Apr.

A week-long extravaganza held in various cinemas, with premières, previews and retrospectives, FFF should appeal to all lovers of horror, fantasy and SF. The Night of Terror, which spotlights some of the goriest movies imaginable in front of an up-for-it crowd, is not to be missed.

## International Documentary Filmfestival Amsterdam

*626 1939/www.idfa.nl.* **Date** last wk in Nov.

Documentaries are the staple of this fascinating annual festival, centred around De Balie (*see p193*). A prestigious prize in the name of the late documentarist Joris Ivens is awarded to the best film.

## International Film Festival Rotterdam

*Information 010 890 9090/reservations 010 890 9000/www.filmfestivalrotterdam.nl).* **Date** late Jan/early Feb.

With around 100 films in both the main programme and in retrospectives, the IFFR is the biggest event of its type in the country. The festival has an emphasis on what can loosely be termed 'art' movies, and is held in a number of different locations, all within walking distance of each other in Rotterdam. The lectures and seminars are normally a highlight, while aspiring moviemakers should visit the afternoon workshops. Check out, too, the eclectic series of events from Exploding Cinema, which also organises alternative events in Amsterdam that show self-produced VHS, 8mm and 16mm films.

## Nederlands Film Festival

*030 230 3800/www.filmfestival.nl.* **Date** Sept.

An all-Dutch affair, the NFF spotlights around 100 features in a variety of venues around Utrecht, along with shorts, docs and TV shows. Every new Dutch production of the year is shown, along with flicks by students from Dutch film and art academies.

## World Wide Video Festival

*420 7729/www.wwvf.nl.* **Date** autumn.

This annual fest takes place at locations including the Paradiso (*see p214*) and the Stedelijk (*see p108*). Aside from videos and DVDs, the festival also features web-based projects, installations and seminars on a plethora of film- and video-related subjects.

# Galleries

Art with a squat edge and the distinguished provenance of Rembrandt.

In the beginning, God made sea and bog. And then the Dutch made some land to sit atop it. This required organisation, and organise they did. Space became the place in which to project one's dreams of order. When they ran out of space, they compensated by turning their attention to paper and canvas, perhaps hoping they could now organise things more perfectly.

Later, Mondriaan would lay out garden plots of colour in the name of simplification, but until then – or, rather, until the camera was invented – Dutch artists tried only to depict reality. And in the Golden Age, not only the rich but also the booming and status-seeking middle classes could afford to invest. Holland offered a very rare milieu: it could actually afford to have a large population of artists. Cash could be made.

Today, little has changed. The average Amsterdammer betrays a shockingly broad knowledge of the arts, and the city retains an abnormally large concentration of galleries and art dealers. Home and workplace are both widely regarded as stark unless they contain at least one work of original art, whether culled from the past or the painfully bleeding edge.

However, creative Amsterdammers are not as spoiled as they once were. Generous subsidies still exist, but it is no longer true – as it was a decade ago – that funding awaits all who call themselves 'artist'. And while the government is spending millions on establishing affordable studio spaces for artists, they're just belated replacements for the organically honed squat scene, pushed out of town in the name of commerce. Ironically, though, with all these new and empty office walls, Amsterdam's locals need their artists now more than ever.

## THE 20TH CENTURY

None of the major art movements of the 20th century grew without being noticed by the Borg-like Dutch artists, but two home-grown – and radically different – movements exerted an enduring influence on the international art scene. The pristine abstraction of De Stijl ('the Style'), founded in 1917 and involving the likes of Theo van Doesburg, Piet Mondriaan and Gerrit Rietveld, sought rules of equilibrium that are as useful in the design of daily life as in art. You just have to surf the web or leaf through *Wallpaper\** magazine to see that it continues to have an impact on modern art and design.

In contrast to De Stijl, some post-war artists followed a messier muse. In the late 1940s, the CoBrA artists interpreted Liberation as a literal rallying call to spontaneity and the expression of immediate urges (for the **CoBrA Museum of Modern Art**, *see p112*). Whereas CoBrA's Surrealist forebears had embraced Freud, these artists, among them Karel Appel and Eugene Brands, had read Jung and sought to wire themselves into the playful unconscious of primitives, children and the mentally deranged.

Even in the 1980s, the abstract expressionism of CoBrA could find semi-descendents in the more figurative work of those Amsterdam artists working under the moniker 'After Nature'. Peter Klashorst, Jurriaan van Hall, Gijs Donker and Ernst Voss were seeking an antidote to the modernist conceptual art that had taken over the market. CoBrA's colourful portraits and nature- and city-scapes, marked with a spontaneous approach, made it no longer a crime to be preoccupied with the figurative.

## THE 21ST CENTURY

In a series of developments that would have pleased adherents of De Stijl, the old boundaries between once-rigid scenes have become blurred. People who were once labelled artists are now

## The best Galleries

### Frozen Fountain
The blurring of arts and the applied.
*See p198.*

### Huis Marseilles
Terrific photography in an epic canalside location. *See p197.*

### Smart Project Space
Broad horizons on the squat scene.
*See p200.*

### Stichting Oude Kerk
The latest art in the oldest church.
*See p196.*

### Torch
A tiny space, but with vast ambitions.
*See p200.*

**Arts & Entertainment**

Space cadets dig the roomy **Huis Marseilles**. *See p197.*

buy directly from the artist, galleries generally sell work on a commission basis. As an artist, which would you choose?

Galleries open and close in Amsterdam all the time. For the most up-to-date list, buy the monthly *Alert* (available at **Athenaeum Nieuwscentrum**; *see p155*); though it's in Dutch, galleries are sorted into areas and clearly marked on maps. Also, check gallery shows in *Uitkrant* (www.uitkrant.nl), or the art listings pamphlet published every two months by AKKA, whose website (www.akka.nl) provides direct links to the websites of the city's more relevant galleries. Many galleries close during July or August and have a relaxed attitude to opening hours the rest of the time, so it's best to call ahead. For **KunstRAI**, an annual art fair, and artists' **Open Studios**, *see p180*. And for more on Dutch art, *see p36*.

## Galleries

### The Old Centre: Old Side

#### Amsterdamse Centrum voor Fotographie

*Bethaniënstraat 9 (622 4899). Tram 16, 24, 25.* **Open** 1-6pm Wed-Sat. Closed July, Aug. **No credit cards. Map** p306 D3.
Photo hounds should go directly to this sprawling exhibition space, within flashing distance of the Red Light District. Besides showing photographers' work, it also has workshops and a black-and-white developing room available for hire.

#### Stichting Oude Kerk

*Oudekerksplein 23 (625 8284/www.oudekerk.nl). Tram 4, 9, 14, 16, 20, 24, 25.* **Open** 11am-5pm Mon-Sat; 1-5pm Sun. **No credit cards. Map** p306 D2.
The 'Old Church' is now the home of World Press Photo (*see p179*), though other shows range from Aboriginal art to artists installing work inspired by the thousands of graves that lie under its stone floor (in one of which lies Saskia Rembrandt). Admission shouldn't be more than €5. *See also p83.*

#### W139

*Warmoesstraat 139 (622 9434/www.w139.nl). Tram 4, 9, 14, 16, 20, 24, 25.* **Open** 1-6pm Wed-Sun. **No credit cards. Map** p306 D2.
In its two decades of existence, W139 has never lost its squat edge. This remarkable space has room to deal with installations, and though the work is occasionally a tad too conceptual, a visit is always worthwhile, especially during one of its chaotic openings.

### The Old Centre: New Side

#### Arti et Amicitiae

*Rokin 112 (623 3508/www.arti.nl). Tram 4, 9, 14, 16, 20, 24, 25.* **Open** 1-7pm Tue-Fri; 1-8pm Sat, Sun. **Admission** free. **No credit cards.**

just as likely to be called photographers (Anton Corbijn, Rineke Dijkstra), VJs (Ottograph, Micha Klein) or architects (Rem Koolhaas)… or is it the other way around? Certainly, global acclaim has been heaped on Dutch graphic and multimedia designers, who have been fundamental in formulating a new universal visual language where stylistic simplicity (De Stijl) does not preclude personal expression (CoBrA). Those with an interest in this area should contact **Baby** (Keizersgracht 676, 530 6666), a foundation and society for designers who put on occasional (and usually excellent) exhibitions in their canalside home.

#### WHAT'S IN A NAME?

In addition to its galleries, the Netherlands boasts five globally notable museums: the **Stedelijk Museum** in Amsterdam (*see p108*), the **Haags Gemeentemuseum** in the Hague (*see p263*), the **Rijksmuseum Kröller-Müller** in Otterlo, the **Groninger Museum** in Groningen and the **Van Abbemuseum** in Eindhoven (for all three, *see p268*). All attempt to curate a mix of established international names and artists of a more local and youthful nature, the result being competition for the smaller galleries that already share the art trade with *kunsthandels* (art dealers). While the *kunsthandels*, who rarely put on exhibitions,

This marvellous building houses a private artists' society, whose illustrious members gather in the first-floor bar. But the public can climb a Berlage-designed staircase to the large space, home to excellent, conversation-inducing temporary shows.

## Western Canal Belt

### Galerie Binnen
*Keizersgracht 82 (625 9603). Tram 1, 2, 5, 13, 17, 20.* **Open** noon-6pm Wed-Sat. **No credit cards.** **Map** p306 C2.
These industrial and interior design specialists have plenty of room in which to show work by unusual names (Starck, Sottsass, Kukkapuro, Studio Atika). Exhibits can include anything from toilet brushes to full-blown installations.

### Galerie Paul Andriesse
*Prinsengracht 116 (623 6237/andriesse@ euronet.nl). Tram 13, 14, 17, 20.* **Open** 11am-6pm Tue-Fri; 2-6pm Sat, 1st Sun of mth. **No credit cards. Map** p306 C2.
While perhaps no longer as innovative as it was in the past, one can interpret a reborn sense of savvy through the early relationship Andriesse forged with the now much-lauded artist Fiona Tan.

### GO Gallery
*Prinsengracht 64 (422 9580/www.gogallery.nl). Tram 13, 14, 17, 20.* **Open** noon-6pm Wed-Sat; 1-5pm 1st Sun of mth. **Credit** AmEx, DC, MC, V. **Map** p305 B2.
Oscar van den Voorn has shown bottomless energy in popularising local art without becoming unfunny-trendy. Expect themed dinners (most Thursdays, it operates the GO Cantina), stained-glass, graffiti art or the work of such local bad boys as Paul Smit.

### Huis Marseilles
*Keizersgracht 401 (531 8989/www.huismarseille.nl). Tram 1, 2, 5.* **Open** 11am-5pm Tue-Sun. **No credit cards. Map** p310 C4.
Located in a monumental 17th-century house, the walls of this foundation for photography might be filled with lunar landscapes or the works of duo Teresa Hubbard and Alexander Birchler. There is usually a token entry fee for exhibitions.

### Montevideo/TBA
*Keizersgracht 264 (623 7101/www.montevideo.nl). Tram 13, 14, 17, 20.* **Open** 1-6pm Tue-Sat. **No credit cards. Map** p306 C3.
Montevideo is dedicated to works that apply new technologies to visual arts, alongside photography and installations. Admire cutting-edge tech in an old world-vibed space, or read up in the reference room.

## Southern Canal Belt

### De Appel
*Nieuwe Spiegelstraat 10 (625 5651/www.deappel.nl). Tram 16, 24, 25.* **Open** noon-5pm Tue-Sun. **Credit** (bookshop only) AmEx, DC, MC, V. **Map** p310 D4.

An Amsterdam institution that showed its mettle early as one of the first galleries in the country to embrace video art. It's maintained a good sense of the modern, and still allows both international and rookie guest curators freedom to follow their muse.

### Clement
*Prinsengracht 845 (625 1656). Tram 16, 24, 25.* **Open** 11am-5.30pm Tue-Sat. **No credit cards. Map** p310 D5.
Clement is best known as a haven for print collectors, having begun as a printing studio in 1958 before the opening of the gallery a decade later. Walk your eyes through a selection that includes work by the likes of Penck, Sierhuis, Lucebert and Cremer.

### Collection d'Art
*Keizersgracht 516 (622 1511). Tram 1, 2, 5, 20.* **Open** 1-5pm Wed-Sat. **No credit cards. Map** p310 C4.
Another old school gallery founded in 1969, which supplements its established Dutch – and often CoBrA-related – names of Westerik, Armando and Constant with a German expressionist or two.

### Espace
*Keizersgracht 548 (624 0802/www.galleries.nl/ espace). Tram 1, 2, 5, 20.* **Open** 1-5pm Wed-Sat; 2-5pm 1st Sun of mth. **No credit cards. Map** p310 C4.
Founded in 1960, Espace has a legendary reputation. Most stories derive from a past when Dubuffet and de Kooning represented the cutting edge, but some recent exhibitions have also been known to surprise.

### Frozen Fountain
*Prinsengracht 629 (622 9375). Tram 1, 2, 5, 20.* **Open** 1-6pm Mon; 10am-6pm Tue-Fri; 10am-5pm Sat. **No credit cards. Map** p309 C4.
A mecca for lovers of contemporary furniture and design items. While staying abreast of innovative young Dutch designers, the 'Froz' also exhibits and sells stuff by the likes of Droog Design and Marc Newsom, modern classics and even photography.

### Galerie Akinci
*Lijnbaansgracht 317 (638 0480/www.akinci.nl). Tram 16, 20, 24, 25.* **Open** 1-6pm Tue-Sat. **No credit cards. Map** p311 E5.
Part of a complex that includes Lumen Traven, Art Affair and Oele, Akinci thrives on surprising with diverse shows that employ every imaginable contemporary media: from the video art of Emmanuelle Antille to the body-hair art of Yael Davids.

### Gallery Delaive
*Spiegelgracht 23 (625 9087/www.delaive.com). Tram 6, 7, 10.* **Open** 11am-5.30pm Mon-Sat. **No credit cards. Map** p310 D5.
An acclaimed, upmarket joint that is renowned for its over-reliance on 'names'. But, hell, it's a top one-stop shop if you're out for a collection of all your favourite CoBrA and Surrealist painters and sculptors, and you can even grab a Picasso or a Warhol while you're at it.

**Arts & Entertainment**

Cold comfort at the **Frozen Fountain**. *See p197.*

## Gate Foundation

*Keizersgracht 613 (620 8057/www.gatefoundation.nl).*
Tram 1, 2, 5. **Open** 10am-5pm Wed-Fri. **No credit cards. Map** p311 E4.

This 'intercultural contemporary art multicultural society' was founded in 1988 to focus on – you guessed it – the role of (multi)cultural identities in (mostly non-Western) arts. Since then it has initiated many projects and websites that promote the exchange of ideas between artists around the world. They might be moving during 2002; call to check.

## Melkweg

*Lijnbaansgracht 234A (531 8181/www.melkweg.nl).*
Tram 1, 2, 5, 6, 7, 10, 20. **Open** 2-8pm Wed-Sun. **No credit cards. Map** p310 D5.

The Melkweg reflects the broad interests of director Suzanne Dechart, with quality shows of contemporary photography. Expect anything from meditative studies of the homeless to portraits of punks or walls of cityscapes. *See also see p194, p213 and p225.*

## Ra

*Vijzelstraat 80 (626 5100/www.gallerie-ra.nl).*
Tram 4, 9, 14, 16, 20, 24, 25. **Open** noon-6pm Tue-Sat. **Credit** AmEx, DC, MC, V. **Map** p310 D4.

Paul Derrez's acclaimed gallery for contemporary jewellery is a healthy antidote to the conservative approach of the city's diamond industry (*see p162*

A girl's best friend). With an equal emphasis placed on both Dutch and international designers, this is the perfect place to put your finger on the pulse while, at the same time, decorating it.

## Reflex Modern Art Gallery

*Weteringschans 79A (627 2832/www.reflex-art.nl).*
Tram 6, 7, 10. **Open** 11am-6pm Tue-Sat. **Credit** AmEx, MC, V. **Map** p310 D5.

A New York flavour exudes from Reflex, which deals with international names such as Christo along with local lads like Dadara and photographers including Erin Olaf. Check out the gallery shop across the street at No.83, where you can score graphics and lithos by Appel while picking up an inflatable Munch *Scream* doll.

# Jodenbuurt, the Plantage & the Oost

## Arcam

*Waterlooplein 213 (620 4878/www.arcam.nl).*
Tram 9, 14, 20/Metro Waterlooplein.
**Open** 1-5pm Tue-Sat. **No credit cards.**
**Map** p307 E3.

Architecture Centrum Amsterdam is obsessed with the promotion of Dutch contemporary architecture, and organises tours, forums, lectures and exhibits on the subject. Besides its central exhibition space, it also has a second spot by the harbour (Oosterdok 14; 620 4878; open 1-5pm Fri-Sun).

## The Waterfront

### Consortium

*Oostelijke Handelskade 29 (421 2408/ www.xs4all.nl/~conso). Bus 32.* **Open** 2-6pm Fri-Sun. **No credit cards.**

Out in the eastern Docklands, Consortium puts on exhibitions dedicated to international up-and-comers. The warehouse in which they're located is being converted; spring of 2002 might see them in the space next door, so call ahead before setting out.

### De Veemvloer

*Van Diemenstraat 410 (638 6894/www.xs4all.nl/ ~veemvlr). Tram 35.* **Open** 1-6pm Wed-Sat. **No credit cards.**

This beautiful waterfront warehouse filled with studios retains something of a squat persona, not only with its evocative location but also through its dedication to younger artists, many culled from Amsterdam's Gerrit Rietveld Arts Academy.

## The Jordaan

### Annet Gelink Gallery

*Laurierstraat 187-9 (330 2066). Tram 13, 14, 17, 20.* **Open** 11am-6pm Tue-Fri; 1-5pm Sat. **No credit cards. Map** p309 B4.

Annet Gelink knew what she wanted in her gallery: space and light, to best reflect some of the latest highways and byways of Dutch and international art. Some notable names: Mat Collishaw, Harmony Korine, Alicia Framis and Kiki Lamers.

### Fuzzy Art

*2e Tuindwarsstraat 11 (626 2780/622 2970/ www.fuzzyart.nl).* Tram 13, 14, 17, 20. **Open** 12.30-5.30pm Thur-Sat, or by appointment. **Credit** MC. **Map** p305 B3.

Located on one of the Jordaan's funkier streets, this gallery appropriately dedicates itself to art with an 'unreal, non-worldly feel', which means they like underground comics and the dizzyingly surreal.

### Galerie Diana Stigter

*Hazenstraat 17 (624 2361/www.dianastigter.nl). Tram 7, 10, 13, 14, 17, 20.* **Open** 1-6pm Tue-Sat; 2-5pm first Sun of mth. **No credit cards. Map** p310 C4.

Formerly of the fêted Bloem Gallery, Diana Stigter has opened her own space. With shows from the likes of Pierre Bismuth, Tariq Alvi and Steve McQueen, it seems that the extreme and the extremely engaged have found another happy home in Amsterdam.

### Galerie Fons Welters

*Bloemstraat 140 (423 3046/www.fonswelters.nl). Tram 13, 14, 17, 20.* **Open** 1-6pm Tue-Sat; 2-5pm 1st Sun of mth. **No credit cards. Map** p305 B3.

Venerable doyen of the scene Fons Welters knows what he likes, and what he likes is to 'discover' the latest new (and often local) talent. For years, he's shown remarkable taste in both sculpture and installation, having provided a home to Atelier van Lieshout, Rob Birza, Jennifer Tee and Aernout Mik. Even the entrance is a *tour de force*.

### Serieuze Zaken

*Elandsstraat 90 (427 5770/malasch@hotmail.com). Tram 7, 10, 17, 20.* **Open** noon-6pm Tue-Sat; 1-5pm 1st Sun of mth. **No credit cards. Map** p310 C4.

Rob Malasch was already known as a quirky theatre type and journalist before opening this gallery in the Jordaan. Shows might feature Brit Art, contemporary Chinese painters or the 'Punk Pictures' of Max Natkiel.

# Going public

There's a case to be made that this fine city is one huge gallery. With a long-held tradition dictating new construction projects having to dedicate a percentage of their costs to public art, one can hardly walk a metre without bumping into some kind of creative endeavour. While not all attempts are successful – please, someone remove the **garishly coloured geometric stacks** acting as lighting poles on Damrak – it's hard to argue with any scheme that produces such gems as Hans van Houwelingen's **bronze iguanas** that frolic in the grass of Kleine Gartmanplantsoen, Atelier van Lieshout's **breast-appended houseboat** floating in the Langer Vonder in Amsterdam Noord, the **stained-glass** of cartoonist Joost Swarte on the buildings along the eastern side of Marnixstraat's northern end, and Rombout & Droste's **demented walking bridges** on Java Eiland (*see p102* **On the waterfront**). All work to make the urban landscape a much richer place indeed.

Amsterdam's public art policy has recently been entrusted to the Amsterdam Fund for the Arts (www.afk.nl), which has been busy not only organising both permanent and temporary installations, but also working to improve the level of dialogue and collaboration between artists, architects, landscape architects and the public. Their excellent book, *2001: A Public Space Odyssey* (available at the likes of **Athenaeum Nieuwscentrum**, for which *see p155*), acts not only as an overview of projects past and future, but as a guidebook of sorts as well.

Take it as read: the **Stedelijk Museum Bureau** is hipper than most.

### Stedelijk Museum Bureau Amsterdam

*Rozenstraat 59 (422 0471/www.smba.nl).*
*Tram 13, 14, 17, 20.* **Open** 11am-5pm Tue-Sun.
**No credit cards. Map** p309 B4.
The Stedelijk's space on Rozenstraat devoted to younger and mostly Amsterdam-based artists has been hipper than its mothership in recent years, with shows including the scary styrofoam sculptures of Folkert de Jong and the cooking-for-kids lessons of Chiko & Toko.

### Steendrukkerij Amsterdam

*Lauriergracht 80 (624 1491/www.steendrukkerij.com).*
*Tram 13, 14, 17, 20.* **Open** 1-5.30pm Wed-Sat;
2-5pm 1st Sun of mth. Closed July, Aug. **No credit cards. Map** p309 B4.
This gallery-cum-printshop in the Jordaan specialises in the hands-on work of woodcuts and lithography, and usually only gives thrills to the initiated. However, more interesting is when guest artists – such as Koen Vermeule and Claes Oldenburg – are asked to collaborate with the more technique-bound printers.

### Torch

*Lauriergracht 94 (626 0284/www.torchgallery.com).*
*Tram 7, 10, 20.* **Open** 2-6pm Thur-Sat.
**Credit** AmEx, DC, MC, V. **Map** p309 D4.
If you like your art edgy, you'll love Torch, which brings the likes of Richard Kern, Annie Sprinkle, Cindy Sherman and Anton Corbijn to Amsterdam. Eerily, their long-planned exhibition of Gregory Green's terrorist art opened mere days after 11 September 2001.

## The Museum Quarter

### Donkersloot Galerie

*PC Hooftstraat 127 (572 2722/www.donkersloot.nl).*
*Tram 2, 3, 5, 12, 20.* **Open** 10am-9pm Mon-Sat; noon-9pm Sun. **Credit** AmEx, DC, MC, V. **Map** p310 C6.
Hyping itself as a 'night gallery', Donkersloot hosts 'live painting events' (such as getting 80 women together to paint each other), VJ-ing artists including REL, and rock 'n' roll types like Herman Brood (*see p215* **Brood swings**). Its openings are a who's who of the city's more potentially decadent artists.

### Smart Project Space

*1e Constantijn Huygensstraat 20 (427 5951/*
*www.smartprojectspace.net).* *Tram 1, 3, 6, 12.*
**Open** 11am-10pm Tue-Sat; 2-10pm Sun. **No credit cards. Map** p310 C5.
Dedicated to 'hardcore art', Smart documents the squattier side of the Amsterdam art spectrum. But don't expect anything low-tech: they have a snazzy website, a TV show, and experimental film nights. Their location is currently under threat; call ahead to check whether they've been forced to move.

## Roving galleries

### Jim Beard Gallery

*06 2888 6505/www.jimbeard.nl.*
A roving, inspired pack of artists and designers who stage events every couple of months in such singular locations as storage containers and karaoke bars. A 2001 show of Bollywood-inspired art in the new cruise ship terminal confirmed their ambition.

# Gay & Lesbian

Cruise around the only place on earth where gay marriage is legal.

'The groom may kiss the groom': same-sex marriage is legal in the Netherlands.

In 2001, the global spotlight fell on the Netherlands as it became the first country in the world to legalise same-sex marriage. This landmark ruling has had some unlikely precedents: as far back as the late 1600s, for example, two lesbians were 'officially' married at the City Hall (now the Royal Palace) on Dam Square, but with one disguised as a man. When the secret came out, the 'groom' was sent to jail, though she soon bailed herself out using money she'd amassed as a brothel owner...

These days, the cloak-and-dagger shenanigans are consigned to the pages of the history books, and Amsterdam has earned itself the enviable title of Gay Capital of Europe. Alongside its forward-thinking attitude to marriage, the city has tons of gay ghettos and boasts an annual pride festival to rival Sydney's famed Mardi Gras. Yet in terms of size and variety, the gay and lesbian scenes couldn't be further apart. Gay men revel in kid-in-candystore luxury, while lesbians enjoy

## The best Gay hangouts

**Backstage**
Coffee, cake, crochet and chat. *See p209.*

**Exit**
No way out at this popular club. *See p207.*

**Getto**
Cocktails and kitsch. *See p208.*

**Saarein II**
Split-level and sweetly Sapphic. *See p210.*

**Soho**
Check out the local body beautiful. *See p208.*

**De Trut**
Cheap entry and cheaper booze. *See p209.*

**Pink Point:** information and souvenirs.

only a handful of women's bars and just one lesbian club, whose greatest claim to fame is its innovatory women's urinals.

That said, the Dutch have a tolerant attitude that's second to none, so both lesbian and gay travellers can relax and enjoy. For information on gay and lesbian resources, including health resources, helplines, meeting groups, libraries and other useful organisations, *see p281.*

## Essential information

Amsterdam's reputation as a liberal city didn't come about by accident. Importantly, though, Amsterdam is also more tolerant of gays and lesbians than most major world cities. The good news: the Netherlands originally decriminalised homosexuality in 1811, with the age of consent for gay men lowered to 16 in 1971; registered partnership between same-sex couples was introduced in 1998; and, three years later, Holland became the first country in the world to legalise same-sex marriages.

**Cruising** used to be generally accepted in Amsterdam, but the last few years have seen a few changes. Vondelpark (by the rose garden: watch out for them thorns!) and the wooded Nieuwe Meer area, in the south-west of the city, are still popular spots for both sunbathing and cruising, although there's an increasingly less tolerant attitude towards cruising now than there once was: Nieuwe Meer has been redesigned to make it more open, and cruising in Vondelpark is now only allowed after dusk. **Darkrooms**, however, are still found in many bars and clubs, and must comply with strict regulations that force proprietors to make both safer sex information and condoms available.

**Marriage** for same-sex couples was made legal in April 2001. However, don't assume you can just fly over and get hitched: to qualify for a 'gay marriage', one of the partners has to officially live, study or work in the Netherlands or be a Dutch national. Anyway, a question-mark remains over whether the marriage is legally recognised abroad. If you are unable to get married officially but would like some form of ceremony, the Remonstrantse Broederschap (Nieuwegracht 27A, 3512 LC Utrecht; 030 231

6970) will bless gay relationships even if you are not Dutch or don't belong to its church. You need to ring six to 12 months in advance.

The super-liberal **prostitution** laws in Amsterdam also apply to gays: there are several male brothels in the city, and rent-boy bars, mainly on Paardenstraat, are legal. However, Paardenstraat is full of exploited, mainly Eastern European boys and can be dangerous, in terms of both personal safety and unsafe sex. Caution is strongly advised.

Since the advent of HIV and AIDS, the Dutch have developed a responsible attitude towards the practice and promotion of **safer sex**, and condoms are available from most gay bars. However, STDs are on the rise, and bareback sex (unsafe sex) is getting more and more popular among gay men. *See p283* for details of HIV- and AIDS-related organisations.

No one blinks an eye when two guys walk hand in hand through the centre of town, but shows of public affection are not so tolerated in the suburbs or in other cities. Queer-bashing has increased recently; in mid-2001, an imam from Rotterdam caused an outcry by stating on national TV that gay people are less than dogs.

### Homomonument

*Westermarkt, Western Canal Belt. Tram 13, 14, 17, 20.* **Map** p306 C3.
The world's first memorial to persecuted gays and lesbians was designed by Karin Daan. Its three tri-angles of pink granite form one large triangle that juts out into the Keizersgracht. Those victimised in World War II are commemorated on 4 May, but flowers are laid daily in memory of more private grief, and also on World AIDS Day (1 Dec).

### Pink Point

*Westermarkt, Western Canal Belt. Tram 13, 14, 17, 20.* **Open** *April-Sept* noon-6pm daily. **Map** p306 C3.
Located by the Homomonument, this funky kiosk serves as both an information point and a souvenir shop. All the free gay publications are stocked here, as are maps, flyers, mags and books. The friendly staff will help with any questions you may have.

## Publications

**Gay News Amsterdam** (www.gaynews.nl), in both Dutch and English, comes out monthly, and is free in many gay establishments (it's around €3 in newsagents). Its main rival is the monthly **Gay & Night** (www.gay-night.nl), free in bars (but around €3 in newsagents).

The best Dutch-language source of national and international news features is the monthly **De Gay Krant**, available from newsagents or online in PDF format at www.gaykrant.nl. In addition, bi-weekly English-language 'zine **Shark**, free across Amsterdam and online at www.underwateramsterdam.com, includes a *Queer Fish* centrefold, regularly updated listings, and a diary of events. The **SAD-Schorerstichting** (*see p282*) produces a free gay tourist map and a safer-sex booklet (with a gay male bias) in English every year.

## Radio & TV

The stations below, all on Amsterdam cable, can be good sources of information and entertainment. Try, too, to check out the gay and lesbian Teletext page on page 447 of NOS Teletext (on Nederland 1, 2 and 3 channels), or **De Gay Krant**'s Teletext service: it has pages 137, 138 and 139 on SBS6. **MVS**'s website, www.mvs.nl, also has some English pages.

### MVS Radio
*Cable 88.1 or 106.8 FM ether (620 0247).*
**Times** 6-8pm Mon-Thur; 6-9pm Fri; 6-7pm Sat, Sun.
Amsterdam's major gay and lesbian radio station, with news, interviews and a gay chart on Saturdays. An English-language show, *Alien*, is broadcast twice a week: Fridays 7-8pm and Sundays 6-7pm.

### MVS TV
*Salto Channel A1: S16 or 264MHz (620 0247).*
**Times** 8-9pm Tue.
This mainly Dutch station covers developments on the scene plus gay culture, events, health, et cetera.

### Radio 5
*747 AM.* **Times** 6pm Sat.
Tune in on Saturdays for gay and lesbian magazine programme *Roze Rijk* (Pink Empire).

## Accommodation

It's illegal for hotels to refuse accommodation to gays and lesbians here, but those detailed below are all specifically gay-owned. The **Gay & Lesbian Switchboard** (*see p282*) has further details of gay- and lesbian-friendly hotels. For more hotels, *see p48*.

### Black Tulip Hotel
*Geldersekade 16, Old Centre: Old Side (427 0933/ www.blacktulip.nl).* Tram 1, 2, 4, 5, 9, 13, 16, 17, 20, 24, 25. **Rates** €48 single; €62-€80 double. **Credit** AmEx, DC, MC, V. **Map** p306 D2.

# The queer year

## Spring
Gay celebrations on **Queen's Day**, every 30 April (*see p181* **A right royal knees-up**), are based at the famous Homomonument, with drag acts, bands and stalls. Most gay and lesbian bars and clubs organise their own parties, so head for your own favourite spot.

**Remembrance Day** takes place on 4 May. Though gay and lesbian victims from WWII are remembered at the event on Dam, the **NVIH/COC** stage their own quiet tribute at the Homomonument. The next day, there's a celebratory open-air party for **Liberation Day**.

**AIDS Memorial Day** is held at the Beurs van Berlage (*see p74*) on the last Saturday of May. Names of deceased loved ones are read and candles lit. Everyone then walks to Dam, where symbolic white balloons are released into the air.

## Summer
The **Midsummer Canal Party** in Utrecht is held on or around 21 June. This three-day extravaganza includes performances on the canals with stages set up on the water.

**Gay Pride Day Nederland** is held on the last Saturday in June in a different town each year. Check ahead with the Gay & Lesbian Switchboard (*see p282*) for details of the cities for 2002 and 2003.

**Amsterdam Diners** is a huge one-day HIV and AIDS fundraiser, usually on the last Saturday of June. However, both venue and date seem to change each year; check www.amsterdamdiners.com for details.

Held on the first weekend in August, **Amsterdam Pride** is probably the most fun event of the year. This three-day extravaganza includes street parties, performances and a gay parade on boats around the canals.

The **Hollywood Party**, held in August at iT (*see p206*), usually brings traffic to a complete standstill. Glitzy transvestite 'stars' gather, before making their way to the club in limos.

## Autumn
**Amsterdam Leather Pride** takes place every November and usually encompasses a week's worth of parties and events. There's also a range of events for women, organised by **Wild Side** (*see p282*). For more details, log on to www.leatherpride.nl nearer the event.

## Winter
Various activities are organised by the Nationale Commissie AIDS-Bestrijding on and around **World AIDS Day** every 1 December, including a series of fund-raising performances, and sometimes auctions, by stars of the stage.

**Arts & Entertainment**

The men-only Black Tulip hotel has mastered the art of serving and accommodating the leather aficionado, effortlessly combining luxury with lust: SM facilities such as sling and bondage hooks are included in all the rooms as standard, as is the more conventional TV and VCR. Located near to Centraal Station and conveniently close to the leather bars that cluster along Warmoesstraat.

### Golden Bear
*Kerkstraat 37, Southern Canal Belt (624 4785/ www.goldenbear.nl). Tram 1, 2, 5.* **Rates** €25-€29 single; €30-€49 double; €53 triple. **Credit** AmEx, MC, V. **Map** p310 D4.
Housed in two 17th-century buildings, the Golden Bear's rooms have plenty of room and are very comfortable, though not all have private bathrooms. All single rooms are decked out with double beds.

### Hotel New York
*Herengracht 13, Western Canal Belt (624 3066). Tram 1, 2, 3, 5, 13, 14.* **Rates** €69 single; €91-€114 double; €125 triple. **Credit** AmEx, DC, MC, V. **Map** p306 C2.
A beautiful, modernised 17th-century building in a particularly charming, picturesque location overlooking the canal. Apparently, it's one of Bette Midler's favourites.

### ITC Hotel
*Prinsengracht 1051, Southern Canal Belt (623 0230). Tram 4, 6, 7, 10.* **Rates** €25-€28 single; €40 double; €69 triple. **Credit** AmEx, DC, MC, V. **Map** p311 E4.
Located within quick and easy reach of Kerkstraat, Reguliersdwarsstraat and the Amstel, this canalside house is one of Amsterdam's more popular stopovers for gays and lesbians.

### Orfeo Hotel
*Leidsekruisstraat 14, Southern Canal Belt (623 1347). Tram 1, 2, 5, 6, 7, 10.* **Rates** €18-€20 single; €27-€43 double; €49 triple. **Credit** AmEx, MC, V. **Map** p310 D5.
The Orfeo is handily located by the Leidseplein. Though the breakfast area looks uninspiring, the rooms are good value.

## Shops & services

### Bookshops
Aside from those listed below, the **American Book Center** (*see p155*) has a well-stocked gay and lesbian section. There is also one charming second-hand women's bookstore, with a large number of English titles: **Vrouwen in Druk** (Westermarkt 5, the Jordaan; 624 5003).

### Intermale
*Spuistraat 251, Old Centre: New Side (625 0009/ www.intermale.nl). Tram 1, 2, 5, 13, 14, 17, 20.* **Open** 11am-6pm Mon; 10am-6pm Tue, Wed, Fri, Sat; 10am-9pm Thur. **Credit** AmEx, MC, V. **Map** p306 C3.
This split-level gay men's bookstore is crammed with literature, porn and books on history and sexuality in different languages, as well as a sexy selection of cards, magazines and newspapers.

### Vrolijk
*Paleisstraat 135, Old Centre: New Side (623 5142/ www.vrolijk.nu). Tram 1, 2, 5, 13, 14, 17, 20.* **Open** 11am-6pm Mon; 10am-6pm Tue, Wed, Fri; 10am-9pm Thur; 10am-5pm Sat. **Credit** AmEx, DC, MC, V. **Map** p306 C3.

'It's just a little thing I flung on this morning...' Dusty at the **Queen's Head**. *See p206.*

Arts & Entertainment

Stockists of a wide range of gay and lesbian books. Many titles are in English, while there are also magazines, CDs, T-shirts and videos. Its monthly newsletter has reviews in Dutch and English.

## Xantippe Unlimited

*Prinsengracht 290, Western Canal Belt (623 5854).* *Tram 1, 2, 5, 10, 13, 14, 17, 20.* **Open** 1-7pm Mon; 10am-7pm Tue-Fri; 10am-6pm Sat; noon-5pm Sun. **Credit** AmEx, DC, MC, V. **Map** p310 C4.
Xantippe has a comprehensive women's studies section (many books are in English), as well as many international women's/lesbian magazines.

## Hairdressers

### Cuts & Curls

*Korte Leidsedwarsstraat 74, Southern Canal Belt (624 6881). Tram 1, 2, 5, 6, 7, 10.* **Open** 10am-8pm Mon-Thur; 10am-7pm Fri; 10am-4pm Sat. **Credit** AmEx, DC, MC, V. **Map** p310 D5.
The leather men here offer 'men's cuts' and 'block-heads' for around €15. No appointments.

## Leather-rubber/sex shops

Within the Red Light District lies the leather district, home to gay leather and rubber shops such as **MR B** (Warmoesstraat 89; 422 0003; www.mrb.nl) and **RoB Accessories** (Warmoesstraat 32; 420 8548; www.rob.nl). Rubber-lovers should also visit **Black Body**, a specialist rubber shop at Lijnbaansgracht 292 in the Jordaan (626 2553) and the main **RoB** shop (Weteringschans 253; 625 4686). Other gay sex shops include the **Bronx** (Kerkstraat 53-5; 623 1548) and **Drakes** (Damrak 61; 627 9544), both of which have a porn cinema.

Women's erotica can be found at **Female & Partners** (*see p176*) and **Mail & Female** (Prinsengracht 489; 623 3916), while **Demask** (Zeedijk 64; 620 5603) is popular with men and women. For erotic and fetish shops, *see p176*.

## Saunas

### Fenomeen

*1e Schinkelstraat 14, Zuid (671 6780).* *Tram 6.* **Open** 1-11pm daily. *Women's day* Mon. **Admission** €3 before 6pm; €4 after 6pm. **No credit cards**.
A relaxed squat sauna popular with lesbians on Monday's women-only day. It's open-plan and split level with a sauna, a steam bath, a cold bath, a chill-out room with mattresses, showers in the courtyard and a café. Extras include massage and a sunbed.

### Thermos Day

*Raamstraat 33, the Jordaan (623 9158). Tram 1, 2, 5, 7, 10.* **Open** noon-11pm Mon-Fri; noon-10pm Sat, Sun. **Admission** €7; €6 under-24s with ID. **Credit** AmEx, DC, MC, V. **Map** p310 C4.

Busy during the week and crowded at weekends, this relaxed sauna has a tiny steam room, a large dry-heat room, a small cinema showing porn, private cubicles, a bar and restaurant, a hairdresser, a masseur, a gym and a roof terrace.

### Thermos Night

*Kerkstraat 58-60, Southern Canal Belt (623 4936).* *Tram 1, 2, 5.* **Open** 11pm-8am Mon-Sat; 11pm-10am Sun. **Admission** €7; €6 under-24s with ID. **Credit** AmEx, DC, MC, V. **Map** p310 D4.
A stone's throw away from De Spijker (*see p208*), Thermos Night's facilities include a spacious bar, a small jacuzzi, a dry sauna and a steam room, a darkroom and a maze of cubicles. Packed on weekends.

## Tattoos

### Eyegasm

*Kerkstraat 113, Western Canal Belt (330 3767/tattoo@eyegasm.org). Tram 1 ,2, 5.* **Open** noon-8pm Tue-Sat. **No credit cards**. **Map** p310 D4.
Europe's only lesbian-owned and -run tattooist, Roxx Mistry specialises in custom designs, tattooing from her beautiful designer, cyber-submarine store.

## Cinema

**Rialto** (*see p193*), **Cinecenter** and **Cavia** (for both, *see p192*) screen gay and lesbian flicks, as does **De Balie** (*see p193*). The latter two are home in December to **De Roze Filmdagen** (or 'Pink Film Days'; www.rozefilmdagen.nl), an event showing underground gay and lesbian shorts and documentaries, while since 2001, De Balie has held the Nederlands Transgender Filmfestival (www.transgenderfilmfestival.com) in October. The **Academie** squat (*see p193*) has occasional gay and lesbian nights in its cinema.

Smaller gay porn cinemas can be found in town; for details, check ads in gay publications. The **Gay & Lesbian Switchboard** (*see p282*) has lists of cinemas and theatres with gay and lesbian programmes.

## Bars & nightclubs

The gay scene is concentrated around four areas, each with its own identity. Clubs and bars are listed by area below, with specialist establishments – restaurants, cafés, coffeeshops and lesbian bars – and the pick of one-off club nights and sex parties listed separately, starting on *p208*. Entry to bars and clubs listed here is free unless stated otherwise.

## Warmoesstraat

The seedy Warmoesstraat, in the Red Light District, may have been renovated in an attempt to smarten up the area, but it still attracts all sorts of lowlife. Despite a high police profile and a nearby police station, it's advisable to take care when walking on your own late at night: act streetwise and avoid talking to the sleazy geezers and junkies that hang around trying to sell you dubious drugs.

Apart from the fabulously kitsch bar-restaurant **Getto** (*see p208*) and trad Dutch brown bar **Casa Maria** (No.60; 627 6848), the strip is dominated by leather bars. **The Web** and **Cuckoo's Nest** (Nieuwezijds Kolk 6; 627 1752), which boasts Europe's largest playroom in its cellar are located nearby, as is the delightfully old-school **Queen's Head** (*see below*).

### Argos

*Warmoesstraat 95 (622 6595). Tram 4, 9, 16, 20, 24, 25.* **Open** 10pm-3am Mon-Thur, Sun; 10pm-4am Fri, Sat. **No credit cards. Map** p306 D2.
The oldest and most famous leather bar in the city, Argos is also the cruisiest; the basement darkroom with cabins is often busier than the upstairs bar. Wednesday night is poppers night, and every last Sunday of the month it hosts SOS (Sex on Sunday): doors are open 3pm-4pm, it costs around €5 to get in, and the dress code is 'nude/shirtless'. Men only.

### Cockring

*Warmoesstraat 96 (623 9604/www.clubcockring.com). Tram 4, 9, 16, 20, 24, 25.* **Open** 11pm-4am Mon-Thur; 11pm-5am Fri, Sat. **No credit cards. Map** p306 D2.
This men-only club is one of a few gay venues for which you need to queue at weekends, particularly after 1am. Though situated in the leather district, the Cockring attracts all types of gays and of all ages. It's a cruisey place, helped by pumping hard house, strip shows, massages and a darkroom. Some Sundays it hosts sex parties, starting at 3pm, with free condoms and sandwiches.

### Eagle

*Warmoesstraat 90 (627 8634). Tram 4, 9, 16, 20, 24, 25.* **Open** 10pm-4am Mon-Thur, Sun; 10pm-5am Fri, Sat. **No credit cards. Map** p306 D2.
Sex and sleaze sum up this cruisey men-only leather bar, which fills up late during the week and gets packed at weekends. Downstairs, the darkroom – watch for those steep stairs – can get as pushy as a sale at Harrods. The upstairs pool table is probably the only one in the world that has an adjustable sling above it. Eagle also co-host regular Rubber Only Parties with rubber shop Black Body (*see p205*).

### Queen's Head

*Zeedijk 20 (420 2475/www.queenshead.nl). Tram 4, 9, 16, 20, 24, 25/Metro Centraal Station.* **Open** 5pm-1am Mon-Thur; 5pm-3am Fri; 4pm-3am Sat; 4pm-1am Sun. **No credit cards. Map** p306 D2.
Action Men and a Dusty doll line the window of this '50s-style Dutch bar, opened by gay couple Johan and Willem (aka Dusty). Monday is cheap beer night, and every Tuesday Dusty drags up to the nines and dons her wig to host her popular bingo night from 10pm onwards. Other nights feature the variety-packed likes of easy tunes, classical music or sports videos. There's also a beautiful view out back on to some old Dutch canal houses.

### The Web

*Sint Jacobsstraat 6 (623 6758). Tram 1, 2, 3, 5.* **Open** 2pm-1am Mon-Thur, Sun; 2pm-2.30am Fri, Sat. **No credit cards. Map** p306 D2.
Another popular leather bar, with DJs most nights playing nu Hi-NRG and disco. However, many come for the darkroom upstairs and the porn in the downstairs bar. Sundays from 5pm is snack afternoon, and Wednesdays from 10pm is lottery night with various sex shop vouchers to be won. Men only.

## Rembrandtplein

The area around Rembrandtplein has traditionally long been associated with Amsterdam's camp scene: most of the gay bars, all within earshot of each other, belt out either oompah music, Dutch pop or cheesy chart hits and feature the occasional drag act. Paardenstraat (packed full of rent boys) is nearby, as are women's bar **Vive la Vie** (*see p210*), café **Le Monde** (*see p209*) and the infamous **iT** (*see below*).

Aside from the spots listed below, there are a cluster of other bars located along the Amstel that provide a bit of a breather from the frantic square located behind. **Gaiety** (No.14; 624 4271) was originally an underground gay bar in the 1950s; **Mix** (No.50; 420 3388) is a nondescript place; and **Hot Spot Café** (No.102; 622 8335) is a less testosterone-laden addition to the scene.

### Amstel Taveerne

*Amstel 54 (623 4254). Tram 4, 9, 14, 16, 20, 24, 25.* **Open** 4pm-1am Mon-Thur, Sun; 4pm-2.45am Fri, Sat. **No credit cards. Map** p307 E3.
For the archetypal Dutch experience, head to this spacious brown café. A TV monitor displays the song being sung: a mix of Dutch singalong songs both old and new get heavy rotation, with the odd Eurovision tune thrown in for bad measure.

### iT

*Amstelstraat 24 (625 0111/www.it.nl). Tram 4, 9, 14.* **Open** 11pm-4am Thur; 11pm-5am Fri, Sat. **Admission** €7-€9 (free for gays Thur). **No credit cards. Map** p307 E3.
This converted cinema, one of Europe's most famous gay clubs, has lost most of its glamorous appeal over the years. That said, it's still packed at weekends (Saturdays are gay men only) and the parties are notorious (such as the Swimming Pool Party in July and Hollywood Party in August). Fancy a souvenir? iT also produces CDs that are compiled by its resident DJs.

Life's a drag at **Lellebel**.

## Lellebel

*Utrechtsestraat 4 (427 5139/www.lellebel.nl). Tram 4, 9, 14, 20.* **Open** *May-Sept* 9pm-3am Mon-Thur, Sun; 9pm-4am Fri, Sat. *Oct-Apr* 9pm-3am Mon-Thur, Sun; 8pm-4am Fri, Sat. **No credit cards. Map** p311 E4.
Lellebel's transvestite staff spontaneously burst into song, and the fun reaches a peak with karaoke evenings and the divine diva Desiree dello Stiletto's terrific live show on Saturdays. Neck a few discounted drinks during happy hour every Sunday (before 10pm), when the music goes multicultural.

## Le Montmartre

*Halvemaansteeg 17 (620 7622). Tram 4, 9, 14, 16, 20, 24, 25.* **Open** 9pm-3am Mon-Thur; 8pm-4am Fri, Sat; 8pm-3am Sun. **No credit cards. Map** p307 E3.
This deliciously cheesy bar is one of the most popular camp bars in the area. The lively crowd loves the pop and Dutch music played here, singing along and strutting their stuff on the tiny raised dancefloor at the back. A good place to start a night out.

## Le Shako's

*Gravelandseveer 2 (624 0209). Tram 4, 9, 14, 16, 20, 24, 25.* **Open** 10pm-3am Mon-Thur, Sun; 8pm-4am Fri, Sat. **No credit cards. Map** p307 E3.
Across the water from the rest of the camp-oriented bars on the Amstel, Shako's is a very friendly and relaxed, late-opening night bar, and a firm favourite among the locals.

## Reguliersdwarsstraat

On the other side of Rembrandtplein is Reguliersdwarsstraat, a tremendously gay street: there are more pansies here than in the flower market on Singel. A posey young crowd hangs out here, and the bars and clubs reflect the trend: **Café April**, **Exit**, **Soho**, **Havana**, and **Downtown** (*see p208*) have the same owner. It's also where the town's only gay coffeeshop, the **Otherside** (*see p209*), and **Reality** (No.129; 639 3012), a multicultural gay bar, can be found.

## Café April

*Reguliersdwarsstraat 37 (625 9572/www.april-exit.com). Tram 1, 2, 4, 5, 9, 14, 16, 20, 24, 25.* **Open** 2pm-1am Mon-Thur, Sun; 2pm-2am Fri, Sat. **No credit cards. Map** p309 D4.
Since Soho opened across the street a few years ago, this bar has lost a lot of its evening clientele. But a

plethora of drinks promos now provide excellent opportunities to drink yourself dizzy. It's also a pleasant place for a spot of afternoon reading.

## Exit

*Reguliersdwarsstraat 42 (625 8788/www.april-exit.com). Tram 1, 2, 4, 5, 9, 14, 16, 20, 24, 25.* **Open** 11pm-4am Mon-Thur, Sun; 11pm-5am Fri, Sat. **Admission** free-€5. **No credit cards. Map** p311 E4.
Voted Best Gay Club 2001 by *De Gay Krant*, Exit is where almost everyone seems to end up at the weekend. The downstairs bar pumps out cheesy pop and gets crowded; upstairs, the R&B bar is mellower, as is the balcony bar. There's an enthusiastic crowd, with women allowed in, but only in small numbers.

## Havana

*Reguliersdwarsstraat 17-19 (620 6788). Tram 1, 2, 5, 16, 20, 24, 25.* **Open** 4pm-1am Mon-Thur; 4pm-2.30am Fri; 2pm-2.30am Sat; 2pm-1am Sun. **Admission** free. *Upstairs* €3. **No credit cards. Map** p310 D4.
The popular Havana is a people-watcher's paradise. However, the Cuban-tinted establishment gets very busy from around 10pm. At weekends, DJs spin soul and R&B upstairs in the small dance area.

# Wanna Bet?

Apart from opening for a brief period during the 1998 Gay Games, **Het Mandje** (Zeedijk 63), one of Amsterdam's first gay and lesbian bars, has remained closed for several years. However, it's still worth a visit for nostalgic reasons, as today it serves as a shrine to its former owner and 'Queen of the Zeedijk', Bet van Beeren.

Van Beeren, the oldest daughter of 11 children, was born in 1902 and, aged just 25, took over Het Mandje in the rough Zeedijk area. The bar was undeniably risqué for its time, though strict rules were still enforced: lesbians and gay men could meet, but weren't allowed to kiss or even dance with a member of the same sex (except on Queen's Day). The openly lesbian, leather-clad Bet would roar around town on her treasured Harley and became a well-known figure, doing her bit for the lesbian movement long before Dykes on Bikes were even on their stabilisers.

Van Beeren went on to earn particular respect for her activities during World War II, not only concealing weapons from the occupying Nazis but sheltering Jews, including the writer Hermijn Heijermans. On her death in 1967, and in inimitable Bet-style, her body was laid out on the bar's billiard table. Way to go, girl!

### Soho

*Reguliersdwarsstraat 36 (330 4400). Tram 1, 2, 4, 5, 9, 14, 16, 20, 24, 25.* **Open** 8pm-3am Mon-Thur; 8pm-4am Fri, Sat; 6pm-3am Sun. **No credit cards.** **Map** p311 E4.

This packed, two-floor English-style boozer is the punter-pulling pub hereabouts. DJs play from 10pm; Cocktail Twilight, 9-11.30pm daily, has half-price cocktails. Be warned, though: Soho can be a little intimidating if you're on your own.

### Kerkstraat

This quiet, innocuous street is home to a variety of gay establishments, and frequented by a larger number of locals than most other areas.

As well as the bars listed below, other hangouts include the **Greenwich Village Hotel** (No.25; 626 9746), the **Aero Hotel** (No.49; 622 7728), sex shop the **Bronx** (*see p205*), sauna **Thermos Night** (*see p205*) and the **Camp Café** (No.45; 622 1506), which serves breakfast, lunch and dinner. Nearby is Arabian gay bar **Habibi Ana** (Lange Leidsedwarsstraat 4-6; no phone), which has regular belly-dancing.

### Cosmo Bar

*Kerkstraat 42 (624 8074). Tram 1, 2, 5.* **Open** 1pm-3am Mon-Thur; 1.30pm-4am Fri, Sat. **Credit** (over €12) AmEx, DC, MC, V. **Map** p310 D4.

A tarty, late-night hangout for those who don't want to go on to a club but don't want to go home, either.

### De Spijker

*Kerkstraat 4 (620 5919). Tram 1, 2, 5.* **Open** 1pm-1am Mon-Thur, Sun; 1pm-3am Fri, Sat. **No credit cards.** **Map** p310 C4.

A friendly and delightfully seedy bar where you won't look out of place in your jeans, leathers or army outfit. Porn vids and cartoons are shown side by side while bare-chested staff serve with smiles. One predominantly male place that also welcomes women.

## Restaurants

### Getto

*Warmoesstraat 51, Old Centre: Old Side (421 5151/www.getto.nl). Tram 4, 9, 16, 20, 24, 25.* **Open** 4pm-1am Tue-Sun. *Kitchen* 6-11pm Tue-Sun. **Main courses** €9-€14. **Credit** DC, MC, V. **Map** p306 D2.

A trendy yet unpretentious spot, with a cool bar and a candlelit restaurant. It's a bit of a rarity: a place where lesbians and gay men genuinely mix. Some nights are mellow, others are clubbier; it also runs a fab mixed-gay evening at the Winston (*see p223*).

### Hemelse Modder

*Oude Waal 9, Old Centre: Old Side (624 3203). Tram 1, 2, 4, 5, 9, 13, 16, 17, 20, 24, 25/Metro Nieuwmarkt.* **Open** 6pm-midnight Tue-Sun. *Kitchen* 6-10pm Tue-Sun. **Set menu** €21-€27. **Credit** AmEx, DC, MC, V. **Map** p307 E2.

You don't expect somewhere with a moniker like 'Heavenly Mud' (the name of a traditional Dutch mousse) to be even remotely romantic. Yet this gay-owned, mixed restaurant's sophisticated interior really enhances the mood. Staff are friendly, the food (Mediterranean with Eastern influences, along with veggie options) is good, and there's a choice wine menu to boot.

### Huyschkaemer

*Utrechtsestraat 137, Southern Canal Belt (627 0575). Tram 4, 6, 7, 10.* **Open** 4pm-1am Mon-Thur, Sun; 4pm-3am Fri, Sat. *Kitchen* 5-11pm daily. **Main courses** €7-€9. **Credit** AmEx, MC, V. **Map** p311 E4.

Huyschkaemer's designer interior – with huge picture windows – attracts a mixed, mainly young and artistic gay and lesbian crowd. Staff at this bar-restaurant are friendly and the good-value food is simply delicious: you can usually turn a starter of your choice into a main dish.

### Raap & Peper

*Peperstraat 23-5, The Waterfront (330 1716). Bus 22, 32, 33, 34, 35, 39.* **Open** 6-11pm Tue-Sun. **Main courses** €5-€9. **Credit** AmEx, MC, V. **Map** p307 E2.

The charming, split-level premises of lesbian-owned and -run 'Turnip & Pepper' were once home to the De Peper squat restaurant. Food here is both delicious and Mediterranean-influenced, so it comes as little surprise that the couple who own it originally ran a restaurant in Portugal.

### La Strada

*Nieuwezijds Voorburgwal 93-5, Old Centre: New Side (625 0276). Tram 1, 2, 5, 13, 17, 20.* **Open** 4pm-midnight Wed, Thur; 2pm-1am Fri, Sat, Sun. **Main courses** €7-€10. **Credit** AmEx, DC, MC, V. **Map** p306 D2.

La Strada is a spacious culinary café in a convenient central location that attracts an arty crowd and is very popular with lesbians. The fine food offers a delicate balance of French, Italian, Spanish and Indonesian influences, and a good selection of vegetarian dishes is always available.

Colourful crochet at **Backstage**. *See p209.*

Party on at Spellbound's **Queer Planet**.

## Cafés

### Backstage
*Utrechtsedwarsstraat 67, Southern Canal Belt
(622 3638). Tram 4, 6, 7, 10.* **Open** *10am-5.30pm
Mon-Sat.* **No credit cards.** **Map** p311 E4.
This multicoloured café-boutique serves almost as
a museum to the half-Mohawk 'Christmas Twins'.
Although Greg died in 1997, identical twin Gary
continues to run the place, selling his unique crochet
wear, chatting to customers and giving spontaneous
horoscope readings. A fabulous place.

### Downtown
*Reguliersdwarsstraat 31, Southern Canal Belt
(622 9958). Tram 1, 2, 4, 5, 9, 14, 16, 20, 24,
25.* **Open** *10am-7pm daily.* **No credit cards.**
**Map** p310 D4.
Snacks, salads and cakes are served by friendly staff
in this small split-level café. Great for eavesdropping
on conversations, but it can be hard to find a seat,
especially at weekends. During summer, the outdoor
terrace provides a temporary solution.

### Le Monde
*Rembrandtplein 6, Southern Canal Belt (626 9922).
Tram 4, 9, 14, 20.* **Open** *8.30am-1am Mon-Thur,
Sun; 8.30am-2am Fri, Sat.* **Kitchen** *8.30am-10.30pm
daily.* **No credit cards.** **Map** p311 E4.
A popular, early-opening and late-closing café, and
a great place to have breakfast, lunch, dinner (includ-
ing vegetarian options), a snack, or a drink.

## Coffeeshop

### The Otherside
*Reguliersdwarsstraat 6, Southern Canal Belt
(421 1014). Tram 1, 2, 5.* **Open** *11am-1am daily.*
**No credit cards.** **Map** p310 D4.
A bright and modern coffeeshop with a good, varied menu that includes single joints, space cake and
cannabis tea. Staff are friendly and informative:
don't hesitate to ask if you have any doubts about
whether you should have your cake and eat it, too.
For more on coffeeshops, *see p147.*

## One-off club nights

Aside from the venues listed below, other bars
and clubs in the city host regular gay nights.
Wednesdays sees popular club Life take over
**More** (*see p227*), while every second Thursday
of the month, **Getto** (*see p208*) hosts the no-frills,
funky, friendly mixed-gay Getto Dance.

Down the street at **Winston International**
(*see p223*), Thursday is also gay night, with
different monthly mixed-gay nights running in
rotation. Among them are the dark **Neues
Nachttierhaus** (first Thursday of the month),
with DJs spinning chilled techno and electro
around videos and visuals; **Wide Open** (third
Thursday of the month; www.wideopen.nu) a

trashy, sexy, anything-goes gig; and **Parking**
(fourth Thursday of the month), a campy
night run by staff from More and the Spijker.
Spellbound, who run Neues Nachttierhaus, also
put on **Queer Planet** parties every two months
at OCCII (Amstelveenseweg 134; 671 7778). For
more, see www.go.to/spellbound-amsterdam.

### Lounge Louche
*NL-Lounge, Nieuwezijds Voorburgwal 169, Old
Centre: New Side (622 7510). Tram 1, 2, 5.* **Open**
*Lounge Louche 3-8pm last Sun of mth.* **Admission**
*call for details.* **No credit cards.** **Map** p306 D3.
Once a month, the infamous Puck proves she's the
lesbian hostess with the mostest with Lounge
Louche's gangsta chic. This decadent late after-
noon/early evening affair offers the perfect ambience
for the post-hangover pre-club party person.

### De Trut
*Bilderdijkstraat 165, Oud West (no phone). Tram 3,
7, 12, 17.* **Open** *11pm-4am Sun.* **Admission** *€1.50.*
**No credit cards.** **Map** p309 B5.
Probably the best gay night in Amsterdam: a mixed
and attitude-free crowd, cheap drinks and great
music. It's also very popular: start queuing outside
no later than 10.40pm to ensure you get in, as doors
open at 11pm and shut when it's full, which could
be just 20 minutes later. The club is held in a basement of a former squat, and is run on a non-profit
basis: proceeds are donated to suitably PC causes.

### Vrankrijk
*Spuistraat, Old Centre: New Side 216 (no phone).
Tram 1, 2, 4, 9, 14, 16, 20, 24, 25.* **Open** *10pm-
2am Mon.* **Admission** *free.* **No credit cards.**
**Map** p306 C3.
This notorious squat near the Royal Palace hosts
mixed-queer night Blue Monday every, er, Monday.

## Lesbian nightlife

Unfortunately, Amsterdam has no lesbian club,
and the tacky **You II** ('bi-het-les lady's dancing
club') is a sorry excuse for one. That said, its
central location at Amstel 178 (421 0900) does
mean many women end up there after **Vive la
Vie** (*see p210*) and **COC** (*see p282*) chuck out.

However, there is a thriving (though small)
lesbian scene in the bars and clubs. Women will
hang out at either Vive la Vie or **Saarein II**
(*see below*), both relatively quiet during the

Wine, women and tapas: **Saarein II**.

week but packed at weekends; or at the mixed **Getto** (*see p208*), an inspired, lesbian-savvy choice where **Getto Dance** (*see p209*) attracts a very good women:men ratio.

On Saturdays, lesbians head along to the women-only night at the COC, though probably more through habit than by choice. On the second Saturday of the month, there's an over-30s party here (they're very strict to the point of being rude about age, so take some ID); younger babes can be found in the upstairs disco area of the building on that night. On Sundays, women often go to the mixed, alternative queer night, **De Trut** (*see p209*).

The women's scene is also boosted by a handful of initiatives organised by the Puck-DJ Natarcia mafia; check out www.wild4women.nl for further details. **Planet Pussy** is their perpetually popular women-only party at the **Melkweg** (*see p225*) on the third Sunday of the month, and every Thursday at **Ministry** (*see p225*) the same posse produces the **Poonani Club**, open to both men and women. Puck also hosts the decadent, mixed **Lounge Louche** at **NL-Lounge** (*see p209*).

Nights and parties come and go, so check the press or in bars for news or contact the **Gay & Lesbian Switchboard** (*see p282*). English-language website www.lesbianamsterdam.com also has up-to-date news about the scene, as well as a wealth of other useful information.

### Saarein II

*Elandsstraat 119, the Jordaan (623 4901).*
*Tram 7, 10.* **Open** 5pm-1am Tue-Thur, Sun; 5pm-2am Fri, Sat. **No credit cards. Map** p310 C4.
Once a women-only bar, Saarein was taken over and reopened as a mixed café in 1999. Still mostly frequented by women (especially on Fridays and Saturdays), this split-level brown bar serves delicious food 6-9.30pm, with tapas available until midnight. Last Sunday of the month is 'Open Podium', for anyone who thinks they can sing.

### Vandenberg

*Lindengracht 95, the Jordaan (622 2716). Tram 3, 10.* **Open** 5pm-1am Mon-Thur, Sun; 5pm-2am Fri; 11am-2am Sat. *Kitchen* 5.30-10pm daily. **Main courses** €5-€7. **No credit cards. Map** p305 B2.
Eel-baiting may have been a popular 'sport' along this canal before it was filled in, but it's one thing you won't find on the menu at this lesbian-owned vegetarian bar-restaurant. Small but glowingly cosy, it attracts a crowd of older locals, though the younger staff pull in a few admirers and contemporaries. The vicious cat is to be avoided at all costs.

### Vive la Vie

*Amstelstraat 7, Southern Canal Belt (624 0114). Tram 4, 9, 14, 20.* **Open** 3pm-1am Mon-Thur, Sun; 3pm-3am Fri, Sat. **No credit cards. Map** p310 E4.
This lively bar has a mainly lipstick/femme clientele, but men are also welcome. Don't be put off by the women dancing and singing along to the trad Dutch music: after a few beers, you'll be joining in. Though the bar is little bigger than a clog box, the pavement terrace offers a solution in summer.

## Sex parties

Apart from **Wild Side** events (*see p282*), there are no women-only sex parties in Amsterdam; just occasional, mixed fetish parties. However, there are regular sex parties for men. The **Stablemaster Hotel** (Warmoesstraat 23; 625 0148) hosts jack-off parties at 8pm most nights, while SOS (Sex on Sunday) is held every last Sunday of the month at the **Argos** (*see p206*) and the **Cockring** (*see p206*) hosts the monthly Nude Club and Horsemen and Knights. The newest kinky/leather club, **Blowbuddies**, is held every first and third Saturday of the month (Warmoesstraat 121; www.blowbuddies.nl); the first Saturday is hardcore, the second is softer.

Just as popular are the larger parties with cabins, slings and golden shower areas. The irregular **Mega Trash** parties, for one, draw a big crowd. The location changes each time, but the dress code is always leather/rubber, and tickets can be bought at www.clubtrash.com or from gay shops such as MR B and Black Body. A less hardcore alternative is the bi-monthly Hot Leather/Rubber Night, held at **COC** (*see p281* or www.stop.demon.nl).

# Music

Where there's sex and drugs, there's rock 'n' roll – but Amsterdam's live music scene also stretches from baroque and bebop to big beat and the blues.

## Rock, Roots & Jazz

Eight years after his 1876 debut with *Deutsches Requiem* in Amsterdam, a dissatisfied Johannes Brahms said farewell to the Dutch music scene, insisting he would only return for food and drinks. How times have changed. Amsterdam has since become somewhere musicians love to perform – and the local cuisine isn't exactly the main attraction. Amsterdam has long been synonymous with sex and drugs, and it's hardly a surprise to find that musicians into both make the most of their visits here. Chet Baker repeatedly visited Amsterdam until he fell from a hotel window here and died, while Jim Morrison legendarily failed to make it on stage at the Doors' only Amsterdam show after passing out in his hotel room. The city's offerings, presumably, had overwhelmed him.

However, Amsterdam has much more to offer than the obvious. The **ArenA** (*see p212*) is capacious enough to accommodate the most famous of bands; the famous **Bimhuis** (*see p216*) is one of many great jazz venues; and the **Paradiso** (*see p214*) is much loved by rock acts both local and of global standing. Now, with the addition of the new **Heineken Music Hall** (*see p213*) and the stylish **Panama** (*see p214*), the possibilities for a great night out have grown still further.

For full listings, check out the **AUB Ticketshop** (0900 0191), and its own free Dutch-listings magazine, *Uitkrant* (*see p279* **Tickets, please**); Dutch-language website *Uitgaanagenda* (http://agenda.welcome.nl); alternative 'zine *Shark* (free in many bars, and online at www.underwateramsterdam.com); or the Dutch national music magazine *Oor* (www.oor.net). Details of the town's more notable gigs are posted on *Time Out*'s website (www.timeout.com/amsterdam).

Few venues make advance tickets available in Amsterdam, and, as a result, most rock, roots and jazz music venues do not accept credit cards. However, at those venues where advance bookings are taken – the Heineken Music Hall, the Paradiso and the Melkweg in particular – tickets can sell out quickly, so try to book as far ahead as possible.

## Rock & roots venues

Aside from the venues listed below, keep an eye out for squat gigs, which may be in *Shark* or on www.squat.net. For details of pop concerts (in Dutch), see the bi-weekly *Oor*.

### Akhnaton

*Nieuwezijds Kolk 25, Old Centre: New Side (624 3396/www.akhnaton.nl). Tram 1, 2, 5, 13, 17, 20.* **Open** 11pm-5am Fri, Sat. **Admission** €5-€7. **No credit cards. Map** p306 D2.
Renowned for world music, regular African dance nights, salsa parties and club nights. It's not exactly palatial, so the club is often bursting at the seams.

### AMP Studios

*KNSM-Laan 13, the Waterfront (418 1111/ www.ampstudios.nl). Bus 28.* **Open** noon-1am daily. **No credit cards.**
AMP Studios started out as a rehearsal space and now offers regular concerts and parties, as well as full recording facilities and a licensed café/bar.

---

**The best** Live music

### Bimhuis

Amsterdam's number one jazz venue is in a great location, but it'll soon be moving to a better one. *See p216.*

### Concertgebouw

Extravagance, beauty and charm combined with the best acoustics on the planet. *See p219.*

### Melkweg

Dairy turned hippie haven turned gallery, cinema, theatre and top music venue. *See p213.*

### Panama

Club, lounge, eat or just enjoy the music in this tastefully decorated place-to-be. *See p214.*

### Paradiso

This legendary venue shouldn't be missed: just ask Prince or the Rolling Stones. *See p214.*

Arts & Entertainment

### ArenA

*ArenA Boulevard 1, Bijlmermeer (311 1333/*
*www.amsterdamarena.nl). Metro Bijlmer.*
**Open** hours vary. **Admission** €18-€27.
**No credit cards**.
This mega-stadium hosts acts so rich they don't need
to tour anymore. It's also home to footie team Ajax
and the annual Sensation dance party.

### Badcuyp

*1e Sweelinckstraat 10, the Pijp (675 9669/*
*www.badcuyp.demon.nl). Tram 4, 16, 20, 24, 25.*
**Open** 5pm-1am Tue-Thur; 5pm-3am Fri; 11am-3am
Sat; 11am-1am Sun. **Admission** free-€15.
**No credit cards. Map** p311 F5.
World music and jazz are the focuses at this small
but friendly venue in the Pijp. There's a session
every Tuesday, often with African musicians.

### De Buurvrouw

*St Pieterpoortsteeg 9, Old Centre: Old Side*
*(625 9654). Tram 4, 9, 14, 16, 20, 24, 25.*
**Open** 8pm-3am Mon-Thur, Sun; 9pm-4am Fri, Sat.
**Admission** free. **No credit cards. Map** p306 D2.
Imaginative decor, occasional live performances
from local bands and a splendidly eclectic back-of-
bar record collection make up this pocket-sized
watering hole. The place draws an alt-rock clientele.

### Café Meander

*Voetboogstraat 3, Old Centre: New Side (625 8430/*
*www.cafemeander.com). Tram 1, 2, 5, 9, 14, 16,*
*24, 25.* **Open** 8.30pm-3am Mon-Thur; 8.30pm-4am
Fri-Sun. **Admission** free-€5. **No credit cards.**
**Map** p310 D4.

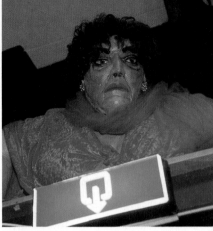

**De Buurvrouw:** eclectic records pull 'em in.

An enthusiastic crowd laps up the mix of live music
(much of it delivered by covers bands, parts of it
jazzy) and DJ sets at this New Side staple, open
almost every night of the week.

### Cruise Inn

*Zuiderzeeweg 29, Zeeburg (692 7188/*
*www.cruise-inn.com). Tram 14/bus 22, 37.*
**Open** 9pm-4am Fri, Sat. **Admission** free-€10.
**No credit cards**.
This tremendously enjoyable and very welcoming
'50s-themed hangout recently moved to a new location, bringing with it Amsterdam's extremely loyal
contingent of bequiffed rockabilly gents and
swingin' hep cats. Daddio!

# Pop tarts

Despite what the ever-cynical Brits might
mutter, decent Dutch rock music is not
as oxymoronic a term as you might expect.
That said, it took a little while to get off the
ground. In the early 1960s, a fledgling scene
emerged, as aspiring locals took to copying
well-known American stars such as Little
Richard and the Everly Brothers.

Within a few years, however, things had
improved dramatically... but not, perhaps
surprisingly, in Amsterdam. The mid to late
'60s saw The Hague become 'Beatcity No.1',
as the Dutch termed it, with bands such as
Shocking Blue ('Venus', later covered to
excruciating effect by Bananarama), Tee
Set ('My Belle Amie') and the mighty Golden
Earring ('Radar Love') all topping the US
charts. Some of The Hague's heavy heritage
lives on even today: the U2-inspired Kane
are the country's most successful new rock
band, while in 1998, singer Anouk had a

Number One with debut single 'Nobody's
Wife'... produced, in neatly circuitous
fashion, by Golden Earring.

Meanwhile, developments on the Dutch
touring circuit have been gloriously varied.
Guitar bands such as Claw Boys Claw, Hello
Venray, Bettie Serveert and Caesar are in
demand at home and abroad; echoes of the
late '60s are heard in critic-pleasers Daryll-
Ann and Johan; while synths and technology
are fundamental to the work of Bauer, Solex
and Arling and Cameron. Amsterdam even
has its own hip hop heroes in the form of
Osdorp Posse, for whom frontman Def P
raps in a local dialect about the beauty
and dirt of his beloved city. However, Junkie
XL are perhaps the biggest indicator of the
Netherlands' international impact on dance
music, and have so far produced two great
CDs of techno with a trancey edge. Shocking
Blue it most certainly ain't.

### Heeren van Aemstel

*Thorbeckeplein 5, Southern Canal Belt (620 2173/
www.deheerenvanaemstel.nl). Tram 4, 9, 14.*
**Open** hours vary. **Admission** free-€30.
**No credit cards. Map** p311 E5.
Located close to Rembrandtplein, this bar offers live
music – usually cover bands or unknowns singing
in Dutch – most nights. Culturally educative.

### Heineken Music Hall

*ArenA Boulevard 590, Bijlmermeer (0900 300
1250/www.heineken-music-hall.nl). Metro Bijlmer.*
**Open** *Box office* from 6.30pm, concert days only.
**Admission** €20-€60. **Credit** AmEx, MC, V.
Acts that've outgrown the Paradiso (*see p214*) and
the Melkweg (*see below*) end up at this newly built
5,000-capacity music hall. What it lacks in ambience
it makes up for with its brilliant acoustics.

### Koninklijk Theater Carré

*Amstel 115-25, Southern Canal Belt (622 5225/
www.theatercarre.nl). Tram 4, 6, 7, 10, 20.*
**Open** *Box office* 10am-7pm Mon-Sat; 1-7pm Sun.
**Admission** €11-€100. **Credit** AmEx, DC, MC, V.
**Map** p311 F4.
Constructed in the late 19th century, this hall lays
on a real mix of performers and music styles. You'll
find everything from opera and flamenco to musi-
cals and singers such as Marianne Faithfull and Lou
Reed. Balcony seats verge on the vertiginous.

### Last Waterhole

*Oudezijds Armsteeg 12, Old Centre: Old Side (624
4814/www.lastwaterhole.nl). Tram 4, 9, 16, 20, 24,
25/Metro Centraal Station.* **Open** 11am-2am Mon-
Thur, Sun; 11am-4am Fri, Sat. **Admission** free.
**No credit cards. Map** p306 D2.
A firm fave with tourists over the years, although
the rock and blues, mostly played by mediocre covers bands, can be hard to get excited about.

### Maloe Melo

*Lijnbaansgracht 163, Western Canal Belt (420
4592/www.maloemelo.com). Tram 7, 10, 13, 14, 17,
20.* **Open** 9pm-3am Mon-Thur, Sun; 9pm-4am Fri, Sat.
**Admission** free-€2. **No credit cards. Map** p311 E5.
Maloe Melo is a cosy hangout for both musicians
and their invariable hangers-on, with a friendly
atmosphere, cheap or sometimes even free admission and music that's both bluesy and rootsy.

### De Meervaart

*Meer en Vaart 300, West (410 7777/
www.meervaart.nl). Tram 1, 17/bus 23, 192.*
**Open** *Box office* 10am-4pm Mon-Fri; 11am-4am
Sat. **Admission** €15-€30. **No credit cards.**
Its modern structure and peripheral location mean
De Meervaart can run a little low on ambience, but
its music programme still has a lot to offer classical,
jazz, blues and world music buffs.

### Melkweg

*Lijnbaansgracht 234A, Southern Canal Belt (531
8181/www.melkweg.nl). Tram 1, 2, 5, 6, 7, 10,
20.* **Open** *Box office* 1-5pm Mon-Fri; 4-6pm Sat,
Sun. *Club* hours vary; usually 9pm-4am daily.
**Admission** €2-€18. *Membership* (compulsory)
€2/mth; €14/yr. **No credit cards. Map** p310 D5.
Once a former dairy (the name translates as 'Milky
Way'), the Melkweg achieved legendary status as
one of the first places in Amsterdam where you
could buy and smoke dope. Thorough renovations,
however, mean that it has lost much of its former
hippie status. The Pepsi-sponsored Max Arena is
large enough to host great international bands,
but the Old Hall still wins out on atmosphere.
Concerts tend to sell out in advance, running the
gamut from corporate rock to world music, and
both halls are home to a variety of regular club
nights (*see p225*). There's a gallery (*see p194*) and
a cinema (*see p198*) here, too.

Jazz and covers bands frequent
**Café Meander.** See p212.

Arts & Entertainment

In full swing at the **Cruise Inn**. *See p212.*

## Mulligans

*Amstel 100, Southern Canal Belt (622 1330/*
*www.mulligans.nl). Tram 4, 9, 14, 16, 24, 25.*
**Open** 4pm-1am Mon-Thur; 4pm-2am Fri; 2pm-2am
Sat; 2pm-1am Sun. **Admission** free.
**No credit cards. Map** p307 E3.
The often excellent live music – more of a feature
here than in similar joints – helps make Mulligans
one of the best Irish pubs in town.

## OCCII

*Amstelveenseweg 134, Museum Quarter (671 7778/*
*www.occii.org). Tram 2, 6.* **Open** 9.30pm-3am Mon-
Thur, Sun; 9pm-2am Fri, Sat. **Admission** free-€5.
**No credit cards.**
A former squat venue, this friendly bar-cum-music
hall has kept some of its aura. Tucked away at the
end of Vondelpark (it's a lovely bike ride), it's a fine
excuse to escape the city centre and enjoy punk,
underground parties, reggae and other alternativalia.

## Paleis van de Weemoed

*Oudezijds Voorburgwal 15, Old Centre: Old Side*
*(625 6964). Tram 4, 9, 16, 20, 24, 25/Metro*
*Centraal Station.* **Open** from 6pm daily.
**Admission** free. **Credit** AmEx, MC, V.
**Map** p306 D2.
Australian-born hostess Fifi l'Amour – not, perhaps,
her real name – welcomes guests to this 'restaurant
chantant', where she strikes up with the songs of
heroes Jacques Brel or Cole Porter. Only diners can
enjoy it, though, and reservations are recommended.

## Panama

*Oostelijke Handelskade 4, the Waterfront (311*
*8686/www.panama.nl). Bus 28, 32, 39.*
**Open** *Box office* noon-6pm daily; also from 1hr
before performance. *Theatre/club* hours vary.
**Admission** €8-€17. **No credit cards.**

This music venue/restaurant/nightclub (*see also*
*p225*) offers a stellar variety of stuff in a plush setting. Thursdays see the 19-piece house band play
everything from the Beatles to surf, with Mondays
and Wednesdays also dedicated to live music.

## Paradiso

*Weteringschans 6-8, Southern Canal Belt (626*
*4521/www.paradiso.nl). Tram 1, 2, 5, 6, 7, 10, 20.*
**Open** hours vary. **Admission** €5-€28. *Membership*
(compulsory) €2/mth; €16/yr. **No credit cards.**
**Map** p310 D5.
What started out as a church, became a hippie hangout in the late '60s, turned into a punk haven in the
mid '70s and then became an all-thing-to-all-people
spot in the 1990s is now Amsterdam's most famous
concert hall. The incredible roster of acts who've
played here reads like a who's who of rock outfits:
even the Rolling Stones have stopped by, recording
much of their live album *Stripped* here. The capacity's only around 1,200, which means that booking
ahead is usually advisable.

## Vondelpark

*Vondelpark, Museum Quarter (open-air theatre*
*673 1499/park office 523 7790). Tram 1, 2, 3,*
*5, 6, 7, 10, 12, 20.* **Open** dawn-dusk daily.
**Admission** free. **No credit cards. Map** p310 C6.
On a pleasant summer's day, this most famous of
Amsterdam parks can be packed, but if you don't
mind a crowd, then check out the stage in its centre;
local musos play Thur-Sun in summer.

## Winston International

*Warmoesstraat 129, Old Centre: Old Side*
*(623 1380/www.winston.nl). Tram 4, 9, 16, 20, 24,*
*25.* **Open** 9pm-3am Mon-Thur, Sun; 9pm-4am Fri,
Sat. **Admission** free-€5. **No credit cards.**
**Map** p306 D3.

# Brood swings

On 11 July 2001, the main headlines of most major Dutch newspapers announced 'Brood is Dood' ('Bread is Dead'). Following in the footsteps of Chet Baker (*see p79*), Herman Brood (*pictured*) ended his life with an appropriately rock 'n' roll thump by stepping off the roof of the **Hilton Amsterdam** (*see p63*). While a suicide note found on his body said that friends, family and fans should just make a party of it, the predominant mood of the Netherlands was that of grief – the country had lost its much cherished personification of sex, drugs and rock 'n' roll.

The funeral didn't fulfil Brood's wish to be flambéed in Grand Marnier, but it did reflect how deeply he was loved by the Dutch. Brood, with his sweet demeanour and two-grams-of-speed-a-day habit, was in effect the nation's cuddle junkie. In Amsterdam in particular, he was a familiar institution. Most locals had seen him wandering about with his pet parrot on his head, or being mothered by waitresses at a local bar.

Brood began his career in the late '60s as the pianist for blues band Cuby & the Blizzards, but only became a household name in 1978 when he and his backing band, the Wild Romance, released *Shpritsz*, from which his biggest hit, 'Saturday Night', was taken. He never made it big on a global scale, but he was famous throughout the Netherlands and in Germany, touring right up until a year before his tragic death.

In 1990, Brood started selling his colourful and funkily figurative paintings and prints. Since his death, prices have rocketed and there is talk of forgeries flooding the market. His studio above his old haunt, **Café Dante** (*see p139*), is now a gallery dedicated to selling all things Herman: artwork, CDs, biographies and memorabilia. A wax likeness, for which he posed a couple of days before his death, has been placed in **Madame Tussaud's Scenerama** (*see p74*) beside another one of his role models: Elvis. Brood, it seems, will live on for a while yet.

Although the recently restyled Winston (*see also p223*) is more of a clubby venue than ever, live music still features every Friday and Saturday around 9pm. In addition, Tuesdays offer either Live on the Low, an open stage for hip hop and R&B acts, or Display, with poets, actors and singer-songwriters.

## Out of Amsterdam

### Ahoy

*Ahoyweg 10, Rotterdam (information 010 293 3300/tickets 0900 235 2469/www.ahoy.nl). NS rail Rotterdam Centraal Station.* **Open** hours vary. **Tickets** prices vary. **Credit** AmEx, MC, V.
This giant complex hosts artists too massive to play Amsterdam's smaller venues. Don't expect a good atmosphere, but do expect to see acts like Jamiroquai or Destiny's Child alongside 10,000 others.

### 013

*Veemarktstraat 44, Tilburg (013 460 9500/ www.013web.nl). NS rail Tilburg.* **Open** hours vary. **Tickets** €3-€25. **Credit** AmEx, MC, V.
With a capacity of 2,200 in its main hall – its smaller spaces hold 350 and 150 respectively – 013 is a step up from intimate haunts like Paradiso (*see p214*) and the Melkweg (*see p213*) and hosts the likes of Underworld and Nick Cave.

## Jazz & blues

Throughout the year, major venues play host to big stars, with local groups and jam sessions sneaking into the early hours in snug bars most nights of the week. For the **IJsbreker**, *see p220*.

### Alto Jazz Café

*Korte Leidsedwarsstraat 115, Southern Canal Belt (626 3249). Tram 1, 2, 5, 6, 7, 10, 20.* **Open** 9pm-3am Mon-Thur, Sun; 9pm-4am Fri, Sat. **Admission** free. **No credit cards**. **Map** p310 D5.
This cosy and relaxed brown bar in an otherwise touristy area offers live jazz and blues.

### Bimhuis

*Oudeschans 73-7, Old Centre: Old Side (623 1361/www.bimhuis.nl). Tram 9, 14, 20/Metro Waterlooplein.* **Open** *Box office* 8-11pm performance nights (usually Thur-Sat). **Admission** €9-€16. **No credit cards**. **Map** p307 E2.
The city's major jazz venue stages a mix of well-known international artists and local talent on most nights of the week. It's often hard to get a seat, so arrive early. Tickets are available on the day from the AUB or Amsterdam Tourist Board, or on the door an hour before showtime. In 2004, the Bimhuis will move to the Eastern Docklands.

### Bourbon Street

*Leidsekruisstraat 6-8, Southern Canal Belt (623 3440). Tram 1, 2, 5, 6, 7, 10.* **Open** 10pm-4am Mon-Thur, Sun; 10pm-5am Fri, Sat. **Admission** €1-€2.50. **No credit cards**. **Map** p310 D5.

Horny! The **Alto Jazz Café**.

A spacious bar with a podium for blues most nights of the week and a very late licence. The friendly staff and customers will make you feel right at home. Performances can border on the poetic.

### Casablanca

*Zeedijk 26, Old Centre: Old Side (625 5685/ www.casablanca-amsterdam.nl). Tram 4, 9, 16, 20, 24, 25.* **Open** 8pm-2am Mon-Thur, Sun; 10pm-4am Fri, Sat. **Admission** free. **No credit cards**. **Map** p306 D2.
Amsterdam's top jazz venue of the '50s still exudes some of its old charm. Music comes from noteworthy local and international names, but don't miss the variety theatre and old-school circus acts.

### Cristofori

*Prinsengracht 581, Western Canal Belt (626 8495/ www.cristofori.nl/salon). Tram 1, 2, 5.* **Open** hours vary. **Admission** prices vary. **No credit cards**. **Map** p310 C4.
Cristofori is worth a visit for the building alone: it's located in a plum canal house that also acts as a piano retailer. At weekends, though, there's live entertainment, from jazz vocalists to chamber music.

Arts & Entertainment

### De Pompoen

*Spuistraat 2, Old Centre: New Side (521 3003/www.pompoen.nl). Tram 1, 2, 5.*
**Open** 10am-1am Mon-Thur, Sun; 10am-3am Fri, Sat. **Admission** free-€15. **No credit cards.** **Map** p306 C2.

A nice restaurant, this, though the live jazz is just as worthwhile as the food. Acts, both local and international, play week-long residencies. Busy at weekends.

## Festivals

Maybe it's the flat terrain. Maybe it's the Netherlands' festival-friendly narcotics legislation (OK, it's almost undoubtedly the latter). It certainly ain't the weather. Whatever the reason, Holland is host to myriad music festivals. Tickets for most are available from **Amsterdam Tourist Board** (0900 400 4040) and the **AUB** (0900 0191). For more events, such as lit-rock event Crossing Border, *see p178.*

### Access to Amsterdam

*320 2119/www.a2a.nl.* **Date** late Sept.
A2A, kind of a Dutch version of Austin's South by Southwest, brings in 350 bands from 20 countries to perform in locations around Leidseplein over four days. All that they have in common is star potential and a desire to be heard.

### Amsterdam Pop Prijs/ Wanted R&B & Hip Hop Prijs Finals

*420 8160/www.grap.net.* **Date** *Pop Prijs* Mar-June. *Wanted* Apr-June.
Pop, R&B and hip hop, all from locals, comes under the spotlight during a series of events around town.

### Amsterdam Roots Festival

*Tickets Uitlijn 0900 0191 premium rate.* **Date** June.
Run by the Melkweg (*see p213*), the Tropeninstituut (*see p248*) and the Concertgebouw (*see p219*), the Roots Festival (tickets up to €27) features some of the greatest world music acts on the planet. A free 'world village' in Oosterpark, with a collection of different podiums, hosts lesser-known names.

### A Camping Flight to Lowlands

*Six Flags, Flevoland (information 015 284 0740/ tickets 0900 300 1250/www.lowlands.nl). NS rail Lelystad.* **Date** last wknd of Aug.
The biggest Dutch alternative festival of the year sees tens of thousands of young indie bucks shell out around €80 on a ticket and descend on Six Flags in Flevoland for three days of camping and moshing. The Dutch Reading, more or less.

### Drum Rhythm Festival

*015 215 7756/www.drumrhythm.com.* **Date** May.
This outdoor festival of danceable – but not always dance – music prides itself on its splendidly eclectic line-ups (2001 featured Basement Jaxx, Badmarsh & Shri and Cameo, among many others). It'll cost around €45 for a two-day pass.

### Dynamo

*06 5097 0737 mobile.* **Date** June.
For years, this headbangers' haven was located near Eindhoven, but it fell victim to the foot-and-mouth epidemic in 2001. Undeterred, the largest hard rock festival in the Low Countries will be back in 2002, probably in the town of Weert.

### North Sea Jazz festival

*Netherlands Congress Centre, Churchillplein 10, the Hague (information 015 215 7756/tickets 010 591 9000/www.northseajazz.nl).* **Date** 2nd wknd in July.
This three-day mega-event (€125 for a pass) in the Hague is a fantastic opportunity to see some bona fide jazz legends: up to a thousand artists perform each year, from big names to a savvy selection of up-and-comers. The three-day pass covers the main hall, where the big names – from the instrumental twiddlings of Oscar Peterson to the croonings of Tony Bennett – take curtain call after curtain call for educated audiences.

### Parkpop

*Zuiderpark, the Hague (0900 340 3505/ www.parkpop.nl).* **Date** late June.
Europe's largest free festival – up to 400,000 turn up annually – is a family-friendly affair. It's also one of the few outdoor events to offer Dutch and international music in equal amounts, but don't expect anything too daring.

### Pink Pop

*Landgraaf (046 475 2500/www.wanadoo.nl/ pinkpop).* **Date** May/June.
This immensely popular three-day outdoor festival (€65 for a pass) has been going strong since the early '70s. Expect an impressive line-up of pop stars: Basement Jaxx, the Hives and Radiohead all played in 2001. Book ahead: the 60,000 tickets always sell out in advance.

### Racism Beat It

*627 7766.* **Date** Aug.
Good intentions are matched by a good atmosphere at this free anti-racism festival. Around 15,000 come to hear lesser-known Dutch rock stars and a slew of DJs. Spaarnwoude was the location in 2001, but it may relocate to Museumplein in the future.

### Sonic Acts

*626 4521.* **Date** varies.
The Paradiso (*see p214*) hosts this three- or four-day festival for new electronic music, which has featured Stockhausen, Scanner and :zoviet*france:. Various workshops and an Image and Sound Lab for remixing complete the cutting-edge ambience. Tickets are usually around €8.

### Turntablized

*420 8160/www.grap.net).* **Date** Nov/Dec.
Talented local cut-and-scratch hip hop DJs get a chance to show off their turntable skills on the decks at this annual c-c-c-competition held at the Melkweg (*see p213*) and the Paradiso (*see p214*).

**Arts & Entertainment**

# Classical & Opera

In an age when governments around the world are slashing arts funding in a frighteningly casual way, it's always a thrill to find a city in which the arts are not only fighting back, but holding their own. Amsterdam is such a city: the local arts scene is on the up-and-up; serious theatre is back on track again despite competition from trashy musicals; and classical music is alive and well following the financial flux of a decade or two ago.

Anyone with a half-decent classical CD collection has at least one disc by the **Royal Concertgebouw Orchestra**. The famed ensemble – based at the **Concertgebouw**, funnily enough – has gone from strength to strength in recent years under Riccardo Chailly's direction. It's not all Chailly, though: despite the fact that the international conducting circuit is starting to get out of hand – how many guest appearances from 'star' conductors do audiences really need? – a roster of visiting baton-wielders that includes Mstislav Rostropovich, Nikolaus Harnoncourt and the orchestra's honorary conductor, Bernard Haitink, cannot fail to catch the eye.

Across town at the Beurs van Berlage, the **Netherlands Philharmonic**, directed by Hartmut Haenchen, plays a symphonic series alongside its regular productions at the Nederlandse Opera, and is normally good value. But the other major ensembles shouldn't be forgotten: the **Rotterdam Philharmonic Orchestra** has as its chief conductor the exceptional Valery Gergiev, while the **Radio Philharmonic Orchestra**, based in Hilversum but a regular visitor to Amsterdam, continues to work at the highest levels under the skilled baton of Edo de Waart.

Almost everyone in Amsterdam has started to forget about the ruckus over the construction of the 'Stopera' – Muziektheater/City Hall – building, which opened in 1985 and is now home to the **Nederlands Opera**. Good thing, too, for the company is on a roll under the acclaimed artistic direction of Pierre Audi, a man who demands much of his audience (as evidenced by his take on Wagner's highly dense 'Ring' cycle).

### ENSEMBLES

Two types of music stand out above all others in this city of extremes. On the one hand, there's the old school. Dutch musicians were the founders of authentic performance practice – performances using authentic period instruments – and the innovation has now almost become a tradition. Ton Koopman holds the torch as harpsichordist and 'director

who doesn't conduct' of the Amsterdam Baroque Orchestra, founded in 1979, while the Amsterdam Bach Soloists, formed by members of the Concertgebouw Orchestra, is led by principle violinist Henk Rubingh when it's not employing a collaborating guest conductor. Recorder-player and director Frans Brüggen extends authentic practice into the classical era with his Orchestra of the 18th Century. Look out for concerts organised by **Organisatie Oude Muziek** – literally, the 'Organisation for Old Music' – whose early music events at the Waalse are often unmissable.

On the flipside, there is a growing modern music scene in Amsterdam. There are about 20 new music ensembles based in the city, with Asko Ensemble, the Combattimento Consort and the Schönberg Ensemble among the most notable. Both the Nieuw Music Ensemble and the Nieuw Sinfonietta are also worth listening out for, as are minimalist eccentrics Orkest de Volharding, while contemporary music fans should check out the Proms. Kind of a down and dirty version of the British festival of the same name, it's a series of contemporary concerts held, oddly, in the **Paradiso** (*see p214*).

### TICKETS & INFORMATION

Ticket prices in Amsterdam are reasonable compared with other European cities. However, this bonus is tempered by the fact that tickets for many of the larger venues are sold on a subscription system, and it can be difficult to get tickets on an ad hoc basis. For big concerts and operas, try to book as far in advance as you can, but if you're just passing through, it's always worth phoning up for returns.

For full listings information, pick up a copy of the free Dutch listings magazine *Uitkrant*, published by the **AUB Ticketshop** (0900 0191; *see p279* **Tickets please**), or call in at the **Amsterdam Tourist Board** (0900 400 4040; *see p289*), which has information on upcoming shows. Discounts on tickets are often available for students and over-65s.

## Concert halls

Where a telephone number is given in the listings below, tickets are sold at the venue's box office. Tickets are also available from the **AUB Ticketshop** and its Uitlijn service (0900 0191) and its website (www.uitlijn.nl). Look out for their annual publication *Uitgids*, which details subscription series concerts.

### Bethaniënklooster

*Barndesteeg 6B, Old Centre: Old Side (625 0078). Tram 4, 9, 14, 16, 24, 25. Tram 4, 9, 16, 20, 24, 25/Metro Nieuwmarkt.* **Open** hours vary. **Tickets** €12. **No credit cards. Map** p306 D2.

# Orchestral manoeuvres

The history of the **Concertgebouw** (*pictured*) is an illustration of just how quickly times change in Amsterdam. When it was built in the 1890s, locals criticised its location for being too far out of town. Soon after its completion, however, population growth led to new neighbourhoods being built outside Amsterdam's original borders. And so it is that today, the area in which the hall sits is one of Amsterdam's most sought-after residential areas.

Over the years, the Concertgebouw's incredible acoustics have encouraged greats such as Cecilia Bartoli, Thomas Hampson and Mitsuko Uchida to perform here, while the house band, the Royal Concertgebouw Orchestra, has also garnered itself something of a longstanding reputation. It wasn't always thus, though. Back in the late 19th century, conductor Willem Kes disliked the informality that used to prevail at the orchestra's concerts here. As Kes led the musicians through the hits of the day, the ungrateful audience would drink, smoke and even chat away, and the social aspect seemed more important than the music. A furious Kes demanded that people quietened down during concerts, which hardly endeared him to the local establishment. However, by the time he quit, attitudes had changed profoundly; these days, visitors even get offered special sweets in a bid to reduce their coughing.

Some things at the Concertgebouw, though, never change. Mahler and Bruckner symphonies have long been one of the Orchestra's great strengths, with Bruckner a particular favourite of conductor Eduard van Beinum, who led the orchestra post-World War II. However, it was the interpretations of his successor Bernard Haitink that firmly linked the orchestra with both Mahler and Bruckner. Present conductor Ricardo Chailly has since picked up on Haitink's fascinations, an influence that has stretched to his including of Mahler's second symphony in a late 2001 programme and inviting Haitink back to become the orchestra's first ever 'Conductor Laureate'. Indeed, Haitink returns to the Concertgebouw in 2002 to lead the orchestra in Mahler's sixth. Kes would no doubt be pleased to note that smoking and drinking will not be permitted in the auditorium.

Hidden in a small alley between Damstraat and Nieuwmarkt, this former monastery caters especially for lovers of chamber music. It's a stage for promising new talents, but you might also find reputed musicians entertaining the crowds.

### Beurs van Berlage: AGA Zaal & Yakult Zaal

*Damrak 213, Old Centre: Old Side (627 0466). Tram 4, 9, 14, 16, 20, 24, 25.* **Open** *Box office* 2.30-5pm Tue-Fri; 12.30-5pm Sat; also from 75min before performance. Closed June-mid Aug. **Tickets** €7-€16. **No credit cards. Map** p306 D2.
This former stock exchange is now a cultural centre, housing a large exhibition hall, two concert halls, one of Holland's dedicated classical radio stations, the Concertzender, and the offices of the resident orchestras: the Netherlands Philharmonic and the Netherlands Chamber Orchestra. Entered from the

Damrak, the medium-sized Yakult Zaal offers comfortable seating, a massive stage and controllable but not ideal acoustics. The 200-seat AGA Zaal is an odd-looking free-standing glass box within the walls of a side-room. *See p74.*

### Concertgebouw

*Concertgebouwplein 2-6, Museum Quarter, (reservations 671 8345/24hr information in Dutch 675 4411). Tram 2, 3, 5, 12, 16, 20.* **Open** *Box office* 10am-7pm daily. *By phone* 10am-5pm daily. **Tickets** €5-€114. **Credit** AmEx, DC, MC, V. **Map** p310 D6.
The Concertgebouw (*see also above*) is the favourite venue of many of the world's top soloists and orchestras, including its own Concertgebouw Orchestra (which, aside from its regular year-round programme, plays a lovely Christmas matinée concert here every 25 December). The acoustics of the Grote

Arts & Entertainment

Zaal (Great Hall) are second to none; the Kleine Zaal (Recital Hall), featuring top-class chamber groups and soloists, is less comfortable but has a nicely intimate atmosphere. Visiting stars push prices up, but for 75% of the remaining concerts, tickets cost less than €20. Throughout July and August, tickets for the Robeco Summer Concerts, featuring high-profile artists and orchestras, are an excellent bargain.

### IJsbreker

*Weesperzijde 23, the Pijp (693 9093/*
*www.netcetera.nl/ysbreker). Tram 3, 6, 7, 10.*
**Admission** €6.50-€16. **No credit cards.**
**Map** p312 G4.
Situated on the picturesque banks of the Amstel, the IJsbreker's café boasts one of the best outdoor terraces in town, with a fantastic view of the Amstel. The music programming here, though, is among Europe's most innovative, concentrating on contemporary classical music and experimental jazz. Like the Bimhuis (*see p216*), it will be moving to the Eastern Docklands in 2004.

## Churches

Many musicians in Amsterdam take advantage of the monumental churches around the city. The bonus for concertgoers is obvious: aside from hearing largely excellent music, you get a chance to see the interiors of these wonderful buildings at the same time. During the summer, the city's many bell-towers resonate to the intricate tinkling of their carillons: thumping the 'keyboard' mechanism triggers a whole array of smaller bells into a clanging and barely melodious nightmare of Hunchbackian proportions. But churches are not just for organ and carillon recitals: the refurbished Amstelkerk and Lutherse Kerk are also used for concerts. Most churches have no box office, but tickets are available from the **AUB**.

### Engelse Kerk

*Begijnhof 48, Old Centre: New Side (624 9665).*
*Tram 1, 2, 4, 5, 9, 14, 16, 20, 24, 25.* **Open**
hours vary. **Admission** free. **No credit cards.**
**Map** p310 D4.
Nestled in an idyllic courtyard, the Academy of the Begijnhof (*see p85*) arranges weekly concerts of baroque and classical music at the English Reformed Church, with particular emphasis on the use of authentic period instruments in performances. The series of free lunchtime concerts in July and August features young players and new ensembles.

### Nicolaaskerk

*Prins Hendrikkade 73, Old Centre: Old Side (624 8749). Tram 1, 2, 4, 5, 9, 13, 14, 16, 17, 20, 24, 25/Metro Centraal Station.* **Open** hours vary.
**Admission** free. **No credit cards. Map** p306 D2.
This recently renovated Catholic church opposite Centraal Station often has a vocal programme on Sundays, offering the likes of Gregorian vespers.

The **Engelse Kerk**: a religious experience.

### Nieuwe Kerk

*Dam, Old Centre: New Side (626 8168). Tram 1, 2, 5, 9, 13, 14, 16, 17, 20, 24, 25.* **Open** 10am-5pm daily.
**Tickets** €6; €5 concessions. **No credit cards.**
**Map** p306 C3.
The Nieuwe Kerk has a magnificent 16th-century organ and hosts organ concerts by top Dutch and international players. Gustav Leonhardt, grandfather of baroque performance practice, is the resident organist. On Saturdays between May and September, it has a programme of guest organists. *See p75.*

### Noorderkerk

*Noordermarkt 48, the Jordaan (427 6163/*
*www.meetingpoint.org/gemeenten/noorderkerk).*
*Tram 3, 10.* **Open** hours vary. **Tickets** prices vary. **No credit cards. Map** p305 B2.
The hardness of the wooden benches in this early 17th-century church is soon forgotten when you're listening to the likes of cellist Pieter Wispelwey playing Bach sonatas. Reservations are recommended.

### Oude Kerk

*Oudekerksplein 23, Old Centre: Old Side (625 8284).*
*Tram 4, 9, 14, 16, 20, 24, 25.* **Open** 11am-5pm
Mon-Sat; 1-5pm Sun. **Tickets** €3-€7; €2-€6
concessions. **No credit cards. Map** p306 D2.
Jan Sweelinck, the Netherlands' most famous 17th-century composer, was once organist here. Concerts (June to August) include organ and carillon recitals, choral and chamber music. The Oude Kerk (*see also p83*) holds a summer 'wandering' concert series together with the Museum Amstelkring (*see p82*).

### Waalse Kerk

*Oudezijds Achterburgwal 157, Old Centre: Old Side (Organisatie Oude Muziek 030 236 2236). Tram 4, 9, 16, 20, 24, 25.* **Open** hours vary. **Tickets** €10;
€8 concessions. **No credit cards. Map** p306 D3.

Small, elegant and intimate, concerts at the Waalse Kerk are organised by the Organisatie Oude Muziek, a group devoted to early music played on period instruments. Musicians from both the Netherlands and abroad play here on a relatively regular basis.

## Opera

### Muziektheater
*Waterlooplein 22, Old Centre: Old Side (625 5455/ www.muziektheater.nl).* **Open** *Box office* 10am-6pm Mon-Sat; 11.30am-6pm Sun; or until start of performance. **Tickets** €12-€18. **Credit** AmEx, DC, MC, V. **Map** p307 E3.
The Muziektheater is home to the Nationale Ballet (*see p250*) and the Nederlands Opera, as well as visiting guest productions. The emphasis is on high-quality opera and dance productions at reasonable prices. The stage's spaciousness invites particularly ambitious ideas from world-famous stage directors like Peter Sellars (*Pelléas et Mélisande*) and attracts respected artists with rock roots such as Björk and Marianne Faithfull.

### Stadsschouwburg
*Leidseplein 26, Southern Canal Belt (624 2311). Tram 1, 2, 5, 6, 7, 10, 20.* **Open** *Box office* 10am-6pm or until start of performance Mon-Sat; from 1½hrs before start of performance Sun. **Tickets** €9-€35. **Credit** AmEx, MC, V. **Map** p310 C5.
This municipal theatre for plays and cabaret usually stages two or three performances of each of the National Travelling Opera's productions, and also hosts operas by visiting companies, often from abroad. The grand surroundings lend a touch of splendour to every aspect of your visit.

## Out of town

### De Doelen
*Kruisstraat 2, Rotterdam (010 217 1717/ www.dedoelen.nl). NS rail Rotterdam Centraal Station.* **Open** *Box office* 10am-6pm Mon-Thur, Sat, Sun; 10am-9pm Fri. **Tickets** €7-€185. **Credit** AmEx, MC, V.
The Doelen, which is best known as home to the Rotterdam Philharmonic Orchestra (RPO), contains both a large and small concert hall. It hosts about two dozen series a year, ranging from contemporary orchestral work to jazz and almost everything in between, including the RPO's own concert season.

### Vredenburg Music Centre
*Vredenburgpassage 77, Utrecht (box office 030 231 4544/information 0900 9203). NS rail Utrecht.* **Open** *Box office* noon-7pm Mon; 10am-7pm Tue-Sat; also from 45min before performance. **Tickets** €16-€25. **Credit** AmEx, MC, V.
Since the opening of the Heineken Music Hall (*see p213*), this venue has more or less ditched its former rock content, focusing instead on classical and jazz, with the occasional pop act. The setting is ugly, but that could all change when Vredenburg relocates to its designated new building, on which construction work will start in 2003.

## Festivals & events

Further details on all the events listed below can be obtained from the **AUB** (0900 0191) and the **Amsterdam Tourist Board** (0900 400 4040). Another festival that features a whole range of arts including classical music is the **Uitmarkt** (*see p181*).

### Grachtenfestival
*Pulitzer Hotel, Prinsengracht, Western Canal Belt (421 4542).* **Date** mid Aug. **Tickets** free.
What started out life as a single free concert by an orchestra floating on a pontoon in front of the Hotel Pulitzer (*see p57*) has gone on to become the 'Canal Festival', involving over 70 chamber concerts in 20 different canalside locations. The line-up balances international names with local up-and-comers. A festival not to be missed.

### International Gaudeamus Music Week
*Postal & telephone enquiries: Stichting Gaudeamus, Swammerdamstraat 38, 1091 RV Amsterdam (694 7349).* **Date** early Sept. **Tickets** €7. **No credit cards**.
An annual competition for young composers, which includes a whole week of intense discussion about the state of the art, plus live performances of selected entries and works by established composers. Also of interest is the International Gaudeamus Interpreters' Competition (usually taking place in Rotterdam during October), a similar competition for performers of contemporary repertoire.

### Utrecht Early Music Festival
*Various venues in Utrecht; information from Organisatie Oude Muziek, Postbus 734 NL, 3500 AS Utrecht (030 236 2236/www.oudemuziek.nl).* **Date** late Aug-early Sept. **Tickets** €7-€31. **No credit cards**.
Top baroque and classical artists and ensembles from around the world, performing in churches and concert halls throughout the city. Many ensembles use period instruments – the kind of meticulous attention to traditional detail which satisfies the trainspotters no end.

## Other organisations

### STEIM (Stichting for Electro-Instrumental Music)
*622 8690.*
Amsterdam's electronic music institution is a unique research team that sets out to examine the interface between man and music. They also organise many bleeding-edge concerts and performances to give clued-up technophiles an intriguing glimpse into the future sound of music.

**Arts & Entertainment**

# Nightclubs

Überclubs, squats, outdoor parties and international DJs –
Amsterdam's after-hours scene rocks the house.

The first day of 2001 changed Dutch clubbing
forever. Eight died and around 200 were injured
in Volendam, a village north of Amsterdam,
as 700 clubbers tried to escape a fire in a three-
storey venue. Midnight sparklers, when coupled
with flimsy paper decorations, created a fire
hazard, exacerbated by the fact that all the
upstairs windows were locked shut. Afterwards,
Dutch officials came under huge pressure to
ensure such a disaster did not occur again.
What ensued was a heavy crackdown on clubs
and bars in Amsterdam, with restrictions on
how many people were permitted inside at any
one time. Some venues had to close temporarily
and implement extra fire-safety precautions.

Otherwise, and despite the addition of new
venues such as glamorous old-skool **Panama**
(*see p225*), überclub **The Zone** and the over-
hyped **More** (for both, *see p227*), it's business
as usual in Amsterdam's clubs circuit. That's not
to say that the scene isn't without its quirks. On
top of admission, you'll need to pay extra to use
the cloakroom or toilet. Guys who want to leave
a good impression with the door staff may need

to tip (the same is not true for the girls); and if
you're travelling in a group of guys, don't expect
to get into any of the good club nights with ease.
To improve your chances, dress well and go to
the door in pairs, and don't show up drunk.

## Club venues

For clubs and venues where the majority of
nights are aimed at the gay community (such as
hetero-friendly **Exit**, and **iT**, where straights
are allowed in on Thursdays and Fridays), *see
p205*. For the **Westergasfabriek**, *see p245*.

### The Old Centre: Old Side

#### Winston International
*Warmoesstraat 129 (623 1380/www.winston.nl).
Tram 9, 14, 25.* **Open** 10pm-3am Mon-Thur, Sun;
11pm-4am Fri, Sat. **Admission** €3.50-€12.
**No credit cards. Map** p306 D2.
When a nightclub proclaims 'goodbye lounge, hello
rococo', you know you're in for something unusual.
The lush Winston (*see p53 and p214*) is no bigger

Get **More** for your money with smart design and international DJs. *See above and p225.*

than a giant living room, but it presents an ace mix of stuff: hip hop, drum 'n' bass, '80s cheese, open-mic poetry, old-skool disco and easy listening (at Sunday's Club Vegas), to name a few. The cocktails are great, and the town's smallest gallery is in the toilets. Its dress code is becoming stricter, so look pretty.

## The Old Centre: New Side

### Dansen bij Jansen
*Handboogstraat 11 (620 1779/ www.dansenbijjansen.nl). Tram 1, 2, 5.* **Open** 11pm-4am Mon-Thur, Sun; 11pm-5am Fri, Sat. **Admission** €1-€4. **No credit cards. Map** p310 D4.
Dansen bij Jansen is run by ex-students for students. You'll need student ID to get inside, where you'll find 500 other students, cheap drinks and a fun, safe-ish party playlist. Unlike most clubs, you get the feeling T-shirts and jeans *are* the dress code here (not to mention male chins with mini stubble-fluff).

### Item
*Nieuwezijds Voorburgwal 163-5 (06 5040 4505 mobile). Tram 1, 2, 5.* **Open** 11pm-4am Tue, Wed, Sun, also some Thur; 11pm-5am Fri, Sat. **Admission** €5-€12. **No credit cards. Map** p306 C3.
The main attraction here is the open-plan layout: the view to the dancefloor through the lighting rig from the third floor is hypnotic. Wednesday is drum 'n' bass night, Friday plays house, and the weekend deals in techno. Leon, whose mobile number is listed above, is happy to give news on late parties, held around every six weeks.

## Western Canal Belt

### Korsakoff
*Lijnbaansgracht 161 (625 7854/www.korsakoff.nl). Tram 10, 13, 14, 17.* **Open** 11pm-3am Mon-Thur, Sun; 11pm-5am Fri, Sat. **Admission** usually free. **No credit cards. Map** p310 C4.
A fantastic down 'n' dirty club that may bring out the crusty goth freak in you. You might feel a little out of place if you're not dreadlocked, pierced or wearing a Marilyn Manson T-shirt, though no one will care much. The venue is small but boozy and friendly, ideal for all-night drinking to the heavy sounds no other club dares play.

## Southern Canal Belt

### Backdoor
*Amstelstraat 32 (620 2333/www.backdoor.nl). Tram 4, 9, 14, 20.* **Open** 11pm-5am Fri, Sat; 9pm-4am Sun. **Admission** €6-€12. **No credit cards. Map** p307 E3.
The erstwhile Soul Kitchen and House of Soul may have undergone name changes in recent years, but the musical offerings remain largely true to its soulful, funky roots. It's an easy-going spot with plenty of room for self-expression on the dancefloor and a nice atmosphere.

**The best** Clubs

**Bloemendaal beach cafés**
Sun's up. Go out and enjoy it. *See p228.*

**Korsakoff**
If you like it rough and ready. *See p223.*

**Panama**
Old skool glam in a mod setting. *See p225.*

**Winston International**
Go retro at Club Vegas (*pictured*). *See p222.*

**The Zone**
Bigger really is better. *See p227.*

### Escape
*Rembrandtplein 11 (622 1111/www.escape.nl). Tram 4, 9, 14, 20.* **Open** 11pm-4am Thur, Sun; 11pm-5am Fri, Sat. **Admission** €12-€20. **No credit cards. Map** p311 E4.
After a 2001 makeover, Escape is safer and looking gorgeous – and with a capacity of 2,000, it's still the town's largest central venue. The door policy is less selective than it was, but it's a popular place: go early or plan on standing in line. Chemistry on Saturdays keeps pulling in the punters with a formula of top local DJs and international guests to help keep the hype and atmosphere at boiling point. Other nights vary from student events to fashion openings.

### Industry
*Pardenstraat 17 (no phone). Tram 9, 14, 20.* **Open** 11pm-4am Thur, Sun; 11pm-5am Fri, Sat. **Admission** €10-€20. **No credit cards. Map** p307 E3.
Industry's music policy is focused on R&B and the occasional theme night; it has two levels, with a bar upstairs and dancefloor downstairs. Baseball caps are not allowed, but – though nasty jewellery seems to be a prerequisite – there are no further dress restrictions and staff are generally attitude-free.

**Arts & Entertainment**

...OUR MISSION IS
TO KEEP A STEP AHEAD
IN THE EVOLUTION OF FASHION

# CYBERDOG

SPUISTRAAT,250
1012 VW-AMSTERDAM
THE NETHERLANDS
t:+3120.3306385
f:+3120.6261996

WWW.CYBERDOG.NET

open:
sun:closed
mon:11-19
tue:11-19
wed:11-19
thu:11-21
fri:11-19
sat:11-19

## Melkweg

*Lijnbaansgracht 234A (531 8181/www.melkweg.nl).*
*Tram 1, 2, 5, 6, 7, 10.* **Open** hours vary.
**Admission** free-€20. *Membership* €2.50/mth
(compulsory). **No credit cards. Map** p310 C5.
In the '70s, a bunch of hippies thought it'd be a neat
idea to turn this milk factory into a cultural venue.
How right they were. Today, the hippies have gone,
replaced by bands, films, theatre, art and clubs. Try
Thursday's 100% Jamaican Crossover with the
Controverse Allstars. *See also p194, p198, and p213.*

## Ministry

*Reguliersdwarsstraat 12 (623 3981/www.ministry.nl).*
*Tram 16, 24, 25.* **Open** 10pm-4am Thur, Sun;
11pm-5am Fri, Sat. **Admission** €3-€12. **No credit
cards. Map** p310 D4.
A small and chic club with a varied music policy.
The thing you can rely on, though, is a funky basis
for everything from phat beats and underground
sounds to live music, jamming and '80s choons.
Expect a ruthless door policy and over-21s age limit.

## Odeon

*Singel 460 (624 9711/www.odeontheater.nl). Tram
1, 2, 5.* **Open** 8.30pm-4am Mon, Tue; 11pm-4am
Wed, Sun; 5pm-4am Thur (students only); 11pm-5am
Fri, Sat. **Admission** €2-€10. **No credit cards.**
**Map** p310 D4.
This beautiful three-storey venue may have seen the
last of its rockin' club days now a severe capacity
limit has been imposed: only 300 people instead of
its previous 800. One of the city's few venues to open
every night, it plays different styles of unchalleng-
ing music on each floor, and attracts both students
and office types out on a knees-up.

Saints and **Sinners in Heaven**.

## Paradiso

*Weteringschans 6-8 (626 4521/www.paradiso.nl).*
*Tram 1, 2, 5, 6, 7, 10, 20.* **Open** 8pm-4am Wed-Fri,
Sun; 8pm-5am Sat. **Admission** €5-€20 (incl
membership). **No credit cards. Map** p310 D5.
Paradiso usually has bands during the week, with a
DJ as the chaser, but among the popular club nights
are Friday's VIP Club and Saturday's Paradisco,
which attracts a youngish, up-for-it crowd. Look
out, too, for off-the-wall happenings courtesy of the
Balloon Company. *See also p214.*

## Sinners in Heaven

*Wagenstraat 3-7 (620 1375/www.sinners.nl). Tram
4, 9, 14, 20.* **Open** 11pm-4am Thur; 11pm-5am Fri,
Sat. **Admission** free-€11.50. **No credit cards.**
**Map** p307 E3.
Sinners in Heaven draws a chic and wealthy crowd:
you may spot a few Dutch soap stars and their beautiful starstruck accessories. Despite being a bit on
the intimate side, the stylish interior and three floors
of different music – hip hop, R&B, garage and disco
– are staples on various nights – should keep you
chilled and thrilled. Entry is free before midnight,
but remember the 11th Commandment: thou shalt
be over 21 and without sportswear on thy body.

# Jodenbuurt, the Plantage & the Oost

## Club Arena

*'s Gravesandestraat 51 (850 2420/www.hotelarena.nl).*
*Tram 3, 6, 7, 10.* **Open** 10pm-4am Fri, Sat.
**Admission** €6-€10. **No credit cards.**
**Map** p312 G3.
Despite its far-flung location – on the edge of
Oosterpark – this spacious ex-chapel is assured of
a devoted public because it's adjoined to a mammoth hotel full of ready-made punters (for more on
the accommodation here, *see p63*). However, the
Arena is also a club in its own right, and plenty of
up-for-it twentysomethings are only too happy to
make the trek all the way across town each weekend to get down to the mostly nostalgic fare played
by the resident DJs.

# The Waterfront

## Panama

*Oostelijke Handelskade 4 (311 8686/*
*www.panama.nl).* **Open** 10pm-3am
Thur, Sun; midnight-4am Fri, Sat.
**Admission** €8-€20. **No credit cards.**
This ambitious nightclub-theatre-restaurant is
impressive: there are plushly carpeted floors, a large
stage and encircling balcony area, a champagne bar,
and small cabaret tables (complete with tea lights)
surrounding the dancefloor. The music, though,
manages to stay contemporary, even with Panama's
ban on techno. Most clubbers are over 30 and while
there's no dress code as such, you'll feel a dork if you
turn up super-casual. Classy and classic.

and Thursday's sound is progressive techno. VJs often play, too. The club fills up fast, so show up in good time and enjoy the unthreatening door policy.

## More

*Rozengracht 133 (528 7459/www.expectmore.nl).*
*Tram 13, 14, 17.* **Open** 11pm-4am Mon, Wed, Thur, Sun; 11pm-5am Fri, Sat. **Admission** €2.50-€11.50.
**No credit cards. Map** p309 B4.
Even with its smart design and enviable ability to draw top club organisers and DJs, newcomer More hasn't quite shaken off the dodgy feel imbued upon it by its bingo hall origins, and has so far failed to live up to its 'expect More' launch hype. Nights vary from two-step, garage and nu-disco to drum 'n' bass. The big point in its favour, though, is that the bar staff are super-cute and kind; otherwise, More is – as they say – less.

## The South

### Vakzuid

*Olympisch Stadion 35 (570 8400/www.vakzuid.nl).*
*Tram 1, 6.* **Open** 10pm-1am Mon-Thur; 10pm-3am Fri, Sat; 3pm-11pm Sun. **Admission** free-€10.
**No credit cards.**
This slick 'n' small restaurant/lounge (*see also p133*) is a multifaceted venue that does cameo appearances as a club. It's nestled under the old grandstands of the stadium built for when Amsterdam hosted the Olympics in 1928. Indeed, there's even a sublime terrace that overlooks the track; and, in a thoughtful touch, blankets are on hand if you get too chilly. For people who wear Prada and those who love them.

### The Zone

*Daniel Goedkoopstraat 1-3 (681 8866/*
*www.thepowerzone.nl). Metro Spaklerweg.*
**Open** 11pm-6am some Fris; 11pm-7am Sat (Comfort Zone 7-11am). **Admission** €10-€35. *VIP membership* €450/yr. **Credit** *VIP's* AmEx, MC, V.
When it comes to the Zone, size really does matter: this roomy megalith holds a staggering 5,000 clubbers. Despite the out-of-the-way location, a beautiful but unpretentious crowd flocks here to groove to happy house. There's no door policy, but look sharp to ensure entry. Incurable show-offs might deplore the breakthrough no-tipping rule, but the rest of us love the fact that everything is included in the fee.

## Outside Amsterdam

Amsterdam's in-town scene doesn't stop some clubbers making a trip out for extra-late events. Though some clubs run free buses to the city, the best way to travel is always by car, so try to befriend someone who has one. However, after two clubbers died drug-related deaths at De Hemkade in late 2001, the out-of-town after-hours scene faced an uncertain future, with the Mayor of Zaanstad imposing a new curfew time on the club. Always check before setting out.

Techno's a real **Mazzo** forte.

## The Jordaan

### Cubic

*Jan van Galenstraat 6-10 (682 3456/www.clubeve.nl/*
*www.kremlin.nl/www.declub.nl). Tram 3/bus 21.*
**Open** 10pm-5am some Fris, Sat; 4pm-midnight Sun.
**Admission** €8-€20. **No credit cards.**
**Map** p309 A4.
No jokes about the clubbers being square, please: this large out-of-centre venue – it's actually a little west of the Jordaan, but not miles away by any stretch – is home to some kicking nights. Sounds range from future disco to trancier stuff, with an early finish on Sunday for those thirtysomethings who love to party but need to be up for their important media jobs on Mondays. Some nights feature a strict dress code.

### Mazzo

*Rozengracht 114 (626 7500/www.mazzo.nl).*
*Tram 13, 14, 17, 20.* **Open** 11pm-4am Wed, Thur, Sun; 11pm-5am Fri, Sat. **Admission** €4-€12.
**No credit cards. Map** p309 B4.
What's not to love about this smallish but friendly club? House, garage and techno are played by residents and an impressive line-up of international guests. On Saturdays, you'll hear mainly techno with resident and visiting DJs; Fridays it's drum 'n' bass;

**Arts & Entertainment**

### De Hemkade

*Hemkade 48, Zaandam (075 614 8154/ www.hemkade.nl). NS rail Zaandam.* **Open** phone to check. **Admission** €10-€20. **No credit cards.**
De Hemkade, north of Amsterdam, is a huge hall with adjoining rooms hosting music of the house/ techno variety. Expect at least one gig a week: check flyers or online to see what's happening, and whether the club has been allowed to open late again after the curfew imposed by the mayor in 2001 (*see p227*).

### Lexion

*Overtoom 65, Westzaan (075 612 3999/ www.lexion.nl). NS rail Zaandam.* **Open** hours vary. **Admission** €10-€30. **No credit cards.**
A new venue/promoter that bills itself as 'the only place to be', although this is, frankly, a little exaggerative. The rules? You have to be over 21, you can't wear jeans or sports gear, and big groups of guys aren't welcome. Oh, and Lexion's speciality is after-hours parties. Sleep? Who needs it?

### De Waakzaamheid

*Hoogstraat 4, Koog aan de Zaan (075 628 5829/ www.waakzaamheid.com). NS rail Koogzanddijk.* **Open** 11pm-10am Sat. **Admission** €11.50-€20. **No credit cards.**
A cosy club in a housing estate in Koog aan de Zaan, whose great DJ line-ups often include top international names. The club opens Saturdays, plus one Friday a month. There's a separate bar area, and in warm weather you can sit outside. A free limousine service runs from Zaandam after 11pm.

Hats off to the **Panama**. *See p225.*

### Bloemendaal beach cafés

*Beach pavilions, Bloemendaal aan Zee (023 573 2152). NS rail to Haarlem, then taxi (€12.50) or train taxi to Bloemendaal aan Zee (order train taxi when buying train ticket).* **Open** May-Oct times vary. **Admission** free. **No credit cards.**
These beach cafés, open in summer, are worth a visit. **Woodstock** caters for up-for-anything regulars, an amiable mix of students, locals, ex-hippies and escaping city slickers. When the dancefloor gets full, the action spills on to the beach.

If Woodstock is like San Francisco, then the less kitschily funksome **Solaris** is a wannabe mini-Ibiza, with techno played for the obvious enjoyment of a younger, more beautiful crowd. **Paradiso aan Zee**, meanwhile, is an extension of Paradiso's in-town venue (*see p225*). Outdoor stages go up in September and October, as all three cafés join forces and throw big beach parties for six straight weeks on Sundays (from 1pm). **Republiek**, meanwhile, tends to be inhabited by people who care more about what they wear than what they hear.

## Underground scene

The powers-that-be have tried to rid this city of all its alternative lifestylers, but underground culture is still blossoming. However, the best thing about Amsterdam's underground is that it doesn't exclude ordinary folk: if you're up for it, they're up for you. Should you be visiting around a full moon or solstice there'll be some sort of celebration. Information on these events is hard to come by, though: look out for flyers, earwig on stoners rambling in coffeeshops or see www.underwateramsterdam.com.

### ADM

*Hornweg 6, Zaandam (411 0081/www.contrast.org/ adm). Tram 3/bus 35.*
Huge parties are staged every couple of months in this out-of-town squat. Events are often geared around the dates of pagan rituals: expect outdoor fires, performances, a dizzying array of music and people your mother warned you about.

### Academie

*Overtoom 301, Oud West (779 4913/ http://squat.net/overtoom301). Tram 1, 6.*
This squat has been part of the low-budget/high-returns party scene for aeons. Especially wonderful are Funk You, an irreverent wink to disco yesteryears put on by the residents, and Inrichting's superbly depressing gothic fests (http://come.to/deinrichting). There's also a restaurant (*see p110* **Baby, let's play house**) and cinema (*see p193*) on site.

### Buitenland

*Oudehaagseweg 51 (408 4570). Tram 2/bus 45.*
It's not exactly the easiest spot to get to – the directions are far too complicated to list in full here; take a cab from Sloten if you can – but in good weather it's well worth the journey. Buitenland (literally, 'the

# On the door

He'll be the first person you see on the way in, and the last person you see on the way out. In between, it's his job to ensure that your night isn't ruined by the wrong kind of people. Welcome to the curious world of the Amsterdam doorman; or, according to the local lingo, 'portier'.

The good news? When you show up at the door, you'll be dealing with professionals. Door staff in Amsterdam are required to undertake a government-regulated portiers course, which involves learning about alcohol restrictions, fire regulations, venue permits and general first aid. It also involves role-playing exercises designed to help you interact with people, especially how to make them do what you want without appearing threatening. Jonathan (*pictured*), who's worked Amsterdam doors since 1995 and now can be found beaming at punters from outside the Melkweg, the Winston International and assorted one-off events, believes the one special skill required is charm. 'You need to be good with people and genuinely enjoy all their little foibles.'

And if you are, you can usually avoid trouble. Perhaps surprisingly, Jonathan hasn't been the victim of any rough stuff, though he has seen a fair bit going down: knives, stabbings, punches thrown. While a fellow portier has had his moped thrown into the canal more than once, the threats Jonathan receives are usually of the empty 'I'm gonna get you' variety.

In Amsterdam, it's always a good idea to tip the doorman if you want to come back. But while Jonathan believes those who do their job well 'should be rewarded', he finds it ridiculous the way certain clubs make portiers behave: some actually have to pay to rent the door space and hope for tips. Jonathan approves of The Zone's no-tip policy, believing it prevents any shady business. However, the days when drug dealers paid doormen not to see them have largely passed. Likewise, the old trend of some brick-shithouse of a man with a low IQ guarding a club's entrance is happily fading away: more and more women can now be found 'manning' the doorways of Amsterdam's clubs.

According to Jonathan, most portiers 'are people who train at the gym every day, and so specifically seek evening work'. Even so, the job takes its toll and doormen normally switch to a day job after a year or two. And does it bother Jonathan that he's working while others are getting down to the serious business of partying? No chance. His favourite thing about being a portier is meeting people; in fact, he even approached his girlfriend of three years while working the door. Awww.

**Arts & Entertainment**

outside land') has food, camping, films, good local DJs and, when sun comes up, breakfast. It's child- and animal-friendly and offers a unique vibe that the likes of London can never hope to match.

### OCCII
*Amstelveenseweg 134 (no phone). Tram 2, 6.*
On the edge of the Vondelpark lies a cultural centre with a satisfying array of parties. Worthy of mention are Spellbound's Queer Planet, an alternative queer night (*see p209*), and Namaste, trancey and artsy and altogether quite special.

## After-hours venues

Clubs in the centre of Amsterdam usually have to close by 5am, but there are some super-early events to keep insomniacs happy. Most clubs have permission to hold about five after-hours parties every year, and there's normally at least one late shindig going on: look out for flyers and keep your ear to the ground. **The Zone** has the only 22-hour drinking licence in town, but they make little use of it. **Lexion**'s Lexcited or After P kick off around 4.30am on most Sundays (*see p228*). However, the after-hours scene was left in limbo after events in late 2001 (*see p227*), so always call ahead to check before setting out.

## Club night organisers

Look out for one-off events organised by the following companies. Flyers can be picked up and tickets bought in the stores under **Tickets & information** (*see below*). Free English 'zine *Shark*, available in bars and clubs and online at www.underwateramsterdam.com, lists many big underground events, as does the **Clubwear House** site (*see p160*) and www.urbanguide.nl.

### Club Risk
*www.clubrisk.nl.*
Risk's resident DJs are Eric de Man and the seemingly ubiquitous Dimitri, with international guests completing the bill. Its website carries news of upcoming events.

### Dance Valley
*Spaarnwoude Recreation Area (0900 300 1250/ www.dancevalley.nl). NS rail to Sloterdijk, then free buses to Spaarnwoude.*
Conceived in 1995, Dance Valley is now the biggest dance festival in Holland. On a Saturday in August, up to 30,000 people gather at Spaarnwoude, outside Amsterdam, to listen to everything from techno and hard house to speed garage, from over 100 DJs and bands. Some party-goers were stranded at the 2001 bash (not enough buses, bizarrely), but that setback's not about to deter Dance Valley, which also organises the monthly HQ at the **Melkweg** (*see p225*) and occasional parties at other venues. Check its site for details on travel, camping and tickets.

Uptown style at **Midtown Records**.

### Healers
*Tickets from Uitlijn, 0900 0191.*
Several times a year, Healers' two Love Boats board near Centraal Station for a clubbing experience on Amsterdam's waterways. On certain holidays – such as Queen's Day, Christmas and New Year – the boats are joined together, with DJs on the decks on deck spinning tunes for an eager and up-for-it crowd.

### Impulz
*www.impulz.nl.*
With high-gloss flyers/booklets and ticket sales from Germany to the UK, Impulz have a firm grasp on what makes party people happy. It organises outdoor events at least twice a year

### Monumental
*0900 300 1250/www.awakenings.nl.*
Monumental hosts the hugely popular Awakenings outdoor party once a year, where a line-up of international DJs play techno until the early hours.

### Q-dance
*www.q-dance.nl.*
Q-dance organise big house parties such as Hardcore Resurrection and Qlub-tempo. Check the website, or look out for them at De Hemkade (*see p228*) or the huge Houseqlassics at the Heineken Music Hall.

### Silly Symphonies
*Tickets from Clubwear House, 622 8766.*
Silly Symphonies hold parties right across Holland. In particular, keep an eye out for the annual beach parties at Scheveningen near the Hague, where DJ Remy and guests spin techno and trance.

## Tickets & information

Flyers and club tickets are offered at a variety of city venues. Chief among them is **Clubwear House** (*see p160*). **Conscious Dreams** (*see p157*), **Cyberdog**, **Housewives on Fire** ( for both, *see p160*), **Midtown Records** (whose specialities is hardcore and gabber; *see p176*), **Outland Records** (which only gives out flyers with record purchases; Zeedijk 22; 638 7576), **Dance Tracks** (which specialises in hardcore house; Nieuwe Nieuwstraat 69; 639 0853) and **Groove Connection** (an underground record store; Sint Nicolaasstraat 41; 624 7234) all also offer flyers and/or tickets for a variety of events.

# Sport & Fitness

Get that endorphin high from a plethora of activities in and around Amsterdam: if only you could play football while cycling on ice...

If these kids are confident enough, don't you think you ought to try **cycling in Amsterdam**?

## The best Sports

**Amstelveen field hockey**
The *other* Dutch pastime. *See p234.*

**Cycling through Amsterdam**
It's exercise and transportation. *See p278.*

**Dutch football**
Glimpse tomorrow's stars today.
*See p232.*

**The Elfstedentoch**
Frozen canals make for a great race.
*See p237.*

**Friday night skate**
A colourful way of seeing the city. *See p236.*

The Dutch's relationship to sport is not unlike their approach to almost everything else: they excel in a few specialised areas and maintain a modest profile in others. The Dutch have traditionally excelled at football, ice skating, hockey, tennis and cycling; more recently, Peter van den Hoogenband's success at the Sydney Olympics increased swimming's profile, just as Raymond van Barneveld's triumph at the 1998 World Darts Championship cemented darts as a growing sport here. Tickets for events in these fields are difficult get your hands on – unless, of course, you plan ages in advance.

That said, there's always another option: participation. If you're keen to release energy rather than just sit back and observe, there's a good chance you'll get what you want. Nearly every sport in Holland operates within rules set out by a national governing organisation; an overview of sports is given in this chapter, along with contact numbers and URLs.

For further details, call the **Municipal Sport and Recreation Department** on 552 2490, or see www.sport.amsterdam.nl (mostly in Dutch) for maps, schedules and links to almost every sport imaginable. The *Amsterdam Yellow Pages* (also mostly in Dutch) is another valuable resource for trying to find out what's on where.

### Nederlands Sportmuseum

*Museumweg 10, Lelystad (0320 261010/ www.olympion.nl). NS rail Lelystad.* **Open** 10am-5pm Tue-Fri; noon-5pm Sat, Sun. **Admission** €4.50; €3.50 under-12s. **No credit cards.**
Aside from all the usual exhibits, the Sportmuseum holds comprehensive archives of books, cuttings and photos, all of which are open by appointment.

## Spectator sports

### American football

American football is taking root in the Dutch sporting psyche. The Admirals are the city's pro team, while the **Amsterdam Crusaders** represent the city in the amateur league, and can be reached on 617 7450. Full details of American football are available from the governing body, the **NAFF**, on 0229 214801 or at www.afbn.nl.

### Amsterdam Admirals

*Amsterdam ArenA, Arena Boulevard 1, Bijlmermeer (465 4545/www.admirals.nl). Metro Strandvliet or Metro/NS rail Bijlmer.* **Season** Apr-June. **Admission** €13.50-€37.50. **Credit** AmEx, DC, MC, V.
Members of NFL Europe, the Admirals regularly draw crowds of 15,000-plus, all the more astonishing given their weak record. Attending an Admirals game may be one of the only ways to actually get into the ArenA.

### Baseball

The dozen or so baseball and softball clubs that compete in and around town deliver a splendid mix of excitement and relaxation during the long days of summer. Baseball is played to a variety of standards, and the season runs April to October. For more, call the regional **KNBSB** on 030 607 7070 or go to www.knbsb.nl.

### Cycling

The Dutch would be quite a different people if it weren't for the *fiets*. Cyclists rarely manage more than 20 kilometres an hour within the city limits, but set loose on the polder, they show what they're made of. The Netherlands has produced many world-class sprinters and climbers: the Dutch still talk with awe about Joop Zoetemelk who, after finishing second six times, finally won the Tour de France in 1985. There's still hope for a future champion.

There's something to do or see nearly every weekend of the year. Dutch cycling fans turn out for stage, *criterium* (road circuit) and one-day road races, plus track, field, cyclo-cross and ATB/mountain biking. The biggest Dutch races are the **Amstel Gold Race** around Limburg in late April; the **RAI Derny Race**, held at the RAI in Amsterdam in mid May; the popular **Acht van Chaam**, a 100-kilometre (62-mile) *criterium* held in Noord Brabant on the first Wednesday after the Tour de France (late July/ early August); and the **Tour de Nederland**, a five-day race – it passes through Amsterdam – held in late August. For more information on what's coming up, contact the **KNWU** (Dutch Cycle Racing Association) at Postbus 136, 3440 AC Woerden (0348 484084/www.knwu.nl).

Alternatively, if you're in on the action yourself and have a racing bike, head for Sportpark Sloten. Two cycle clubs are based here – **ASC Olympia** (617 7510/secretary 617 3057/www.ascolympia.nl), the oldest club in Europe, and **WV Amsterdam** (secretary 619 3314) – and there is a 22-kilometre (12-mile) circuit round the park. The 200-metre track has recently been rebuilt as a modern velodrome.

For a more leisurely yet organised approach to cycling, try the Dutch Tour Bike Association (**NTFU**) on 0318 581300, at www.ntfu.nl, or by post to Postbus 326, 3900 AH Veenendaal. It offers its members advice on routes and cycling groups. NTFU activities are mostly held at weekends, both in the day and at night.

### Football

The outstanding reputation Dutch football enjoys is still merited, though Dutch clubs have been hard pressed to hold on to star players in recent years. Star salaries don't seem to fit within the budgets of most Dutch clubs, and so economics lures players in their prime to south European and English clubs (Manchester United's Ruud van Nistelrooy being the most recent high-profile example). This dynamic doesn't sit well with Dutch fans, who are meant to be appeased with the argument that Dutch training is still superior and offers an excellent preview of up-and-coming players. These factors ensure disappointment but also unpredictability. The former is predictable in itself, but the latter demands football enthusiasts keep their eyes on Dutch leagues: last year's losers are this year's stars. Still, it may be some time before the nation recovers from the humiliation of failing to qualify for the 2002 World Cup after a stunning defeat at the hands of the underdog Irish.

There's a huge gap between the big clubs in the Netherlands and the smaller teams. After Ajax, PSV and Feyenoord, it's a long way down. The Dutch season starts in late August and runs until late May, with a short break from Christmas until early February. Thanks to current attempts at keeping a tight rein on hooliganism, a problem here for years, buying tickets for pro matches has become nearly impossible, with possession of a **Personal Club Card** now a prerequisite for securing tickets to any league event. The waiting lists for the cards are discouragingly long, and you'll be lucky if you get in. Pleasingly, you can still watch the big games on network TV, though following games at local cafés surrounded by partisan supporters may prove a viable and exciting alternative if you can manage to peer over the heads.

### Ajax

*Amsterdam ArenA, Arena Boulevard 1, Bijlmermeer (311 1444/www.ajax.nl). Metro Strandvliet or Metro/NS rail Bijlmer.* **Tickets** €11.50-€41. **Credit** AmEx, DC, MC, V.

The losers in 2000 had a good run for 2001's honours. The starting line-up seems to change every other month, but Ajax remains a club to watch nonetheless. Getting your hands on tickets may prove more tougher than marking alumnus Dennis Bergkamp.

### Feyenoord

*De Kuip, Van Zandvlietplein 3, Rotterdam (information 010 292 6888/tickets 010 292 3888/ www.feyenoord.nl). NS rail Rotterdam Centraal Station, then bus 49 or tram 23.* **Tickets** €12.50-€27.25. **Credit** AmEx, DC, MC, V.

Rotterdam's home team has certainly been shining brightly of late, but although it's no longer a true underdog, it still experiences some trouble trying to keep up with its arch-rivals Ajax (*see above*). Rotterdammers are unswervingly loyal to everything Rotterdam, and Feyenoord fans epitomise this loyalty. De Kuip doesn't always sell out, yet match tickets may still be hard to come by: ownership of a Personal Club Card is the unpromising solution to this predicament.

# Game on

It had been growing for a while. On TV (SBS-6 had been screening the big events) and in a few pubs and bars, where people could play. But this sly spurt in popularity was nothing compared to the explosion that can be traced back to the evening of Sunday 11 January 1998. For it was then that, after a thrilling tussle with Welshman Richie Burnett that went down to a final set, a burly former postman from the Hague by the name of Raymond van Barneveld (*pictured*) won the Embassy World Darts Championship. And the Netherlands went beserk.

Recently, darts in the UK has struggled to scale the peaks of popularity it enjoyed in the 1980s. But in the Netherlands, it's never been bigger, and a lot of that is down to Barney (as he's universally known). The day after his triumph, Barney arrived back at Schiphol Airport to an unseemly media scrum. The TV news that evening was full of reports on the conquering hero, who looked endearingly shell-shocked at all the attention. When he retained the title the following year, though – becoming the first player since Eric 'Crafty Cockney' Bristow in the mid 1980s to do so – he stayed more composed... unlike his vociferous pack of supporters at the Lakeside in Frimley Green, Surrey. Having flown over for the week-long tournament, the orange army were determined to celebrate in the most vocal (not to mention alcoholic) fashion possible.

Barney's by no means the only Dutch darter to have seen success. Hague native Roland Scholten has run neck and neck with Barney the last couple of years as the leading Dutch player, and pencil-thin Amsterdam tram driver Co Stompe is not far behind. Vincent van der Voort, one of many young players looking to follow in Barney's footsteps, made his Embassy debut in 2002, while the Dutch also have one of the best female players in the world in the shape of Francis Hoenselaar.

The Dutch Darts Federation (NDF) looks after the sport, but regional affiliates do much of the work. Some 150 Amsterdam cafés boast 180 teams and 1,300 members affiliated to DORA (408 4184/www.dora.nl), which runs leagues from September to May; with 400 members, the ADB (634 1738) is smaller. It's easy to find a café in which to play, but if you're serious, try De Vluchtheuvel (Van Woustraat 174; 662 5665) or Matchroom Sloten (Slimmeweg 8; 617 7062). Barney won't be there in person, but he'll be there in spirit.

### PSV

*Philips Stadium, Frederiklaan 10A, Eindhoven (040 250 5501/www.psv.nl). NS rail Eindhoven, then bus 4, 13.* **Tickets** €16-€38.50. **No credit cards.**
It's not the force it used to be, but PSV is still a club to watch. Eindhoven's team has what it takes to draw the crowds and tickets are hard to come by.

### Other teams

Though stadiums may not be full, the Personal Club Card will prove an obstacle for any visitors keen to see a Premier League game. Instead, try the First Division, which has a more flexible policy on the card. Failing that, some of the city's top amateur clubs – such as **Blauw Wit**, **DGC** and **Elinkwijk** – play decent football. For details, or if you fancy a game, call Amsterdam's **KNVB** on 487 9130 or see www.knvb.nl.

## Hockey

Playing hockey on ice is a novel and respected idea to the Dutch, but for real action head to carefully tended pastures with stick in tow. Field hockey is hugely popular and the Dutch are fantastic at it: men and women's teams consistently rank at the top. The Dutch Hockey Association (**KNHB**) boasts the largest number of affiliated teams of any equivalent association in the world. Wagener Stadium in Amstelveen has a capacity of 7,000 and is used for club games and internationals. The many clubs in the area welcome players and spectators; details of the local teams are available from the KNHB Bunnik (030 656 6444/www.knhb.nl). The season runs from September until May.

The **Jaap Edenhal** (694 9652), meanwhile, is home to all things icy, including ice hockey. Call the rink or the **Dutch Ice Hockey Union** (079 341 7574/www.nijb.nl) for information on when Amsterdam's own Boretti Tigers are playing.

Recent variations on hockey combine Dutch field prowess with new twists. Ever heard of salibandy, innebandy or stockey? These are all legitimate hockey-style games that are drawing more and more enthusiasts. Some Dutch men's teams have competed internationally. For further information, contact the **Netherlands Floorball and Unihockey Federation** on 053 434 2422, or visit www.nefub.nl.

## Kaatsen

A forerunner to tennis, but using the hands to hit the ball, kaatsen was banned between 1500 and 1750 because of the nuisance it caused. However, this authentic Dutch sport – played on a 60-metre by 32-metre (197-foot by 105-foot) field, with two teams of three players – is still

popular in Friesland, where many competitions are held. Contact governing body the **KNKB** (0517 397300/www.knkb.nl) or the **KC Amsterdam Kaatsclub** (613 5679) for details.

## Korfball

Korfball was developed by an Amsterdam teacher in 1902, and is best described as a quirky form of basketball. Its appeal has always been strong here, but it has grown considerably abroad. The season has three stages: from September to mid November and from April to June, games are played outdoors, while from mid November to March, it heads indoors. Contact the **North Holland KNKV** (075 656 6350/www.knkv.nl) for more details.

## Motor sport

### TT Races

*De Haar Circuit, Assen (0592 321321/raceday information 0592 380367/www.tt-assen.com/ advance tickets from TT Assen, Postbus 150, 9400 AD Assen, fax 0592 356911). Exit Assen south off A28, then follow signs.* **Date** *Grand Prix* late June. **Tickets** €40-€70. **No credit cards.**
Track renovations set for completion in March 2002 promise faster and more exciting races than ever. Grand Prix mania takes over Assen in late June.

### Zandvoort

*Circuit Park Zandvoort, Burgermeester van Alphenstraat, Zandfoort (023 574 0740/ www.circuit-sandvoort.nl). NS rail Zandvoort.* **Tickets** €7-€21. **No credit cards.**
This racing track, about 40 minutes' drive from Amsterdam, was once a venue for Formula One racing. A programme of international races runs every other weekend from March to October, with tickets available from 8am on the day.

## Rugby

Both men's and women's teams have decent reputations and more than 100 clubs take part in various competitions throughout the country, with four clubs active in Amsterdam. The season runs September to May. For information on the Heineken Rugby Sevens tournament, matches or clubs that welcome new members, contact the **National Rugby Board** on 480 8100 or by email at info@rugby.nl.

## Volleyball

Thanks to the success of men's and women's national teams, volleyball is increasingly popular here. For details of events and local clubs, contact the **NeVoBo** on 0348 411994 (national office) or 693 6458 (Amsterdam office) or at www.holland.volleyball.nl.

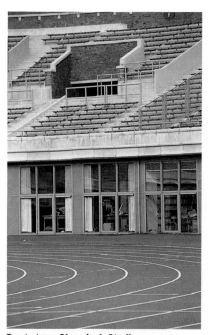

Track down **Olympisch Stadion**.

## Fitness & leisure

### Athletics

There are four tracks in the city – Elzenhagen, Olympiaplein, Ookmeer and Chris Bergerbaan – along with the recently renovated Olympisch Stadion. August's *Trimloopboekje* lists all running events in the country. The four major events in Amsterdam are the **Vondelparkloop** in January; June's **Grachtenloop** around the city's canals (*see p180*); the **Dam tot Damloop** from Amsterdam to Zaandam in late September (*see p183*); and the **Amsterdam Marathon** in October. Further details are available from the **KNAU** on 030 608 7300 or see www.knau.nl.

### Badminton

Contact the **Amsterdam Badminton Union** on 697 3758 for more on badminton in the city.

### Basketball

While public courts are a rarity in the city centre, there are several clubs in Amsterdam that welcome players: call the **NBB** Amsterdam district office on 675 0462 for more information.

## Golf

Golf, anyone? Golf, everyone! The popularity now enjoyed by this once-exclusive sport is remarkable. Courses fill up quickly during weekends with players of all standards. A safety certificate is required for private courses, but public courses are open to all, with many offering driving ranges. You can play at a private club if introduced by a member, or if you belong to a British club. For details, see the *Amsterdam Yellow Pages*, or contact the **Amsterdam Golf Club** (497 7866).

### Golfbaan Sloten

*Sloterweg 1045, Sloten (614 2402). Bus 145.* **Open** *Mid June-mid Aug* 8.30am-dusk daily. *Mid Aug-mid June* 8.30am-6pm Mon-Fri. **Rates** €30/day. **No credit cards**.
A nine-hole public course, with a driving range and practice green. Booking is advisable on weekends.

### Golfpark Spaarnwoude

*Het Hogeland 2, Velsen-Zuid, Spaarnwoude (023 538 5599). Bus 82.* **Open** *Summer* 6.30am-8.30pm daily. *Winter* 8.30am-3.30pm daily. **Rates** *18-hole course* €23. *9-hole courses* €12. *Pitch & putt* €5. **No credit cards**.
An 18-hole course, plus 9-holers and a pitch and putt. Reservations can be made up to three days ahead.

### De Hoge Dijk

*Abcouderstraatweg 46, Zuid-Oost (0294 281241/285313). Metro Nieuw Gein; from Holendrecht stop, take bus 120, 126 to Abcoude.* **Open** dawn-dusk daily. **Rates** *Winter* €16/18 holes; €13/9 holes. *Summer* €35/18 holes; €20/9 holes; €40/wknd. *Club hire* from €2.50. **Credit** AmEx, DC, MC, V.
A public 18-hole polder course on the edge of town. Reservations are required.

## Health & fitness

Look under 'Fitnesscentra' in the *Amsterdam Yellow Pages* for a full listing of health centres.

### Barry's Fitness Centre

*Lijnbaansgracht 350, Southern Canal Belt (626 1036).* **Open** 8am-11pm Mon-Fri; 9am-6pm Sat, Sun. **Admission** €10/day; €23/wk; €57/mth. **No credit cards**. **Map** p311 E5.
This excellent club has earned itself a stellar rating from *Men's Health*. You'll find free weights and machines, cardiovascular equipment, aerobics, massage and a sauna. Individual trainers can help if required (by appointment).

### The Garden

*Jodenbreestraat 158, Jodenbuurt (626 8772). Tram 9, 14, 20/Metro Waterlooplein.* **Open** 9am-11pm Mon, Wed, Fri; noon-11pm Thur; 11am-6pm Sat; 10am-7pm Sun. **Admission** €9/day; €32/wk; €58/10 visits. **No credit cards**. **Map** p307 E3.

The cheapest all-in-one price in town gives you the choice of high- and low-impact and step aerobics, bodyshape, callisthenics and stretching. There's also a sun studio, a hairdresser and masseurs.

### Sporting Club Leidseplein

*Korte Leidsedwarsstraat 18, Southern Canal Belt (620 6631/www.clubsportive.nl). Tram 1, 2, 5, 6, 7, 10, 20.* **Open** 9am-midnight Mon-Fri; 10am-6pm Sat, Sun. **Admission** €12/day; €28/wk; €53/mth. **No credit cards**. **Map** p310 C5.
A central club with weights, aerobics and a sauna. Individual training programmes can be put together.

## Horse riding

The two main centres – **De Amsterdamse Manege** (643 1342) and **Nieuw Amstelland Manege** (643 2468) – both offer rides daily in the Amsterdam Bos at €15 an hour for adults; lessons are available for kids. For more details, see 'Maneges' in the *Amsterdam Yellow Pages*.

## Saunas

Most Dutch saunas are mixed, and covering up is frowned upon. But most offer women-only times as well. See also the *Amsterdam Yellow Pages* under 'Saunas'.

### Deco Sauna

*Herengracht 115, Western Canal Belt (623 8215/ www.saunadeco.nl). Tram 1, 2, 5, 13, 17, 20.* **Open** noon-11pm Mon-Sat; 1-6pm Sun. **Admission** €11 before 3pm; €14 after 3pm. **No credit cards**.
The most beautiful sauna in town, with art deco glass panels and murals. Facilities include a Turkish bath, a Finnish sauna, a cold plunge bath and a solarium. Massages, shiatsu and skin and beauty care are by appointment.

### De Keizer

*Keizersgracht 124, Western Canal Belt (622 7504). Tram 1, 2, 5, 13, 17, 20.* **Open** noon-11pm Mon, Wed, Fri, Sat; 10am-11pm Tue, Thur; noon-8pm Sun. *Women only* 10am-3pm Tue, Thur. **Admission** from €12.50. **No credit cards**. **Map** p306 C2.
Tucked away in the servants' quarters of this 18th-century canal house is a full sauna that conjures up Hollywood interpretations of ancient Rome.

## Skateboarding, inlining & roller-skating

Skater dudes and dudettes flaunt their skills on the half-pipe at Museumplein and in parks elsewhere in the city. Inline skating is hugely popular as a sport and mode of transportation, with bike paths doubling as skating paths (be

# A whole new ballgame

You had to be there. Sadly, few were. But if it had been the final of the World Cup, the game held in Toronto on 15 July 2001 would have gone down as one of the greatest internationals ever played.

They were struggling at 112-6, with a massive 84 runs needed from only ten overs. Through a mix of luck and judgment, they got it down to ten from the final over, five from two deliveries and then three from the last ball of the match. A good ball it was, too, but JJ Esmeijer got his bat on it. An inside edge, a misfield by the man at short fine leg, and Esmeijer and Asim Khan scrambled three runs to jubilant scenes from the sparse crowd. Thrilling stuff; and with it came the ICC Trophy and qualification for the World Cup in 2003. Losers Namibia were as distraught as the victors were ecstatic. Dutch cricket had never experienced such a high.

Yep, you read that right. Dutch cricket is no oxymoron; of all the countries not yet granted full test status by the International Cricket Council, the Dutch are among the strongest. Led by former Somerset fast bowler Roland Lefebvre, the sport has grown speedily in the last decade, a ten-year span that's seen them qualify for the World Cup once before (1996, when they failed to win a match), stage a World Cup game (1999, when South Africa beat Kenya at Amstelveen during a tournament held mostly in England) and even beat the English.

And again, you read that correctly. Granted, it wasn't an official international, but in Haarlem in 1993, the Dutch still defeated an England XI that included Darren Gough and Nasser Hussain by seven wickets. In England, it was seen as the nadir of a particularly sorry stretch of failures; in the Netherlands, the result gave the first oxygen of publicity to a sport thus far starved of it.

It's been growing ever since, too. There are now over 100 teams affiliated to the Royal Dutch Cricket Board (KNCB; 645 1705/ www.kncb.nl), including several in Amsterdam; the best is the VRA (312 8729). Most Dutch clubs also have junior, veteran and women's teams as well as their main sides, and welcome new players. And thanks in part to JJ Esmeijer, they may be welcoming many more come 2003.

Vondelpark is home to many sporting types, with **skaters** everywhere. *See p236.*

wary of irritated cyclists though). Vondelpark is Mecca for skaters. If weather conditions are dry enough, then check out the **Friday Night Skate**, an informal and popular tour that takes place around Amsterdam (for more, see www.fridaynightskate.nl). Wearing protective gear and blinkers is strongly encouraged, and you must be able to stop at intersections.

Consult the *Amsterdam Yellow Pages* (under 'Sport en Spelartikelen') for a complete list of specialist shops and rental locations.

### Balance

*Overtoom 464-6, Museum Quarter (489 4723). Tram 1, 6.* **Open** *Apr-Dec* 1-6pm Mon; 10am-6pm Tue, Wed, Fri; 10am-9pm Thur; 9.30am-5pm Sat; *Jan-Mar* 1-6pm Mon; 6-9pm Thur; 10am-5pm Sat. **Rates** from €6. **Credit** MC, V.

The rates for skate hire here include protection for the wrists, knees and elbows, but not helmets, which cost €1.25 a day or €5 a week to hire.

### Rent A Skate

*Vondelpark 7; entrance at Amstelveenseweg, Museum Quarter (06 5466 2262 mobile). Tram 1, 2, 3, 5, 6, 12, 20.* **Open** *Apr-Oct* 11am-9.30pm Mon-Fri; 10.30am-8pm Sat, Sun. **Rates** from €4.50. **No credit cards. Map** p310 C6.

Vondelpark has two branches of Rent a Skate: one at the café by the Amstelveenseweg, the other over at the Melkgroothuis.

## Skating

Locals have been skating on frozen canals and ponds since the sea was pumped out. But whatever its roots, fanaticism is skating's legacy: the Dutch are mad about long-distance and speed skating. Unfortunately, conditions are rarely right nowadays: the scenes depicted by the old masters of people skating on the canals are, in general, a thing of the past.

If conditions are right – the ice must be very thick, which is why the race hasn't been held since 1997 – look out for the **Elfstedentocht**, a 200-kilometre (124-mile) race round Friesland. With up to 10,000 people taking part, it's a massive national event. You must be a member of the Elfstedenvereniging association to compete, and even then lots are drawn as numbers are limited. However, exceptions are sometimes made for foreigners.

If the canals freeze over in Amsterdam and you fancy a skate, then be careful: the ice is often weak. If in doubt, ask a local. The reflection pool at Museumplein is meant to accommodate ice skaters who can't wait for frozen canals. If winter's too balmy for ice, head to the **Jaap Edenhal** ice track at Radioweg 64 (694 9652/www.jaapeden.nl). Some of the ponds and lakes in and around Amsterdam may offer

Shooting strikes at **Knijn Bowling**. Big Lebowski not pictured. *See p239.*

safe opportunities: contact the **KNSB** in Amersfoort (0334 621784/www.knsb.nl) for details on conditions and organised events.

## Snooker & carambole

There are several halls in Amsterdam where you can play snooker or pool fairly cheaply. Carambole, played on a table without pockets, is a popular variation. Traditionally, billiards (*biljart*) has been associated with cafés: outside the centre of town, there are many cafés with billiards and pool tables. In town, many bars have pool tables, though they're often scruffy.

### De Keizer
*Keizersgracht 256, Western Canal Belt (623 1586). Tram 13, 14, 17, 20.* **Open** 1pm-1am Mon-Thur, Sun; 1pm-2am Fri, Sat. **Rates** €5-€6 pool; €5-€7.50/hr snooker. **No credit cards**. **Map** p306 C3.
There are two pro-size pool tables and seven snooker tables here, all in separate rooms. There are phones in all rooms, so players can phone orders down to the bar and have drinks or sandwiches sent up. Members pay less for tables, but all are welcome.

### Snookercentre Bavaria
*Van Ostadestraat 97, the Pijp (676 4059). Tram 3, 12, 20, 24, 25.* **Open** 2pm-1am Mon-Thur, Sun; 2pm-2am Fri, Sat. **Rates** €7/hr pool; €7.50/hr snooker. **No credit cards**.
Spread over four floors here, the Bavaria boasts one carambole table, 26 billiards tables and seven snooker tables, with the first floor a pool hall. Some nights are reserved for members only.

## Squash

For details of clubs, phone the **Amsterdam Squash Rackets Club** on 662 8767. Details of squash courts can be found in the *Amsterdam Yellow Pages* under 'Squashbanen'.

### Squash City
*Ketelmakerstraat 6, West (626 7883). Bus 18, 22.* **Open** 8.45am-midnight Mon-Fri; 8am-9pm Sat, Sun. **Rates** €7/45min before 5pm; €9/45min after 5pm. **No credit cards**.
The place to head if you see squash as more of a hobby than a battle. There are 12 courts here.

## Swimming

Public pools usually have rigidly scheduled programmes for babies, toddlers, women, families, nude swimmers and those who want to swim lengths. Opening times vary for both indoor and outdoor pools; some indoor pools close in summer. While it's best to phone ahead, most pools set aside lanes for swimming lengths in the early morning, mid-afternoon and evening. Look in the *Amsterdam Yellow Pages* under 'Zwembaden' for a full list of pools.

### Flevoparkbad (outdoor)
*Insulindeweg 1002, Oost (692 5030). Tram 14.* **Open** *May-early Sept* 10am-5.30pm (10am-7pm in hotter weather) daily. **Admission** from €2. **No credit cards**.
This good outdoor choice provides two huge swimming pools alongside kids' areas, a playground and a sunbathing area.

Arts & Entertainment

### Marnixbad (indoor)
*Marnixplein 9, the Jordaan (625 4843/
www.marnixbad.nl). Tram 3, 7, 10.* **Open** daily, times
vary. **Admission** from €2.50. **No credit cards.**
As well as a 25m indoor pool with water slides and
a whirlpool, Marnixbad also boasts a sauna.

### Mirandabad (indoor & outdoor)
*De Mirandalaan 9, Zuid (546 4444/restaurant
546 4457/www.mirandabad.nl). Tram 15/bus
169.* **Open** times vary. **Admission** €2.50.
**No credit cards.**
The city's only sub-tropical pool – with waterslide,
whirlpool and outdoor pool – is for fun rather than
serious swimming. There are also squash courts here.

### Zuiderbad (indoor)
*Hobbemastraat 26, Museum Quarter (671 0287).
Tram 1, 16, 24, 25.* **Open** times vary.
**Admission** from €2.50. **No credit cards.**
One of the country's oldest pools, the Zuiderbad was
built in 1912. Nude swimming on Sundays, 4-5pm.

## Table tennis

For details of clubs, contact the **Nederlandse
Tafeltennis Bond** on 079 341 4811.

### Amsterdam 78
*Schoolstraat 2, Museum Quarter (683 7829).
Tram 1, 6.* **Open** 7-11am Mon, Tue, Thur-Sat;
2-7pm Wed, Sun. **Rates** €2.50/per person (incl
bats and balls). **No credit cards.**
One of the few places where you can both ping and
pong in town. Booking is advisable.

Row, row, row your boat...

## Tennis

For details on competitions – including August's
Dutch Open – and clubs, call the **KNLTB North
Holland Office** on 023 643 4920; the national
office is at www.knltb.nl or on 033 454 2600. For
a full listing of courts see the *Amsterdam Yellow
Pages* under 'Tennisparken en-hallen'.

### Amstelpark
*Koenenkade 8, Amstelveen (301 0700). Bus 170,
171, 172 from Amsterdam Centraal Station/169
from Amstel Station.* **Open** 8am-11.30pm Mon-Fri;
8am-10pm Sat, Sun. **Rates** *Apr-Sept* €16/hr.
*Oct-Mar* €21/hr. **Credit** AmEx, DC, MC, V.
All in all, 42 courts: both indoor and outdoor. There
are also 12 squash courts, a Turkish bath, a sauna, a
swimming pool and a shop. Racket hire is €2.50.

### Tennishal Kadoelen
*Sportpark Kadoelen 5, Kadoelenweg, Noord (631
3194). Bus 92.* **Open** 9am-11pm daily. **Rates**
*Mid Sept-mid Apr* €14-€19/hr. *Mid Apr-mid Sept*
€13/hr. **No credit cards.**
Kadoelen is subsidised by the local council, so the
nine indoor courts cost less to hire than elsewhere.
Tennis lessons can be arranged in advance.

## Ten-pin bowling

There are a fair few bowling lanes in
Amsterdam; see the *Amsterdam Yellow
Pages* under 'Bowlingbanen'. Phone the
**Nederlandse Bowling Federatie** on 010
473 5581 for more information, including
details of competitions and leagues.

### Knijn Bowling
*Scheldeplein 3, Zuid (664 2211/www.knijnbowling.nl).
Tram 4.* **Open** 10am-1am Mon-Fri; noon-1am Sat;
noon-midnight Sun. **Rates** €15/lane before 5pm;
€19.50/lane after 5pm; Sun €20.50/lane; twilight bowl
(Fri 10pm-12.30am) €10/person. **No credit cards.**

## Watersports

Holland has loads of water, and watersports
are accordingly very popular. If you want to go
sailing, visit Loosdrecht (25km/15 miles south-
east of Amsterdam) or go to the IJsselmeer. For
details on canoeing, phone the **NKB** (033 462
2341/www.nkb.nl). Most schools ask for a
deposit and ID when you rent a boat.
   There are rowing clubs on the Amstel and
at the Bosbaan (the former Olympic rowing
course) in the Amsterdam Bos. For details, call
the Dutch Rowing Union (**KNRB**) on 646 2740.

### Gaasperplas Park
*Gaasperplas Park, Zuid-Oost. Metro Gaasperplas/
bus 59, 60, 174.* **Open** 24hrs daily.
This park's large lake is a centre for watersports and
windsurfing. There's also a campsite.

# Theatre, Comedy & Dance

Traditional drama, futuristic performance art, sparky stand-up, world-class dance: whichever way you look at it, Amsterdam has stage presence.

## Theatre

Forward-thinking to the last, the Dutch have long been keen to embrace an international presence in their theatre, an enthusiasm tangible throughout the scene. Their willingness to welcome global influences into their local drama leads to a tension between homegrown projects and those from abroad that is almost always productive. And although the majority of productions are in the local tongue, you'll find a surprising amount of offerings, from both Dutch and international companies, in English.

Many of the larger venues offer a variety of different styles in their programming, though it's usually tied to a particular theme: comedy or cabaret, say, or even socially informed drama. Smaller theatres, meanwhile, are often inclined to strive towards freedom from genre conventions, a continuation of trends dating from the 1960s. Their shows tend to incorporate a greater variety of different styles, from music

### The best Theatre, etc

**Boom Chicago**
Americans bring comedy to the Dutch. Cue laughter. *See p246.*

**Dogtroep/Warner & Consorten**
You're looking for classic plays, traditionally performed? Keep looking. *See p243* **Location, location, location....**

**Muziektheater**
Whether old school or modern, dance here will be a feast for the eyes. *See p248.*

**Parade**
Theatre festivals are rarely this sprawling, ambitious and fun. *See p245.*

**Uitmarkt**
Amsterdam's annual inauguration of the cultural season. *See p181.*

to improvisation. The less venue-tied tradition of open-air theatre has a long history in the Netherlands, and is still seen in festivals such as **Parade** and **Boulevard** (for both, *see p245*), as well as in the summer-long outdoor programme at **Vondelpark** (*see p246*). And then there are groups not tied to any specific space, whose work is both uncategorisable and unpredictable (*see p243* **Location, location, location...**).

You'll find theatres throughout Amsterdam, but the majority are concentrated around two main areas. Urban planners originally intended **Leidseplein** to be the new recreational focus of Amsterdam, which resulted in a number of theatres being built on and around it. The most important are the **Stadsschouwburg** and the **Bellevue** (for both, *see p243*), but theatre has since flourished and other buildings in the area have been converted into venues. Most theatres on **Nes**, meanwhile, were established during or after the 1960s, and offer a refreshing contrast to the polished venues on Leidseplein. Further afield, the two most vital venues are perhaps the **Muziektheater** on Waterlooplein (*see p248*), and **De Kleine Komedie** on Amstel (*see p242*).

Traditionally, the Dutch government has subsidised theatre in an effort to stimulate the average Dutchman's exposure to performances and to encourage production companies to take shows outside large cities. However, financial assistance was cut in the '80s and '90s, forcing smaller companies to pool resources and look for alternative venues. This has led to some interesting collaborations in unconventional venues, including the **NDSM Shipyard** (*see p245*) in Amsterdam Noord, a complex intended to accommodate many small groups.

### TICKETS AND INFORMATION

For further information about what's on in Amsterdam, call or visit the **Uitburo** on Leidseplein (*see p279* **Tickets, please**) or the **Amsterdam Tourist Board** (*see p289*). Browsing through the former's free monthly *Uitkrant* will give you a sound idea of programming in and around the city.

Arts & Entertainment

Winding down from Dam Square, **Nes** is a hotbed of theatrical activity.

# Theatres

## Badhuis Theater de Bochel

*Andreas Bonnstraat 28, Oost (668 5102). Tram 3, 6, 7, 10, 20.* **Box office** open 30min prior to performance; advance reservations taken until 30min before start of performance. **Tickets** €2-€4. **No credit cards. Map** p312 G4.

Located in a square, this old bathhouse is now a cultural centre of sorts. On Fridays and Saturdays, the venue hosts cult dance parties, but at other times of the week – albeit only sporadically in recent years – there are multicultural events including children's theatre activities and workshops. The space has now been classified as a state monument.

## De Balie

*Kleine Gartmanplantsoen 10, Southern Canal Belt (553 5100/www.balie.nl). Tram 1, 2, 5, 6, 7, 10, 20.* **Box office** 1-6pm or until start of performance Mon-Fri; 5pm-start of performance Sat; 90min before performance Sun. **Tickets** €6-€9. **No credit cards. Map** p310 D5.

Theatre, new media, cinema (*see p193*) and literary events sit alongside lectures, debates, discussions and political projects at this cultural centre; all informally influence public opinion among the intelligensia. There's a café here, too.

## De Brakke Grond

*Nes 45, Old Centre: Old Side (622 9014/ www.brakkegrond.nl). Tram 4, 9, 14, 16, 20, 24, 25.* **Box office** 1-5pm Mon, Sun; 10am-8.30pm Tue-Sat. **Tickets** €2-€5. **Credit** AmEx, MC, V. **Map** p306 D3.

De Brakke Grond is part of the clunkily named Stichting [NES]theaters, which aims to spread the word about progressive theatre and Flemish culture in an intimate setting. Expect more of the former than the latter here.

## Cosmic Theater

*Nes 75, Old Centre: Old Side (622 8858/ www.cosmictheater.nl). Tram 4, 9, 14, 16, 20, 24, 25.* **Box office** *By phone* 10am-6pm Mon-Fri. *In person* from 1hr before performance. **Tickets** €2-€6. **Credit** AmEx, MC, V. **Map** p306 D3.

Cosmic formed 15 years ago in the Caribbean and, after a spell in New York, ended up here. The company has toured widely and developed an international reputation for its productions addressing the multicultural realities of the modern world.

## De Engelenbak

*Nes 71, Old Centre: Old Side (information 626 3644/box office 626 6866/www.engelenbak.nl). Tram 4, 9, 14, 16, 20, 24, 25.* **Box office** *By phone* 1-7.30pm Mon-Sat. *In person* from 1hr before performance. **Tickets** €6-€8. **No credit cards. Map** p306 D3.

The famous draw here is Open Bak, an open-stage event (Tuesdays at 10pm) where virtually anything goes. It's the longest-running theatre programme in the Netherlands, where everybody gets their 15 minutes of potential fame; arrive at least half an hour before the show starts in order to get a ticket. Otherwise, the best amateur groups in the country perform between Thursday and Saturday.

## Felix Meritis

*Keizersgracht 324, Western Canal Belt (623 1311/ www.felixmeritis.nl). Tram 1, 2, 5, 13, 17, 20.* **Box office** 9am-7pm Mon-Fri, or until start of performance; 1hr before start of performance Sat, Sun. **Tickets** €5-€15. **No credit cards. Map** p310 C4.

The Felix Meritis stages a variety of international dance and theatre performances alongside its noted programme of discussions, lectures and courses about Europe and other subjects. Worth visiting, if just to see the building: built in 1787, it's a handsome structure overlooking the Keizersgracht.

## Frascati

*Nes 63, Old Centre: Old Side (626 6866/
www.nestheaters.nl). Tram 4, 9, 14, 16, 20, 24, 25.*
**Box office** 1-5pm Mon, Sun; 10am-8.30pm Tue-Sat.
**Tickets** €2-€5. **Credit** AmEx, MC, V. **Map** p306 D3.
Stichting [NES]theaters set up two small alternative
theatres in the '60s – the other is De Brakke Grond;
*see p241* – and has been running them ever since.
Frascati's three stages provide both actor and audience member with a pleasingly intimate setting.
Check out the 250 Kuub, a freestyle production that
allows actors to make up their performance as they
go along, albeit under certain preset conditions.
Members of the audience are free to come and go as
they please, and there's no cover charge.

## Gasthuis Werkplaats & Theater

*Marius van Bouwdijk Bastiaansestraat 54; entrance
opposite 1e Helmerstraat 115, Museum Quarter
(616 8942/www.theatergasthuis.nl). Tram 1, 3,
6, 12.* **Box office** *By phone* noon-5pm Mon-Fri.
*In person* from 1hr before performance. **Tickets**
€3-€4. **Credit** AmEx, MC, V. **Map** p305 B6.
This adaptable, stageless space on the grounds of
an old squatted hospital is now fully legit and may
receive monument status. Gasthuis Werkplaats is
often used by young theatre students to try out their
talent, as well as being home to smaller productions.
The programme is mainly experimental; check
beforehand whether the production is in English.

## De Kleine Komedie

*Amstel 56, Southern Canal Belt (624 0534). Tram
4, 9, 14, 16, 24, 25.* **Box office** noon-6pm Mon-Sat.
**Tickets** €2-€6. **Credit** AmEx, DC, MC, V.
**Map** p307 E3.
One of Amsterdam's oldest and most important theatres, De Kleine Komedie is the country's premier
cabaret stage, though it also offers a wide range of
musical acts. Wildly popular among locals, it's one
of the more characterful Amsterdam venues.

## Koninklijk Theater Carré

*Amstel 115-25, Southern Canal Belt (622 5225/
0900 252 5255 premium rate/www.theatercarre.nl).
Tram 4, 6, 7, 10, 20/Metro Weesperplein.* **Box
office** 10am-7pm Mon-Sat; 1-7pm Sun. **Tickets**
€12-€16. **Credit** AmEx, MC, V. **Map** p311 F4.
Formerly home to a circus, the Carré now hosts some
of the best Dutch comedians and cabaret artists
around, and also stages opera. However, if mainstream theatre is more your thing, look out for Dutch
versions of popular musicals such as *42nd Street*,
*Cats* and *Oliver*, which usually end up here.

## De Nieuw Amsterdam

*Grote Bickersstraat 2/4, Westerdok, the Waterfront
(627 8672/www.denieuwamsterdam.nl). Bus 18, 22.*
**Box office** 10am-5pm Mon-Fri; also 7.30pm-start
of performance. **Tickets** €7; €6 students.
**No credit cards. Map** p305 B1.
The brainchild of director Rufus Collins, De Nieuw
Amsterdam is the leading socially concerned theatre
company in the Netherlands. Aside from its shows,

it also runs a programme for young people set on
becoming the next big thing, known as ITS DNA.
The ensemble of actors and teachers from ITS are
overseen by Aram Adriaanse.

## Het Rozentheater &
## Het Compagnietheater

**Het Rozentheater** *Rozengracht 117, the Jordaan
(620 7953/www.rozentheater.nl). Tram 13, 17, 20.*
**Box office** 10am-5pm Mon-Sat, and from 1hr before
start of performance. **Tickets** €2-€8. **No credit
cards. Map** p305 B3.
**Het Compagnietheater** *Kloveniersburgwal 50, Old
Centre: Old Side (520 5320/www.theatercompagnie.nl).
Tram 4, 9, 14, 16, 24, 25.* **Box office** 10am-5pm
Mon-Sat, and from 1hr before start of performance.
**Tickets** €2-€8. **No credit cards. Map** p306 D3.
A few years ago, two production companies – De
Trust and Art & Pro – allied themselves in a bid to
increase their profile. Now working under the name
De Theatercompagnie, they produce culturally and
politically aware programmes for three theatres: Het
Rozentheater, where the schedule is tilted towards
15- to 30-year-olds; Het Compagnietheater, where the
focus is on the work of modern Dutch writers; and
a third touring group, who aren't bound to one type
of production or site, though De Stadsschouwburg
(*see p243*) is home to most of their premieres.

From ancient to modern at
**De Stadsschouwburg.** *See p243.*

# Location, location, location...

The Netherlands' most interesting and exportable theatre groups have been boldly exploring space, the final frontier. From prison to shipyard, no space is deemed too strange to be used as an inspiring performance location.

The most acclaimed of such groups is **Dogtroep** (*pictured*; www.dogtroep.nl). For the last 25 years, the company has been putting on absurd multimedia spectacles that almost defy the imagination: driven by technical wizardry, highlighted by wild costumes and topped off by exploding stuff. Each show is developed by an array of designers, painters, actors, builders, techies and musicians in response to the performance's location and context. Although the group began by performing in squats and other abandoned buildings, it's now entered the mainstream so convincingly that it's been allowed to use such unique locations as Moscow's Red Square and Belgium's highest security prison. Dogtroep's art is something approximating to guerrilla street theatre, albeit evolved to its outer limits.

Likewise, **Warner & Consorten** (www.warnerenconsorten.nl), which started as an offshoot of Dogtroep, brings together creatives of various disciplines to react to

a specific site, staging dialogue-free shows in 20 different locations around the world each year. Shows such as *Drempelhonger* ('Threshold Hunger'), which took place in a monumental former factory reminiscent of the set from *Brazil*, are marked by a blurring of boundaries: dancers might make music while the musicians act, for example.

Dogtroep and Warner & Consorten have long headlined festivals such as **Oerol** and **Over Het IJ** (*see p245*), but head to **Robodock** (www.robodock.org), a newer and much edgier festival that takes place at the end of September in the former ADM shipping yards, for up-and-coming performers in a similar vein. As essentially the last 'free space' in town – at least since the closure of such mega-squats as Silo and Vrieshuis Amerika – this industrial complex is the perfect setting in which to view orchestral pyrotechnics and brain-melting projections, battling robots and frolicking mutants.

In freeing theatre from the theatres, it seems that a lot of pretentious baggage is also dispatched. The net result is a type of theatre that owes little to Shakespeare and his ilk, but that is a purer, more immediately accessible form of entertainment. Don't miss.

## De Stadsschouwburg

*Leidseplein 26, Southern Canal Belt (624 2311/ www.stadsschouwburgamsterdam.nl). Tram 1, 2, 5, 6, 7, 10, 20.* **Box office** 10am-6pm or until start of performance Mon-Sat; from 1½hrs before start of performance Sun. **Tickets** €10-€18. **Credit** AmEx, MC, V. **Map** p310 C5.

The Stadsschouwburg (or Municipal Theatre) is into its third incarnation, the first two buildings having been destroyed by fire in the 17th and 18th centuries. The present theatre, which opened in 1894, is a beautiful and impressive baroque building, built in the traditional horseshoe shape and seating about 950. Aside from nurturing traditional Dutch theatre, it

also stages a decent variety of contemporary national and international productions. The programme consists of mostly theatre but there is also dance, modern music and light opera. The theatre's Bovenzaal space plays host to small-scale productions that are often in English.

## Theater Bellevue & Nieuwe de la Mar Theater

**Theater Bellevue** *Leidsekade 90, Southern Canal Belt (530 5301/www.theaterbellevue.nl). Tram 1, 2, 5, 6, 7, 10, 20.* **Box office** 11am-6pm or until start of performance daily. **Tickets** €7.50-€15. **Credit** AmEx, DC, MC, V. **Map** p310 C5.

If you build it, they will come: **Kinetic Noord at the NDSM Shipyard**. *See p245.*

**Nieuwe de la Mar Theater** *Marnixstraat 404, Western Canal Belt (530 5302/ www.nieuwedelamartheater.nl). Tram 1, 2, 5, 6, 7, 10, 20.* **Box office** 11am-6pm or until start of performance daily. **Tickets** €10-€25. **Credit** AmEx, DC, MC, V. **Map** p310 C5.

They may have fused in 1987, but these two theatres close to Leidseplein have very distinctive histories and specialities even today. The Bellevue dates from 1840 and deals in popular theatre over its three stages: one for modern theatre, dance and music, one devoted to cabaret and a third for literary events. The younger Nieuwe de la Mar, which was founded in 1947, offers dance, serious spoken theatre and cabaret, performed by a mix of hot Dutch talent and imported international artists.

### Theater de Cameleon

*3e Kostverlorenkade 35, West (489 4656/ http://sites.netscape.net/cameleonidae). Tram 1, 6.* **Box office** noon-6pm daily. **Tickets** €2.50-€11. **No credit cards. Map** p305 A3.

A relatively new theatre in the old western part of town. Besides a wide variety of theatre performances, often in English, the Cameleon hosts music productions every Sunday at 3.30pm, and also offers theatre and voice workshops.

### Theater Pompoen

*Spuistraat 2/Kattegat 10, Old Centre: New Side (521 3000/www.pompoen.nl). Tram 1, 2, 5.* **Box office** 10am-5pm daily; also from 1hr before start of performance. **Tickets** €3-€5. **Credit** AmEx, MC, V. **Map** p306 C2.

A small, multi-functional theatre on the New Side that offers a good deal of productions in English, Pompoen is also home to a café/restaurant with Internet and computer games available (*see p85*). On offer is a tour of Amsterdam's most haunted sites; basically, it's a scripted play in which you meet witnesses of Amsterdam's most heinous crimes. Fun.

### Zaal 100

*De Wittenstraat 100, Westerpark (688 0127). Tram 3, 10/bus 18, 22.* **Box office** from 1hr before start of performance. **Tickets** prices vary. **No credit cards. Map** p305 A2.

This neighbourhood cultural centre, in an ex-squat building beyond the Jordaan, offers a sporadic programme in its small but cosy theatre space. The in-house group, Sub Theatre, usually performs one show a month. There are live jazz nights on Tuesdays, a big band gig every third Wednesday of the month, and performance poetry every third Thursday of the month.

## Cultural complexes

### Kinetic Noord at the NDSM Shipyard
*TT Neveritaweg 15, Noord (330 5480/www.ndsm.nl). Ferry from Centraal Station/bus 35, 94.*
The redevelopment of this old abandoned shipbuilding site is one of Amsterdam's most ambitious recent projects. The construction of Kinetic Noord began at the NDSM Shipyard in mid-2000; when finished – construction has been delayed and postponed so often that no one knows when that might be – it'll be an enormous cultural centre, maybe the biggest of its kind in Europe. There'll be two main halls on the site: one for large events and concerts, and the other housing a labyrinth of spaces that will include studios, a cinema, a theatre, a gallery, an art market, a skate park, performance areas and cafés. The large outdoor area, meanwhile, will afford spectacular views over the IJ river of Amsterdam. For details of events, contact the Uitburo on 0900 0191.

### Westergasfabriek
*Haarlemmerweg 8-10, West (www.westergasfabriek.nl). Bus 18, 22.*
This former gas factory originally supplied all of Amsterdam with gas for its street lighting. But when huge gas reserves were discovered north of Holland, it became redundant, and is now being converted into a multimedia arts complex. The site consists of 13 monumental buildings of various sizes and shapes, which have been redesigned to play host to film and theatre groups, fashion shows, corporate functions, movie shoots, operas, techno parties and assorted festivals, plus nightclubs, restaurants and bars (including Café West Pacific; *see p144*).

The site is a classic visual example of the changes that occurred in the 20th century, specifically that from industrial age to information age. Westerpark is being expanded to encompass the buildings and, when it's completed, the complex will be able to hold outdoor events, an exhibition area and café terraces. Renovation work looks set to continue throughout 2002 and 2003, though, and – with the exception of the still-open Café West Pacific – there will be no events here until late 2003 at the earliest. For more background information on the project, including details of when it will reopen, log on to its website, of which there's a basic English version available.

## Theatre festivals

### Boulevard
*'s Hertogenbosch (073 613 7671/www.bossenova.nl). Date Aug.*
Boulevard finds actors, musicians, dancers and performers of visual arts taking over the centre of the medieval town of Den Bosch ('s Hertogenbosch) each summer. The main festival venues are tents erected in the square next to St Jan Cathedral, though performances are also staged in theatres and in other,

more unlikely locations. Among the companies who've taken part in recent years are Circus Oz (Australia), Vis à Vis (Netherlands) and Stomp (UK). Tickets for the festival are available at Theater aan de Parade/Bosch (073 612 5125) and at all Amsterdam Tourist Board and GWK offices.

### ITs Festival
*Around Amsterdam (527 7613/www.its.ahk.nl). Date June.*
Something of a theatrical talent-spotter's dream, the International Theaterschool Festival is where students from all over the world show what they've learned during their studies. A mix of cabaret, dance, mime and drama takes place in the Theaterschool (*see p247*) and at several other venues in town. During the festival, many congregate at the ITs lounge in the Theaterschool building.

### Oerol
*PO Box 327, 8890 AA Midsland, Terschelling (0562 448448/www.oerol.nl). Date June.*
Terschelling, one of the five Frisian islands that sit off the north coast of Holland, has a unique landscape shaped by wind dunes, dykes and woodlands. It's usually a peaceful place, but for ten days each year, it's transformed into a cultural free state for the Oerol festival. Around 200 different acts perform, from international theatre groups creating their own environments influenced by the landscape to world music events on the beaches, theatre expeditions through the woods to bicycle tours. There are regular ferries to the island.

### Over het IJ
*NDSM Shipyard, TT Neveritaweg 15, Noord (0900 0191 premium rate/www.ijfestival.nl). Ferry from Centraal Station/bus 35, 94. Date July-Aug.*
A summer festival of large-scale theatrical projects and avant-garde mayhem, Over het IJ is usually interesting and frequently compelling. Dogtroep (*see p243* **Location, location, location…**) stole the show at 2001's festival; past highlights have included Vis à Vis's predictably large-scale Picnic, and Dansgroep Krisztina de Châtel (*see p249*) in a theatrical deconstruction of *Tomb Raider*'s Lara Croft. In other words, expect the unexpected.

### Parade
*Martin Luther Kingpark, Zuid (033 465 4577/www.mobilearts.nl). Date Aug.*
This unique event has captured the essence of the old circus/sideshow atmosphere that's so conspicuous by its absence in today's commercial fairgrounds. Parade offers a plentiful selection of bizarre shows, many in beautiful circus tents; spread between them are cafés, bars and restaurants, as well as the odd roving performer. The event has become very popular, and many shows sell out quickly: go early, have dinner and book your tickets at the Parade Kiosk for the night (some smaller shows, however, sell their own tickets separately). For more, *see p180*; for **Winter Parade**; *see p184*.

## Vondelpark Openluchttheater

*Vondelpark (673 1499/www.openluchttheater.nl).*
*Tram 1, 2, 3, 6.* **Date** late May-Aug.
Theatrical events have been held in Vondelpark since 1865, and the tradition continues each summer with a variety of free shows. Wednesdays offer a lunchtime concert and a mid-afternoon children's show; Thursday nights find a concert on the bandstand; there's a theatre show every Friday night; various events (including another theatre show) take place on Saturdays; and theatre events and pop concerts are held on Sunday afternoons.

## Bookshop

### International Theatre & Film Books

*Leidseplein 26, in the Stadsschouwburg building,*
*Southern Canal Belt (622 6489). Tram 1, 2, 5, 6, 7,*
*10, 20.* **Open** noon-6pm Mon; 10am-6pm Tue, Wed, Fri, Sat; 10am-7pm Thur. **Credit** (min €45) AmEx, DC, MC, V. **Map** p310 C5.
A wide variety of international magazines and books on stage, screen, dance and opera. There's everything from books on circuses and musicals to production and technical manuals, often in English, plus texts of current theatre productions. The store also has the biggest collection of dance books and videos in Europe. A great place for a browse, but be warned: it's hard to leave without buying something.

## Comedy

While the Dutch have a hilarious history of their own thanks to their very singular take on cabaret, stand-up comedy is a fairly recent import. However, the last few years have seen it become popular in Amsterdam, and it continues to grow. Shows often feature a mix of foreign and local acts who may or may not do their schtick in English (call ahead to check).

### Boom Chicago

*Leidseplein Theater, Leidseplein 12, Southern Canal*
*Belt (423 0101/www.boomchicago.nl). Tram 1, 2,*
*5, 6, 7, 10, 20.* **Box office** noon-8.30pm Mon-Thur, also Sun in summer; noon-11.30pm Fri, Sat.
**Shows** 8.15pm Mon-Fri, also Sun in summer; 7.30pm, 10.45pm Sat. *Heineken Late Nite* 11.30pm Fri. **Tickets** €15-€17.50. *Heineken Late Nite* €10. **Credit** AmEx, MC, V. **Map** p310 D5.
American improv troupe Boom Chicago is one of Amsterdam's biggest success stories. With several different shows running seven nights a week (except Sundays in winter), all in English, the group offers a mix of rehearsed sketches and audience-prompted improvisation. New show *Rock Stars* will open here in May 2002, running through until February 2003. The bar offers cocktails and DJs (for more on this, *see p142*), and is something of an unofficial meeting point for wayward Americans; a restaurant serves noon-9pm daily; and they even publish a free magazine for visitors to the city. A winner.

## Comedy Café Amsterdam

*Max Euweplein 43-5, Southern Canal Belt (638*
*3971/www.comedycafe.nl). Tram 1, 2, 5, 6, 7, 10,*
*20.* **Box office** 9am-5pm Mon-Fri. **Shows** 9pm Tue, Thur, Fri, Sun; 9.30pm Wed; 9pm, 11.30pm Sat.
**Tickets** €7 Tue, Sun; free Wed; €12 Thur-Sat.
**Credit** AmEx, MC, V. **Map** p310 C5.
Stand-up has never been as popular in Amsterdam as it is in, say, London or New York, but the Comedy Café has been doing a decent job at getting the art a wider audience. From Thursday to Saturday, there's a stand-up show in a mix of Dutch and English. On Wednesdays, comics try out new material at the venue's Open Mic Night, while Sundays offer an improv show, Off Your Head.

### Toomler

*Breitnerstraat 2, Zuid (670 7400/www.toomler.nl).*
*Tram 2, 5, 16, 24.* **Box office** from 7pm Tue-Sun.
**Shows** 8.30pm. **Tickets** €2-€5. **No credit cards**.
Located next to the Hilton, this café has something going on six nights a week. Most programming is stand-up in Dutch, but it's the monthly Comedy Train International – when English takes over – that has come to be most closely associated with the venue. They also offer live music.

## Dance

Like its theatre, Dutch dance doesn't operate in a bubble of isolationism. International companies stage productions in the Netherlands and shows are often imported from abroad and performed by Dutch troupes. Keep an eye out, too, for collaborations during local festivals.

Dynamic collaborations such as these serve as a magnet for talent, ensuring a surplus of top dancers, trainers and choreographers, as well as a healthy exchange of ideas. Everyone benefits from this situation, especially smaller companies and the audience, who are spoiled for choice by productions that stretch from the stiffly traditional to the out-there avant-garde. Nor is the art limited to exclusively dance-centred events: a great deal of fringe theatre incorporates a lot of dance into its productions and vice versa. In turn, these are influenced by factors such as the media and technology. Annual festivals (*see p248* **Dance festivals**) offer excellent opportunities to catch some of the Netherlands' innovative work.

But though many associate Dutch dance with a mere two names – the **Nationale Ballet** and **Nederlands Dans Theater** (for both, *see p250*) – there's a lot more to the scene. It's impossible to give a full list here, but among the Amsterdam-based choreographers worth checking out are **Krisztina de Châtel, Beppie Blankert, Truus Bronkhorst, Shusaku Takeuchi, Andrea Leine and Harijono Roebana, Marcello Evelin** and **Katie Duck**.

Five live: the **Nationale Ballet** performs Hans van Manen's *Five Tangos. See p250*.

## TICKETS AND INFORMATION

Tickets for the majority of performances can be bought at the venues themselves, or from any of the various phone, online or drop-in **AUB** operations (*see p279* **Tickets, please**); their *Uitkrant* offers information on dance in the city.

# Venues

Dance is performed at a variety of venues in Amsterdam, the biggest of which are detailed below. Other primarily theatrical venues also stage some dance, such as the **Theater Bellevue**, the **Stadsschouwburg** (for both, *see p243*) and the **Cosmic Theater** (*see p241*).

## Danswerkplaats Amsterdam

*Arie Biemondstraat 107B, Museum Quarter (689 1789/www.euronet.nl/~dwa). Tram 1, 17.* **Box office** *By phone* 10am-5pm Mon-Fri. *In person* 7.30pm-15min before start of performance. **Tickets** €5.50-€7. **No credit cards**.

Danswerkplaats' dance studio has been staging performances once a month, both here and elsewhere in the city or country, since 1993. Plans to take part in the Huis voor de Dans (House for Dance) are still under discussion. For further information, consult their website which was launched in English towards the end of 2001.

## International Theaterschool

*Jodenbreestraat 3, Old Centre: Old Side (527 7700/ 527 7620/www.ahk.nl/the). Tram 4, 9, 14, 16, 20, 24, 25/Metro Waterlooplein.* **Box office** times vary. **Tickets** prices vary, though many performances are free. **No credit cards. Map** p307 E3.

ITs brings together students and teachers from all over the world to learn and create in the fields of dance and theatre. Performances – some of which are announced in *Uitkrant* – vary from studio shots to evening-long events in the Philip Morris Dans Zaal. Keep an eye open for Summerdance, which fell through in 2001 but is slated to take place again.

## Melkweg

*Lijnbaansgracht 234A, Western Canal Belt (531 8181/www.melkweg.nl). Tram 1, 2, 5, 6, 7, 10, 20.* **Box office** 1-5pm Mon-Fri; 4-6pm Sat, Sun; also 7.30pm-start of performance. **Tickets** €7-€14. *Membership* (compulsory) €2/mth; €14/yr. **No credit cards. Map** p310 C5.

This multidisciplinary venue – *see also p194, p198, p213 and p225* – opened its doors to national and international dance and theatre groups in 1973. For many years, the small stage hosted mainly dancers and choreographers at the start of their careers. However, the renovated theatre now has capacity for more ambitious projects; and there's a café here, too. As befits its under-one-roof eclecticism, special focus is placed on multimedia performances.

## Muiderpoorttheater

*2e Van Swindenstraat 26, Oost (668 1313).*
*Tram 4, 6, 9, 14.* **Tickets** €7. **No credit cards.**
**Map** p312 H2.
Muiderpoorttheater is known primarily for its performances by international acts. Every January, the small space hosts the Go Solo festival, a showcase of solo works. The monthly MAD interdisciplinary improvisation event, in which pioneers of dance and music invite and get invited to perform by new faces on the scene, is worth checking out.

## Muziektheater

*Waterlooplein 22, Old Centre: Old Side (625 5455/*
*www.muziektheater.nl).* Tram 9, 14, 20/Metro
Waterlooplein. **Box office** 10am-6pm or until start
of performance Mon-Sat; 11.30am-6pm or until start
of performance Sun. **Tickets** €11-€63. **Credit**
AmEx, DC, MC, V. **Map** p307 E3.
The Muziektheater is Amsterdam at its most ambitious. This plush, crescent-shaped building, which opened in 1986, has room for 1,596 people and is home to both the Nationale Ballet (*see p250*) and the Nederlands Opera (*see p221*), though the stage is also used by visiting companies such as the Royal Ballet and the Martha Graham Company. On top of that, the lobby's panoramic glass walls offer impressive views of the Amstel.

## Tropeninstituut Theater

**Kleine Zaal** *Linnaeusstraat 2, Oost;*
**Grote Zaal** *Mauritskade 63, Oost (568 8500/*
*www.kit.nl/theater).* Tram 9, 10, 14, 20.
**Box office** noon-4pm, from 1hr before start of
performance Mon-Sat. **Tickets** €12-€16.
**Credit** MC, V. **Map** p312 H3.
The Tropeninstituut, just by the Tropenmuseum
(*see p99*), organises performances in music, dance
and occasionally theatre that are related to or drawn
from non-Western cultures. The dance programme
varies from classical Indian to South African, from
Indonesian to Argentinian.

---

## Out of town venues

### Lucent Danstheater

*Spuiplein 152, the Hague (information 070 360*
*9931/box office 070 360 4930/www.ldt.nl). NS*
*rail Den Haag Centraal Station.* **Box office** 10am-
6pm Mon-Sat. **Tickets** €14-€30. **Credit** AmEx,
DC, MC, V.
The Lucent Danstheater, located in the centre of the
Hague, is the home of the world-famous Nederlands
Dans Theater (*see p250*). As well as staging high-
quality Dutch productions in dance and opera, it's
also become one of the country's most important

# Dance festivals

In July each year, the **Stadsschouwburg** (*see*
*p243*) hosts **Julidans**, a month-long showcase
of international dance. The **International**
**Concours for Choreographers** in Groningen,
meanwhile, is a competition event at
which prizes are awarded for ensemble
choreographies. Details about festivals,
competitions, performances, courses and
workshops are available from the **Theater**
**Instituut**, for which *see p88*.

For details of the **Holland Festival** and
**Uitmarkt**, two multicultural festivals that
both include a number of noteworthy dance
performances from around the world in their
pleasingly eclectic calendars, *see p180* and
*p181* respectively.

### Cadans

*Korzo Theater, Postbus 13407, 2501 EK*
*the Hague (070 363 7540/www.korzo.nl).*
**Dates** biennial; next held in Nov 2002.
The Hague's exciting international festival
of contemporary dance takes place every
other winter in the Hague (it alternates
years with the Holland Dance Festival).
Each and every work is choreographed
specifically for the festival.

### Holland Dance Festival

*Nobelstraat 21, 2513 BC the Hague (070*
*361 6142/www.hollanddancefestival.com).*
**Date** biennial; next held in Nov 2003.
Held every two years in November, the
Holland Dance Festival takes place at
three different venues, including the Hague's
Lucent Danstheater (*see p248*), and is easily
the biggest and most important festival
on the Dutch dance calendar. Many of the
world's larger companies are attracted to
the event – 2001's festival featured
companies from almost 20 countries –
and the quality of the work is consistently
high. Though a variety of Dutch acts usually
perform at the event, Nederlands Dans
Theater (*see p250*) is invariably the country's
main representative.

### Spring Dance

*Postbus 111, 3500 AC Utrecht*
*(030 233 2032).* **Dates** Apr-May.
Spring Dance, held annually in Utrecht in
late April and early May, attempts to give
an overview of recent developments in
contemporary dance, film and music from
around the world.

Might as well jump: **Nederlands Dans Theater**. *See p250.*

venues in which to see international companies. With its excellent acoustics, fine visibility and stage that compares favourably in size to the Metropolitan in New York, the theatre offers wonderful facilities to go with its exceptional performances. A real treat.

### Rotterdamse Schouwburg

*Schouwburgplein 25, Rotterdam (010 411 8110/www.schouwburg.rotterdam.nl). NS rail Rotterdam Centraal Station.* **Box office** 11am-7pm Mon-Sat; noon-5pm Sun. **Tickets** €5-€18. **Credit** AmEx, DC, MC, V.

This large, square-shaped theatre opened in 1988 and quickly became known as Kist van Quist (Quist's box) after its architect. Rotterdamse Schouwburg offers a large variety of classical ballet and modern dance, from both Dutch and international troupes, in its two auditoriums (one of 900 seats, the other of 150 seats). There's also a bar, a café and a shop.

### Toneelschuur

*Smedestraat 23, Haarlem (023 531 2439/ www.toneelschuur.nl). NS rail Haarlem Centraal Station.* **Box office** 3-7pm or start of performance Mon-Sat; 1.30-2.30pm Sun. **Tickets** €7-€14. **No credit cards.**

Many dance- and theatre-lovers from Amsterdam head to Haarlem for shows at the Toneelschuur. There are two halls here (plus a bar and café, if you arrive early) and the venue is nationally renowned for its programmes of theatre and modern dance.

## Companies

The following companies are all based in Amsterdam, but perform only sporadically and are not tied to any one venue. For details on shows, call the numbers listed, check online or pick up a copy of *Uitkrant*.

### Dance Company Leine & Roebana

*489 3820.*

Harijono Roebana and Andrea Leine's company performs its exciting, inventive modern dance works at various venues across Amsterdam.

### Dansgroep Krisztina de Châtel

*669 5755/www.dechatel.nl.*

Over the last quarter-century, Hungarian Krisztina de Châtel's company has grown into an internationally recognised dance group. Most productions last an entire evening, and combine elements of dance, music and visual art.

## Het Internationaal Danstheater
*Box office 623 5359/company 623 9112/*
*www.intdanstheater.nl.*
This Amsterdam-based company performs original dance from all over the world. The corps of 24 dancers works with guest international choreographers on a regular basis.

## Magpie Music Dance Company
*616 4794/www.xs4all.nl/~magpie.*
Magpie uses improvisation to mix up a remarkable blend of dance, music and text into surprising whole-night events. Founded by dancer Katie Duck and musician Michael Vatcher in 1994, the company has toured extensively both in Europe and the USA, though it maintains a season of performances at the Melkweg (*see p247*).

## Nationale Ballet
*Muziektheater box office 551 8225/*
*www.het-nationale-ballet.nl.*
The largest company in the Netherlands boasts over 20 Balanchine ballets in its repertoire, the largest collection outside New York. However, since moving to the Muziektheater (*see p248*) in 1986, its repertoire has included the more popular classical ballet as the company attempts to fill the theatre on a regular basis. Toer van Schayk and Rudi van Dantzig have been instrumental in developing its distinctive style within contemporary ballet.

## Nederlands Dans Theater
*Lucent Danstheater box office 070 360 9931/*
*www.ndt.nl.*
Nederlands Dans Theater was founded in 1959 and is now one of the most successful modern dance companies in the world. With two world-famous choreographers leading it – Jiri Kylian and Hans van Manen – the company has a very firm foundation. Apart from the main company, look out for NDT2, made up of novices and up-and-coming dancers, and NDT3, which comprises veterans.

# Out of town companies

Amsterdam performances by the companies below are usually held in the Stadsschouwburg.

## RAZ/Hans Tuerlings
*013 583 5929/www.raz.nl.*
Hans Tuerlings regards his performances as narratives without a set story through a language of nonchalant, yet pure and especially well-measured, precisely timed movement. The RAZ company, meanwhile, consists of international dancers and performs regularly at the Bellevue.

## Rotterdamse Dansgroep
*010 436 4511/www.drd.org.*
The Rotterdamse Dansgroep is one of the most vigorous exponents of New York modern dance in the Netherlands. Imported dance routines are mixed with work by young Dutch choreographers.

## Scapino Ballet
*010 411 8110/www.scapinoballet.nl.*
Scapino is the oldest dance company in the country. Until recently, the company's work was more oriented towards youth dance and family programmes, but Scapino's image is now more in tune with current, modern trends.

# Movement theatre groups

Movement theatre is more popular here than in most cities, though it's frequently fused with other art forms in larger, multimedia theatrical spectacles.

## Griftheater
*419 3088/www.grif.nl.*
Griftheater is a giant on the international mime scene. The company produces both location movement theatre and productions for existing theatre spaces. An excellent combination of plastic arts and modern mime.

## Shusaku & Dormu Dance Theater & Bodytorium
*662 4692.*
Veteran Japanese choreographer Shusaku Takeuchi has been producing fascinating work for over 20 years. He specialises in massive location spectacles, often on or near bodies of water – perfect for Amsterdam, in other words – that also feature impressive lighting and live music. His indoor work is less grandiose, and is influenced by his background in plastic arts.

# Courses & workshops

## Dansstudio Cascade
*Koestraat 5, Old Centre: Old Side (623 0597/*
*689 0565). Tram 4, 9, 14, 16, 20, 24/Metro*
*Nieuwmarkt.* **Open** 6-10.30pm Mon-Fri. **Cost**
€3-€6/class. **No credit cards. Map** p306 D3.
Modern dance technique, capoeira, contact improvisation and Pentjak Silat are all taught at Dansstudio Cascade, just a stone's throw from Nieuwmarkt. Most teachers work within the new dance technique.

## Henny Jurriens Foundation
*Gerard Brandtstraat 26-8, Museum Quarter*
*(412 1510/www.euronet.nl/~hjs). Tram 1, 6.*
**Classes** 9-11am, 11am-12.30pm, 12.30-2pm Mon-Fri;
11am Sat. **Cost** €7 per class; €55 ten-class card.
**Map** p309 B3.
The Henny Jurriens Foundation provides open training for professional dancers in both classical and modern dance techniques throughout the year, with modern classes taking place at Danswerkplaats Amsterdam (*see p247*). Teachers are a mix of locals and guest teachers from abroad, and the foundation also offers workshops (pre-registration is necessary); phone for more information.

# Trips Out
of Town

# Introduction

From cheesy cliché to the urban unique, Holland's best is just a tulip away.

So untypical is Amsterdam of the rest of the Netherlands that you can barely say you've visited the country until you've taken at least one trip out of town. Not hard: it's a small place, and even the remotest corners are less than a day's drive or train ride away. Many of the towns and cities worth visiting are under an hour away from Amsterdam.

## TRAVEL INFORMATION

The **Netherlands Board of Tourism** or VVV (Vlietweg 15, 2266 KA Leidschendam; 070 370 5705/www.visitholland.com) can help with general information and also accommodation, as can the **Netherlands Reserverings Centrum** (*see p48*). For all national transport information and timetables (trains, buses and the Metro), call the **OV Reisinformatie** information line (premium rate 0900 9292) or go to www.ns.nl, in Dutch but decipherable.

## Getting around

### Driving

The Netherlands' road system is extensive, well maintained and clearly signposted. For driving advice and details of the motoring organisation **ANWB**, *see p277*.

### Buses & coaches

The national bus service is reasonably priced, but not as easy to negotiate as the railway. For information and timetables, phone **OV Reisinformatie** (*see above*).

### Cycling

The Netherlands is flat (though windy), so it's no surprise that the bike is the country's favourite mode of transport. Cycle paths can be found in abundance and the ANWB and VVV offices sell cycle tour maps. Most major railway stations have bike hire depots and offer discounts to rail ticket holders. Road bikes cost around €5 per day and €20 per week, mountain bikes something over twice that. Both are in short supply in summer; book at least a day ahead. You'll need proof of identity and a cash deposit (ranging from €50 to €200). It'll also cost money to take a bike on a train. For bike hire in Amsterdam, *see p278*.

**The best** Trips

**For cheesy grins**
Alkmaar (*see p253*).

**For Holland in miniature**
Madurodam (*see p264*).

**For the other great Dutch city**
Rotterdam (*see p267*).

## Rail

Nederlandse Spoorwegen (aka NS, and translatable as Netherlands Railway) offers an excellent service in terms of cost, punctuality and cleanliness. Aside from singles and returns, you can also buy family and group passes, tickets that entitle you to unlimited travel on any given day (Dagkaarten), one that also entitles you to use buses, trams and the Metro (OV Dagkaarten) and, for selected places, NS Rail Idee tickets, all-in-one tickets that'll get you to a destination and also include the admission fee to one or more of the local sights. Services are frequent, and reservations are unnecessary.

As a rule, tickets are valid for one day only: if you make a return journey spanning more than one day you need two singles. A weekend return ticket is the exception to the rule: it's valid from Friday night until Sunday night. Credit cards are seldom accepted at ticket offices.

With a rail ticket, you can avail yourself of **Treintaxi**, a special cab that takes you to any destination within a fixed distance of 110 stations for under €5.

### DISABLED TRAVELLERS

NS produces a booklet called *Rail Travel for the Disabled* (in English), available from all main stations or from the above number. There is disabled access to refreshment rooms and toilets at all stations. For special assistance, call **030 230 5566** at least a day in advance.

### Centraal Station Information Desk

*Stationsplein 15, Old Centre: New Side (0900 9292/ www.ns.nl).* Tram 1, 2, 4, 5, 9, 13, 16, 17, 20, 24, 25. **Open** *Information desk* 6.30am-10pm daily. *Bookings* 24hrs daily. **Credit** MC, V. **Map** p306 D1.

# Excursions in Holland

Cheese, tulips, windmills... Holland just wouldn't be Holland without them.

Think of the Netherlands and the chances are its most enduring, popular and stereotypical sights spring to mind – most of which are concentrated in Noord and Zuid Holland. The good news is that these two provinces are both small, close to Amsterdam and readily accessible by public transport. Note that none of the establishments listed in this chapter take credit cards.

## Charming Clichés

### Cheese

Ah, yes. Cheese. It gives you strange dreams, apparently. Not that the Dutch seem to mind. When they're not munching it or selling it abroad – more than 400,000 tonnes of it are exported annually – they're making a tourist industry of it, too. Visit in the summer and you can experience a taste of how this commodity used to be made and sold at various cheese markets, museums and traditional farms.

One ritual for both tourists and members of the cheese porters' guild is the **Alkmaar Cheese Market**, which runs 10am-noon every Friday (mid Apr to mid Sept). First, porters – clad in pristine white uniforms and straw hats with coloured ribbons denoting their competing guilds – weigh the cheeses and carry them on wooden trays hung from their shoulders. Then buyers test a core of cheese from each lot before the ceremony, which takes place at the Waag (weighhouse); here you can also find craft stalls and a **Cheese Museum**. Yet Alkmaar has a lot more than cheese to offer. The VVV provides a written walking tour of the medieval centre, which dates from 935. You'll find a beer-tasting cellar at the **Biermuseum**, and impressive art and toy collections at the **Stedelijk Museum**.

The Netherlands' famous red-skinned cheese is sold at **Edam**'s cheese market, held every Wednesday in July and August from 10am until noon. The town was a prosperous port during the Golden Age, and you can still see some exquisite façades and bridges.

Meanwhile, over in **Gouda**, golden wheels of cheese are for sale at the cheese market every Thursday from 10am in July and August in front of the Gothic city hall of 1450 and the 1668 Waag, whose gablestone depicts cheese-weighing. There are also many thatched-roof

*kaasboerderijen* (cheese farms) near Gouda, several of which are on the picturesque River Vlist. Look for signs that indicate a farm shop: see *kaas te koop* ('cheese for sale') and you may well be able to peer behind the scenes as well as buy freshly made Gouda.

But though the cheese is justly famed the world over, Gouda does have other things to recommend it beside the yellow stuff. Its other famous products include clay pipes and pottery, which can be seen in the **De Moriaan Museum**; interested visitors shouldn't miss the popular pottery festival, held each year in the second week of May. Gouda's candles are another city classic: 20,000 of them illuminate the square during the Christmas tree ceremony.

### Alkmaar Biermuseum

*Houttil 1, Alkmaar (072 511 3801/ www.biermuseum.nl).* **Open** 10am-4pm Tue-Sat; 1-4pm Sun. **Admission** €2; €1 concessions.

Dream on... **Alkmaar Cheese Market.**

## Alkmaar Cheese Museum

*De Waag, Alkmaar (072 511 4284).* **Open** *Mid Apr-mid Sept* 10am-4pm Mon-Thur, Sat; 9am-4pm Fri. Closed Nov-Mar. **Admission** €2; €1 under-11s.

## De Moriaan Museum, Gouda

*Westhaven 29, Gouda (0182 588444).* **Open** 10am-5pm Mon-Sat; noon-5pm Sun. **Admission** €2; €1.50 over-65s; free children.

## Stedelijk Museum, Alkmaar

*Canadaplein 1, Alkmaar (072 511 0737/ www.stedelijkmuseumalkmaar.nl).* **Open** 10am-5pm Tue-Fri; 1-5pm Sat, Sun. **Admission** €1.50; free MJK, 10-17s.

## Getting there

### Alkmaar

*By car* 37km (22 miles) north-west. *By train* direct from Amsterdam Centraal Station.

### Edam

*By car* 10km (5 miles) north. *By bus* 110, 112, 114 from Amsterdam Centraal Station.

### Gouda

*By car* 29km (18 miles) south-west. *By train* direct from Amsterdam Centraal Station.

## Tourist information

### Alkmaar VVV

*Waagplein 2, Alkmaar (072 511 4284/ www.vvv.alkmaar-nh.nl).* **Open** 10am-5.30pm Mon; 9am-5.30pm Tue, Wed; 9am-9pm Thur; 9am-6pm Fri; 9.30am-5pm Sat.

### Edam VVV

*Stadhuis, Damplein 1, Edam (0299 315125/www.vvv-edam.nl).* **Open** *Apr-June, Sept, Oct* 10am-5pm Mon-Sat. *July, Aug* 10am-5pm daily. *Nov-Mar* 10am-3pm Mon-Sat.

### Gouda VVV

*Markt 27, Gouda (0900 4683 2888 premium rate/www. vvvgouda.nl).* **Open** 9am-5pm Mon-Fri; 10am-4pm Sat.

## Flowers

Want a statistic that boggles the mind? Try this: the Netherlands produces a staggering 70 per cent of all the world's flowers. Once you know that, it's less surprising that so many varieties can be seen all year round in markets, botanical gardens, auctions and parades. For export rules on bulbs and flowers, *see p165*.

The world's biggest flower auction is the **Verenigde Bloemenveilingen** in Aalsmeer, which handles more than 3.5 billion cut flowers and 370 million pot plants each year, mostly for export. The unusual sales method gave rise to the English phrase 'Dutch auction'. Basically,

dealers bid by pushing a button to stop a 'clock' that counts from 100 down to one: thus the price is lowered – rather than raised – until a buyer is found. Bidders risk either overpaying or not getting the goods if time runs out. The best action here is usually before 9am, except on Thursdays.

**Broeker Veiling**, the oldest flower auction in the world, is a bit of a tourist trap. Bidding is in 'proper' auction style, and the admission price includes a museum of old farming artefacts, and – for a small fee – a boat trip.

The greenhouse and extensive fields of the 200-year-old **Frans Rozen Nursery** are open to the public, and allow visitors an insight into commercial cultivation and the development of new hybrids. You can buy bulbs for export, and there's a tulip show in April and May.

There have been flowers everywhere at the **Keukenhof Bulb Gardens** since 1949. This former 15th-century royal 'kitchen garden' contains 500 types of tulip and over six million bulbs in 1.25 square miles (over three square kilometres), but the glass flower pavilion – all 6,500 square metres (70,480 square feet) of it – is just as interesting. Follow a VVV map and tour the bulb district (in bloom March to late May), from which over half the world's cut flowers and pot plants originate. Arrive early, as the gardens get overrun. For more on the bulb district's history, visit the **Museum de Zwarte Tulp**.

### Broeker Veiling

*Museumweg 2, Broek-op-Langerdijk (0226 313807/ www.broekerveiling.nl).* **Open** *Apr-Nov* 10am-5pm Mon-Fri; 11am-5pm Sat, Sun. Closed Dec-Mar. **Admission** *Auction & museum* €5; €3 under-15s. *Auction, museum & boat trip* €8; €4 under-15s.

### Frans Rozen Nursery

*Vogelenzangseweg 49, Vogelenzang (023 584 7245).* **Open** *Mid Mar-mid May* 8am-6pm daily. *Mid May-Sept* 9am-5pm Mon-Fri; 10am-5pm Sat, Sun. Closed Oct-mid Mar. **Admission** €4; €2-€3 concessions.

### Keukenhof Bulb Gardens

*Keukenhof, near Lisse (0252 465555).* **Open** *Mid Mar-mid May* 8am-7.30pm daily. Closed late May-early Mar. **Admission** €11; €5.50 4-11s.

### Museum de Zwarte Tulp

*Grachtweg 2A, Lisse (0252 417900).* **Open** 1-5pm Tue-Sun. **Admission** €4; €3 under-12s.

### Verenigde Bloemenveilingen

*Legmeerdijk 313, Aalsmeer (0297 393939).* **Open** 7.30-11am Mon-Fri. **Admission** €3.50; €2 under-12s.

## Getting there

### Aalsmeer

*By car* 15km (9 miles) south-west. *By bus* 172 from Amsterdam Centraal Station.

### Broek-op-Langerdijk
*By car* 36km (22 miles) north. *By train* from
Amsterdam Centraal Station to Alkmaar, then
bus 155; from Amsterdam Centraal Station to
Heerhugowaard, then taxi.

### Keukenhof/Lisse
*By car* 27km (17 miles) south-west. *By train* from
Amsterdam Centraal Station to Leiden, then bus 54.

### Vogelenzang
*By car* 25km (16 miles) west. *By train* from
Amsterdam Centraal Station to Heemstede, then
bus 90 to Café Rusthoek.

---

# Dutch Traditions

Small historic towns in the Netherlands – which
depend on the tourist business – have become
expert at capitalising on their traditions, right
down to the lace caps, wooden shoes and
working windmills that churn out souvenirs
like flour and mustard. Authentic it ain't, but
lovers of kitsch should head here immediately.

## Zuid-Holland & Utrecht

It's hardly catwalk glamour, but a sizeable
minority of **Bunschoten-Spakenburg**
residents still strut their stuff in traditional
dress on midsummer market Wednesdays
between mid July and mid August; some older
people wear it every day. Costumes are also
worn at the special summer markets in Hoorn
(*see p258*), Medemblik (*see p257*) and Schagen,
and on folkloric festival days in Middelburg.

An amazing sight can be seen over in
Alblasserdam, where 19 **Kinderdijk
Windmills** form a group called a *gang*.
Although they were originally clustered in
order to drain water from reclaimed land, they
are now under sail specifically for the benefit
of tourists (2-5pm Saturdays in July and Aug,
and the first Saturday in May and June). During
the second week in September, you'll find them
illuminated, and a spectacular sight it is, too;
from April to September, you can take a boat
trip out to see them (€2).

**Schoonhoven** has been famous since the
17th century for its silversmiths, who crafted
items to be worn with traditional costume.
You can see antique pieces in the **Nederlands
Goud-, Zilver- en Klokkenmuseum** and
the **Edelambachtshuis** (Museum of Antique
Silverware). Olivier van Noort, the first
Dutchman to sail around the world, and Claes
Louwerenz Blom, who locals believe introduced
the windmill to Spain in 1549, are buried in the
14th-century **Bartholomeuskerk**, the tower
of which leans 1.6 metres (five feet).

**Kinderdijk:** Do you want to be in my gang?

Dating from the 11th century, **Oudewater**
(north of Schoonhoven) was once known for
its rope-making. However, locals began witch-
hunting during the 1480s, a fashion that didn't
die out until the beginning of the 17th century,
and Oudewater achieved fame for its weighing
of suspected witches and warlocks in the
**Witches' Weigh House** ('Heksenwaag');
today, swarms of tourists step on to the scales.

### Edelambachtshuis
*Haven 13, Schoonhoven (0182 382614).*
**Open** 10am-5pm Tue-Sat. **Admission** 50¢.

### Kinderdijk Windmills
*Molenkade, Alblasserdam (078 691 5179/
www.kinderdijk.nl).* **Open** Apr-Sept 9.30am-5.30pm
daily. Closed Oct-Mar. **Admission** Windmills €1.50;
€1 under-16s.

### Nederlands Goud-, Zilver-
en Klokkenmuseum
*Kazerneplein 4, Schoonhoven (0182 385612/
www.home.hccnet.nl/a.vuijk/gnngouda/ngzkm).* **Open**
noon-5pm Tue-Sun. **Admission** €3.50; €2 under-12s.

### Witches' Weigh House
*Leeuweringerstraat 2, Oudewater (0348 563400).*
**Open** Apr-Oct 10am-5pm Tue-Sat; noon-5pm Sun.
Closed Nov-Mar. **Admission** €1.50; €1 MJK, over-
65s; 50¢ 4-12s; free under-4s.

**Trips Out of Town**

Fishermen at **Volendam** await the tourists.

## Getting there

### Alblasserdam
*By car* 55km (34 miles) south-west. *By train* from Amsterdam Centraal Station to Utrecht, then bus 154.

### Bunschoten-Spakenburg
*By car* 35km (22 miles) south-east. *By train* from Amsterdam Centraal Station to Amersfoort, then bus 116.

### Oudewater
*By car* 40km (25 miles) south. *By train* from Amsterdam Centraal Station to Utrecht, then bus 180.

### Schoonhoven
*By car* 50km (31 miles) south. *By train* from Amsterdam Centraal Station to Utrecht, then bus 195.

## Tourist information

### Alblasserdam VVV
*Cortgene 2, inside City Hall, Alblasserdam (078 692 1355).* **Open** 9am-4pm Mon-Fri.

### Bunschoten-Spakenburg VVV
*Oude Schans 90, Spakenburg (033 298 2156/ www.vvvspakenburg.nl).* **Open** *Apr-Sept* 10am-5pm Mon-Fri; 10am-4pm Sat. *Oct-Mar* 1-5pm Mon-Fri; 10am-3pm Sat.

### Oudewater VVV
*Kapellestraat 2, Oudewater (0348 564636/ www.vvvgroenehart.nl/vvv_nl/index_dag_nl.html).* **Open** *Apr-Oct* 10am-4.30pm Tue-Sat; noon-3.30pm Sun. *Nov-Mar* 10am-1pm Tue-Sat.

### Schoonhoven VVV
*Stadhuisstraat 1, Schoonhoven (0182 385009).* **Open** *May-Sept* 1.30-5pm Mon; 9am-5pm Tue-Fri; 10am-3pm Sat. *Oct-Apr* 9am-4pm Tue-Fri; 10am-3pm Sat.

# Waterland

Until the IJ Tunnel opened in 1956, the canal-laced peat meadows of Waterland north of Amsterdam were accessible mainly by ferry and steam railway. This isolation preserved much of the area's heritage, best seen from a bicycle: for a prime view, look around the old wooden buildings at **Broek in Waterland**.

**Marken**, reached via a causeway, was once full of fishermen, but is now awash only with tourists. Visit off-season, however, and you'll likely find it quieter and more authentic than Volendam (*see below*). To protect against flooding, many houses are built on mounds or poles. The **Marker Museum** offers a tour of the island's history.

The number of preserved ancient buildings, from Golden Age merchants' houses to its famous herring smokehouses, is what makes **Monnickendam** special. Music-lovers will want to close their ears, but fans of cutesy decorative stuff may like the music boxes at the **Stuttenburgh** fish restaurant (Haringburgwal 3-4, 0299 651869), and there's a fine antique carillon on the bell-tower of the old town hall.

Such was **Volendam**'s runaway success as a fishing village that it's said the town flag was flown at half-mast when the Zuider Zee was enclosed in 1932, cutting off access to the sea. The village's enterprise was soon applied to devising a theme park from its fascinating historic features, but, sadly, the cheerily garbed locals can barely be seen for the coachloads of tourists that are dumped there every day.

**De Zaanse Schans** is not your typical museum village. The difference? People live in it. One of the world's first industrial zones, the small Zaan district was once crowded with 800 windmills that powered the manufacture of paint, flour and lumber. Today, amid the gabled green and white houses, attractions include an old-fashioned Albert Heijn store.

### Marker Museum
*Kerkbuurt 44-7, Marken (0299 601904).* **Open** *Apr-Oct* 10am-5pm Mon-Sat; noon-4pm Sun. Closed Nov-Mar. **Admission** €2; 75¢ under-12s.

### De Zaanse Schans
*Information from Zaandam VVV; see p257 (www.zaanseschans.nl).* **Open** times vary, generally: *Museums* 10am-5pm Tue-Sun. *Shops & windmills* 9am-5pm Tue-Sun. **Admission** free-€10; free-€4 under-13s.

## Getting there

### Broek in Waterland
*By car* 10km (6 miles) north-east. *By bus* 110, 111, 114 or 116 from Amsterdam Centraal Station.

## Marken
*By car* 20km (12 miles) north-east. *By bus* 111 from Amsterdam Centraal Station to Marken, or 110, 114 or 116 to Monnickendam, then boat to Marken.

## Monnickendam
*By car* 15km (9 miles) north-east. *By bus* 110, 114 or 116 from Amsterdam Centraal Station.

## Volendam
*By car* 20km (12 miles) north-east. *By bus* 110 from Amsterdam Centraal Station.

## De Zaanse Schans
*By car* 15km (9 miles) north-west. *By train* to Koog-Zaandijk. *By bus* 89 from Marnixstraat.

## Tourist information

### Monnickendam VVV
*Nieuwpoortslaan 15, Monnickendam (0299 651998).* **Open** 9am-5pm Mon-Fri; 10am-5pm Sat.

### Volendam VVV
*Zeestraat 37, Volendam (0299 363747/www.vvv-volendam.nl).* **Open** *Mid Mar-Oct* 10am-5pm daily. *Nov-mid Mar* 10am-3pm Mon-Sat.

### Zaandam VVV
*Gedempte Gracht 76, Zaandam (075 616 2221).* **Open** 9am-5.30pm Mon-Fri; 9am-4pm Sat.

## West Friesland

West Friesland faces Friesland across the northern IJsselmeer. Despite being a part of Noord Holland for centuries, it has its own customs, and fewer visitors than its near-neighbour. One scenic way to get there is to take a train to Enkhuizen, then a boat to Medemblik. From here, take the **Museumstoomtram** ('Steam Railway Museum') to Hoorn.

The once-powerful fishing and whaling port of **Enkhuizen** has many relics of its past, but most people come here for the remarkable **Zuider Zee Museum**. Wander either the indoor Binnenmuseum, which has exhibits on seven centuries of seafaring life around the IJsselmeer, or the open-air Buitenmuseum, a reconstructed village of authentic late 19th- and early 20th-century buildings transplanted from towns around the Zuider Zee.

The Gothic Bonifaciuskerk and Kasteel Radboud dominate **Medemblik**, a port dating from the early Middle Ages. The 13th-century castle is smaller than when it defended Floris V's realm, but retains its knights' hall and towers. Glassblowers and leatherworkers show off their skills at the Saturday market in July and August. Nearby is the 'long village' of Twisk, with its pyramid-roofed farm buildings, and the circular village of Opperdoes, built on a mound.

# Floral calendar

## Spring
The flower trade's year kicks off in mid- to late February with the indoor **Westfriese Flora** (0228 511644) at Bovenkarspel, near Enkhuizen. From late March to late May, the bulb district from Den Helder to Den Haag is carpeted with blooms of the principal crops: daffodils, crocuses, gladioli, hyacinths, narcissi and – of course – tulips.

The **Noordwijk-Haarlem Flower Parade** (0252 434710) is held on the first Saturday after 19 April, departing Noordwijk at 10am and arriving in Haarlem (via Sassenheim) at 7pm. The florid floats are on show in Lisse and Hobahohallen for two days prior to the parade.

## Summer
In mid- to late May, golden fields of rapeseed brighten Flevoland, Friesland and Groningen. In The Hague, the Japanese Garden at **Clingendael Gardens** is in full flower from early May to mid-June, while the rose garden in Westbroek Park (which contains 350 varieties) bursts into colour during July and August.

In late June, there's the Floralia exhibition at the Zuider Zee Museum in **Enkhuizen**. And on the first weekend in August, it's the **Rijnsburg Parade** (071 409 4444). The floats leave Rijnsburg at 11am on Saturday, reach Leiden at 1pm and journey to Nordwijk by 4pm, where they show at the Boulevard that evening and the next day.

## Autumn
Heather purples the landscape – especially in **Veluwe**, in the province of Gelderland – during August and September, when greenhouse flowers also emerge. The **Bloemen Corso** (0297 325100), Europe's biggest flower parade, winds from Aalsmeer to Amsterdam and back on the first Saturday in September, with float viewing taking place the day before and after the parade in Aalsmeer.

## Winter
In November, the public and florists from all over the world view new varieties at the Professional Flower Exhibition at **Aalsmeer Flower Auction**. At Christmas, there's the Kerstflora show at Hillegom near Lisse.

**Trips Out of Town**

The pretty port of **Hoorn**, which dates from around 1310, grew rich on the Dutch East Indies trade; its success is reflected in its grand and ancient architecture. Local costumes and crafts can be seen at the weekly historic market, Hartje Hoorn (10am-5pm Wednesdays in July and August only), and the **Museum van de Twintigste Eeuw** ('Museum of the 20th Century'), while hardly living up to its unsuitably grand name, does have plenty of interest in its permanent exhibit. The Statencollege (council building), built in 1632, houses the **Westfries Museum**, which focuses on art, decor and the region's past.

### Museum van de Twintigste Eeuw
*Bierkade 4, Hoorn (0229 214001/ www.museumhoorn.nl).* **Open** 10am-5pm Tue-Sun. **Admission** €2; €1.50 concessions.

### Museumstoomtram Hoorn-Medemblik
*Hoorn-Medemblik; tickets behind the station at Van Dedemstraat 8, Hoorn (0229 214862/ www.museumstoomtram.nl), or* **Hoorn VVV** *below.* **Admission** €6.50-€11.

### Westfries Museum
*Rode Steen 1, Hoorn (0229 280028/www.wfm.nl).* **Open** 11am-5pm Mon-Fri; 2-5pm Sat, Sun. **Admission** €2.50; €1 concessions; free MJK.

### Zuider Zee Museum
*Wierdijk 12-22, Enkhuizen (0228 351111/ www.zuiderzeemuseum.nl).* **Open** *Apr-Jun, Sept, Oct* 10am-5pm Mon-Sat, 10am-6pm Sun; *July, Aug* 10am-6pm daily; *Nov-Mar* 10am-5pm daily. **Admission** €4; €2.50 concessions.

## Getting there

### Enkhuizen
*By car* 55km (34 miles) north-east. *By train* direct from Amsterdam Centraal Station.

### Hoorn
*By car* 35km (22 miles) north-east. *By train* direct from Amsterdam Centraal Station.

### Medemblik
*By car* 50km (31 miles) north. *By train* direct from Amsterdam Centraal Station.

## Tourist information

### Enkhuizen VVV
*Tussen Twee Havens 1, Enkhuizen (0228 313164/ www.enkhuizen.nl).* **Open** *Apr-Oct* 9am-5pm daily. *Nov-Mar* 9am-5pm Mon-Fri; 9am-2pm Sat.

### Hoorn VVV
*Veemarkt 4, Hoorn (0229 218343/ www.vvvhoorn.nl).* **Open** *Apr, May* 1-5pm Mon; 9.30am-5pm Tue-Sat; 1-5pm Sun. *June-Aug* 1-6pm Mon; 9.30am-6pm Tue-Fri; 9.30am-5pm Sat; 1-5pm Sun. *Sept-Mar* 1-5pm Mon; 9.30am-5pm Tue-Sat.

### Medemblik VVV
*Dam 2, Medemblik (0227 542852).* **Open** *Apr-Jun, Sept, Oct* 10am-5pm Mon-Sat. *July, Aug* 10am-5pm Mon-Sat; noon-5pm Sun. *Nov-Mar* 10am-noon, 2-4pm Mon-Sat.

# Ancient Castles

What Amsterdam lacks in palaces and castles, the rest of Holland makes up for in spades. The Netherlands is studded with 400 castles, and many fortress towns retain large parts of their defences. Some of the best are in the province of Utrecht, within half an hour of Amsterdam. Almost 100 of the castles are open for tourists or business conferences: the 15th-century **NJHC Slot Assumburg** at Heemskerk, between Haarlem and Alkmaar, is a youth hostel (025 123 2288), while the ultimate power lunch can be had at either **Château Neercanne** in Maastricht (043 325 1359) or **Kasteel Erenstein** in Kerkrade (045 546 1333).

The fairy-tale splendour of **De Haar** is appealing but misleading. While it looks like the quintessential medieval castle, its ornate embellishments are actually relatively recent

**Zuider Zee Museum.** *See p257.*

recreations. In 1892, the baron who inherited the ruins of De Haar (dating from 1391), and his Rothschild wife, recreated the original building on a majestic scale, moving the entire village of Haarzuilens 850 metres (259 feet) to make room for the formal grounds. The lavish interior boasts medieval weaponry, stone carvings, ancient tapestries, Louis XIV-XVI furniture and Far Eastern art, and spectacular stained-glass in the hall. The castle is open by guided tour only.

Many Dutch historical events took place in the legendary **Muiderslot**. This moated castle, situated at the mouth of the River Vecht, was originally built in 1280 for Count Floris V, who was murdered nearby in Muiderberg in 1296. Rebuilt in the 14th century, the fortress has been through many sieges and frequent renovations. The 17th-century furnishings may seem out of context, but they originate from the period of its most illustrious occupant, PC Hooft, who entertained in the castle's splendid halls.

The star-shaped stronghold of **Naarden** is not only moated, but also has arrowhead-shaped bastions, and a very well-preserved fortified town; it was in active service only in 1926. All is explained in the **Vestingmuseum**, located partly underground in the Turfpoortbastion (Peat Gate). The fortifications date from 1675, after the inhabitants were massacred by the Duke of Alva's son in 1572; the slaughter is depicted above the door of the Spaanse Huis (Spanish House), now a conference venue.

Meandering up the River Vecht into **Utrecht**, boat passengers can glimpse some of the plush country homes built in the 17th and 18th centuries by rich Amsterdam merchants. Two of the trips afford close-up views of castles. The first stops on the way back downriver for a one-hour tour of Slot Zuylen, a 16th-century castle that was renovated in 1752. The boat company, **Rondvaartbedrijf Rederij Schuttevaer**, can arrange an English guide in advance. The collection of furniture, tapestries and objets d'art gives insight into the lives of the residents. Another boat drops passengers in the charming town of Loenen, which has the restored castle of Loenersloot; sadly, it's not open to the public.

### De Haar

*Kasteellaan 1, Haarzuilens, Utrecht (030 677 3804/ www.kasteeldehaar.nl).* **Open** *June-Sept* 11am-4pm Mon-Fri; 1-4pm Sat, Sun. *Mid Mar-May, Oct-mid Nov* 1-4pm Tue-Sun. *Jan-mid Mar, late Nov* 1-4pm Sun. *Dec* groups only. *Grounds* 10am-5pm daily. **Admission** *Castle & grounds* €7; €5 5-12s (no under-5s); free MJK. *Grounds only* €2.25; €1.25 5-12s; free MJK, under-5s.

### Muiderslot

*Herengracht 1, Muiden (0294 261325/ www.muiderslot.demon.nl).* **Open** *Apr-Oct* 10am-4pm Mon-Fri; 1-4pm Sat, Sun. *Nov-Mar* 1-3pm Sat, Sun. **Admission** €4.50; €3 concessions; free MJK.

Swim for it… **Muiderslot**.

### Rondvaartbedrijf Rederij Schuttevaer

*Oudegracht, opposite No.85, Utrecht (030 272 0111/ 030 231 9377/www.schuttevaer.com).* **Times** *June-Sept* to Slot Zuylen 10.30am Tue, 11.30am Thur, returning 4pm. *June-Sept* to Loenen 10.30am Wed *(July, Aug* also Fri), returning 6pm. **Tickets** €15-€22; €13-€21 under-13s; reservations mandatory.

### Vestingmuseum Turfpoortbastion

*Westvalstraat 6, Naarden (035 694 5459/ www.vestingmuseum.nl).* **Open** *Mar-Oct* 10.30am-5pm Tue-Fri; noon-5pm Sat, Sun. *Nov-Feb* noon-5pm Sun. **Admission** €4.50; €3 -€4 concessions; free MJK, under-4s.

## Getting there

### De Haar

*By car* 30km (19 miles) south. *By train* Amsterdam Centraal Station to Utrecht, then bus 127.

### Muiderslot

*By car* 12km (7.5 miles) south-east. *By bus* 136 from Amstel Station.

### Naarden

*By car* 20km (12 miles) south-east. *By train* direct from Amsterdam Centraal Station. *By bus* 136 from Amstel Station.

## Tourist information

### Naarden VVV

*Adriaan Dortsmanplein 1B, Naarden (035 694 2836).* **Open** *May-Oct* 10am-5pm Mon-Fri; 10am-3pm Sat; noon-3pm Sun, public holidays. *Nov-Apr* 10am-2pm Mon-Sat.

# City Breaks

The Netherlands has more urban appeal than the bright lights of Amsterdam: check out the Randstad for life on the Edge.

**The Randstad** – or 'Edge City', named for its coastal location on the Netherlands' western edge – is a ring-shaped conurbation bounded by Amsterdam, Delft, Haarlem, the Hague, Leiden, Rotterdam and Utrecht, though in recent years, Gouda (*see p253*) and Dordrecht have come to be considered part of it. Though separately administered and fiercely independent, the individual towns work together by choice for their common good. Surprisingly, it's also one of the most densely populated areas in the world: no less than 40 per cent of the Dutch population inhabit this urban sprawl.

The road, rail and waterway networks are impressive, and the area's economy is strong. The Randstad's importance is based on several factors: Rotterdam's enormous port; Amsterdam's Schiphol Airport and the city's role as financial and banking centre; the seats of government and royalty at the Hague; and a huge agricultural belt.

Regarded with a mix of awe, indifference and resentment from the outlying provinces, the Randstad is often accused of monopolising government attention and funds. However, it has no formally defined status and is still prone to bitter rivalries between cities and municipalities: Amsterdam and Rotterdam in particular, a feud that's only growing sharper as Amsterdam moves towards Disneyfication while Rotterdam grows more individual. The smaller cities in the Randstad can be exploited as peaceful day-trip escapes from the swirling vortex of Amsterdam.

## Delft

Imagine a miniaturised Amsterdam – canals reduced to dinky proportions, bridges narrowed down, merchants' houses shrunken – and you have the essence of Delft. However, though it's small, scoffed at for its seeming sleepiness, Delft is also a student town with social carryings-on if you care to look for them.

Everything you might want to see is in the old centre. As soon as you cross the road from the station towards the city centre, you encounter the first introduction to Delft's past: a modern representation of Vermeer's *Melkmeisje* ('Milkmaid') in stone on the junction of Phoenixstraat and Binnen Watersloot.

Delft, though, is of course most famous for its blue and white tiles and pottery, known as Delft Blue (or internationally as Royal Blue). There are still a few factories open to visitors – among them **De Delftse Pauw** and **De Porceleyne Fles** – but for a historical overview of the industry, head for the **Museum Lambert van Meerten**. The huge range of tiles, depicting everything from battling warships to randy rabbits, contrasts dramatically with today's mass-produced trinkets.

Delft was traditionally a centre for trade, producing and exporting butter, cloth, Delft beer – at one point in the past, almost 200 breweries could be found beside the canals – and, later, pottery. Its loss in trade since has been Rotterdam's gain, but the aesthetic benefits can be seen in the city's centuries-old gables, hump-backed bridges and shady canals. To appreciate how little has changed, walk to the end of Oude Delft, the oldest canal in Delft (it narrowly escaped being drained in the 1920s to become a sunken tram-line), which has some impressive mansions incorporated into its terrace. Cross the busy road to the harbour, for it was on the far side of this canal that Johannes Vermeer (1632-75) stood when painting his famous *View of Delft*, now on display in the Mauritshuis in the Hague (*see p263*).

Delft also has two spectacular churches. The first, the Nieuwe Kerk (the New Church), stands in the Markt (the Market) and contains the mausoleums of lawyer-philosopher Hugo de Groot and William of Orange (alongside his dog, who faithfully followed him to his death by refusing food and water). It took almost 15 years to construct and was finished in 1396. Across the Markt is Hendrick de Keyser's 1620 Stadhuis (or City Hall); De Keyser also designed Prince William's black and white marble mausoleum. Not to be outdone, the town's other splendid house of worship, the Gothic Oude Kerk (c1200), is known as 'Leaning Jan' because its tower stands two metres off-kilter. Art-lovers should note that it's the last resting place of Vermeer.

Museums in Delft have the air of private residences and are pretty much crowd-free. **Het Prinsenhof Municipal Museum**, located in the former convent of St Agatha, holds ancient and modern art exhibitions along with the permanent displays about Prince William of

Orange, who was assassinated in 1584 by one of many who had tried to earn the price put on his head by Philip II of Spain in the midst of Holland's 80-year fight for independence. The bullet holes are still visible on the stairs.

But while the museums are grand, it's fun to simply stroll around town. The historic centre has more than 600 national monuments in and around the preserved merchants' houses. Pick up a walk guide from the VVV and see what the town has to offer: the country's largest military collection at the **Legermuseum** (Army Museum), for example, or western Europe's largest collection of poisonous snakes at the **Reptielenzoo Serpo**. One of the many places that may draw you in is the Oostpoort (East Gate), dating from 1394. And while at the VVV, ask if you can visit the Windmill de Roos and the torture chamber in Het Steen, the 13th-century tower of the historic city hall in the market square. Both will fascinate and enchant.

### De Delftse Pauw

*Delftweg 133 (015 212 4920/www.delftsepauw.com).* **Open** *Apr-Oct* 9am-4.30pm daily. *Nov-Mar* 9am-4.30pm Mon-Fri; 11am-1pm Sat, Sun. **Admission** free. **Credit** AmEx, DC, MC, V.

### Legermuseum

*Korte Geer 1 (015 212 4920/www.legermuseum.nl).* **Open** 10am-5pm Mon-Fri; noon-5pm Sat, Sun. **Admission** €5; €2.50 4-12s; free MJK, under-4s. **Credit** MC, V.

### Museum Lambert van Meerten

*Oude Delft 199 (015 260 2358).* **Open** 10am-5pm Tue-Sat; 1-5pm Sun. **Admission** €2.50; €2 12-18s; free under-12s. **Credit** AmEx, MC, V.

### De Porceleyne Fles

*Rotterdamseweg 196 (015 251 2030/ www.royaldelft.com).* **Open** *Apr-Oct* 9am-5pm Mon-Sat; 9.30am-5pm Sun. *Nov-Mar* 9am-5pm Mon-Sat. **Admission** €2.50. **Credit** AmEx, DC, MC, V.

### Het Prinsenhof Municipal Museum

*Sint Agathaplein 1 (015 260 2358).* **Open** 10am-5pm Tue-Sat; 1-5pm Sun. **Admission** €3.50; €3 12-16s; free under-12s. **Credit** AmEx, MC, V.

### Reptielenzoo Serpo

*Stationsplein 8 (015 212 2184/www.serpo.nl).* **Open** 10am-6pm Mon-Sat; 1-6pm Sun. **Admission** €5; €3 4-12s; free under-4s. **Credit** MC, V.

## Where to eat & drink

Though many bars and cafés may appear to outsiders as survivors of a bygone era – white-aproned waiters and high-ceilinged interiors – it's the norm in Delft. Other cities offer hot chocolate finished with whipped cream; cafés here use real cream and accompany it with a fancier brand of biscuit.

Don't miss local institution **Kleyweg's Stads Koffyhuis** (Oude Delft 133, 015 212 4625), which has a terrace barge in the summer and serves Knollaert beer, a local brew made to a medieval recipe. **De Wijnhaven** (Wijnhaven 22; 015 214 1460) and **The V** (Voorstraat 9; 015 214 0916) provide delicious meals at nice prices.

## Where to stay

**De Ark** (Koornmarkt 65; 015 215 7999, www.deark.nl) is upmarket, with rooms priced from €93 to €117. **De Plataan** (Doelenplein 10; 015 212 6046/www.hoteldeplataan.nl) is more reasonable, costing €68 for a single, €80 for a double. Budget travellers should try the campsite at **Delftse Hout** (Korftlaan 5; 015 213 0040), where a site for two costs €22. During the colder weather, try **De Kok** (Houttuinen 14; 015 212 2125), where singles cost €66-€86, and doubles go for €71-€115.

## Getting there

### By car

60km (37 miles) south-west on A4, then A13.

### By train

1hr from Amsterdam Centraal Station, changing at the Hague if necessary.

## Tourist information

### VVV

*Markt 83-5 (0900 335 3888 premium rate/ www.vvvdelft.nl).* **Open** *Apr-Sept* 9am-5.30pm Mon-Sat; 11am-3pm Sun. *Oct-Mar* 9am-5.30pm Mon-Fri; 9am-5pm Sat.

A night on the tiles in **Delft**.

**Trips Out of Town**

**De Hallen** in Haarlem.

## Haarlem

Lying between Amsterdam and the beaches of Zandvoort and Bloemendaal, Haarlem – a kinder, gentler and older Amsterdam – is a stone's throw from the dunes and the sea, and attracts flocks of beach-going Amsterdammers and Germans every summer. All trace of Haarlem's origins as a 10th-century settlement on a choppy inland sea disappeared with the draining of the Haarlemmermeer in the mid-19th century. But the town hasn't lost its appeal: the historic centre, with its lively main square, canals and some of the country's most charming almshouse courtyards, is beautiful.

To catch up with Haarlem's history, head to **St Bavo's Church**, which dominates the main square. It was built around 1313 but suffered fire damage in 1328; rebuilding and expansion lasted another 150 years. It's surprisingly bright inside: cavernous white transepts stand as high as the nave and make for a stunning sight. The floor is made up of 1,350 graves, including one featuring only the word 'Me' and another long enough to hold a famed local giant, plus a dedication to a local midget who died of injuries from a game he himself invented: dwarf-tossing. Music buffs will swoon at the sight of the famed Müller organ (1738): boasting an amazing 5,068 pipes, it's been played by both Handel and the young Mozart.

Haarlem's cosy but spacious Grote Markt is one of the loveliest squares in the Netherlands. A few blocks away is the former old men's almshouse and orphanage that currently houses

the **Frans Halsmuseum**. Though it holds a magnificent collection of 16th- and 17th-century portraits, still lifes, genre paintings and landscapes, the highlights are eight group portraits of militia companies and regents by Frans Hals (who's buried in St Bavo's). The museum also has collections of period furniture, Haarlem silver and ceramics and an 18th-century apothecary with Delftware pottery. Nearby is **De Hallen**, whose two buildings, the Verweyhal and the Vleeshal, house modern art.

Though it's rather in the shadow of the Frans Halsmuseum, the **Teylers Museum** is equally excellent. Founded in 1784, it's the country's oldest museum; fossils and minerals sit by antique scientific instruments, while there's also a superb collection of 10,000 drawings by 16th- to 19th-century masters including Rembrandt, Michelangelo and Raphael. However, Haarlem is more than just a city of nostalgia: it's one of vision. Local illustrator/cartoonist Joost Swarte, for example, has spread his wings and designed the Tonelschuur Theatre in the town.

### Frans Halsmuseum

*Groot Heiligland 62 (023 511 5775).* **Open** 11am-5pm Mon-Sat; 1-5pm Sun. **Admission** €5; €3.50 over-65s; free under-19s. *Combination ticket with De Hallen* €6; free MJK, under-19s. **No credit cards**.

### De Hallen

*Grote Markt 16 (023 511 5840).* **Open** 11am-5pm Mon-Sat; noon-5pm Sun. **Admission** €3.50; €2.50 over-65s; free MJK, under-19s. *Combination ticket with Frans Halsmuseum* €6; free MJK, under-19s. **No credit cards**.

### Teylers Museum

*Spaarne 16 (023 531 9010).* **Open** 10am-5pm Tue-Sat; noon-5pm Sun. **Admission** €5.50; €1.50 5-18s; free MJK, under-5s. **No credit cards**.

## Where to eat & drink

If you have money to burn, don't miss French-inspired **De Componist** (Korte Veerstraat 1; 023 532 8853), located in a refurbished art nouveau warehouse. The pick of the many spots on Groot Markt is the **Loft** (Grote Markt 8; 023 551 1350). Cosier is **Jacobus Pieck Drink & Eetlokaal** (Warmoesstraat 18; 023 532 6144), while the riverside **Eclectic Bar Restaurant Willendorf** (Bakenessergracht 109; 023 531 1970/www.willendorf.nl) is a hip space with regular DJs. If you're into wooden panelling, leather wallpaper, chaotic conviviality and infinite beer choices, head to In **Den Uiver** (Riviervismarkt 13, 023 532 5399). Finally, you'll find bands and/or DJs at the **Patronaat** (Zijlsingel 2; 023 532 6010/www.patronaat.nl), Haarlem's answer to Amsterdam's Melkweg.

## Where to stay

The beautiful **Carlton Square Hotel** (Baan 7; 023 531 9091/www.carlton.nl) is posh and pricey, with rooms from €192. For a real splurge, however, book one of the two mind-blowingly sumptuous suites – one at €290, the other €350 – at design hotel **Spaarne 8** (Spaarne 8; 023 551 1544/www.spaarne8.com). The **Carillon** (Grote Markt 27; 023 531 0591/www.hotelcarillon.com) has doubles for €53, while outside the centre, the **NJHC Hostel Jan Gijzen** (Jan Gijzenpad 3; 023 537 3793/www.njhc.org) offers B&B from €18.

## Getting there

### By car
10km (6 miles) west on A5.

### By train
15min, direct from Amsterdam Centraal Station.

## Tourist information

### VVV
*Stationsplein 1 (0900 616 1600 premium rate).*
**Open** *Summer* 9.30am-5.30pm Mon-Fri; 10am-2pm Sat; 10am-4pm Sun. *Winter* 9.30am-5.30pm Mon-Fri; 10am-2pm Sat.

## The Hague

While never officially a city – in days of yore, powers-that-be did not want to offend its more ancient neighbours, Leiden and Utrecht – the Hague (aka Den Haag) is the nation's power hub and centre for international justice. It began life as the hunting ground of the Counts of Holland before being officially founded in 1248 when William II built a castle on the site of the present parliament buildings, the **Binnenhof**. It was here that the De Witt brothers were lynched after being accused of conspiring to kill William of Orange; they were brutalised nearby in what is now the most evocatively gross torture museum in the country: **Gevangenpoort**.

Queen Beatrix arrives at the Binnenhof in a golden coach every Prinsjesdag (third Tuesday in September) for the annual state opening of parliament. Guided tours are organised daily to the Knights' Hall, where the ceremony takes place. The **Mauritshuis**, a former regal home, is open to the public with one of the most famous collections in the world: works by the likes of Rubens, Rembrandt and Vermeer.

The Hague's city centre is lively, with a good selection of shops lining the streets and squares around the palaces and along the lovely and more upmarket Denneweg. Architects have

Losing your religion? **St Bavo's Church** may help you get it back. *See p262.*

Trips Out of Town

Gone fishin': **Scheveningen**.

worked to bring the city into a bigger and brighter cultural sphere – with mixed success – yet the Hague is also one of the greenest cities in Europe, and has a number of lovely parks. Clingendael has a Japanese garden; Meijendael, further out, is part of an ancient forest; and the Scheveningse Bosje is big enough to occupy an entire day. Between the Bosje and the city is Vredes Paleis (the Peace Palace), a gift from Andrew Carnegie that is now the UN's Court of International Justice and will be the setting for Milosevic's sulky theatrics for years to come.

Beyond Scheveningse Bosje is Scheveningen, a former fishing village and now a huge resort. The architectural highlight is the Steigenberger Kurhaus Hotel: built in 1887, it's a legacy of Scheveningen's days as a bathing place for European high society. The town's history as a spa has been resurrected with the opening of Kuur Thermen Vitalizee (Strandweg 13F; 070 416 6500/www.vitalizee.nl), a spa bath that offers a range of treatments. Also here is the 'Sculptures by the Sea' exhibition, a multi-dimensional collection of statues at the **Museum Beelden aan Zee**. The renovated **Panorama Mesdag** houses not only the largest painting in the country – from which it takes its name – but also works from the Hague (marine style) and Barbizon (peasant life and landscape) schools.

None, though, is worth as much as *Victory Boogie Woogie*, Piet Mondriaan's last work, which went for a cool ƒ80 million (€36 million) in 1998. It's now at the **Gemeentemuseum**, which holds the world's largest collections of works by Mondriaan and MC Escher in newly restored buildings. The Gemeentemuseum is linked to the Museon, an excellent science museum that induces wonder in both kids and adults, and the Omniversum IMAX Theatre, a state-of-the-art planetarium, while Gemeente's sister museum, **Het Paleis** on the Lange Voorhout, has special temporary exhibitions and, during the summer only, a fine selection of 20th-century sculptures along the tree-lined avenue out front. One way of exploring Holland speedily is by visiting **Madurodam**, an insanely detailed miniature city that every Dutch cliché in the book. Windmills turn, ships sail and modern trains speed around on the world's largest model railway.

The Hague offers a decent calendar of events, the most entertaining of which is Queen's Day on 30 April (though it's not as wild as Amsterdam's celebrations). The North Sea Regatta is held at the end of May, falling in the middle of the International Sand Sculpture Festival (early May to early June). Add to this the Hague Horse Days, equestrian displays held in the Lange Voorhout (late May), Parkpop, Europe's largest free pop festival (June), and the mammoth North Sea Jazz Festival (July), and the old cliché about there being something for everyone rears its ugly but relevant head.

### Binnenhof

*Binnenhof 8 (070 364 6144).* **Open** 10am-3.45pm Mon-Sat. **Admission** €5; €4 under-13s. **No credit cards.**

### Gemeentemuseum

*Stadhouderslaan 41 (070 338 1111/ www.gemeentemuseum.nl).* **Open** 11am-5pm Tue-Sun. **Admission** €7; €2.50 13-18s; free MJK, under-13s. **No credit cards.**

### Gevangenpoort Museum

*Buitenhof 33 (070 346 0861/www.gevangenpoort.nl).* **Open** 11am-5pm Tue-Fri, noon-5pm Sat-Sun. **Admission** €4; €3 under-12s. **No credit cards**.

### Madurodam

*George Maduroplein 1 (070 355 3900/ www.madurodam.nl).* **Open** *Mid Mar-June* 9am-8pm daily. *July, Aug* 9am-10pm daily. *Sept-mid Mar* 9am-6pm daily. **Admission** €10; €9.50 over-60s; €7 4-11s; free under-4s. **No credit cards**.

### Mauritshuis

*Korte Vijverberg 8 (070 302 3456/ www.mauritshuis.nl).* **Open** 10am-5pm Tue-Sat; 11am-5pm Sun. **Admission** €7; free MJK, under-18s. **No credit cards.**

### Museum Beelden aan Zee
*Harteveltstraat 1 (070 358 5857/*
*www.beeldenaanzee.nl).* **Open** 11am-5pm
Tue-Sun. **Admission** €4; €2.50 5-12s; free
under-5s. **No credit cards.**

### Het Paleis Museum
*Lange Voorhout 74 (070 362 4061/*
*www.gemeentemuseum.nl).* **Open** 11am-5pm
Tue-Sun. **Admission** €6; €5 over-65s; free MJK,
under-18s. **No credit cards.**

### Panorama Mesdag
*Zeestraat 65 (070 310 6665/www.mesdag.nl).*
**Open** 10am-5pm Mon-Sat; noon-5pm Sun.
**Admission** €4; €3 over-65s; €2 4-13s; free
under-4s. **No credit cards.**

The **Binnenhof** in the Hague. *See p263.*

## Where to eat & drink

**Juliana's** (Plaats 11; 070 365 0235) is where
the beautiful people enjoy lunch and dinner,
whereas **De Klap** (Koningin Emmakade
118A; 070 345 4060) is a more down-to-earth
café with cheap meals. For inspired Indonesian
cuisine in a swish setting, try **Surakarta
Indonesische Brasserie** (Prinsestraat 13;

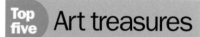

## Top five Art treasures

### Johannes Vermeer, *View of Delft* (c1660)
Transplanted to the Hague's excellent
**Mauritshuis** museum (*see p263*).

### Rembrandt van Rijn, *Palamedes before Agamemnon* (1626)
The only Rembrandt still in his hometown
of Leiden, at the **Stedelijk Museum de
Lakenhal** (*see p266*).

### Hieronymus Bosch, *The Prodigal Son* (c1510)
On permanent display at the **Museum
Boijmans-Van Beuningen** in Rotterdam
(*see p267*).

### Frans Hals, *Banquet of the Officers of the Civic Guard of St Adrian* (1623)
Now to be found at – where else? – the
**Frans Halsmuseum** in Haarlem (*see p262*).

### Marlene Dumas, *Brides of Dracula* (1997)
This striking Dumas can be seen at the
glorious **Centraal Museum** in Utrecht
(*see p271*).

070 346 6999/www.surakarta.nl). In the
remarkably atmospheric catacombs under
the old City Hall, **Catacomben** (Grote
Halstraat 3; 070 302 3060) offers reasonably
priced Caribbean, French, Asian and Middle
Eastern eats.

Beer fans should try **De Paas** (Dunne
Bierkade 16A; 070 365 2633/www.depaas.nl),
while the living-room feel and occasional jazz
at **Murphy's Law** (Dr Kuyperstraat; 070 427
2507) attracts an odd but friendly mixture of
vaguely alternative folk and drunk diplomats.
**De Zwart Ruiter** (Grote Markt 27; 070 364
9549), a revamped brown café with stylish
decor, is located next door to the more grubby
and down-at-heel **September** (Grote Markt
26; 070 362 3862); regulars at both often head
on to **Jetlag** (Kettingstraat 12B; www.jetlag-
lounge.nl) for dancing. Coffeeshop connoisseurs
should try **Cremers** (Prinsestraat 84; 070 346
2346), which attracts a diverse crowd with its
fully stocked bar (complete with absinthe).

## Where to stay

**Des Indes InterContinental** (Lange Voorhout
54-6; 070 361 2345/www.desindes.com) is
arguably the most luxurious hotel in town,
with prices to match its facilities: singles cost
€230, doubles €295. The **NJHC City Hostel
Den Haag** (Scheepmakersstraat 27; 070 315
7878/www.njhc.org/english/denhaag) charges
€18 to €27 per person, plus €2.50 extra if you
are not a member .

## Getting there

### By car
50km (31 miles) south-west on A4, then A44.

### By train
50min from Amsterdam Centraal Station to Den
Haag Centraal Station; change at Leiden if necessary.

**Trips Out of Town**

A small country is rendered even tinier at **Madurodam**. *See p264.*

## Tourist information

### VVV

*Koningin Julianaplein 30, outside Centraal Station
(0900 340 3505 premium rate/www.denhaag.com).*
**Open** *July-Aug* 9am-5.30pm Mon-Fri; 10am-5pm Sat;
11am-3pm Sun. *Sept-June* 9am-5.30pm Mon-Fri;
10am-5pm Sat.

## Leiden

Canal-laced Leiden derives a good deal of its
charm from the Netherlands' oldest university,
which was founded here in 1575 and which
boasts alumni such as Descartes, US president
John Quincy Adams and many a Dutch royal.
The old town teems with bikes and bars, boasts
the most historic monuments per square metre
in the country, and is, accordingly, a rewarding
place for a stroll and a short weekend away
from the relative madness of Amsterdam.

In the Dutch Golden Age of the late 16th and
17th centuries, Leiden grew fat on the textile
trade. It also spawned three great painters of
the time: Rembrandt, Jan van Goyen and Jan
Steen. Although few works by these three
masters remain on display in Leiden today,
the **Stedelijk Museum de Lakenhal**
(Lakenhal Municipal Museum), where the
Golden Age clothmakers met, does have a
Rembrandt, as well as other Old Masters
and collections of pewter, tiles, silver and
glass. Perhaps Leiden's most notable museum,
though, is the **Rijksmuseum van Oudheden**
(National Museum of Antiquities), which houses
the largest archaeological collection in the
Netherlands: the Egyptian mummy collection
should not be missed. The **Rijksmuseum
voor Volkenkunde** (National Museum of

Ethnology), meanwhile, showcases the
cultures of Africa, Oceania, Asia, the
Americas and the Arctic.

The ten million fossils, minerals and
stuffed animals exhibited at the **Naturalis**
(Natural History Museum) make it the country's
largest museum collection, while the **Hortus
Botanicus**, one of the world's oldest botanical
gardens, is worth a visit: its 6,000 species
include descendants of the country's first
tulips. If Dutch clichés are your schtick, head
to the **Molenmuseum de Valk** (the Falcon
Windmill Museum), a windmill-turned-museum
where you can see living quarters, machinery
and a picturesque view of Leiden. An even
better view can be had from the top of the
Burcht, a 12th-century fort on an ancient
artificial mound in the city centre.

### Hortus Botanicus Leiden

*Rapenburg 73 (071 527 7249/www.hortus.leiden.nl).*
**Open** *Summer* 10am-6pm daily. *Winter* 10am-4pm
Mon-Fri, Sun. **Admission** €4; €2 concessions; free
MJK. **Credit** AmEx, MC, V.

### Molenmuseum de Valk

*2e Binnenvestgracht 1 (071 516
5353/www.molenmuseum.nl).* **Open** 10am-5pm
Tue-Sat; 1-5pm Sun. **Admission** €2.50; €1.50
concessions; free MJK, under-6s. **No credit cards.**

### Naturalis, Nationaal
Natuurhistorisch Museum

*Darwinweg (071 568 7600).* **Open** noon-6pm Tue-
Sun. **Admission** €7.50; €4.75 4-12s; free under-3s.
**No credit cards.**

### Rijksmuseum van Oudheden

*Rapenburg 28 (071 516 3163/www.rmo.nl).*
**Open** 10am-5pm Tue-Fri; noon-5pm Sat, Sun.
**Admission** €6; €5.50 6-18s; €5 over-65s; free
MJK. **Credit** AmEx, DC, MC, V.

### Rijksmuseum voor Volkenkunde
*Steenstraat 1 (071 516 8800).* **Open** 10am-5pm
Tue-Sun. **Admission** €6.50; €3.50 concessions;
free MJK. **No credit cards.**

### Stedelijk Museum de Lakenhal
*Oude Singel 28-32 (071 516 5360/www.lakenhal.nl).*
**Open** 10am-5pm Tue-Fri; noon-5pm Sat, Sun.
**Admission** €4; €2.50 over-65s; free MJK, under-18s.
**No credit cards.**

## Where to eat & drink

A trad cosy atmosphere is to be had at **De
Hooykist** (Hooigracht 49; 071 512 5809) and
**In Den Bierbengel** (Langebrug 71; 071 514
8056), which specialises in meat, fish and wines.
Bar-restaurant **Annie's Verjaardag**
(Hoogstraat 1A; 071 512 5737) occupies eight
candlelit cellars underneath a bridge in the
centre of town: its main selling point is the
canal barge terrace. For something ultra-cheap
and cheerful, try **La Bota** (Herensteeg 9; 071
514 6340) near the Pieterskerk. It's really a fun
studenty bar that does home-style meat and
veggie dishes, salads and snacks for around €7.

For a walk on the grungey side, try another
student standby, **WW** (Wolsteeg 4-6; 071 512
5900/www.deww.nl), which has dartboards and
graffiti. The **Duke** (Oude Singel 2; 071 512
1972) offers live jazz, and **LVC** (Breestraat 66;
071 566 1059/www.lvc.nl) hosts smaller touring
acts. Traditional bars are dotted along Nieuwe
Beestenmarkt, Nieuwstraat and Breestraat.

## Where to stay

The **Golden Tulip** (Schipholweg 3; 071
522 1121/www.goldentulip.nl) is the town's
poshest hotel, with rooms from €80 to €170.
Cheaper is the **Mayflower** (Beestenmarkt 2;
071 514 2641), where rooms are €85-€110,
while the **Pension De Witte Singel** (Witte
Singel 80; 071 512 4592) is cheaper still, at
€46-€58 for a double.

## Getting there

### By car
40km (24 miles) south-west on A4.

### By train
35min from Amsterdam Centraal Station, direct.

## Tourist information

### VVV
*Stationsweg 2D (0900 222 2333 premium rate).*
**Open** *Summer* 9.30am-6pm Mon-Fri; 10am-4.30pm
Sat; 11am-3pm Sun. *Winter* 9.30am-6pm Mon-Fri;
10am-4.30pm Sat.

## Rotterdam

A skate city, a harbour city; a multicultural
fusion, an artists' haven; hometown to
humanism, an architectural inspiration; the
2001 Cultural Capital of Europe, a historical
museum centre, a jazz-lover's dream…
There's no pinning Rotterdam down.

There's a case to be made that Rotterdam
is the Netherlands' only real city, but you
shouldn't mention that to an Amsterdammer.
Neither should you hint at the possibility that
within a decade Rotterdam may surpass the
'Dam in pure happeningness. This 'Manhattan
on the Maas' had a clean slate to play with after
its almost complete destruction in World War II
and has recently managed to fill in the massive
and long-standing gaps in both its urban and
cultural landscape. Rotterdam is a city to watch,
so head to the VVV for a complete overview of
its offerings, including excellent architectural,
harbour and industry tours.

The imposing, futuristic skyline along the
banks of the River Maas is certainly a success
story with the Oude Haven (Old Harbour) now
a work of imaginative modernism, the pinnacle
of which is Piet Blom's witty **Kijk-Kubus**.
These bright yellow cubic houses are tilted
cater-corner and stand, a little goofily, on
stilts. Of the houses, No.70 is open to visitors.
Across the epic bridge **Erasmusbrug** (named
after famous local boy, the humanist Erasmus)
the renovation of the old harbour districts
of Kop van Zuid and Entrepot is nearing
completion. Don't miss the cutting-edge
multimedia art on display in the Los Palmas
warehouse complex (010 402 2001).

Across town, architectural wizard Rem
Koolhaas designed Rotterdam's cultural heart,
the Museum Park, where you'll find outdoor
sculptures and five museums. The three best
are the **Netherlands Architecture
Institute**, which gives an overview of the
history and development of architecture,
especially in Rotterdam; the **Museum
Boijmans-Van Beuningen**, with a
beautiful collection of traditional and
contemporary art (including works by
Van Eyck and Rembrandt) and a sizeable
design collection; and the **Kunsthal**, which
deals with art, design and photography of a
more modern persuasion. The enjoining street
Witte de Withstraat has many smaller but
no less cutting-edge galleries along with
some excellent restaurants and bars. A bird's
eye view of all the modern development can
be had from the nearby **Euromast**, if you
can handle the height (185 metres, or 607 feet).
The park at its base is where many locals
hang out when the weather holds up.

**Trips Out of Town**

Rotterdam's **Erasmusbrug**. *See p267.*

# Beyond Holland

The country's attractions don't begin and end with the province of Holland and the cities of the Randstad. The other provinces offer a variety of attractions that provide a cultural education for those looking to explore the Netherlands beyond all the usual stops.

## Drenthe

Fens, moors and forests highlight this historical province: humans have lived here for some 50,000 years. The **Drents Museum** in Assen (Brink 1, Assen; 0592 312741) offers a glimpse of the area's past with its terrific prehistoric artefacts; while those bored of Rembrandts will treasure the **Museum of Fake Art** (Brink 1, Vledder, Westerveld Drenthe; 052 138 3352/www.museums-vledder.nl).

For information on attractions in Drenthe, call the **Provincial VVV** (0592 373755) or visit the **Assen VVV** (Brink 42, Assen; 0592 314324).

## Friesland

Once an independent tribal nation located along the coast from North Holland to East Germany, Friesland's main attraction is its network of waterways; boating is now focused around the town of **Sneek**. To the north and west of Friesland are the desolate **Frisian Islands** with nature and bird reserves.

The **Provincial VVV** is at Stationsplein 1 in Leeuwarden (0900 202 4060 premium rate). The **Sneek VVV** can be found at Markstraat 18

(0515 414096). For information on the Frisian Islands, visit the **Texel VVV** at Emmelaan 66 on the island of Texel (0222 312847).

## Gelderland

The largest of the Dutch provinces, Gelderland is dominated by the **Veluwe**, a massive stretch of forest and moorland. It's here you'll find the country's biggest national park, the **Hoge Veluwe** (entrances at Otterlo, Schaarsbergen and Hoenderloo, visitors' centre 0318 591627), and the terrific **Rijksmuseum Kröller-Müller** (just near Otterlo entrance of Hoge Veluwe; 0318 591041).

The **Provincial VVV** can be reached on 026 333 2033, and offers full information on the area's attractions.

## Groningen

Arguably the most staid and conservative of the Dutch provinces, Groningen does sport a studenty and scenic-y capital with the epic church **Martinikerk**, a notorious nightlife and a globally statured modern art gallery. Towns such as **Garmerwold**, **Ten Boer**, **Stedum**, **Appingedam** and **Uithuizen** have ancient and wonderful rural churches.

The **Provincial VVV** and the **Groningen VVV** are located in the same building at Gedempte Kattendiep 6 in Groningen (0900 202 3050 premium rate).

The **Historical Museum de Dubbelde Palmboom** (Double Palm Tree) is housed in an old granary in Delfshaven, and features life and work in the Meuse delta from 8000 BC to the present. As part of the Rotterdam City Museum, it's also linked to **Het Schielandshuis**, a 17th-century palatial mansion and another of the few buildings spared in the bombing. Now placed in bizarre juxtaposition to Quist's Robeco Tower built in 1992 and the giant Hollandse Bank Unie, it displays rooms and clothing from the 18th century to the present. Old world charm also abounds at the neighbouring village of Schiedam (VVV 010 473 3000), which sports both the world's tallest windmill and the planet's largest collection of Dutch gins and liqueurs in the tasting house of its museum.

One of the shopping areas, Beurstraverse, is a modern development itself; it has the usual bright international chains along with the Bijenkorf department store. At the base of the oval World Trade Center on Coolsingel is the Koopgoot – 'the buying gutter', as it was dubbed by the playful local tongue – which was the country's first underground shopping mall. Nieuwe Binnenweg is a shopping paradise for clubbers, Van Oldenbarneveltstraat offers more upmarket fare, and Jan Evertsenplaats is a green square where you can take a rest from all that spending.

One can perhaps best experience Rotterdam as the only city in the Netherlands that is experiencing a growth in youth population by renting inline skates or roller-skates and trying out the largest outdoor skate park in the country on West-Blank; get your skates on at Rotterdam Sport Import (Witte de Withstraat 57; 010 461 0066). Where Amsterdam has bikes, Rotterdam seems to prefer smaller wheels.

If you're a backpacker, take advantage of Use-it (Conradstraat 2; 010 240 9158/ www.jip.org/use-it), located outside the station on an island surrounded by Eurolines bus bays.

## Limburg

Limburg is arguably most notable – besides, of course, for their frolicsome Carnival celebrations – for the town of **Maastricht**, a lovely spot to explore quite aside from its European political ties. The **Maastricht VVV** is at Kleine Straat 1 (043 325 2121), while the **Provincial VVV** can be found at Kerkstraat 31 in Valkenburg (043 601 7321).

## Noord Brabant

Bordering Belgium to the south, Noord Brabant's main attractions are the **Safaripark Beekse Bergen** in Hilvarenbeek (0900 233 5732 premium rate) and **De Efteling Theme Park** in Kaatsheuvel (0416 288111). However, it's also home to the city of **Eindhoven**, which offers a fine football team (PSV) and an even better modern art museum (the **Stedelijk van Abbemuseum**, Vonderweg 1; 040 275 5275).

The **Provincial VVV** can be found in the town of Tilburg (Stadhuisplein 128; 013 535 1135); the **Eindhoven VVV** is at Stationsplein 17 (0900 112 2363 premium rate).

## Overijssel

Known as the 'Garden of the Netherlands', Overijssel is criss-crossed by long, winding rivers and 400 kilometres (249 miles) of canoe routes. Among its attractions are the **Hellendoorn Adventure Park** (0548 655555), the splendid modern art museum, the **Rijksmuseum Twenthe** in Enschede (Lasondersingel 129-31; 053 435 8675) and the summer carnivals that are held in almost every town in the province.

For more information, contact the **Enschede VVV** (Oude Markt 31; 053 432 3200) or the **Provincial VVV** (0546 535535).

## Utrecht

Utrecht's main attractions – the province's capital (*see p271*) and the assorted castles (*see p259*) – have been covered elsewhere in this chapter. The beautiful medieval town of **Amersfoort** is also worth a look; its **VVV** can be found at Stationsplein 9-11 (0900 112 2364 premium rate).

## Zeeland

Many old buildings and farms in Zeeland were swept away in the floods of 1953. As a result, the province is now home to the Delta Works, the world's biggest flood barrier that was completed in 1986 at a cost of ƒ14 billion (€6.4 billion). Among the province's less useful but more entertaining attractions are the **Stedelijk Museum** in Vlissingen (Bellamypark 19, 0118 412498) and the historical **Zeeus Museum** in Middelburg (Abdij, 0118 626655). The **Provincial VVV** is at Nieuwe Burg 42 in Middelburg (0118 659965).

Alternative living at
**Kijk-Kubus**. *See p267.*

### Historical Museum de Dubbelde Palmboom
*Voorhaven 12 (010 476 1533/
www.hmr.rotterdam.nl/nl/ddp/ddp.htm).* **Open** 10am-
5pm Tue-Fri; 11am-5pm Sat, Sun. **Admission** €2.70;
€1.35 concessions. **No credit cards.**

### Kunsthal
*Westzeedijk 341 (010 440 0301).* **Open** 10am-5pm
Tue-Sat, 11am-5pm Sun. **Admission** €6; €3.50
concessions. **No credit cards.**

### Kijk-Kubus
*Overblaak 70 (010 414 2285/www.cubehouse.nl).*
**Open** 11am-5pm daily. **Admission** €1.75; €1.25
concessions; free under-4s. **No credit cards.**

### Museum Boijmans-Van Beuningen
*Museumpark 18-20 (010 441 9400).* **Open** 10am-
5pm Tue-Sat; 11am-5pm Sun. **Admission** free-€6;
free-€2 4-16s; free MJK, under-4s. **No credit cards.**

### Netherlands Architecture Institute
*Museumpark 25 (010 440 1200/www.nai.nl).* **Open**
10am-9pm Tue; 10am-5pm Wed-Sat; 11am-5pm Sun.
**Admission** €4; €2 4-16s; free MJK, under-4s. Free
to all 5-9pm Tue. **No credit cards.**

### Het Schielandshuis
*Korte Hoogstraat 31 (010 217
6767/www.hmr.rotterdam.nl).* **Open** 10am-5pm
Tue-Fri; 11am-5pm Sat, Sun. **Admission** €3; €1.50
4-16s; free under-4s. **No credit cards.**

## Where to eat & drink

**Oude Haven**, the **Entrepot** district and
**Delfshaven** all offer a wide choice of (grand)
cafés and restaurants. For veggies, **Bla Bla**
(Piet Heynsplein 35; 010 477 4448) is expensive
but busy, so book ahead. **Foody's** (Nieuwe
Binnenstraat 153; 010 436 5163) is the latest in
fine international eateries; **Colosseo** (Rodezand
36; 010 414 7030) is a fine and cheap purveyor
of Indonesian cuisine; **El Faro Analuz**
(Leuvehaven 73-74; 010 414 6213) serves stellar
Spanish tapas; while the best Chinese in town
can be found by cruising the **Katendrecht**.

Bars-wise, **De Schouw** (Witte de Withstraat
80; 010 412 4253) is a stylish brown café, a
former journalists' haunt that now attracts a
mix of artists and students. Lofty ceilings give
**Café Duodok** (Meent 88; 010 433 3102) an
artsy feel, making it a mellow spot for lunch.
Jazz fiends should try **Dizzy** ('s Gravendijkwal
127; 010 477 3014), one of the best jazz venues
in the country, while for bands and club-nights
venture to **Nighttown** (West-Kruiskade 26-8;
010 436 1210), located on a multicultural road
filled with inexpensive global eating treats.
The cavernous but socially cosy **Now & Wow**
(Lloydstraat 30; 010 477 1074) is regarded as
one of the best dance clubs in Benelux.

Kind of a young person's VVV, it offers a
feast of ideas for stuff to do in the city, as
well as free lockers if you want to ditch your
backpack and take the weight off your
shoulders as you roam around.

Besides the terrific International Film
Festival Rotterdam (www.iffr.com; *see p194*)
that starts at the end of January, it's one
festival after another from the beginning of
June until late September. The summer
carnival, Streetlife, a sporty lifestyle event
for young people, takes place at Blaak in late
June (029 734 444). Don't miss the Dunya
Festival (World Festival), with music, poetry,
stories and street theatre, held at the Park
(near the Euromast) in June. For De Parade
(033 465 4577), the Museumpark is taken over
by a travelling theatre, and on the occasion of
the Fast Forward Dance Parade in mid-August,
almost the entire city becomes one massive
street party.

### Euromast
*Parkhaven 20 (010 436 4811/www.euromast.nl).*
**Admission** €7.50; €5 4-11s. **Open** *Apr-June,
Sept* 10am-7pm daily. *July, Aug* 10am-10.30pm
daily. *Oct-Mar* 10am-5pm daily. **Credit** AmEx,
DC, MC, V.

## Where to stay

Housed in the former Holland-American Line offices, the **Hotel New York** is one of the most luxurious places in town (Koninginnenhoofd 1; 010 439 0500): doubles cost from €90. Wven if you don't stay here, pop in for a coffee or even a full blown plate of *fruits de mer*. One unusual way to spend the night in Rotterdam is on **De Clipper** (Leuvehaven, accessible via Terwenakker; 065 185 7380), a boat moored in the centre of the city. It'll set you back around €25 a night with breakfast. **Hotel Bazar** (Witte de Withstraat 16; 010 206 5151) is a little out of the ordinary, too: it sports an Arabian nights decor and a fine Middle Eastern restaurant. Their prices for a double range from around €75 to €125. For budget travellers, there is the **NJHC City Hostel Rotterdam** (Rochussenstraat 107-9;, 010 436 5763); for €15 a night, you also get the use of a kitchen.

## Getting there

### By car
73km (45 miles) south on A4, then A13.

### By train
1hr from Amsterdam Centraal Station, direct.

## Tourist information

### VVV
*Coolsingel 67 (0900 403 4065 premium rate/ www.vvv.rotterdam.nl).* **Open** *Apr-Sept* 9.30am-6pm Mon-Thur; 9.30am-9pm Fri; 9.30am-5pm Sat; noon-5pm Sun. *Oct-March* 9.30am-6pm Mon-Thur; 9.30am-9pm Fri; 9.30am-5pm Sat.

## Utrecht

One of the oldest cities in the Netherlands, Utrecht was also, in the Middle Ages, its biggest, and was a religious and political centre for centuries. At one point, there were around 40 houses of worship in the city, all with towers and spires. From a distance, Utrecht must have resembled a giant pincushion.

However, there's more to Utrecht than history and scenery. Utrecht University is one of the largest in the Netherlands – continuing to expand and provide work for cutting-edge architects such as Rem Koolhaas (who designed the Educatorium) – and the city centre is bustling with trendy shops and relaxed cafés. Happily, too, the Hoog Catharijne, the country's biggest shopping mall but also one of the biggest eyesores, is soon to be destroyed. But for some time yet, you'll have to wander its labyrinthine layout following signs to 'Centrum' in order to exit Central Station. Lovers of luxury should instead head for the boutiques and galleries tucked down the streets along the canals. Linger especially on Oudkerkhof, where there is a concentration of designer shops; La Vie, the shopping centre on Lange Viestraat; and the flower and plant markets along Janskerkhof and Oudegracht on Saturdays.

Though bikes can be hired from Rijwiel Shop (030 296 7287), the city is so compact that practically everything is within walking distance. A good place to start a stroll around town is the Domtoren (the French gothic-style cathedral tower). At over 112 metres (367 feet), not only is it the highest tower in the country, but with over 50 bells it's also the largest musical instrument in the Netherlands. Visitors are allowed to climb the tower. The panoramic view is worth the effort expended on climbing its 465 steps: vistas stretch 40 kilometres (25 miles) to Amsterdam on a clear day. Buy tickets across the square at the Information Center for the Cultural History of Utrecht (Domplein 9; 030 233 3036) where you can also get details on the rest of the city and the castles located on its outskirts.

The space between the tower and the Domkerk was originally occupied by the nave of the huge church, destroyed in a freak tornado in 1674. Many other buildings were damaged, and the exhibition inside the Domkerk shows interesting 'before' and 'after' sketches. Outside is the Pandhof, a cloister garden planted with many medicinal herbs. The garden, with its beautiful statuette of a canon hunched over his writing, is a tranquil spot to sit and rest a while. Another fascinating place to explore is the Oudegracht, the canal that runs through the centre of the city. Unlike Amsterdam, where the water is at street level, the people of Utrecht have been blessed with waterside footpaths and cellars, which allow them to use the basements of their canalside houses. Many of those cellars now house cafés and shops, and are excellent places to have a snack and watch boats navigate their way under the narrow bridges.

Of Utrecht's several museums, the **Museum Catharijnecovent** (St Catharine Convent Museum) is located in a beautiful late medieval building and gives an account of the country's religious history, while the excellent and sprawling **Centraal Museum** harbours not only paintings by 17th-century masters but also the largest Rietveld collection in the world. The **Nationaal Museum van Speelklok tot Pierement** has the world's biggest collection of automated musical instruments, and the **Universiteitsmuseum** (University Museum) focuses on the interaction between science and education. At the **Nederlands**

**Trips Out of Town**

Spoorwegmuseum (Dutch Railway Museum), visitors can drive a train simulator and look at old locomotives, while the country's biggest rock garden is a striking part of **Fort Hoofddijk**; on a cold day, the tropical greenhouse is a perfect place to thaw out and absorb such themes as 'plants as clocks' or 'magic and religion'. Look out, too, for the few special days throughout the year when monuments and museums throw their doors open to the public for free (check with the VVV); also, during July and August, there are informative walking tours through the city.

Utrecht is located in an area abundant with castles, forests and arboretums. In the outskirts of the city, Slot Zuylen (Zuylen Castle, Tournooiveld 1, Oud Zuilen, 030 244 0255) presides over exquisite ornamental waterfalls and gardens. Check the concerts and shows in Kasteel Groeneveld's gorgeous gardens (Groeneveld Castle, Groeneveld 2, 035 542 0446/www.kasteelgroeneveld.nl), just north-east of Utrecht. Stroll in the lovely Arboretum von Gimborn (Vossensteinsesteeg 8, 030 253 1826) in Doorne, then pop across the town to Kasteel Huis Doorn (Doorn Castle, Langbroekerweg 10, 034 341 2244/www.kasteeldehaar.nl) to see how royalty lived at the end of the 19th century.

### Centraal Museum

*Nicolaaskerkhof 10 (030 236 2363/ www.centraalmuseum.nl).* **Open** 11am-5pm Tue-Sun. **Admission** €8; €4 concessions. **No credit cards**.

### Fort Hoofddijk

*Budapestlaan 17, De Uithof (030 253 5455).* **Open** *Mar, Apr, Oct, Nov* 10am-4pm daily. *May-Sept* 10am-5pm daily. **Admission** €3.50; €1.50 4-12s; €2.50 over-65s; free MJK. **No credit cards**.

### Museum Catharijneconvent

*Lange Nieuwstraat 38 (031 231 3835/7296/ www.catharijneconvent.nl).* **Open** 10am-5pm Tue-Fri; 11am-5pm Sat, Sun. **Admission** €6; €3-€5 concessions; free MJK, under-6s. **No credit cards**.

### Nationaal Museum van Speelklok tot Pierement

*Buurkerkhof 10 (030 231 2789/ www.museumspeelklok.nl).* **Open** 10am-5pm Tue-Sat; noon-5pm Sun. **Admission** €6; €4-€5 concessions. **No credit cards**.

### Nederlands Spoorwegmuseum

*Maliebaanstation 16 (030 230 6206/ www.spoorwegmuseum.nl).* **Open** 10am-5pm Tue-Fri; 11.30am-5pm Sat, Sun. **Admission** €7; €4.50 4-18s; €5.75 over-65s; free MJK, under-4s. **No credit cards**.

### Universiteitsmuseum

*Lange Nieuwstraat 106 (030 253 8008/www.museum.ruu.nl).* **Open** 11am-5pm Tue-Sun. **Admission** €4; €2-€3 concessions; free MJK. **No credit cards**.

## Where to eat & drink

**De Winkel van Sinkel** (Oudegracht 158; 030 251 0693/www.dewinkelvansinkel.nl), located in a former department store, is a grand setting for a coffee or a meal: especially at night, when its canal-level catacombs open for club nights and to act as a late-night restaurant. **Stadskasteel Oudaen** (Oudegracht 99; 030 231 1864/www.oudaen.nl), the only existing urban medieval castle left in the country, is even posher. **Casas Sanchez** (Springweg 64; 030 231 9566) serves tapas, while top Japanese sushi can be munched at **Konnichi Wa** (Mariaplaats 9; 030 241 6388). If you want a local speciality, try the delicious offerings at the **Pancake Bakery de Oude Munt Kelder** (Oudegracht aan de Wer; 030 231 6773).

Most bars in the city centre are busy with students. **ACU** (Voorstraat 71; 030 231 4590) is a legendary squat with cheap eats (6-7.30pm Mon-Thur, Sun) and some of the city's edgier musical events; **Belgie** (Oudegracht 196; 030 231 2666) serves over 300 types of beer; and the trying-hard-to-be-hip **'t Hart van Utrecht** (Voorstraat 10; no phone) has the coolest crowd of all. The **Tivoli** (Oudegracht 245; 030 231 1491/www.tivoli.nl) is the best place to check for club nights and touring bands of every imaginable genre.

## Where to stay

The four-star **Malie Hotel** (Maliestraat 2; 030 231 6424/www.hotelmalie.nl) is a beautiful old merchant's house: if you really want to pamper yourself, a double costs €115 to €130 a night. Those on a tighter budget should take a ten-minute bus ride out from the city centre to Bunnik, where the **NJHC Youth Hostel** (Rhijnauwenselaan 14, Bunnik; 030 656 1277/ www.njhc.org/english) offers a night in a shared room for €16 to €18.

## Getting there

### By car

40km (25 miles) south-east.

### By rail

30min from Amsterdam Centraal Station, direct.

## Tourist information

### VVV

*Vinkenburgstraat 19 (0900 128 8732 premium rate/www.12utrecht.nl).* **Open** 9.30am-6.30pm Mon-Wed, Fri; 9.30am-9pm Thur; 9.30am-5pm Sat; 10am-2pm Sun.

# Directory

## Features

# Directory

## Getting Around

Getting around Amsterdam is easy. The city has an efficient and cheap tram and bus system, though if you're staying in the centre of town, most places are reachable on foot. Locals tend to get around by bike: the streets are busy with cycles all day and most of the evening. There are also pleasure boats, commercial barges and water taxis.

If you're thinking of bringing a car, don't. The roads aren't designed for them, and parking places are elusive. Unfortunately, public transport provision for those with disabilities is dire: though there are lifts at all Metro stations, staff can't always help people in wheelchairs.

### Arriving & leaving

### By air

For general airport enquiries, ring Schiphol Airport on 0900 0141 or go to www.schiphol.nl.

**British Airways**
346 9559/www.britishairways.nl.
**British Midland**
346 9211/www.britishmidland.com.
**EasyJet**
023 568 4880/www.easyjet.co.uk.
**KLM**
474 7747/http://nederland.klm.com.

### KLM Hotel Bus Service

*Main exit, Schiphol Airport, Zuid (653 4975).* **Times** every 40min 7am-3pm, then on the hr 3-9pm daily. **Tickets** €8 single; €14 return. This service is available to anyone prepared to pay, not just KLM passengers or hotel guests. The route starts at Schiphol Airport, then goes to the Golden Tulip Barbizon (Leidseplein), Pulitzer (Westermarkt-Keizersgracht), Krasnapolsky (Dam Square), Holiday Inn and Renaissance (Nieuwezijds Voorburgwal), Barbizon Palace (Zeedijk) and back to Schiphol again. There is also a route that

leaves from the south of the city: details from the above number or the Amsterdam Tourist Board (*see p289*).

### Schiphol Airport Rail Service

*Schiphol Airport/Centraal Station (information 0900 9292/ www.ns.nl/reisinfo).* **Times** Trains every 15min 4am-midnight, then every hr from 12.44am daily. **Tickets** *Single* €2.95; €1.70 under-12s with adult; free under-4s. *Return* €5.22; €3.06 under-12s with adult; free under-4s.
The journey to Centraal Station takes about 20 minutes. Note that a return ticket is valid only for that day.

### Taxis

There are always plenty of taxis outside the main exit. It's pricey, however: about €30-€35 from the airport into Amsterdam is average.

### Public transport

For information, tickets, maps and an English-language guide to the city's ticket system, visit the GVB, Amsterdam's municipal transport authority. A basic map of the tram network is on *p316*.

*See p252* for details of NS, the Netherlands' rail network.

### GVB

*Prins Hendrikkade 108-14, Old Centre: New Side (0900 9292). Tram 1, 2, 4, 5, 9, 13, 16, 17, 20, 24, 25.* **Open** *Telephone enquiries* 6am-midnight Mon-Fri; 7am-midnight Sat, Sun. *Personal callers* 7am-9pm Mon-Fri; 8am-9pm Sat. **Map** p306 D1.
The GVB runs Amsterdam's Metro, bus and tram services, and can provide information on all.
**Branches**: GVB Head Office, Prins Hendrikkade 108, Old Centre: New Side; Amstel Railway Station, Julianaplein, Zuid.

### Fares & tickets

Beware of travelling on a bus or tram without a ticket. Uniformed inspectors make

regular checks and passengers without a valid ticket – or an exceptional excuse – will be asked for ID and fined €29.10 on the spot. Don't even think about playing the ignorant foreigner. It won't work.

### Strippenkaarten

A 'strip ticket' system operates on trams, buses and the Metro. It's initially confusing, but ultimately good value for money. Prices range from €1.40 for a strip of two units to €5.90 for 15 units and €17.40 for 45 units; children under four travel free, and older children (aged 4-18) pay reduced fares (€3.70 for a 15-strip card). Prices increase annually.

Tickets can be bought at GVB (public transport) offices, post offices, train stations and many tobacconists. The tickets must be stamped upon boarding a tram or bus and on entering a Metro station. The city is divided into five zones: Noord (north), West, Centrum, Oost (east) and Zuid (south); most of central Amsterdam falls, not surprisingly, within zone Centrum. Strip tickets are also valid on trains that stop at Amsterdam stations, with the exception of Schiphol.

For travel in a single zone, two units must be stamped, while three are stamped for two zones, four for three zones and so on. On trams, you can stamp your own tickets in the yellow box-like contraption near the doors: fold the ticket so that the unit you need to stamp is at the end. Some trams, though, will now only allow passengers to enter at the rear, where a conductor will stamp the ticket for you. On buses, drivers stamp the tickets, and on the Metro there are stamping machines located at the entrance to stations.

An unlimited number of people can travel on one card, but the appropriate number of units must be stamped for each person. The stamps are valid for one hour, during which time you can transfer to other buses and trams without having to stamp your card again. If your journey takes more than an hour, you have to stamp more units, but no single tram journey within central Amsterdam is likely to take that long. Strippenkaarten remain valid for one year from the date of the first stamp.

## Dagkaarten

A cheaper option for unlimited travel in Amsterdam, a 'day ticket' costs €5.20. Dutch pensioners, the unwaged and children aged four to 18 pay €3.60. Child day tickets are valid on night buses. A day ticket is valid on trams, buses and the Metro on the day it is stamped until the last bus or tram runs. You need to buy a new ticket for night buses. Only the one-day ticket can be bought from drivers on trams and buses. After you've stamped the day ticket on your first journey, you do not need to stamp it again.

The extended form of the day ticket costs around €16: aside from entitling the bearer to use trams, buses and the Metro, it also includes all-day use of the Canal Bus network (*see p274*) and offers almost €150 worth of vouchers valid in museums, attractions and restaurants.

And if you only want to make one journey, no problem: for under €2 single, you can get a single ticket valid for two hours; returns, valid for four hours, cost around €3.50.

## Sterabonnement

'Season tickets' can be bought from GVB offices, tobacconists and post offices, and are valid for a week, a month or a year. A weekly pass for the central zone (Centrum) costs €8.90, a monthly one €29.40 and a yearly one €294. Children aged from four to 18 get cheaper season tickets: €5.65 for a day, €18.65 for a month and €186.50 for a year. You'll need a passport photo to get a season ticket.

## Trams & buses

As a visitor to Amsterdam, you will find buses and trams a particularly good way to get around the city centre. Tram services run from 6am Monday to Friday, 6.30am on Saturday and 7.30am on Sunday, with a special night bus service taking over late in the evening. Night buses are numbered from 71 to 79; all go to Centraal Station, except 79. Night bus stops are indicated by a black square at the stop with the bus number printed on it. Night buses run from 1am to 5.30am from Monday to Friday, and until 6.30am on weekends.

Yellow signs at tram and bus stops indicate the name of the stop and further stops. There are usually maps of the entire network in the shelters and diagrams of routes on board the trams and buses. The city's bus and tram drivers are generally courteous and will give directions if asked; most are sufficiently fluent to do this in English.

The yellow and decorated varieties of tram are as synonymous with Amsterdam as the red double-decker bus is with London. The vehicles make for fast and efficient travel, but other road users should be warned that they will stop only when absolutely necessary. Cyclists should listen out for tram warning bells – as well as being careful to cross tramlines at an angle that avoids the front wheel getting stuck – and motorists should try to avoid blocking tramlines: cars are allowed to venture on to them only if they're turning right.

To get on or off a tram, wait until it has halted at a stop and press the yellow button by the doors, which will then open. On some trams you can buy a ticket from the driver at the front; on others from either a machine in the middle, or a conductor at the back.

Tram 20, also known as the Circle Line tram, departs from two stops outside Centraal Station. Its route stays within a fairly central area and is convenient for all the major museums and sights. It's been rumoured for two years that the 20 route may be cancelled due to financial losses, so don't make plans to rely on it.

Note that Metro 51, 53 and 54 are, confusingly, fast trams that run on Metro lines. This is not the same as the number 5 tram, actually called a *sneltram* (which translates literally as 'fast tram').

## Metro

The Metro system uses the same ticketing system as trams and buses (*see p274*), and serves suburbs to the south and east. There are three lines, all terminating at Centraal Station (which is sometimes abbreviated to CS). Trains run from 6am Monday to Friday (6.30am Sat, 7.30am Sun) to around 12.15am daily.

## Taxis

There are a few ground rules that visitors would do well to follow. Be sure to check that the meter initially shows no more than the minimum charge (€2.18). Always ask the driver for an estimate of how much the journey will cost before setting out. Even short journeys are expensive: on top of €2.18, you will be expected to pay €1.54 per kilometre for the first 25 kilometres, then €1.27 per kilometre thereafter.

If you feel you have been ripped off, ask for a receipt, which you are entitled to see before handing over cash. If the charge is extortionate, phone the central taxi office (677 7777) or contact the police. Rip-offs are relatively rare.

You're not supposed to hail a taxi in the street – though occasionally one may stop for you – as there are ranks dotted around the city. The best of the central ones are found outside Centraal Station, by the bus station at the junction of Kinkerstraat and Marnixstraat, Rembrandtplein and Leidseplein. You can book cabs on the central taxi office number above. The line is often busy on Friday and Saturday nights, but there's a telephone queuing system.

Wheelchairs will only fit in taxis if they are folded. If you're in a wheelchair, phone the car transport service for wheelchair users on 633 3943 (generally open 9am to 5pm, Monday to Friday). You'll need to book your journey one or two days in advance and it costs around €2 per kilometre.

# Driving

If you absolutely must bring a car to the Netherlands, join a national motoring organisation beforehand. These should provide you with international assistance booklets, which explain what to do in the event of a breakdown in Europe.

To drive in the Netherlands you'll need a valid national driving licence, although the Dutch motoring club, **ANWB** (*see below*), and many car hire firms favour a photocard licence (Brits should note that you need the paper version as well for this to be legal, and that the photocard takes a couple of weeks to come through if you're applying from scratch).

Major roads are usually well maintained and clearly signposted. Motorways are labelled 'A'; major roads 'N'; and European routes 'E'. Brits in particular should note that the Dutch drive on the right, while everyone should remember that drivers and front-seat passengers must always wear seatbelts. Speed limits are 50kmh (31mph) within cities, 70kmh (43mph) outside, and 100kmh (62mph) on motorways. If you're driving in Amsterdam, look out for cyclists, who'll come at you from every which way. To complicate things further, many Amsterdam streets are now one-way.

To bring your car into the Netherlands, you'll need an international identification disk, a registration certificate, proof of the vehicle having passed a road safety test in its country of origin and insurance documents.

## Royal Dutch Automobile Club (ANWB)

*Museumplein 5, Museum Quarter (070 314 1414/customer services 0800 0503/24hr emergency line 0800 0888/www.anwb.nl). Tram 2, 3, 5, 12, 16, 20.*

**Open** *Customer services* 8am-10pm Mon-Fri; 8am-5pm Sat, Sun. **Credit** MC, V. **Map** p310 D6.
If you haven't joined a motoring organisation, enrol here for an annual €48-€74, which covers the cost of assistance should your vehicle break down. If you're a member of a foreign motoring organisation, you may be entitled to free help. Emergency crews may not accept credit cards or cheques at the scene.

# Car hire

Dutch car hire (*autoverhuur*) companies generally expect at least one year's driving experience and will want to see a valid national driving licence (with photo) and passport. All companies will require you to pay a deposit through a credit card, and you'll generally need to be over 21. Prices given below are for one day's hire of the cheapest car available excluding insurance, unless otherwise stated.

## Adam's Rent-a-Car

*Nassaukade 344-6, Oud West (685 0111). Tram 7, 10, 17, 20.* **Open** 8am-6pm Mon-Fri; 8am-8pm Sat. **Credit** AmEx, DC, MC, V. **Map** p310 C5.
One-day hire costs from €34; the first 100km (62 miles) are free, and after that the charge is 13¢/km.

## Dik's Autoverhuur

*Van Ostadestraat 278-80, the Pijp (662 3366). Tram 3, 4.* **Open** 8am-7.30pm Mon-Sat; 9am-12.30pm, 8-10.30pm Sun. **Credit** AmEx, DC, MC, V. **Map** p311 F6.
Prices start at €29 per day. The first 100km are free, then it's 10¢/km.

## Hertz

*Overtoom 333, Oud West (612 2441/www.hertz.nl). Tram 1, 6.* **Open** 8am-6pm Mon-Fri; 8am-2pm Sat; 9am-2pm Sun, public holidays. **Credit** AmEx, DC, MC, V. **Map** p309 B6.
Prices start at €54 per day including insurance and mileage.

## Ouke Baas

*Van Ostadestraat 362-72, Oost (679 4842). Tram 3, 4.* **Open** 7am-7.30pm Mon-Fri; 8am-8.30pm Sat; 8am-1pm, 7-10pm Sun. **Credit** AmEx, DC, MC, V. **Map** p312 G5.
Inclusive of VAT and the first 100km, Ouke Baas' cheapest car costs €35 per day. After the first 100km, it costs 10¢/km.

# Clamping & fines

Amsterdam's wheel-clamp (*wielklem*) teams are swift to act and show little mercy if they see a car parked illegally. A yellow sticker on the windscreen informs you where to go to pay the fine (just over €60). Once you've paid, return to the car and wait for the traffic police to remove the clamp. Luckily, the declampers normally arrive promptly.

If you park illegally and fail to pay your parking fine within 24 hours, your car will be towed away. It'll cost around €135, plus parking fine, plus a tariff per kilometre to reclaim it from the pound if you do so within 24 hours, and around €45 for every 12 hours thereafter. The pound is at Daniel Goedkoopstraat 7-9. Take your passport, licence number and enough cash or travellers' cheques to pay the fine. All major credit cards are accepted. If your car has been clamped or towed away, head to any of the following offices to pay the fine.

## Head office

*Weesperstraat 105A, Old Centre: Old Side (553 0300). Tram 6, 7, 9, 10, 14, 20.* **Open** 8.30am-4.30pm Mon-Sat. **Map** p307 F3.

## Branches

*Weesperstraat 105A, Old Centre: Old Side (553 0333). Tram 6, 7, 9, 10, 14, 20.* **Open** 8am-8pm Mon-Sat. **Map** p307 F3.
*Beukenplein 50, Oost (553 0333). Tram 9, 14.* **Open** 8am-8pm Mon-Sat. **Map** p312 H4.
*Jan Pieter Heijestraat 94, Oud West (553 0333). Tram 3, 12.* **Open** 8am-8pm Mon-Sat.
*Daniel Goedkoopstraat 7-9, Oost (553 0333). Metro Spaklerweg.* **Open** 24hrs daily.

# Parking

Parking in central Amsterdam is a nightmare: the whole of the town centre is metered from 9am until at least 7pm – and in many places up to 11pm – and meters are difficult to find. Meters will set you back up to

**Directory**

€3 an hour depending on how central you are. Illegally parked cars get clamped or towed away without any warning (*see p277*). Car parks (*parkeren*) are indicated by a white 'P' on a blue square. After controlled hours, parking at meters is free. Below is a list of central car parks where you're more likely to find a space during peak times. Be sure to empty your car completely of all valuables and the radio: cars with foreign number plates are vulnerable to break-ins.

### ANWB Parking Amsterdam Centraal
*Prins Hendrikkade 20A, Old Centre: New Side (638 5330).* **Open** 24hrs daily. **Rates** €2.50/hr; max €25/day; €125/wk (from noon Sat to noon following Sat). **Credit** AmEx, DC, MC, V. **Map** p306 D2.
Many nearby hotels offer a 15% discount on parking here.

### Europarking
*Marnixstraat 250, Oud West (623 6694).* **Open** 6.30am-1am Mon-Thur; 6.30am-2am Fri, Sat; 7am-1am Sun. **Rates** €2.50/hr; €25/24hrs. **Map** p309 B4.

### De Kolk Parking
*Nieuwezijds Voorburgwal 12, Old Centre: New Side (427 1449).* **Open** 24hrs daily. **Rates** €2.50/hr; €25/24hrs. **Map** p306 C2.

## Petrol

The main 24-hour petrol stations (*benzinestations*) within the city limits are at Gooiseweg 10-11, Sarphatistraat 225, Marnixstraat 250 and Spaarndammerdijk 218.

## Boats to rent

### Canal Bike
*Weteringschans 24, Southern Canal Belt (626 5574/www.canal.nl).* **Open** *Summer* 10am-9.30pm daily. *Winter* 10am-6pm daily. **Moorings** Leidsekade at Leidseplein; Stadhouderskade, opposite Rijksmuseum; Prinsengracht, by Westerkerk; Keizersgracht, on corner

of Leidsestraat. **Hire rates** *4-person pedalo* if 1 or 2 people, €7/person/hr; if 3 or 4 people, €6/person/hr. **Deposit** €45/canal bike. **No credit cards**. **Map** p310 D5.

### Roell
*Mauritskade 1, by the Amstel, the Plantage (692 9124).* Tram 6, 7, 10. **Open** *Apr-Sept* 11am-7pm Tue-Fri; 11am-4pm Sat. *Oct-Feb* 11am-6pm Wed-Fri; also by appointment. **Hire rates** *2-person pedalo* €13/hr; *4-person pedalo* €17/hr; *4-person motor boat* €25/1hr (€45 for 2hrs). **Group boat** (Mar-Dec only; max 30 persons incl captain) €105/1hr; €90/hr for subsequent hours. **Deposit** *Pedalos* €25; *motor boat* €125 (ID required). **No credit cards**. **Map** p312 H2.

## Canal buses

### Canal Bus
*Weteringschans 24, Southern Canal Belt (623 9886/www.canal.nl).* Tram 6, 10. **Open** 10am-7pm daily. **Cost** *Day ticket* €14; €10 under-12s. *Combination day ticket incl entrance to Rijksmuseum* €20 (not available during special exhibitions); *All Amsterdam Transport Pass* €17. **Credit** AmEx, MC, V. **Map** p310 D5.

## Water taxis

### Water Taxi Centrale
*Stationsplein 8, Old Centre: New Side (622 2181).* Tram 1, 2, 4, 5, 9, 13, 16, 17, 20, 24, 25. **Open** 8am-midnight daily. **Cost** *8-person boat* €60 for first 30min, then €35/30min. *16-person boat* €110 for first 30min, then €60/30min. *25-person boat* €120 for first 30min, then €70/30min. **Credit** AmEx, MC, V (accepted only prior to boarding). **Map** p305 D1.
Try to book in advance.

## Cycling

Cycling is the most convenient means of getting from A to B: there are bike lanes on most roads, marked by white lines and bike symbols. Some drivers insist on parking in bike lanes (often paved red), but most are used to the abundance of cyclists and collisions are rare. However, cycling two abreast is illegal, as is going without reflector bands on front and back wheels. Also watch out for pedestrians stepping off the pavement into your path.

Never leave your bike unlocked: there's a thriving trade in stolen bikes, so use a sturdy lock. Always lock your bike to something immovable, preferably using two locks: one around the frame and one through the front wheel. If someone in the street offers you a bike for sale ('fiets te koop'), don't be tempted: it's almost certainly stolen, and there's no shortage of firms where a good bike can be hired for €6-€8 a day. Aside from the firms listed below, check the *Amsterdam Yellow Pages* (*Gouden Gids*) under 'Fietsen en Bromfietsen Verhuur'.

### Bike City
*Bloemgracht 68, the Jordaan (626 3721/www.bikecity.nl).* Tram 10, 13, 14, 17, 20. **Open** 9am-6pm daily. **Rates** €6-€10/1st day; €4.5-€9/extra days; €23-€45/wk; plus €23 deposit and passport/ID card or credit card imprint. **Credit** AmEx, DC, MC, V. **Map** p305 B3.
Opening times may vary in winter.

### Mike's Bike Tours
*302A Lijnbaansgracht, Southern Canal Belt (622 7970/ www.mikesbiketours.com).* Tram 6, 7, 10, 16, 24, 25. **Open** *May-Aug* 9am-9pm daily. *Sept-Apr* 9am-6pm daily. **Rates** from €7/day; passport, national ID or €136 as deposit. **No credit cards**. **Map** p305 D5.
Rent lovely comfortable cruisers at good rates from this well-reputed tour company (daily guided tours in the city and out into the countryside).

### Rent-A-Bike
*Damstraat 20-22, Old Centre: Old Side (625 5029/www.bikes.nl).* Tram 4, 9, 14, 16, 20, 24, 25. **Open** 9am-6pm daily. **Rates** €15-€30/day; plus €23 deposit and passport/ID card or credit card imprint. **Credit** AmEx, DC, MC, V. **Map** p306 D3.
A 10% discount (excluding deposit) on bike hire if you mention *Time Out*.

### Take-A-Bike
*Centraal Station, Stationsplein 12, Old Centre: New Side (624 8391).* Tram 1, 2, 4, 5, 9, 13, 16, 17, 20, 24, 25. **Open** *Hire* 8am-10pm daily. *Storage* 6am-midnight Mon-Fri; 7am-midnight Sat; 8am-midnight Sun. **Rates** €6/day; €24/wk; plus €91 deposit and passport/driving licence. **Credit** MC, V. **Map** p306 D1.
Here you can either hire a bike (until 10pm) or store one (until midnight).

# Resources A-Z

## Addresses

Amsterdam's street layout
is cluttered and chaotic,
especially in the centre of town.
However, it's a small city, and
you should soon get the hang
of finding your way around.
Addresses take the form of
street then house number,
such as Damrak 1.

## Age restrictions

In the Netherlands, only those
over the age of 16 can purchase
alcohol, while you have to be
16 to purchase cigarettes (18 to
smoke dope). Driving is limited
to those aged 18 or over.

## Attitude & etiquette

Amsterdam is a relaxed city.
However, while some assume
anything goes, not everything
does. While smoking dope is
decriminalised, for example,
it's not accepted everywhere:
spliffing up in restaurants is
usually frowned upon. And
while most restaurants don't
operate a dress code, many
nightclubs do, with sportswear
and trainers banned.

## Business

The forthcoming construction
of a new Metro line linking
north and south Amsterdam –
the Noord–Zuidlijn – is
indicative of the city's status
as a business centre. The south
of Amsterdam is where most
of the action is, with corporate
hotels such as the Hilton
rubbing shoulders with the
World Trade Center and the
RAI convention centre.

## Banking

The branches listed below are
head offices. Most do not have
general banking facilities, but
staff will be able to provide a
list of branches that do. For
information about currency
exchanges, *see p285*.

### ABN-Amro

*Vijzelstraat 68, Southern Canal Belt
(628 9393/www.abnamro.nl). Tram
6, 7, 10, 16, 24, 25.* **Open** 9am-5pm
Mon-Fri. **Map** p310 D4.
Branches all over Amsterdam.

### Fortis Bank

*Singel 548, Old Centre: New Side
(624 9340/www.fortisbank.com).
Tram 4, 9, 14, 16, 20, 24, 25.*
**Open** 1-5pm Mon; 9.30am-5pm
Tue-Fri. **Map** p310 D4.
Full banking facilities in 50 branches.

### ING Group

*Bijlmerplein 888, Bijlmermeer (563
9111/www.ing.com). Metro Bijlmer/
bus 59, 60, 62, 137.* **Open** 9am-4pm
Mon-Fri.
ING incorporates the 50 Amsterdam
branches of the Postbank (*see below*).

### Postbank

*Postbus 94780, 1090 GT (565 5010/
www.postbank.nl).* **Open** *Enquiries*
8.30am-5pm Mon-Fri.
One in every Amsterdam post office.

### Rabobank

*Dam 16, Old Centre: New Side (777
8899/www.rabobank.nl).* Tram 1, 2,
5, 9, 13, 14, 16, 17, 20, 24, 25.
**Open** 9.30am-5pm Mon-Wed, Fri;
9.30am-6pm Thur. **Map** p306 D2.
Some 30 branches in Amsterdam.

## Conventions & conferences

Most major hotels offer full
conference facilities, with the
**Krasnapolsky**'s the best in
town. The **World Trade
Center** (*see p280*) will offer
fine facilities when renovations
are completed in 2002.

### Congrex Convention Services

*AJ Ernststraat 595K, Southern Canal
Belt (504 0200/www.congrex.nl).
Tram 5/Metro 51.* **Open** 9am-5.30pm
Mon-Thur, 9am-5pm Fri. **Credit**
AmEx, DC, MC, V. **Map** p311 E4.
Specialists in teleconferencing.

# Tickets, please

Though the Amsterdam Tourist board and the
GWK sell tickets for concerts, plays and other
events, the main ticket retailer in Amsterdam
is the **AUB**. It offers a variety of services,
ranging from online sales to personal service
at its Leidseplein shop.

Before you go about buying tickets, it helps
to know what's on when. For this, pick up
the AUB's free monthly magazine *Uitkrant*,
available in many theatres and bookshops
(as is *Uitgids*, an annual publication offering
details of subscription series and the like).
It's only in Dutch – as is the online version
(*see below*) – but it's easy to decipher.

*Uitkrant* (pronounced 'out-krant') is
also available at the **AUB Ticketshop** in
Leidseplein, which is open from 10am to
6pm daily except Thursday, when it closes
at 9pm. Expect to pay a commission fee
of around €2 on each ticket.

You can also buy tickets by phone, though
the commission is about 50 per cent higher
and you'll also be paying for premium-line
phone rates. The Uitlijn ('out-line') service
is on 0900 0191 (+31 20 621 1288 from
abroad), and is open 9am to 9pm daily.
Finally, for a commission of around €3 per
ticket, you can book online at www.uitlijn.nl.

## RAI Congresgebouw

*Europaplein 8-22, Zuid (549 1212/
www.rai.nl). Tram 4, 25/NS rail RAI
Station.* **Open** *Office* 9am-5.30pm
Mon-Fri.

A self-contained congress and trade
fair centre in the south of the city. The
building contains 11 halls totalling
87,000 sq m of covered exhibition
space and 22 conference rooms that
can seat up to 1,750 people.

## Stichting de Beurs
## van Berlage

*Damrak 277, Old Centre: Old Side
(530 4141/www.beursvanberlage.nl).
Tram 4, 9, 14, 16, 20, 24, 25.* **Open**
9am-5pm Mon-Fri. **Map** p306 D2.

Used for cultural events and smaller
trade fairs (up to 2,500 visitors can
be provided with buffet dinners).
Berlage Hall is a conference venue
for between 50 and 2,000 people.

## Couriers & shippers

### FedEx

*0800 022 2333 freephone/500 5699/
www.fedex.com/nl_english).* **Open**
*Customer services* 8am-6.30pm Mon-
Fri. **Credit** AmEx, DC, MC, V.

### TNT

*0800 1234/www.tnt.com.* **Open** 24hrs
daily. **Credit** AmEx, DC, MC, V.

## Office hire &
## business services

Lots of tobacconists and copy
shops also have fax facilities.

### Avisco

*Stadhouderskade 156, the Pijp
(671 9909/www.acsavcompany.com).
Tram 3, 4, 16, 20, 24, 25.* **Open**
8am-5pm Mon-Fri. **Map** p311 F5.

Slide projectors, video equipment,
screens, cameras, overhead
projectors, microphones and tape
decks hired out or sold.

### Euro Business Center

*Keizersgracht 62, Western Canal
Belt (520 7500/www.ebc.nl). Tram 1,
2, 5, 13, 14, 17, 20.* **Open** 8.30am-
5.30pm Mon-Fri. **Credit** AmEx,
DC, MC, V. **Map** p306 C2.

Fully equipped offices for hire (long
or short term) including the use of
fax, photocopier, phone and mailbox
services plus multilingual secretaries.

### World Trade Center

*Strawinskylaan 1, Zuid (575 9111/
www.wtcamsterdam.com). Tram
5/NS rail RAI Station.* **Open** *Office
& enquiries* 9am-5pm Mon-Fri.

Offices here are let either long or
short term; call 575 2044 for details.

---

Assorted business services are also
offered here. When renovations are
completed in mid-2002, conference
facilities should be outstanding.

## Translators &
## interpreters

### Berlitz GlobalNET

*Nieuwezijds Voorburgwal 142,
Old Centre: New Side (344 5757/fax
344 5767/www.berlitzglobalnet.com).
Tram 1, 2, 5, 13, 17.* **Open** 9am-
6pm Mon-Fri. **Map** p306 C2.

Specialists in commercial, technical,
legal and scientific documents.

### Mac Bay Consultants

*PC Hooftstraat 15, Museum Quarter
(24hr phoneline 662 0501/fax 662
6299/www.macbay.nl). Tram 2, 3, 5,
12, 20.* **Open** 9am-7pm Mon-Fri.
**Map** p310 C6.

Specialists in financial documents.

## Useful organisations

Many of the agencies listed
below are in The Hague,
though they are able to deal
with basic enquiries on the
telephone or by post. For full
information on embassies and
consulates, *see p281.*

### American Chamber
### of Commerce

*Van Karnebeeklaan 14, 2585 BB
The Hague (070 365 9808/
www.amcham.nl).* **Open** 9am-5pm
Mon-Fri.

### British Embassy

*Commercial Department, Lange
Voorhout 10, 2514 ED The Hague
(070 427 0427/fax 070 427 0345/
www.britain.nl).* **Open** 9am-1pm,
2-5.30pm Mon-Fri.

### Commissariaat
### voor Buitenlandse
### Investeringen
### Nederland

*Bezuidenhoutseweg 2, 2500 EC
The Hague (070 379 8818/fax 070
379 6322/www.nfia.nl).* **Open** 8am-
6pm Mon-Fri.

The Netherlands Foreign Investment
Agency is probably the most useful
first port of call for business people
wishing to relocate to Holland.

### Effectenbeurs
### (Stock Exchange)

*Beursplein 5, Old Centre: New
Side (550 4444/www.euronext.com).
Tram 4, 9, 14, 16, 20, 24, 25.*
**Open** for free tours. **Map** p306 D2.

---

Stock for listed Dutch companies is
traded here, and for Nederlandse
Termijnhandel, the commodity
exchange for trading futures, and
Optiebeurs, the largest options
exchange in Europe.

### EVD: Economische
### Voorlichtingsdienst

*Bezuidenhoutseweg 181, 2594
AH The Hague (070 379 8933/
www.hollandtrade.com).* **Open**
8am-5pm Mon-Fri.

The Netherlands Foreign Trade
Agency incorporates the Netherlands
Council for Trade Promotion (NCH),
both of which are handy sources of
information. Don't turn up on spec:
make an appointment in advance.

### Home Abroad

*Weteringschans 28, Southern Canal
Belt (625 5195/fax 624 7902/
www.homeabroad.nl). Tram 6, 7,
10.* **Open** 10am-5.30pm Mon-Fri.
**Map** p311 E5.

Assistance in all aspects of living and
doing business in the Netherlands.

### Kamer van Koophandel

*De Ruijterkade 5, the Waterfront
(531 4000/fax 531 4799/
www.kvk.nl). Tram 1, 2, 4, 5, 9, 13,
16, 17, 24, 25.* **Open** 8.30am-5pm
Mon, Tue, Thur, Fri; 8.30am-8pm
Wed. **Map** p306 C1.

Amsterdam's Chamber of Commerce
has lists of import/export agencies,
government trade representatives
and companies by sector.

### Ministerie van
### Buitenlandse Zaken

*Bezuidenhoutseweg 67, Postbus
20061, 2500 EB The Hague
(070 348 6486/fax 070 348
4848/www.bz.minbuza.nl).*
**Open** 9am-5pm Mon-Fri.

The Ministry of Foreign Affairs.
Detailed enquiries may be referred
to the EVD (*see above*).

### Ministerie van
### Economische Zaken

*Bezuidenhoutseweg 30, 2594 AV
The Hague (070 379 8911/fax
070 379 4081/www.minez.nl).*
**Open** 8am-5.30pm Mon-Fri.

The Ministry of Economic Affairs can
provide answers to general queries
concerning the Dutch economy.
Detailed enquiries tend to be referred
to the EVD (*see above*).

### Netherlands–British
### Chamber of Commerce

*Oxford House, Nieuwezijds
Voorburgwal 328L, Old Centre:
New Side (421 7040/fax 421 7003/
www.nbcc.co.uk). Tram 1, 2, 5, 13,
14, 17.* **Open** 9am-5pm Mon-Fri.
**Map** p306 D3.

## Consumer

If you have any complaints about the service you received from Dutch businesses that you were not able to resolve with the establishment, contact the National Consumentenbond on 070 445 4000.

## Customs

EU nationals over the age of 17 may import limitless goods into the Netherlands for their personal use. Other EU countries may still have limits on the quantity of goods they permit on entry. For citizens of non-EU countries, the old limits still apply. These are:
● 200 cigarettes or 50 cigars or 250g (8.82oz) tobacco;
● 2 litres of non-sparkling wine plus 1 litre of spirits (over 22 per cent alcohol) or 2 litres of fortified wine (under 22 per cent alcohol);
● 60cc/ml of perfume;
● other goods to the value of €167.

The import of meat or meat products, fruit, plants, flowers and protected animals to the Netherlands is illegal.

## Disabled

The most obvious difficulty people with mobility problems face here is negotiating the winding cobbled streets of the older areas. Poorly maintained pavements are widespread, and steep canal house steps can present problems. But the pragmatic Dutch can generally solve any problems quickly.

Most large museums have facilities for disabled users but little for the partially sighted and hard of hearing. Most cinemas and theatres have an enlightened attitude and are accessible. However, it's advisable to check in advance.

The Metro is accessible to wheelchair users who 'have normal arm function'. There is a taxi service for wheelchair

users (*see p275*). Most trams are inaccessible to wheelchair users due to their high steps.

The AUB (*see p279* **Tickets, please**) and the Amsterdam Tourist Board (*see p289*) produce brochures listing accommodation, restaurants, museums, tourist attractions and boat excursions with facilities for the disabled.

## Drugs

The locals have a relaxed attitude to soft drugs, but smoking isn't acceptable everywhere, so use discretion. Outside Amsterdam, public consumption of cannabis is largely unacceptable. For more, *see p44*.

Foreigners found with harder drugs should expect prosecution. Organisations offering advice can do little to assist foreigners with drug-related problems, though the **Drugs Prevention Centre** is happy to provide help in several languages, including English. Its helpline (626 7176; open 1-5pm Mon, Tue, Thur) offers advice and information on drugs and alcohol abuse.

## Electricity

The voltage here is 220, 50-cycle AC and compatible with British equipment, but because the Netherlands uses two-pin continental plugs you'll need an adaptor. American visitors may need to buy a transformer, plus a new plug: Dutch sockets require a larger plug than those used in the USA.

## Embassies & consulates

### American Consulate General
*Museumplein 19, 1071 DJ (664 5661/visas 0900 872 8472 premium rate/www.usemb.nl). Tram 3, 5, 12, 16, 20.* **Open** *US citizens & visa applications* 8.30am-noon Mon-Fri.
**Map** p310 D6.

### Australian Embassy
*Carnegielaan 4, 2517 KH The Hague (070 310 8200/ www.australian-embassy.nl).* **Open** 8.45am-4.55pm Mon-Fri.
*Visa enquiries* 8.45-11.45am Mon-Fri.

### British Consulate General
*Koningslaan 44, 1075 AE (676 4343/www.britain.nl). Tram 2.* **Open** *British citizens* 9am-noon, 2-3.30pm Mon-Fri. *Visa enquiries* 9am-noon Mon-Fri.

### British Embassy
*Lange Voorhout 10, 2514 ED The Hague (070 364 5800/ www.britain.nl).* **Open** 9am-5.30pm Mon-Fri.
For visa and tourist information, contact the Consulate General (*see above*).

### Canadian Embassy
*Sophialaan 7, 2514 JP The Hague (070 311 1600).* **Open** 10am-noon Mon-Fri. *Canadian nationals* 2.30-4pm Mon, Tue, Thur, Fri.

### Irish Embassy
*Dr Kuyperstraat 9, 2514 BA The Hague (070 363 0993).* **Open** 10am-12.30pm, 2.30-5pm Mon-Fri. *Visa enquiries* 10am-noon Mon-Fri.

### New Zealand Embassy
*Carnegielaan 10, 2517 KH The Hague (070 346 9324/visas 070 365 8037/www.immigration.govt.nz).* **Open** 9am-12.30pm, 1.30-5.30pm Mon-Thur; 9am-12.30pm, 1.30-5pm Fri.

## Emergencies

In an emergency, call **112**, free from any phone, and specify if you need ambulance, fire service or police. For helplines, *see p283*; for hospitals, *see p282*; for addresses of police stations, *see p287*.

## Gay & lesbian

### Help & information

### COC Amsterdam
*Rozenstraat 14, the Jordaan (626 3087/www.cocamsterdam.nl). Tram 13, 14, 17, 20.* **Open** *Telephone enquiries* 10am-5pm Mon-Fri. *Info-Coffeeshop* 1-5pm Sat.
**Map** p305 B3.
The Amsterdam branch of the COC deals largely with the social side of gay life. The Info-Coffeeshop is a useful place to make enquiries about the COC or the gay scene in general.

**Directory**

## COC National

*Rozenstraat 8, the Jordaan
(623 4596/textphone 620 7541/
www.coc.nl).* Tram 13, 14, 17,
20. **Open** 9am-5pm Mon-Fri.
**Map** p306 C3.
COC's head office deals with all
matters relating to gays and lesbians;
the organisation has strong social
and activist tendencies.

## Gay & Lesbian Switchboard

*Postbus 11573, 1001 GN (623
6565/www.switchboard.nl).*
**Open** 2-10pm daily.
Whether it's information on the
scene or safe-sex advice you're after,
the friendly English-speakers here
are well informed.

## Homodok–Lesbisch Archief Amsterdam

*Nieuwpoortkade 2A, Westerpark
(606 0712/fax 606 0713/
www.homodok-laa.nl).* Tram 10, 12,
14. **Open** 9.30am-4pm Mon-Fri.
Books, journals, articles and theses
are housed here, as is a large video
collection. However, the location is
by no means permanent; call or check
the website before visiting.

## IIAV

*Obiplein 4, Oost (665 0820/
www.iiav.nl).* Tram 3, 6, 10, 14/
bus 15, 22. **Open** noon-5pm Mon;
10am-5pm Tue-Fri.
This women's archive was confiscated
during World War II and removed
to Berlin, where it vanished. In 1992,
it was found in Moscow, but the
Russians are still refusing to return
it. The current collection, started after
the war, is officially an archive,
but there are a lot of other resources,
including several online databases.

## Het Vrouwenhuis (the Women's House)

*Nieuwe Herengracht 95, Southern
Canal Belt (625 2066/fax 538 9185/
www.vrouwenhuis.nl).* Tram 7, 9,
14, 20/Metro Waterlooplein. **Open**
*Office* 10am-5pm Mon-Fri. *Info-Café*
noon-5pm Wed, Thur. **Map** p307 F3.
There's a well-stocked library here
(around 4,000 books; membership is
€9 a year) plus free Internet facilities
(noon-5pm Wed, Thur). Most classes
are held in Dutch.

## Other groups & organisations

### Amsterdam Stetsons

*683 7333/http://people.a2000.nl/
tfokker/saloon/eng/saloon.html.*
A gay country and western club that
meets at the Cruise Inn *(see p212).*

## Dikke Maatjes

*c/o COC Amsterdam, Rozenstraat
14, the Jordaan (0343 531791/
www.dikkemaatjes.nl/uk).*
'Dikke Maatjes' means 'close friends',
though its literal translation is 'fat
friends'. That's exactly what this gay
club is for: chubbies and admirers.

## Groep 7152

*PO Box 1402, 3500 BK Utrecht
(023 527 4299/www.geocities.com/
WestHollywood/Stonewall/2951/
engels.html#algemeen).*
This national organisation for
lesbians and bisexual women meets
monthly (except June-Aug) at the
Crea Café, Turfdraagsterpad 17,
Grimburgwal (627 3890).

## Long Yang Club

*PO Box 1172, 1000 BD (30 254
0776/www.longyangclub.nl).*
The Dutch branch of this worldwide
organisation for Asian and oriental
gays and their friends meets often.

## Mama Cash

*PO Box 15686, 1001 ND
(689 3634/fax 683 4647/
www.mamacash.nl).* **Open** 9am-5pm
Mon-Fri.
This group supplies funding
for women-run businesses, and
has sponsored many lesbian
organisations and events in the city.

## Netherbears

*c/o Le Shako, Postbus 15495, 1001
ML (625 1400/www.xs4all.nl/
~elza/netherbears/club.htm).*
This hairy men's club meets at Le
Shako's *(see p207)* every second
Sunday of the month, 5-9pm.

## Sjalhomo

*Postbus 2536, 1000 CM (023 531
2318 evenings only).*
This national organisation for
Jewish gays, lesbians and bisexuals
organises regular activities on
and around Jewish feast days.

## Sportclub Tijgertje

*Postbus 10521, 1001 EM (673
2458/664 3922/www.tijgertje.nl).*
Tijgertje organises a wide variety
of sports activities, from yoga to
wrestling, for gays and lesbians,
including an HIV swimming group.

## Wild Side, Women to Women SM Group

*c/o COC Amsterdam, Rozenstraat
14, the Jordaan (070 346 4767/
www.wildside.dds.nl).*
A group for woman-to-woman SM,
which holds workshops, meetings
and parties, and publishes a free
bi-monthly, bilingual newsletter
available from the COC Amsterdam
*(see p281)* and the Vrolijk *(see p204).*

As with any trip abroad, it's
advisable to take out medical
insurance before you leave. If
you're a UK citizen, you should
also get hold of an E111 *(see
p284)* to facilitate reciprocal
cover. For emergency services,
medical or dental referral
agencies and AIDS/HIV
information, *see p283.*

## Afdeling Inlichtingen Apotheken

*694 8709.*
A 24-hour service that can direct you
to your nearest chemist.

## Centraal Doktorsdienst/Atacom

*592 3434/atacom@xs4all.nl.*
A 24-hour English-speaking line for
advice about medical symptoms.

## Accident & emergency

In the case of minor accidents,
try the outpatient departments
at the following hospitals
(*ziekenhuis*), all open 24 hours
a day year-round.

## Academisch Medisch Centrum

*Meibergdreef 9, Zuid (switchboard
566 9111/first aid 566 3333).
Bus 59, 60, 120, 126, 158/Metro
Holendrecchp.*

## Boven IJ Ziekenhuis

*Statenjachtstraat 1, Noord (634
6346). Bus 34, 36, 37, 39, 171, 172.*

## Onze Lieve Vrouwe Gasthuis

*'s Gravesandeplein 16, Oost
(switchboard 599 9111/first aid
599 3016). Tram 3, 6, 10/Metro
Weesperplein or Wibautstraat.*
**Map** p312 G4.

## St Lucas Andreas Ziekenhuis

*Jan Tooropstraat 164, West
(switchboard 510 8911/first aid
510 8161). Tram 13/bus 19, 47,
80, 82, 97.*

## VU Ziekenhuis

*De Boelelaan 1117, Zuid
(switchboard 444 4444/first
aid 444 3636). Bus 142, 147,
148, 149, 170, 171, 172/Metro
Amstelveenseweg.*

# Contraception & abortion

## MR '70

*Sarphatistraat 620-26, the Plantage (624 5426). Tram 6, 9, 10, 14/ bus 22.* **Open** 9am-12.30pm, 1.30-4pm Mon-Thur; 9am-1pm Fri. **Map** p312 G3.
An abortion clinic that offers help and advice.

## Polikliniek Oosterpark

*Oosterpark 59, Oost (693 2151). Tram 3, 6, 9.* **Open** *Advice services* 9am-5pm daily. *Phonelines* 24hrs daily. **Map** p312 H4.
Advice on contraception and abortion. Non-residents without appropriate insurance will be charged from €327 for an abortion. The process is prompt and backed up by sympathetic counselling.

## Rutgersstichting

*Aletta Jacobshuis, Overtoom 323, Museum Quarter (616 6222/ www.rutgers.nl). Tram 1.* **Open** *By appointment* 9am-4.30pm Mon, Wed, Fri; 6-8pm Tue, Thur. **Map** p310 C6.
Besides giving information on health issues, the staff at this family planning centre can help visitors with prescriptions for contraceptive pills, morning-after pills and condoms, IUD fitting and cervical smear tests. Prescription costs vary.

# Dentists

For a dentist (*tandarts*), call the dentist administration bureau on 0900 821 2230. Operators can put you in touch with your nearest dentist; lines are open 24 hours. Alternatively, make an appointment at one of the clinics listed below.

## AOC

*Wilhelmina Gasthuisplein 167, Oud West (616 1234). Tram 1, 2, 3, 5, 6, 12.* **Open** 9am-4pm Mon-Fri. **Map** p309 B5.
Emergency dental treatment.

## TBB

*570 9595.*
A 24-hour service that can refer callers to a dentist. Operators can also give details of chemists open outside normal hours.

# Opticians

For details of opticians and optometrists in Amsterdam, *see p159.*

# Pharmacies

For pharmacy hours, *see below* **Prescriptions**. For pharmacies, *see p176.*

# Prescriptions

Chemists (*drogists*) sell toiletries and non-prescription drugs and are usually open 9.30am to 5.30pm, Monday to Saturday. For prescription drugs, go to a pharmacy (*apotheek*), usually open 9.30am to 5.30pm Monday to Friday.

Outside these hours, phone the **Afdeling Inlichtingen Apotheken** (*see p282*) or consult the daily newspaper *Het Parool*, which publishes details of which *apotheken* are open late that week. Details are also posted at local *apotheken*.

# STDs, HIV & AIDS

The Netherlands was one of the first countries to pour money into research once the HIV virus was recognised. But though the country was swift to take action and promote safe sex, condoms are still not distributed free in clubs and bars as they are in the UK.

Aside from the groups listed below, the **AIDS Helpline** (0800 022 2220/689 2577; open 2-10pm Mon-Fri), part of the Stichting AIDS Fonds (*see below*), offers advice by phone (including on STDs).

## HIV Vereniging

*1E Helmersstraat 17, Oud West (616 0160/fax 616 1200/www.hivnet.org). Tram 1, 2, 3, 5, 6, 12.* **Open** 9am-5pm Mon-Fri. **Map** p310 C5.
The Netherlands HIV Association supports the interests of all those who are HIV positive, including offering legal help, and produces a bi-monthly Dutch magazine, *HIV Nieuws* (€36 per year). There's an HIV Café every Tuesday and Sunday, plus regular lunches and dinners for people with HIV.

## SAD-Schorerstichting

*PC Hooftstraat 5, Museum Quarter (662 4206/www.schorer.nl). Tram 2, 3, 5, 6, 7, 10, 12, 20.* **Open** 9am-5pm Mon-Fri. **Map** p310 D5.

This state-funded agency offers psycho-social support, education and HIV prevention advice for gays and lesbians. Examinations and treatment of sexually transmitted diseases, including an HIV test, are free. The clinic is held at the city's health department, the GG&GD (Groenburgwal 44); call to make an appointment. Staff speak English.

## Stichting AIDS Fonds

*Keizersgracht 390, Western Canal Belt (626 2669/fax 627 5221/ www.aidsfonds.nl). Tram 1, 2, 5.* **Open** 9am-5pm Mon-Fri. **Map** p310 C4.
This group, which runs fundraisers such as the Amsterdam Diners (*see p203* **The queer year**), channels money into research and safe sex promotion. It also runs a helpline for gay and lesbian-specific health questions (662 4206/0900 204 2040; open 10am-5pm Mon-Thur) and organises workshops such as F*CKSH*P, on anal sex. Parts of its website are in English.

# Helplines

## Alcoholics Anonymous

*625 6057.* **Open** 24hr answerphone.
A lengthy but informative message details times and dates of meetings, and contact numbers for counsellors.

## Narcotics Anonymous

*662 6307.* **Open** 24hr answerphone with phone numbers of counsellors.

## SOS Telephone Helpline

*675 7575.* **Open** 24hrs daily.
A counselling service – comparable to the Samaritans in the UK and Lifeline in the US – for anyone with emotional problems, run by volunteers. English isn't always understood at first, but keep trying and someone will be able to help you.

# ID

Regulations concerning identification require that everyone carries some form of ID when opening accounts at banks or other financial institutions, when looking for work, when applying for benefits, when found on public transport without a ticket and when going to a professional football match. You then have to register with the local council, in the same building as the Aliens' Police (*see p290*).

**Directory**

## Insurance

EU countries have reciprocal medical arrangements with the Netherlands. British citizens will need form E111, obtained by filling in the application form in leaflet SA30, available from the Post Office. Read the small print so you know how to get treatment at a reduced charge: you may have to explain this to the Dutch doctor or dentist who treats you. If you need treatment, photocopy your insurance form and leave it with the doctor or dentist concerned. Not all treatments are covered by the E111, so take out private travel insurance covering both health and personal belongings. Citizens of other EU countries should make sure they have obtained one of the forms E110, E111 or E112; citizens of almost all other countries should take out insurance before their visit.

## Internet

Among Amsterdam's ISPs are **Xs4all** (www.xs4all.nl), **Cistron** (www.cistron.nl) and **Chello** (www.chello.nl). All of the main global ISPs, such as **AOL** and **Compuserve**, have a presence here (check websites for a local number). Local hotels are increasingly well equipped for surfing, whether with dataports in the rooms or a terminal in the lobby.

### Internet cafés

### EasyEverything
*Reguliersbreestraat 22, Southern Canal Belt (320 6289/ www.easyeverything.com). Tram 16, 24, 25.* **Open** 24hrs daily. **Rates** from €2.50/unit. **Map** p311 D4.
The amount of time one unit allows depends on how busy it is: as little as a half-hour or as much as six hours. There's a branch at Damrak 33.

### Freeworld
*Nieuwendijk 30, Old Centre: New Side (620 0902/www.freeworld.nl). Tram 1, 2, 5, 13, 17, 20.*

**Open** 10am-1am Mon-Thur, Sun; 10am-3am Fri, Sat. **Rates** €1.15/30min. **Map** p306 D2.
If you want to surf here, you'll have to drink: refreshments are compulsory. Coffee/tea is €1.20, beer €1.70.

### Internet Café
*Martelaarsgracht 11, Old Centre: New Side (627 1052/ www.internetcafe.nl). Tram 4, 9, 16, 20, 24, 25.* **Open** 9am-1am Mon-Thur, Sun; 9am-3am Fri, Sat. **Rates** around €1.15/30min. **Map** p306 D2.
Funky spotlighting and speedy connections, but compulsory drinks: beware of seemingly oh-so-courteous refills by staff pushing a point.

## Left luggage

There is a staffed left-luggage counter at Schiphol Airport, open from 7am to 10.45pm daily. There are also lockers in the arrival and departure halls, while in Amsterdam there are lockers at Centraal Station with 24-hour access. Expect to pay €2.50-€6 per item per day.

## Legal help

### ACCESS
*Plein 24, 2511 CS The Hague (070 346 2525/www.euronet.nl/users/ access).* **Open** 10am-4pm Mon-Fri;
The Administrative Committee to Coordinate English Speaking Services is a non-profit organisation, which provides assistance in English through a telephone information line, workshops and counselling.

### Bureau Voor Rechtshulp
*Spuistraat 10, Old Centre: New Side (520 5100/www.bvr.rechtsbijstand.net). Tram 1, 2, 5.* **Open** *Telephone enquiries* 9am-5pm Mon-Fri. *By appointment* 9am-1pm Mon-Fri. **Map** p306 C3.
Qualified lawyers who give free legal advice on a variety of matters.

### Legal Advice Line
*444 6333.* **Open** *Telephone enquiries* 9pm-5pm Mon-Thur. Free advice from student lawyers.

## Libraries

You'll need to present proof of residence in Amsterdam and ID if you want to join a library (*bibliotheek*) and borrow books. It costs €18.60 (23-64s) or

€11.12 (18-22s, over-65s) per year and is free for under-18s. However, in public libraries (*openbare bibliotheek*) you can read books, papers and magazines without taking out membership. For university libraries, *see p288*.

### American Institute
*Plantage Muidergracht 12, the Plantage (525 4380). Tram 7, 9/Metro Waterlooplein.* **Open** Call for details. **Map** p312 G3.

### British Council Education Centre
*Oxford House, Nieuwezijds Voorburgwal 328L, Old Centre: New Side (421 7040/fax 421 7003/ www.nbcc.co.uk). Tram 1, 2, 5, 13, 14, 17.* **Open** 9am-5pm Mon-Fri. **Map** p306 D3.

### Centrale Bibliotheek
*Prinsengracht 587, Western Canal Belt (523 0900/www.oba.nl). Tram 1, 2, 5.* **Open** 1-9pm Mon; 10am-9pm Tue-Thur; 10am-5pm Fri, Sat. *Oct-Apr* also 1-5pm Sun. **Map** p310 C4.
Anyone is welcome to use this, the main public library, for reference purposes. There is a variety of English-language books.

## Lost property

For the sake of insurance, report lost property to the police immediately; *see p287*. If you lose your passport, inform your embassy or consulate as well. For anything lost at the Hoek van Holland ferry terminal or Schiphol Airport, contact the company with which you're travelling. For lost credit cards, *see p286*.

### Centraal Station
*Stationsplein 15, Old Centre: Old Side (557 8544). Tram 1, 2, 4, 5, 9, 13, 16, 17, 20, 24, 25.* **Open** 8am-8pm Mon-Fri, 9am-5pm Sat. **Map** p306 D1.
Items found on trains are kept here for four days and then sent to NS Afdeling Verloren Voorwerpen, 2e Daalsedijk 4, 3500 HA Utrecht (030 235 3923; open 8am-8pm Mon-Fri, 9am-5pm Sat).

### GVB Lost Property
*Prins Hendrikkade 108-14, Old Centre: New Side (460 5858). Tram 1, 2, 4, 5, 9, 13, 16, 17, 20, 24, 25.* **Open** 9am-4pm Mon-Fri. **Map** p306 C1.

**Directory**

Where to head for items lost on a bus, metro or tram. If you're reporting a loss from the previous day, phone after 2pm to allow time for the property to be sorted.

### Police Lost Property

*Stephensonstraat 18, Zuid (559 3005). Tram 12/Metro Amstel Station/bus 14.* **Open** *In person* 9.30am-3.30pm Mon-Fri. *By phone* noon-3.30pm Mon-Fri.
Report any loss to the police station in the same district: it holds items for a day or so before sending them here for up to three months.

## Media

### Newspapers & magazines

*De Telegraaf*, a one-time collaborationist and still right-wing daily, is the Netherlands' biggest-selling paper, the nearest the country has to a tabloid press. *Het Parool* was the main underground wartime journal, but is now a hip afternoon rag; its sister morning paper, *De Volkskrant*, also enjoys a relatively young, progressive readership. *Trouw*, the other Amsterdam-published national daily, is owned by Perscombinatie, the same company that owns *Het Parool* and *De Volkskrant*.

For Anglophones, there's the *Financieele Dagblad*'s sole English page each day, and, as of late 2001, a new four-page English-language paper focusing on Dutch news, business and events, given away Monday to Saturday with the *International Herald Tribune*. The Amsterdam Tourist Board publishes the monthly *Day by Day*, a basic listings guide. However, *Shark*, a freesheet found in bars and clubs, does a fine job of picking up the slack with round-ups of films and music, as well as a section for gay and lesbian events. For more, check www.underwateramsterdam.com.

Foreign magazines and papers are widely available here, but they're pricey; British papers are around €2 for a daily, €4 for a Sunday. **Athenaeum** is a browser's dream; 100 metres away, **Waterstone's** stocks UK publications, and the **American Book Center** nearby has plenty of American magazines. For all, *see p155*.

## Broadcast media

After reform in the late 1990s, the city currently has ten commercial stations, most of which are as short on viewers as they are on style; they include Veronica and SBS6 (both painfully commercial), TV10 (old repeats, such as *Blackadder*), RTL5 (series and films from the US) and the Music Factory (a Europop-heavy, Dutch-language MTV clone). There are now about 30 extra channels on cable, including non-commercial stations in German, French, Italian and Belgian, various local channels, and English-language multinationals such as CNN and MTV. The basic deal also includes BBC1, so there's no need to miss out on *EastEnders*. The wall-to-wall porn is an urban myth, so don't expect any late-night thrills unless your hotel has the 'extended service', which usually also features film channels, Discovery, the Cartoon Network, Eurosport and others. Dutch radio is generally as bland as the TV.

## Money

Since January 2002, the Dutch currency has been the euro. For more on this, *see p286* **The euro files**.

## ATMs

Cash machines are only found at banks here: as yet, no bank has been resourceful enough to set any up in shops or bars, as is increasingly the case in the UK and parts of the US. If your cashcard carries the Maestro or Cirrus symbols, you should be able to withdraw cash from ATMs here, though it's worth checking with your bank first.

## Banks

Banks and bureaux de change offer similar rates of exchange, but banks tend to charge less commission. Most banks are open from 9am to 5pm Monday to Friday, with the Postbank opening up on Saturday mornings. Dutch banks buy and sell foreign currency and exchange travellers' cheques, but few of them will give cash advances against credit cards. For a list of banks, *see p279*, or check the *Amsterdam Yellow Pages* under 'Banken'.

## Bureaux de change

Bureaux de change can be found in the city centre, especially on Leidseplein, Damrak and Rokin. Those listed offer reasonable rates, though they charge more commission than banks. Hotel and tourist bureau exchange facilities generally cost more.

### American Express

*Damrak 66, Old Centre: New Side (504 8777). Tram 4, 9, 14, 16, 20, 24, 25.* **Open** 9am-5pm Mon-Fri; 9am-noon Sat. **Map** p306 D2.
A number of facilities here.

### Change Express

*Damrak 86, Old Centre: New Side (624 6681/624 6682). Tram 4, 9, 14, 16, 20, 24, 25.* **Open** 8am-11pm daily. **Map** p306 D2.
**Branch**: Leidseplein 123 (622 1425).

### GWK

*Centraal Station, Old Centre: Old Side (627 2731). Tram 1, 2, 4, 5, 9, 13, 16, 17, 20, 24, 25.* **Open** 7am-10.30pm daily. **Map** p306 D1.
**Branch**: Schiphol Airport (in the railway station; 653 5121).

### Thomas Cook

*Dam 23-5, Old Centre: New Side (625 0922). Tram 4, 9, 14, 16, 20, 24, 25.* **Open** 9.15am-6.15pm daily. **Map** p306 D3.
**Branches**: Damrak 1-5 (620 3236); Leidseplein 31A.

## Credit cards

Credit cards are widely used here, but not every establishment accepts them. The majority of restaurants will take at least one type of card; they're less popular in bars and shops, so always carry some cash. The most popular cards, in descending order, are Visa, Mastercard (aka Eurocard), American Express and Diners Club.

If you lose your cards, call the following relevant 24-hour numbers immediately.

**American Express** 504 8666.
**Diners Club** 651 4821.
**Mastercard/Eurocard** 030 283 5555 if card was issued in the Netherlands; otherwise, freephone 0800 022 5821.
**Visa** 660 0611 if card was issued in the Netherlands; otherwise, freephone 0800 022 4176.

## Tax

Sales tax (aka BTW; 19 per cent on most items, six per cent on goods such as books and food, more on alcohol, tobacco and petrol) will be included in the prices quoted in shops. If you live outside the EU, you are entitled to a tax refund on purchases of up to €150 from one shop on any one day. Get the clerk to give you an export certificate, and then present it to a customs official as you leave the country, who'll stamp it; you can then collect your cash at the ABN-AMRO bank at Schiphol Airport or via post at a later date (ask the official for information).

There's an additional tourist tax of five per cent levied on hotels, though in all but the priciest spots, this will be included in the prices quoted.

# The euro files

As of 1 January 2002, Europe has had a new currency. The franc, the peseta, the lira, the guilder and a handful of other currencies are history, and 12 European countries now recognise only the **euro**.

The new currency has been a long time in the making. Its genesis was implicit in the 1958 Treaty of Rome, which aimed to create a common European market that would increase economic prosperity and contribute to 'an ever closer union among the peoples of Europe'. Building on this, the Single European Act (1986) and the Treaty on European Union (1992) introduced Economic and Monetary Union (the slightly unfortunately acronymed EMU) and laid the foundations for a single currency.

On 1 January 1999, the third stage of EMU began, with the setting of exchange rates against the currencies of the participating countries – one euro is equivalent to 2.20371 old Dutch guilders; or, put another way, the old guilder was worth 0.45378 euros – and the implementation of a common monetary policy in each state. Three years later the euro was introduced as a legal currency and the 11 currencies that it replaced (after a brief overlap period) – those of Germany, France, Spain, Portugal, Italy, the Netherlands, Belgium, Luxembourg, Ireland, Austria and Finland – all became subdivisions of the euro. Greece threw the drachma into the euro ring in January 2001, making a total of 12 member states that share a single interest rate set by the European Central Bank (ECB).

### RECOGNISING THE EURO

**One euro** is made up of **100 cents**. The euro symbol is **€**. There are seven new banknotes, and eight coins.

The **notes** are of differing colours and sizes (€5 is the smallest, €500 the largest). They were designed by Austrian artist Robert Kalina to represent different periods and styles of European architecture. They are:

**€5** (grey; classical)
**€10** (red; Romanesque)
**€20** (blue; Gothic)
**€50** (orange; Renaissance)
**€100** (green; baroque and rococo)
**€200** (yellow-brown; iron and glass)
**€500** (purple; 20th century)

The eight denominations of coins, designed by Luc Luycx of the Royal Belgian Mint, vary in colour, size and thickness. They share one common side, showing a map and flag; the other side features a country-specific design (note: all can be used in any participating state). They are:

**€2** (outer part white, inner part yellow; fine milled edge with lettering)
**€1** (outer part yellow, inner part white; interrupted milled edge)
**50 cents** (yellow; shaped edge, fine scallops)
**20 cents** (yellow; plain edge)
**10 cents** (yellow; shaped edge, fine scallops)
**5 cents** (red; smooth edge)
**2 cents** (red; smooth edge with a groove)
**1 cent** (red; smooth edge)

For more information on the euro, check online at **www.euro.ecb.int**.

## Opening hours

For all our listings in this Guide we give full opening times, but as a general rule, shops are open from 1pm to 6pm (if they're open at all; many shops are closed Mondays); 10am to 6pm Tuesday to Friday, with some staying open until 9pm on Thursdays; and 9am to 5pm on Saturdays. Smaller shops tend to open at varying times; if in doubt, phone first. For shops that open late, *see p168*.

The city's bars open at various times during the day and close at around 1am throughout the week, except for Fridays and Saturdays, when they stay open until 2am or 3am. Restaurants are generally open in the evening from 5pm until 11pm (though some close as early as 9pm); many are closed on Sunday and Monday.

## Police stations

The Dutch police are under no obligation to grant a phone call to those they detain – they can hold people for up to six hours for questioning if the alleged crime is not serious, 24 hours for major matters – but they'll phone the relevant consulate on behalf of a foreign detainee.

If you are a victim of theft or assault, report it to the nearest police station. For emergencies, *see p281*.

### Hoofdbureau van Politie (Police Headquarters)

*Elandsgracht 117, the Jordaan (559 9111). Tram 7, 10, 20.* **Open** 24hrs daily. **Map** p310 C4.

## Postal services

For post destined for outside Amsterdam, use the *overige bestemmingen* slot in letter boxes. The logo for the national postal service is *ptt post* (white letters on a red oblong). Most post offices – recognisable by their red and blue signs – are open 9am to 5pm, Monday to Friday. The postal information phoneline is 0800 0417. Housed in every post office is the Postbank, a money-changing facility.

It costs 50¢ or 54¢ to send a postcard from Amsterdam to anywhere in Europe, and 75¢ outside Europe. Stamps (*postzegels*) can be bought with postcards from tobacconists and souvenir shops.

## Post offices

### Centraal Station Post Office

*Oosterdokskade 3, Old Centre: Old Side (622 8272). Tram 1, 2, 4, 5, 9, 13, 16, 17, 20, 24, 25.* **Open** 8.30am-9pm Mon-Fri; 9am-noon Sat. **Map** p307 E1.

### Main Post Office

*Singel 250, Old Centre: New Side (330 0555). Tram 1, 2, 5, 13, 14, 17, 20.* **Open** 9am-6pm Mon-Wed, Fri; 9am-8pm Thur; 10am-1.30pm Sat. **Map** p306 C3.

## Post restante

*Post Restante, Hoofdpostkantoor, Singel 250, 1016 AB Amsterdam.* **Map** p306 C3.

If you're not sure where you'll be staying in Amsterdam, people can send your post to the above address. You'll be able to collect it from the main post office (*see p287*) with ID.

## Religion

### Catholic

**St John and St Ursula** *Begijnhof 30, Old Centre: New Side (622 1918). Tram 1, 2, 4, 5, 16, 20, 24, 25.* **Open** 1-6pm Mon; 8.30am-6pm Tue-Sat. **Services** in Dutch and French; phone for details. **Map** p306 D3.

### Dutch Reformed Church

**Oude Kerk** *Oudekerksplein 33, Old Centre: Old Side (625 8284). Tram 4, 9, 16, 20, 24, 25.* **Open** 11am-5pm Mon-Sat; 1-5pm Sun. **Services** in Dutch; 11am Sun. **Map** p306 D2.

### Jewish

**Liberal Jewish Community Amsterdam** *Jacob Soetendorpstraat 8, Zuid (642 3562/office rabbinate 644 2619). Tram 4.* **Open** 9am-3pm Mon-Fri. *Rabbi's office* 10am-3pm Mon-Thur. **Services** 8pm Fri; 10am Sat.

**Orthodox Jewish Community Amsterdam** *Postbus 7967, Van der Boechorststraat 26, Zuid (646 0046). Bus 69, 169.* **Open** 9am-5pm Mon-Fri by appointment only. Information on orthodox synagogues and Jewish facilities.

### Muslim

**THAIBA Islamic Cultural Centre** *Kraaiennest 125, Zuid (698 2526). Metro Gaasperplas.* Phone for details of prayer times and cultural activities.

### Quaker

**Religious Genootschap der Vrienden** *Vossiusstraat 20, Museum Quarter (679 4238). Tram 1, 2, 5.* **Open** 11am-4pm Tue; on other days call 070 363 2132. **Service** 10.30am Sun.

### Reformed Church

**English Reformed Church** *Begijnhof 48, Old Centre: New Side (624 9665/minister Mr John Cowey 672 2288/www.ercadam.nl). Tram 1, 2, 4, 5, 9, 16, 20, 24, 25.* **Open** May-Sept 2-4pm Mon-Fri. Closed Oct-Apr. **Services** in English 10.30am Sun; Dutch 7pm Sun. **Map** p306 D3. The main place of worship for the local English-speaking community.

### Salvation Army

**Meeting Hall** *Oudezijds Achterburgwal 45, Old Centre: Old Side (520 8422). Tram 1, 2, 4, 5, 9, 13, 16, 17, 24, 25.* **Service** 10am Sun. **Map** p306 D2.

## Safety & security

Amsterdam is a relatively safe city, but that's not to say you shouldn't take care when walking through it. The Red Light District is rife with undesirables who, if not necessarily violent, are expert pickpockets; be vigilant, especially on or around bridges, and try to avoid making eye contact with anyone who looks like they may be up to no good (a relative term in the Red Light District, but the point stands).

Take care on the train to Schiphol, where there has been a recent spate of thefts, and, if you cycle in town, lock your bike super-securely. Otherwise, just use your common sense, keeping valuables in a safe place, not leaving bags unattended, and so on.

**Directory**

## Smoking

Smoking is widely tolerated in Amsterdam. You'll have no problems sparking up in a bar or most restaurants. For smoking dope, *see p147*.

## Study

Amsterdam's two major universities are the **UvA** (Universiteit van Amsterdam), which has around 27,000 students, and the **VU** (Vrije Universiteit), with about half that. Many UvA buildings across town are historic and listed (recognise them by their red and black plaques), whereas the VU has just one big building at de Boelelaan, in the south of Amsterdam.

Students are often entitled to discounts at assorted shops, attractions and entertainment venues; presenting an ISIC card is usually enough.

### Courses

A number of UvA departments offer international courses and programmes at all levels. Details are available from the Foreign Relations Office (Spui 25, 1012 SR). Most postgraduate institutes of the UvA also take foreign students.

#### Amsterdam Summer University

*Felix Meritis Building, Keizersgracht 324, Southern Canal Belt (620 0225/ www.amsu.edu). Tram 1, 2, 5.* **Courses** mid July-early Sept. **Map** p310 C4.
The ASU offers an annual summer programme of courses, workshops, training and seminars in the arts and sciences, plus international classes.

#### Crea

*Turfdraagsterpad 17, Old Centre: Old Side (525 1400/www.crea.uva.nl). Tram 4, 9, 14, 16, 20, 24, 25.* **Open** 10am-11pm Mon-Fri; 10am-5pm Sat; 11am-5pm Sun. Closed July (phone to check). **Map** p306 D3.
Inexpensive creative courses, lectures and performances, covering theatre, radio, video, media, dance, music, photography and fine art. Courses are not in English.

## Foreign Student Service (FSS)

*Oranje Nassaulaan 5, Zuid (671 5915). Tram 2.* **Open** 9am-5.30pm Mon-Fri.
The Foreign Student Service promotes the well-being of foreign students, providing personal assistance and general information on studying in the Netherlands.

### UvA Service & Information Centre

*Binnengasthuisstraat 9, Old Centre: Old Side (525 8080). Tram 4, 9, 16, 20, 24, 25.* **Open** *In person* 10am-4pm Mon-Wed, Fri; 10am-7pm Thur. *Telephone enquiries* 9am-5pm Mon-Fri. **Map** p306 D3.
Personal advice on studying and everything that goes with it.

### VU Student Information

*Office 444 7777/direct line 444 5000.* **Open** 9am-5pm Mon-Fri.
The VU's helpline provides advice on courses and accommodation.

## Student bookshops

Because English textbooks are widely used in colleges, they are sold everywhere, often cheaply. *See p155* for more bookshops.

### VU Boekhandel

*De Boelelaan 1105, Zuid (644 4355). Tram 5/Metro 51.* **Open** 9am-7pm Mon-Fri; 10am-3.30pm Sat. **Credit** AmEx, MC, V.
The VU Academic Bookshop has a large selection of books relating to all sciences, plus novels, tourist guides and children's books.

## Students' unions

### AEGEE

*Vendelsstraat 2, Old Centre: Old Side (525 2496). Tram 4, 6, 9, 24, 25.* **Open** 2-5pm Mon-Fri. **Map** p306 D3.
The Association des Etats Généraux des Etudiants de l'Europe basically organises seminars, workshops, summer courses and sporting events in Amsterdam and around 170 other European university cities.

### ASVA-OBAS

*Binnengasthuisstraat 9, Old Centre: Old Side (623 8052). Tram 4, 9, 14, 16, 20, 24, 25.* **Open** *July, Aug* 11am-4pm Mon-Fri. *Sept-Jun* 12.30-4pm Mon-Wed, Fri; 12.30-6pm Thur. **Map** p306 D3.
ASVA offers assistance to foreign students, including help in finding accommodation.

## SRVU

*De Boelelaan 1183A, Zuid (444 9424). Tram 5/Metro 51.* **Open** *Mid Aug-June* 12.30-3.30pm Mon-Fri. *July-mid Aug* irregular hours.
SRVU is the union for VU students. Its accommodation service can also help foreign students find a place to stay, and offer general advice. Membership is €10 per year.

## University libraries

Both libraries below hold many academic titles and also provide access to the Internet.

### UvA Main Library

*Singel 425, Old Centre: New Side (525 2326). Tram 1, 2, 5.* **Open** *Study* 9am-midnight Mon-Fri; 9.30am-5pm Sat. *Borrowing* 9.30am-5pm Mon, Wed, Fri; 9.30am-8pm Tue, Thur; 9.30am-1pm Sat. **Map** p310 D4.
To borrow books you need a UB (Universiteit Bibliotheek-University Library) card (€18): foreign students can get one if they're in Amsterdam for three months or more. Cards can be issued for one day, one month or one year.

### VU Main Library

*De Boelelaan 1105, Zuid (444 5200). Tram 5/Metro 51.* **Open** *Study* Sept-Jun 9am-9pm Mon-Thur; 9am-5pm Fri. July-Aug 9am-5pm Mon-Fri. *Borrowing* 10am-4pm Mon-Fri. **Membership** €15 per year.
Not one big library, but several small ones. Membership is open to foreign students.

## Telephones

All Amsterdam numbers within this book are listed without the city code, which is 020. To call Amsterdam from within the city, you don't need the code: just dial the seven-digit number. To call an Amsterdam number from elsewhere in the Netherlands, add 020 at the start of the listed number. Numbers in the Netherlands outside of Amsterdam are listed with their code in this Guide.

In addition to the standard city codes, three other types of numbers appear from time to time in this book. 0800 numbers are freephone numbers; those prefixed 0900 are charged at premium rates (20¢ a minute or more); and 06 numbers are for mobile phones. If you're in any doubt, call directory enquiries (0900 8008).

## Dialling & codes

### From the Netherlands

Dial the following code, then the number:
**To Australia**: 00 61
**To Irish Republic**: 00 353
**To UK**: 00 44, plus number (drop first '0' from area code)
**To USA**: 00 1

### To the Netherlands

Dial the relevant international access code listed below, then the Dutch country code 31, then the number; drop the first '0' of the area code, so for Amsterdam use 20 rather than 020. To call 06 (mobile) numbers from abroad, there is no city code: just drop the first '0' from the 06 and dial the number as it appears. However, 0800 (freephone) and 0900 (premium rate) numbers cannot be reached from abroad.
**From Australia**: 00 11
**From Irish Republic**: 00
**From UK**: 00
**From USA**: 011

### Within the Netherlands

**National directory enquiries**: 0900 8008
**International directory enquiries**: 0900 8418
**Local operator**: 0800 0101
**International operator**: 0800 0410

## Making a call

Listen for the dialling tone (a hum), insert a phonecard or money, dial the code (none is required for calls within Amsterdam), then dial the number. A digital display on public phones shows the credit remaining, but only wholly unused coins are returned. Phoning from a hotel is pricey.

### International calls

International calls can be made from all phone boxes. Off-peak rates apply 8pm to 8am Monday to Friday and all weekend. For more information on off-peak rates, phone international directory enquiries (0900 8418).

### Telephone directories

Found in post offices (see p287). When phoning information services, taxis or train stations you may hear

the recorded message, 'Er zijn nog drie [3]/twee [2]/een [1] wachtende(n) voor u.' This tells you how many people are ahead of you in the telephone queuing system.

## Public phones

Public phone boxes are mainly glass with a green trim. There are also telephone poles all over the city, identifiable by their blue and green KPN logo. Most phones take phonecards rather than coins, available from the Amsterdam Tourist Board, stations, post offices and tobacconists. You can use credit cards in many phones.

## Mobile phones

Amsterdam's mobile network is run on a mix of the 900 and 1800 GSM bands, which means all dual-band UK handsets should work here. However, it's always best to check with your service provider that it has an arrangement with a Dutch provider. US phone users should always contact their provider before departure to check compatibility.

## Time

Amsterdam is one hour ahead of Greenwich Mean Time (GMT). All clocks on Central European Time (CET) now go back and forward on the same spring and autumn dates as GMT. For the speaking clock in Dutch, phone 0900 8002.

## Tipping

Though a service charge will be included in hotel, taxi, bar, café and restaurant bills, it's polite to round your payment up to the nearest euro for small bills and to the nearest five euros for larger sums, leaving the extra in change rather than filling in the blank on a credit card slip. In taxis, the most common tip is around ten per cent for short journeys.

## Toilets

Using the green metal urinals that have been 'enhancing' the streetscape for over a century should be a part of any visiting boy's agenda. On weekends, the city also places 'grey rockets' in which to piss on nightlife-oriented squares such as Leidseplein. And if you choose to ignore either of these options and get busted for 'wild pissing' – as it's known here – you may find yourself having to pay a €40 ticket. For the ladies, it's a sadder story: public toilets are rare, and you may be forced to seek a bar or a café and buy something before you can use their facilities.

## Tourist information

### Amsterdam Tourist Board (VVV)

*Stationsplein 10, Old Centre: New Side (0900 400 4040/ www.visitamsterdam.nl). Tram 1, 2, 4, 5, 9, 13, 16, 17, 20, 24, 25.* **Open** 9am-5pm daily. **Map** p306 D1.
The main office of the Amsterdam Tourist Board is right outside Centraal Station. English-speaking staff can change money and provide details on transport, entertainment, exhibitions and day-trips in the Netherlands. They also arrange hotel bookings for a fee of €2.75, and excursions and car hire for free. There is a good range of brochures for sale detailing walks and cycling tours, as well as cassette tours, maps and, for €1.15, a monthly listings magazine *Day by Day*. The information line features an English-language service but note that it is charged at premium rates. **Branches:** Leidseplein 1 (open 9am-5pm daily); Centraal Station, Platform 2 (open 8am-7.45pm Mon-Sat; 9am-5pm Sun); Schiphol Airport (open 7am-10pm daily).

## Visas & immigration

A valid passport is all that is required for a stay in the Netherlands of up to three months if you're from the EU, the USA, Canada, Australia or

New Zealand. Citizens of other countries should apply in advance for a tourist visa from their country of origin.

As with any trip, you should confirm visa requirements well before you plan to travel, with your local Dutch embassy or consulate or on www.immigratiedienst.nl.

For stays of longer than three months, apply for a residents' permit (MVV visa), generally easier to get if you're from one of the countries listed above. (Technically, citizens of EC member countries don't need a residents' permit, but they will be required for all sorts of bureacratic functions like opening a bank account.)

When you have a fixed address, take your birth certificate to the **Dienst Vreemdelingenpolitie** (Aliens' Police; Johan Huizingalaan 757, Slotervaart; 559 6300/ www.immigratiedienst.nl), pick up a form and wait to hear if you've been accepted for interview.

## When to go

### Climate

Amsterdam's climate is very changeable, and often wet and windy. January and February are coldest, with summer often humid. The average daytime temperatures range from around 2-3°C (36-38°F) December through February, up to 14-17°C (57-62°F) from June to September.

If you can understand Dutch, try calling the weather line on 0900 8003.

### Public holidays

Called 'Nationale Feestdagen' in Dutch, they are as follows: New Year's Day; Good Friday; Easter Sunday and Monday; Koninginnedag (Queen's Day, 30 April); Remembrance Day (4 May); Liberation Day (5 May); Ascension Day; Whit (Pentecost) Sunday and Monday; Christmas Day, and the day after Christmas.

## Women

Aside from some pockets of the Red Light District late at night, central Amsterdam is fairly safe for women, as long as usual common-sense safety precautions are observed.

### De Eerstelijn

*613 0245.* **Open** 9.30am-11pm Mon-Fri; 4-11pm Sat, Sun.
This helpline is for victims of rape, assault, sexual harassment or threats.

### Meldpunt Vrouwenopvang

*611 6022.* **Open** 9.30am-11pm Mon-Fri; 4-11pm Sat, Sun.
Victims of abuse will be referred to a safe house or safe address.

## Working in Amsterdam

EU nationals can work here, but only with a residents' permit (*see above*); non-EU citizens will find it difficult to get a visa without a job in place. Jobs are not easy to come by, particularly without a visa.

# Moving in

As moving around Europe gets easier, so Amsterdam's accommodation situation gets tougher. It's all down to supply and demand in this four-storey sardine can of a city: not enough of the former, and too much of the latter.

To get a flat, you need friends, money and tons of luck. In Amsterdam, there are two main price sectors: below €450 per month, and above €450 per month. Anything above €450 is considered free sector housing and can be found through agencies or in newspapers (in particular, the Wednesday, Thursday and Saturday editions of *De Telegraaf* and *De Volksrant*, and every Tuesday and Thursday in the ads paper *Via Via*). Unfortunately, flatshares are not common, and agency commission is high.

If you're looking for properties under the €450 mark, you have two main choices. Both require a residents' permit (*see above*). If you're studying in the city, register with

one of the three main housing co-ops: **Woning Net** (0900 8210 premium rate), **Archipel** (511 8911) and **Spectrum** (489 0085). For a charge of around €16 (registration is an extra €11 or so with Archipel), these agencies supply information on available accommodation. However, this method can take forever given the shortage of properties and surfeit of clients.

The other alternative is to register with one of the many non-profit housing agencies that hold property lotteries among would-be tenants. This may seem bizarre, but they do at least give you a chance of eventually getting a room in a house. Call **ASW Kamerbureau** on 523 0130.

Holders of residents' permits can also apply for council (public) housing. Register with the **Stedelijke Woning Dienst** (City Housing Service; Stadhuis, Waterlooplein; 552 7511/www.swd.amsterdam.nl). Bank on a very long wait.

# Vocabulary

The vast majority of people you'll meet in Amsterdam will speak good English, and you'll probably be able to get by without a word of Dutch during your stay. However, a little effort goes a long way, and the locals are appreciative of those visitors polite enough to take five minutes and learn some basic phrases. Here are a few that might help.

## PRONUNCIATION GUIDE

**ch**  like 'ch' in 'loch'
**ee**  like 'ay' in 'hay'
**g**  similar to 'ch'
**ie**  like 'ea' in 'lean'
**ei**  like 'i' in 'line'
**j**  like 'y' in 'yes' except when preceded by 'i', when it should be said as a 'y'
**oe**  like 'o' in 'who'
**oo**  like 'o' in no
**ou**  like 'ow' in 'cow'; same for *au* and *ui*
**tie**  like 'tsy' in 'itsy bitsy'
**tje**  like 'ch' in 'church'
**v**  like 'f' in 'for'
**w**  like 'w' in 'which', with a hint of the 'v' in 'vet'
**y/ij**  (written as either) a cross between 'i' in 'hide' and 'ay' in 'way'

## WORDS

**hello**  hallo (*hullo*) or dag (*daarg*)
**goodbye**  tot ziens (*tot zeens*)
**bye**  dag (*daarg*)
**yes**  ja (*yah*)
**yes please**  ja, graag (*ya, graag*)
**no**  nee (*nay*)
**no thanks**  nee, dank je (*nay, dank ye*)
**please**  alstublieft (*als-too-bleeft*); also used to replace phrase 'there you are' when exchanging items with others
**thank you**  dank u (*dank-oo*)
**thanks**  bedankt

**excuse me**  pardon
**good**  goed
**bad**  slecht
**big**  groot
**small**  klein (*kline*)
**waiter**  ober
**nice**  mooi (*moy*)
**tasty**  lekker (*lecker*)
**open**  open
**closed**  gesloten/dicht
**inside**  binnen
**outside**  buiten (*bowten*)
**left**  links
**right**  rechts (*reks*)
**straight on**  rechtdoor
**far**  ver (*fair*)
**near**  dichtbij (*dikt-bye*)

## PLACES

**street**  straat (*straart*)
**square**  plein (*pline*)
**canal**  gracht
**shop**  winkel
**bank**  bank
**post office**  postkantoor
**pharmacy**  apotheek
**hotel**  hotel
**hotel room**  hotelkamer
**bar**  bar
**restaurant**  restaurant
**hospital**  ziekenhuis

## DAYS

**Monday**  Maandag
**Tuesday**  Dinsdag
**Wednesday**  Woensdag
**Thursday**  Donderdag
**Friday**  Vrijdag
**Saturday**  Zaterdag
**Sunday**  Zondag
**today**  vandaag
**yesterday**  gisteren
**tomorrow**  morgen

## PHRASES

**excuse me, do you speak English?**
sorry, spreekt u Engels? (*sorry, spraykt oo Engels?*)
**sorry, I don't speak Dutch**
het spijt me, ik spreek geen Nederlands (*et spite meh, ik spraykhane nayderlants*)
**I don't understand**
Ik begrijp het niet (*ik begripe et neet*)
**what is that?**
wat is dat? (*vot is dat?*)

**where is...?** waar is...?
**what's the time?**
hoe laat is het?
**my name is...**
mijn naam is... (*mine naam is...*)
**I want...** Ik wil graag...
**how much is...?**
wat kost...?
**could I have a receipt?**
mag ik een bonnetje alstublieft?
**how far is it to...?**
hoe ver is het naar...?
**I am sick** Ik ben ziek
**I think I ate too much spacecake**
Ik denk dat ik te veel spacecake heb opgegeten

## INSULTS

**kut**  female private parts (use as 'fuck!')
**lul**  male private parts (use as 'asshole!')
**boer**  farmer (term of abuse used by locals, often by cyclists at car drivers)
**moederneuker** motherfucker
**volgescheten palingvel**
shit-filled eel-skin (directed towards skinny person)

## NUMBERS

| | |
|---|---|
| **0** nul | **1** een |
| **2** twee | **3** drie |
| **4** vier | **5** vijf |
| **6** zes | **7** zeven |
| **8** acht | **9** negen |
| **10** tien | **11** elf |
| **12** twaalf | **13** dertien |
| **14** veertien | **15** vijftien |
| **16** zestien | **17** zeventien |
| **18** achttien | **19** negentien |
| **20** twintig | |
| **21** eenentwintig | |
| **22** tweeëntwintig | |
| **30** dertig | |
| **31** eenendertig | |
| **32** tweeëndertig | |
| **40** veertig | **50** vijftig |
| **60** zestig | **70** zeventig |
| **80** tachtig | **90** negentig |
| **100** honderd | |
| **101** honderd een | |
| **200** tweehonderd | |
| **1,000** duizend | |

**Directory**

# Further Reference

## Books

### Fiction

**Baantjer** *De Cock* series
This ex-Amsterdam cop used his experiences to write a series of crime novels set in town. Also a TV series.
**Martyn Bedford** *The Houdini Girl*
A terrific thriller that roams from Oxford to Amsterdam.
**Rudi van Dantzig**
*For a Lost Soldier*
An autobiographical story set in the years following 1944.
**Arnon Grunberg** *Blue Mondays*
Philip Roth's *Goodbye Columbus* goes Dutch in this cathartic 1994 bestseller.
**John Irving** *A Widow for One Year*
Classic Irving, partly set in the Red Light District.
**Lieve Joris** *Back to the Congo*
A historical novel about Belgium and its ex-colony.
**Tim Krabbé** *The Vanishing*
A man's search for his vanished lover. Twice made into a feature film (the first is the best).
**Marga Minco** *Bitter Herbs*
An autobiographical masterpiece about a Jewish family falling apart during and after the war.
**Margriet de Moor**
*First Grey, Then White, Then Blue*
A compelling story of perception, love and mortality.
**John David Morley**
*The Anatomy Lesson*
Morley's novel is about two very different American brothers growing up in Amsterdam.
**Harry Mulisch** *The Assault*
A boy's perspective on World War II.
**Multatuli**
*Max Havelaar or the Coffee Auctions of the Dutch Trading Company*
The story of a colonial officer and his clash with the corrupt government.
**Cees Nooteboom**
*The Following Story*
An exploration of the differences between platonic and physical love.
**Heleen van Royen**
*The Happy Housewife*
A fine debut from this Dutch writer, about a woman coming to terms with having a baby.
**Renate Rubinstein**
*Take It or Leave It*
Diary of one of the Netherlands' most renowned journalists and her battle against MS.
**Irvine Welsh** *The Acid House*
Short stories, one set – perhaps predictably – in Amsterdam's druggy underworld.
**Janwillem van der Wetering**
*The Japanese Corpse*

An off-the-wall police procedural set in Amsterdam, and one of an excellent series.
**Manfred Wolf (ed)** *Amsterdam: A Traveller's Literary Companion*
The country's best writers tell tales of the city.

### Non-fiction

**Rudy B Andeweg & Galen A Irwin** *Dutch Government & Politics*
An introduction to Dutch politics that assumes no prior knowledge.
**Kathy Batista & Florian Migsch** *A Guide to Recent Architecture: The Netherlands*
Part of the excellent pocket series, with great pictures.
**Derek Blyth** *Amsterdam Explored*
Nine walks around the city.
**CR Boxer**
*The Dutch Seaborne Empire*
The Netherlands' wealth and where it went.
**Peter Burke** *Venice & Amsterdam*
A succinct comparative history of these two watery cities.
**Simon Carmiggelt**
*I'm Just Kidding: More of a Dutchman's Slight Adventures*
An Amsterdam columnist famous for sucking his readers in to take a closer look at Amsterdam.
**Anne Frank**
*The Diary of Anne Frank*
The still-shocking wartime diary of the young Frank.
**RH Fuchs** *Dutch Painting*
A comprehensive guide.
**Miep Gies & Alison Leslie Gold** *Anne Frank Remembered*
The story of the woman who helped the Frank family during the war.
**Paul Groenendijk** *Guide to Modern Architecture in Amsterdam*
What the title suggests.
**Zbigniew Herbert**
*Still Life with a Bridle*
The Polish poet and essayist meditates on the Golden Age.
**Jonathan I Israel**
*The Dutch Republic and the Hispanic World 1606-1661*
How the Dutch Republic broke free.
**Maarten Kloos (ed)**
*Amsterdam, An Architectural Lesson*
Architects and town planners on the city.
**EH Kussmann**
*The Low Countries 1780-1940*
Good background reading.
**Geert Mak**
*Amsterdam: A Brief Life of the City*
The city's history told through the stories of its people, both acclaimed and plain.
**Paul Overy** *De Stijl*
Modern art examined.

**Geoffrey Parker** *The Thirty Years' War; The Dutch Revolt*
The fate of the Netherlands and Spain in descriptive, analytical but readable history.
**Simon Schama**
*The Embarassment of Riches*
A lively social and cultural history of the Netherlands. His biog of sorts, *Rembrandt's Eyes*, is also worth a look.
**William Z Schetter**
*The Netherlands in Perspective*
An essential book that goes beyond the usual stereotypes.
**Peter van Straaten**
*This Literary Life*
A highly amusing collection of one of the Netherlands' most popular cartoonist's works.
**Jacob Vossestein**
*Dealing with the Dutch*
Netherlanders explained in fascinating fashion.
**Wim de Wit**
*The Amsterdam School: Dutch Expressionist Architecture*
Early 20th-century architecture.
**Various**
*Dedalus Book of Dutch Fantasy*
Contemporary Dutch short stories.

## Music

### Albums

**Arling & Cameron**
*Music for Imaginary Films* (2000)
Showered with acclaim, eclectic duo reinvent the history of film soundtracks.
**Chet Baker** *Live at Nick's* (1978)
Accompanied by his favorite rhythm section, Chet soars in one of his best live recordings.
**The Beach Boys** *Holland* (1973)
Californians hole up in Holland and start recording.
**Bettie Serveert** *Palomine* (1993)
Alt.rock guitar with perfect pop songs and angelic vocals.
**Herman Brood & His Wild Romance** *Shpritsz* (1978)
The nation's cuddle junkie rocker scored international hit with 'Saturday Night'.
**The Ex** *Starters Alternators* (1998)
Anarcho squat punks/improv-jazzsters team up with Steve Albini.
**Focus** *Hocus Pocus: the Best of Focus* (1975)
Prog rock with yodelling!
**George Baker Selection**
*Little Green Bag* (1970)
Part of the 'Dutch Invasion' who exchanged the rocking riffs of this album for softer moods a few years later with the icky 'Una Paloma Blanca'.

**Golden Earring** *Moontan* (1974)
The Hague's answer to The Who;
includes hit 'Radar Love'.
**Human Alert** *Dirty Dancing* (2002)
Hysterically funny punk legends
go orchestral.
**Junkie XL**
*Saturday Teenage Kicks* (1997)
The Lowlands' answer to the
Chemical Brothers.
**Osdorp Posse**
*Origineel Amsterdams* (2000)
Nederhop maestros offer a primer in
local street talk for 'moederneukers'.
**Outsiders**
*Capital Collectors Series* (1996)
Dutch take on '60s beat and garage
punk whose legend goes beyond their
four-year existence.
**Lee 'Scratch' Perry**
*The Return of Pipecock Jackxon* (1980)
Godfather of dub burns down studio
and comes to Amsterdam to drop
acid and record this brain-melter.
**Oscar Peterson Trio**
*At Concertgebouw* (1958)
One of many jazz legends who've
taken advantage of the ace acoustics
to record a live set.
**Shocking Blue**
*The Best of…* (1994)
Killer bubblegum riffs in songs like
'Send Me a Postcard'. Bananarama
covered 'Venus'.
**Solex** *Pick Up* (1999)
Amsterdam record-store owner
Elisabeth Esselink turns dance
music on its head.
**Treble Spankers**
*Araban* (1994), *Hasheeda* (1996)
Inspired surf, taking the genre back
to Middle Eastern roots.
**Urban Dance Squad**
*Mental Floss for the Globe* (1990)
Rude Boy and gang produce
influential crossover album.
**Various** *Als Je Haar Maar
Goed Zit, Vols.1 & 2* (1982/1983)
Documents Amsterdam's early
'80s hardcore scene with tracks
recorded by the likes of BGK,
Amsterdamned, Null, Frites
Moderns and Nitwitz.
**Various** *Amsterdammers* (1996)
Local bands of every genre,
including Solid Ground, pay
tribute to their hometown.

## Songs

**assorted singers**
'Aan de Amsterdamse Grachten'
**Bone Thugs-N-Harmony**
'The Weed Song'
**Bertus Borgers** 'Red Red Lebanon'
**Brainbox** 'Amsterdam, the
First Days'
**Jacques Brel** 'Amsterdam'
**John Cale** 'Amsterdam'
**Kevin Coyne** 'Amsterdam'
**Cypress Hill** 'Spark Another Owl'
**Dorus** 'Het Mooiste van Mokum';
'Hij Vindt Amsterdam wel Aardig'

**Drukwerk** 'Hey Amsterdam'
**Eminem** 'Under the Influence'
**Herman Emmink**
'Tulpen uit Amsterdam'
**Green Day** 'Misery'
**Ruud Gullit & Revelation Time**
'Not the Dancing Kind'
**Tol Hansse** 'Big City'
**Ronnie Hilton** 'A Windmill
in Old Amsterdam'
**Rika Jansen** 'Amsterdam Huilt
(Waar het Eens Heeft Gelachen)'
**Jesus & the Gospelfuckers**
'Amsterdam'
**Jasperina de Jong** 'De Rosse Buurt'
**Johnny Jordaan** 'Geef Mj Maar
Amsterdam'; 'Bij Ons in de Jordaan'
**Kirsty MacColl**
'Here Comes That Man Again'
**NRA** 'Amsterdam Surf Song'
**Mojo Nixon**
'Amsterdam Dogshit Blues'
**Porn Kings** 'Amsterdam XXX'
**Willem Breuker Kollectief
meets Djazzex**
'Amsterdam Thoroughfare'
**Van Halen** 'Amsterdam'

## Films

**Amsterdam Global Village**
*dir. Johan van der Keuken* (1996)
A meditative and very long arty
cruise through Amsterdam's streets
and peoples.
**Amsterdamned**
*dir. Dick Maas* (1987)
Thriller with psychotic frogman
and lots of canal chase scenes, made
only slightly worse by continuity
problems that result in characters
turning an Amsterdam corner and
ending up in Utrecht.
**The Fourth Man**
*dir. Paul Verhoeven* (1983)
Mr *Basic Instinct* films Gerard Reve
novel with Jeroen Krabbe seething
with homoerotic desire. Better than
it might sound.
**Hufters en Hofdames
(Bastards and Bridesmaids)**
*dir. Eddy Terstall* (1997)
Twentysomethings use Amsterdam
as backdrop against which to have
relationship trouble.
**Karacter (Character)**
*dir. Mike van Diem* (1997)
Oscar winner for Best Foreign
Language film: an impeccably
scripted father-son drama.
**Naar de Klote! (Wasted!)**
*dir. Ian Kerkhof* (1996)
An appropriately hallucinogenic
trip through Amsterdam's techno
clubland. This was the first feature
film to be made on DV.
**De Noorderlingen
(The Northerners)**
*dir. Alex van Warmerdam* (1992)
Absurdity and angst in a lonely
Dutch subdivision.
**Puppet on a Chain**
*dir. Geoffrey Reeve* (1970)

Based on Alistair MacLean's
spy novel, the film documents
a swinging Amsterdam and
psychotic clog dancers.
**Still Smokin'**
*dir. Tommy Chong* (1989)
Cheech and Chong visit their
spiritual homeland of Amsterdam
**Turks Fruit (Turkish Delight)**
*dir. Paul Verhoeven* (1973)
Sculptor Rutger Hauer witnesses the
brain tumour of his babe
**Zusje (Little Sister)**
*dir. Robert Jan Westdijk* (1995)
A family affair with voyeuristic
overtones.

## Websites

**www.amsterdam.nl**
An accessible site with advice
on living in, as well as visiting,
Amsterdam. The searchable maps
are terrific.
**www.amsterdambackdoor.com**
An attention-grabbing e-zine
and database of Amsterdam
unconventionality, drug tip-offs
included. Cute sound, nice content.
**www.amsterdamhotspots.nl**
An upbeat review-based site of, uh,
Amsterdam's hotspots.
**www.amsterdamlinks.nl**
Thorough, if conventional.
**www.amsterdamlive.nl**
Get a close look at the city's venues
with the webcam, or make use of the
excellent links. In Dutch only.
**www.amsterdam-webcams.com**
Some personal, some public, all in
Amsterdam.
**www.archined.nl**
News and reviews of Dutch
architecture, in both Dutch and
English. Informative and interesting.
**www.bmz.amsterdam.nl/adam/
nl/monum.html**
Fantastically detailed site devoted to
Amsterdam's architectural heritage.
Some pages in English.
**www.channels.nl**
Takes you, virtually, through
Amsterdam's streets with reviews
of their sights, hotels, restaurants
and clubs.
**www.gayamsterdamlinks.com**
What it says on the packet.
**www.simplyamsterdam.nl**
Aimed at the backpacker.
**www.uitlijn.nl**
Event listings for Amsterdam, in
Dutch but fairly easy to navigate.
**www.underwateramsterdam.com**
The web home of alternative listings
mag *Shark*, in whose shallows
several *Time Out* writers lurk.
**www.visitamsterdam.nl**
Factual and comprehensive (if a little
drab) tourist guide.
**www.xs4all.nl/~4david**
An anatomy of the mind,
Amsterdam-style (ie left brain). Drug
techniques you never knew existed.

**Directory**

# Index

Numbers in **bold** indicate the key entry for the topic; numbers in *italics* indicate illustrations. Dutch personal names are indexed under the last element: eg Beeren, Bet van.

# Advertisers' Index

Please refer to the relevant pages for
addresses and telephone numbers.

# Maps

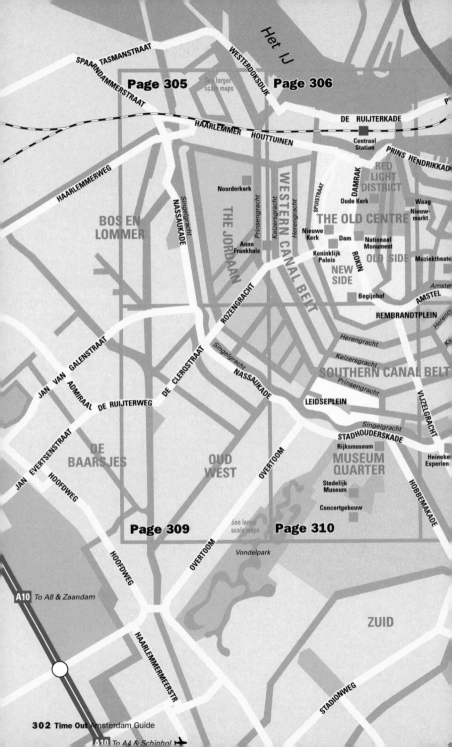

Het IJ

TASMANSTRAAT

SPAARNDAMMERSTRAAT

WESTERDOKSDIJK

See larger scale maps

HAARLEMMER HOUTTUINEN

DE RUIJTERKADE

P

Centraal Station

PRINS HENDRIKKAD

HAARLEMMERWEG

Noorderkerk

Prinsengracht

Keizersgracht

Herengracht

SPUISTRAAT

DAMRAK

Oude Kerk

RED LIGHT DISTRICT

Waag Nieuw- markt

BOS EN LOMMER

Singelgracht

NASSAUKADE

THE JORDAAN

WESTERN CANAL BELT

Nieuwe Kerk

THE OLD CENTRE

Anne Frankhuis

Dam

Nationaal Monument

OLD SIDE

Muziektheate

Koninklijk Paleis

ROKIN

NEW SIDE

Amste

AMSTEL

Begijnhof

REMBRANDTPLEIN

ROZENGRACHT

Heren

Herengracht

JAN VAN GALENSTRAAT

DE CLERQSTRAAT

Singelgracht

NASSAUKADE

Keizersgracht

SOUTHERN CANAL BELT

Ke

Prinsengracht

ADMIRAAL DE RUIJTERWEG

VIJZELGRACHT

JAN EVERTSENSTRAAT

LEIDSEPLEIN

DE BAARSJES

Singelgracht

STADHOUDERSKADE

HOOFDWEG

OUD WEST

OVERTOOM

Rijksmuseum

MUSEUM QUARTER

Heineke Experien

HOBBEMAKADE

Stedelijk Museum

Concertgebouw

See larger scale maps

HOOFDWEG

OVERTOOM

Vondelpark

A10 To A8 & Zaandam

ZUID

HAARLEMMERMEERSTR

A10 To A4 & Schiphol

# Amsterdam Overview

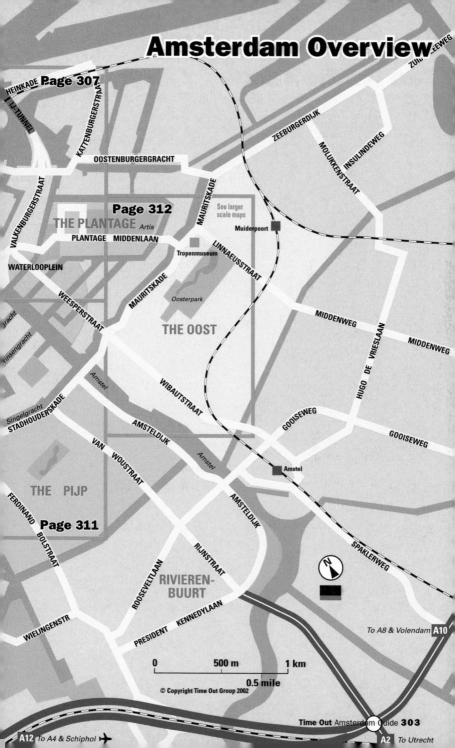

Page 307

ZUID...EWEG

HEINKADE

IJ-TUNNEL

KATTENBURGERSTRAAT

OOSTENBURGERGRACHT

ZEEBURGERDIJK

MOLUKKENSTRAAT

INSULINDEWEG

MAURITSKADE

See larger
scale maps

Page 312

THE PLANTAGE    *Artis*

Muiderpoort

PLANTAGE  MIDDENLAAN

VALKENBURGERSTRAAT

Tropenmuseum

LINNAEUSSTRAAT

WATERLOOPLEIN

MAURITSKADE

*Oosterpark*

WEESPERSTRAAT

THE OOST

MIDDENWEG

MIDDENWEG

...racht

...insengracht

*Amstel*

WIBAUTSTRAAT

HUGO  DE  VRIESLAAN

Singelgracht

STADHOUDERSKADE

AMSTELDIJK

*Amstel*

VAN  WOUSTRAAT

GOOISEWEG

GOOISEWEG

THE  PIJP

FERDINAND BOLSTRAAT

Page 311

AMSTELDIJK

Amstel

ROOSEVELTLAAN

RIJNSTRAAT

RIVIEREN-
BUURT

SPAKLERWEG

N

WIELINGENSTR

PRESIDENT  KENNEDYLAAN

*To A8 & Volendam* **A10**

| 0 | 500 m | 1 km |

0.5 mile

© Copyright Time Out Group 2002

**A12** *To A4 & Schiphol* ✈

**A2** *To Utrecht*

# The Netherlands

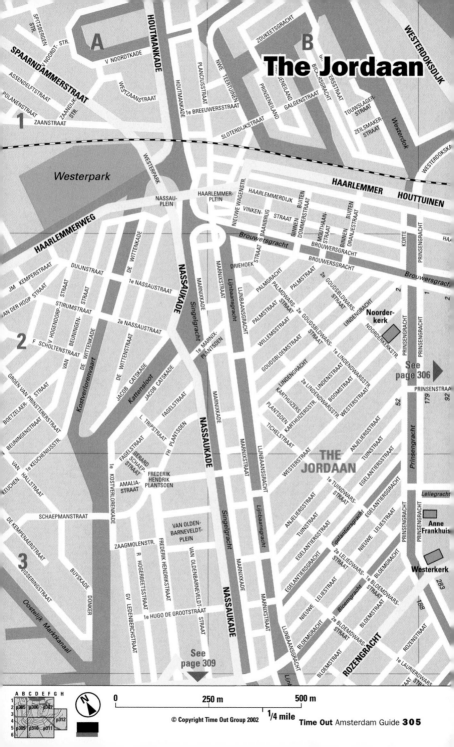

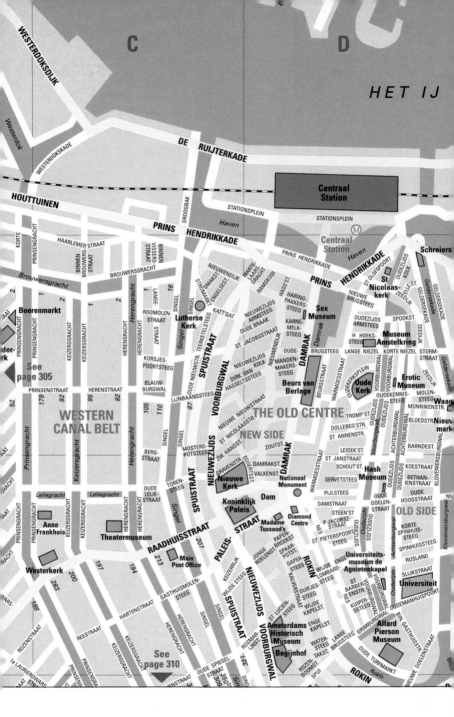

DE RUIJTERKADE

Centraal
Station

STATIONSPLEIN

HOUTTUINEN

PRINS

Haven

STATIONSPLEIN

Centraal
Station

Schreiers

HENDRIKKADE

PRINS HENDRIKKADE

Haven

PRINS

HENDRIKKADE

St
Nicolaaskerk

DROOGBAK

NIEUWE
BRUGSTEEG

Boerenmarkt

Brouwersgracht

HAARLEMER STRAAT

BROUWERSGRACHT

Nieuwendijk

BINNEN
BROUWERS
STRAAT

KORTE
PRINSENGRACHT

BINNEN
VISSERS
STRAAT

HERENGRACHT

LANGE-
NIEUWE
STRAAT

ROOMOLEN-
STRAAT

SINGEL

16

Lutherse
Kerk

KATT'GAT

MARTE
LAARS-
GRACHT
GRACHT

JAN ENGELSCHESTR.

NIEUWEZIJDS
ARMSTEEG

OUDE BRAAK

MASS ST.

HARING-
PAKKERS-
STEEG

Sex
Museum

KARNE-
MELK-
STEEG

Damrak

OUDEZIJDS
ARMSTEEG

OUDEZIJDS
KOLK

St OLOFSPOORT

ST OLOFSTEEG

GELDERSEKADE

GELDERSEKADE

SPOOKST.

Museum
Amstelkring

H HOEKS-
STEEG

LANGE NIEZEL

KORTE NIEZEL

ZEEDIJK

STORM-
STRAAT

ZEEDIJK

GELDERSEKADE

See
page 305

52

2

KEIZERSGRACHT

KEIZERSGRACHT

HERENGRACHT

HERENGRACHT

SINGEL

TEERKETELSTEEG

OUDE NIEUWSTR.

ST JACOBSSTRAAT

NIEUWEZIJDS

DIRK. VAN KOLK

HASSELTSSTEEG

OUDE-
MANDEN-
MAKERS-
STEEG

BRUGSTEEG

H HOEKS-
STEEG

Beurs van
Berlage

WARMOESSTRAAT

Oude
Kerk

OUDEKENNIS-
STEEG

Erotic
Museum

MOLEN-
STEEG

Waag

PRINSENGRACHT

179

92

HERENSTRAAT

95

82

KORSJES-
POORTSTEEG

BLAUW-
BURGWAL

LIJNBAANSSTEEG

SPUISTRAAT

VOORBURGWAL

NIEUWE NIEUWSTRAAT

BEURSSTRAAT

OUDEZIJDS

VOORBURGWAL

OUDEZIJDS

ACHTERBURGWAL

BLOEDSTR.

Nieuwmarkt

MONNIKENSTR.

WESTERN
CANAL BELT

Prinsengracht

105

110

SINGEL

ST NICOLAASSTR.

ZW. HANDSTR.

NIEUWE NIEUWEZIJDS

MOSTERD-
POTSTEEG

BERG-
STRAAT

GRAVENSTR.

NIEUWEZIJDS

ZOUTST.

TROMP'ST.

DOLLEBEG'STR.

ST ANNENSTR.

LEIDEK'ST.

ST JANSTRAAT

ST ANNENSTR.

VOORBURGWAL

OUDEZIJDS

ACHTERBURGWAL

BARNDEST.

KOESTRAAT

KLOVENIERSBURGWAL

THE OLD CENTRE

NEW SIDE

DAMRAK

SCHOUT'ST.

Hash
Museum

SERVETSTEEG

BETHAN-
IENSTRAAT

OUDE
HOOGSTRAAT

Leliegracht

Leliegracht

KEIZERSGRACHT

HERENGRACHT

EGGERTSST.

Nieuwe
Kerk

DAMRAKST.

VALKENST.

Nationaal
Monument

WARMOESSTRAAT

PIJLSTEEG

OUDE
DOELEN-
STRAAT

OLD SIDE

Anne
Frankhuis

TOREN-
STEEG

OUDE
LELIE-
STRAAT

SINGEL

Koninklijk
Paleis

Dam

Madame
Tussaud's

Diamond
Centre

DAMSTRAAT

STEEN'ST

P JACOBSZ-
STRAAT

KORTE
SPINHUIS-
STEEG

SPINHUISSTEEG

RUSLAND

Theatermuseum

Westerkerk

200

197

194

213

Main
Post Office

RAADHUISSTRAAT

207

KEIZERSGRACHT

PALEIS-
STRAAT

PAPEN-
BROEKST.

JONGE
ROELENSTR.

GAPER
STEEG

NES

WIJDE
LOMBARD-
STEEG

DUIFJES-
STEEG

ST
PIETERSPOORT
STEEG

Universiteits-
museum de
Agnietenkapel

ST
BARBER-
STR.

SLIJKSTRAAT

Universiteit

SLIJKSTRAAT

Oudezijds

KUIPER-
STEEG

ROKIN

283

188

ROZENGRACHT

te LAURIERDWARS

PRINSENGRACHT

KEIZERSGRACHT

HERENGRACHT

GASTHUISMOLEN
STEEG

HARTENSTRAAT

REESTRAAT

SINGEL

NIEUWEZIJDS

SPUISTRAAT

VOORBURGWAL

OUDE SPIEGEL
STRAAT

WIJDE
KAPELST.

ST LUCIEN-
STEEG

Amsterdams
Historisch
Museum

Begijnhof

WATER-
STEEG

ROZEN-
STEEG

SPUI

OUDE TURFMARKT

KOLK

ENGE
KAPELST.

LANGE
BRUGSTEEG

GRIMBURGWAL

OUDEMANHUISPOORT

BIN GASTHUISSTR.

NIEUWE DOELENSTRAAT

Allard
Pierson
Museum

ROKIN

Rokin

See
page 310

350 STR.

309

ROKIN

RISMAR-
LJNST.

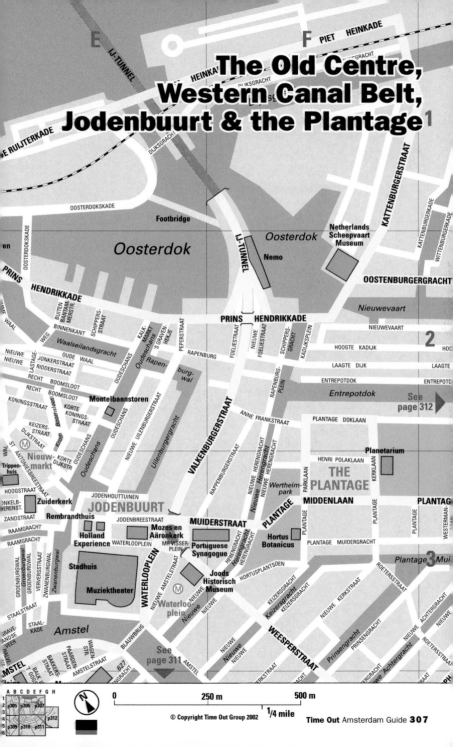

# Teamsys.

## A WORLD OF SERVICES

 Teamsys is always with you, ready to assure you all the tranquillity and serenity that you desire for your journeys, 365 days a year.

Roadside assistance always and everywhere, infomobility so not to have surprises, insurance... and lots more.

To get to know us better contact us at the toll-free number **00-800-55555555**.

...and to discover Connect's exclusive and innovative integrated infotelematic services onboard system visit us at:

www.targaconnect.com

# Oud West

© Copyright Time Out Group 2002

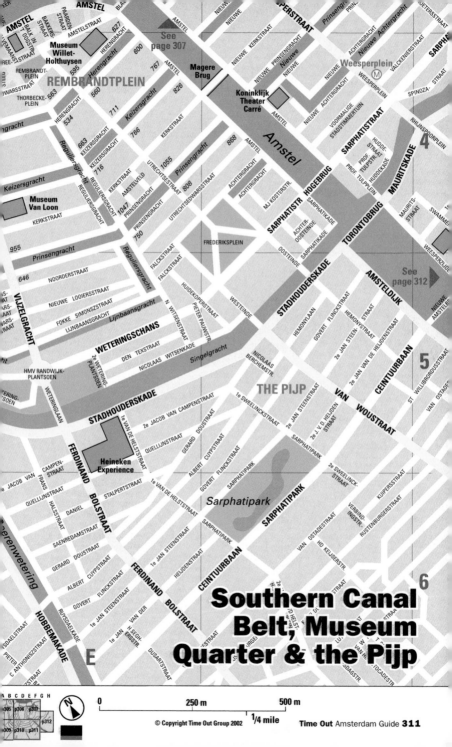

# Southern Canal Belt, Museum Quarter & the Pijp

# The Oost

**ARTIS**
See
page 307

Entrepotdok

GE DOKLAAN

ANTAGE MIDDENLAAN

Aquarium

PLANTAGE MUIDERGRACHT

Plantage Muidergracht

SARPHATISTRAAT

KAZERNE-STRAAT

ALEXANDERKADE

Singelgracht

MAURITSKADE

VON ZESENSTRAAT

COMMELINSTRAAT

DAPPERSTRAAT

WAGENAARSTRAAT

1e v SWINDENSTRAAT

2e v SWIND-ENDWARS-STRAAT

P. NIEUWLANDERSTRAAT

REINWARDTSTRAAT

V. VAN SWIND-ENDWARS-STRAAT

WESTERMAN-LAAN

PLANTAGE LEPELLAAN

PLANTAGE BADLAAN

PLANTAGE MUIDERGRACHT

ALEXANDER-PLEIN

LINNAEUSSTRAAT

Muidergracht

Tropenmuseum

WITTENBACHSTR.

SARPHATISTRAAT

NIEUWE ACHTERGRACHT

VALCKENIERSTRAAT

MAURITSKADE

Arena

KORTE 'S-GRAVESANDE-STRAAT

'S-GRAVESANDE-STRAAT

Singelgracht

OOSTERPARK KASTAN-JEWEG

KASTAN-JERLEIN

**Oosterpark**

EIKENWEG

EIKEN-PLEIN

SARPHATISTRAAT

MAURITSKADE

SCHENBROEKSTRAAT

MUNTENDAM-STRAAT

MARY ZELDENRUSTSTRAAT

SAJET-PLEIN

OOSTERPARK

2e OOSTERPARKSTRAAT

OOSTERPARK

VROLIKSTRAAT

POPULIERENWEG

BONNSTRAAT

TILANUSSTRAAT

RUYSCHSTRAAT

BEUKENWEG

BEUKEN-STRAAT

**THE OOST**

TUGELAWEG

RETIEFSTRAAT

ANDREAS

CAMPENSTRAAT

2e BOERHAAVESTRAAT

MUSV.

Gasthuis
(Hospital)

BEUKENWEG

1e OOSTERPARKSTRAAT

PLEIN-STRAAT

BEUKENWEG

MARITZSTRAAT

SMITSTR.

MAJUBA-STR.

TRANSVAALST

SPOORPLEIN

TILANUSSTRAAT

2e BOERHAAVESTRAAT

CAMPENSTRAAT

2e OOSTERPARKSTRAAT

3e OOSTERPARK-STRAAT

VROLIKSTRAAT

TUGELAWEG

PRETORIUSSTRAAT

**WIBAUTSTRAAT**

1e BOERHAAVE-STRAAT

DEYMANSTRAAT

RUYSCHSTRAAT

BLASIUSSTRAAT

IEPENWEG

1e OOSTERPARKSTRAAT

2e OOSTERPARKSTRAAT

POPULIERENWEG

PRESIDENT BRAND-STRAAT

REITZSTRAAT

CHRISTIAAN DE WETSTRAAT

KRUGERSTRAAT

TRANSVAALK

SWAMMERDAMSTRAAT

2e OOSTERPARKSTRAAT

2e VROLIKSTRAAT

REITZSTRAAT

WEESPERZIJDE

IJsbreker

See
page 311

NIEUWE AMSTELBRUG

BLASIUSSTRAAT

1e OOSTERPARKSTRAAT

OETGENSSTRAAT

BURMANDWARS-STRAAT

BURMANSTRAAT

GRENSSTRAAT

WEESPERZIJDE

**Wibautstraat**

Ⓜ

PLATANENWEG

VROLIKSTRAAT

TUGELAWEG

JOUBERTSTRAAT

DE LA REIJSTR.

VAALRIVIERSTR.

KRUGERSTRAAT

**Amstel**

LLIBRORDUSSTRAAT

VAN OSTADESTRAAT

KUIPERSTRAAT

MUIDERSTRAAT

**AMSTELDIJK**

**G**

GV AMSTELSTR.

GRAAF FLORISSTR.

MARCUSSTR.

**H**

BEN VILJOENSTRAAT

D THERONSTR.

HORMEYSTRAAT

PRES STEYNPLANT

TRANSVAALKADE

**WIBAUTSTRAAT**

2

3

4

5

N

0    250 m    500 m

1/4 mile

© Copyright Time Out Group 2002

A B C D E F G
1
2  p305  p306  p307
3
4
5  p309  p310  p311
6

# Street Index

## About the maps

This index has been designed to tie in with other available maps of Amsterdam, and certain principles of the Dutch language have been followed for reasons of consistency and ease of use:
● Where a street is named after a person – Albert Cuypstraat, for example – it is alphabetised by surname. Albert Cuypstraat, therefore, is listed under 'C'.
● Where a street takes a number as a prefix, it has been listed under the name of the street, rather than the number. 1e Bloemdwarsstraat, then, is alphabetised under 'B'.

● The following prefixes have been ignored for the purposes of alphabetisation: Da, De, Den, 's, Sint (St), 't, Van, Van der. Where street names contain one of these prefixes, they have been alphabetised under the subsequent word. For example, Da Costakade can be found under 'C', and Van Breestraat is listed under 'B'.
● In Dutch, 'ij' is essentially the same as 'y'. Streets containing 'ij' – Vijzelstraat, for example – have been alphabetised as if 'ij' was a 'y'.

# Street Index

# Amsterdam Transport

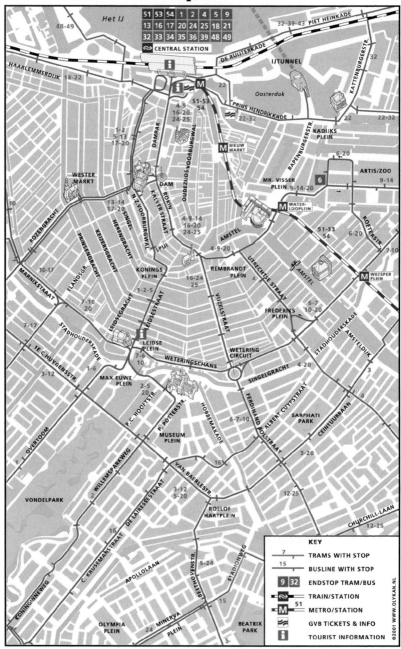

Het IJ

| 51 | 53 | 54 | 1 | 2 | 4 | 5 | 9 |
| 13 | 16 | 17 | 20 | 24 | 25 | 18 | 21 |
| 32 | 33 | 34 | 35 | 36 | 39 | 48 | 49 |

48-49

32-39-43 PIET HEINKADE

CENTRAL STATION

DE RUITERKADE

HAARLEMMERDIJK 18-22

IJTUNNEL

Oosterdok

KATTENBURGERSTR.

32

22

PRINS HENDRIKKADE

4-9
51-53
54

22-32

22-32

22

24-25

DAMRAK

RAPENBURGERSTR.

KADIJKS
PLEIN

1-2
5-13
17-20

N. Z. VOORBURGWAL

OUDEZIJDS VOORBURGWAL

NIEUW
MARKT

6-20

ARTIS/ZOO

WESTER
MARKT

KALVERSTRAAT

ROKIN

MR. VISSER
PLEIN 9-14-20

6

9-14

13-14
17-20

SINGEL

HERENGRACHT

DAM

4-9-14
16-20
24-25

AMSTEL

WATER-
LOOPLEIN

51-53
54

6-20

ROETERSTR.

ROZENGRACHT

SPUI

4-9-20

7-10

KEIZERSGRACHT

10

PRINSENGRACHT

10-17

ELANDSGR.

KONINGS
PLEIN

REMBRANDT
PLEIN

UTRECHTSE STRAAT

AMSTEL

WEESPER
PLEIN

MARNIXSTRAAT

LEIDSEGRACHT

LEIDSESTRAAT

16-24
25

1-2-5

VIJZELSTRAAT

FREDERIKS
PLEIN

6-7
10-20

7-17

7-10
20

LEIDSE
PLEIN

WETERING
CIRCUIT

STADHOUDERSKADE

AMSTELDIJK

STADHOUDERSKADE

1E C. HUYGENSSTR.

1-6

7-9
10.

WETERINGSCHANS

SINGELGRACHT

4-20

3

3-12

MAX EUWE
PLEIN

2-5
20

FERDINAND BOLSTRAAT

ALBERT CUYPSTRAAT

SARPHATI
PARK

4

P.C. HOOFTSTR.

HOBBEMAKADE

6-7-10

CEINTUURBAAN

1 OVERTOOM

MUSEUM
PLEIN

3-20

VAN BAERLESTR.

16

WILLEMSPARKWEG

DE LAIRESSESTRAAT

3-12
5-20

VONDELPARK

ROELOF
HARTPLEIN

12-25

CHURCHILL-LAAN

16

12-25

C. KRUSEMANSTRAAT

BEETHOVENSTR.

5-24

STADIONWEG

KONINGINNEWEG

APOLLOLAAN

15

OLYMPIA
PLEIN

MINERVA
PLEIN

24

BEATRIX
PARK

## KEY

| | |
|---|---|
| 7 | TRAMS WITH STOP |
| 15 | BUSLINE WITH STOP |
| 9  32 | ENDSTOP TRAM/BUS |
| ⌁ | TRAIN/STATION |
| M  51 | METRO/STATION |
| | GVB TICKETS & INFO |
| i | TOURIST INFORMATION |

©2001 WWW.OLYKAN.NL

# Amsterdam Please let us know what you think

## About this guide...

**1. How useful did you find the following sections?**

|  | Very | Fairly | Not very |
|---|---|---|---|
| In Context | ☐ | ☐ | ☐ |
| Accommodation | ☐ | ☐ | ☐ |
| Sightseeing | ☐ | ☐ | ☐ |
| Eat, Drink, Smoke, Shop | ☐ | ☐ | ☐ |
| Arts & Entertainment | ☐ | ☐ | ☐ |
| Trips Out of Town | ☐ | ☐ | ☐ |
| Directory | ☐ | ☐ | ☐ |
| Maps | ☐ | ☐ | ☐ |

**2. Did you travel to Amsterdam...?**

| Alone ☐ | With children ☐ |
|---|---|
| As part of a group ☐ | On vacation ☐ |
| On business ☐ | To study ☐ |
| With a partner ☐ | I live here ☐ |

**3. How long was your trip to Amsterdam?**
(write in) _____ days

**4. Where did you book your trip?**

*Time Out* Classifieds ☐
On the Internet ☐
With a travel agent ☐
Other (write in) ☐

**5. Where did you first hear about this guide?**

Advertising in *Time Out* magazine ☐
On the Internet ☐
From a travel agent ☐
Other (write in) ☐
_____

**6. Is there anything you'd like us to cover in greater depth?**
_____
_____
_____

**7. Are there any places that should/ should not\* be included in the guide?**
(\*delete as necessary)
_____
_____
_____
_____

**8. How many other people have used this guide?**

none ☐  1 ☐  2 ☐  3 ☐  4 ☐  5+ ☐

**9. What city or country would you like to visit next? (write in)**
_____
_____

## About other Time Out publications...

**10. Have you ever bought/used *Time Out* magazine?**

Yes ☐   No ☐

**11. Have you ever bought/used any other Time Out City Guides?**

Yes ☐   No ☐

If yes, which ones? _____

**12. Have you ever bought/used other Time Out publications?**

Yes ☐   No ☐

If yes, which ones? _____

## About you...

**13. Title (Mr, Ms etc):** _____

First name: _____
Surname: _____
Address: _____
_____
_____  P/code: _____
Email: _____
Nationality: _____

**14. Date of birth:** ☐☐/☐☐/☐☐

**15. Sex:**  male ☐  female ☐

**16. Are you...?**
Single ☐
Married/Living with partner ☐

**17. What is your occupation?**
_____

**18. At the moment do you earn...?**

under £15,000 ☐
over £15,000 and up to £19,999 ☐
over £20,000 and up to £24,999 ☐
over £25,000 and up to £39,999 ☐
over £40,000 and up to £49,999 ☐
over £50,000 ☐

☐ Please tick here if you do not wish to receive information about other Time Out products.
☐ Please tick here if you do not wish to receive mailings from third parties.

**Time Out Guides**

FREEPOST 20 (WC3187)
LONDON
W1E 0DQ